Words

A User's Guide

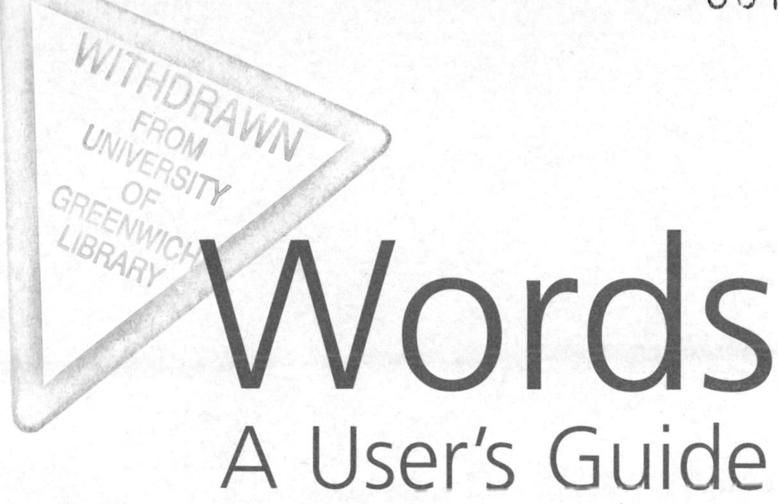

Words
A User's Guide

Stewart Clark and
Graham Pointon

Harlow, England • London • New York • Boston • San Francisco • Toronto
Sydney • Tokyo • Singapore • Hong Kong • Seoul • Taipei • New Delhi
Cape Town • Madrid • Mexico City • Amsterdam • Munich • Paris • Milan

PEARSON EDUCATION LIMITED

Edinburgh Gate
Harlow CM20 2JE
United Kingdom
Tel: +44 (0)1279 623623
Fax: +44 (0)1279 431059
Website: www.pearsoned.co.uk

First edition published in Great Britain in 2009

ISBN: 978-1-4058-5915-8

British Library Cataloguing in Publication Data
A CIP catalogue record for this book can be obtained from the British Library.

Library of Congress Cataloging in Publication Data
Clark, Stewart.
Words : a user's guide / Stewart Clark and Graham Pointon. – lst ed.
p. cm.
Includes bibliographical references and index.
ISBN 978-1-4058-5915-8 (pbk. : alk. paper) 1. English language–Great Britain–Usage.
2. English language–Great Britain–Pronunciation. I. Pointon, G. E. (Graham E.) II. Title.
PE1460.C4855 2009
428—dc22

2008048400

10 9 8 7 6 5 4 3 2 1
12 11 10 09 08

Typeset in 8.5/10.5pt Linoletter Roman by 35
Printed in Great Britain by Henry Ling Ltd., at the Dorset Press, Dorchester, Dorset

The publisher's policy is to use paper manufactured from sustainable forests.

Contents

Introduction

Words: A User's Guide is a practical guide to English usage. It gives clear recommendations about using the language to ensure that the message you send – whether you are writing an essay, an email or a business presentation – is clear and understandable. The book considers questions of usage, levels of formality, pronunciation, spelling and style. Although it is primarily addressed to the British English market, many entries focus on differences in usage between British English (BE) and American English (AE). Non-native speakers will also find the book invaluable as it presents contemporary English usage in a systematic way.

Most entries consider pairs or groups of words that may be confused. Each entry is structured as groups of words (technically called 'headwords') that sound alike, look alike or are frequently mixed up. For instance, when a writer describes a group of people on a beach, are they *naturalists* watching out for unusual creatures in the sand, or *naturists* wanting to soak up the sun without leaving any pale patches where their clothing has been? Is the bomb disposal squad trying to *defuse* the mine in the harbour, or *diffuse* it over a wide area? A monarch in the modern world *reigns*, but the Prime Minister often holds the *reins* of power.

Some will ask what purpose a guide such as this one can possibly serve in an age of technological advancement and the ubiquitous spellchecker. Well, both *defuse* and *diffuse* from the paragraph above would have passed clean through any spellchecker. They are, after all, spelt correctly. It is in the area of usage – how to employ these seemingly close but quite different words – that some will need guidance. *Words: A User's Guide* does exactly this: its comparative approach allows you to see immediately the differences between words in each entry. It provides clear and straightforward definitions of each of the headwords, and each definition is followed by examples of how the word can be used in a sentence.

All of the examples we offer are adapted from databases of contemporary English, such as dictionaries or the British National Corpus – a vast collection of 100 million words of English in actual use, taken from many varied sources: novels, newspapers, recorded conversations and lectures. This comparative approach is what sets this book apart from dictionaries. There are few that question the excellence of most dictionaries on the market such as the *Longman Dictionary of Contemporary English* (also available online **http://www.ldoceonline.com**), but dictionaries are limited by the structure of an alphabetical listing of single words. Consequently it is difficult for them to focus on the contrast between words that are frequently confused but may be a hundred or more pages apart: *abuse* and *misuse*, for instance.

Language usage is one of the most hotly debated subjects in the English-speaking world. Scarcely a week goes by without some newspaper or other printing an angry letter from a reader complaining about the so-called 'greengrocer's apostrophe', or a similar example of (alleged) language misuse. Whole books are devoted to attacks on modern trends, such as text speak (or should that be txt spk?), and their writers seem to assume that no worse catastrophe can befall the human race than the inability to spell correctly. Those who hold these views can be called *prescriptivists*, who believe that the language has strict, unchanging rules, and that everyone who uses English for public purposes (that is by writing in newspapers, making speeches or broadcasting) should follow these rules very carefully. Such attacks are often answered by equally forthright claims that usage is king, which is the same as saying that 'if this is the way people speak and write these days, then it is correct'. If you meet someone holding this view, you would be within your rights to call them a *descriptivist*. Descriptivists dismiss any thought of imposing rules on language, and point out that the published grammar of any newly discovered language is a description of its speakers' practice, and not what the linguists think it ought to be. To borrow a cliché, we see both sides of the story. Nonetheless – and in the absence of an English equivalent to the Académie française – there are some things worth knowing.

The English language is now the most important language in the world. It has about 375 million native speakers. This is many millions fewer than Mandarin Chinese, but in addition to the native speakers, English is the second language (the foreign language of choice) of at least twice as many again, and in contrast to Mandarin, its speakers and learners come from all corners of the world. The Internet is overwhelmingly written in English, not only by those for whom it is the first language, but also by native speakers of hundreds if not over a thousand other languages. At the most basic level, then, the English language is our most effective tool for navigating a way through the world. If we are not comfortable with our ability to use it effectively, we may find that our navigation goes off course, with all the consequences that can bring.

So, despite the cheerful spirit in which the book is written, the lack of precision in one's native language is a serious matter. The Provost of University College London, Malcolm Grant, predicted three years ago that British students will struggle to win places at university in future because of their poor command of English compared to that of European applicants (*The Sunday Telegraph*, June 2006). It is a point worth dwelling on – and we hope that this book will contribute in some small measure to an improvement in the scenario outlined by Professor Grant.

International English

This is a book that will also help native English speakers communicate successfully with others. With good reason, native speakers often fail to appreciate that the nuances of a language may be lost on some non-native speakers. This book warns how idiomatic phrases may be misunderstood when ideas are expressed in sporting phrases like *level playing fields, sticky wickets, moving the goalposts* and *ballpark figures*. Informalities such as *let's hit the sack* or *to be given the sack* may also be misleading for many non-native speakers of English. In business communication, punctuation in currencies can be misleading: full stops and commas are used in different ways around the world. Confusions can also arise from the way dates are written in different countries. Most people in Europe put the day first, most people in the US put the month first and a quarter of mankind – the Chinese – write the year first. This book will help you to use international standards such as ISO (International Organization for Standardization), and point out areas in which your effective communication with non-native speakers might be improved.

User friendly

Some books on English usage are formidable and inaccessible due to grammatical and linguistic terminology that creates problems for the general reader. This book avoids such terms but remains, to a degree, prescriptive in recommending what a careful writer would do. It points out non-standard usage if this is relevant. Many of the entries are followed by a small box which adds a general comment or two on that entry as a quick reminder. When there are generalizations to be made such as the avoidance of sexist language or tautology (repeating the same thing in different words), there is an entry that discusses the issue. In addition, there are sections giving some of the basic rules of English grammar, on word formation and on punctuation, and also a section on writing skills, providing guidance on modern email standards, on how to construct an effective CV (with web links to templates). This book can also be used by those who want to do some exercises for self-study and the web pages at **www.pearsoned.co.uk/words** will open up another dimension.

Words: A User's Guide has its origins in many years of teaching, working with, and thinking about the English language. We cannot claim to have written the final word, and we may even have made errors of our own. We are certain, however, of the debt we owe to Philip Langeskov who commissioned the book and was unfailingly enthusiastic about it, and Liz Potter, who has painstakingly questioned many of our preconceptions about English usage and has provided careful editorial assistance. The book is written with a cheerful spirit, one that sees the English language as a wonderful and ever-evolving platform for self-expression. The way we choose to use words is part of what makes us unique, and part of the charm of the English language. There are conventions of usage that are worth knowing and we draw attention to them throughout the book. Ultimately, however, this is a guide to usage and not a rule book. Take from it what you will, in other words, and if the book does nothing more than alert you to the wonders of language – or makes you more confident in your ability to express yourself – then it will have achieved its aim.

Guide to pronunciation

Most of the words included in this book present no problem with their pronunciation. However, there are cases where we have thought it useful to provide some guidance.

We have adopted a 'belt and braces' approach: pronunciations are given first in a 'respelling' system, and then in a transcription using the alphabet of the International Phonetic Association (IPA), which is placed between slashes: /. . ./. Occasionally, also, we have added a 'rhymes with . . .' or 'sounds like . . .' where there may still be some doubt.

The symbols used are as follows:

Respelling	*IPA*	*As in*	*Respelling*	*IPA*	*As in*
a	æ	h**a**t	o	ɒ	h**o**t
aa	ɑː	ban**a**na	ō	əʊ	n**o**
air	eər	h**air**	oo	uː	m**oo**n
ar (or aar)	ɑːr	p**ar**t	ŏŏ	ʊ	f**oo**t
aw	ɔː	l**aw**	or	ɔːr	b**or**n
ay	eɪ	d**ay**	ow	aʊ	n**ow**
b, bb	b	**b**at, ra**bb**it	oy	ɔɪ	b**oy**
ch	x	Scottish lo**ch**	p, pp	p	**p**e**pp**er
ck	k	ha**ck**	r, rr	r	**r**at, na**rr**ow
d, dd	d	**d**ab, la**dd**er	s, ss	s	**s**at, ma**ss**
e	e	g**e**t	sh	ʃ	**sh**ut
ee	iː	m**ee**t	t, tt	t	**t**ap, bi**tt**en
eer	ɪə	b**eer**	tch	ʧ	ha**tch**
er	ɜː	h**er**d	th	θ	**th**in
ew	juː	f**ew**	th	ð	**th**at
f, ff	f	re**f**er, e**ff**ort	u	ʌ	b**u**t
g, gg	g	**g**et, da**gg**er	ur	ɜːr	f**ur**
h	h	**h**at	v, vv	v	**v**et, 'bo**vv**er'
hl	ɬ	Welsh **Ll**ane**ll**i	w	w	**w**et
i	ɪ	b**i**t	y	j	**y**ellow
ī	aɪ	f**i**ve	z, zz	z	**z**oo, da**zz**le
īr	aɪər	f**ire**	zh	ʒ	the 's' of 'mea**s**ure'
j	ʤ	**j**ar	ă, ĕ, ŏ, ŭ	ə	the neutral vowel of
k	k	**k**itchen			b**a**nan**a**, cel**e**ry,
l, ll	l	**l**u**ll**			t**o**mato, p**u**rsue
m, mm	m	**m**arry, su**mm**er	(ng)	~	nasalized vowels
n, nn	n	**n**ature, fu**nn**y			found in words
ng	ŋ	si**ng**, si**ng**er			borrowed from
ng-g	ŋg	fi**ng**er			French

Double consonant letters are used in the respelling to emphasize that the preceding vowel is short but not the neutral vowel: **salon** sálonn /'sælɒn/.

The stress is shown in the respelling by means of an acute accent above the stressed vowel, and in the IPA by a vertical apostrophe before the beginning of the stressed syllable, e.g. **pastoral** paástŏrăl /'pɑːstərəl/.

Sounds that may be left out are written in italics in the IPA transcription. This mostly affects the letter 'r', which is pronounced in Southern British English only when the following sound is a vowel, e.g. **radar** ráydaar /'reɪdɑː*r*/, but is pronounced in all positions in most forms of American English, Scots and Irish.

What has become known as the 'happy' vowel, which occurs in some unstressed syllables mostly spelt with 'i' or 'y', is represented in the IPA by /i/, following most current pronouncing dictionaries, but is not separately shown in the respelling.

Syllabic consonants are indicated in the IPA by placing a short vertical line beneath the consonants, e.g. **abyssal** ăbíssăl /ə'bɪsl̩/; **corporation** korpŏráyshŏn /kɔː*r*pə'reɪʃn̩/.

Guide to features

Part of speech: each headword is classified by its part of speech given in italics.

Pronunciation is shown in two ways: in a re-spelling system, and then using the IPA alphabet. Both are explained in the Guide to pronunciation on pages x–xi. Sometimes this is also shown by giving a word that rhymes with the headword.

lead, led

lead[1] *noun*, is a soft metal, with the chemical symbol Pb: *From the late 1980s, lead was gradually eliminated from petrol.* **Lead** rhymes with 'fed'. *Lead pencils* actually contain graphite.

lead[2] *noun*, means the front of a group of moving people or animals: *As the procession reached the corner, we could see the school band in the lead*; or the advantage of one person or team in a competition: *The home team took the lead from a fifth-minute penalty*. Note that **lead** in this sense rhymes with 'feed'.

lead *verb*, means to be in charge of something: *Last year's captain will continue to lead the club this season*; or to be at the front: *The Irish horse was leading as they came to the last furlong marker. Lead to* can also mean to cause: *Excess stress on the body can ultimately lead to prolonged illness and possible death*. In another sense, **lead** means to experience: *She wanted to live in a flat, lead an ordinary life, and wait*. Note that **lead** in this sense also rhymes with 'feed'.

led *verb*, is the past tense and past participle of the verb *lead*: *Ahead of me was a glass-panelled oak door which led out to the sun terrace*.

> Never confuse the spellings of *lead* (metal) and *led* (past tense of the verb *to lead*), although they are pronounced the same.

Grey boxes cover points that apply to all the words in the group immediately above.

learned, learnt

learned[1] *adjective*, means scholarly, or refers to a person with much knowledge: *a learned author*. It can also be applied to publications: *In Britain, a learned journal about the impact of global warming has just been launched*. Note that with this meaning, the word is always pronounced as two syllables: lérnid /ˈlɜːrnɪd/.

learned[2] *adjective*, refers to knowledge that has been acquired: *Affirmative assessment must go beyond seeing anxiety, anger, guilt and sadness as simply newly learned reactions*. With this meaning, the word is pronounced as one syllable: lernd /lɜːrnd/.

learned *verb*, is the past tense and past participle of the verb *to learn* in BE and AE. In AE, **learned** is the only past participle form. *Learn* means to acquire knowledge through study or experience: *I learned a great deal from Fred*. When used as a past tense or past participle, **learned** is pronounced as one syllable: lernd /lɜːrnd/.

learnt *verb*, is an alternative form of the past tense and past participle of *to learn* but as the past participle is only used in BE: *I never went to drama school, but have learnt my craft the hard way*. See LEARN (TEACH).

learning difficulty, mental handicap

learning difficulty *noun*, means a mental problem that may affect how well a person can learn something: *Dyslexia is a common*

References send the reader to another entry for more information or comparison. If the word or topic indicated is not the first in a group, then the first word of the group is included in brackets. So to find LEARN, look under TEACH.

Headwords in italics indicate that the headwords are pronounced alike or very nearly alike.

leak, leek

leak *noun & verb*, refers to the accidental loss of gas or liquid from a pipe or container: *A gas leak at Bhopal, India, killed 2,500 people.* Figuratively, **leak** refers to the disclosure of confidential information: *The leader denied that any member of the party was connected with the leak; I can't carry on employing staff who might have been able to leak sensitive information.*

leek *noun*, is a vegetable related to the onion. It is also the Welsh national emblem: *The soup of the day is leek and cauliflower served with a crusty roll.*

Example sentences are given in italics.

Blue boxes give general information about grammatical terms.

Latin abbreviations in English

Many of the abbreviations used in formal written English are the short forms of Latin words. See entries for: **ca**, **cf.**, **e.g.**, **etc.**, **et al.**, **ibid.**, **i.e.**, **op. cit.**, **viz.** for some tips about how to use some of the most common ones.

'Use it or loose it.'
(Newspaper review of book that encouraged the elderly to have an active sex life) **!**

Blue-edged boxes are either jokes or examples of poor usage. Note that poor usage is flagged by an exclamation mark inside the margin of the box.

Spelling

laborat**ory**	Note -ory at the end
la**cq**u**er**	Note the -cq- and the -er ending
la**t**i**t**ude	Note the single -t- each time
le**ag**u**e**	Remember the -a- and the -u-
le**a**rner	Remember the -a-
legi**tim**ate	Note -tim-
l**ei**sure	Note -e- before -i-
len**g**th	Remember the -g-
leni**e**nt	Note the -ent ending
l**eop**ard	Remember the -o-, and the single -p-
lett**uce**	Note the ending -uce

Spelling box at the end of each letter gives some words where the spelling may cause problems. The problems themselves are spelt out after the word.

A

a, an

See ARTICLES (GRAMMAR TIPS).

abaft

See ASTERN.

abandon

See EVACUATE.

abbreviation, acronym

An **abbreviation** is usually formed by taking the initial letters of a phrase or name and reading them letter by letter, such as *IBM* or *ASAP* (for 'as soon as possible'). However, there are other forms of abbreviation, which are mentioned below. An **acronym** is a word formed from the initial letters of other words but pronounced as a word, such as *AIDS* aydz /eɪdz/ and *NATO* náytō /ˈneɪtəʊ/. When using an unfamiliar abbreviation or acronym, it is normal to write the name in full the first time it is mentioned, followed by the abbreviation or acronym in brackets. Later references only need the shorter version: *This is called Finite Element Modelling (FEM). Engineering design now uses FEM widely.*

abbreviation

There are two types of abbreviation. The first type is formed by using the first letter of one or more words. Abbreviations formed from the initial letters of the names of companies, organizations and states, such as *IBM*, the *EU* and the *USA*, are written in modern dictionaries without stops, and pronounced as individual letters. Some Latin abbreviations, such as *e.g.* are also of this type, although the stops are retained. See LATIN ABBREVIATIONS. Alternative names for this type of abbreviation are alphabetism or initialism. Some alphabetisms are written as if they were words in their own right, such as *deejay* for *DJ* (disc jockey, but not dinner jacket), or *emcee* for *MC* (master of ceremonies). The second type of abbreviation is formed by leaving out some of the letters of a word or name. Examples of this type are *dept* (for department), *bros* (brothers), *Fri.* (Friday), *Mr* (Mister) and *Dr* (Doctor). In speech, these abbreviations are pronounced as if the full word had been written (but for an exception, see LTD (PLC)). There is a difference in usage between the British and American English spelling of this second type of abbreviation. In British English, no full stop is written if the final letter of the word is included in the abbreviation (e.g. *Mr*), while a full stop is written if the final letter is missing (e.g. *Fri.*) American usage insists on a full stop in all cases (*Mr.*, *Fri.*). It is rare for a new abbreviation of this type to be invented nowadays. The same distinction applies to the abbreviations of university degrees: *BA*, *MSc* in BE, and *B.A.* or *M.Sc.* in AE.

Plurals of abbreviations are often formed with an 's' as in: *no.*, *nos.* (number/s); *fig.*, *figs.* (figure/s); *eq.*, *eqs.* (equation/s). The plural of *p.* (page), however, is *pp.* (pages). These abbreviations keep the stop in BE, even though the final letter is now *s*. The ISO standard concerning basic scientific units states that abbreviations such as *cm*, *h*, *kg*, *km*, *m*, *s* are to remain unaltered in the plural and are to be written without a final stop (ISO 31-0: 1992).

Some abbreviations have become so familiar that the words the letters stand for have been forgotten, with the result that the final word may be repeated in full. A common example is *HIV*: the V stands for 'virus', so it is unnecessary to add the complete word again after the abbreviation. See CLIPPED WORDS (WORD FORMATION), CONTRACTIONS.

acronym

With familiarity, an abbreviation may change into an acronym. An example is *U.N.E.S.C.O.*, written originally as initial letters with stops, and read letter by letter. It has now developed into the acronym ➡

UNESCO, pronounced **yoonéskō** /juːˈneskəʊ/.

An acronym is written without stops and read as a word. Most acronyms are written in capital letters, but a few are often seen in lower case and are scarcely recognizable as acronyms because they are treated as everyday words. Examples of these are *laser* (**l**ight **a**mplification by **s**timulated **e**mission of **r**adiation), pronounced **láyzĕr** /ˈleɪzər/ and *radar* (**ra**dio **d**etection **a**nd **r**anging), **ráydaar** /ˈreɪdɑːr/. These are sometimes called anacronyms. Other examples, such as *AIDS* (**a**cquired **i**mmune **d**eficiency **s**yndrome) and *PIN* (**p**ersonal **i**dentification **n**umber) have become so familiar that people forget what the letters stand for, and this leads to the word *syndrome* or *number* being repeated after the acronym. Some people prefer PIN code to PIN number. Market researchers have produced many acronyms such as *YUP* (**y**oung **u**rban **p**rofessional) some of which survive and generate everyday words, written in lower case, such as the noun *yuppie*. Some of the acronyms that have been widely adopted are carefully chosen to make catchy words, such as the American term *WASP* (**w**hite **a**nglo-**s**axon **p**rotestant). Most dictionaries of computing terms are full of acronyms such as *GIGO* **gī́gō** /ˈgaɪgəʊ/: '**g**arbage **in**, **g**arbage **o**ut'.

non-English abbreviations and acronyms

International institutions often follow the practice of the UN, and retain the abbreviation or acronym from one language, French or German for instance, while using an English version of the full name. An example of this is Système International d'Unités, called the International System of Units in English, for which the abbreviation *SI* is used in all languages. Another example is *CERN*, originally standing for **C**entre **E**uropéen pour la **R**echerche **N**ucléaire in French, and European Council for Nuclear Research in English. Even though the French name has now changed to Organisation Européenne pour la Recherche Nucléaire, the acronym has remained the same. See ISO.

abeam

See ASTERN.

abet

See AID.

abide, abode

abide *verb*. When it is followed by *by*, **abide** means to accept or obey: *Seeing the consequences, the government had to abide by the rules*. In this sense the past form is *abided*. **Abide** used with the negative of *can* or *could* means that the speaker cannot tolerate a person or idea: *I cannot abide him or his family*. An archaic meaning of **abide** is to dwell or reside. The past tense for this meaning is *abode*.

abode *noun*, means a dwelling and is used in the legal phrase for someone who is homeless: *A person of no fixed abode*. It is most commonly used in poetry and other formal contexts or in the humorous expression: *My humble abode*.

ability, capacity

ability *noun*, means the skill and intelligence to do something: *If you are to move about in the senior echelons of industry, this is an important ability to develop*.

capacity *noun*, means the talent for doing something that requires skill: *He met one of the crucial tests of leadership – the capacity to be both firm and flexible*. **Capacity** also means the maximum amount that may be produced by a machine: *This photocopier has the capacity to print 50 pages a minute*, or the

A British speaker once told a group of Americans how he was rescued by the AA (Automobile Association). Unfortunately most of the audience thought he meant Alcoholics Anonymous.

amount that a container can hold: *He recommended the version with a 10-litre capacity to the customer*.

One distinction between these two terms is that *ability* is something acquired and *capacity* is something inborn: *His ability as a pianist was helped by his capacity for memorizing complex scores*.

abjure, adjure, renounce

abjure *verb*, means to promise in public to give up a belief: *He abjured any further ties to Catholicism*. This is a formal word and *renounce* is more commonly used.

adjure *verb*, means to ask or command someone to do something: *The government adjured him not to reveal that he had had any contact with the British authorities*. This is a formal word.

renounce *verb*, means either to give up a belief or no longer behave in a particular way: *In front of the court, the teenagers renounced any further violent behaviour*. **Renounce** also means to state in public that you no longer wish to have a position or title: *She renounced her claim to the throne*.

-able, -ible

These suffixes are added to verbs to form adjectives, meaning 'that can be . . .', e.g. *eatable*: 'that can be eaten'. Most verbs add **-able** to form the adjective, especially those of native English origin, and in most cases, the adjectives ending in **-ible** cannot simply lose the ending to recover the verb, e.g. *feasible* (there is no verb to 'fease'), but there is a list of about 50 reasonably common exceptions, such as *suggestible*. They are listed below. Where a word may be spelt with either **-able** or **-ible**, e.g. *collectable~collectible*, this is indicated in the list.

accessible
coercible
collapsible
collectable, -ible
combustible
compactible
comprehensible
compressible
condensable, -ible
connectable, -ible
controvertible
convertible
corruptible
deductible
descendible
destructible
detectable
diffusible
digestible
discernible
discussable, -ible
dismissible
dispersible
distractible
evincible
exhaustible
explosible
expressible
extendable, -ible
extractable, -ible
flexible
forcible
ignitable, -ible
immersible
impressible
includable, -ible
infer(r)able, -ible
interruptible
invertible
perfectible
preventable, -ible
producible
reducible
repressible
reproducible
resistible
reversible
sensible
submergible
suggestible
suppressible

abnormal, subnormal

abnormal *adjective*, describes something that differs from what is considered usual: *Many consider that global warming has resulted in abnormal weather conditions*.

subnormal *adjective*, describes something below the norm: *Many winters had subnormal temperatures* (meaning colder than average). This is sometimes used for people whose mental capacity is assessed as being below normal. In such contexts, it is now considered a derogatory term, and is best avoided. See POLITICAL CORRECTNESS.

abode

See ABIDE.

abolish

See ELIMINATE.

aborigine, aboriginal

aborigine abbŏríjjini /æbəˈrɪdʒɪni/ *noun*, means someone belonging to the race or people who were the original inhabitants of an area and in this sense it is not capitalized. When written with an initial capital A, it used to be the normal way to refer to the pre-European inhabitants of Australia. Both 'native Australian' and 'Koori' (original inhabitants of south-eastern Australia) are preferred by such people to **Aborigine**.

aboriginal abbŏríjjinăl /æbə'rɪʤənəl/ *adjective & noun*, describes the people, animals or plants native to an area from the earliest times. In this sense the word is not capitalized: *The call went out to help dismantle the myths that continue to belittle aboriginal people throughout the world*. When capitalized as an adjective or noun it describes the people already living in Australia before the Europeans arrived in the eighteenth century: *The selection illustrates 200 years of Australian painting from the earliest colonial art to contemporary Aboriginal work*.

> *Indigenous* or *indigenous people* are suitable – and preferred – replacements for both of these terms.

abort, abortion, miscarriage

abort *verb*, means to terminate a pregnancy: *After the blood test, the hospital recommended her to abort the pregnancy*. This may be either from natural causes or by deliberate intervention. **Abort** also means to terminate a process, especially if it is likely to fail in any case: *The rocket launch had to be aborted due to a technical fault*.

abortion *noun*, means the termination of a pregnancy by deliberate intervention: *The question whether to legalize abortion is still undecided in many countries*. In a general sense, **abortion** can mean something that is badly made or poorly constructed: *That building is an abortion and should be pulled down*. This is informal usage.

miscarriage *noun*, means the termination of a pregnancy by natural causes: *The woman was depressed after her third miscarriage*. In non-medical use, *miscarriage of justice* is a phrase commonly used to express the wrongful conviction of an innocent person.

about, around, round

about *adverb*, is a term of approximation often used before quantitative amounts, particularly with reference to distance or size: *We had to walk about 12 miles when the car broke down*. In informal speech, *round about* is often used in this sense. See SOME (ANY).

around *adverb*, is a term of approximation that usually refers to time, cost or number: *He'll be home around six o'clock*; *There were around 12,000 people at the concert*. In informal speech, *around about* is often used in this sense. In another sense, it also means in many parts of an area: *We backpacked around Scandinavia last summer*; or on or to the other side of something: *You will find the supermarket just around the corner*.

round *adverb*, is most commonly used for direction or movement, not approximation. Thus it can mean travelling in a circle: *The moon goes round the earth*; or surrounding: *Chairs are drawn up round the table*. **Round** can also be used to refer to reversing direction: *She turned the car round before going to bed*. In all these cases, AE would use *around*.

> Note that *round* on its own cannot be used for approximation.

above, below (in reports)

above *adverb*, is often used to refer to something mentioned earlier on the same page or on a previous page: *The above comments can be questioned, however, as . . .* An alternative is *the preceding comments . . .*

below *adverb*, is used to refer to something mentioned later on the same page or on a later page in a report: *The information below is attributed to a BBC Insight report last June*. An alternative is *the information that follows . . .* See UNDERNEATH.

abrogate, arrogate

abrogate *verb*, means to annul a law or abolish a custom: *This is a totalitarian government which disregards individual liberty and abrogates human rights*. See ANNUL.

arrogate *verb*, means to seize power without justification: *He arrogated to himself the authority to disregard the Supreme Court*.

> These are both formal words.

absorb, adsorb

absorb *verb*, means to soak up or to take in an idea or substance: *The CO_2 will be absorbed by the porous sandstone rock*. Figuratively it means to be engrossed: *She was absorbed in her book*.

adsorb *verb*, is a technical word meaning to retain something on a surface layer: *This* *chemical will adsorb on rock surfaces and will lead to rupturing of the water film.*

abstract, extract

abstract ábstrakt /'æbstrækt/ *noun, adjective & verb* ăbstrákt /əb'strækt/ *verb*. As a noun, this means a summary of a report or paper usually in about 250 words (half a page of A4). As an adjective it means existing in thought or just as an idea: *The state – like communism – was too abstract, too vague for her.* **Abstract** can also refer to an art movement, and artistic expression, which does not try to represent the world in a naturalistic way. Note that the stress is on the first syllable. As a verb in a formal sense, **abstract** means to take out, or remove something: *The water company plans to abstract five million gallons from the river.* Note that the stress is on the second syllable.

extract éckstrakt /'ekstrækt/ *noun &* ickstrákt /ɪk'strækt/ *verb*. As a noun, this means a short passage from a book that provides a sample of its style and content: *He allowed an extract from his latest novel to appear in the Sunday papers.* As a verb, it means to remove one substance from another and also to obtain evidence or information: *The journalists managed to extract some crucial evidence from the smokescreen of the official report.*

abuse, misuse

abuse ăbéwss /ə'bjuːs/ *noun*, ăbéwz /ə'bjuːz/ *verb*, as a noun means poor treatment, the violent and improper use of something, or the insulting use of language: *He was imprisoned after being found guilty of repeated child abuse.* As a verb, **abuse** means to mistreat someone or something, either physically, or in words: *I expect people to regard this as my house and not to abuse my privacy.*

misuse miss-éwss /mɪs'juːs/ *noun*, miss-éwz /mɪs'juːz/ *verb*, means the use of something incorrectly or for a purpose it was not designed for: *The guarantee does not cover the misuse of this vacuum cleaner for gardening.*

> Note that as nouns, *abuse* and *misuse* rhyme with 'juice', but as verbs they rhyme with 'news'.

abysmal, abyss, abyssal

abysmal ăbízmăl /ə'bɪzməl/ *adjective*, means very bad: *The food in that hotel is abysmal.* In this sense it is an informal term not to be used in formal writing. Both uneatable and inedible are alternatives in the above context. In its original meaning referring to a very deep or bottomless pit, **abysmal** is only used in poetic contexts.

abyss ăbíss /ə'bɪs/ *noun*, means a hole or chasm with no apparent bottom: *He gazed into the smoking abyss of the volcanic crater.* In a figurative sense, it means a very dangerous situation: *Unless the congress takes the correct decisions, it will plunge the country into an abyss of confrontation.*

abyssal ăbíssăl /ə'bɪsl̩/ *adjective*, is a technical term that describes the ocean depths, especially those between 3,000 and 6,000 metres: *Abyssal mapping operations.*

> Note that all these words are stressed on the second syllable.

academic, scientist

academic *adjective & noun*. As an adjective, this normally means anything associated with university education such as *academic standards, academic freedom.* In this sense it is a positive word. More negatively, it also describes something that is without practical application or relevance: *We have already won the overall competition, so the result of this match is purely academic.* As a noun, **academic** is used to mean a teacher or researcher in higher education. See SCHOLAR.

scientist *noun*, is someone who is trained in or works in science, especially the natural sciences: *He's a world-famous scientist searching for a cancer cure.*

academic record

See TRANSCRIPT.

accede

See AGREE.

accent, accentuate

accent áksĕnt /'æksənt/ *noun &* ăksént /ək'sent/ *verb*. As a noun this has many meanings relating to the study of language.

First, it means the way a person speaks, in particular the features that show where a person comes from, geographically, historically or socially: *Queen Victoria spoke with a typical nineteenth-century upper-class English accent*. It also means the little mark added to letters in some languages to change the pronunciation, or to show where the stress of a word comes, for instance the acute accent written above the two e's of *résumé* to distinguish it from the verb *resume*. Third, it is used to mean the stress that emphasizes one syllable of a word more than the others. In a more general sense, it means emphasis on one aspect of something: *These areas of special planning control have a strong accent on the environmental effects of any development*. As a noun, **accent** is stressed on the first syllable. As a verb, **accent** means to emphasize something: *Heels click and stamp to accent the appropriate beats*. When it is used as a verb, **accent** is usually stressed on the second syllable in BE.

accentuate *verb*, means to draw attention to something in order to make it noticeable: *The thickness of some lines on these maps accentuates the importance of these roads*. The related noun is *accentuation*.

accept, except

accept *verb*, means either to take something that is offered: *As it was his only job offer, he decided to accept the offer of employment*; or to agree to something that cannot be changed: *We have to accept that this is not an ideal world*.

except *preposition & verb*. As a preposition, this means not including, or omitting something: *The room above the pub was quiet except on Saturday nights*. It can often be replaced by 'apart from'. As a verb, to **except** means to leave out or exclude: *If we except the years at Harvard, this was the best period of his life*. This is a formal word.

access, excess, excessive

access *noun & verb*. As a noun, this means entry or admittance: *There is no way to gain access to the gallery from this lift*. As a verb, it is widely used to mean open an electronic file: *Email messages can also be accessed from your mobile*, as well as to enter a physical location. The associated adjective is *accessible*, which refers to something that can be reached or entered: *The well-lit, easily accessible car park is reserved for managers*. See ENTRY.

excess écksess /'ekses/, or ěkséss /ɪk'ses/ *noun*, écksess /'ekses/ *adjective*. As a noun, this means something more than is permitted or needed: *About 20 per cent of these children had levels of mercury in excess of the safety limit*. In insurance terminology, the **excess** is the amount the policy holder will have to pay before the insurance company meets any claim. As an adjective, this means additional and not needed: *Blot wet hair with a towel to remove excess water*. The phrase *excess baggage* refers to the weight of baggage that is above the permitted limit.

excessive *adjective*, means more than is reasonable: *Ten pints of beer regularly night after night seems to me like excessive drinking*.

accessory

See AUXILIARY.

accommodation, accommodations

accommodation *noun*, means a room or building where someone can live or stay: *Student accommodation in town is always hard to find at the beginning of term*. It is an uncountable noun when used in this sense. As a countable noun, **accommodation** means a settlement, agreement or compromise: *The two sides came to an accommodation*. In BE this word is only used in the singular.

accommodations is the plural of accommodation, but is used only in AE: *Overnight accommodations available this summer*.

> Note that the correct spelling has double -cc- and double -mm-.

accomplish

See ACHIEVE.

accord

See TREATY.

accountable

See RESPONSIBLE.

accumulate, cumulative, accumulative, acquisitive

accumulate *verb*, means to build up or collect something: *As a student, she accumulated a lot of debt*. In this context of gathering together, amass is an alternative term. However, only **accumulate** is possible in a sentence such as: *Debts began to accumulate*, where there is no object.

cumulative *adjective*, means increasing in strength or importance as successive amounts are added: *The cumulative effect of the drug started to cause concern*. Here, the focus is on qualitative results. In financial accounts the *cumulative total* refers to a running total.

accumulative *adjective*, also means increasing gradually and focuses on quantitative aspects: *The Baltic is very susceptible to the accumulative effects of pollution*.

acquisitive *adjective*, means wanting to obtain and keep lots of possessions: *Many museums have benefited from the acquisitive habits of rich donors who collected anything and everything*.

accuracy

See PRECISION.

accurate

See PRECISE.

acetic

See AESTHETIC.

achieve, accomplish, attain

achieve *verb*, means to reach an objective or standard, especially over a period of time: *A time limit is set, usually three months, within which it is hoped to achieve the goals*.

accomplish *verb*, can mean the same as *achieve*, but has an additional sense of successfully completing something: *This kind of resourcefulness can accomplish a lot in business*. The related adjective, *accomplished*, describes a person who does something with great skill: *She is an accomplished pianist*. Remember that this word is spelt with double -cc-.

attain *verb*, means to reach a certain standard or goal, and is particularly used when referring to levels, sizes and ages: *These benefits are payable for those who have attained the age of 65*. In another sense it means to succeed in *achieving* something after a long period of trying: *Minorities are gradually attaining more power in Australia*. This is a formal word.

acid, acrid, pungent

acid *adjective*, means having a sharp, bitter taste: *The strong lemon tea left an acid taste in her mouth*. An *acid comment* is an unkind one, and an *acid test* means a crucial trial: *The acid test of a good leader is how well they select a style to suit the circumstances*.

acrid *adjective*, means unpleasantly bitter in taste or smell: *The old man ignited his pipe and a cloud of acrid smoke rose to the low, blackened beams*. Figuratively, an *acrid parting* means an angry and bitter one.

pungent *adjective*, means strong in taste or smell: *The pungent smell of curry hit him as he walked into the kitchen*.

acknowledge, admit

acknowledge *verb*, means to confirm that something has been received: *I should be grateful if you would acknowledge receipt of this letter*. It also means to recognize or accept a truth: *Many animal rights campaigners acknowledge that they too may have to compromise*. **Acknowledge** is used in more formal contexts to mean to thank: *The Scottish Council is pleased to acknowledge the support of the European Commission*. The related noun *acknowledgement* can also be spelt *acknowledgment*. See ACKNOWLEDGEMENTS (WRITING SKILLS).

admit *verb*, means to accept the truth of something: *They were reluctant to admit that the project had influenced them*. It also means to allow access: *This voucher will admit two adults and up to three children to the theme park*. See ACCESS.

acoustic, acoustics

acoustic *adjective*, refers to hearing, sound or the science of sound. The *acoustic nerve* is one of the nerves in the head, which controls hearing and balance. **Acoustic** is also found in expressions such as *acoustic guitar*, meaning one in which the sound is not amplified electronically. Many technical expressions use the related adjective *acoustical* in terms such as *acoustical measurement* and *acoustical shadow*. In AE, *acoustical* means the same as **acoustic**.

acoustics *uncountable noun*, has two meanings. First, it is the science of sound, when, like other academic subjects ending in '-ics', it always takes a singular verb: *Acoustics is an important subject for phoneticians to study*. Second, it means the sound properties of a room or a building. Here it takes a plural verb: *The acoustics of the hall seem admirably suited to this music*. See **-ICS**.

acquaintance, friend

acquaintance *noun*, is someone you know, but not very well: *Mr Hunter is just a business acquaintance*. *Acquaintance* also means a slight friendship: *He hoped their acquaintance would develop into something more*.

friend *noun*, is used for a person you have developed affection for: *Imagine that you had just met an old friend*. A *close friend* or a *special friend* may imply a person you are sexually intimate with. See **BOYFRIEND, GUY (MATE), PARTNER**.

acquiesce

See **AGREE**.

acquisitive

See **ACCUMULATE**.

acrid

See **ACID**.

acronym

See **ABBREVIATION**.

acumen, acuity

acumen áckyoŏmĕn /ˈækjʊmən/ *uncountable noun*, means the ability to understand matters correctly and act quickly: *The PM's acumen enabled him to ride the storm*.

acuity ăkéw-iti /əˈkjuːɪti/ *noun*, means the ability to think, see or hear clearly: *The acuity of his perception was impressive*. This is a formal word and keenness is a more common alternative.

acute, chronic (medical uses)

acute *adjective*, refers to a sudden illness or a very serious medical condition as in a crisis: *In a very acute illness the treatment may need to be repeated every hour or two*.

chronic *adjective*, refers to a serious medical disease or other condition that persists for a long time and may be difficult to cure: *Seven years after the accident, the pilot was still suffering from chronic pain*.

AD, BC, BCE, CE

AD stands for *Anno Domini* (Latin for 'in the year of our Lord') and is written before the year: *Pompeii was destroyed in AD 79*. Although some people argue that it is incorrect to use '*in* AD 79' as in Latin *anno* means '*in* the year', the combination '*in* AD 79' is in general use. Another criticism is that **AD** should not be combined with *century*, because a century cannot be in the year of anything. Nevertheless, when combined with the name of a century, **AD** comes at the end: *The church dated back to the fourth century AD*.

BC stands for *before Christ* and is written after the year: *Julius Caesar was assassinated in 44 BC*. Note that **AD** and **BC** are generally written in small capitals in published text.

BCE stands for *before Common Era*, and is increasingly used as a replacement for **BC**, since many of the countries now using the Western (formerly Christian) calendar do not have a Christian heritage.

CE stands for *Common Era*, and may be seen particularly in AE. The numbering is identical to that in **AD** terms, so that *2008 CE* is the same exactly as *AD 2008*. This is a way of avoiding using Christian terminology in a worldwide calendar.

adapt, adopt, adept

adapt *verb*, means to adjust to something: *In Western Australia he had to adapt to a climate with extreme summer temperatures*. When **adapt** has an object, it means to change something to suit new requirements: *She adapted the recipe to suit her vegetarian daughter-in-law*. See **CONFORM (COINCIDE)**.

adopt *verb*, means to start to use a new method or attitude: *The town adopted the idea of recycling domestic waste*. In another sense it means to take on the legal responsibility for someone else's child: *When his parents were killed in a car crash, an aunt adopted him.* **Adopt** also means to select a new name: *For his own safety, the witness had to adopt a new name after the court found his attackers guilty.* This word must have an object.

adept *adjective & noun*. As an adjective, this means highly skilled: *He became adept at inventing excuses for not doing his homework.* As a noun, it means someone who is highly skilled: *Adepts of karate can smash concrete with their limbs.* In BE, the adjective is usually stressed on the second syllable, and the noun on the first.

adaptation, adoption

adaptation *noun*, means a change from one form or use to a different one: *The most common type of conversion project at the present time is the adaptation of a mill or warehouse into a block of dwellings.* In another context this refers to the conversion of a novel or stage play into a television programme or film.

adoption *noun*, means the taking of legal responsibility for someone else's child. A person who adopts a child is most commonly called an *adoptive parent*. The more general meaning, the acceptance and carrying out of a particular course of action, is less common: *This may work against your adoption of a more effective and efficient approach to note-making.*

adapter, adaptor

adapter *noun*, is a person who changes something from one form to another, for instance, making a television series out of a novel.

adaptor *noun*, is a piece of equipment that allows two otherwise incompatible items to be connected, for instance an unearthed electrical plug with an earthed socket.

added value

See VALUE CREATION.

addendum, addenda

addendum *noun*, means an inserted section of a book containing supplementary information. It is an additional element to the main text: *Addendum 1. This contains the list of typographical errors.*

addenda *plural noun*, is the plural of *addendum* and is often used as a heading: *Addenda: Since the publication of these recommendations a number of extensions have been published.* See APPENDIX.

address

See TALK.

addresses in letters

See WRITING SKILLS.

adept

See ADAPT.

adequate

See ENOUGH.

adhesion, adherence

adhesion *noun*, means the quality of sticking to a surface: *If you go into a corner too fast the tyres will lose their adhesion.* In medical use, **adhesion** means the sticking together of internal body surfaces as a result of surgery or inflammation.

adherence *noun*, means support for a particular party or ideology: *Fidel Castro declared his formal adherence to Marxism-Leninism in 1961.*

adjective

See GRAMMAR TIPS.

adjourn, postpone

adjourn *verb*, means to break off a meeting that has started: *We adjourn the meeting until next week*, or, more informally, it can also mean to move somewhere else: *After the wedding ceremony they adjourned to the hotel for the reception.* See CANCEL (ANNUL).

postpone *verb*, means to rearrange a meeting, seminar or other arrangement that has not yet started for a later date: *The takeover negotiations were postponed because of the director's sudden illness.* See RAIN CHECK.

adjure

See ABJURE.

administration

See GOVERNMENT.

admission, admittance, admissible

admission *noun*, means the confession and acceptance of responsibility: *He made the following admission of guilt to the court.* It also means the right to enter a place, especially when referring to the cost of entry to something: *The gallery does not charge for admission*.

admittance *uncountable noun*, means the permission to enter a place: *No admittance after 5 p.m.* Note that it is often used in a negative sense: *Admittance is prohibited.* Although the related verb *admit* can refer to confession, **admittance** is not used in this sense.

admissible *adjective*, means something that can be allowed in court, or more generally in a legal sense: *The police expected that this would be admissible evidence*.

admit

See ACKNOWLEDGE.

adopt

See ADAPT.

adoption

See ADAPTATION.

adsorb

See ABSORB.

advantageous, beneficial

advantageous *adjective*, means bringing advantage that gives practical benefit such as more profit or better results: *Travel in low season is highly advantageous for those who are not tied to 9–5 jobs.*

beneficial *adjective*, means having a general good influence, or bringing benefit to a situation: *Aerobic exercise is beneficial to the heart.*

adverb

See GRAMMAR TIPS.

adverse, averse

adverse *adjective*, means unfavourable, or harmful: *Other people can also help by noting the beneficial and adverse effects of treatment.* **Adverse** is used with abstract nouns such as *adverse climate conditions, adverse effects.* The word is stressed on the first syllable: ádverss /'ædvɜːrs/.

averse *adjective*, means opposing or having a strong dislike for something, or for people. Also note that *not* is commonly used with **averse**, so care has to be taken not to write the opposite of what you mean: *As a former MI5 operative, he was not averse to secrecy.* This means that he was happy to keep things secret. **Averse** is almost always used with the preposition *to*. **Averse** generally follows the verbs *to be* or *to feel*. Note that this word is stressed on the second syllable: ăvérss /ə'vɜːrs/.

advertisement, advertorial, documercial, infotainment

advertisement *noun*, means an announcement or public notice giving details of an event, or of goods or services for sale: *The advertisement says, 'write for application form'*. In this sense it is often abbreviated to *advert* or *ad*. **Advertisements** placed in newspapers by individuals or small companies offering goods or services, or requesting the supply of goods or services, are usually grouped together by type in a section called *classified ads*, or *small ads*. In another sense, **advertisement** means the process of making announcements: *This post involves being available to assist in the advertisement of fund-raising activities*.

advertorial *noun*, means an advertisement that is written in the style of a newspaper article, and that may be intended to mislead readers into thinking that it is part of the editorial material: *The advertorial is intended to look as much like the other editorial pages as possible*. See BLEND WORDS (WORD FORMATION).

documercial *noun*, means a film made in the style of a documentary that is in fact an advertisement. See BLEND WORDS (WORD FORMATION).

infotainment *uncountable noun*, means radio or television broadcasting that uses an entertaining method of putting across information. See **BLEND WORDS (WORD FORMATION)**.

advice, advise

advice *uncountable noun*, means a recommended course of action. Since it is an uncountable noun, an amount of advice is expressed by the phrase *a piece of advice* or *some advice*. It always takes a singular verb and determiner: *Women's Aid: provides advice, support and accommodation for abused women and children*. Note that **advice** is replaced by a singular pronoun. The ending rhymes with 'ice'.

advise *verb*, means to make recommendations: *Can you advise me how to go about this and what bits I need?* The ending rhymes with 'eyes'.

adviser, advisor

adviser *noun*, is a person who gives advice. This spelling is usual in BE: *If your car is damaged or stolen, please contact your Insurance Adviser*. Note that the related adjective is spelt *advisory*.

advisor is an alternative BE spelling for *adviser* and is the usual spelling in AE.

AE

AE means American English and is the abbreviation used throughout this book. See **AMERICAN ENGLISH (BRITISH ENGLISH)**.

ae, e, oe

In words of Greek and Latin origin, the sounds ee [iː] and i [ɪ] are sometimes spelt **ae** or **oe** in BE. The joined **æ** spelling is rarely used today in AE, except in the plural suffix -ae.

Examples:

BE	*AE*	*Pronunciation*	
aesthetic	esthetic	eess-théttick	iːs'θetɪk
amoeba	ameba	ăméebă	ə'miːbə
anaemic	anemic	ănéemik	ə'niːmɪk
anaesthetic	anesthetic	annĕs-théttik	ænəs'θetɪk
archaeology	archeology	aarki-ólŏji	ɑːrki'ɒlədʒi
diarrhoea	diarrhea	dī-ărée-ă	daɪə'rɪə
faeces	feces	féesseez	'fiːsiːz
oesophagus	esophagus	issóffăgŭss	ɪ'sɒfəgəs
oestrogen	estrogen	éeströjĕn	'iːstrədʒən
paedophile	pedophile	péedŏfīl	'piːdəfaɪl

See **PLURAL NOUNS (WORD FORMATION)**.

aeon

See **ERA**.

aerial, antenna

aerial *adjective & noun*. As an adjective, this describes something which is in or comes from the air, or that involves the use of aircraft: *Most aerial photographers are pilots who have taught themselves photography*. As a noun, in BE an **aerial** is a wire to transmit or receive radio waves: *If you adjust the aerial, you'll get better radio reception*.

antenna[1] *noun*, refers to the sense organ on the heads of insects: *The beetle's antenna helps it to locate prey by sensing the telltale vibrations of any small insect*. It can also be used figuratively to refer to a person's intuition: *He never allows his natural optimism to put his acute political and economic antenna out of action*. The plural form **antennae** is pronounced **anténnee** /æn'teniː/ in both BE and AE: *Usually insects smell by tuning their antennae to scents in the air*.

antenna[2] *noun*, in technical use means an arrangement of aerials. In this sense, the plural is **antennas**: *Antennas around the top of the ship pick up the radar signals*. In AE, **antenna** is used instead of the BE term *aerial*.

aero-

See **AIR-**.

aesthete, esthete

aesthete *noun*, means a person who understands and appreciates beauty. It is old-fashioned to spell this with 'æ'. See **AE- E- OE-**.

esthete is the usual AE spelling of *aesthete*.

aesthetic, ascetic, acetic

aesthetic *adjective*, describes that which is concerned with beauty, or something made in an artistic way: *Few people would choose* *to decorate a room without considering its aesthetic appeal*. In another sense, **aesthetic** describes something made in an artistic manner rather than a functional one: *The design of the chairs was more aesthetic than functional*. The usual AE spelling is *esthetic*.

ascetic ăsséttik /əˈsetɪk/ *adjective*, means living a simple life, or holding to very strict principles, especially for religious reasons: *His ascetic determination led him to sell his non-Christian books*.

acetic ăsséetik /əˈsiːtɪk/ *adjective*, refers to the type of acid that gives vinegar its sharp taste: *The chef has used diluted acetic acid coloured with caramel rather than a true vinegar*. See ACID.

a few

See FEW.

affect

See EFFECT.

affectation, affection

affectation *noun*, means behaviour that shows either insincerity: *He was not fooled by her rural affectation of innocence*; or artificiality: *This is an affectation as it is not necessary to wear jeans, baseball boots and earrings to devise good advertising*.

affection *noun*, means the feeling of liking or loving someone or something: *He is a typical hacker who is obsessed with programming but has a deep affection for the machine itself*. The plural form **affections** refers to a person's feelings: *She transferred her affections to someone who was not interested in computer science*.

affiliation, affinity

affiliation *noun*, is used mostly in a political or religious sense, and means that people belong to a particular group: *The European Parliament arranges the seating of delegates by political affiliation rather than by nationality*; or the official connection of one organization with another: *At the Edinburgh Conference of the Labour Party in 1936 a request for affiliation from the Communist Party was refused*.

affinity *noun*, means a relationship or the sense of belonging that one person or group has for another: *I personally felt a great affinity with the people of the highlands and islands*.

affix

See WORD FORMATION.

afflict

See INFLICT.

affluent

See RICH.

affront, effrontery

affront *noun*, means a remark or action that is usually deliberately offensive: *In his view, the paintings were an affront to public morality*.

effrontery *noun*, means shameless and impudent behaviour: *A member of the jury had the effrontery to challenge the judge's authority*.

African American

See BLACK.

afterwards, afterward

afterwards *adverb*, means at a later time. *We must find that child and look for the dog afterwards*. This is the normal BE spelling.

afterward *adverb*, is the normal AE form of *afterwards*.

age

See ERA.

aged

See OLD.

agenda, agendas, hidden agenda

agenda *noun*, means the subject matter to be discussed, usually in a meeting: *Make sure that there is a logical sequence to the items on the agenda*. In a broader sense, **agenda** refers to policy issues: *The agenda for integration is entirely determined by the government*. Note that although **agenda** is a Latin plural, in modern English it is a singular noun which takes a singular verb. The Latin singular *agendum* is not recommended.

agendas is the plural of **agenda**: *The agendas for the three spring meetings will be decided today.*

hidden agenda *noun*, means that the reason for an action or expression is kept secret because of ulterior motives: *We don't see how the company can survive with such a small workforce unless they have a hidden agenda.* Although most centres of power have one or more *hidden agendas* the last thing they will ever do is admit it in public.

aggravate, exacerbate

aggravate *verb*, means to make an unpleasant situation worse: *The proximity of Allied warships will only aggravate the situation in the Middle East.* It is also often used to mean deliberately irritate or annoy: *You shouldn't aggravate the person who will be marking your essay.* This is informal usage, and should be avoided in formal writing. See ANNOY.

exacerbate *verb*, in many cases means the same as aggravate, but is used only for situations, diseases or problems – never for people: *If this development is allowed to go ahead it will exacerbate the already serious parking problems in the village.* Note that this is stressed on the second syllable.

aggressive, offensive, forceful, vigorous

aggressive *adjective*, means behaving in a threatening and angry manner: *The aggressive behaviour of some pupils led to three teachers resigning.* In another sense, it means pushing certain aims and interests assertively and with determination: *Without aggressive and persistent action by our solicitors the Council would never have come to a decision.* Alternatives include active and dynamic.

offensive *adjective & noun*. As an adjective, this describes behaviour or language that causes hostility or distress: *Those who find press bias offensive can change their newspaper.* **Offensive** can also mean disgusting if associated with an unpleasant smell: *Herrings, although cheap and nutritious, added yet another offensive smell to poorly ventilated rooms.* As a noun, **offensive** is used in a military sense, to mean a sustained attack: *The rebels captured the country's second-largest city after an all-out offensive.*

forceful *adjective*, means dynamic and assertive. It is commonly used about people and their behaviour: *She was a forceful personality who did not suffer fools gladly.*

vigorous *adjective*, means very active and full of energy: *A free, honourable and vigorous press played a central role in exposing the president.* Note that **vigorous** is spelt with only one 'u'.

> *Vigorous* is the only word in this group that is free of negative associations.

agoraphobia

See CLAUSTROPHOBIA.

agree, accede, acquiesce

agree *verb*, means to have the same opinion as another person: *We agreed that it would be a good idea to write this book. Agree with* means have the same opinion about something: *I agree with the principles underlying freedom of speech.* Figuratively, if food does not *agree with* someone, it makes them ill. *Agree to* means accept a suggestion made by somebody else: *They agreed to the new pension plan.*

accede *verb*, means to agree or consent to something: *The dictator was forced to accede to their demands.* This is a formal word and *agree* is a less formal alternative.

acquiesce *verb*, means to accept something without argument, even if you do not agree: *It has to be made more dangerous to acquiesce than to dissent and this is not an easy trick to turn.* This is a formal word.

agreement, agrément, gentleman's agreement

agreement *noun*, means a negotiated arrangement between two or more parties. An **agreement** can be written or oral: *The plan looks unlikely to get agreement given the opposition by two of the bank's largest shareholders.* See TREATY.

agrément *noun*, borrowed from French, is found on a product's label to show that it has been approved by the relevant EU authority. Hence its meaning in English is approval.

gentleman's agreement means an unwritten, but binding agreement, based on trust and usually confirmed by a handshake. This may also be called a *gentlemen's agreement*.

> *'It is a written gentleman's agreement.'*
> (House of Representatives, 1989) **!**

agreement between subject and verb

See **GRAMMAR TIPS**.

aid, aide (nouns)

aid *uncountable noun*, means assistance, usually financial, that is often given by charities, governments or international organizations: *Considerable aid is always necessary for orphans in war zones*. More generally, **aid** means help, and in this sense is a countable noun: *The writer has used the plan as an aid to memory*. A *hearing aid* is a device to help the deaf to hear better.

aide *noun*, means an assistant in the armed forces, government and diplomatic corps: *It was announced that the president had appointed his brother as a presidential aide*. An *aide-memoire* is a document compiled, as it says, to assist the memory. In a diplomatic context, this is called a memorandum. See **MEMORANDUM (NOTE)**.

aid, abet (verbs)

aid *verb*, means to help to make something possible or easier: *Footballers and boxers, too, often have their entry into the sports world aided by zealous schoolteachers*.

abet *verb*, also means to help or encourage, but when the result is illegal or wrong: *Reports said that the Dec. 6 attack on the mosque was effectively abetted by the guards*. Note the 'tt' in the past and present participles. The phrase *aid and abet* means to help someone do something illegal.

AIDS

See **SYNDROME**.

aim, objective, goal, target

aim *noun*, means a desired purpose or intention: *The aim of the challenge was to encourage children to think for themselves*.

objective *noun*, means the overall purpose of an action. This word is frequently used in reports and more formal types of English: *The objective to reduce global carbon emissions was agreed at the international conference*.

goal *noun*, means the object of a precise ambition: *Marriage and motherhood need not be a girl's only goals in life*. Note that this is less formal than *objective*.

target *noun*, means something aimed at, and frequently occurs in connection with other terms: *target date, production target*. A value is often attached to **target**: *The government set an initial target of recycling 25 per cent of household waste*.

air-, aero-

air- is the prefix used in most of the words connected with aviation in BE and AE. Examples: *airborne, aircrew, aircraft* and *airport*.

aero- is the prefix used in a few words connected with aviation, or the properties of air. Examples: *aeronautics, aerodynamics, aerospace* and *aeroplane* (BE).

aircraft, plane, airplane

aircraft *noun*, means a flying vehicle. This includes aeroplanes, gliders and helicopters. It is often used in BE as an alternative for aeroplane. Note that in BE, **aircraft** is used for both the singular and plural forms: *Six aircraft were on the runway*.

plane *noun*, is the usual BE form for a powered flying vehicle with fixed wings. It is short for *aeroplane*.

airplane *noun*, is the AE form for a fixed-wing aircraft (in BE *aeroplane*). The usual plural is *aircraft*, but *airplanes* is a possible plural in AE.

airspace, aerospace

airspace *uncountable noun*, is the area of sky above a country that is legally controlled by that country: *The passenger plane inadvertently drifted into North Korean airspace*.

aerospace *uncountable noun*, is the industry that builds aircraft and equipment for use in space: *The aerospace industry is still doing extremely well*.

aisle

See ISLE.

alcohol, liquor, liqueur

alcohol *noun*, is a liquid that forms the intoxicating element in wine, spirits and beers. *Low alcohol* drinks include wines and beers from which most of the **alcohol** has been removed. *Non-alcoholic* drinks include soft drinks, which do not contain **alcohol**.

liquor líckŏr /ˈlɪkər/ *noun*, in a non-technical sense means a distilled spirit. Occasionally, **liquor** may refer to any alcoholic drink. **Liquor** is commonly used in AE to mean drinks such as vodka and whisky: *They do not touch hard liquor or even coffee*. The BE term for this is generally seen in the plural: spirits. **Liquor** may also refer to the non-alcoholic liquid in which food is cooked: *Gently reheat the leek sauce with the cooking liquor*.

liqueur lick-yŏŏr /lɪˈkjʊər/ *noun*, is a strong, sweet alcoholic drink that may be drunk in small quantities at the end of a meal: *Here you can browse through the book-lined shelves or simply relax with an after-dinner liqueur by the roaring log fire*. Note that the second syllable is pronounced like the word 'cure'.

ale

See BEER.

alien

See STRANGER.

alike

See SIMILAR.

allegation

See ASSERTION.

alleviate, assuage, ameliorate

alleviate *verb*, means to make pain or a problem less severe. This tends to be used for physical conditions and states: *More water should be recycled in order to alleviate shortages, according to a recent report*.

assuage *verb*, means to reduce the intensity of an unpleasant feeling, or to satisfy one's appetite: *Obsessive spending can assuage feelings of inner emptiness among compulsive shoppers*.

ameliorate *verb*, means to make something that is bad or unsatisfactory better. This term is generally used to talk about physical conditions such as poverty and widespread disease: *The United Nations is taking steps to ameliorate the situation for those suffering drought in the Sahel region*.

alley

See STREET.

all of

See MOST OF.

all ready, already

all ready *adverb + adjective*, means completely prepared: *Your brother's upstairs all ready to go*. As a noun, **all** may also be followed by **ready** as an adverb, meaning that everything is prepared: *I've just cleaned them all ready for this afternoon*.

already *adverb*, refers either to something that has happened before now: *I've already seen everything that's on offer*; or before a time in the past: *Outside the window the day was already darkening*.

> A clue to which spelling is correct is in the pronunciation: two stresses means two words.

all right, alright

all right *pronoun + adverb*, means satisfactory, without problems, or suitable. It can also be used to ask for permission: *Will it be all right if I move the meeting forward?* It is also commonly used as an alternative to OK, which means agreed, or as a statement of reasonable health: *I calmed down and I was all right after about 10 minutes*.

alright *adverb*, is another spelling of *all right*, that many people consider incorrect. However, it is approved by some major dictionaries. It may therefore be better to avoid using **alright** in formal contexts.

all together, altogether

all together *pronoun + adverb*, means a number of things or people, taken as a group: *When all the fledglings have left the nest, it is rare to have them all together again*.

altogether *adverb*, means in total, completely or entirely: *This year the fund sponsored 10 sick children, and their parents, making a total of 32 altogether to date*. Note that **altogether** is often used to reduce the strength of a negative statement: *The warning notices pointing out the danger of bullets are not altogether a bluff*. The phrase *in the altogether* is used humorously to mean naked, but is only used following a verb. See **NAKED**.

allude, elude

allude ălléwd or ălo͝od /ə'ljuːd/ *verb*, means to mention or refer to something indirectly: *The reporter alluded to the President's secret fortune*. **Allude** is always followed by the word *to*, although an adverb may come between the two. See **ALLUSION (ILLUSION)**.

elude ĕléwd or ĕlo͝od /ɪ'ljuːd/ *verb*, means to evade or escape from someone or something, usually by skill: *Be quick, watchful, clever, like a wild creature that must elude the hunters*. If something **eludes** a person, it means that he or she has failed to achieve or understand it: *The note of mild panic in her voice did not elude him*. See **DELUSION (ILLUSION)**.

aloud

See **LOUD**.

already

See **ALL READY**.

alright

See **ALL RIGHT**.

altar, alter

altar *noun*, means the holy table or surface used in religious ceremonies: *The bride and groom walked towards the altar*.

alter *verb*, means to make something different: *Winning the lottery altered his bank balance, not his character*.

altercation

See **ARGUMENT**.

alternative, alternate

alternative *noun & adjective*. As a noun, this originally meant a choice between two options, but now it is increasingly common to see references to 'several alternatives': *The alternative for a manager if he does not like what is on offer in his present job is to move to a different one*. As an adjective, this describes a different approach, idea or plan that can be used instead of the present one: *This alternative plan will generate far more renewable energy*. It also describes something that is not conventionally or officially approved such as *alternative medicine* or an *alternative lifestyle*, which means an unconventional way of lifc.

alternate awltérnăt /ɔːl'tɜːrnət/ *adjective*, refers to two things that follow each other in a repeated pattern: *They practise these two methods of reproduction, sexual and asexual, in alternate generations*. Note that the stress is on the second syllable. In AE, **alternate** is also used where BE prefers *alternative*: *Our policy is having alternate suppliers*.

alternate áwltĕrnayt /'ɔːltərneɪt/ *verb*, means to vary regularly between two or more things: *Scenes of peace and meditation, enacted in a cemetery, alternate with chaos and consternation*. Note that the stress is on the first syllable, and that the final syllable rhymes with 'late'.

although, even though, though

although and **even though** *conjunctions*, both mean in spite of the fact that, or but, and are mainly used at the beginning of a sentence: *Although/Even though we ran, we did not catch the bus*; or, by turning the sentence round, in the middle: *We didn't catch the bus, although/even though we ran*.

though *conjunction & adverb*. As a conjunction, **though** is used at the beginning, middle or end of a sentence. It has the same meaning as *although* and *even though*, but is more common in spoken English. As an adverb, **though** may be used at the end of a sentence, where it means however: *We did not catch the bus, though*. Note that a sentence that starts with one of these words should *not* contain the word *however*. See **HOWEVER**.

altitude

See **HEIGHT**.

altogether

See **ALL TOGETHER**.

A

aluminium, aluminum

aluminium alyŏŏmíni-ŭm /æljʊ'mɪnɪəm/ *uncountable noun*, is a lightweight metal with the chemical symbol Al. This is the BE spelling and pronunciation, with stress on the third syllable.

aluminum ălóominŭm /ə'luːmɪnəm/ is the AE spelling and pronunciation of *aluminium*. Note that there is only one 'i' in the AE spelling, and that the stress is on the second syllable.

alumni, former student

alumni ălúm-nī /ə'lʌmnaɪ/ *plural noun*, strictly speaking means only the former male students of a university. However, **alumni** is also used for former students of both sexes. The singular forms, *alumnus* (male) and *alumna* (female) are not very common. In BE, it is more common to refer to 'graduates' than to **alumni**. The *alumni association* is the organization in a university to keep in touch with the **alumni** (of both sexes). The final syllable is pronounced 'nigh'.

former student *noun*, means someone who has attended courses at a college or university, and is a more general term than graduate or *alumni*. See STUDENT.

ambassador, legate

ambassador *noun*, means the senior diplomat sent to another country to represent his or her government: *The South Korean ambassador in Washington visited the State Department on 20 January*. In a more general sense, an **ambassador** is anyone who represents or promotes the interests of a group or activity: *He has made some good films and is a good ambassador for the industry*. See EMBASSY, ENVOY.

legate léggăt /'legət/ *noun*, is the word used for an ambassador appointed by the Pope to represent him abroad: *The Pope, who had agreed to be godfather, sent a Legate to represent him at the christening*. See LEGATION (EMBASSY).

ambivalent, ambiguous

ambivalent ambívvălĕnt /æm'bɪvələnt/ *adjective*, means having simultaneous opposing feelings: *Governments have an ambivalent attitude towards defectors*. The related noun is *ambivalence*: *Most of us feel some ambivalence towards computer games and their effects on child health*.

ambiguous *adjective*, describes something that can be understood in different ways: *Some legal principles tend to remain highly ambiguous and not worth the paper they are printed on*. In another sense it can mean not clearly defined: *His gesture to the referee was ambiguous*. The related noun is *ambiguity*: *The key terms should be clear and defined so as to avoid ambiguity*.

ameliorate

See ALLEVIATE.

amend, *emend*, correct

amend *verb*, means to change something, usually in order to correct a mistake or to avoid confusion: *A proposal was put forward to amend the resolution by adding the following. . . .*

emend *verb*, means to correct a mistake, without necessarily making the text easier to read or understand: *Software and support should take account of the possible need to emend the data after it has been released*.

correct *verb*, means to change something by removing the errors: *Proofread your work and correct any mistakes you find*.

America, (The) Americas, North America, Central America, Latin America, South America

America *noun*, can be used to mean either the political unit: the United States of America, or the geographical land mass comprising North and South America joined by Central America. Canadians and citizens of other American countries may be annoyed if they are referred to as 'Americans'.

(The) Americas *plural noun*, means the geographical land mass comprising North and South America joined by Central America. This is usually preceded by the definite article and always takes a plural verb.

North America *noun*, consists of Canada, the United States of America (excluding Hawaii) and Mexico.

Central America *noun*, consists of all those states to the south of Mexico and to the north of Colombia.

Latin America *noun*, comprises all the states of South, Central and North America where the principal language is either Spanish or Portuguese, i.e. almost the whole of South and Central America (excluding Suriname, Guyana, French Guiana and Belize), and Mexico.

South America *noun*, comprises all the states to the south of Panama.

American English

See BRITISH ENGLISH.

American Indian

See NATIVE AMERICAN.

American plan

See PENSION.

American road types

divided highway *noun*, is an AE term for the BE dual carriageway, meaning a road with two lanes in each direction, separated by a central raised part, making it impossible for vehicles to cross from one side to the other.

expressway *noun*, is an AE term for an urban highway.

freeway *noun*, is an AE term for a dual carriageway with limited access. The term 'free' means that such roads are without toll charges.

interstate *noun*, also called *interstate highway*, is a major US highway that crosses state borders. It is a dual carriageway with limited access. Interstates are numbered with I- followed by the road number, which are even from east to west, and odd from north to south. For instance, I-90 runs from Boston to Seattle, while I-65 starts in Mobile, Alabama, and ends in Gary, Indiana. See INTESTATE.

throughway *noun*, is a general AE term for a main highway. An alternative spelling is *thruway*.

turnpike *noun*, is an AE term for a main highway. **Turnpike** was originally another term for tollgate. Thus it is used for a highway where a road toll is charged.

Americanisms

Americanisms are usually defined as words or other features of English that are characteristic of American rather than British usage. This means that some terms have different meanings in AE and BE, such as *corn, gas*. Many terms like *live wire, rain check* and *third degree* that were originally Americanisms are now widely used elsewhere. In other cases the terms are common only in AE, such as *sidewalk* and *traffic circle*. The same can be said for AE idioms and spellings. See AMERICAN ENGLISH (BRITISH ENGLISH).

amiable, amicable

amiable *adjective*, describes people and expressions that appear good-natured and friendly: *He was a very kind, youngish, amiable scholar of great distinction.*

amicable *adjective*, is used to describe an agreement reached without argument or a friendly relationship: *Jack agreed on her having custody of the child, and an amicable arrangement was made regarding visiting.*

amnesty, moratorium

amnesty *noun*, means an official order by a government that frees a specific group of prisoners: *The new president agreed to sweeping reforms and an amnesty for political offenders.* In another sense it is a period in which people can admit to doing something illegal without being punished: *The weapons amnesty resulted in 341 knives being handed in at police stations across the county.*

moratorium *noun*, means the official halt to an action for a specified period of time: *The organization is mobilizing support for a moratorium on executions in Texas.*

among(st), amid(st), between

among(st) *preposition*, is used about people or things in a group: *Patel is now among the commonest names in British telephone directories.* **Among** is used when there are more than two people or things in the group. **Amongst** is an alternative form, mainly used in BE. See PREPOSITIONS (GRAMMAR TIPS).

amid(st) *preposition*, means in the middle of, or surrounded by: *They stood amid the station* *crowds, arguing; Cornelius climbed from the cab and stood amidst the rubble*. **Amidst** is used in more literary contexts than **amid**. See **MID-**.

between *preposition & adverb*, is used for people or things. **Between** is properly used just for two, but it is increasingly used to mean more than two, in constructions such as: *She shared the food equally between her six cats*. A better alternative here would be *She shared the food equally among her six cats*. If there are measurements or dates etc. after **between**, these should always be linked by the word *and*. Example: *Voters born between 1975 and 1979*.

amoral, immoral

amoral *adjective*, describes actions that are outside moral standards or ethics: *We live in an amoral age – no one cares about moral standards today*.

immoral *adjective*, describes actions that go against accepted moral standards or what most people regard as good and honest: *We would consider it immoral to treat animals as if they had no ecological value*. See **IMMORALITY**.

amount of, number of

amount of *noun + preposition*, is used to describe a quantity and only applies to uncountable nouns; that is nouns that do not have a plural, such as *furniture* and *butter* or abstract terms like *influence* and *knowledge*: *The book attempts to compress a large amount of information into just a few hundred pages*.

number of *noun + preposition*, means several or some and applies to countable nouns; that is nouns that have a plural. When **a number of** is followed by a plural noun, it takes a plural verb: *A number of voters are undecided*. However, when the definite article is used instead, **the number of**, this means the size of the total and always takes a singular verb: *The number of voters outside is increasing*.

One way to remember whether to use a plural or singular verb with *number* is the codeword **PAST**. This stands for **P**lural with **A** number, **S**ingular with **T**he number.

ampersand

See **AND, SYMBOLS**.

amulet

See **TALISMAN**.

anaemia, anemia

anaemia *noun*, means the condition of suffering from a deficiency of red blood cells. This is the BE spelling. See **AE- E- OE-**.

anemia *noun*, is the usual AE spelling of *anaemia*.

anaemic, anemic

anaemic *adjective*. This is the related adjective to *anaemia* and is the BE spelling. See **AE- E- OE-**.

anemic *adjective*, is the usual AE spelling of *anaemic*.

anaesthesia, anesthesia

anaesthesia *noun*, is the state of being unable to feel pain. This is the BE spelling. See **AE- E- OE-**.

anesthesia *noun*, is the usual AE spelling of *anaesthesia*.

anaesthetic, anaesthetics, analgesic

anaesthetic *noun & adjective*. As a noun, this is a substance that creates insensitivity to pain. A *general anaesthetic* makes the patient unconscious, while a *local anaesthetic* makes only a part of the body insensitive to pain. As an adjective, **anaesthetic** describes a substance that makes a person or animal insensitive to pain in any part of their body: *The dentist administered an anaesthetic spray*. This is the BE spelling. The usual AE spelling is *anesthetic*. See **AE- E- OE-**.

anaesthetics *uncountable noun*, is the study or practice of *anaesthesia*. This is the BE spelling. The usual AE spelling is *anesthetics*.

analgesic annăljeéezik /ænəlˈdʒiːzɪk/ *noun*, is a drug that relieves pain: *Paracetamol is an effective analgesic in cases of headache*.

anal

See **ANNALS**.

analyse, analyze

analyse *verb*, means to examine methodologically and in detail. This is the BE spelling. See **-ISE -IZE, -YSE -YZE**.

analyze is always the AE spelling.

analyst, annalist

analyst *noun*, is a person who analyses, i.e. who makes a detailed examination of data in order to give an opinion on them: *City analysts look for signs of recession*. By itself, **analyst** is often used to mean *psychoanalyst*.

annalist *noun*, is a person who writes annals, i.e. the historical records of a period (originally year by year): *The main annalist's fondness for tales of woe in this case led him to distort the facts*.

ancient, antique, antiquated

ancient *adjective*, describes very old things that belong to the distant past, such as an *ancient civilization*. Informally, it can refer in a humorous way to people who are considered old: *My Dad's ancient: he's just had his thirtieth birthday*.

> *'Beef broth with ancient bohemian meat balls.'*
> (Restaurant menu) **!**

antique *adjective & noun*, describes things made valuable by age: *A beautiful grade II listed Regency building, it is furnished in both an antique and modern style*.

antiquated *adjective*, describes ideas and things that are outdated and not in favour: *This is a modern health services research unit with a director who has an antiquated view of science*.

ancillary

See **AUXILIARY**.

and, ampersand

and *conjunction*, is used in several ways. The most common is connecting two or more elements or things: *They played a trio for violin, cello and piano*. Note that the determiner before **and** is not repeated before the second term if the two are closely connected. Compare: *His father and mother; His socks and shoes* with: *His father and <u>his</u> nephew* and *His socks and <u>his</u> umbrella*. Another use of **and** is in mathematics to mean plus: *Two and two equal four*. And what about using **and** at the beginning of a sentence? It is not incorrect, but in writing should be restricted to some special effect such as summing up matters: *And now, we come to how much the loan will cost*. Do not overuse this construction as it is likely to be irritating to some readers. See **OXFORD COMMA (PUNCTUATION GUIDE), AGREEMENT (GRAMMAR TIPS)**.

ampersand *noun*, is the symbol **&**. This is used either informally to replace *and* in short notes and in set phrases like *R&D* (research and development); or formally in the names of companies: *Procter & Gamble; AT&T; Johnson & Johnson*. Note that unless specific reference is being made to the symbol **&** itself, this is always read as 'and'. It is a useful symbol to use when groups are being written about. For instance, writing *Oliver & Boyd and Hodder & Stoughton* rather than *Oliver and Boyd and Hodder and Stoughton* makes it clear that there are two publishing houses involved, not three or four.

annalist

See **ANALYST**.

annals, anal

annals *plural noun*, means a chronicle of events: *In the annals of British maritime history there are few heroes more dazzling than Captain James Cook*. The singular, *annal*, also exists, but is rare.

anal áynăl /'eɪnəl/ *adjective*, describes anything relating to the anus. *Anal retentive* is a term used in psychology to describe someone who is obsessively tidy or fussy about something: *There was no way I was going to come across as an anal retentive simply because I had pride in my appearance*.

annex, annexe

annex[1] ănécks /ə'neks/ *verb*, means to acquire territory by force: *In 1939, Germany and the Soviet Union each annexed part of Poland*. Note that the verb is stressed on the second syllable.

A

annex[2] ánnecks /ˈæneks/ *noun*, refers to an addition to a document or report: *One way of attempting to assess the situation is to look at the list of unfair terms set out in the annex to the Directive*. **Annex** is also an alternative spelling in BE and AE for *annexe*. Note that the noun is stressed on the first syllable. See APPENDIX.

annexe ánnecks /ˈæneks/ *noun*, means an additional part of something, such as an extra building: *The hotel annexe is across the road*. This spelling is mainly used in BE.

annoy, exasperate, infuriate

annoy *verb*, means to make a person upset or irritated: *If Hyde returns while I am writing this confession, he will tear it to pieces to annoy me*. Aggravate is often used in this sense, but it is better to distinguish between aggravating a situation, and *annoying* a person. See AGGRAVATE.

exasperate *verb*, means to make someone very annoyed or irritated: *One of the things most likely to exasperate staff and reduce hygiene standards in the kitchen is a cabinet that is difficult to clean*.

infuriate *verb*, means to make someone extremely angry: *The idea of providing more money for road-building will infuriate environmentalists*. An alternative term that expresses the same degree of anger is enrage.

In a scale of irritation, *annoy* is less intense than *exasperate*, which is less intense than *infuriate*.

annual, perennial

annual *adjective & noun*. As an adjective, this means something that happens each year: *Annual profits have slumped from over £100 million to an expected £45 million this year*. In business English, **annual** is often used in phrases such as *annual report* and *annual general meeting* (AGM). In the noun form, an **annual** is a plant that has a one-year life cycle. An **annual** can also be a special edition of a book for that year: *He bought the children a Mad annual for Christmas*. See BIANNUAL.

perennial *adjective & noun*, means lasting or recurring through the years: *An image of perennial conflict between science and religion is inappropriate as a guiding principle*. As a noun, a **perennial** is a plant that flowers annually and may live for many years: *This is a hardy herbaceous perennial with leafy stems that are 6 ft tall*. See BIENNIAL.

annul, cancel, invalidate, rescind

annul *verb*, is a legal term meaning to declare officially that something is no longer considered as having ever been legally valid: *The Pope refused to annul the King's first marriage, to Catherine of Aragon, so he could marry Ann*. Note that this word is stressed on the second syllable.

cancel *verb*, means to decide or announce that a planned event will not take place: *The Queen was forced to cancel two engagements yesterday and another today because she has flu*. In another sense, it means to terminate, as in the phrase *cancel an agreement*. See ADJOURN.

invalidate *verb*, means to make something officially ineffective, or no longer correct: *A mattress used with the wrong base may be uncomfortable and would invalidate the guarantee*. The stress is on the second syllable. See INVALID (DISABLED).

rescind *verb*, means to make an official declaration that something is no longer valid: *The proposal to rescind the ban came from New Zealand, and was seconded by Australia*.

answer

See REPLY.

-ant, -ent (adjective and noun suffixes)

As adjective suffixes, these indicate that the whole word means 'that is or does something', e.g. *different* = that differs, *abundant* = that abounds.

As noun suffixes, these mean 'a person or thing that . . .' e.g. *inhabitant* = a person who inhabits, *defendant* = a person who defends, *adherent* = a person who adheres, i.e. belongs. In a few cases, both **-ant** and **-ent** spellings are used, e.g. *dependant* is the usual BE spelling in the sense of 'a person who depends on another', with *dependent* as the AE spelling. Note that the adjective is spelt *dependent* in both varieties of the language.

The spelling of each individual word is the result of its etymology, and is governed by the spelling of the Latin word it is derived from. Therefore the only way to be certain of the correct spelling is to consult a dictionary in each case. Here are some of the most common words beginning with A and ending **-ant** or **-ent**, to illustrate the problem: *aberrant, abhorrent, absent, absorbent, abstinent, abundant, accelerant, accident, accountant, acquiescent, adamant, adherent, adjutant, adolescent, affluent, ambient, annuitant, antecedent, antidepressant, antioxidant, antiperspirant, apparent, applicant, ardent, arrant, arrogant, ascendant, assailant, assistant, astringent, attendant.*

ante-, anti-

ante- ánti- /'æntɪ-/ *prefix*, means before and also in front of. It can be added to adjectives, verbs and nouns: *antenatal* (adjective) means before birth, *antediluvian* (adjective) means before the (biblical) Flood and is sometimes used to describe very antiquated concepts; *antedate (verb)* means to precede in time or come before (for an invention, idea, etc.); an *antechamber* (noun) is a small or minor room leading to a larger or more important one. **Ante-** is pronounced the same in BE and AE.

anti- ánti- /'æntɪ-/ (BE), ánti-, ántī- /'æntɪ-, 'æntaɪ-/ (AE) means against or opposed to. An *antiseptic* is an agent which destroys bacteria. Other words with **anti-** are: *antibiotic, antibody, anticyclone*. **Anti-** in the sense of *opposed to* is the basis of words like *Antichrist, anti-hero* and *antimatter*. Most words with the **anti-** prefix are stressed on the stem of the word (e.g. *antiséptic, anticýclone*) but there are a few stressed on the first syllable, for example: *ántibody, Ántichrist, ánti-hero*. Note that the pronunciation may be different in BE and AE in these cases. However, a few other words are stressed on the second syllable, such as: *antipathy* antípăthi /æn'tɪpəθi/ and *antipodes* antíppŏdeez /æn'tɪpədiːz/ where the pronunciation is the same in both BE and AE. See **HYPHENATION IN INDIVIDUAL WORDS (PUNCTUATION GUIDE)**.

In BE *ante-* and *anti-* are pronounced the same and rhyme with 'scanty'. In AE, *anti-* is often pronounced with the second syllable rhyming with 'tie'.

antenna

See **AERIAL**.

anticipate, expect

anticipate *verb*, means to foresee and make preparations for a response to a future event: *Before the job interview, try to anticipate the questions you will be asked*. In another sense, it means to think about something that is going to happen, particularly something that is pleasant: *They were anticipating that the film would win the Oscar*. In a third sense, it means to do something before anyone else, that is later proved to be correct: *Some early astronomers anticipated the theories that proved the Earth was not the centre of the universe*.

expect *verb*, means to believe that something will happen in the future because it seems likely: *Expect events in the coming week to cost you money, stretch your patience and strain your brain*. In another sense, it means to demand an action that is required or reasonable: *This university expects a lot from its students*.

antiquated, antique

See **ANCIENT**.

antisocial, unsocial, unsociable

antisocial *adjective*, means hostile or harmful to society: *Criminal acts tend to be antisocial rather than conscious acts against 'the state'*.

unsocial *adjective*, means outside the hours of the normal working day: *Thomas arose at 3 a.m., for the hours of a baker are notoriously unsocial*. It can also mean causing harm to society, but is less common than *antisocial* in this sense.

unsociable *adjective*, describes someone who is unfriendly or who does not seek or enjoy the society of others: *I remember Grandpa as a grumpy, unsociable old sourpuss*. It also means unsocial: *Rowdy crowds in the street at unsociable hours have left the family bleary-eyed*.

anxious, nervous, nervy, on edge

anxious *adjective*, means worried about something that may happen in the future and feeling that you have little control over events: *Roger and Sally had spent an anxious hour waiting for the doctor*. A second meaning is keen, or eager: *Explain that you are anxious to learn their language as well as possible*.

nervous *adjective*, means worried, frightened and not relaxed. When it refers to worry it is caused by something that you have to do: *I was really nervous about going for my first job interview*. When it relates to the nerves, **nervous** is used in phrases such as *nervous condition* and *nervous twitch*.

nervy *adjective*. In BE this means suffering from nervousness and easily frightened: *She is an extremely nervy type*. It also means excitable: *She was as nervy as a wildcat*. This is an informal word. In AE, it describes a brave and confident person who can easily cause offence: *He was a boxer, a coiled, nervy guy who started asking us hostile questions*.

on edge *adjective phrase*, means nervous, or tense through anticipation of something unpleasant that is expected: *I have been on edge all day waiting to hear more news about the crash*.

any, some

any *determiner & pronoun*. As a determiner, this means an indefinite amount or number of things: *Any student of this university who feels that they have grounds for complaint must ensure that their tutor is also informed*. Note how **any** is followed by the plural 'they' . . . 'their' in order to avoid the possibly sexist 'he' . . . 'his' for any student or the awkward construction 'he or she' . . . 'his or her'.

some *determiner, adverb & pronoun*. As a determiner, **some** means an indefinite amount or number of things. **Some** can also indicate certain groups: *Some people still think that the Earth is flat*. Note that in this sense the pronunciation is always the strong form with a full vowel. As an adverb, when a number follows **some**, it should be a round number ending in a zero: *Some 500 soccer fans were arrested*, not *Some 498 fans*. . . . As a pronoun, **some** is used when making a statement and in questions when the expected answer is 'yes', or you want to encourage a 'yes' answer: *I've made fresh coffee. Would you like some?*

anyone/anybody, *any one*, someone/somebody

anyone/anybody *pronoun*, means any person. Note that **anyone** or **anybody** always takes a singular verb, because it refers to any single person, and 'one' or 'body' is the subject, but it is often followed by a plural pronoun, *their*, in order to avoid writing either the possibly sexist 'he' or the heavy construction 'he or she': *Anybody taking this examination can use their calculator*.

any one *determiner + pronoun*, means a specific person or thing from a group: *Each scrap of news any one of them had about themselves or their immediate family was as fascinating to each other as if it were their very own*. Note that **any one** always takes a singular verb, because it refers to 'any single person', and 'one' is the subject. Both words are stressed.

someone/somebody *pronoun & noun*. As a pronoun, this means a person who is unspecified or unknown: *Someone is at the door*. In questions like: *Is someone at the door?* the expected answer is 'Yes'. Note that **someone/somebody** always takes a singular verb, because it refers to 'some single one', and 'one' is the subject. As a noun, **someone** or **somebody** means a person who either is important, or is considered important: *The world is full of nobodies who want to become a somebody*. See **NO ONE**.

> In spoken language, *anybody* and *somebody* are more common than *anyone* and *someone* respectively. It is recommended to use *anyone* and *someone* in formal written contexts.

any way, *anyway*

any way *determiner + noun*, means in any direction or method: *Any way we go there is a river to cross*. In this sense it is always written as two words.

anyway *adverb*, is used to add something to an idea: *No time for a holiday and anyway it is going to be too expensive*. It also means even so or besides: *It was pouring with rain but we* *walked anyway*. This is always written as one word.

anywhere, anyplace

anywhere *adverb*, means in, at or to any place: *You may sit anywhere you like*. Note that **anywhere** is used in negative sentences such as *I can't find my keys anywhere*, unlike somewhere, which occurs in positive sentences. See SOMEWHERE.

anyplace *adverb*, means the same as **anywhere** but is used only in AE.

a posteriori

See A PRIORI.

apostrophe (')

See PUNCTUATION GUIDE.

apparent, manifest

apparent *adjective*. When it comes before the noun, **apparent** describes something that appears to be true, but may not be: *The apparent reluctance of the education authorities to take action is understandable*. When **apparent** comes after the verb, it means obvious: *In such circumstances the opportunity to improve is much less apparent*.

manifest *adjective*, describes things that are easy to see or perceive: *This criticism of referees could be extended to their manifest errors of judgement in a fair proportion of games*.

appeal, plea

appeal *verb & noun*. As a verb, in a legal sense, to **appeal** means to call on a higher authority to review a decision: *He decided to appeal against the long prison sentence*. In AE, the word *against* may be omitted. As a noun, an **appeal** is this process to review something in court. This use is always followed by *against*: *She was granted bail pending an appeal against the sentence*. Note that the **appeal** is made *to* the authority: *The issue might be resolved by an appeal to the European Court of Justice*.

plea *noun*. In a legal sense, a **plea** is a statement made by someone accused of a crime, or on behalf of that person: *Her solicitor entered a plea of guilty on her behalf*. In a more general sense, **plea** is an urgent request often with emotion: *His fiftieth goal came with a plea to the fans to 'Bring the house down'*. See PLEA-BARGAINING.

appendix/appendices, appendix/appendixes

appendix[1] *noun*, is something added to a report and placed at the end. In this sense it has the plural **appendices** ăpéndisseez /ə'pendɪsiːz/: *The amount of traffic on the route (see Appendix D) never increased following the improvements*. Many style guides suggest that **appendices** are numbered A, B, C and D (as in the example above). If there are sections within an **appendix**, these are usually numbered A.1, A.2 etc. A neat way to refer to Table 2.1 in Appendix B is *See Table B.2.1*. Similarly, Figure 2.2 in Appendix C is referred to as *See Figure C.2.2*. See ADDENDUM, ANNEX.

appendix[2] *noun*, is an internal bodily organ: *He was rushed to hospital with a burst appendix*. This meaning of **appendix** has the plural **appendixes** ăpéndicksiz /ə'pendɪksɪz/. The 'k' sound in this plural should be pronounced.

appointment

See MEETING.

appraise, apprise

appraise *verb*, means to assess or evaluate someone's performance in a task, especially professionally: *It is the responsibility of internal audit to review, appraise and report upon the following matters: . . .*

apprise *verb*, means to inform someone of something: *I thought it right to apprise Cyril of what had happened*. This is a formal word, and inform and let someone know are alternatives.

approve, authorize, empower

approve *verb*, means to officially agree to a request: *The board took six months before approving the new factory plans*. In another sense, it means to be acceptable or suitable: *The government must approve the appointment of all members of the Committee*. The phrasal verb *approve of* means to find something acceptable or suitable: *Her parents would approve of her latest partner*.

authorize *verb*, also means to give official permission to someone to take decisions on their own: *Each bank manager can authorize mortgages up to £100,000.*

empower *verb*, means to give permission to someone to make decisions without referring to a higher authority: *Its aim is to empower women to control their own lives.*

approximately, approx.

approximately *adverb*, is used before quantitative amounts: *Approximately 25 kilo. Approximately EUR 2 million.*

approx. is usually written after the approximation and is often in brackets: *The price is EUR 2 million (approx.).* Although the abbreviation is acceptable in formal written English, read this as **approximately**. The pronunciation ăprócks /ə'prɒks/ should only be used in informal contexts, not in formal presentations.

a priori, a posteriori

a priori ay prī-áwrī /eɪ praɪ'ɔːraɪ/ *adjective*, means theoretical reasoning that looks ahead to the cause and the likely effect: *An a priori assumption means that if it rains, I will need an umbrella.*

a posteriori ay possteeri-áwrī /eɪ pɒstɪərɪ'ɔːraɪ/ *adjective*, means reasoning that uses empirical facts to look back at the cause: *An a posteriori assumption means that if the umbrella is wet, it must have been raining.*

> One way to keep these apart is to remember that they are Latin phrases meaning from what precedes (prior) and from what follows (posterior).

apt, liable

apt *adjective*, means either likely to occur: *With the right contacts, such graduates are apt to end up with careers in the media*; or appropriate: *Dressed to kill would have been an apt description of his appearance.*

liable *adjective*, also means likely to occur but it invariably refers to negative consequences: *Unless there are exceptional circumstances you are liable to be sacked straight away for such behaviour*; or an imminent threat: *The region is volcanic and is liable to severe earthquakes.* In another sense, **liable** refers to legal responsibility: *Under the Social Security Act 1971, a man is liable to maintain his wife and children.* See PRONE.

Arab, Arabia, Arabic, Arabian

Arab *adjective & noun*, refers to a member of one of the Semitic peoples inhabiting parts of the Middle East and North Africa: *All the key players in the Arab world were gathered at the meeting.* See NATIONALITY WORDS.

Arabia *noun*, refers to the geographic area between the Red Sea and the Persian Gulf: *Saudi Arabia is just one of the states in this region.* See FOREIGN PLACE NAMES.

Arabic *adjective & noun*, refers to the language and literature of the Arabs. The number symbols we use were introduced to Europe by the Arabs, and are called *Arabic numerals*.

Arabian *adjective & noun*. As an adjective, this refers to Arabia or its people: *the Arabian peninsula*. As a noun, this is a historical term except when referring to the nationality of a person from Saudi Arabia who is called a *Saudi Arabian*.

archaeology, archeology

archaeology *uncountable noun*, means the study of human history through excavation. This is the BE spelling. Remember that 'a' occurs twice in this word. See AE- E- OE-.

archeology *uncountable noun*, is the usual AE spelling of *archaeology*.

archetype, stereotype

archetype *noun*, means the original example of something that contains its most important qualities: *The Model T Ford was the archetype of mass production.*

stereotype *noun*, means a belief or idea of what a particular thing or person is like, and implies criticism: *'Brokeback Mountain' has questioned the macho stereotype of the American cowboy.*

area

See FIELD, STRETCH.

arena

See STAND.

argument, altercation

argument *noun*, means a discussion where there is disagreement, often with anger: *Ten minutes later, the manager was still having a heated argument with an official*. In another sense **argument** can be reasons or a line of reasoning: *There are strong arguments for more optional courses in the third year*.

altercation *noun*, means noisy argument or disagreement: *The spark that led to the riot was when a black youth became involved in an altercation with an officer over a parking ticket*. This is a formal word and quarrel or row are more common alternatives.

arise, arouse, rouse

arise *verb*, means to happen or start to exist: *You should refer your complaint to the manager at the branch or office where the problem has arisen*. It is only in songs and poetry that **arise** means to get out of bed.

arouse *verb*, means to awaken a feeling or attitude, or generate a response: *Our recommendations for the teaching of literature aroused a great deal of controversy*. **Arouse** also means to wake someone up, and in this sense it is a literary word. In another sense, *aroused* can mean sexually stimulated. Do not confuse **arouse** with *arose*, which is the past tense of *arise*. See **WAKE**.

rouse *verb*, means to wake a person up, especially if they are in deep sleep: *The burning midday sun roused him from a feverish sleep*. This is a formal word, and wake is the usual word to use in this context. Like *arouse*, **rouse** can refer to the generation of interest, anger, suspicion, action and sexual stimulation: *He shouted at the fighters with him, and roused them to stand by his side*.

> Note that *arise* does not take an object, but that both *arouse* and *rouse* do.

arithmetic

See **EXPONENTIAL**.

arithmetical progression, geometrical progression

arithmetical progression *noun*, is a sequence of numbers where the difference between each number is the same amount, for example: 5, 7, 9, 11.

geometrical progression *noun*, is a sequence of numbers where the difference between each pair of numbers has the same ratio, for example: 5, 10, 20, 40.

around

See **ABOUT**.

arouse

See **ARISE**.

arrant

See **ERRANT**.

arrogant

See **IMPERIOUS**.

arrogate

See **ABROGATE**.

artefact, artifact

artefact *noun*, is a product of human art or workmanship: *Flint tools are typical artefacts of the early Stone Age*. **Artefact** also means a typical but unintended consequence, often resulting from experimentation: *These temperature fluctuations are an artefact of voltage instability*. A modern meaning is a typical negative consequence: *Alcoholism is an artefact of business entertainment*. This is the BE spelling.

artifact is the usual AE spelling of *artefact*.

articles: indefinite and definite

See **GRAMMAR TIPS**.

artifice, cunning, crafty

artifice *noun*, means the clever use of tricks to give a false impression: *In many Elizabethan plays, the world was seen as a stage, life as artifice and such ideas became part of the culture*.

cunning *adjective & noun*. As an adjective, this describes obtaining an objective in a clever way, especially by trickery. As a noun, it means the clever use of trickery or cheating somebody to obtain an advantage. In this sense, it is usually disapproving. In another sense, **cunning** means cleverness and skill: *He admired the traditional style of Scottish football for its finesse and cunning*. This is not disapproving.

crafty *adjective*, means clever at obtaining an objective using indirect or dishonest methods: *He was sent off after the crafty forward took a dive at his feet.*

artificial, synthetic

artificial *adjective*, describes something that is not natural: *The artificial division of people into age groups has a damaging effect on society.* An **artificial** product imitates the real thing. *Artificial intelligence* is not true intelligence, but the development of computer software that can simulate intelligent human behaviour.

synthetic *adjective*, describes manufactured products that are identical to the natural ones. Thus *synthetic rubber* or *synthetic oil* are rubber and oil produced by the chemical industry, rather than by refining a natural product.

artist, artiste

artist *noun*, in a general sense means a gifted and skilled person such as a painter, craftsperson or performer who creates works of art. In a narrower sense, an artist is a person who creates visual art such as paintings: *Please could you recommend a book on horse anatomy for the artist, rather than the vet.*

artiste *noun*, means a performing dancer or singer, particularly on the stage or in a circus: *Many circus artistes belong to different generations of the same family.* Note that the last syllable rhymes with 'beast', and is stressed.

arts, humanities, liberal arts

arts *plural noun*, includes subjects such as literature, language, philosophy and history as opposed to science and technology: *The arts have flourished in recent years, due to a growing interest in modern foreign languages.*

(the) humanities *plural noun*, means academic fields such as literature, language, history and philosophy that are concerned with the way people think and act: *The study of the humanities is essential to society as a whole, since the humanities are concerned with a truthful understanding of where we are and where we come from.* Although **the humanities** were originally restricted to classical studies in Latin and Greek, today they mean all arts subjects. See **HUMANITY (HUMANISM)**.

liberal arts *plural noun*, is a term that sometimes has wider scope than the arts or humanities. In the US, where the term is frequently used, **liberal arts** courses cover a range of arts and science subjects intended to develop students' general knowledge and cultural awareness.

> These terms are often combined with the definite article.

-ary, -ery, -ory

-ary *noun & adjective suffix*, means connected with. Typical examples of nouns and adjectives with this ending are: *dictionary, boundary, budgetary, capillary, centenary, imaginary, military, momentary, ordinary, primary, stationary* (not moving).

-ery *noun suffix*, refers to a place, condition, or class. Some common words ending in **-ery** are: *adultery, bakery, cemetery, confectionery, distillery, jewellery* (BE), *monastery, slavery* and *stationery* (writing material).

-ory *noun & adjective suffix*, may have the meaning of relating *to*, or resembling: *accessory, accusatory, advisory, allegory, auditory, category, celebratory, circulatory, compulsory, conciliatory, congratulatory, conservatory, consolatory, contradictory, contributory, derisory, dilatory, factory, mandatory, observatory, signatory.*

> These suffixes can all mean a place or object – *dictionary, bakery, cemetery, distillery, factory*; but **-ary** and **-ory** can also refer to a quality – *momentary, contradictory*.

as a matter of fact

See **FACT**.

ascent, ascension

ascent *noun*, means physical movement upwards: *He paused, as if gathering breath for an ascent up a steep mountainside.* **Ascent** also means the process of becoming more powerful or successful: *The dictator's ascent to power was extremely rapid.* In this sense, **ascent** is an uncountable noun.

ascension *noun*, describes the action of rising. It is used in formal and religious contexts: *Ascension Day is when the Church observes the bodily ascension of Christ into heaven.*

> *'Guests are requested not to perambulate the corridors in the hours of repose in the boots of ascension.'*
> (Mountain hotel)
> !

ascertain

See FIND OUT.

ascetic

See AESTHETIC.

ashamed, embarrassed

ashamed *adjective*, means feeling shame because of something that has been done, and for which a person believes they are responsible. Only use **ashamed** for someone who feels guilty about something of importance: *The genuine supporters were genuinely ashamed that no one stopped the racist comments from the crowd.*

embarrassed *adjective*, describes the feelings of a person in a difficult social situation who feels awkward especially following a stupid mistake: *The football manager was embarrassed by the newspaper article and clearly sorry over the impact of his remarks.* A person who is **embarrassed** may also feel shy and inadequate: *He looked embarrassed and said he didn't have the faintest idea.* Note the spelling with -rr- and -ss-. See EMBARRASS.

Asian, Asiatic

Asian *adjective & noun*. As an adjective, this describes something or someone connected to Asia or originating in Asia, such as *Asian American*, or *Asian flu*. As a noun, in Britain, **Asian** means a person from the Indian subcontinent. In the USA, **Asian** means a person from the Far East. Elsewhere, the term **Asian** means a person who is a native or inhabitant of the continent of Asia. This term is appropriate for both the people and the culture.

Asiatic *adjective*, can be used to refer to geographical features in Asia: *The Himalayas originated when the Indian continental plate started to slide under its Asiatic counterpart.* Note that it should not be used to refer to people as this is racially offensive. Use **Asian** or the specific nationality of the person when referring to someone from Asia. See ORIENT (ORIENTAL).

as if

See SIMILAR.

Asperger's syndrome

See AUTISM.

assent, consent

assent *noun & verb*. As a noun, this means the acceptance of a decision: *Vernon was nodding his assent when he tripped.* As a verb, **assent** means to accept or acquiesce in a decision taken by someone else: *The architect agreed with Margaret that it would make the room much lighter and in the end Matthew assented.* Note that this is a formal word as both a noun and a verb. Do not confuse this word with its soundalike ascent.

consent *noun & verb*. As a noun, this means agreeing to something being carried out: *Jones, of London Road, admitted taking a car without consent.* As a verb, **consent** means to agree to something suggested or decided by other people: *He consented to give the address at the funeral.*

assertion, allegation, claim

assertion *noun*, means a forceful statement about the truth of something made with confidence: *Ian found William's assertion hard to believe but he conceded defeat nevertheless.*

allegation *noun*, means an accusation that some wrongdoing has occurred, but without any evidence being provided: *The world champion stuck to his allegation that someone had deliberately tried to push him off the track.*

claim *noun & verb*. As a noun, this is an unproven statement that something is true: *His claim that the voting had been manipulated was supported by an independent observer.* As a verb, **claim** means either to present a request for compensation: *If you only claim for broken glass in your car's windscreen, it will not affect your insurance premium*; or to state confidently that something is true, often without proof: *Researchers claim that their system has resulted in lower truancy rates.*

assuage

See **ALLEVIATE**.

assume, presume

assume *verb*, means to suppose without evidence: *This appears to assume that most secondary school departments have scrapped all their previous work, which of course is not the case.* In another sense, **assume** means to take over responsibility: *Turkey assumed the presidency of the Council of Europe for six months.* Note that if someone **assumes** a name, this is a pseudonym or one that has been adopted: *He was living in Chelmsford under an assumed name.*

presume *verb*, means to draw a conclusion from some evidence: *Dr Livingstone, I presume?* In another sense, **presume** means to behave without showing respect: *Do you presume to be prouder than your father?* Here, **presume** is a formal word.

assurance, insurance

assurance *noun*, means promise, and is used in BE insurance terminology for insuring against certainties such as death, and so frequently appears in the names of companies: *Prudential Assurance Company.* Nevertheless, most native English speakers use **insurance** as a general term irrespective of whether a life is *assured* or a car is *insured*.

insurance *noun*, provides protection against loss, and is the term used when referring to property, belongings, health and travel: *Many criteria are used to determine motor vehicle insurance premiums.* In AE usage, *life insurance* is the term preferred over the BE *life assurance*.

assure, *ensure*, *insure*

assure *verb*, means to tell someone something with absolute certainty: *I've been to both places, and can assure you there is a great difference.* **Assure** also means to inform someone of something to their benefit: *The Welfare Officer assured her that temporary accommodation had been arranged.*

ensure *verb*, means to make sure or make certain: *Always ensure the ideal environmental conditions for the fish you wish to breed.*

insure *verb*, means to take out insurance either on something: *You will also have to insure the property*, or against an unexpected and unwelcome event: *No one can insure against all eventualities.* In AE, **insure** is commonly used instead of the BE *ensure*: *I will do all I can to insure it doesn't happen again.* See **INSURANCE**.

> Note that in spoken English *ensure* and *insure* are often pronounced the same.

astern, abaft, abeam

astern *adverb*, means towards the back of a ship or aircraft or anything directly behind a ship or aircraft.

abaft *adverb*, describes something in the stern of a ship or behind it.

abeam *adverb*, describes a line at right angles to the length of a ship or aircraft at its midpoint: *The lighthouse will soon be abeam of us.*

astronomy, astrology

astronomy *noun*, is the scientific study of the heavens: *He was very interested in astronomy and he used to lecture on the stars and that sort of thing.*

astrology *noun*, is the study of the heavens in an attempt to predict the future. See **HOROSCOPES**.

ATM

See **CASH MACHINE**.

at present

See **SOON**.

attain

See **ACHIEVE**.

attorney

See **SOLICITOR**.

attribute

See **IMPUTE**.

auburn

See **HAIR COLOUR**.

audience

See **PUBLIC**.

auditor

See **EXTERNAL STUDENT**.

au pair

See **MAID**.

aura, aurora

aura *noun*, in its non-medical sense means a distinctive quality that seems to surround someone or something: *His appearance gave an aura of military training*. The plural form is *auras*.

aurora *noun*, literally means the dawn, but is mostly used in connection with *aurora borealis*, the northern lights and *aurora australis*, the southern lights. The term *aurora polaris* covers both polar regions. The plural form is either *auroras* or *aurorae*.

aural

See **VERBAL**.

authentic, genuine

authentic *adjective*, describes something that is real and not an imitation: *The builders are not using any nails in the construction, in an effort to build an authentic cultural centre*.

genuine *adjective*, describes something that is exactly what it appears to be, and not artificial: *The investigation revealed six genuine paintings and five forgeries*. In another sense, it means sincere and honest: *It's not often that I am moved to feel genuine sympathy for a Cabinet Minister*.

> *'Genuine replica Swiss watches'*
> (Online advert) **!**

author, authoress

author *noun*, means a writer of books or articles. An **author** can be either male or female. Writers of poems and plays are called poets and playwrights, respectively. Avoid the verb *to author* by using to write instead. See **'WE' TIPS FOR AUTHORS (WRITING SKILLS)**.

authoress *noun*, means a female *author* and most women writers prefer to be called *author*. The term **authoress** tends to have derogatory overtones, and *author* is the neutral form for both sexes. See **SEXIST LANGUAGE (WRITING SKILLS)**.

authoritarian, authoritative

authoritarian *adjective*, means demanding that others show obedience to those in charge: *Fewer and fewer subordinates will tolerate authoritarian power, at least in democratic societies*. As **authoritarian** describes something that hinders personal freedom, it is now considered a negative word in Western democracies.

authoritative *adjective*, means having authority in the sense of being trustworthy and reliable: *Since he acknowledges that he has no formal medical expertise, there is no reason to take his remarks as authoritative*.

authorize

See **APPROVE**.

autism, Asperger's syndrome

autism *noun*, is a mental disorder that causes someone to have difficulties in communicating and forming relationships with others.

Asperger's syndrome *noun*, is the name of one of the syndromes associated with *autism*. Sufferers may be obsessive, lack social skills, and prefer things always to remain the same. It is pronounced either **áspergĕrz** /ˈæspɜːrgərz/ or **ásperjĕrz** /ˈæspɜːrdʒərz/. See **SYNDROME**.

automatic, automated, mechanical

automatic *adjective*, describes a device or unit that works by itself without human control or intervention: *Automatic inspection is preferable to human inspection where accurate measurement is possible*.

automated *adjective*, means converted to work entirely automatically or with some manual assistance: *This factory has an automated production line with robots and mechanical sorters*.

mechanical *adjective*, means having to do with machines, or capable of being operated by engine power: *Lives were at risk from mechanical defects, including faulty brakes*.

autumn, fall (season)

autumn *noun*, is the BE term for the season between summer and winter: *The summer ended in a spell of autumn showers.* **Autumn** is only capitalized when it is the first word in a sentence. In figurative use, **autumn** means a period of mellowness, often with reference to the later period of a person's life: *The politician became more tolerant in the autumn of his life.* See SEASONS.

fall *noun*, is the AE term for *autumn*. It is only capitalized when it appears as the first word of a sentence.

auxiliary, ancillary, accessory

auxiliary awgzíl-yări /ɔːg'zɪljəri/ *adjective & noun*. As an adjective, this refers to a position where someone is helping or supporting the main group of workers: *She worked as an auxiliary nurse for six years, until she was given a permanent position.* The word can also refer to a piece of equipment that is used as a standby. The standby engine on a boat is called the *auxiliary engine*. As a noun, it means a worker who provides additional help for a group: *He started working for the fire and rescue service as an auxiliary.*

ancillary ansíllări /æn'sɪləri/, *adjective*, means having a secondary or minor role, or helping someone more highly qualified: *One of the areas I looked at first was the ancillary services; that is cleaning, catering and laundry.*

accessory *noun*. In a general sense, an **accessory** is something additional that improves the look or performance of an object, such as women's shoes that match a dress, or extra loudspeakers in a car: *A traditional jug and bowl set is the essential accessory for a Victorian-style bedroom.* It is also a legal term for a person who assists criminals in carrying out a crime: *He terrified her, but if she failed to go to the police, she could be charged as an accessory.* The alternative spelling *accessary* may be found, especially in legal contexts.

> The first two of these words have very similar meanings, so their spelling (auxiLlary, anciLLary) and pronunciation differences should be carefully remembered.

available

See VACANT.

avenge, avenger, revenge, vengeance

avenge *verb*, means to punish or hurt someone for something done earlier: *He planned how to avenge his wife's death.* **Avenge** is a literary term and is often used in constructions like *seek to avenge*.

avenger *noun*, means the person who *avenges* a harmful action, or less drastically, a sporting defeat: *Following the team's defeat away from home, their expensive striker acted as avenger in the return match, scoring two goals.*

revenge *uncountable noun & verb*. As a noun, this usually means a single act of harm done to someone in return for an injury or wrong done by them earlier: *Other people were trying to locate the driver to take revenge for their injuries.* Note that **revenge** often occurs with verbs such as seek, exact and take. As a verb, this means to punish someone who has done something to harm you or another person who is close to you: *John revenged the murder of his brother by planting a bomb in their car.*

vengeance *uncountable noun*, is the act of punishing someone for the harm they have done to you: *They took the law into their own hands in order to wreak vengeance on their fellow-citizens.* The phrase *with a vengeance* means to a greater extent than would be expected: *I took up dancing again with a vengeance; grinding through as many as six lessons a week.*

avenue

See STREET.

average, mean, median

average *noun & adjective*. This means the result of the addition of mathematical units and the division of the total by the number of units. For example: 3 plus 6 plus 12 equals 21, 21 divided by 3 equals 7. Thus 7 is the **average**. It can also refer to something which lies between two extremes: *Particularly there is a balance between courage and cowardice and the average between the two.*

mean *noun & adjective*. This means the figure halfway between the highest and lowest of a group of numbers: five students are aged 18, 19, 21, 24 and 26. The **mean** age is 22 being the mid-point between the two extremes: 18 plus 26 equals 44. Divided by 2 makes 22.

median *noun & adjective*. This refers to the middle value of a series. If a group of students are aged 18, 19, 21, 24 and 26, then the **median** is 21 as there are two students younger and two students older than this age. See CENTRAL RESERVATION.

averse

See ADVERSE.

avert, hinder, inhibit, prevent

avert *verb*, means to ward off an unwanted event or occurrence: *A last-ditch plea to avert a world trade war was made last night*. It also means to look away from something that is unpleasant: *He averted his eyes from the embarrassing scene*.

hinder *verb*, means to slow down or stop the progress of something: *Unhelpful behaviour like this will hinder your career in this company*. An alternative term is impede.

inhibit *verb*, means to stop the proper development of something: *Our procedures are intended to foster and not inhibit the exercising of creative problem solving*. If **inhibit** refers to restraining someone's action, this means that moral or social pressure is being applied: *At that time, TV and newspapers were inhibited by public policy from displaying too much naked flesh*.

prevent *verb*, means to make it impossible for someone to do something. If **prevent** refers to hindering an action by someone, this means that physical or legal force may be involved: *The fouling of footways by dogs will be prevented by the fines in the 'poop-scoop' bye-laws*.

> Note that all these verbs apart from *avert* are often followed by the preposition 'from' and an -ing form. A planned action becomes more impossible when using *prevent* rather than *hinder*. Compare *His broken leg prevented him from climbing the steps* with *His broken leg hindered him from climbing the steps*.

avoid, evade

avoid *verb*, means to keep away from something: *He left early to avoid the rush-hour traffic*. In another sense, it means to deliberately not do something: *He avoided using his credit card in order not to get into debt*.

evade *verb*, means to escape from something unpleasant, usually by deception: *She had lied to him because she wished to evade the unpleasant truth of her life as a rich heiress*. In another sense, it means to find a way of not doing something that legally or morally should be done: *He evaded paying taxes in both Britain and the USA*.

avoidance, evasion

avoidance *noun*, is the failure to do something in order to arrive at a satisfactory situation: *This avoidance of conflict became the key to the much-vaunted 'harmony' of the Japanese social system*.

evasion *noun*, is the manipulation of a situation to gain an advantage, usually in an underhand or illegal way: *After they broke up, she accused him of evasion of his responsibilities towards her and his children*.

> *Tax avoidance* means a legal way of not paying tax; *tax evasion* is illegal, as it involves concealment in one form or another, and is therefore fraud.

await

See WAIT.

awake

See WAKE.

axe, axis, axes

axe *noun*, means a tool used for chopping wood. This is the BE spelling. The usual AE spelling is *ax*.

axis *noun*, means a line that a body rotates around: *The Earth revolves on its axis every 24 hours*. There are numerous other mathematical and scientific uses of this word.

axes *noun*, is the plural spelling of both *axe* and *axis*. However they are pronounced differently: **axes** (chopping tools) is pronounced ácksiz /ˈæksɪz/ to rhyme with 'taxes', while **axes** (the mathematical term) is pronounced áckseez /ˈæksiːz/, which rhymes with 'Jack sees'.

aye, no (politics)

aye *noun*, means an affirmative answer in some dialects, e.g. Scots, and is also used in Parliament to indicate the total number of people voting 'yes' in a formal debate: *The ayes have it*, which means the aye or 'yes' vote has won. See YEA.

no *noun*, means a negative answer. In Parliament it indicates the total number of people voting 'no' in a formal debate. The plural is spelt with -es: *The noes have it*, which means the 'no' vote has won. See NAY (YEA).

Spelling

a**b**a**tt**oir	Note single -b- but double -tt-
a**bb**reviate	Note double -bb-
ab**s**en**c**e	Note -s- following -b-, but -c- at the end
accede	See *-cede, -ceed, -sede*
a**cc**o**mmo**date	Note double -cc-, double -mm-, and -mod-
a**cc**omplish	Note double -cc-
a**cc**umulate	Note double -cc-
ach**ie**ve	Remember -i- before -e-
adap**ta**tion	Note that this word has four syllables
alle**g**e	Note there is no 'd' in this word
allo**tt**ed	Remember the double -tt-
a**m**endment	Note the single -m- following the a-
anal**o**gous	Note -log-
anci**ll**ary	Note -ll-, but no 'i' following the -ll-
a**n**e**m**o**n**e	Remember -n- comes before and after the -m-
a**pp**rove	Remember the double -p-
auxi**li**ary	Note single -l-, and -i- following it

B

baby boom, baby boomer

baby boom *noun*, means a period when more babies are born than the average.

baby boomer *noun*, means a person born during a baby boom, particularly the one following the end of the Second World War.

back burner

See **PENDING**.

back-formation

See **WORD FORMATION**.

background

See **ENVIRONMENT**.

back-handed compliment, left-handed compliment

back-handed compliment *noun*, refers to a statement that seems to say something flattering but could also be understood as an insult: *The Press made a back-handed compliment about the independence of the judiciary*. This is a BE expression.

left-handed compliment *adjective phrase*, is the AE equivalent of a back-handed compliment: *The senator paid her a left-handed compliment, calling her quite competent for someone so inexperienced.*

backhander

See **BRIBE**.

backlog (in BE and AE)

backlog *noun*, means work or goods that are not completed: *We will start to tackle the backlog of school repairs*. In BE this is a negative term.

backlog means the same in AE as in BE, but without the negative idea of having too much to do: *We have a comfortable backlog of orders*. In this sense, **backlog** reflects its origin as a log at the back of a fire to be used as a reserve.

backpack

See **RUCKSACK**.

backside, back

backside *noun*, means the buttocks or bottom in BE. It is generally used when the speaker wants to be critical: *He planted his backside in the director's chair, and refused to move*. This is an informal word in BE. In AE, **backside** can also mean the rear of an object, like the **backside** of a mountain. If it is spelt as two words, *back side*, it means the other side of something in both BE and AE.

back *noun*, means the other side of something: *The safety instructions are on the back of this folder*. In a building such as a cinema, the **back** is the part of the auditorium furthest from the screen: *There are seats available at the back*. See **REVERSE**.

backward, backwards

backward *adjective*, means towards the rear: *A backward glance in his mirror*. **Backward** also describes a lack of progress: *She feels that returning to live with her parents would be a backward step*. **Backward** was formerly used about people who are slow at learning or developing, but this is no longer considered acceptable. See **LEARNING DIFFICULTY**.

backwards *adverb*, means a reverse direction of movement: *He drove backwards*. In another sense, it means lack of progress: *She felt her new job would be a step backwards in her career*. This is the BE spelling. *Backward* is an alternative form, especially in AE.

bacterium, bacteria

bacterium *noun*, is a single-cell micro-organism. This is the singular form of *bacteria*.

bacteria *noun*, is the plural of *bacterium*. **Bacteria** must have a plural verb and pronoun: *The bacteria are starting to spread and they must be contained.*

B

bad – a word to use sparingly

Bad is a word that lacks precision. Often *poor* (quality) and *weak* (strength) are better alternatives. Other possibilities are *unpleasant, foul, disgusting, appalling, traumatic* or *frightening*. A bad person can be *horrible, wicked, evil* or *malicious*. A bad road crash can be *serious* or *terrible*. A bad situation can be described as *awful, dreadful, awkward* or *difficult*. However, bad weather is the normal phrase and severe weather describes more exceptional conditions.

badge, patch, button

badge *noun*, is a piece of metal or cloth attached to clothing to show membership of or rank in an organization: *He wore the winged dagger badge of the SAS with pride*; or to a piece of equipment to indicate the manufacturer's name: *At last, a sensible coupé with terrific looks and a main car-maker's badge*.

patch *noun*, means a small area that contrasts with a larger one that surrounds it. This can be a piece of cloth covering damage in clothing; a covering for a damaged part of the body (an *eyepatch*); a small area of clouds in a blue sky, or conversely a small area of blue in an otherwise overcast sky; or an area of baldness on someone's head. In AE it also means the piece of cloth sewn to clothing as part of a uniform, equivalent to BE *badge*.

button *noun*, means a small, usually round object used as a fastener on clothing. In computing, it means the small area on a computer screen that is clicked on to perform an action: *Click on the top right button to close this program*. In AE, it means a small metal or plastic badge with a message or picture on it: *Millions of presidential campaign buttons were distributed during the primaries*.

bail, bale

bail *noun and verb*. As a noun this means a sum of money either used as a guarantee to a court: *He had to ask his partner to post bail*, or for the temporary release of an accused person who has not been tried by law: *He was then released on bail*. As a verb, it means either to be released from a court on bail or to be helped out of a difficult situation: *The bank bailed him out*. The process of scooping water out of a boat or ejecting pilots from damaged aircraft is *bailing out*. In BE, a variant spelling of the verb in this second meaning is *bale*.

bale *noun and verb*. As a noun, this means a material that is compressed and tied such as a *bale of cotton* or a *bale of hay*. As a verb it means to compress such material. It is also the BE variant spelling of the verb *bail* in the sense of *bale out*.

bait, bated

bait *noun and verb*. As a noun it is used in fishing to mean a lure on a hook: *We used worms as bait*. More generally, **bait** refers to a person or thing that is used to catch vermin or people. It is also something used to attract people, often dishonestly: *The bait she used was the promise of a sexual adventure*. As a verb, **bait** means to use food to capture fish or animals: *Let me bait up your hook*, or to tease and deliberately make someone angry: *Stop baiting your sister*.

bated *adjective*. This is only used in the phrase *with bated breath*, where it means anxious or in suspense: *The American people listened to the president's confession with bated breath*.

Many people confuse the past tense of the verb *baited* with the soundalike adjective *bated*. This is to be avoided.

'The world waited with baited breath for the return of Michael Jackson.'
(www.bbc.co.uk/6music)

balance, scales

balance *noun*. In the context of something remaining, the **balance** is the outstanding amount that is to be paid: *I enclose a cheque for £34 as payment for the outstanding balance on my last instalment*. A **balance** is an instrument for weighing objects and as a figurative extension of this sense contrasts two related categories: *As labour markets tightened, the balance of industrial power tilted towards the workers*. See **BALANCE SHEET (PROFIT & LOSS ACCOUNT)**.

scales *plural noun*, means an instrument for weighing objects: *He stood on the bathroom scales every Monday morning*. In AE this is also called a *scale*. Figuratively, people refer to the *scales of justice* which are represented by the two dishes on a balance.

bale

See BAIL.

baleful, baneful

baleful *adjective*, means threatening to cause evil or do harm to someone: *She shot him a baleful look, which made him quake in his shoes*.

baneful *adjective*, describes something that is evil and destructive: *In order to counteract such baneful influence, they should be moved into a religious education programme*. **Baneful** is derived from the noun *bane*, which means something that causes trouble or unhappiness, that is used in the phrase *the bane of someone's life*: *Spam mails were the bane of his life*.

These are both mainly literary terms.

ball game, state of play

ball game *compound noun*, means any game played with a ball, but in AE it especially refers to baseball. **Ball game** has also become an informal term in both AE and BE to mean a very different situation from that which existed before: *Today's IT world is a whole new ball game*.

state of play *noun phrase*, means an interim stage that has been reached in the course of a process: *Added together, the BBC1 and ITV election results specials will take up a mere 12–14 hours, depending on the state of play at 4 a.m.* As this phrase originated in the game of cricket, it may confuse international audiences. See STATE OF AFFAIRS (SITUATION).

ballot

See ELECTION.

ballpark figure

See ESTIMATE.

balmy, barmy

balmy *adjective*, describes a temperature that is pleasantly warm and is used only in the context of the weather: *This balmy airmass gave most places their warmest day of the month*.

barmy *adjective*, means mad, silly or foolish: *It's driving me barmy, it is*. This is an informal word most often used in BE.

baluster, balustrade

See BANISTER.

band-aid solution

See TEMPORARY SOLUTION.

bandwagon, cause

bandwagon *noun*, means an activity that attracts people to join: *More and more MPs are climbing/jumping on the bandwagon*. This is an overused phrase with negative connotations as it is seen as a move to gain popular support and thereby hinder people from thinking independently. The **bandwagon** used to be a wagon for a circus band to travel on, not the winning side.

cause *noun*, means an idea or organization that people support. It is a more neutral term than *bandwagon*: *At least some of the MPs are working for a good cause*. If the venture cannot succeed or is doomed to failure it is a *lost cause*. See CAUSE (REASON).

baneful

See BALEFUL.

banister, baluster, balustrade

banister *noun*, is a handrail along a staircase inside a building.

baluster *noun*, is a stone support to the railings along an outside flight of steps.

balustrade *noun*, is a decorative row of posts with a horizontal bar along the edge of a balcony or bridge. It naturally acts as a safety feature too.

bank, left and right (of a river)

left bank *noun*, means the left-hand side of any river looking downstream: *Situated on the left bank of the Rhine, Cologne's mighty Gothic cathedral dominates the city*. It also means the artistic and cultural people and their way of life to the south of the River Seine in Paris. In the latter sense it is capitalized: *The bohemian atmosphere of the Left Bank attracts many young people to Paris.*

right bank *noun*, means the right-hand side of a river, looking downstream: *The street-lamps lining the promenade on the right bank glittered in the waters below the bridge.*

bank card, cash card, charge card, credit card, debit card, store card

bank card is sometimes called a *cheque card* or *banker's card* and is frequently used in BE in connection with a cheque. This is a more general term than the others in this group.

cash card is a type of *bank card* which is used to take money from a cash machine. These are called ATM cards in AE (ATM stands for automated [or automatic] teller machine). See CASH MACHINE.

charge card is used to purchase goods or services on credit, but the bill, once received, must be paid in full. American Express and Diners Club issue **charge cards**.

credit card is used to purchase goods on credit. Only a percentage of the bill has to be paid each month, but interest is charged on the outstanding balance.

debit card is used like a *charge card* or *credit card*, but the money is taken direct from the user's account, with no period of free credit.

store card is a restricted type of *credit card*, valid only in outlets of the retail store that issues the card.

As banking regulations vary around the world, these definitions describe the situation in the UK.

bank holiday

See PUBLIC HOLIDAY.

banknote, bill

banknote *noun*, means paper money issued by a bank: *I just thought there might be a fifty-pound banknote in that envelope.* **Banknote** is usually shortened to *note*: *I paid with a twenty-pound note.* This is the usual BE term. See NOTE.

bill *noun*, means a *banknote* in AE: *All dollar bills are the same size.* Note that **bill** in the BE sense of a piece of paper showing the cost of food and drink consumed in a cafe or restaurant is called a *check* in AE.

bar

See EXCLUDE.

barbaric, barbarous

barbaric, *adjective*, means violently cruel, savage, and implies the behaviour of uncivilized people: *To the outsider, the way the whales are killed is nothing short of barbaric.*

barbarous, *adjective*, also means extremely cruel: *This punishment was the most disgusting and barbarous thing I had ever seen*; it may also be used to refer to uncivilized people or ungrammatical language: *The editor of that dictionary maintains certain rules on the grounds of avoiding barbarous sentences or ambiguities.*

bare

See NAKED.

barely, hardly, scarcely

barely *adverb*, means either just possible, but with difficulty: *He was barely able to stand upright in the wind*, or not more than: *She was barely three when her father died.* In another sense, **barely** describes something that almost does not exist: *The rash may be barely visible.*

hardly *adverb*, means either only just: *The music was so loud, I could hardly hear her speak*; or almost not at all: *I'd hardly been back for a month when Mother died.* It also means with difficulty: *He could hardly believe that he had flown solo for the first time.* **Hardly** can never replace *hard*. Compare: *She hardly worked* and *She worked hard.*

scarcely *adverb*, also means only just, or almost not at all. **Scarcely** and *hardly* are often interchangeable in the sense of almost not at all, but **scarcely** is more formal: *You can scarcely/hardly ever see the mountains because of all the pollution.*

All these words are negatives, and care should be taken when they are combined with other negative words such as *not* or *never*. Compare *He could hardly say who was the killer* and *He could hardly not say who was the killer*. See NEGATIVES.

barmy

See BALMY.

barrister

See SOLICITOR.

basal

See BASIC.

base, bass

base *noun, adjective & verb*. As a noun, a **base** is a physical foundation or support: *The base of the statue*. It is also a location used by the military or the starting point for a trip or expedition: *It makes an ideal base from which to tour the Central Highlands*. The phrase *off base* also means off target or out of order, especially in AE: *The Supreme Court is way off base with a one-day sentence for murder*. As an adjective, **base** means low in morality: *She was a base liar who did not know right from wrong*. A *base metal* is one that is not precious, such as lead or iron. As a verb, **base** means select a specific location as the main one for an activity such as a holiday or business: *We are going to be based in Brussels next year*.

bass bayss /beɪs/ *adjective & noun*, means low, but is only used in musical terms: *bass guitar, bass voice*. As a noun, **bass** refers to musical instruments or singers. Note that this rhymes with 'face'. But when it is pronounced to rhyme with 'lass', this is the name of several species of fish. In this sense, the usual plural is also **bass**.

basement, cellar

basement *noun*, is a whole storey of a building that is partly or entirely below ground level: *The basement flat is often the cheapest one in a house*.

cellar *noun*, is a room below ground level, usually one used for storing things: *He has an excellent cellar for his woodworking tools*. In modern usage, a *wine cellar* need not be underground.

Basements are often used for accommodation but a *cellar flat* conjures up the idea of wet walls and impoverished living conditions.

basic, basal

basic *adjective*, describes the fundamental part of something, from which other things can develop: *Students must take the basic organic chemistry course in their first year*. It can also mean at the simplest level: *The hotel in Paris was extremely basic and spartan*. It can also mean fundamental to everyone, such as *basic human rights*.

basal *adjective*, means at an initial or bottom level: *Heat generated in the main part of the nest above the basal plate causes the air to rise through the passageways and chambers*. This word is used mostly in technical senses.

bass

See BASE.

bated

See BAIT.

bath, bathe

bath *noun & verb*. As a noun, this usually means a long narrow container that people sit or lie in to wash themselves, and is the normal word for this container in BE. In AE, both *bathtub* and *tub* are commonly used. **Bath** can also refer just to the water: *Anna was running a bath*. A *Turkish bath* is a complex of rooms for various sorts of relaxation and washing. In the plural, **bath** can also mean the building where a swimming pool is found: *We all went swimming on Tuesday nights at Hamilton baths*. As a verb, **bath** means to wash someone else in a **bath**: *You need to dress, undress and bath your baby gently, with lots of soothing noises to reassure him*. In BE, people *have a bath*, in AE they *take a bath*. Figuratively, to *take a bath* means to suffer a large financial loss, as in: *We took a bath in Hong Kong last year*.

bathe *verb*. In BE, this means to swim in a pool, river, lake or the sea. In AE, **bathe** and swim are used as in Britain, but **bathe** also means to wash in a *bathtub*. **Bathe** is also used in both BE and AE for washing something carefully: *bathe a wound* or *bathe your eyes*. Note that **bathe** has the same vowel as 'bay'.

bathetic

See PATHETIC.

bathos

See PATHOS.

bathroom

See TOILET.

batter, pound, pummel

batter *verb*, means to hit very hard and often, usually causing a lot of damage: *Behind him was a broom which could have been used to batter him.*

pound *verb*, means to hit repeatedly, often with a lot of noise: *She pounded the door, trying to make them hear that she was there.*

pummel *verb*, means to hit repeatedly, usually with the fists: *They pummelled the pillows back into shape.*

bay

See PLATFORM.

bazaar

See BIZARRE.

BC, BCE

See AD.

bcc

See CC.

BE

BE stands for British English, and is an abbreviation used throughout this book. See BRITISH ENGLISH.

beach, beech

beach *noun & verb*. As a noun, **beach** means a shelving shoreline, which can be sandy or rocky. As a verb it means to bring something, usually a boat or ship, out of the sea on to the shore: *The admiral ordered his fleet to be either sunk or beached.* A *beached whale* is one that is stranded on the shore and unable to return to the sea.

beech *noun*, is a type of hardwood tree: *Fifty years ago this entire area was planted with beech trees.*

bear market, bull market

bear market is a market in which share prices are either falling or expected to fall: *In a bear market you normally expect shares to drop 15 to 25 per cent over 18 months.* The related adjective is *bearish*.

bull market is a market in which share prices are either rising or expected to rise. The related adjective, *bullish*, also has a general meaning of feeling confident about the future.

beat, beet

beat *verb & noun*. As a verb, this means to defeat someone in a game or competition: *Away teams always love to beat Man Utd on their home ground.* It also means to hit someone or something repeatedly. As a noun, **beat** means the basic rhythm of a piece of music: *They were all tapping out the beat with their feet*; the striking of something such as a drum: *The six beats on the drum were the signal they were waiting for*; or the regular movement of something such as a heart. See BATTER.

beet *noun*, is a type of plant that is cultivated for human or animal food: *Fields of sugar beet are found all over this part of the country.*

Beaufort scale, Richter scale

Beaufort scale bőfŏrt /ˈbəʊfərt/. This is the scale used internationally to indicate wind speed measured in knots – nautical miles per hour. It was invented by Sir Francis Beaufort, an English admiral. It ranges from 0 to 12, where the lowest number means that there is no wind, and the highest is a hurricane. Each of these numbers is called a 'force'. A force 5 wind means a fresh breeze. When describing storms, it is common to use 'on the Beaufort scale': *The wind was NW, gale force 8 gusting to 9 on the Beaufort scale*.

Richter scale rícktĕr /ˈrɪktər/. This is the scale used to measure the magnitude of earthquakes. It was invented by Charles Richter, an American geologist. It is a logarithmic scale, so an earthquake of magnitude 6 is twice as strong as one of magnitude 5: *There are about 120 earthquakes each year that are between 6 and 7 on the Richter scale*.

bedsit, studio, efficiency apartment

bedsit *noun*, means a small room for living and sleeping in. This and the alternative *bedsitter* are terms mainly found in BE. Formally this is called a *bedsitting room*.

studio *noun*. Apart from the room where TV and radio programmes are made, or where painters and photographers work, it is also used in the plural for the place where film companies make films. In the context of accommodation, it means a small one-room flat, commonly known as a *studio flat* in BE, and a *studio apartment* in AE.

efficiency apartment *noun*, means a room for living and sleeping in, with a separate bathroom. This and the alternatives *efficiency unit* and *efficiency* are the equivalent of the *bedsit* and are only AE terms.

beech

See BEACH.

beer, ale, lager

beer *noun*, is an alcoholic drink made from fermented malt, usually barley, and flavoured, most often, with hops. In this sense it is uncountable: *Consuming too much beer on a regular basis can cause health problems*. **Beer** used as a countable noun means a *glass of beer*.

ale *noun*, is a type of beer brewed using top-fermenting yeast. It is now used in names like *pale ale, brown ale, mild ale*. In AE, the terms *beer* and **ale** are used to distinguish different fermentation processes. See FERMENT.

lager *noun*, is a type of pale beer brewed using bottom-fermenting yeast.

beet

See BEAT.

behalf

See ON BEHALF OF.

behaviour, behavior

behaviour *uncountable noun*, means the way a person acts: *The class structure affects people's attitudes and behaviour significantly*. **Behaviour** can also be applied to animals, plants and chemicals: *The behaviour of the horse was studied carefully before the race*. For things that are not living, it is more usual to use the word performance.

behavior *noun*, is the AE spelling of *behaviour*.

Belgium, Belgian

Belgium *noun*, is the name of the country bordered by the Netherlands, Germany, Luxembourg and France.

Belgian *adjective & noun*. As an adjective, this refers to the culture and people of *Belgium*. As a noun, it means a person who is a citizen of *Belgium*.

belligerent, bellicose

belligerent *adjective & noun*. As an adjective, this means either hostile or aggressive: *He stopped, jammed his hands on his hips and leaned forward from the waist in a belligerent posture*. As a noun, **belligerent** is used for a state or country engaged in a war.

bellicose *adjective*, means aggressive and warlike: *Americans, threatened by nothing more bellicose to their north and south than Canada and Mexico, are not accustomed to thinking they are in a battle zone*.

> These words are very close in meaning but *belligerent* usually refers to a hostile attitude while *bellicose* usually refers to engagement in war or warlike intention.

B

below

See **ABOVE**, **UNDERNEATH**.

benchmark

See **BEST PRACTICE**.

beneficial

See **ADVANTAGEOUS**.

bereaved, bereft

bereaved *adjective* means having lost a close relative, but the word has no emotional overtones: *A mother who lost her twin daughters has set up a counselling agency to help bereaved families*.

bereft *adjective*, is lacking something and as a result feeling sad, lonely and miserable. This is a very emotional word: *Bereft of hope, some people seek an end to their misery in suicide*. In another sense, it means without any hope: *At 6–0 down at half-time, the team seemed bereft of inspiration*.

berry

See **BURY**.

berth

See **DOCK**.

best practice, benchmark

best practice *compound noun*, means a way of doing something that is the best example that others can copy. This term is widely used in business: *The boards of all listed companies should comply with the code of best practice*.

benchmark *noun & verb*. As a noun, this means a standard against which other organizations can be measured or compared: *Ranking lists are a benchmark of the standards of universities across the world*. As a verb, this means using the performance of an organization as a standard for comparison: *Our institution is benchmarked against other leading-edge research institutes*.

between . . . and, from . . . to

between . . . and . . . . This pair of words is used to indicate the space in the middle of something: *between the devil and the deep blue sea*; *between eight o'clock and half past nine*; *between ten and twenty pounds*; or *between London and Coventry*. See **AMONG(ST)**.

from . . . to . . . . This pair of words is more concerned with the journey involved in travelling the distance, whether it is a physical journey in space or time, or a transition: *From here to eternity*; *from Monday to Saturday*; or *from London to Coventry*.

> These two constructions are often confused, the most common mistake being to use *between . . . to . . .* with amounts of money. By thinking of examples in which figures are not used, such as *between London and Coventry*, it becomes clear that *between . . . to . . .* is non-standard.

be used to

See **USED TO**.

bewitch

See **ENTRANCE**.

bi-, duo

bi- *prefix*, means two, or having two. Note that measurements of time such as *biweekly* and *bimonthly* can be ambiguous, as they mean either once every two weeks/months or twice a week/month. It is best to avoid such combinations and write *every two weeks/months* and *twice a week/month*. See **BIMONTHLY**, **DUAL**.

duo *noun*, means two people or things acting together, especially in entertainment or sport: *Experienced guitarist/backing vocalist seeks dedicated partner, main vocals and guitar, for duo work*.

biannual, biennial, biennale

biannual *adjective*, means twice a year. In order to avoid potential confusion with *biennial*, it is often advisable to replace **biannual** with semi-annual, half yearly or every six months. See **ANNUAL**.

biennial *adjective & noun*, means once every two years: *Every other spring, New York's social climbers battle for tickets to the biennial*. To avoid potential confusion with *biannual*, it is possible to replace **biennial** with every second year or every other year. **Biennial** is also used to mean a plant that lives for two years, and flowers only in the second, before dying: *This is the time to sow biennial flower seeds, to flower next spring and early summer.* See ANNUAL.

biennale *noun*, pronounced bi-ĕnaálay /biːəˈnɑːleɪ/, means a large exhibition or music festival held every two years: *The first Biennale was held in Venice in 1895.*

biased

See UNBALANCED.

bibliography

See REFERENCES (WRITING SKILLS).

bicentenary, bicentennial

bicentenary *noun*, means a two-hundredth anniversary. This is the usual term in BE: *The bicentenary of the French Revolution was in 1989.* Note that the third syllable rhymes with 'teen': bīssĕnteénări /baɪsənˈtiːnəri/.

bicentennial *noun*, is the usual term for *bicentenary* in AE: *The bicentennial of the Declaration of Independence was celebrated in 1976.* Note that the third syllable rhymes with 'ten': bīssĕnténni-ăl /baɪsənˈtenɪəl/, and that **bicentennial** has three n's.

bid

See TENDER.

biennial, biennale

See BIANNUAL.

big

See LARGE.

bilateral

See UNILATERAL.

bill

See BANKNOTE.

billion, billions, trillion

billion *noun*, means a thousand million (10^9). When **billion** follows an exact number or the words 'a', 'few' or 'several': *400 billion kilometres, a few billion litres, several billion litres*, a plural verb is used: *One point two billion people were watching the match on TV.* When **billion** is used with a unit of time, distance, temperature, money, etc., it takes a singular verb: *£2.5 billion is required.* The abbreviation is *bn*.

billions is the plural of *billion* and refers to an inexact very large number. Often it is immediately preceded by 'tens of' or 'hundreds of'. Thus **billions** can range from a few **billions** to many **billions**: *The budget deficit is likely to increase into the billions.* It is often followed by *of* and informally, it can mean very many times: *He has done this billions of times.*

trillion *noun*, means a million million (10^{12}). This is the standard meaning of **trillion** in international scientific English and modern BE and has always been the meaning in AE.

In BE, *billion* used to mean a million million (10^{12}). Similarly *trillion* used to be a million million million (10^{18}), but these meanings are now considered old-fashioned. In some other European languages, *billion* still has the value 10^{12}, and *trillion* 10^{18}. To express 10^9, these languages use the term 'milliard'.

bimonthly

See FORTNIGHTLY.

binder

See FILE.

bird's-eye view, vantage point

bird's-eye view *noun*, means a general view from a very high position: *A map is a flat plan of an area – a sort of bird's eye view made into a diagram.* It may also be used figuratively: *A good selective bibliography gives a bird's eye view of the subject literature.*

vantage point *noun phrase*, means a place or position providing a good view of something: *From my second-floor vantage point I could see my classmates.* This is sometimes used figuratively for considering matters in time as well as space: *From a present-day vantage point, the First World War formed a juncture in social relations.* See OVERLOOK.

B

'The crowds are gathering to get a bird's-eye view of the funeral.'
(Radio reporter, London)

birthday, date of birth, birthday suit

birthday *noun*, is the anniversary of a person's birth, but in AE, **birthday** may also mean a person's date of birth: *To enter this website, you must enter your birthday to confirm that you are over 18.*

date of birth *noun*, is the date on which a person was born: *Is your date of birth the fourth of September nineteen fifty-four?* This is abbreviated to *dob* or *DOB* on some forms.

birthday suit *noun*, is a humorous and informal expression meaning the clothes one was born in, i.e. none: a state of nakedness: *The man ran into the Olympic stadium in his birthday suit.*

> As the way of writing dates in digital form differs around the world, this may give rise to confusion. See DATES.

biscuit

See CRACKER.

bisect, dissect

bisect bīssékt /baɪ'sekt/ *verb*, means to divide something into two parts, which in technical senses are exactly equal. In a more general sense, it means to divide: *The county council plans to build a bypass so that the road will no longer bisect the village.*

dissect dissékt /dɪ'sekt/ *verb*, means to cut something up in order to examine its structure, or figuratively to examine something in detail: *We will explain how to dissect owl pellets to find out what barn owls eat.* Although many people pronounce this word to rhyme with *bisect*, it is preferable to follow the advice of most dictionaries, where the first syllable is shown to rhyme with 'miss', not 'my'.

bit, byte (computer science)

bit *noun*, is the smallest unit of information used by a computer. It has the capacity of one binary digit (bit = Binary digIT). It is like a light switch with two different states: either on (1) or off (0). For example, the number 10011001 is 8 bits long, which is normally called a *byte*.

Here are some common multiples of **bit**, with their standard abbreviations and the quantity of bits:

kilobit	kb	10^3
megabit	Mb	10^6
gigabit	Gb	10^9
terabit	Tb	10^{12}

byte *noun*, is a unit of measurement of information storage. It is pronounced 'bite'.

Here are some common multiples of **byte**, with their standard abbreviations and the quantity of bytes:

kilobyte	kB	10^3
megabyte	MB	10^6
gigabyte	GB	10^9
terabyte	TB	10^{12}

> As the abbreviations of these terms are only differentiated by capitalization, in certain contexts it is recommended to write the terms out in full before using the abbreviations.

biweekly

See **SEMI-WEEKLY**.

bizarre, bazaar

bizarre *adjective*, means odd and weird: *In our society it is considered bizarre for men to wear women's clothing*.

bazaar *noun*, means either a market area in some Asian or Middle Eastern countries, or in Western countries the sale of goods, often handmade, for charity: *'I'm helping to set out the stalls for the hospital bazaar,' she called*.

black, African American, people of color, coloured, Negro

black *adjective & noun*. As well as its meaning as a general colour term, **black** refers to races of people with dark skin, especially of African and Australian aboriginal origin. Among Black Africans and West Indians in Britain, **black** is the politically correct word to describe their appearance. It can be capitalized for a group but not for an individual: *A black police officer was promoted to inspector*. See **ABORIGINE, HAIR COLOUR, NATIVE AMERICAN.**

African American is the currently accepted term in the US for Americans of African origin.

people of color *noun*, is a recently revived AE term now used to describe anyone who is not white. However, it has not yet gained acceptance in all groups in American society. The phrase *women of color* has also been introduced as an alternative to 'minority women'.

coloured *adjective & noun*, means wholly or partly of non-white descent. In the UK and US, this is considered to be an offensive term and *black* is an alternative. However, in South Africa **coloured** is a technical term for those of mixed race. In the US, the term is disliked by most black people and it is mainly found today in organizational names, such as *the National Association for the Advancement of Colored People (NAACP)*. Note that *colored* is the AE spelling.

Negro *noun*, is an ethnic or historical term for Black Africans and is used today only in contexts like *Negro spirituals*. **Negro**, together with the female form *Negress*, is offensive, and should be avoided elsewhere, and replaced by *Black* (BE) or *African American* (AE).

blackmail

See **BRIBE**.

blatant, obvious

blatant *adjective*, means apparent or clear, and refers to a hostile or unwelcome action that is performed openly and deliberately, often in order to shock, and without regard to the consequences: *There were blatant violations of electoral procedure in the presidential election*. This is a disapproving term. See **FLAGRANT**.

obvious *adjective*, also means clear or apparent: *The most obvious difference between the PC and the Mac is their architecture*.

> Note that in the first example above, an obvious violation would be transparent but not necessarily deliberate.

bleach, blench, blanch, whiten

bleach *noun & verb*, as a noun is a powerful household cleaning agent. As a verb, it means to clean, and also to make something white or paler by removing its colour: *Sunbathing can bleach your hair within a few days*.

blench *verb*, means to react in a frightened way: *They blenched when the street artist dressed as a marble statue waved at them*.

blanch *verb*, means to make something such as food white by removing its colour: *Cover the stems of leeks and trench celery with earth in order to blanch them*. In another sense, it means to become pale through fear or shock: *He blanched as he looked at Colin's blood-drenched uniform*. This is only used in literary contexts.

whiten *verb*, means to turn something white by adding something to it: *Elizabeth I used highly toxic lead powder to whiten and enhance her complexion*.

blend words

See **WORD FORMATION**.

blink, wink

blink *verb*, means to open and shut both eyes in order to clear them of tears or dust: *Alan* *saw him blink away the tears which pricked his eyes.* **Blink** can be used negatively to indicate a lack of surprise: *He did not blink at the price they wanted for the house. On the blink* means not working: *The fuel gauge had gone on the blink shortly after the start.*

wink *verb*, means to close and open one eye as a signal which may imply humour, affection or that something is secret: *At the door his father turned to wink familiarly at Madeleine.*

bloc, block

bloc *noun*, means a group of countries or political bodies with common interests: *The former Soviet bloc was a world force.* **Bloc** is also used in the expression *en bloc*, which means as a whole: *If this is the only decision they can come up with, they should resign en bloc.*

block *noun*, has numerous meanings. It can be a quantity of something regarded as a unit: *a block of ice* or *a block of shares*. In BE, it is used to mean a building that is part of a hospital or school: *Our next class is in the science block*. The terms *tower block* and *block of flats* both relate to housing. In AE, **block** means a group of buildings surrounded by roads on all sides. Note that distance in urban areas in the US is often indicated in **blocks**: *Walk three blocks, then take a left.* See QUARTER.

blog, log

blog *noun*, means a diary or record of activities, thoughts, or beliefs from an individual or a group that appears on a web page or website, and is an abbreviation of *weblog*. Apart from being frequently updated, a **blog** invites readers to comment on matters that are presented, unlike a normal web page which is a finished document on the Internet. The person who writes a **blog** is a *blogger* and the process is termed *blogging*.

log *noun*, means an official record of events particularly during voyages by sea or air: *The captain's log explained the causes of the shipwreck. Logbook* is an old-fashioned alternative, although in BE it is the correct term for a vehicle's registration document.

blond, blonde

See HAIR COLOUR.

blue-collar

See WHITE-COLLAR.

blueprint, scheme

blueprint *noun*, means a detailed design produced in the early stages of a project setting out the way in which it should be carried out: *The European Commission produced a detailed blueprint for the accession of Eastern European countries into the Union.* Originally a **blueprint** was a plan printed with white lines on a special blue paper.

scheme *noun & verb*. As a noun, this is a plan that lays out the stages or system by which a project should be carried out: *An employee profit-sharing scheme is open to all UK full-time employees of the company*. In another sense, it means a devious plan to obtain something illegally: *This spam mail from Nigeria is one of those get-rich-quick schemes*. As a verb, it is only found with this second meaning. See PLAN.

blue-sky, hypothetical, horizon scanning

blue-sky *adjective*, describes innovative thinking or research that has no immediate practical applications: *Research is being used to stimulate blue-sky thinking on how to improve levels of literacy.*

hypothetical *adjective*, describes situations that are theoretically possible rather than existing in reality: *This contingency plan describes the hypothetical situation of severe flooding in central London.*

horizon scanning has been defined by the Office of Science and Technology of the British government as *the systematic examination of potential threats, opportunities and likely future developments, including (but not restricted to) those at the margins of current thinking and planning*.

blush, flush

blush *verb & noun*. As a verb, this means to become red in the face from embarrassment or shame: *'I was more shocked than embarrassed and so I did not blush'*. As a noun, it means the red colouring that appears on the cheeks when someone is embarrassed or ashamed.

flush *verb & noun*. As a verb, this means to become red, due to anger, embarrassment or over-exertion: *Robbie felt her cheeks flush scarlet*. In another sense, it also means to clean out a pipe with liquid. As a noun, a **flush** is the red colouring that appears on the body: *She hoped the hectic flush would be put down to the exertion of bending nearly double*. In another sense, it can also mean a strong feeling: *He felt a sudden flush of anger*.

Note that the *blush* is controlled by signals from the brain when people feel embarrassed or shamed, while a *flush* is due to physical stimuli.

board

See **PENSION**.

boat, ship

boat *noun*, usually means a small vessel for travelling on water: *I took the bag to my boat and sailed out to sea*. It can also be used to describe travel in larger vessels such as ferries: *They crossed the Baltic by boat*. Submarines are also termed **boats**.

ship *noun & verb*. As a noun, this means a large vessel for transporting passengers or goods. It is also possible to travel *by ship*. As a verb, to **ship** usually means to transport goods or people. Some use this verb only for **ships**. Nevertheless, *shipping* by air, road or rail is widely used: *Ship this consignment by air*. See **FREIGHT**.

bobby pin

See **HAIRPIN**.

body politic

See **POLITIC**.

bolder, boulder

bolder *comparative adjective*, describes behaviour in a person or animal that is braver or more confident than that in another: *After the pep talk, the manager felt bolder and returned to the press conference*. It can also describe something that stands out more: *On this animal the markings were much bolder and more complex*.

boulder *noun*, means a very large rock: *Progress was prevented as a large boulder blocked the road*. See **ROCK**.

bona fide, bona fides

bona fide *adjective*, means genuine and real: *British Actors' Equity exists so that only bona fide members of the profession may apply for work*. This is pronounced bōnă fídi /bəʊnə ˈfaɪdi/.

bona fides *noun*, means good standing. Though the final letter of the second word is 's', this is not a plural and takes a singular verb: *His bona fides is completely legitimate*. This is pronounced bōnă fídeez /bəʊnə ˈfaɪdiːz/.

bookish words

Are you a *bibliophage* (bíbbli-ōfayj /ˈbɪblɪəʊfeɪʤ/)? If so, this means that you devour books and are a keen reader or bookworm. Here are some other words for book-lovers and a few for book-haters:

Bibliophile (bíbbli-ōfīl /ˈbɪblɪəʊfaɪl/) means a person who is either a collector or a lover of books. If this becomes a passion, one may suffer from *bibliomania* (bibbli-ōmáyni-ă /bɪblɪəʊˈmeɪnɪə/) and even become a *bibliomaniac* (bibbli-ōmáyni-ack /bɪblɪəʊˈmeɪnɪæk/), a passionate collector or possessor of books. If you can never sell a book and your library overflows into the hall and bedroom you may be a *bibliotaph* (bíbbli-ōtaaf /ˈbɪblɪəʊtɑːf/). This means someone who hoards books. Another term is *biblioklept* (bíbbli-ōklept /ˈbɪblɪəʊklept/), meaning a person who steals books. People who are *bibliolaters* (bibbli-ólătěrz /bɪblɪˈɒlətərz/) are devoted either to all types of books, or just to the Bible. Informal and derogatory alternatives to the latter are *bible-puncher* or *bible-basher*.

If, on the other hand, you prefer a paperless society and hate books, you may be a *bibliophobe* (bíbbli-ōfōb /ˈbɪblɪəʊfəʊb/). If you go even further and physically attack books, you are a *biblioclast* (bíbbli-ōklasst /ˈbɪblɪəʊklæst/) – a person who destroys, cuts up or mutilates books.

B

border, bounds, boundary, frontier

border *noun*, means the edge of something: *Measure a border 2 cm in along all four sides*. **Border** also means the demarcation line between two countries or smaller administrative areas, such as counties. This often follows a natural division, such as a river, or range of mountains. **Border** is a less formal and less restrictive term than *frontier*: *There is no border in the accepted sense between Norway, Sweden and Finland*. In AE, the term *state line* is used for **borders** between states of the Union.

bounds *plural noun*, means limits, the furthest one can go with permission. It is most often found in the expression *out of bounds*, meaning beyond the permitted limits: *The east wing was not out of bounds*.

boundary *noun*, is a limit, or a line that marks a division between two areas: *Many of the county boundaries in England and Wales were changed in recent years*.

frontier *noun*, means a formal *border* separating two countries: *The geographical position of the frontier fluctuated with the fortunes of war*. **Frontier** is also used to refer to the limit of settled land, beyond which lies a wild and unknown territory: *A long way from anywhere, Kununurra has all the atmosphere of a frontier town*. A **frontier** can also be used figuratively to mean the limit of what is known about something or between two differences of opinion: *The frontier between liberalism and socialism remained open*.

born, borne

born *past participle & adjective*. As a verb, this means existing as a result of birth: *Andy Warhol was born in 1928 to Slovakian parents*. Figuratively, it can describe the origins of ideas or an organization: *During a brainstorming session in Chicago, the idea of Internet2 was born*. As an adjective, it means having a natural ability or quality: *Her mother was a born worrier*.

borne *adjective & past participle*. As an adjective, this means carried by a substance such as air, water or sea: *Water-borne diseases are going to lead to an epidemic in this area*. As a past participle of the verb to *bear*, it refers to the fact of having given birth: *His wife died at the age of thirty-three, having borne him nine sons*. It also means having endured something, as in: *It would look officious, and that could not be borne*. See BEAR.

Both of these words are past participles of the verb *bear*.

'I am a borne and bread Swede.'
(Student CV)

borrow, lend, loan

borrow *verb*, means to gain the temporary use of something that belongs to someone else: *You should be able to borrow these books from a library*. It also means to be *lent* money by a financial institution, which must be paid back at a specified rate of interest: *You can borrow a lump sum or you can borrow money in stages as you need*. The person who *borrows* is the *borrower*. Note that things are *borrowed from* people.

lend *verb*, means to let someone else use a possession temporarily: *Daniel had been offering to lend her his favourite book of poetry*. *Lent* is the past tense: *She lent me her copy of Anaïs Nin's most famous book*.

loan *noun & verb*. As a noun, this means something that a person or organization is given temporarily: *Some companies demand heavy charges for paying a loan off quickly*. Apart from its use with books and other objects, **loan** can also refer to sportsmen and sportswomen who sometimes move from one team to another *on loan*: *He has already been on loan at Middlesbrough and Stoke this season*. As a verb, **loan** is used as an alternative to *lend*: *He had loaned £5,000 to one of the most notorious crooks in Paddington*.

bosom

See BREAST.

both

See EACH.

bottom line, bottom out, rock bottom

bottom line *noun*, refers to the final total on a balance sheet or financial document that shows the profit or loss for the year: *The bottom line showed a pre-tax profit of £851,000 on sales of £18m*. In more general use, the **bottom line** means the final price that can be offered or the most important thing that will lead to a decision: *The bottom line is that the hydrogen-powered car is not profitable today*. The expressions fundamental issue or crux of the matter are alternatives to **bottom line** used in this sense.

bottom out *phrasal verb*, with reference to the price of goods or a difficult situation means to level off or not get any worse: *The price of bank shares bottomed out after the government stepped in*. Note that prices are likely to rise, but unlikely to fall further after they **bottom out**.

rock bottom *noun*, means the lowest point or level possible. The reference is to someone digging who hits bedrock and cannot dig any further: *House prices will fall another 15 per cent before they hit rock bottom*. When the price of goods or a relationship between people hits **rock bottom** this is the lowest level it can reach.

bought

See BROUGHT.

boulder

See BOLDER.

boulevard

See STREET.

boundary, bounds

See BORDER.

boyfriend, girlfriend

boyfriend *noun*. If a woman talks about her **boyfriend**, she means a romantic or sexual partner, not just a male friend: *Wendy's boyfriend was pleased with the idea of being a father*. However, since this word can be associated with adolescent relationships, partner is often regarded as a more adult choice. A man's **boyfriend** means his homosexual partner, although partner is a more common term. See FRIEND (ACQUAINTANCE), PARTNER.

girlfriend *noun*, can mean either a female romantic or sexual partner, or, especially in AE, a female friend. See FRIEND (ACQUAINTANCE).

boyish, girlish, *girlie/girly*

boyish *adjective*, means characteristic of a young man. It may be used to refer to women as well as men. It is a positive and flattering description: *The boyish grin is the same and at fifty-seven, he looks ten years younger*.

girlish *adjective*, means characteristic of a young woman. This is often negative: *Her mother regarded Sarah's feelings for him as a girlish infatuation*. See FEMALE, WOMANLY.

girlie/girly *adjective*, has two meanings: first to describe magazines that contain photos of naked or semi-naked women; and second as a description of clothing suitable for girls. It can also describe female behaviour which is usually in a disapproving way: *She lay on her back and spoke in a little girly voice*. Both spellings are equally acceptable.

brace

See PAIR.

brackets, parentheses

brackets *noun*, is the word used to describe a pair of marks that enclose words or figures in a text, adding an extra piece of information. They have various shapes and names. See PUNCTUATION GUIDE.

parentheses *noun*, is an alternative term for *round brackets*, especially in AE. Note that the stress comes on the second syllable, and that the last syllable rhymes with 'seas': părénthĕsseez /pə'renθəsiːz/. The singular form is *parenthesis* părénthĕssiss /pə'renθəsɪs/ which is sometimes used in a wider sense to indicate an afterthought or a digression: *He describes the three months of coalition government as 'a lamentable political parenthesis'*.

Brahman, Brahmin

Brahman *noun*, means a member of the highest caste in the Hindu caste system.

Brahmin *noun*, is an alternative spelling to *Brahman* and in AE is used for the members of socially important families in

New England: *The term Boston Brahmin came to connote great wealth, political influence, old New England roots.*

brain surgery

See ROCKET SCIENCE.

brake, break

brake *noun & verb*. As a noun, this is the device that slows down or stops a vehicle or other machinery: *Use the gears to slow down rather than making sudden brake stops*. As a verb, **brake** means to stop something: *She had to brake hard to avoid a milk float*. The word may also be used figuratively as both noun and verb: *Higher interest rates will put a brake on consumer spending*.

break *noun & verb*, has numerous meanings. As a noun, it means a pause or interval: *We will have a break in an hour*; or a change in continuity: *There was a break in style between Tony Blair and his predecessors*. As a verb, **break** means to disobey something such as a law. It also means to destroy something.

brand, brand name

See TRADEMARK.

bravery, bravado

bravery *uncountable noun*, means an attitude that shows courage: *Rescuing the child from the burning house demonstrated his extraordinary bravery*.

bravado *uncountable noun*, means behaviour that is deliberately intended to make others believe that you are brave: *About 30 recruits sat around wearing a variety of expressions from sickly smiles to tough bravado*.

breach

See BREECH.

breakdown, break down

breakdown *noun*, means either a collapse: *The poor woman had a nervous breakdown, and never returned to good health*, or an analysis, especially relating to statistics. When **breakdown** means collapse, it is often followed by *in*: *There was a real risk of a major breakdown in the emergency service*, but when it means classification or analysis, it is followed by *of*: *The breakdown of scores is shown in Table 3.3*.

break down *verb*, means to analyse; to stop functioning: *Lifts tend to break down when they are full of people*; to lose self-control due to emotional distress: *Her daughter's attack made her break down and weep*; or to divide into its parts: *Scientists have found a way to break down nitrates to nitrogen gas*. This phrasal verb is always written as two words, and pronounced with equal stress on both.

breakfast, power breakfast, wedding breakfast, dog's breakfast, dog's dinner

breakfast *noun*, means the first meal of the day: *She brings me breakfast in bed every day*. Note that the first syllable rhymes with 'neck'. A derived word is *brunch*, a blend of *breakfast* and *lunch* which is a meal for late risers at about 11 a.m.

power breakfast *noun*, means an early meeting of influential people to discuss business while eating breakfast.

wedding breakfast *noun*, means the meal served after a wedding. It is called the **wedding breakfast**, regardless of the time of day when it is eaten.

dog's breakfast *noun*, means a mess or muddle of people doing something extremely badly: *That group made a complete dog's breakfast of that number*.

dog's dinner *noun*, means something that is meant to be fashionable or impressive but appears to others to be a complete mess: *She was dressed up like a dog's dinner*. It is also widely used like *dog's breakfast* to mean a mess: *The government's policy in this area has been dismissed as a dog's dinner by an influential think tank*.

breaking and entering

See BURGLARY.

breast, bust, bosom, chest

breast *noun*, is a milk-producing organ in mammals. It also means the part of the body between the neck and the stomach: *He held her to his breast*. In another sense it means the cut of meat taken from the front of a lamb or from a bird between its forelegs or wings.

bust *noun*, either means the distance around a woman's body at the level of the *breasts*, used in measuring the sizes of clothes, or refers to a head-and-shoulders sculpture of either sex: *It was a terracotta bust of his father*.

bosom bo͝ozŏm /ˈbʊzəm/ *noun*, means a woman's *breasts*: *She held the baby close to her bosom*. It is also used figuratively to refer to a situation where someone is held in great affection, and is considered central: *Jerry returned to the bosom of his family*. **Bosom** is generally used in the singular when referring to an individual woman: *Her bosom heaved with pride as her dog won Best in Show*.

chest *noun*, is the anatomical and medical term for the front of the body in both males and females: *I was here the other day and had an X-ray of my chest*. It is also the figure given as a measurement for men's or children's clothes: *His chest size was out of stock*.

breath, breathe

breath *noun*, means the air coming into or out of the lungs: *He stared at her while drawing in a deep breath*. It also means fresh air: *Bring a breath of country air into your home*.

breathe *verb*, means to inhale and exhale: *The air we breathe is shared by all life on our planet*. When the '-ing' form is written, the final 'e' is omitted: *His breathing was irregular*.

breech, breach

breech *noun*, means the back part of a rifle or cannon where ammunition is loaded: *He pumped a shot into the breech and laid the gun down*. In a medical sense, a *breech birth* is one in which the lower part of the baby's body comes out of the mother first. This is also known as *breech delivery*. *Breeches* are special trousers that come just below the knee and are used for riding or as a part of ceremonial dress.

breach *noun & verb*. As a noun, this means the breaking of a contract or agreement: *This may give rise to a civil claim for breach of contract*. In another sense, it means a hole made in a wall: *Once more into the breach, dear friends* (Shakespeare). It is also used in phrases such as *breach of security* (e.g. obtaining classified information) and, in BE, *breach of the peace* (the crime of making too much noise, or fighting in public). As a verb it means either to break an agreement: *The company regularly breached the minimum wage regulations*, or to make a hole or opening: *The dam was breached in six places*.

> *'Failure to accept the wastes might be considered a breech of contract.'*
> (Republican Policy Committee, USA) **!**

brethren

See **BROTHER**.

brew, distil

brew *verb & noun*. As a verb, this means to make a drink such as tea or coffee by soaking and boiling the dry ingredients. Beer is first **brewed**, then fermented with hops for flavouring. Figuratively, **brew** can also be used to mean develop: *A storm is brewing* – which may mean literally stormy weather, or figuratively an argument. As a noun, this is in BE a drink such as tea that is brewed: *We've been working for two hours: it's time for a brew*. In AE it means a beer or can of beer: *A cold brew in a frosted glass*.

distil *verb*, means to produce a concentrated substance by boiling and condensation. Alcoholic spirits are produced by fermenting and then *distilling* the substance. **Distil** is the BE spelling. The AE spelling is *distill*. The forms *distilled* and *distilling* have the same spelling in both BE and AE.

> *'Brewed from genuine Scottish grapes.'*
> (Advert for a counterfeit 'Scotch' whisky) **!**

bribe, backhander, bung, blackmail

bribe *noun & verb*. As a noun, this means money or other benefits given to somebody to persuade them to partake in an illegal transaction: *He attempted to kill the mayor for refusing to pay an immense bribe*. As a verb, it means to give a public official money or other inducements in order to carry out an action: *We had to bribe the customs official to get into the country*. Children are often **bribed** with sweets or ice cream to make them behave well.

backhander *noun*, means an illegal payment to someone in exchange for favours: *The government is insisting on these changes, and* *some people are hinting that a backhander is involved*. This is an informal term.

bung *noun*. As a noun, this is an informal term in BE for a bribe. It is commonly used in connection with transfers in football and other sports: *The agent claimed that he had never paid bungs to any manager, but the court found him guilty on three counts of bribery*. See KICKBACK.

blackmail *uncountable noun & verb*. As a noun, this means money demanded from someone who threatens to reveal secret information about you: *The politician said that the threat was just blackmail, and rang the police*. As a verb it means to attempt to force someone to pay money by threatening to reveal a secret. *Moral* or *emotional blackmail* does not demand money, but tries to persuade someone to behave in a particular way.

bridal, bridle

bridal *adjective*, refers to a bride or things connected to a wedding: *The bridal suite was very popular in the hotel*.

bridle *noun & verb*. As a noun, this means the headgear on a horse that is used to control it. As a verb it means to put the headgear on a horse: *She bridled the horse quickly*. The phrasal verb *bridle at* means to show resentment: *She bridled at his accusation*.

bring, take

bring *verb*, means to move something or someone towards the speaker or the place referred to where the speaker will be: *When are you going to bring Julie home?* **Bring** can also be the cause of something: *The cold weather will bring icy roads with it*. The past tense and participle is *brought*. See BROUGHT.

take *verb*, means to move something or someone away from the speaker: *When are you going to take Julie home?*

> These two words focus on the physical position of the speaker: *She brought the children to Canada* means that the speaker is in Canada. *She took the children to Canada* means that the speaker is not in Canada. There are numerous phrasal verbs that modify the meaning of both these words, and the *Longman Dictionary of Contemporary English* has an extensive selection.

bring up, touch upon

bring up *phrasal verb*, means to raise children: *I am trying to bring up these girls to be strong, patient and unselfish*; or a topic for discussion: *Don't bring up the subject of money immediately!* In another context, **bring up** means to vomit.

touch (up)on *phrasal verb*, means to mention, or discuss something briefly, without going into detail: *I wish to touch on three proposals*. See BROACH.

Britain/Great Britain, England, United Kingdom/UK, British Isles

Britain/Great Britain is the island which includes England, Scotland and Wales. These are officially geographical terms but are often used to mean the *United Kingdom*.

England is the largest of the four countries which make up the United Kingdom. Note that **England** may mean the English: *England expects that every man will do his duty* (Lord Nelson's signal to his fleet before the Battle of Trafalgar, 1805). Many English people forget that **England** is not a political entity, but merely part of the *United Kingdom*. The English refers to people born or living in England, not to their nationality. See BRITISH.

(The) United Kingdom or **the UK** means Britain and Northern Ireland. This is a political unit, formally named *the United Kingdom of Great Britain and Northern Ireland*. The definite article is always used in running text: *Contributions came from all over the United Kingdom*. See DEFINITE ARTICLE (GRAMMAR TIPS).

British Isles is a geographical term which covers Great Britain and the whole of Ireland, and smaller offshore islands from Shetland to the Channel Islands: *Geographically peripheral communities in the British Isles, such as Shetland, Tory Island and the Isle of Lewis*.

> These terms all refer to different geographical or political areas.

British, Briton, Britisher, Brit, English

British *adjective*, describes people from the United Kingdom, and is the official nationality of such people. The word **British** is always capitalized.

Briton *noun*, means an individual *British* person, but it is rare for **Britons** to use it about themselves. It occurs in newspapers to save space: *Briton given top military job in NATO*, and is correct for the *ancient Britons* (the inhabitants of Britain before the Roman invasion of AD 43).

Britisher *noun*, is an old-fashioned AE term for a British subject. It is rarely found in BE.

Brit *noun & adjective*, is an abbreviation of *British*, *Britisher* or *Briton* and is an informal term used in AE and BE, especially in the popular press: *Holiday Brit dies in jet ski tragedy*. It should be avoided in serious writing.

English *noun & adjective*. As a noun, this is the main language of most British people but it also means the people who come from England. Remember that many British people are Scottish, Welsh or Northern Irish, not **English**. As an uncountable noun, **English** refers to literature written in English and to the academic subject: *She has taken a Master's degree in English*. As an adjective, it relates to England or its people: *This is according to English law*; or it relates to the language used in Britain, the US and many other countries.

British English (BE), American English (AE)

BE and AE are the two main varieties of English. They are classified as different in dictionaries and are defined with different spellcheckers in computer software. They should always be distinguished. It is best to be consistent and use one variety only.

This book has listed some of the differences between BE and AE usage under the respective headwords. Though BE and AE are about 80–90 per cent the same, the main differences can be summarized as follows:

Pronunciation

There are wide regional differences of pronunciation even within both BE and AE. The way BE and AE speakers pronounce the vowels of words like *new, Tuesday, clerk, data* and *dance/grass* (in southern BE), reveals some of the main differences between BE and AE. Also, the pronunciations of *fertile* and *missile* are a good indication of BE/AE differences (fúrtīl /ˈfɜːrtaɪl/, míssīl /ˈmɪsaɪl/ in BE and fúrtl /ˈfɜːrtl̩/, míssl /ˈmɪsl̩/ in AE). For those with a particular interest in pronunciation differences between BE and AE, the major pronunciation dictionaries all include comprehensive coverage.

Stressing

Many words are stressed differently in BE and AE. Some typical differences are BE *advértisement* and AE *advertísement*; BE *alumínium* and AE *alúminum* (note also the difference in spelling); and BE *labóratory* and AE *láboratory*.

Grammar

The AE past participle of *get* is *gotten* when it means acquired; in BE it is *got*. AE: *I've gotten a new automobile*; BE: *I've got a new car*. There are some other irregular verb differences, such as *dived* (past participle and past tense of *dive* in BE) and *dove* (AE); *leapt* (mostly BE) and *leaped* (mostly AE); *pleaded* (BE) and *pled* (AE); *sank* (BE) and *sunk* (AE); *shrank* (BE) and *shrunk* (AE); *spelt* (BE) and *spelled* (BE and AE). For a complete list see lists of irregular verbs in dictionaries or on the Internet.

Many differences occur in the use of prepositions. Examples:

BE	*AE*
a quarter past three	a quarter after three
a quarter to four	a quarter of four
at school	in school
fill in a form	fill out a form
Friday to Sunday	Friday through Sunday
meet somebody	meet with somebody
stay at home	stay home
visit somebody	visit with somebody

Spelling

Some of the most common differences, by type:

BE		AE	
-ce	defence*	*-se*	defense*
-eable	saleable	*-able*	salable
-ll-	travelling	*-l-*	traveling
-mme	programme (program in EDP)	*-m*	program
non-	non-profit		nonprofit
-oe-	diarrhoea	*-e-*	diarrhea
-ogue	catalogue	*-og*	catalog
-oul-	mould	*-ol-*	mold
-our	colour	*-or*	color
	neighbour		neighbor
-re	centre	*-er*	center
	metre		meter
	litre		liter
-yse	analyse	*-yze*	analyze

* Ministry of Defence (BE) and Department of Defense (AE) should always be spelt in these ways, as they are proper names.

Note that both *-ize* and *-ise* are used at the end of verbs in BE and AE. See **-IZE, -ISE**.

Spelling differences in some common words:

BE	AE
aluminium	aluminum
cheque	check
cosy	cozy
crayfish	crawfish
draught	draft
grey	gray
kerb (pavement)	curb (sidewalk)
manoeuvre	maneuver
pyjamas	pajamas
skilful	skillful
speciality	specialty
storey	story
sulphur	sulfur
tyre	tire

Note that some words that are hyphenated in BE are written as one word in AE. Example: non-linear (BE) and nonlinear (AE). See **HYPHENATION IN INDIVIDUAL WORDS (PUNCTUATION GUIDE)**.

Vocabulary

Some of the most common differences:

BE	AE
aeroplane	airplane
anywhere	anyplace
autumn	fall
badge (on a blazer)	patch
banknote (note)	bill
barrister, solicitor	attorney
bill (in a restaurant)	check
bonnet (of a car)	hood
boot (of a car)	trunk
bumbag	fanny pack
bumper (of a car)	fender
biscuit	cookie
car	automobile
carriage (railway)	car (railroad)
chemist	drugstore
cupboard	closet
diary	datebook
draughts	checkers
drawing pin	thumbtack
dustbin, rubbish bin	garbage can, trash can
estate (car)	station wagon
estate agent	realtor
first floor	second floor (and so on)
flat	apartment
gear lever	gearshift
ground floor	first floor
handbag	purse
hoarding	billboard
lift (for people)	elevator
maize	corn
maths	math
motorway	expressway, freeway
nappy	diaper
off-licence	liquor store
pants	underwear, shorts
paraffin	kerosene
pavement	sidewalk
petrol	gas/gasoline
purse	wallet
railway(s)	railroad
return ticket	round-trip ticket
road surface	pavement
roundabout	traffic circle
saloon (car)	sedan
single ticket	one-way ticket
spanner	wrench
sweets	candy
tap	faucet
toll road	turnpike, toll road
trousers	pants
turn-up (on trousers)	cuff
vest	undershirt
waistcoat	vest
wallet	billfold

Note the difference in weights and measures:

British/metric scale	*American scale*
tonne (1000 kg)	
also called metric ton	
long ton (2240 lb or 1016 kg)	short ton (2000 lb or 907 kg)
fluid ounce (28.4 ml)	fluid ounce (29.6 ml)
pint (20 fl.oz or 0.57 l)	pint (16 fl.oz. or 0.47 l)
gallon (4.55 l)	gallon (3.79 l)

British place names

Place names can tell us a lot about the history and geography of a country, so long as we can untangle the spelling and pronunciation problems. In Britain we have names of Celtic, Roman, Anglo-Saxon, Viking and Norman (French) origins, as well as modern inventions. There are even a few which probably date back to before the time in the eighth century BC when the Celtic languages arrived in Britain. Many of these names tell us something about the local geography, as well as indicating the ownership or function of settlements.

Dover is Celtic in origin, and is derived from a word meaning 'waters', while **London**, although it first appears in its Latin form *Londinium*, is also of pre-Roman date, and has not yet had its meaning definitely confirmed. The many place names ending in *-chester*, *-caster* or *-cester* indicate Roman settlements (*castra* is the Latin word for camp), although the form in which we have these names is Anglo-Saxon, and the names themselves are Anglo-Saxon (**Chester**, for instance, was known as *Deva* during the Roman period).

The Angles, Saxons and Jutes overran the whole of England except for Cornwall between the fifth and eighth centuries, giving their names to places as they settled the land (including **England** – Angle-land), but also often leaving the Celts alone in their own settlements. The *Wal-* of the many places called **Walton** is often, although not always, the same 'wal' that we find in the word *Wal*es (meaning country of the Celts). The Anglo-Saxon word *burh*, meaning a fortified place (much like the Latin *castra*), is found in many place names which now end in *-borough*, *-brough*, *-burgh* (**Scarborough**, **Middlesbrough**, **Edinburgh**). The endings *-ham*, *-ing*, *-ton* are also typical Anglo-Saxon place name endings: **Rotherham**, **Reading**, **Preston**.

The area of Viking settlement in the ninth to eleventh centuries is clearly shown on maps from the distribution of the endings *-by* (**Grimsby**), *-thorp* (**Scunthorpe**), *-thwaite* (**Slaithwaite**) and *-toft* (**Lowestoft**). These are almost all restricted to an area north of a line drawn roughly from the Thames estuary to the Wirral peninsula just south of Liverpool.

The Normans, who invaded and conquered England in 1066, have left less of a mark on place names, but **Richmond** ('rich mountain') is one example of a Norman name. Many Anglo-Saxon place names have their Norman owner's name attached to help distinguish them: **Milton Keynes** for instance (the middle settlement belonging to the Keynes family).

In Wales and Scotland, many of the place names are Welsh or Scots Gaelic, and these present their own problems for people from elsewhere, especially of pronunciation: **Llanelli** hlannéhli /ɬæ'neɬi/, **Caersws** kīrssoóoss /kaɪər'suːs/, **Kirkcudbright** kĭrkoóobri /kər'kuːbri/, **Milngavie** mŭlgī́ /mʌl'gaɪ/.

In modern times, owners of large businesses have sometimes built villages for their workers, and given them what they thought were appropriate names: **Saltaire** pronounced sawltáir /sɔːl'teər/ was built by Sir Titus Salt in the Aire Valley; and **Port Sunlight** was built by the Lever brothers and named after their 'Sunlight' soap.

Pronunciation

It is important, both out of courtesy, and in order to be understood, to pronounce place names correctly. A particular problem is the ending *-wich*: in **Ipswich** the 'w' is pronounced: íps-witch /ˈɪpswɪʧ/, but in **Norwich** and **Greenwich** it is silent: nórritch /ˈnɒrɪʧ/ or nórrij /ˈnɒrɪʤ/, grínnij /ˈgrɪnɪʤ/. Another problem is the names ending in -cester: **Leicester** léstĕr /ˈlestər/, **Worcester** wŏŏstĕr /ˈwʊstər/, **Bicester** bístĕr /ˈbɪstər/, etc. Wherever possible, check the pronunciation of place names in a pronouncing dictionary – or ask a long-time resident.

> *A foreign radio broadcast included a 5-minute report from a place in London that the speaker called 'Green witch'.* **!**

broach, brooch

broach *verb*, means to mention a matter for discussion. It is often used about a delicate topic: *How can I broach the subject with some degree of sensitivity?* This is a formal word and bring up, touch on or raise are alternatives. See BRING UP.

brooch *noun*, is a decorated pin usually worn by women: *She wore her pearl and diamond brooch because he wanted everyone to see it.* Pin is the AE term for a **brooch**: *She wore a pin with three diamonds set in gold on her blouse*. See BADGE.

These two words are pronounced identically, and rhyme with *coach*.

broad, broadly, wide, widely

broad *adjective*, describes the distance from side to side of an area or object. It gives the impression of spaciousness: *To my left were the broad muddy reaches of the Severn*. In figurative uses, it means wide-ranging or general: *The Party needs the trade unions to provide broad and representative support*.

broadly *adverb*, means in a general way, focusing on the main facts rather than the details. In another sense, it means a range of different things, such as a *broadly based* education.

wide *adjective*, describes the distance from side to side of an area or object, but it is generally used to refer to openings or distances between limits: *By the time the storm is fully formed it may be as much as 400 miles wide.*

widely *adverb*, means either occurring in many places or to a large extent: *He was Oxford educated, widely travelled, and still more widely read*. The phrase *widely read* may mean either read by a lot of people: *a widely read novel*, or as in the quotation above, having read many books.

broadcast

See TRANSMIT.

broil

See GRILL.

brother, brethren

brother *noun*, means a male who has the same parents as a sibling. In another sense, it means a male member of certain groups, such as religious orders or trade unions. Black males often use this as a form of address for other black males. See SIBLING.

brethren *noun*, is the old plural of *brother*, and is especially used for members of religious groups: *Apart from the monks, there were frequently large numbers of lay brethren*. When used in organizations or sects such as the *Plymouth Brethren*, the term **brethren** may include women: *Our Brethren in the Labour Party*. See PLURAL NOUNS (WORD FORMATION).

brought, bought

brought *verb*, is the past tense and past participle of *bring*: *The pain brought him out of his unconsciousness*. See BRING.

bought *verb*, is the past tense and past participle of *buy*: *New potatoes should be bought in small amounts*. The phrase *he cannot be bought* implies that a person cannot be bribed: *She couldn't be bought and she wouldn't be forced out of here*.

Because of the similar contexts in which these verbs may be used, they are frequently confused. It may help to remember that the present tense of *bring* contains an 'r', while the present of *buy* does not.

brown

See HAIR COLOUR.

brownstone

See **TOWN HOUSE**.

brunet, brunette

See **HAIR COLOUR**.

buffet (noun and verb)

buffet *noun*, is a meal where you serve yourself from a central table rather than be served where you sit: *The dining-room was crowded as she made her way to the cold buffet*. A *buffet car* is a railway carriage where food and drink can be bought. It may be pronounced either **búffay** /'bʌfeɪ/ or **bóofay** /'buːfeɪ/. Note that the last vowel is pronounced as in the word 'day', and that the 't' is silent.

buffet *verb*, means to hit something and cause it to move unsteadily. **Buffet** usually refers to the action of natural phenomena, such as air or sea currents. It is commonly used in the passive: *The plane was buffeted by the strong winds*. Note that the final 't' is pronounced: **búffět** /'bʌfɪt/.

bug, bugger

bug *noun & verb*. As a noun, this means either an insect or an electronic listening device: *There was a bug planted in the phone*. In computer terminology, **bug** means a defect: *We have to remove the bugs in this software*. As a verb it means to bother someone: *Stop ringing me, you are bugging me*. This is an informal word.

bugger, *verb*, means either to spoil: *The storm buggered our weekend*, or to be exhausted: *I was buggered after that long drive*. **Bugger** also means to commit an act of sodomy and in AE only this sexual meaning is common. As a result some BE slang expressions may lead to transatlantic misunderstandings. Some people may find this word offensive, so it should not be used in formal contexts.

building

See **HOUSE**.

bull market.

See **BEAR MARKET**.

bung

See **BRIBE**.

bungalow, ranch house

bungalow *noun*, means a single-storey house in BE. It may also mean a large house with more than one storey in some parts of Asia.

ranch house *noun*, means either any type of house on a ranch or in AE a *bungalow*.

burglary, housebreaking, breaking and entering

burglary *noun*, means the illegal entry of a house or building, usually by forcing open a door or window, with the intent to steal something, cause damage, or injure a person: *He also admitted burglary at another house in Kensington Road*.

housebreaking *noun*, means the illegal entry of a house or building, usually by forcing open a door or window, with the intent to steal something, cause damage, or injure a person. This is mostly used in BE, and generally refers to actions during daylight hours: *Housebreaking on this scale deserves a long prison sentence*.

breaking and entering *noun*, means the illegal entry of a house or building, usually by forcing open a door or window. If there is no intent to steal something and this was done in order to find shelter in a storm, it is still illegal but in most countries is not the same as *burglary* or *housebreaking*. *Break-in* is an alternative term.

burgle, rob, steal, thieve

burgle *verb*, means to enter a house or building illegally, usually by forcing open a door or window, in order to *steal* something: *We were burgled three times last year*. *Burglarize* is an AE alternative to **burgle**. It is a back-formation from the noun *burglar*. See **BACK-FORMATION (WORD FORMATION)**.

rob *verb*, means to take property from a person or place by force or threat of force: *The gang robbed the bank at lunchtime*; *A man has been charged with attempting to rob two shop assistants*. **Rob** is used to indicate that a person or place has been the victim of thieves. It does not tell us what has been taken.

steal *verb*, means to take property belonging to a person or place without any legal right to ownership: *Thieves had used a chainsaw to cut off and steal a petrol pump*. The thing that is taken is *stolen*, not *robbed*. If something is *stolen*, this means it is physically removed: *The cash machine was stolen by a gang using a fork-lift truck*. **Steal** does not tell us who the victims of the crime are.

thieve *verb*, means to *steal* something: *Two weeks after he was released, he started thieving again*. This is an informal usage in BE.

burial, funeral

burial *noun*, means the practice of burying the dead: *Six weeks after his burial, the soldiers discovered his grave*. See INTERMENT.

funeral *noun*, means the ceremony at which a dead person is buried or cremated: *They would be given a proper funeral in the parish church*. **Funeral** is also used informally in a wider sense to advise someone that they are responsible for any negative outcome: *If you get involved in illegal activities, that is your funeral*.

bursary

See SCHOLARSHIP.

bury, berry

bury *verb*, means to cover something with earth, sand or snow: *George decided to bury the girl's body in the gravel*. It is also used figuratively: *The government should take advantage of the world crisis to bury any controversial decisions*. See BURIAL.

berry *noun*, means a small fruit that grows on a plant: *The berries were delicious with cream*.

bus, coach

bus *noun & verb*. As a noun, this is a vehicle for public transport on a fixed route: *There is a regular bus service into Oxford*. In BE, a **bus** is normally reserved for the local public transport of people and is not the same as a *coach*. In AE, **bus** covers both the BE sense of the term and the term *coach*: *The Greyhound bus only takes 5 hours to Boston*. The plural of **bus** is *buses* in BE: *Special buses will run every Sunday from the end of May*, but may also be *busses* in AE. As a verb, it means to transport by **bus**: *In parts of the US, busing students has political significance*. The verb forms in both BE and AE may be spelt with either single 's': *buses, bused*, or double 'ss': *busses, bussed*.

coach *noun*, usually means a single-decker bus that is used for transport for medium-distance and long journeys. This is a BE term: *Travel is by luxury coach with an experienced driver*. **Coach** in BE is associated with luxury, but in AE, **coach** means economy class when referring to air or train fares: *We enjoyed the trip even though we only paid coach-class fares*. In another sense in BE, a **coach** is a railway carriage. In AE this would be called a car.

business, firm, enterprise, company, concern, undertaking

business *noun*, and **firm** *noun*, both mean a commercial organization, which can be of any size. **Business** is used as a countable noun to mean a specific shop or a *company*: *She has a small hair salon business*. This has the plural *businesses*. **Business** as an uncountable noun means commerce and trade: *He was responsible for an enormous amount of business*. In another sense, **business** means a series of events or actions that are typically seen as negative or scandalous: *The people on the stock market are up to their usual monkey business*.

enterprise *noun*, means a commercial organization. A *small* or *medium-sized enterprise (SME)* may differ considerably in size or in the number of staff from one country to another.

company *noun*, is the term used for registered *enterprises* with shareholders: *Limited company* (*Ltd*), or *Public Limited Company* (*PLC*). See PLC.

concern *noun*, means any type of commercial organization such as a *business, enterprise* or *firm*. Note that this term can refer to enterprises of all sizes. A *going concern* is an organization that is making a profit: *The company was turned around last year, and is now a going concern*. See GROUP.

undertaking *noun*, means an important job or piece of work: *This project will be a risky undertaking*. In another sense it means a formal promise: *I give an undertaking that* *we shall not attempt to delay its progress unduly*. In documents from the European Commission it is often used as a synonym for *enterprise*, which makes many native English speakers think of the business of an undertaker.

bust

See **BREAST**.

button

See **BADGE**.

by, by-, bye

by *preposition & adverb*. As a preposition, this is often used to indicate who is responsible for an action: *The car was washed by hand*. **By** can also refer to what causes something: *He crossed the road and was hit by a bus*. In a third sense, it denotes proximity: *He was standing by the window*. As an adverb, it refers to something that is passing: *As he looked out of the window, a bus went by*. See **PREPOSITIONS (GRAMMAR TIPS), VIA**.

by- *prefix*, is used in combination with nouns to mean secondary or local. It is sometimes joined with a hyphen in BE: *by-election, by-product*. There are other words with a **by-** prefix, where the adverb **by** is placed first, and there is no hyphen: *bygone, bystander, bypass*. *Bye-* is an alternative BE spelling for some of these words such as *bye-law*. Note that *byname* and *byline* are written as one word.

bye *exclamation*, is an informal way of saying *goodbye*, and may be repeated as *bye-bye*. See **GOODBYE**.

by means of

See **VIA**.

byte

See **BIT**.

Spelling

ba**ll**oon	Note the double -ll-
ba**rr**acks	Note the double -rr-
bas**in**	Note the -in ending
ba**zaa**r	Note the single -z- followed by double -aa-
begi**nn**er	Remember the double -nn-
bicente**nn**ial	Remember the double -nn-
bi**s**ect	Note the single -s-
bi**zarr**e	Note single -z-, single -a- and double -rr-
bound**ary**	Note the -ary ending
br**ie**f	-i- before -e-
bro**cc**o**l**i	Note the double -cc- and single -l-
b**uo**yant	Remember the -u-

C

c, ca

See CIRCA.

cabbage

See VEGETABLE.

cache, cachet

cache kash /kæʃ/ *noun*, means a hidden store or hoard: *Maisie had concealed her cache of sweets under her jumper*. This is pronounced like the word 'cash'.

cachet káshay /ˈkæʃeɪ/ *noun*, means prestige: *It was a university without the cachet of Oxford, but it had produced many eminent scholars*. Note that this word has two syllables, and that the second rhymes with 'may'. This is a formal word.

cacophony

See EUPHONY.

cafeteria, canteen

cafeteria *noun*, means a restaurant where people select food and drink from a counter and then pay before taking it to a table. *Cafeterias* are often found in office buildings, colleges and hospitals. See CAFÉ (RESTAURANT).

canteen *noun*, means either a place where food and drink are served in schools, offices, military bases and factories, or a small container for carrying water typically used by soldiers or people on expeditions. As **canteen** in the sense of a place where food is served is typically BE, use *cafeteria* when addressing an international audience.

calculus, calculuses, calculi

calculus *noun*, is the branch of mathematics that deals with the properties of derivatives and integrals: *Calculus is the basis of the software that measures the speed of falling objects*. **Calculus** is also used to means a stone in the medical sense, e.g. a kidney stone.

calculuses is the plural form of *calculus* in mathematics.

calculi kálkyŏŏlī /ˈkælkjʊlaɪ/ is the plural form of *calculus* in its medical sense: *His pain was caused by calculi in the gall bladder*.

calendar, calender, colander

calendar *noun*, is a monthly list of dates that is often hung on a wall as a reminder or a presentation of a seasonal timetable: *The new racing calendar was eagerly awaited*.

calender *noun*, is a machine that presses a material such as cloth or paper between rollers.

colander kúllănděr /ˈkʌləndər/ *noun*, is a perforated bowl used for draining vegetables or pasta. *Cullender* is an alternative spelling for **colander**.

call

See PHONE.

callus, callous

callus *noun*, is hardened skin: *After 20 years as a guitarist, he had a callus on his right thumb*.

callous *adjective*, means cruel and unfeeling: *This must be a deliberate, callous attempt to inflict hurt*.

calm, tranquil

calm *adjective & noun*. As an adjective, this means showing no emotion, not excited, worried or angry: *The voice was calm and soft and the words were ordinary*. **Calm** is also used to describe a stretch of water when there are no large waves, or weather that is not stormy: *When we entered the harbour, we finally had some calm water*. As a noun, **calm** means a peaceful situation: *The city returned to calm after the recent violence*. It also means an unflustered character: *She had always prided herself on her calm, her coolness under pressure*. The phrase *the calm before the storm* describes a situation in which everyone is expecting something dramatic to happen. The phrase is used particularly in economic and political writing: *Until April 1940, there was little action in the West, but this was just the calm before the storm*.

tranquil *adjective*, describes a place or a situation that is quiet and peaceful: *The hotel has a sun terrace and swimming pool set in the peaceful and tranquil gardens on the lakeside*. This is a formal word that is usually found in written English.

campus, grounds (of universities)

campus *noun*, means the land and buildings of a university, which may be in different locations: *The university chaplains contribute to community life at each campus*. In BE, a *campus university* is one which is outside a town or city, with all teaching facilities, student accommodation and some shops on one site. The plural is *campuses*. In AE, **campus** is commonly used to refer to the land and buildings of a range of institutions, including schools, hospitals and large companies.

grounds *plural noun*, means the enclosed land or gardens around a large building, usually a large house: *Parking space can be found within the hospital grounds*. See also **GROUNDS (REASON)**.

can[1], could, may, might

can *verb*, indicates ability: *He can play the piano very well*. Informally, it is also used for asking and giving permission: *'Can I use your phone, please?' 'Yes, of course you can'* – but refer to *may* below. In another sense, **can** refers to predictable behaviour: *The train can get very full at rush hour*. It is also used with verbs expressing the five senses, i.e. hear, see, touch, taste and smell: *Since the operation, he can touch his toes again*. *Cannot* is the usual negative form in formal written English. Note that it is normally written as one word. It is only written as two words: *can not*, when there is equal stress on both parts, as in: *I can* not *agree, I can refuse to do it*. *Can't* is a contraction of *cannot*. This is an oral expression which should be avoided in formal English and in general written English for business or academic purposes. See **CONTRACTIONS**.

could *verb*, is the past of *can*, but also has other uses, including making a request: *Could I use your phone, please?* This is more polite and formal than *can*, but unlike *can* and *may*, **could** is not used for giving permission. Use *may* instead. **Could** is also used either to make a suggestion: *If you think it would help, we could go and see him*; or to show annoyance: *How could you be so rude?*

may *verb*, is used to ask for and to give permission in more formal contexts than *can*, and therefore **may** sounds more polite: *'May I use your phone, please?'* **May** is also used to express a possibility: *The train may be late this morning because of engineering work on the line*. However, it is more common and less formal to use *might* in this sense. The phrase *may have* is used to indicate the possibility of a past action which may still be true: *I don't know where John is. He may have gone home*. This should not be confused with *might have* (see below). The only negative form is *may not*.

might *verb*, normally expresses possibility: *'Are you coming to the party?' 'Yes, I might'*. The phrase *might have* is often used in a similar way to *may have*, but they have different meanings: *might have* refers to a possible result of a past action, which we now know did not happen: *If John had not disappeared, we might have managed to catch the last bus home*. The negative forms are *might not* and, informally, *mightn't*.

can[2], tin (noun)

can *noun*, is a sealed metal container, in BE for drinks or other liquids, or in AE, for drinks or solid food: *In 1988 a total of 5.6 billion drinks cans were sold in the UK*. Other types of **can** may be made of other materials: *'Professional Grade Plastic Watering Can' (advertisement)*.

tin *noun*, is an uncountable noun when referring to the metal itself (chemical symbol Sn): *The bottom surface of the enclosure is lined with tin*. However, it is a countable noun when used to mean a sealed metal container for food (BE): *She bought four tins of beans for the children's party*. A **tin** is also a food container, such as a *biscuit tin*, or a cooking utensil used without a lid for roasting or baking food, such as a *cake tin* (in AE this is called a *cake pan*).

canal, channel

canal *noun*, is an artificial waterway either for shipping, or for the movement of water for irrigation: *The Panama Canal was opened in 1914*. **Canal** also has an anatomical use:

the *alimentary canal* and the *birth canal* are both used to describe passages within the body.

channel *noun*, is a natural waterway, typically a narrower long stretch of water that joins two larger areas: the *English Channel*. An even narrower stretch of water is known as a strait. **Channel** also has several other meanings such as the band of frequencies used for radio and television transmission, which has been broadened to mean the particular radio or TV station itself: *Channel 4*; and a medium for communication: *If a proper legal system existed there would be official channels of redress*. When **channel** is used as a verb, the past and present participle forms are spelt *channelled* and *channelling* in BE, but *channeled* and *channeling* in AE. See STRAIT.

cancel

See ANNUL.

cancer, Cancer

cancer *noun*, (not capitalized) is a disease which may affect almost any part of the body: *A court has ruled that passive smoking causes lung cancer, asthma and respiratory problems in children*.

Cancer *noun*, (capitalized) is the name of a constellation, and also the fourth sign of the zodiac: *People born under the sign of Cancer are supposed to be romantic, imaginative and sympathetic*. This is symbolized by a crab. See HOROSCOPES.

Cantab, Oxon

Cantab *abbreviation*, is short for *Cantabrigiensis*, the Latin for *of Cambridge* (University), and is placed in brackets after the abbreviation for a person's degree.

Oxon *abbreviation*, is short for *Oxoniensis*, the Latin for *of Oxford* (University), and is placed in brackets after the abbreviation for a person's degree. Stephen Hawking has degrees from both Oxford and Cambridge, so that he may be referred to as Stephen Hawking BA (Oxon), PhD (Cantab). See OXBRIDGE.

canteen

See CAFETERIA.

canvas, canvass

canvas *noun*, is a type of cloth used for sails, large tents and oil paintings: *The artist moved into the countryside with his paints, brushes, and a good supply of canvases*. When referring to the material in general, **canvas** is an uncountable noun.

canvass *verb*, means to attempt to gather votes and get support: *David systematically canvassed the independent members of Parliament*. In another sense it means to determine people's opinions on a specific issue.

capacity

See ABILITY.

capital, capitol

capital *noun*, refers to the city or town in any country or state that is the seat of government. It is often, but not always, the city that is either the largest in terms of population or the most important economically. As an uncountable noun, it can refer to an amount of money that has been invested: *The redundancy payment was an important source of capital*.

capitol *noun*, is a building where the legislature of each state in the US meets. In general use it is not capitalized, but when it refers to a specific building it is: *Straight ahead of him he could see the dome of the Texas State Capitol*. If no other state is mentioned, then *The Capitol* (capitalized) refers to the building in Washington, DC where the US Congress meets.

capital letters

See WRITING SKILLS.

capital punishment, corporal punishment

capital punishment *noun*, means the execution of a person following a legal procedure: *After 1977, capital punishment was reinstated in the United States courts*. The method of execution may vary, but the origin of the term (Latin *caput* – the head) implies beheading. The death penalty is a more informal term for **capital punishment**.

corporal punishment *noun*, means a beating, flogging, slapping or smacking given for misbehaviour. Caning was a common form of **corporal punishment** in British schools until the late twentieth century: *Instead of inflicting corporal punishment on the children maybe the parents should face a heavy fine or a jail sentence.*

carat, caret

carat *noun*, is a unit of weight used for gems and also the unit of purity of gold: *A 22 carat gold ring*. In AE, the unit of purity in gold is also spelt *karat*.

caret *noun*, is a proofreader's mark such as ^ below text to show that something has been omitted and needs to be added.

Both these words are pronounced the same as the vegetable (carrot).

'The proofreader must be tired: he asked me to have a careful look at his carrots.' !

caravan, trailer, mobile home

caravan *noun*, means an unpowered vehicle towed behind a car that is used for holidays or temporary accommodation: *The caravans stretched for miles along the cliffs*. In AE this is called a camper, camper van or motor home.

trailer *noun*, means an unpowered vehicle towed behind a car or truck for transporting cargo, goods or pleasure craft: *They moved the boat to winter storage on a trailer*. In AE, **trailer** also means a *mobile home*. A caravan site in AE is termed a *trailer park*.

mobile home *noun*, means an unpowered vehicle towed by a truck to be used as a home or an office.

car boot sale, garage sale

car boot sale *noun*, is an outdoor gathering where people place objects that they wish to sell in the boot of their car or on a table. This is typically a BE term.

garage sale *noun*, is a sale of furniture, household goods or used clothes that is held in the garage of a house or on the drive. This is also called a yard sale in AE.

cardinal number

See **NUMBERS**.

care about, care for

care about *verb*, means to be interested or concerned. It is mostly used in negative sentences and in questions: *He did not care about what happened to him.*

care for *verb*, means either to like or love: *I do not care for your cat*. With this meaning, **care for** is very formal. It also means to look after: *He is caring for three orphans in India*. In another sense, **care for** with the auxiliary *would* is a formal way of saying like, or wish: *Would you care for a drink?* See **WANT**.

career, careen (verbs)

career *verb*, means to move quickly in an uncontrolled way: *Debbie had a lucky escape when a milk tanker careered into her cottage.*

careen *verb*, means to turn a boat or ship on to its side in order to scrape the hull clean: *The men only had to scrape the ship and careen her, recaulk her seams and overhaul her rigging*. In AE, it means to move forward quickly and suddenly but unsteadily: *The economy careened from crisis to crisis.*

careful, cautious, prudent

careful *adjective*, means being thoughtful about an activity or paying particular attention in order to avoid damage or injury: *We passed some overgrown roses and were careful not to let the thorns rip our clothes.*

cautious *adjective*, means taking care to say or do the right thing and avoid mistakes: *When the reporter asked about the financial situation, the company spokesperson was deliberately cautious*. A person who is **cautious** does not take risks: *John is such an extremely cautious driver that he never goes above 30 miles an hour.*

prudent *adjective*, means being sensible and taking care when making decisions to avoid unnecessary risks: *The army commander who led his troops over the top of the trenches agreed that it might have been more prudent to stay put.*

careless, casual

careless *adjective*, means not paying attention so that mistakes are made: *We made a careless* *mistake when we sent that email to the newspaper.* **Careless** is often combined with *with* when it refers to possessions: *He is extremely careless with his credit card.*

casual *adjective*, relates to attitudes of mind; for instance showing a lack of care or thought, or seeming to be unworried: *She appeared so casual when she told us that she had lost her job.* **Casual** is often combined with *about*: *She was furious that the police were so casual about her stolen handbag.*

cargo

See FREIGHT.

carnivorous

See CONIFEROUS.

carousal, carousel

carousal kărówzăl /kə'raʊzḷ/ *noun*, is a drinking bout, particularly one that becomes noisy and lively: *The pub was closed due to complaints about the carousals and heavy drinking that went on every night.*

carousel karro͝ossél /kærʊ'sel/ *noun*, is originally the AE word for what BE calls a merry-go-round: *In the park is a children's playground with a carousel.* It is now also used for many objects that rotate, such as the machinery that delivers luggage to passengers at an airport: *I waited at the carousel, and by the time she got back the bags had already come up.* It also means a circular holder for photographic slides attached to a projector.

Note that *carousal* is stressed on the second syllable, while *carousel* is stressed on the last.

carriageway

See LANE.

carry out

See IMPLEMENT.

case, instance

case *noun*, means either somebody's line of argument: *He put forward a good case for lower speed limits in towns*, or a legal action: *There are 36 cases of libel pending against 'The Sun'.* It also means a specific situation that relates to a person or organization: *I think this is just a case of taking one game at a time.* See VERBIAGE.

instance *noun*, means a situation that provides an example: This is the worst *instance* of sexual discrimination I have ever come across.

Note that the example sentence in *instance* is more formal than *This is the worst case of sexual discrimination I have ever come across.*

caseworker

See SOCIAL WORKER.

cash card

See BANK CARD.

cash machine, cash dispenser, cashpoint, ATM

These are all terms that mean a machine for getting money out of a bank account or for accessing other automatic banking services. Another informal name for all of these is a hole in the wall. All these terms are common in BE. In parts of Europe this machine is called a minibank, bankautomat or bancomat. **Cash machine and ATM (automatic teller machine)** are common terms used in AE.

cashier, teller

cashier *noun*, means a person in a bank, shop, restaurant, hotel or similar whose job is to receive and pay out money: *The second copy is handed to the cashier who uses it to prepare the customer's bill and the third copy is retained in the waiter's book.*

teller *noun*, means either a person in a bank whose job is to receive and pay out money (this is dated in BE but still current in AE) or is the name of a machine that pays out money automatically – an ATM (*automatic teller machine*): *They introduced cheque book and ATM facilities.*

cashmere, Kashmir

cashmere *uncountable noun*, means a type of fine soft wool made from goat hair and used for making expensive clothes.

Kashmir *noun*, is the disputed territory in Asia that is now divided between India, Pakistan and China.

cast, caste

cast *noun and verb*. As a noun, this means the actors in a play or film: *After two years in the West End, the cast had to be changed*. As a verb it can mean to select suitable actors for a specific play or film: *They are going to start casting in the autumn*. It also means to form something in a mould: *The statue was cast in bronze*, and to throw something attached to a line, such as a net or hook when fishing. The past form and past participle are identical with the present.

caste *noun*, is a hereditary social system most associated with Hinduism. In a wider context it means any system where one social group has exclusive advantages: *The training of the diplomatic corps often helps to breed a special caste*.

> *'Buddhism marriage and family under the Hindu cast system'.*
> (History 101: Possible Topics for the Research Paper, US University) **!**

caster, castor

caster *noun*, means either one of a set of small swivelling wheels such as on a tea trolley or piano; or a container with holes in that is used for sprinkling sugar and the like. In AE the latter is called a shaker. Note that *castor* is an alternative spelling in both senses of the word. *Caster sugar*, a fine sugar used for sprinkling over food, or for cooking, can also be spelt *castor sugar*.

castor *noun*, meaning an oily substance or the beans of a *castor oil* plant always has the 'or' spelling: *He felt constipated and bought some castor oil at the chemists*.

casual

See **CARELESS**.

casualty

See **VICTIM**.

Catholic, catholic

Catholic *noun*, is a member of the Roman Catholic Church or one who follows the Roman Catholic faith. This is always capitalized.

catholic *adjective*, means wide-ranging: *He had very catholic tastes in music: everything from Gregorian chant to rap was in his CD collection*. This is not capitalized unless it is the first word in the sentence.

Catseyes, road reflectors

Catseyes *noun*, is a reflector system fitted in a road to reflect a car's lights to guide traffic in conditions of poor visibility or at night. This is a trademark written in one word and capitalized.

road reflectors *noun*, is a general term for various types of reflecting material embedded in or on the side of roads to help guide traffic in conditions of poor visibility or at night.

> As *Catseyes* is mostly used in Britain, *road reflectors* is the term to use when addressing an international audience.

catsup

See **KETCHUP**.

cause

See **BANDWAGON, REASON**.

cautious

See **CAREFUL**.

caveat

See **WARNING**.

cc, bcc

cc is an abbreviation for *carbon copy* used on business correspondence (letters and emails), to indicate that a copy (originally a copy made on carbon paper) has been sent to someone else: *To Stewart Clark, cc Graham Pointon*.

bcc is an abbreviation for *blind carbon copy* used in business correspondence to remind the sender that a copy has been sent to a third party without the knowledge of the main recipient: *To Stewart Clark's Anglophone Movement (SCAM), bcc The British Council, London.*

CE

See AD.

-cede, -ceed, -sede

As all these endings are pronounced the same: **seed** /siːd/, care must be taken with their spelling.

-cede is the normal spelling in almost all words ending with this syllable: *precede, recede.*

-ceed is used in a few words such as: *exceed, proceed* and *succeed.*

-sede is used in only one word: *supersede.*

celibate, chaste

celibate *adjective*, means being neither married nor having any sexual relations. This is usually because of a religious vow: *The candidate for holy orders must formally declare his intention of remaining celibate.* **Celibate** may also be used as a noun to mean an unmarried person who does not have sexual relations. The associated state is called *celibacy*.

chaste *adjective*, means not having sex with anyone, or only having sex with the person you are married to or in a partnership with. The associated noun is *chastity*.

cellar

See BASEMENT.

cellphone

See MOBILE[1].

Celsius, centigrade

Celsius sélssi-ŭss /'selsɪəs/ is the scientific name of the temperature scale in which water boils at 100 degrees and freezes at 0 degrees at normal atmospheric pressure. **Celsius** is widely used nowadays in technical and scientific contexts for giving temperatures. It is also the standard term elsewhere when stating the temperature. **Celsius** is capitalized, as it is the name of the inventor of the scale, *Anders Celsius*, an eighteenth-century Swedish astronomer.

centigrade is a nineteenth-century French term, for the Celsius scale of temperature. Modern scientific use is always Celsius, and this is preferred in writing.

C

The abbreviation C is used for both: *A warm spell will follow, and the temperature will reach 25 °C on Sunday* (read as twenty-five degrees Celsius).

Celt, celtic

Celt kelt /kelt/ *noun*, in the British context refers to the earliest known inhabitants of the British Isles, whose culture now survives mainly on the western fringes of Great Britain and in Ireland, and the extreme north-west of France (Brittany). **Celt** was formerly often spelt *Kelt*, which reflects the pronunciation.

celtic kéltik /'keltɪk/ *adjective*, is derived from *Celt*. There are two exceptions to the pronunciation with initial **k**: these are the names of the Glasgow and Belfast football clubs originally founded by Catholic organizations, which are both pronounced séltik /'seltɪk/, and have capital letters.

cement

See PLASTER.

censor, sensor, censer

censor *noun & verb*. As a noun, this means a moral judge, or a person who removes objectionable words or scenes from any text or film production for moral or political reasons: *The censor cut so much out of the film that it was difficult to follow.* As a verb, **censor** means to remove items from any document which are regarded as unacceptable for any reason: *Letters sent by prisoners from this prison are always censored.*

sensor *noun*, is a device that senses movement, heat, sound or light: *The fire alarm goes off every time a guest has a shower in that room. We must adjust the sensor.*

censer *noun*, is a holder for incense: *A priest began walking through the congregation swinging a censer and filling the church with a pungent aroma.*

censure, criticism

censure sénshŭr /ˈsenʃər/ *noun & verb*. As a noun, this is often used in parliamentary procedure to refer to negative criticism: *The House passed a vote of censure and stopped the government's plans to change taxation law*. As a verb, **censure** means to criticize someone officially for having done something wrong: *Use the report to criticize specific behaviour and situations rather than to censure a specific person*.

criticism *noun*, is the expression of disapproval: *The constant unjustified criticism from his managers led to Peter's resignation*. In another sense, **criticism** means the positive assessment of literature and the like: *Literary criticism should stimulate our appreciation of works of literature*.

census, consensus

census *noun*, is an official count, usually of a population: *The first national British census was in 1801*. Note that the plural is *censuses*. See FOREIGN PLURALS (WORD FORMATION).

consensus *noun*, means agreement that is reached in a group. Note the spelling with three s's. As a **consensus** has to be general, the phrase *general consensus* is unnecessary. See VERBIAGE.

centenary, centennial, century

centenary sentéenări /senˈtiːnərɪ/ *noun & adjective*, is the word used in BE for the hundredth anniversary of a significant event: *The company celebrated its centenary in 2007*. The second syllable is pronounced teen /tiːn/. See BICENTENARY, MILLENNIUM.

centennial senténni-ăl /senˈteniəl/ *noun & adjective*, is the AE equivalent of *centenary*. Note the correct spelling of **centennial** and that the second syllable is pronounced ten /ten/.

century *noun*, means either a period of 100 years: *The amateur ethic ruled games in Britain for a century and more*; or one of the periods of 100 years expressed as an ordinal number: *In the late nineteenth century the cathedral was extensively restored and altered*. The first century AD covered the years 1–100, so subsequent centuries carry the number of the last year in the century, not the first, and the twentieth century ended at the end of 2000. The expression *turn of the century* means the period within four or five years either side of the year ending in 00, and can be ambiguous: does *the turn of the nineteenth century* mean 1795–1805, or 1895–1905? People interpret this differently, so always make it clear which is meant by writing *the end of the nineteenth century*, or *the beginning of the twentieth century*, or give the exact dates. The word **century** is also used in cricket to mean 100 runs scored by a single batsman in an innings. See AD, BC.

centigrade

See CELSIUS.

Central America

See AMERICA.

central reservation, median (roads)

central reservation *noun*, is a narrow area of land that separates the two sides of a dual carriageway or motorway. This is the BE term. See RESERVATION (NATURE RESERVE).

median *noun* is an AE term for the central reservation. This is also known as the *median strip*. See AMERICAN ROAD TYPES, MEDIAN (AVERAGE).

centre, *center*, middle

centre *noun & verb*. As a noun, this means a precise midpoint: *The village was exactly in the centre of England*. As a verb, **centre** means to move into the middle: *This headline should be centred on the page, not left justified*. This is the BE spelling.

center *noun & verb*, is the AE spelling of *centre*. *Centered* is the past form of the verb in AE.

middle *noun*, means the region furthest from the boundaries or edges: *She was in the middle of the forest*. *Centre* is more exact than **middle** when indicating a midpoint.

centre in, centre on, revolve around

centre in *verb*, is used in the passive to refer to the place where an activity or event is concentrated: *The computer industry is still centred in Silicon Valley*.

centre on *verb*, means to focus attention on an event, situation or concern: *Every fourth year global attention is centred on the Olympic*

Games. Careful writers avoid the phrase *centre around*, as a central point cannot go around something else.

revolve around *verb*, means to move around a central point, like a planet around a star. In a figurative sense it means to treat a person or thing as the most important element: *Hugh's entire life revolved around one thing – Manchester United*.

century

See **CENTENARY**.

CEO

See **MANAGING DIRECTOR**.

cereal

See **SERIES**.

ceremonious, ceremonial

ceremonious *adjective* means behaving or being carried out in a very formal manner: *The schools preserved the ceremonious standards and the traditional academic curriculum*.

ceremonial *adjective*, refers to the traditional items, actions and words associated with or used on special occasions: *We are delighted that the Princess has agreed to conduct the ceremonial opening*. This can also be used as a noun as an alternative to *ceremony*.

certain

See **SATISFIED**.

certificate

See **DEGREE**.

certified

See **CHARTED**.

cession, session

cession *noun*, means the passing over of rights or territory from one authority to another: *The cession of Alaska to the USA*. . . .

session *noun*, is a period of time during which an event occurs: *Parliament is in session*. It also means a period devoted to a particular activity such as a jazz *jam session* or a *training session*.

cf., ref.

cf. sée éff /ˈsiː ˈef/ *abbreviation*, means compare with. It is used in writing to refer a reader to another book or to a different part of the same book or report: *Cf. pages 12 to 24*.

ref. *abbreviation*, means reference. It is used in business English to refer to something in a document: *We refer to our order, ref. 12345, and your invoice dated 2009-04-23*. This is read as 'reference'. See **RE, REFEREE**.

chafe, chaff

chafe chayf /tʃeɪf/ *verb*, means to be impatient about something that prevents someone doing what they want. *She did not chafe at the confinement as once she had*. It also means to rub the skin until it becomes sore or rub a part of the body in order to make it warm.

chaff chaaf /tʃɑːf/ *verb & noun*. As a verb this means to poke fun at or tease others in a good-natured way. This verb is considered old-fashioned. As an uncountable noun it means the outer cover of seeds of grain such as wheat. Since the **chaff** is discarded, it is commonly referred to in the idiom 'separating the wheat from the chaff': *This gives the courts a useful power to separate the wheat from the chaff among the pending cases*.

chair, chairperson, chairman, chairwoman (meetings)

chair, chairperson *noun*, means either someone who is in charge of a meeting, or the position of being in charge: *The delegates who were talking were asked kindly to address the chair*. **Chair** is a neutral term that avoids the accusation of sexist language that may be made against the word *chairman*. **Chairperson** is another neutral alternative. See **SEXIST LANGUAGE (WRITING SKILLS), PROFESSOR**.

chairman *noun*, means the person in charge of a meeting, and can be either a man or a woman: *Madam Chairman* is not impossible but *chair* or *chairperson* is a neat way of avoiding this apparently contradictory phrase.

chairwoman *noun*, must be a female who is chairing a meeting.

chamber

See **ROOM**.

champ

See **CHOMP**.

championship, tournament

championship *noun*, means a series of contests which may last for up to a year with the aim of finding a champion: *The UEFA Championship qualifiers start in July*. On the other hand, a golf championship is usually settled after only four days.

tournament *noun*, is also a championship but is often more concentrated in time.

> While a *championship* is always designed to find a winner, there are *tournaments* that are intended as simply demonstrations of skills.

chance

See **OPPORTUNITY**.

channel

See **CANAL**.

chapter

See **STYLE GUIDELINES (WRITING SKILLS)**.

character

See **FONT**.

characteristic

See **TYPICAL**.

charge card

See **BANK CARD**.

charm

See **TALISMAN**.

charted, chartered, certified

charted *verb*, is the past tense and past participle of *chart*, and is used particularly of the sea: *They charted a course which would avoid the most dangerous waters*. The phrase *uncharted waters* is used to describe a situation whose outcome is uncertain. See **CHART (MAP)**.

chartered *adjective*, describes a member of a professional organization appointed by a Royal Charter: *She was the youngest chartered engineer in the company*. Note that a *chartered accountant* in the UK is the equivalent of a *certified accountant* in the US. In another sense, a ship or plane that is hired is described as **chartered**: *Chartered yachts available on a monthly basis*.

certified *adjective*, refers to qualifications that are officially recognized: *He was a certified accountant with 20 years of experience*. Ships, planes and films are also **certified** by authorized bodies. In another sense, **certified** refers to a person who has been officially declared insane. See **MAD (INSANE)**.

chaste

See **CELIBATE**.

chat line, chat room, web forum, electronic mailing list

chat line *noun*, is a telephone service that allows people to talk, or to listen to others talking.

chat room *noun*, is a text-based way to share information on a specific topic with others on the Internet. The users are often termed the *chat group*. New technology opens up other possibilities such as file sharing: *With a webcam you can see the people in the chat room*.

web forum *noun*, is an Internet website for text-based discussion. The content is composed of member-written contributions, known as threads. There are many other terms in use for the **web forum** including message board, discussion board, (electronic) discussion group, discussion forum and bulletin board. Many forums have topic-based sub-forums which are referred to as a message board or one of the other terms.

electronic mailing list *noun*, is usually an email-based system that automatically delivers a new message to all the subscribers. This is unlike a web forum, where the members have to visit the website, and check for new entries.

chat show, phone-in

chat show *noun*, is a TV or radio programme where a host gathers a group of people to discuss one or more topics. Some **chat shows** are serious and gather learned authorities on a subject. Others are purely for entertainment, featuring writers or showbiz people in the news. Sometimes such shows are supplemented by comments from viewers or listeners. *Talk show* is the usual AE term for a **chat show** and is an alternative BE term.

phone-in *noun*, is a TV programme or more often a radio programme usually concerned with a particular subject that encourages telephone comments from viewers or listeners. An AE term for this is a *call-in show/program*.

cheap, inexpensive

cheap *adjective*. As well as meaning low in cost, **cheap** often also suggests poor quality: *He was carrying a cheap suitcase*. As the price of something is its cost expressed as a number, careful writers avoid using **cheap** to describe the price, as **cheap** is a comparative expression. Objects, such as vegetables, hats and cars may be **cheap**, but their price should be described as low or reasonable.

inexpensive *adjective*, also means low in cost, but as it avoids the connotation of poor quality, it is often a better choice of word than *cheap*, even though the sum of money involved may be the same: *He was carrying an inexpensive suitcase*.

> *'Nokia 6600 at cheap price.'*
> (www.cellular-news) **!**

checkers

See DRAUGHTS.

cheque, check (money)

cheque *noun*, means a printed form that is used as a way of paying for goods. This is the BE spelling: *He checked whether he still had his cheque book and his traveller's cheques*. The expression *blank cheque* (BE) and *blank check* (AE) is either a signed cheque without an amount of money written on it, or permission to take whatever action is necessary in a particular situation: *He was effectively granted a blank cheque to conduct a war without Congressional authorization for up to 90 days*.

check *noun*, means the same as the BE *cheque*. This is the AE spelling. Note the AE spelling of *traveler's check*. See CHECK (CONTROL).

chest

See BREAST.

chesterfield

See SOFA.

chickpea, garbanzo

chickpea *noun*, is a type of light-brown pea that is cooked and eaten as a vegetable. This is the BE term.

garbanzo gaarbánzō /gɑːrˈbænzəʊ/ *noun*, is the AE term for *chickpea*. The plural is *garbanzos*. This is also called the *garbanzo bean*.

chicory, endive

chicory chíckŏri /ˈtʃɪkəri/ *noun*, is a green plant with bitter leaves that can be cooked as a vegetable or eaten raw. The roasted and ground root can be used as a coffee substitute. This is the BE name for the plant whose specific Latin name is *Cichorium intybus*.

endive éndīv /ˈendaɪv/ or éndiv /ˈendɪv/ *noun*, is the BE name for the vegetable whose specific Latin name is *Cichorium endivia*. In AE this is known as *chicory*, or *chicory crown*. The leaves may be blanched and eaten in salads.

childlike, childish

childlike *adjective*, means having the qualities of a child or something that is typical of a child: *The traffic warden looked at her wide blue eyes and childlike innocence and let her park on the double yellow lines for five minutes*. **Childlike** nearly always has positive connotations.

childish *adjective*, means having the qualities of a child or behaving in a way that is typical of a child: *The teachers found the childish enthusiasm of the youngest pupils stimulating*. In this context **childish** is being used without any suggestion of approval or disapproval. However, when it is applied to adults, **childish** is always disapproving: *The traffic warden said that it was childish to get angry about being given a ticket for parking on double yellow lines*.

Chinese[1], Chinaman

Chinese *noun & adjective*, refers to the people, language and culture of China: *We met 10 Chinese doctoral students*. Informally, *a Chinese* may be either a meal of Chinese food, or a Chinese restaurant. See NATIONALITY WORDS.

Chinaman *noun*, as a reference to a native of China is old-fashioned and has become offensive. It is also a technical term in cricket for a particular way of bowling the ball: *Smith was bowled by a chinaman*. In this case it is not capitalized, and has no offensive overtones.

Chinese[2], Pinyin (language)

Chinese *uncountable noun*, is the language of China. In its various dialects, it is the world's most commonly spoken first language and has many thousands of characters in its written form.

Pinyin *uncountable noun*, is the standard system for the writing or transliteration of Mandarin Chinese in the Roman alphabet. This has given us the spellings *Beijing* instead of *Peking*, *Chang Jiang* not *Yangtze* River, and the chairman *Mao Zedong* rather than *Mao Tse-tung*.

chip and PIN

See PIN.

chips, crisps

chips *noun*, in BE are narrow strips of deep-fried potato as found in the national dish of *fish and chips*. In AE, these are known as French fries or just fries. See FRY (ROAST).

crisps *noun*, in BE are cold wafer-thin slices of fried potato eaten as a snack, as in *a packet of crisps*. They are called *potato chips* in AE.

> *'German Bytes, French Chips and Swiss Software.'*
> (Siliconvalley Internet News) !

chomp, champ

chomp *verb*, means to eat food noisily: *Britons now chomp their way through more than 27,000 tonnes of pizza a year*.

champ *verb*, also means to eat noisily, and in another sense means to bite and grind teeth. This verb is usually applied to horses and is commonly used in the informal phrase *champing at the bit* which means impatient to start doing something.

> Google registers three times as many hits for *chomping at the bit* as for *champing at the bit*, so both forms are common.

chord, cord

chord *noun*, is a combination of musical notes played simultaneously, or as a mathematical term, a straight line joining the ends of an arc.

cord *noun*, is any type of string, rope or similar: *This electric cord needs to be replaced*. It also refers to parts of the body that resemble string such as *umbilical cord*, *spinal cord* and *vocal cords* (note that the latter can also be spelt *vocal chords*, although this spelling is now rarely seen).

choose, select, pick

choose *verb*, means to decide on a preference, often between two items: *The type of frame you choose can either make or spoil the photo*. The past tense is spelt *chose* and the past participle is *chosen*.

select *verb*, means to make a careful decision from a range of possibilities (where there are more than two): *You should not select a technique just to get the desired answer*.

pick *verb*, means to decide a preference among more than two things, and is a less formal word than either *choose* or *select*: *What type of curtains are you going to pick?* **Pick** suggests a more random procedure than *choose* or *select*: *Pick any number between 1 and 36*. In another sense, **pick** means to gather fruit, vegetables etc., that grow above the ground: *He picked a large bunch of wild flowers while she was resting*.

> *Choose* is the only one of these three terms that can be used without an object: *You can choose whether to buy them or not*.

Christian name

See **FIRST NAME**.

chronic

See **ACUTE**.

circa, c, ca

circa súrkă /ˈsɜːrkə/ *preposition*, means approximately. **Circa** is restricted to certain specific contexts, such as job advertisements: *circa £35k plus car* (meaning round about £35,000 plus car). In running text it is better to use about, roughly, approximately or approx., rather than **circa** or its abbreviations.

c and **ca** are both abbreviations for *circa*, and are used in dates given on captions to museum exhibits or churches: *Norman, c 1100* (meaning built around AD 1100). **Ca** is more common than **c** in AE. They are both pronounced in full, as *circa*.

cite

See **SITE**.

citizen

See **RESIDENT**.

city

See **TOWN**.

civic, civics, civil

civic *adjective*. In the main sense, this relates to a town or city, particularly its administration: *The tourist office is in the civic centre* (which will be a building). In another sense, **civic** relates to the activities and duties of those living in a town or local area: *The mayor was the natural centre of civic life*.

civics *noun*, means the study of the rights and duties of citizenship: *Civics is taught well in the college*. Note that this takes a singular verb and follows the pattern of other nouns with *-ics* endings. See **-ICS**.

civil *adjective*, refers to matters concerning ordinary citizens as opposed to religious or military groups. **Civil** also means behaving correctly and politely. It is a fairly formal word: *I will speak to you when you have learned to be more civil*. **Civil** appears in several compound nouns, such as *civil war*, meaning a war between the citizens of a single country; *civil aviation* in contrast to military activities; and *civil rights*, the political and social rights of a citizen.

civil partnership

See **SAME-SEX MARRIAGE**.

claim

See **ASSERTION**.

clarification, elucidation

clarification *noun*, means the clearing up of a problem by making it easier to understand: *He asked for some clarification of what this decision actually means*. See **CLARIFY (EXPLAIN)**.

elucidation *noun*, means giving or getting an explanation of something in a clear and easily understandable manner: *A light was beginning to dawn in my mind, an elucidation of why their relationship was so perfect*. This is a formal word. See **ELUCIDATE (EXPLAIN)**.

> Although these words are very close in meaning, a *clarification* is often a more limited explanation of a minor point while an *elucidation* may mean a flash of light and reveals what something really means or represents. As a politician once pointed out: *This clarification needs clarification*.

classic, classical

classic *adjective & noun*. As an adjective, this refers either to lasting high quality: *He was wearing a suit with a classic cut*; or to something that is typical of a category: *This is a classic example of the Oedipus complex*. As a noun, it means a good example of its kind: *Humphrey Bogart played in many films that are now regarded as classics*. See **-IC**.

classical *adjective*, refers to certain historical genres or periods as in *classical music* or *classical literature* (Latin and Greek). Many films, such as 'Casablanca', are *classics*, but only a film about life in ancient Rome or Greece will be **classical**.

claustrophobia, agoraphobia

claustrophobia *uncountable noun*, means fear of being in confined spaces: *The men said that they suffered from claustrophobia and tried to kick open the lift doors*.

agoraphobia aggŏrŏfṓbi-ă /ægərəˈfəʊbɪə/ *uncountable noun*, means fear of being in open spaces where there are many other people: *An estimated half a million people in Great Britain suffer from agoraphobia and fear to leave their homes*. See PHOBIA (MANIA).

clean, cleanse

clean *verb & adjective*. As a verb, this means to remove dirt and dust by washing or rubbing: *It took a week to clean the house*. As an adjective, it refers to the state of not being dirty: *The house was extremely clean and tidy*. Things that are not harmful or offensive are also **clean**: *The show was just good clean fun*.

cleanse *verb*, means to remove all impurities. Thus a wound is cleansed when this is a more thorough process than if it had been simply cleaned: *The wound was cleansed with disinfectant*. **Cleanse** is used figuratively to mean make free from guilt: *Cleanse us of our sins*, or get rid of criminal elements: *The Governor decided to cleanse the city of drug dealers*. Advertisers often prefer the word **cleanse** to help sell cleaning liquids and skin treatment products, as it implies a more thorough process.

clergy, clergyman, minister, priest, vicar

clergy *plural noun*, means the body of ordained members of any of the Christian churches, who are authorized to administer the sacraments. The word has no singular.

clergyman *noun*, is a general term for a male member of the clergy. The female equivalent is *clergywoman*.

minister *noun*, in the religious sense is usually a member of the Protestant or Nonconformist *clergy*. See MINISTER.

priest *noun*, in the Christian Church means a *clergyman* of the Orthodox, Roman Catholic and Anglican churches. In churches where women are admitted to the Christian priesthood, they are called *priests* too. The feminine form *priestess* is only used for female *priests* of some non-Christian religions.

vicar *noun*, is a member of the clergy in the Church of England who has the responsibility for a parish: *I was waiting at the back of the church because I wanted a word with the vicar*. See REVEREND (REVERENT).

clerk, office staff

clerk *noun*. In the BE sense, a **clerk** is a person employed in an office or bank for administrative work. In AE, **clerk** can also mean someone at a sales or service counter, or in the reception of a hotel. **Clerk** is pronounced **klark** /klɑːrk/ in BE and **klurk** /klɜːrk/ in AE. See SHOP ASSISTANT.

office staff *noun*, means the staff in offices. This is a wider term than *clerk* as it covers secretaries, clerks, management and other office workers.

clever

See SMART.

cliché

A **cliché** is a phrase or idea that has been used so much that it has lost all or much of its value. Typically they are parts of, or even entire proverbs or sayings. Examples: *Many hands make light work*; *Dead as a doornail*; *For love or money*; *A stitch in time saves nine*; *Don't count your chickens before they're hatched*. Many modern style guides accept that using the occasional cliché is fairly common. They can scarcely be avoided and are known ways of reinforcing an idea. Many modern phrases like *bottom line*; *rain check* are used widely, and a few are included in this book. For some, these phrases are new, for others they are clichés. It is best not to overdo the use of the cliché as too many of them make what is said appear trite and unexciting. Consider the example of a sports broadcast that contained 12 clichés in just five minutes, including: *The home team may pull this off . . . It's a real pressure cooker down there . . . It's a nail biter . . . It's a see-saw game . . . At least the fans are getting their money's worth*.

In business English it is best to avoid clichés if you can. It does not sound very impressive to end all correspondence with clichés like: *Thanking you in advance* (perhaps you should thank people afterwards); *Yours in anticipation of an early reply* (an alternative here is *Looking forward to your comments by the end of . . .*). See VERBIAGE, CORRESPONDENCE (WRITING SKILLS).

C

click, clique

click *noun & verb*, as a noun this means a short, sharp noise: *The door closed with a click*. As a verb, it means to make such a noise, and also to have a sudden realization: *James had been learning to drive for months, but suddenly everything clicked, and he passed his test the next week*. If two people **click**, they get on very well with each other.

clique *noun*, means a small group of people with similar interests who exclude outsiders: *His friends were an exclusive clique*. **Clique** is usually pronounced kleek /kliːk/.

client, clientele, customer, patron

client *noun*, is a person who pays to obtain professional advice, for example from an accountant, architect, engineer or lawyer. Medical practitioners such as doctors and dentists have *patients*, not *clients*. **Client** is a word that makes the recipient of the service feel respected as it stresses the individual relationship. The term *social client* is used by social workers to stress the professional nature of their relationship to give dignity to the people they are helping.

clientele klee-ĕntéll /kliːən'tel/ *noun*, is a body of clients but it needs to be used with care as **clientele** is associated with clubs, pubs, shops, etc. The people who use a professional person's services should be called *clients*.

customer *noun*, means a person or organization that buys things from a shop or business, but pays only for the goods supplied, not for the use of that service: *The regular customers at the local supermarket were mostly women*. It is a term used by business instead of *shoppers* and *passengers* to underline the customer's power of choice. **Customer** is used where there is no individual relationship. Note that the term *custom* can mean the number of *customers* or the amount of business: *How is custom at this time of year?*

patron *noun*, means a person who eats in a particular restaurant or drinks in a particular pub: *This bar has facilities for disabled patrons*. This is a more formal word than *customer*. In other senses, a **patron** is a benefactor of a charity, or a *patron saint*, such as St Christopher who gives protection to travellers.

client-server

See PEER-TO-PEER.

climatic, climactic

climatic *adjective*, is derived from the noun *climate*, and so refers to the weather in a specific area: *The climatic conditions in this part of Spain have changed over the last 100 years*.

climactic *adjective*, is derived from the noun *climax*, and so refers to the peak of excitement that has been built up. This is nearly always restricted to written English: *The battle was the climactic scene of* Star Wars Episode IV: A New Hope.

climax, crescendo

climax *noun*, is a peak of excitement or most intense event: *The series of public meetings came to a climax on the weekend of 30 March with a large protest march*.

crescendo *noun*, is a musical term meaning an increase in intensity or loudness: *A murmur rose in a crescendo and drowned him out*. It is often used figuratively: *The papers stimulated a crescendo of complaint about the latest rulings from Brussels*.

> As *crescendo* means a change in intensity or loudness, careful writers use the phrase *reach a climax*, not *reach a crescendo*.

clipped words

See WORD FORMATION.

clique

See CLICK.

cloakroom, wardrobe

cloakroom *noun*, is a room in a building where coats and luggage can be left: *He asked the cloakroom attendant for his briefcase*. In AE, this is also called the checkroom or coatroom. In BE, a **cloakroom** may also be a room in a public building with toilets. See TOILET.

wardrobe *noun*, is a large piece of furniture used for storing clothes: *They bought a beautiful fitted wardrobe for their new* *bedroom*. **Wardrobe** also means a collection of clothes: *Her spring wardrobe was bought in Paris*. It is also the name of the department in a theatre, or a film production, which deals with the costumes.

close, near, nearby

close *adverb & adjective*, means only a short distance from the point of reference: *This hotel is close to all the cafés and restaurants*. **Close** is also used to indicate emotional ties: *He is a close friend of the family*.

near *preposition*, indicates places a short distance away from the point of reference: *The better houses were near the church*. Objects or people that are **near** are further away than those that are called *close*. **Near** is also used before place names: *I used to live near Cambridge*.

nearby *adjective & adverb*, means at a short distance from the person who is the subject of the sentence or clause: *Guests have free access to the nearby lakeside swimming area*. Note that the adverb form may also be spelt as two words: *From various tables near by she could hear a handful of languages being spoken*.

clothes, clothing, garment, cloth

clothes *plural noun*, are items that are worn to cover the body: *Summer clothes are now in the shops*.

clothing *uncountable noun*, means clothes in a collective sense: *Items of clothing were strewn around the room*.

garment *noun*, means an item of clothing: *He claimed that the garment was handmade*. This is a formal word that may apply to any item of *clothing*. More informal alternatives are **suit**, dress or outfit, but they are also more specific.

cloth *noun*, means a piece of fabric, and is often used in compounds: *This is a beautiful tablecloth*. A *man of the cloth* is a formal term for a clergyman.

co, co-

The prefix **co-** means joint, mutual, together with. Words beginning with **co-** fall into three groups:

1. Those in which the prefix is not followed by a hyphen: *cohabit*, *coincide*, *cooperate* and *coordinate*. Although the latter two may have a hyphen in BE, the most common spelling is without one.
2. Those in which the prefix is followed by a hyphen in BE, but is often written without one in AE. These are words that are newly introduced or that may be confusing. Here the sense is joint and mutual. Examples include: *co-driver*, *co-editor*, *co-pilot* and *co-worker*.
3. Those in which the prefix is always followed by a hyphen, in both BE and AE. This is found in some words when **co-** is followed by 'o'. Examples: *co-opt*, *co-own* (but not *cooperate/cooperation*).

If two words may be confused, then hyphenation will help clarify the distinction.
See CO-RESPONDENT, HYPHENATION (PUNCTUATION GUIDE).

coach

See BUS.

cohabit, live together, live-in

cohabit *verb*, means to live together in a sexual relationship without being married to each other: *They met in 1988 and began to cohabit in 1989, although they did not marry until 1998*. This is more formal than the other phrases in this group.

live together *verb*, means to occupy the same room, flat or house and it usually implies a sexual relationship between the people concerned: *He took her out, they fell in love and started to live together*. People who live in the same flat but do not have a sexual relationship are best described as sharing the house or flat. This focuses on the flat and says nothing about the relationship between the people.

live-in *adjective*, refers to a sexual relationship: *The last time I heard from her she was planning to marry her live-in partner*. It can also refer to a domestic helper who lives in the employer's home: *His chateau was spacious and the meals laid on by the live-in girl were top quality*.

C

coincide, conform, correspond

coincide *verb*, means to occur at the same time or place as something else: *Thanks to careful planning, the conference and the trade fair coincided.*

conform *verb*, means to agree to an established pattern or idea. In another sense, it means to behave in a similar way to other people or follow established rules: *After a phase of rebellion, he eventually conformed to the rules.*

correspond *verb*, means to be the equivalent of: *The spelling of aluminium in BE corresponds to the AE spelling aluminum*. Avoid the preposition *with* here, as *correspond with* means to write to and receive letters from someone.

colander

See CALENDAR.

collaborate

See COOPERATE.

colleague

See ET AL.

collective nouns

See GRAMMAR TIPS.

college

See SCHOOL.

collocation (word partnerships)

This is the way words combine with each other to form idiomatic language. People will probably understand what you mean if you talk about 'strong rain' or a 'heavy wind' but both are unlikely combinations. English is a predictable language in many ways and 'heavy rain' and 'strong wind' are normal idiomatic collocations. This book has systematically included the most normal collocations with the entry word (this is based on the results of computerized studies of collocation). This means that you get a lot of extra information about how words can be used together with others enabling you to easily generate idiomatic phrases. Consider the entry on *control*. The example sentence: *The government failed to establish effective control over inflation* contains a lot of information about how to use *control*. It points out which verbs can be used (*failed to control* or *establish control*), which adjective can be used with *control* (*effective*), and the position of *control* in the sentence. Also you can see which preposition to use together with *control* (*over*).

collude

See COOPERATE.

colon (:)

See PUNCTUATION GUIDE.

colour, color

colour *noun and verb*, has numerous meanings from the property of light to skin tone. This is the BE spelling.

color is the AE spelling of *colour*.

colour words

Words to describe colours are often used by advertisers to make their products more attractive. Compare a *brown car* or one in *bronzed sand* or *with a bronzed metallic finish*. Some manufacturers have a colour associated with their products, like Ferrari (red), Levis (faded blue) and IBM (dark blue). *Biscuit, marmalade* and *oyster* are examples of colour words that are also the names of objects. There may be problems using colour words to describe the colour of hair. See HAIR COLOUR.

Words for skin colour must be used with care. See BLACK, NATIVE AMERICAN.

coloured

See BLACK.

come out in the wash

See FIND OUT.

comic, comical

comic *adjective & noun*. As an adjective, this means funny and amusing: *He is a comic actor who has been very successful on TV.*

It is also used in the phrase *comic opera*. As a noun, a **comic** is an alternative term for comedian: *He is a stand-up comic*; and also a children's magazine, often containing cartoons. See FUNNY, -IC.

comical *adjective*, means unintentionally amusing: *He is such a strange little man, and really quite comical*.

comma (,)

See PUNCTUATION GUIDE.

commendable

See CREDITABLE.

comment, commentary

comment *noun*, means an opinion or an explanation: *We would like your comments on the last election*.

commentary *noun*, means an expression of opinion that consists of many comments: *This commentary on the recent bomb attacks put the conflict in perspective*.

committed, commitment, committal, commit

committed *adjective*, means pledged to carry out an action: *Doctors are committed to the practical care of all those who are ill*. It can also mean dedicated: *He was a committed amateur, and refused to accept the prize money*.

commitment *noun*, means dedication: *The high standard of this product shows our commitment to quality*. In this sense, **commitment** is an uncountable noun. It also means a promise: *A commitment of extra funds to this project would be very welcome*. Here it is a countable noun.

committal *noun*, means the placing of a body in a grave, or of a person in a prison or other institution: *An order was made for his committal to a mental hospital*.

commit *verb*, means to carry out a crime: *'Did the accused commit the assault as charged?'* and also to imprison: *The judge committed him to a long term in prison*. **Commit** can also mean to pledge or promise: *They expressed reluctance to commit further funds to the projects because of the ongoing costs involved*; come to a definite decision: *The police are not prepared to commit themselves yet, but they must have their suspicions*; or just remember something: *Commit it to memory*.

commodity

See RAW MATERIAL.

common, normal, ordinary

common *adjective*, refers to things that occur frequently, or exist in large amounts: *Pollution is a common problem in large cities like Beijing*. Things that are related or shared are **common**: *The problems with the Common Agricultural Policy are well known*. When **common** is used before a noun this refers to a category with low status as in *a common criminal*. However, it is old-fashioned and insulting to describe someone from a low social order as **common**.

normal *adjective*, means typical and expected. A person who feels normal or who acts in a normal way should cause no surprises. If the word **normal** is used to make a contrast with someone who is physically or mentally disabled this may be considered offensive.

ordinary *adjective*, refers to something that is not a special or unusual example: *The hire car was just an ordinary family car*. A person who is average, and not unusual, special, famous or rich can be termed **ordinary**: *Millions of pounds have been given by ordinary people in response to appeals for help*. In a negative context **ordinary** means plain, dull and not especially interesting.

> All these words can cause negative reactions: a *common* person (low status), a *normal* person (not disabled), an *ordinary* person (uninteresting). See PLAIN.

common sense, commonsense

common sense *noun*, means sensible behaviour and judgement and is written in two words: *It is a matter of sound common sense*.

commonsense *adjective*, is written as one word: *It was a commonsense matter*.

communication, communications

communication *noun*, means the exchange of information by speech or in writing. It can also be a formal term used in diplomacy and military contexts, or a way of communicating, as in: *Communication between the sexes is not always easy*. In computer science **communication** rather than *communications* is recommended in the term *information and communication technology (ICT)*.

communications *noun*, is a means of connection between people or places: *Communications in this part of Scotland are poor*. **Communications** has a plural verb when it means ways of transmission or transmitting ideas: *There is so much static, communications are poor*. However, as an academic subject it has a singular verb. This is often used in compounds: *Telecommunications is taught at master's level there*.

company

See BUSINESS.

compare to, compare with

compare to *verb*, is used to show likeness. This may be between two people but is often between a person and an object: *Shall I compare thee to a Summer's day?* (Shakespeare). With **compare to** there is a likeness that may be figurative. You can compare a person's voice to thunder, an unfortunate face to the back of a bus, or again like Shakespeare, the world to a stage.

compare with *verb*, is used to show the similarity or dissimilarity between things that are usually in the same category, or between people of the same stature: *The essay topic was to compare Henry James' work with that of H.G. Wells*.

compatriot

See PATRIOT.

compel, impel, propel

compel *verb*, means to make someone else do something: *The police had guns and compelled him to surrender*.

impel *verb*, means to force something forward, or make something happen, often due to internal motivation: *He claimed that it was the voices in his head that impelled him to steal*.

propel *verb*, means to drive something forward: *They used a long fishing vessel propelled by six oars*.

Note that the past tense and present participle of all these words have a double 'll' in both BE and AE.

compelling, compulsive, impulsive

compelling *adjective*, refers either to something that is very interesting that holds someone's attention: *The impact of the television screen is very compelling*; or to something that is completely convincing: *The conclusion of an argument is compelling if its reasoning is accepted*.

compulsive *adjective*, refers to behaviour caused by a strong impulse that is difficult to control: *TV series try to make us into compulsive viewers*.

impulsive *adjective*, refers to sudden action or behaviour carried out without careful consideration of the consequences: *A good way to avoid impulsive spending is to agree on a limit that can be spent without consulting your partner*.

compensation

See DAMAGE.

competence, competency

See EXPERTISE.

compile

See COMPOSE.

complacent, complaisant, compliant

complacent kŏmpláyssĕnt /kəm'pleɪsn̩t/ *adjective*, means being self-satisfied with one's own achievements or being uncritically satisfied about a group's performance: *A good manager cannot be complacent when staff continually complain about working conditions*.

complaisant kŏmpláyzĕnt /kəm'pleɪzn̩t/ *adjective*, means willing to please other people without any signs of protest: *We expect the workers to react, not remain complaisant about the proposed wage cuts*.

compliant *adjective*, means either obeying other people's wishes or manufactured or carried out according to existing standards: *Future DVD recorders will be compliant with the new industry standard*.

complement, compliment

complement kómpliment /ˈkɒmplɪmənt/ (*noun*) kómpliment /ˈkɒmplɪment/ (*verb*). As a noun, this means something which, when added to something else, improves its quality or makes it complete. **Complement** also means the required total or quota, particularly relating to the number of staff in a company. It is often used in the phrase *the full complement*: *With a nearly full complement of 673 passengers, the ship cast off from the city dock*. Note that the last syllable is pronounced with a neutral vowel. As a verb, **complement** means to add an element to make something complete or perfect: *These terracotta pots complement the herbs very well*. As this word is often confused with its soundalike *compliment*, think of the 'e' in the middle as meaning something 'extra'. Note that there is a full vowel in the pronunciation of the last syllable of the verb.

compliment kómpliment /ˈkɒmplɪmənt/ (*noun*) kómpliment /ˈkɒmplɪment/ (*verb*). As a noun, this is a remark or action that expresses praise for something: *It's a great compliment to be compared to her, as she is very beautiful*. This word is often used in the phrase *pay a compliment*. As a verb, **compliment** means to pay respect, praise, or say something admiringly: *He complimented John and Mary by inviting them to be godparents*. Note the difference in pronunciation between the noun and verb.

complementary, complimentary

complementary *adjective*, refers to the combination of things that are usually different to form a whole: *Summer conferences were a complementary activity to winter sports in the mountain resort*. In a technical sense, **complementary** can refer to two angles that fit together and form 90°.

complimentary *adjective*, means either praising: *His complimentary remarks to the students fired their enthusiasm*; or describes something given away free as a favour: *An accompanying person can be given a complimentary ticket for the screenings*.

> *'Honeymooners receive a complementary bottle of champagne.'* **!**
> (Hotel notice, Crawley)

compliant

See COMPLACENT.

compose, compile

compose *verb*, means to combine elements together to create a whole such as a poem or symphony or even a letter: *She began to compose a letter in her head*. The related noun is *composition*. In the passive, *to be composed of* means to be made up of several parts of things, or people: *The minority government is composed of three non-Socialist parties*. See CONSTITUTE.

compile *verb*, means to use existing material from elsewhere to produce a list or new collection such as a book, report or anthology of poetry: *This self-assessment list will also be useful when you compile your CV*. The related noun is *compilation* which means the process or result of making a book or CD from already existing material.

compounds

When to use one word, a hyphen or two words?

In a recent dictionary of British English, entries like *oilfield*, *oil-tanker* and *oil well* show that selecting when to write a single word, use a hyphen or write the words separately is not straightforward. American English tends to write many such constructions as a single word, where BE uses two words or a hyphen.

Guidelines to compounds in BE:

1. Two words in a phrase are kept as separate words until they become treated as one unit. Then either a hyphen will be used or they become one word (e.g. *off-shore activities, off-shore racing* have now developed into *offshore activities, offshore racing* in recent dictionaries). The original concept of a position off the coast is still used but is no longer written as two words.
2. If the first words in a phrase act as adjectives and describe the subject, hyphenation should be used to help the reader understand your meaning (e.g. *a*

big-headed politician does not mean one with a large head). *A state-of-the-art concept* is hyphenated as the four words all function together as an adjective phrase to say something about the concept.

3. In conference proceedings etc., hyphens can distinguish between:
   - *the non-French-speakers* (those who do not speak French) and
   - *the non-French speakers* (the speakers who are not French citizens).

See HYPHENATION (PUNCTUATION GUIDE).

comprehensive, comprehensible, understandable

comprehensive *adjective*, means including everything or everybody, such as a comprehensive school, where pupils of all abilities attend, or a comprehensive explanation, which deals with all possible aspects of a problem.

comprehensible *adjective*, means capable of being understood: *His accurate description of the route was comprehensible to all the competitors in the cross-country race*. In spoken English and general written English, *understandable* is more commonly used than **comprehensible**.

understandable *adjective*, when it refers to behaviour, feelings, reactions, etc. means normal and reasonable in a particular situation: *They cannot talk to the press at the moment, which is perfectly understandable*. It also means easy to understand: *Safety notices must be readily understandable*.

comprise

See CONSTITUTE.

compulsive

See COMPELLING.

compulsory, mandatory

compulsory *adjective*, refers to behaviour and to actions that have to be carried out in order to follow laws or other rules: *In many countries compulsory education is from 6 to 16*.

mandatory *adjective*, refers to behaviour or something that is required by law: *It is also tightening its mandatory requirements of the local education systems particularly in respect of the curriculums*. In AE, **mandatory** is often used where *compulsory* would be used in BE: *A mandatory course in scientific writing* (AE); *the MSc student must take four compulsory courses* (BE).

Although these words overlap, in BE when something is required by rules and regulations *compulsory* is commonly used. *Mandatory* is reserved for things that are required by law.

computerate

See LITERATE.

computer fraud

See PHISHING.

con

See PRO.

concern

See BUSINESS.

concrete

See PLASTER.

condom

See CONTRACEPTIVE.

conduct (noun & verb)

conduct kóndukt /ˈkɒndʌkt/ *noun*, means the way a person behaves in a particular situation: *I do not believe that the principal cause of last week's riots was the conduct of the police*. It is often used in fixed expressions such as *professional conduct* and *code of conduct*: *The use of chemical weapons offends international codes of conduct*. Note that the stress is on the first syllable.

conduct kŏndúkt /kənˈdʌkt/ *verb*, means either to lead: *Did you ever conduct the Leningrad Philharmonic?* or to manage: *He has hired consultants to help him conduct his appeal*. It is also used reflexively to mean behave: *He always conducted himself as a*

Christian and a gentleman. Note that the stress is on the second syllable.

conference

See CONGRESS.

confident, confidant(e)

confident *adjective*, means self-assured, certain of being right, or of success: *They made her feel so confident that she was utterly convinced she would win*.

confidant(e) kónfidant /ˈkɒnfɪdænt/ *noun*, means a special trusted friend, who knows one's secrets: *He had been the only really close friend and confidant of George*. **Confidant** refers to a male, while **confidante** refers to a female. The last syllable of both forms usually rhymes with 'ant', although some speakers prefer a more French pronunciation: kónfidaant /ˈkɒnfɪdɑːnt/.

confine, contain

confine *verb*, means to keep or restrict someone or something to within recognized limits: *The soldiers were all confined to barracks after a weekend of trouble*. Although **confine** is usually associated with something that is forbidden, an invalid in a wheelchair may be *confined* in terms of movement and a speaker may also **confine** himself/herself to a particular issue.

contain *verb*, means to prevent something from escaping or going beyond its boundary or limitation: *The captured soldiers were contained by the vicious guard dogs*. **Contain** centres on the idea of physical restraint and control. Thus diseases and tempers may be *contained*. However, feelings may be more difficult to **contain**: *The children clapped their hands and could hardly contain themselves when Santa Claus entered the room*.

conform

See COINCIDE.

congenial

See GENIAL.

congregation

See PUBLIC.

congress, conference, symposium, seminar, workshop

congress *noun*, is a large formal meeting where delegates discuss ideas. When it refers to the lawmaking assembly of elected representatives in the USA or some other countries, **congress** is capitalized: *The US Congress refers to both the House of Representatives and the Senate*.

conference *noun*, means a large formal meeting or gathering and is an alternative term for a *congress*: *The twentieth International Conference of the Red Cross confirmed principles for action*. The phrase *to be in conference* means to be in a meeting where the participants do not expect to be disturbed: *The managers are in conference with the board* (note there is no definite article in this sense).

symposium *noun*, means a small conference or meeting of experts on a particular issue. The plural is either *symposia* or *symposiums*.

seminar *noun*, means a small meeting for teaching or training in which the participants are expected to play an active part.

workshop *noun*, means a meeting on a specific theme involving practical work to improve skills.

coniferous, carnivorous

coniferous *adjective*, refers to cone-bearing trees such as pines and firs: *The coniferous forests in Finland seem to stretch for ever*.

carnivorous *adjective*, means meat-eating: *Only a few plants are carnivorous: they trap insects*.

> *'We have carnivorous trees in the garden.'*
> (Student essay) !

connection

See INTERFACE.

connections, relations

connections *noun*, are the people with whom one has social contact, particularly those who have influence in society: *Thanks to his connections, officially he had never been in trouble with the police*.

relations *noun*, has two meanings. In a physical sense **relations** are relatives: siblings, cousins, etc. The second, more abstract meaning, is the way people or countries feel about each other and the dealings they have with each other: *For Macedonia–Slovenia diplomatic relations see p. 383*. Note that with this meaning, there is no article before **relations**. In another sense, **relations** can refer to sexual activities.

> *'. . . the seating is limited to those who have relations with the police.'* !
> (Translation of a French notice on Eurostar, Daily Telegraph)

connotations

The meaning of a word is often more than its dictionary definition. These added values are termed its **connotations**. For example, if you are thinking about a person who is clever, it is possible to divide the connotations into three classes:

- favourable: *bright, gifted, intelligent, talented, wise*
- neutral: *able, capable*
- unfavourable: *artful, brainy, crafty, cunning, foxy, knowing, wily*

connote, denote

connote *verb*, means to suggest something implied or in addition to the literal meaning of a term: *The word 'home' connotes warmth and security*.

denote *verb*, means to give the explicit meaning of something: *The word 'home' denotes a structure such as a flat or bungalow*.

consensus

See CENSUS.

consent

See ASSENT.

conservation, preservation

conservation *noun*, is the practice of keeping something in good condition and undamaged. It is often applied to the natural environment: *The country has no institutions dedicated to soil conservation*.

preservation *noun*, is the maintenance of something in its present condition, even if that is less than perfect: *The exterior wall is in a fair state of preservation*.

Conservative, conservative

Conservative *adjective & noun*. As an adjective (capitalized) this refers to the policies of a particular British political party or a similar one in other countries. As a plural noun, it is the name of a British political party: *The Conservatives are also known as the Tory Party*.

conservative *adjective* (not capitalized), means against change and in favour of tradition: *He was a person of conservative dress and behaviour*.

conservatory, conservatoire

conservatory *noun*, is a room attached to a house, but with glass walls and roof, used as a sun lounge. In AE it is also used as an alternative to *conservatoire*.

conservatoire *noun*, is a college for the teaching and study of the arts, principally classical music.

conserve, preserve, reserve

conserve *verb*, means to protect. This is used especially for environmental or culturally important things or places: *When the weather is good, water supplies may be restricted to conserve stocks*.

preserve *verb & noun*. As a verb, this means either to maintain something in its original or existing state: *It is meaningless to want to preserve these slums, the people are without schools or health care*; or to prevent any decay: *A mixture of petals was collected to preserve the perfume of the flowers*. As a noun, it means an area kept for hunting or fishing, or figuratively an area designed for a specific group: *The laboratory was a male preserve*. It is also a formal term for jam: *This strawberry preserve is available exclusively from us*.

reserve *verb & noun*. As a verb, this means to keep for future use: *We have reserved a table for you at eight o'clock tonight*. As a noun, a

reserve is an area of land kept for the benefit of the natural world rather than humans: *We visited the osprey reserve at Loch Garten, where the birds flew free*. See NATURE RESERVE.

consider

See DELIBERATE.

considerable

See LARGE.

consist

See CONSTITUTE.

consternation, worry

consternation *noun*, means anxiety, shock or fear: *To the vicar's consternation, the ice on the river suddenly gave way*. This is a formal term.

worry *verb & noun*. As a verb, **worry** means to feel anxious or uneasy about something: *You have every reason to worry about the effects of asbestos*. As a noun, it means something that causes anxiety: *Although sufferers appear to have lost their appetite, their chief worry is weight increase*.

constitute, comprise, consist

constitute *verb*, means to make up or form: *It was proposed that the meeting elect a number of people who would constitute a new committee*.

comprise *verb*, means to include a number of items that make up a whole: *Art criticism is a many-levelled activity that comprises the historical, the recreative and the judicial*. Note that **comprise** should never be followed by *of*.

consist *verb*. When followed by *of*, this means to be formed of a number of items: *The Maldives in the Indian Ocean consist of 1196 atolls that would disappear if sea level rose by one metre*. When followed by *in*, it refers to an essential feature: *Happiness does not consist in eating out every day*.

In most sentences *comprise* and *consist of* are interchangeable, but *comprise* is more formal.

consulate

See EMBASSY.

contagious, infectious

contagious *adjective*, refers to diseases that are transmitted either by direct physical contact with a diseased person or animal, or by contact with something that carries the infection, such as clothing. **Contagious** can also refer to the person or animal with the disease: *Sufferers from tuberculosis of the lung can be contagious all their life*. When used figuratively, **contagious** refers to both pleasant and unpleasant things, such as *contagious laughter* and *contagious panic*.

infectious *adjective*, refers to diseases that are spread by germs or viruses in the air or water: *The Asian flu is highly infectious*. **Infectious** can also refer to the agent or person that carries the disease: *The drinking water was infectious; People with flu are already infectious before they show signs of the illness*. When used figuratively, only pleasant things are referred to, for instance *infectious laughter*.

contain

See CONFINE.

contaminate

See POLLUTE.

contemptible, contemptuous

contemptible *adjective*, refers to a person's actions as being nasty, or unworthy: *Last month our production fell because of your contemptible idleness*.

contemptuous *adjective*, means having a low opinion of someone, often without good reason: *The new manager was contemptuous of most of his staff, and tried all sorts of methods to persuade them to leave*.

Both these words imply a negative attitude by the speaker towards the person referred to.

continuing education, further education, lifelong learning

continuing education *uncountable noun*, means education provided for adults after they have completed their formal education: *Our continuing education programme offers a series of short courses tailored to working life*. Normally university credits or a vocational qualification are the result of this training. See COURSES AT COLLEGE OR UNIVERSITY.

further education *uncountable noun*, in the British sense, means courses below degree level taken outside the university sector for those who are above compulsory school age: *She is studying at the local further education college*. Elsewhere in Europe, **further education** can refer to courses taken at higher education level, i.e. at university level, equivalent to refresher courses in the UK.

lifelong learning *uncountable noun*, is a more general term than the others in this group, and is the name of a new EU education programme – the Lifelong Learning Programme 2007–2013. This comprises four sectoral programmes: Comenius for schools, Erasmus for university students, Leonardo da Vinci for industrial training and Grundtvig for adult education.

continual, continuous

continual *adjective*, refers to something that either never stops or reoccurs frequently: *The continual changing of public expenditure targets has made planning impossible*.

continuous *adjective*, refers to an unbroken and uninterrupted sequence: *To mark his continuous service to the company Charles was presented with a set of crystal glasses*.

contraceptive, condom, prophylactic

contraceptive *noun*, means a method, technique or device that is used to avoid pregnancy: *The World Health Organization is promoting the use of contraceptives all over the world*.

condom *noun*, is a general term for a type of contraceptive. In Britain a well-known brand is called Durex, but Australians in Britain, and Britons in Australia need to be careful: Durex is the name of a brand of sticky tape in Australia. Another source of confusion is the word *rubber*, which in BE means an eraser, but in AE is a colloquial term for **condom**. See DUREX (ERASER).

prophylactic proffilácktik /prɒfɪˈlæktɪk/ *noun & adjective*. As a noun, this means a medicine or course of action to prevent disease. In AE, it also means *condom*. As an adjective, it refers to actions taken to prevent disease: *Prophylactic measures have improved treatments considerably over the last 20 years*.

contractions

The word *not* as part of a negative verb form, and forms of auxiliary verbs such as *be, do, have*, are often shortened in speech, and may also be shortened in informal writing (but not in formal essays or dissertations). These shortened forms, usually known as **contractions** rather than abbreviations, are indicated in writing by an apostrophe written in the place where the letters have been omitted.

As scientific and academic writing uses formal English, this does not allow **contractions**, except in written dialogue. Informal letters to friends and informal emails often use contractions to stress the lack of formality.

Examples of contractions including ***not*** are: *aren't, can't, couldn't, doesn't, don't, hasn't, haven't, isn't, shan't, wasn't, weren't, won't* and *wouldn't*.

Forms of the verb ***to be*** are contracted: *I'm, you're, he's, she's, it's, we're, they're* and *who's*.

Shall is not generally contracted, since it is mostly used as an emphatic first-person form.

Will is contracted in speech and written dialogue to *'ll*: *I'll, you'll, he'll, she'll, it'll, we'll* and *they'll*.

Has is often contracted to *'s*: *John's got a new car*. (See below for *is* and *has*.)

Does may be contracted to *'s*: *What's he want?*

confusing contractions and their soundalikes

it's (it is or it has) is often confused with the possessive ***its***. Compare: *It's time to land* (contraction), *the plane lost its wheels* (possessive).

they're (they are) may be confused with the possessive ***their*** or even the adverb ***there*** (all of which may be soundalikes).

you're (you are) may be confused with the possessive ***your*** (*You're late; has your watch stopped again?*)

who's (who is or who has) may be confused with the possessive ***whose***. Compare: *Who's driving to town?*

(contraction), *Whose car is that?* (possessive).

It is also necessary to be careful with *is* and *has* when used as auxiliary verbs, since their contracted forms are the same. Compare: *He's finished* (he is finished) and *He's finished* (he has finished). The context should make it clear which verb is being used, but if there is any potential ambiguity, it is safer to use the full form of the verb.

Remember that the apostrophe in the contraction indicates that letters have been omitted. See **ABBREVIATION, APOSTROPHE (PUNCTUATION GUIDE), FORMAL ENGLISH (WRITING SKILLS)**.

contradiction

See **DICHOTOMY**.

contrastive, distinctive, distinct

contrastive *adjective*, makes a comparison between two things that are usually related but very different: *This is a contrastive analysis of Eastern and Western folk music.*

distinctive *adjective*, refers to a characteristic that makes something easily noticed or different: *The distinctive sound of Peruvian music, with its pan pipes, can be heard in many European cities during the summer.*

distinct *adjective*, means either separate and different: *Average wages in the urban and rural regions were completely distinct*; or easily sensed: *There was a distinct smell of curry in that part of town.*

contrive

See **ENGINEER**.

control, check

control *verb & noun*. As a verb this means to have the power to influence the behaviour or action of other people or things: *She could not control her dog.* It can also mean to hold oneself back from doing something: *She counted to ten and managed to control her anger.* As an uncountable noun it means the power to make decisions about how to manage a country or organization: *The government failed to establish effective control over inflation.* **Control** can mean the ability to make others or an object do what you want: *The passengers took over the control of the ship.* It can also mean the place where regulations are checked such as *immigration and passport control*. As a countable noun it means the buttons, etc. that are needed to operate a mechanical device: *An experienced pilot is at the controls.* See **QUALITY CONTROL**.

check *verb & noun*. As a verb, this means to examine and make sure either that something is accurate or that its quality and condition are satisfactory: *We will check and see if the bill has been paid.* In BE **check** can mean to inspect something. In AE it also means to deposit something. Thus, *to check your bag* may cause some transatlantic confusion. As a noun, **check** means the examination of something. A *check-up* means an examination or inspection: *His doctor gave him a thorough check-up.* See **CHEQUE**.

convince, persuade

convince *verb*, means to make someone believe that something is true: *I had to convince myself that my grasp of reality was not slipping away.*

persuade *verb*, means to make someone or something take action by giving good reasons or a convincing argument: *Our aim is to persuade countries to reduce their output of greenhouse gases.*

cookie

See **CRACKER**.

cooperate, collaborate, collude

cooperate kō-óppĕrayt /kəʊ'ɒpəreɪt/ *verb*, means to work together with others towards the same end. It is used to express approval that often indicates a willingness to work together: *NATO has adopted a common structure in which to cooperate.* **Cooperate** is not hyphenated in modern BE or in AE.

collaborate *verb*, means to cooperate in the production or creation of something that often involves joint scientific or literary activity: *The department collaborates closely with two distinguished Centres for Speech Research.* Note that *cooperate* and **collaborate** can often be used interchangeably, but that **collaborate** can also mean to help an enemy, and thus may be disapproving. A person who collaborates is a *collaborator*, whichever sense of the word is intended.

collude *noun*, means to cooperate illegally or in secret in order to cheat or deceive others. Terrorists and criminals may **collude** but scientists and students *cooperate*. **Collude** and its related noun *collusion* have strong negative associations. The University of Texas, Austin has written that *'"Scholastic dishonesty" includes, but is not limited to, cheating, plagiarism, collusion, falsifying academic records.'* It is best to use this word with care.

cooperation, corporation

cooperation kō-oppĕráyshŏn /kəʊɒpəˈreɪʃn̩/ *uncountable noun*, is the act of two or more people or organizations working together to achieve the same end: *If interviewers find cooperation difficult the selection procedure will be inefficient*. Note that there is no hyphenation in modern English, and as it is an uncountable noun, it always takes a singular verb.

corporation korpŏráyshŏn /kɔːrpəˈreɪʃn̩/ *noun*. In BE, a corporation may be an elected town council, or a company such as the BBC (British Broadcasting Corporation), either operating without a profit motive, or as a nationalized industry (for instance the former British Steel Corporation, before it was privatized). In AE, it is a large commercial company.

coordinate, coordinates

coordinate kō-órdinayt /kəʊˈɔːrdɪneɪt/ *verb*, means to organize an operation so that its separate parts work well together: *We need to provide new, highly committed leadership that will coordinate all our manufacturing efforts*. It also means to choose clothes that match each other: *Her wardrobe was full of trousers, skirts and tops – none of which coordinated*.

coordinates kō-órdinăts /kəʊˈɔːrdɪnəts/ *noun pl*, means the latitude and longitude used to fix a position such as on a map. In computing it can mean the set of numbers that determine a position on a computer screen. It also means clothing that is well matched: *This shop specialized in coordinates – skirts and tops that matched*.

> This spelling (without a hyphen) is the usual one in modern BE and in AE.

cord

See CHORD.

co-respondent, correspondent

co-respondent kō-rispóndĕnt /kəʊrɪˈspɒndənt/ *noun*, means the alleged lover of the person accused of adultery in a divorce action: *It will be difficult to decide on the co-respondent, of course, as we have such a rich and varied choice*. **Co-respondent** is the preferred spelling, but *corespondent* is sometimes used in AE. The stress is on the third syllable, and the first syllable rhymes with 'so'.

correspondent korrispóndĕnt /kɒrɪˈspɒndənt/ *noun*, means a person who writes and receives letters, or is a contributor to a newspaper or broadcasting network: *The Guardian's Washington correspondent was a close friend of the President*. The first two syllables rhyme with 'sorry'.

corn, sweetcorn, *maize*, *maze*

corn *uncountable noun*, in BE means any grain crop, such as wheat, oats or barley: *It is possible to store hay, straw and corn outside*. In AE, **corn** means *maize*, which has given the name to the breakfast cereal, *cornflakes*, that is made from *maize*. Other *maize* products are *sweetcorn* and *corn on the cob*.

sweetcorn, *uncountable noun*, means the yellow seeds of maize that are eaten as a vegetable: *Many people do not realize that peas and beans and sweetcorn are such valuable vegetables*.

maize *uncountable noun*, is the BE name for the plant called *corn* in AE: *There is some dispute about when maize was introduced to Europe*.

maze *noun*, is a labyrinth: *Most of the town consisted of a picturesque maze of narrow, rambling streets*.

corporal punishment

See CAPITAL PUNISHMENT.

corporation

See COOPERATION.

corpse, corps

corpse *noun*, means a dead body. The plural, *corpses*, is pronounced **kórpsiz** /ˈkɔːrpsɪz/.

corps kor /kɔːr/ *noun*, is an organized group of people, particularly a military formation: *The Royal Army Educational Corps*. **Corps** is also used in phrases such as *press corps, diplomatic corps*. Note that the singular and plural are spelt the same, but that the plural is pronounced **korz** /kɔːrz/.

correct

See AMEND, RIGHT.

correspond

See COINCIDE.

correspondence – emails and letters

See WRITING SKILLS.

cost

See PRICE.

cost-benefit, cost-effective

cost-benefit *adjective*, refers to a process that compares the cost of an action with the value of the resulting benefits: *Cost-benefit analysis is widely used to assess a new project*. This is sometimes abbreviated to CBA.

cost-effective *adjective*, refers to something that is effective or productive in relation to its cost: *Cost-efficient is another term for cost-effective*.

cosy, cozy

cosy *adjective*, means warm and comfortable due to being in a confined space: *It all looked delightfully cosy, with an en suite bathroom*. When matters become *too cosy*, this refers to a situation that is not always honest or correct: *The auditors became too cosy with their clients and failed to pick up the problems*.

cozy *adjective*, is the AE spelling of *cosy*.

cotton

See THREAD.

couch

See SOFA.

could

See CAN[1].

councillor, counsellor

councillor *noun*, means a member of a council. The AE spelling is *councilor*.

counsellor *noun*, means an adviser or lawyer. The AE spelling is *counselor*.

counsel

See SOLICITOR.

country, state

country *noun*, means either an area of land that is controlled by its own government: *The country has just celebrated its five-hundredth anniversary*, or an area of land with distinctive features: *This is fine hunting and fishing country*. In this second sense, **country** usually follows an adjective. When people refer to *the country* this may mean a unit such as England or France, or an area that is not a town or city. The expression 'To go to the country' in British politics means to call a general election: *The Prime Minister went to the country over the issue and lost the general election*.

state *noun & verb*. As a noun, this means the political organization of a country or a country considered as a political organization: *EU terminology tends to refer to member states not countries*. **State** in BE means the government and public administration at national level, but in AE it only refers to government in any of the 50 **states** in the USA. The term is often written without a capital: *The meeting of heads of state and government spelled out new strategies*. **State** is capitalized in the titles of countries, or organized political entities or parts of a federal republic: *The State of California*. Also some proper nouns containing the word are capitalized such as *State Registered Nurse*. *The States* is normally understood as an informal reference to the USA. **State** in other senses means a condition: *He was in a confused state of mind*. As a verb, **state** means to express something definitely and clearly in speech or writing: *We have to state clearly what the problem is*. When used as an adjective, *stated* means declared or fixed: *This was the stated aim of the talks*. See GOVERNMENT.

countryside

See RURAL AREA.

couple

See PAIR.

coupon

See VOUCHER.

courses at college or university

correspondence course means a course of study that is taken at home using books and exercises sent by post or email, or accessed through the Internet.

degree course means a programme that enables students to take a bachelor's or master's degree. The length of such courses varies from university to university, and also according to the level of the degree.

foundation course is a general course to prepare students for more advanced courses.

refresher course means a short period of training to improve skills or be updated on developments in an area of specialization.

sandwich course means a course of study which combines study and periods of work in industry.

co-worker

See ET AL.

cozy

See COSY.

cracker, cookie, biscuit

cracker *noun*. The most common meaning is a savoury crispy biscuit, but it also means the coloured paper tube that makes a bang at parties.

cookie *noun*. This is the usual word in AE for a sweet biscuit. In computing, a **cookie** is information that a website leaves in a computer in order to recognize that computer the next time the site is accessed.

biscuit *noun*, is the most common word in BE for a *cracker* or a *cookie* in the AE sense of the words: *We have both sweet and savoury biscuits*. Note that in AE a **biscuit** is a type of soft bread baked in small round pieces.

crafty

See ARTIFICE.

-crat, -cratic

-crat *combining form in nouns*, means a member, representative or supporter of one type of political system: e.g. *democrat*; form of organization: *bureaucrat*; social status: *aristocrat*; or type of expertise: *technocrat*.

-cratic *combining form in adjectives*, refers to a type of political system: e.g. *democratic*; a form of organization: *bureaucratic*; social status: *aristocratic*; or a type of expertise: *technocratic*.

The *-crat* ending can imply criticism of a group, particularly if the word is a recent construction.

crayfish, crawfish

crayfish *noun*, means a variety of edible freshwater or saltwater lobster. This is the BE spelling.

crawfish *noun*, is the AE spelling of *crayfish*.

credible, credulous

credible *adjective*, means believable or convincing: *It hardly seemed credible that such events could occur*. The opposite is *incredible*. See INCREDIBLE.

credulous *adjective*, is usually applied to people who are gullible and easily believe things: *It is easy to sneer at the credulous pilgrims*. See INCREDULOUS (INCREDIBLE).

credit card

See BANK CARD.

creditable, commendable, praiseworthy

creditable *adjective*, refers to something of satisfactory standard and deserving praise: *The Braintree team worked hard and produced a creditable performance*. This is a formal word. The opposite is discreditable which means harmful to a person's reputation.

commendable *adjective*, means deserving of praise: *All in all, this is a commendable book, packed with sound information and wise opinion.*

praiseworthy *adjective*, means worth praising: *To have achieved our budgeted turnover was in itself a praiseworthy effort*. See LAUDABLE.

crepuscular

See DIURNAL.

crescendo

See CLIMAX.

crevasse, crevice

crevasse krĕváss /krɪˈvæs/ *noun*, is a large deep crack in ice, usually in a glacier: *Spacing must eliminate the risk of more than one member falling into the same crevasse*. In AE, a **crevasse** is also a breach in the embankment of a river or canal.

crevice kréviss /ˈkrevɪs/ *noun*, means a narrow cleft or crack, usually in rock: *The grey wagtail nests in ledges and crevices of rocks upstream*.

crippled

See DISABLED.

crisis, crises

crisis *noun*, means a turning point or a time of great danger and difficulty. **Crisis** should only be used for a decisive event, not for a persistent state of difficulty. **Crisis** is the singular form and has the last syllable pronounced as 'sis'.

crises *noun*, is the plural of *crisis* and the last syllable is pronounced 'seas'. In both the singular and plural the first syllable is stressed, and pronounced 'cry'. See FOREIGN PLURALS (WORD FORMATION).

crisps

See CHIPS.

criterion, criteria

criterion *noun*, means a standard of judgement: *This is a criterion that we always use when recruiting new staff*. This is the singular form, and always takes a singular verb.

criteria *noun*, is the plural of *criterion*: *These criteria gave a very positive profile of the new member of staff*. This is a plural noun and always takes a plural verb. See FOREIGN PLURALS (WORD FORMATION).

> *'This criteria is set by the Border and Immigration Agency.'* !
> (UK government website)

critic, critique

critic *noun*, is someone who assesses an artistic performance or exhibition. It is often used for people who have this as their job: *He was a drama teacher at a London school and the theatre critic for a national newspaper*. However, it can be used more generally to mean a person who voices disapproval of others in public.

critique kriteék /krɪˈtiːk/ *noun*, means a detailed review of a book, film or play. Note that the stress is on the second syllable.

critical, crucial

critical *adjective*, has a general meaning concerned with criticism, expressing disapproval of someone's behaviour or appearance: *It is very strange that the slimmer we get the more critical we become of our body*. **Critical** also has a more specific meaning referring to something that is extremely important or decisive: *Economic survival and the profit line are of critical importance to us all*.

crucial *adjective*, also means extremely important for having a decisive effect on other things: *Parental involvement is crucial in terms of developing relevant language teaching practice*.

criticism

See CENSURE.

cross-disciplinary, interdisciplinary, multidisciplinary

cross-disciplinary *adjective*, relates to the involvement of two or more academic disciplines. A key distinction between this term and the other two grouped here is the degree of involvement. *Interdisciplinary* and *multidisciplinary* cooperation normally mean more formalized involvement than **cross-disciplinary** cooperation. See DISCIPLINE (FIELD).

interdisciplinary *adjective*, refers to the involvement or combination of two or more academic disciplines in a common approach or issue. *Our environmental energy programme combines mechanical and electrical engineering in an interdisciplinary degree.*

multidisciplinary *adjective*, refers to the involvement or combination of more than two academic disciplines in a common approach or issue.

crosswalk

See PEDESTRIAN CROSSING.

crotch, crutch

crotch *noun*, is the part of the human body between the tops of the legs where they join the torso. **Crotch** can also refer to the piece in an item of clothing such as tights that covers this part of the body.

crutch *noun*, is a piece of wood or metal that supports the body of someone who is having difficulty walking, by allowing the armpit to rest on it. The word may also be used figuratively for something that helps make someone happier or more confident. **Crutch** is also an alternative spelling of *crotch*.

crucial

See CRITICAL.

cumulative

See ACCUMULATE.

cunning

See ARTIFICE.

curb, kerb

curb *verb & noun*, as a verb, means to control or restrain something: *She tried to curb her temper when she was given a parking ticket.* As a noun, **curb** is the AE spelling for the edge of a pavement (BE) or sidewalk (AE): *His arm tightened around her as they stepped off the curb again.*

kerb *noun*, is the BE spelling for the edge of a pavement (BE) or sidewalk (AE): *My taxi drew to the kerb and she climbed in beside me.*

currant, current

currant *noun*, is the dried fruit of a small variety of seedless grape: *She bought two packets of currants for her Christmas cake.*

current *adjective & noun*. As an adjective, this means happening at the present time: *The current budget for these activities is low and we need to be as cost-effective as possible.* As a noun, **current** means a flow of liquid, gas or electricity: *The Gulf Stream is the current that brings warm water to much of western Europe.*

currency units

The national symbols for currency units such as $ and £ can be misunderstood internationally, as there are many dollars and pounds used around the world. The three-digit currency codes listed in ISO 4217 are preferred by some because they are easier to write and give greater precision. In international business life, these ISO currency codes such as USD (US dollar) and NZD (NZ dollar) should always be used to avoid confusion. Consult the latest ISO listings of currency codes on website www.iso.ch.

Note that the ISO currency code is always written before the amount, but read after the amount.

Written as:	*Read as:*
EUR 55.50	Fifty-five euro fifty (cent)
USD 25.50	Twenty-five US dollars fifty (cents)
GBP 3.20	Three pounds sterling twenty (pence)

When there are decimals, the currency unit is read where the decimal point is. (Note that *euro* and *eurocent* are invariable.)

The use of 'k' for 'kilo' and 'm' for 'million' with an ISO currency code may cause confusion. It is safer to write EUR 25 thousand than EUR 25k.

curriculum, syllabus

curriculum *noun*, means the subjects included in a course of study at school, college or university: *The National Curriculum* *stipulates the core subjects and foundation subjects to be taught in state schools in England and Wales.* **Curriculum** is the singular and *curricula* or *curriculums* are the plural forms. The adjective is *curricular*.

syllabus *noun*, means the list of topics that a student will be required to study in a particular subject at school, college or university: *The French literature option has a very extensive syllabus.* Note that **syllabus** means the content of one subject and *curriculum* means the content of a complete course of study. The plural can be either *syllabuses* or *syllabi*.

curriculum vitae, résumé, resume

curriculum vitae *noun*, is a brief written record of a person's life, education and career that is commonly required with job applications or as career documentation. *CV* is the usual abbreviation of **curriculum vitae**. The plural form is *curricula vitae*, although the abbreviated form *CVs* is more widely used: *Enclose the CVs from the research team.* CV(s) is read as sée vée(z) /ˈsiː ˈviː(z)/. See CV WRITING (WRITING SKILLS).

résumé or **resume** rézyoŏmay /ˈrezjʊmeɪ/ *noun*, means a summary: *I will now give a quick résumé of the results from the initial meeting.* In AE, **résumé** is an alternative to *curriculum vitae*: *Applicants are invited to submit their résumés.* The spelling with accents over the two e's is recommended to prevent confusion with the verb *resume*.

resume *verb*, means to start to do something again after a pause: *After the strike it took two days before production resumed.* The related noun is *resumption*.

custodian

See GUARDIAN.

customary

See TYPICAL.

customer

See CLIENT.

cutting edge

See STATE OF THE ART.

CV writing

See WRITING SKILLS.

cyclic, cyclical

cyclic *adjective*, refers to patterns recurring in the same order at intervals: *Cyclic fluctuations in population numbers occur in many species of small mammal.* In mathematics and geometry it means related to circular patterns. It also has specialist meanings in the natural sciences especially in chemistry and botany.

cyclical *adjective*, refers to cyclic patterns and is often an alternative to *cyclic*. However, **cyclical** cannot be used in the mathematical or natural science contexts where *cyclic* is used.

cyclone

See HURRICANE.

cynic, sceptic, sceptical, septic

cynic *noun*, means a person who takes a pessimistic view of events: *Even hardened cynics agreed that the conference may help the peace process in the region.* The corresponding adjective is *cynical*.

sceptic *noun*, means someone who doubts or mistrusts other people's opinions that are generally thought to be true: *This sceptic claims to have better knowledge about the cause of global warming than the rest of us.* This is the BE spelling. Despite the spelling with initial 'sce-' the pronunciation is sképtik /ˈskeptɪk/. *Skeptic* is the AE spelling.

sceptical *adjective*, means tending to disagree with the opinions of other people: *To deny that pollution is part of the problem with global warming is excessively sceptical.* The AE spelling is *skeptical*.

septic *adjective*, refers to anything that is infected or poisoned by bacteria: *Two weeks later the cut on the patient's leg became septic.* A *septic tank* is a drainage system that uses bacterial action to break down organic waste: *The house drains are directed into septic tanks.*

> *'I am just septical about ordering over the Internet.'* **!**

C

Spelling

C**ae**s**a**r	-a- before -e-, and -a- before the final -r
calend**a**r	As a list of dates, note the final -ar
ca**nn**ibal	Note the double -nn-, but single -b-
Ca**r**i**bb**ean	Note single -r-, but double -bb-
cata**rrh**	Note single -t-, but double -rr-, and final -h
cat**e**gory	Remember the -e- between -t- and -g-
c**ei**ling	-e- before -i-
cem**e**t**e**ry	Every vowel is -e-
cen**s**us	Note the -s- in the middle
co**mm**e**m**orate	Note double -mm- followed by single -m-
co**mm**itment	Note the double -mm-
co**mm**i**tt**ee	Note -mm-, -tt-, -ee
compuls**ory**	Note the -ory ending
con**cede**	See *-cede, -ceed, -sede*
confid**ent**ly	Note the -e-
co**nn**oi**ss**eur	Note the double -nn- and double -ss-
con**sc**ience	Note the -sc-
con**sc**ious	Note the -sc-
con**s**ensus	Note the second syllable begins with -s-
co**rr**ect	Remember the double -rr-
co**rr**espond**e**nce	Note the double -rr-, and final -ence
co**rr**espond**e**nt	Note the double -rr-, and final -ent
co**rr**ob**o**rate	Note the double -rr-, and the -o- before the last -r-
curs**o**r	Note this ends in -or

D

daily

See EVERYDAY.

dairy, diary

dairy *noun*, means a place to process cheese, butter or milk: *New Zealand's dairy farmers have become the cheapest producers in the OECD*.

diary *noun*, means a record of events and experiences that is often kept on a daily basis: *Most teenagers keep a diary at some stage*. In AE, the term *daybook* is used to mean a **diary**.

damage, damages, compensation

damage *uncountable noun & verb*. This refers to physical harm caused to things or to parts of the body: *The damage to both houses was considerable*. In BE, but not AE, the question 'What is the damage?' in a pub or café is an informal way of asking how much the bill comes to. As a verb, **damage** means to harm or injure: *Pumping operations are threatening to damage the site beyond repair*. Things are **damaged**, but people are physically *injured*, although their reputation or health may be **damaged**: *Smoking will damage your unborn child*. Machinery is **damaged** if the cause is external; otherwise it is said to *malfunction* or *break down*. See INJURE (WOUND), MISTAKE (FAULT).

damages *plural noun*, is the legal term for an amount of money claimed or received for injury or harm to a company's or person's reputation. It is not the plural of *damage*: *The defendants accepted that damages could be awarded for mental distress*. Note that in AE, **damages** can be used informally about the cost of something: *What are the damages for the repair job?*

compensation *uncountable noun*, is the legal term for an amount of money claimed or received for physical injury or material loss to a person or company: *Victims will be eligible for compensation from the Criminal Injuries Board*.

Dame

See SIR.

dash

See PUNCTUATION GUIDE.

data, datum

data *uncountable* or *plural noun*, means facts and statistics collected for analysis or reference. **Data** is the plural form of *datum*. However, **data** is often used as an uncountable noun, especially in computer science and data processing: *There is no data to show that first babies really do cry more*. **Data** is used as a plural noun in scientific and formal writing or when referring to different types of data: *Birthplace data show that only 40 per cent of those had been born in the town they lived in*.

datum *noun*, means one piece of information. It is rarely used, except as a standard of comparison or as a reference point in surveying: *The top line in this diagram is called the datum line or datum level*.

date of birth

See BIRTHDAY.

dates (digital and non-digital)

digital dates

Suppose there is a project deadline, a delivery date or payment date written as 12/04/10 or 12.04.10. What date will international readers think is meant?

Here are the possibilities:

- The European system, day-month-year, gives: 12 April 2010
- The US system, month-day-year, gives: December 4, 2010
- The ISO system, year-month-day, gives: 2012 April 10. This is the standard order that is used for dates in China.

Many companies set up their standard letter/fax/report title page so that they automatically generate dates in digital form according to the ISO 8601 standard (ccyy-mm-dd or, as an example, 2010-04-12) in the date space on the first page and on following pages. Unfortunately, many people fail to follow this standard and write 12.4.2010 or 12/4/2010 elsewhere in emails and reports. This can lead to expensive misunderstandings.

When writing digital dates it is therefore best to follow the ISO 8601 standard and systematically use the model ccyy-mm-dd or 2010-04-12 (i.e. 12 April 2010). It is stipulated in this standard that two digits are used for days and months and four digits should be used for years (i.e. 2010) and that hyphens, not dots or slashes, should be used to separate the units. If it is necessary to give a time interval, then an en dash can be used (e.g. 2005-06-01–2010-04-12). ISO 8601 only specifies digital notations and does not cover dates where words are used in the representation. The ISO format means that you can refer to exact time by adding the hours, minutes and time zone: 2010-04-12:21.45 CET. See TIME ZONES.

non-digital dates

Another way of avoiding confusions with digital dates is always to write the month in words. The two main customs are *12 April 2010*, which is common in BE and *April 12, 2010*, which is common in AE (do not forget the comma). The ordinal form (1st, 2nd, 3rd, 4th etc.) is now considered old-fashioned for written dates in business English. However, when reading dates out loud, use the model: *the twelfth of April 2010* in BE and *April twelfth 2010* in AE.

weeks and months

These abbreviations for the names of months are generally used: *Jan., Feb., Mar., Apr., Jun., Jul., Aug., Sept., Oct., Nov., Dec.* (*May* is written in full). In parts of Europe, the 52 or 53 weeks of the year are numbered, and in these places it is common to refer to a meeting, for instance, as being in 'Week 47', rather than in 'late November'. See EMAILS AND LETTERS (WRITING SKILLS), NUMBERS.

'Contract settlement date 3/9/10'. Is this 3 September 2010 or March 9, 2010? **!**

davenport

See SOFA.

day, daytime, 24 hours, 24–7, round-the-clock

day *noun*, means both the 24-hour period starting at midnight, and the time spent at work or office hours: *Work on this during the day* (during office hours). Most office staff now work a *five-day week*, meaning Monday to Friday, or are given one of these days off, if they have to work on Saturday or Sunday.

daytime *noun & adjective*. As a noun, this means the hours of daylight, as opposed to night-time: *Do not take naps in the daytime if you feel tired*. As an adjective, **daytime** is most commonly used to describe the entertainment programmes (game shows, chat shows, etc.) broadcast by television stations during office hours (between approximately 9 a.m. and 5 p.m.) for people who are at home at that time.

24 hours *noun*, means **day** in the sense of a 24-hour period or refers to a facility that is never closed: *The security office is manned 24 hours a day*. Note that when this phrase is used adjectivally, such as *24-hour service*, it is hyphenated and has no final -s.

24–7 *adverb*, means something that is open 24 hours a day and 7 days a week: *That petrol station is open 24–7*. It was originally an AE term, but is now becoming more familiar in BE.

round-the-clock *adjective*, refers to something that operates permanently, both day and night: *The RSPB organizes a round-the-clock watch of nests at breeding times*. Note that when this phrase is used adjectivally, as here, it is hyphenated. When it is used as the object of a sentence, it is not hyphenated: *She worked round the clock to bring up a young family by herself*.

deadly, deathly, mortal, lethal

deadly *adjective & adverb*. As an adjective, this means causing death, or having the potential to do so: *More than 3,800 people have died since deadly gas escaped from a pesticide plant*. As an adverb, **deadly** can be combined with dull or serious to mean extremely: *Life in a small village can be deadly dull*. See FATAL.

deathly *adjective & adverb*. As either an adjective or an adverb, this refers to something that resembles death and is normally used figuratively: *When the objector stood up, there was a deathly silence* (adjective); *His face was deathly white* (adverb).

mortal *adjective*, means certain to die, referring to all living things: *She saw all the bodies in the morgue and realized that she too was mortal*. It also means causing death, but it is used only in formal contexts: *There are some injuries that are mortal however hard you fight*. The phrase *mortal remains* refers to a dead body.

lethal *adjective*, refers to a substance capable of causing death: **lethal** is the word to choose in formal contexts: *Damaged leads and incorrectly wired equipment can be lethal*.

dead zone

See **NO-GO AREA**.

debit card

See **BANK CARD**.

deca-, deci-

deca- means ten, or ten times something. For instance, the *decathlon* involves ten separate events for the same competitor at an athletics meeting.

deci- is used in the decimal system to mean a tenth: *A blood alcohol level of 200 micrograms per decilitre is twice the legal limit in the US*.

decade

See **NUMBERS**.

deception, deceit

deception *noun*, means something that deceives, or the act of deceiving: *He was charged with obtaining property by deception*.

deceit *noun*, is either behaviour intended to mislead, or a fraud: *The police were clearly engaged in a trick or deceit*.

deceptive, deceitful

deceptive *adjective*, means giving an impression that is not correct: *The clumsy repair was skilfully disguised by deceptive restoration*.

deceitful *adjective*, means deliberately misleading others, usually on a regular basis: *He was frequently deceitful in his deliberate misrepresentations of the cash flow in the company*.

decide, determine, resolve

decide *verb*, means to come to a conclusion, either quickly or based on careful consideration: *She could not yet decide which bits were real and which were dreams*.

determine *verb*, means to establish the facts about something: *Exploration is under way to determine whether the life of the mine can be extended*. See **DETERMINED (OBSTINATE)**.

resolve *verb*, means to make a firm decision: *By the spring of 1527, Henry had resolved to put Catherine aside and to marry Anne Boleyn*. It also means to find a satisfactory solution to an issue or problem: *Most labour directors have resolved this conflict by operating as responsible managers*.

decimate

See **MASSACRE**.

deck of cards

See **PACK (PACKAGE)**.

decline

See **REFUSE**.

de facto, de jure

de facto dee fácktō /diː 'fæktəʊ/ *adjective & adverb*, is a Latin phrase that describes a situation as it exists, even though this may not be the official or legal state of affairs: *Long-term foster placements may turn into de facto adoptions*.

de jure dee jŏ́ori /diː 'dʒʊəri/ *adjective & adverb*, is a Latin phrase that describes the legal situation: *A fostered child is still in the de jure control of the social services*.

> These expressions are both technical phrases, and often occur together as a contrast: *De jure, the Baltic states gained their independence in 1918, but de facto, they were part of the USSR from 1940 to 1990*.

defect, defection

defect deéfekt /'diːfekt/ *noun*, means a fault: *Laura was born with a rare heart defect which prevented enough oxygen reaching her blood*.

Note that the stress is on the first syllable. See **MISTAKE (FAULT)**.

defect diffékt /dɪˈfekt/ *verb*, means to change one's allegiance from one country or organization to another: *Rebels said that many government troops had defected to their side*. Note that the stress is on the second syllable.

defection *noun*, is the act of leaving a country or (usually) a political organization in order to join an opposing country or body: *The party must face up to the defection of some members to the main social democratic party*.

defective, deficient

defective *adjective*, means faulty: *The seed was defective and the resulting crop was useless*. It is old-fashioned and offensive to use **defective** for someone with a mental illness. See **LEARNING DIFFICULTY**.

deficient *adjective*, means not enough, or not good enough: *We now know that these cereals are deficient in some of the more important nutrients*.

defence, defense

defence *noun*, means protection from attack, criticism or the elements; and the government organization Ministry of Defence. This is the BE spelling. Note that the related adjectives *defensive* and *defensible* are spelt with an 's' in BE and AE, while *defenceless* has a 'c' in BE.

defense noun, is the AE spelling: *Department of Defense*. One way to remember the correct spelling is to think of defen<u>s</u>e and the U<u>S</u>A.

(the) defence, (the) prosecution (law)

defence *noun*, means the lawyer or lawyers who have the task of proving to a court that a person charged with a crime is innocent: *The case for the defence was that the revolver went off accidentally in the course of a struggle*. Note that in AE this is spelt *defense*.

prosecution *noun*, means the lawyer or lawyers who have the task of proving to a court that a person charged with a crime is guilty: *The prosecution made such a poor presentation that there was no case for the defence to answer*.

> Note that these words both take the definite article in this sense.

defer

See **RAIN CHECK**.

deficient

See **DEFECTIVE**.

definite, definitive

definite *adjective*, means clearly stated or decided, without any room for doubt: *Additional tests are needed to reach a more definite conclusion*. It is not necessary to use **definite** in order to give emphasis to something: *We want your definite answer* underlines that the immediate answer is likely to change. Always remember the word 'finite' to avoid the common misspelling of this word.

definitive *adjective*, refers to conclusions that are reached decisively and with authority: *The question 'What is History?' beloved of university examiners, has no definitive answer*. Books are also **definitive** when they are authoritative works and provide the final word on a subject: *This is likely to remain the layman's definitive Celtic history book for some time to come*.

definite article

See **ARTICLES (GRAMMAR TIPS)**.

deflation, devaluation

deflation *noun*, means the reduction of money available in an economy in order to

> *'We apologize for the error in last week's paper in which we stated that Mr Arnold Dogbody was a defective in the police force. We meant, of course, that Mr Dogbody is a detective in the police farce.'*
> (Correction notice, *Ely Standard*) !

lower prices and wages or to keep them at the same level: *The result will be a general deflation of both money wages and prices which will leave real wages unchanged*. The opposite is inflation.

devaluation *noun*, means the lowering of the value of one currency in relation to others as an attempt to slow the rate of inflation or to increase exports, or both: *The devaluation of the pound has added 15 per cent to the value of housing abroad for British investors*. The opposite is revaluation.

These terms are used in economics, and it is important not to confuse them.

defuse, diffuse

defuse dee-féwz /ˈdiːˈfjuːz/ *verb*, means to remove a fuse: *Experts then moved in to defuse the 'large explosive device'*. Figuratively it means to remove tension: *The authorities promised to look into the complaints in order to defuse the situation*. For clarity, the word should be stressed on each syllable.

diffuse difféwz /dɪˈfjuːz/ *verb &* difféwss /dɪˈfjuːs/ *adjective*. As a verb, this means to disperse or scatter: *If you put a drop of soluble dye in a glass of water, it will slowly diffuse outwards until the water is uniformly coloured*. As an adjective, **diffuse** means difficult to understand: *His diffuse arguments left the audience no wiser when he sat down*. It also means scattered and less concentrated: *Sometimes, occupation-specific skills are called for; on other occasions, more diffuse skills are sought*.

> *'Keanu Reeves stars as Jack Traven, an L.A.P.D. SWAT team specialist who is sent to diffuse a bomb.'*
> (Amazon.com) **!**

degenerate

See **REPROBATE**.

degree, diploma, certificate

degree *noun*, is the academic qualification given by a college or university after the successful completion of a programme of study, usually involving examinations: *She was awarded a bachelor's degree in 2002*. It also refers to higher education in progress: *He is taking a degree at Oxford*. See **DIPLOMA MILL**.

diploma *noun*, means an official document awarded by an educational body to show that someone has successfully completed a course of study at school, college or university level. It also refers to the course that is being followed: *She's taking a diploma in healthcare*. In addition, it may be a postgraduate qualification, or one taken instead of a degree: *The Diploma in Education is a one-year full-time course for graduates*.

certificate *noun*, means an official document awarded by a body to show that someone has successfully completed a course, not necessarily an academic one. **Certificates** are used to document other things such as birth (*birth certificate*), marriage (*marriage certificate*) or death (*death certificate*), or even vehicle roadworthiness (*MOT certificate*). **Certificate** is also the name of a qualification after a programme of study, and is also used for the course of study itself. In this sense, it is specifically a term used in BE but not AE: *The General Certificate of Secondary Education (GCSE) is usually taken at the age of 15 or 16*.

de jure

See **DE FACTO**.

delete

See **ERASE**.

deliberate, consider

deliberate dĕlíbbĕrăt /dɪˈlɪbərət/ *adjective &* dĕlíbbĕrayt /dɪˈlɪbəreɪt/ *verb*. As an adjective, this refers to something done on purpose, not accidentally: *He would read out my favourite stories, sometimes with deliberate mistakes for me to correct*. **Deliberate** may also mean careful and painstaking: *Lute-making is a slow, deliberate craft to which precision is the key*. Note that the final syllable contains a neutral vowel. As a verb, **deliberate** means to think about something carefully and to discuss it at length: *The military council deliberated for 24 hours on their response to this incident*. Note that when this word is used as a verb, the final syllable is pronounced 'rate'.

consider *verb*, means either to think about something carefully, particularly when a decision has to be made: *The military council is seriously considering the invasion plans;* or to say how something or somebody is regarded: *He is considered a leading expert in military strategy*.

delicate

See FRAIL.

delicious

See TASTEFUL.

delightful

See NICE.

delimit

See LIMIT.

deliver

See SUPPLY.

deliverables, delivery

deliverables *noun*, means a product or something provided at the end of a development process: *They agreed on the terms of payment for the deliverables*. Note that this noun usually occurs in the plural.

delivery *noun*, means the act or date of delivering something: *Delivery of the interim report is to be on 12 April 2010*. **Delivery** can also refer to the process of childbirth, or to the way in which a person speaks or sings: *Pitch and pace should be varied to avoid a monotonous and uninteresting delivery*.

delusion

See ILLUSION.

de luxe, deluxe

de luxe *adjective*, means luxury. This is the BE spelling.

deluxe *adjective*, is an alternative spelling of *de luxe* in AE.

demand, demands

demand *noun*, means a firm request for something: *Air traffic controllers are making a demand for higher wages*. In another sense, **demand** means the pressure from customers for a product: *Reporters are always looking for new ways to meet the demand for entertainment*.

demands *plural noun*, means the pressures imposed on people: *Safety regulations place considerable demands on air traffic controllers*.

D

demi-

See SEMI-.

demolish

See DISMANTLE.

demure

See HUMBLE.

denominator

See NUMERATOR.

denote

See CONNOTE.

deny

See REFUSE.

dependant, dependent, independent

dependant *noun*, means a person who is given financial or in-kind support by others: *About 20 per cent of all households have a dependant in need of care*. This is spelt *dependent* in AE.

dependent *adjective*, means either relying on or determined by: *The stability of the rural economy may, in part, be dependent on the effects of climatic change*. In another sense it can mean addicted to: *Misusing drugs in pregnancy may lead to the birth of a baby who is dependent on drugs*. **Dependent** takes the prepositions *on* or *upon*.

independent *adjective*, means free of outside control, particularly when followed by the preposition *from*: *It has been independent from Britain for over 200 years*. The expression *independent of* means generally or financially separate: *In many countries, you are legally independent of your parents at 18*.

depreciate, deprecate, deplore

depreciate *verb*, usually means to fall in value: *Because of the 2.9-litre engine, the latest* *cars will depreciate heavily in the first year.* A second and more formal meaning is to play down the importance of something: *Those who put greater emphasis on technology depreciate the importance of art in education.*

deprecate *verb*, means to disapprove strongly or criticize something: *We strongly deprecate the current moral standards in the UK.* **Deprecate** also means to dismiss or reduce the importance of something. Note that the adjective *self-deprecating* refers to playing down one's own achievements: *He began his talk with several self-deprecating comments which made the audience feel at ease.* This is a formal word.

deplore *verb*, means to disapprove of something very strongly or criticize it severely: *The international press deplored the escalation of violence in Tibet.*

Note that while *deprecate* is used reflexively for personal comments (*self-deprecating*), *deplore* cannot be used in this way.

derisive, derisory

derisive *adjective*, means showing in an unkind way that you think someone or something is ridiculous: *His mouth twisted in a derisive smile.* This is also an infrequent synonym for *derisory*.

derisory *adjective*, means very small and unimportant: *The pay rise that was offered was a derisory 2 per cent.*

descendant, descendent

See **HEIR**.

desert, deserts, dessert

desert dĕzért /dɪˈzɜːrt/ *verb* & dézzĕrt /ˈdezərt/ *noun*. As a verb, this means to abandon and leave without support: *He deserted his family and fled the country.* Someone who runs away from the army is a *deserter*. As a noun, this is a dry, barren region. It is also used figuratively to refer to a situation that is lacking some quality, such as a *cultural desert*. *Deserts*, pronounced dézzĕrts /ˈdezərts/, is the plural of **desert** in this sense.

deserts dĕzérts /dɪˈzɜːrts/ *plural noun*, is used as part of the idiom to *get one's just deserts*. This means to receive what one deserves, often because of having done something evil: *The convicted killer got his just deserts: life imprisonment.* Note that this is stressed on the second syllable.

dessert dĕzért /dɪˈzɜːrt/ *noun*, is the sweet course at the end of a meal. This is one of the very few words spelt with '-ss-' but pronounced '-z-'. It is stressed on the second syllable.

'Today's special desert: "Mixed fruit and whalenuts."'
(menu item) **!**

destiny, fate, providence

destiny *uncountable noun*, means a power that controls events, often one that makes people feel they can achieve great acts: *MacArthur was spurred on by a strong sense of destiny and ambition.*

fate *uncountable noun*, means a power that controls events, often one that makes people feel they are helpless: *It was fate that decided my future in Indonesia.*

providence *uncountable noun*, means fate controlled by a divine being or God-like force that is usually positive for the believers: *Many Protestants found their trust in divine providence to be a source of great comfort.*

destroy

See **WRECK**.

determine

See **DECIDE**.

determined

See **OBSTINATE**.

detract

See **DISTRACT**.

devaluation

See **DEFLATION**.

develop, exploit

develop *verb*, means to become, or cause something to become, more mature or advanced: *Mobiles have developed faster than anyone could have thought a decade ago.* It can also mean to expand the potential of something, especially in the context of resources: *We have decided to develop the forestry resources in this region.* Note that there is no 'e' after the 'p' in **develop**. See USE.

exploit ĕksplóyt /ɪks'plɔɪt/ *verb &* écksployt /'eksplɔɪt/ *noun*. As a verb, this means to make full use of a possibility, often at the expense of others: *Manufacturers of mobiles have exploited new possibilities for earning money.* Although **exploit** usually has a negative connotation, it is the correct word to use for deriving benefit from a resource: *They are going to begin exploiting another mine in the area.* However, because of this potential ambiguity, *develop* is often a better choice here. As a noun, **exploit** means a brave or exciting undertaking: *The Range Rover is the perfect vehicle for serious cross-country exploits.*

device, devise

device *noun*, means a piece of equipment designed for a specific task: *This is a new credit card protection device for home shoppers.*

devise *verb*, means to plan or think up something: *You must devise a promotional campaign for next Christmas.* Note that the spelling of the verb is **-ise** in both BE and AE.

diaeresis

See SYMBOLS.

diagnose, diagnosis

diagnose *verb*, means to identify a mechanical problem or a disease: *They developed a new test that could diagnose a disease in ten minutes.* Note that the form *diagnoses* is pronounced dī-ăg-nőziz /daɪəg'nəʊzɪz/, rhyming with 'noses'.

diagnosis *noun*, is the identification of a medical or mechanical problem: *The doctor said that exact diagnosis would require numerous tests.* Note that the plural is *diagnoses* dī-ăg-nősseez /daɪəg'nəʊsiːz/ with the final syllable pronounced 'seas'.

diagram, technical drawing

diagram *noun*, means a simplified drawing to show how something works or is located. Note that it is only spelt with a single 'm'. As a verb, **diagram** means to represent something graphically. Note that the past form, *diagrammed* and the present participle, *diagramming*, have a double 'm' in BE and a single 'm' in AE.

technical drawing *noun*, is a graphical representation of structures, machines and components to give exact information about the parts to those who make a product.

diary

See DAIRY.

dice

See DYE.

dichotomy, paradox, contradiction

dichotomy dīkóttŏmi /daɪ'kɒtəmi/ *noun*, means a division into two distinct groups that are completely different with opposing features: *They believe aid fails due to the dichotomy between theory at a distance and practical reality at the local level.* Note that a **dichotomy** stresses the difference between two things such as good and evil.

paradox *noun*, means a statement with two opposing ideas that may seem contradictory, but are probably true: *Man learns from history that man learns nothing from history* (Hegel). A person or situation with two opposite features that are puzzling can also be termed a **paradox**: *He was a paradox – a loving father and yet a murderer.* Note that a **paradox** accounts for the strangeness found in idioms like *more haste, less speed*.

contradiction *noun*, means a discrepancy between two statements or states of affairs such that they cannot both be valid.

die

See DYE.

dietician, dietitian

See NUTRITIONIST.

different, various

different *adjective*, means unlike in nature, shape, form and quality: *He was so different from John in every way that it was amazing to think the human race could contain them both.* In BE, although *different to* is in common use, some careful writers prefer *different from*. In AE *different than* is the most common construction.

various *adjective*, means a number of different things or types that are not distinctly different. When discussing a range of things, use **various** rather than *different*: *There are various languages that have evolved from Latin.* **Various** is usually placed before a plural noun. See FEW.

diffuse

See DEFUSE.

dilemma, predicament, quandary, Hobson's choice

dilemma *noun*, means facing a difficult choice between two or more alternatives of equal importance that are usually undesirable: *He faced the dilemma of choosing between his girlfriend and his career.* The Greek prefix (di- = two) means that careful writers restrict **dilemma** to two alternatives.

predicament *noun*, means being in a difficult and unpleasant situation. The term is often used in the context of an embarrassing financial position: *No one envied the financial predicament the club was in.*

quandary *noun*, means a problem or situation that is difficult to resolve: *He was in a quandary about accepting the new job or not.*

Hobson's choice *noun*, means a situation in which you have no choice. It is 'take it or leave it'. The origin of **Hobson's choice** is a Cambridge innkeeper called Thomas (or Tobias) Hobson *ca* 1600 who hired out horses. Customers were told to take the one nearest the door, or walk.

diner

See RESTAURANT.

dinner jacket, tuxedo

dinner jacket *noun*, is a type of suit for men with a short jacket without tails that is worn at a formal dinner. This is usually black or white, and a bow tie (often black as well) is normal. The expression 'Dress: black tie' on an invitation means a **dinner jacket** for men and an evening dress for women. The abbreviation is DJ. See DRESS CODES.

tuxedo *noun*, is mainly an AE word for a **dinner jacket**. It can also mean a formal evening suit. The usual plural is *tuxedos*.

diploma

See DEGREE.

diploma mill, degree mill

diploma mill *noun* (also known as a **degree mill**), is an organization that is a non-existent or non-accredited university that sells degrees or diplomas often based on life experience rather than academic study. *Webster's Third New International Dictionary* defines a diploma mill as *'An institution of higher education operating without supervision of a state or professional agency and granting diplomas which are either fraudulent or because of the lack of proper standards, worthless'.*

disabled, crippled, handicapped, invalid

disabled *adjective*, refers to someone who has a physical illness or mental condition that restricts actions and mobility. Note that *disabled person* and *disabled people* are alternatives to the term *the disabled*. **Disabled** has replaced old-fashioned terms like *handicapped*. It is widely accepted, and not considered offensive, although some feel it has negative associations. New terms are being introduced to replace **disabled**. Two of these are *differently abled* and *physically challenged*.

crippled *adjective*, means disabled in such a way that a person cannot walk or move easily. More generally, **crippled** can be used to describe something that is seriously damaged: *The crippled plane circled above the densely populated suburb, dumping fuel in a lake.* The related noun *cripple* is old-fashioned and offensive.

handicapped *adjective*, refers to a person who is mentally or physically *disabled*. This is becoming old-fashioned and is often considered an offensive term. *Disabled* is an accepted general alternative. If the person has a mental handicap, it is acceptable to say that he or she is suffering from a learning disability. See LEARNING DIFFICULTY.

invalid *noun & adjective*. As a noun this means someone who needs another person to care for them due to illness: *He developed epilepsy at the age of 15 and spent the rest of his life as an invalid.* In this sense of the word, the stress is on the first syllable: **ínvălid** /ˈɪnvəlɪd/. As an adjective it means not legally accepted: *He had an invalid driving licence*. In computing it refers to a command that is not accepted. Note that the adjective has the stress on the second syllable: **inválid** /ɪnˈvælɪd/. A notice such as 'invalid access' can mean the entry point for those in wheelchairs (**ínvălid** /ˈɪnvəlɪd/): *The Plitsch Platsch provides invalid access to the pool as well as invalid showers*; or that it is impossible to access a database or a server on the Internet (**inválid** /ɪnˈvælɪd/): *I've been getting an 'invalid access' error message all day*.

disapprove

See DISPROVE.

disburse, disperse

disburse *verb*, means to pay money from a fund: *A system that gives the university complete freedom to decide how to disburse the whole of the national settlement*.

disperse *verb*, means to distribute or scatter over a wide area: *The presidential guard yesterday used tear gas and clubs to disperse about 1,000 student protesters*.

disc, disk

disc *noun*, means a round flat shape or object: *The dog's name was on a disc hanging from its collar*. This spelling is generally preferred in BE: *compact disc, disc brake, disc jockey* and a *slipped disc* (cartilage that has moved out of position).

disk *noun*, is the usual spelling of the word in most contexts in AE: *compact disk, disk brake* and *disk jockey*. This spelling is also used in BE in connection with computer equipment such as *floppy disk, hard disk* and *disk drive*.

discipline

See FIELD.

discount, reduction, rebate

discount *noun*, means a deduction from the usual price of some goods: *There is a 50 per cent discount on these goods during the sale*. **Discount** is often, but not always, referred to in terms of a percentage.

reduction *noun*, means an arrangement that makes the prices of goods lower: *Special reduction on ice cream, all week*. In shops, this is often termed a special offer or just a special.

rebate *noun*, means a refund, often from the tax authorities: *After several letters to the tax office, his claim for a tax rebate was accepted*.

D

discovery

See INNOVATION.

discreet, discrete

discreet *adjective*, means tactful and taking care with what one says or does: *A discreet waiter tries to be as invisible as possible*. A related noun is *discretion*: *All benefits are at the discretion of the company*.

discrete *adjective*, means separate and individually distinct: *The enhanced processing of the tape revealed the discrete units of sound*. This is a technical term.

discrepancy, disparity, imbalance

discrepancy *noun*, means a difference between amounts or reports that should have been the same. Consequently it focuses on the lack of factual accuracy: *There's a substantial discrepancy between your account and his*.

disparity *noun*, means a difference between two or more things, especially due to inequality: *The most publicized aspect of the North–South divide has been the wide disparity between house prices*.

imbalance *noun*, means a difference between two or more things that are out of proportion or are not being treated fairly or equally: *A pressing need in higher education is addressing the imbalance between teaching, research and administration*.

discriminate, discrimination, discriminating

discriminate *verb*. When used with the preposition *against*, this means to block or make an unfavourable distinction between people based on factors over which they have no control such as social background, race or sex: *Apartheid formed a legal basis to discriminate against the non-white races in South Africa*. The phrase *discriminate between* means to recognize a difference between two or more things: *It is important for young learners to be able to discriminate between the shapes of letters and their sounds.*

discrimination *uncountable noun*, means the unfair treatment of people because of their race or sex, for instance. The term *positive discrimination* refers to a means of favouring a group that had previously been excluded, through a special measure or quota: *The university is using positive discrimination to attract girls to computer science studies.* In another sense it means the ability to select high quality due to good taste: *Chosen with discrimination, it was a welcome addition to parish church music.*

discriminating *adjective*, refers to a person who is able to judge what is good quality and what is not: *He was a discriminating art critic who worked for 'The Times' for 36 years.*

discussion

See TALKS.

disguise, guise

disguise *noun & verb*. As a noun, this means a false appearance: *No one recognized him in his Father Christmas disguise.* As a verb, **disguise** means to change one's appearance, in order to deceive: *The bank robber disguised himself as Father Christmas.* It can also refer to hiding a fact or feeling: *No one could disguise the fact that the President was in deep trouble.*

guise *noun*, means the way someone or something appears to be in order to hide the truth: *At the factory, the children were subjected to an obligatory, unpaid form of child labour, under the guise of education.* This is a formal word.

disinterested, uninterested

disinterested *adjective*, means impartial and not have anything to win or lose from the result of a situation: *A solicitor's ability to give impartial and disinterested advice is a fundamental element of his or her relationship with the client.*

uninterested *adjective*, means apathetic and showing no sign of enthusiasm or interest in someone or something: *The public is completely uninterested in knowing whether the contest is rigged or not, and rightly so.*

Although many people regard these words as synonyms, one hopes that the members of a jury in a court of law are *disinterested* rather than *uninterested*.

disk

See DISC.

dismantle, demolish

dismantle *verb*, means to take something apart carefully: *Plans are afoot to dismantle the control tower brick by brick and reassemble it on another plot of land.*

demolish *verb*, means to break something up, with no intention of preserving the elements in the construction: *They hope to demolish the store and build a bar extension in its place.* Figuratively, arguments can be *demolished*, meaning that they are shown to be completely wrong, in a sporting event the opposition can also be *demolished*. The informal BE use of **demolish** meaning to eat something very quickly may puzzle people from other parts of the world.

dismiss, fire, sack, notice (give someone notice)

dismiss *verb*, is the word used for officially terminating someone's employment, typically following unsatisfactory performance or dishonourable conduct by the employee: *You will be dismissed at the end of this week.*

fire *verb*, is an informal equivalent of dismiss: *You are fired as of now.*

sack *verb & noun*, is another informal equivalent of dismiss. When used as a verb, it is possible to say to **sack** someone. As a noun, **sack** is normally used in set phrases with *to give*, such as *He was caught stealing and given the sack*.

notice (give someone notice) *noun*, means the formal announcement of termination of employment and can be from either the employer or the employee: *She was required to give three months' notice*. Between the announcement and the last day of employment the employee is *working his (or her) notice*. See **REDUNDANT**, **RESIGN**.

disparity

See **DISCREPANCY**.

disperse

See **DISBURSE**.

dispersal, dispersion

dispersal *noun*, is the process of distributing or spreading something over a wide area: *The dispersal of the crowd was left in the hands of the police*.

dispersion *uncountable noun*, is either the process or the result of distributing or spreading something over a wide area: *The dispersion of the crowd led to several injuries among both the rioters and the police*. In some academic subjects, such as physics, **dispersion** has a specialist meaning such as the separation of white light into colours.

> Note that *dispersal* can only be used for the process, while *dispersion* can be used to cover both the process and result of being dispersed.

dispose of, disposal

dispose of *verb*, means to throw away something that is no longer wanted: *Most urban areas have problems in finding a way to dispose of their refuse*. **Dispose of** can also mean to remove an opponent, such as in tennis or politics, or to defeat an argument: *He disposed of the minister's arguments within five minutes*. As **dispose of** can also be used as a euphemism for killing someone, it should be used with care: *The minister once boasted that he disposed of all of his opponents*.

disposal *uncountable noun*, means the act of removing something: *The disposal of nuclear waste is a severe global problem*. **Disposal** also appears in two phrases with opposite meanings: *for disposal* means that something is to be thrown away: *When used, these batteries are for disposal only. Do not recharge*. However, *at one's disposal* means that something is available for use: *Each of the officials had a chauffeured limousine at their disposal during the Olympics*.

disprove, disapprove

disprove *verb*, means to prove something to be untrue or false: *One of the conclusions of the Chiefs of Staff was soon disproved by events*.

disapprove *verb*, means to consider something or someone unsuitable, or to dislike them, often for moral reasons: *The world disapproved of the decision made by the Chiefs of Staff*. In a formal sense, it also means to fail to agree to something.

disrespectful

See **RESPECTABLE**.

dissatisfied

See **UNSATISFIED**.

dissect

See **BISECT**.

dissertation

See **THESIS**.

dissolve, melt

dissolve *verb*, means to mix a solid in a liquid so that it becomes part of the liquid: *Dissolve the stock cube in 450 ml of boiling water*. Figuratively, it means to bring an association to an end, for instance a parliament, marriage or business: *In theory, the British monarch may dissolve Parliament without taking advice*. See **SOLUBLE**.

melt *verb*, means to turn from a solid to a liquid following an increase in temperature: *In a globally warmed world the ice caps will melt and sea level will rise*. If a crowd *melts away*, this means that a group of people is gradually disappearing. See **MOLTEN**.

distil

See **BREW**.

distinct, distinctive

See **CONTRASTIVE**.

distract, detract

distract *verb*, means to divert someone's attention way from an activity: *Police said the message was a decoy to distract attention from the real danger area*.

detract *verb*, means to take away something that was wanted or make something less good: *The few reservations I have expressed about the encyclopaedia are not intended to detract from its excellence*.

distress, hardship

distress *uncountable noun*, means severe unhappiness or pain: *He suffered emotional distress after being demoted and was awarded £5,000 in compensation*.

hardship *noun*, means suffering or severe lack of comfort or something that causes this: *The austerity period after the war brought more years of appalling hardship*.

distrust, mistrust

distrust *uncountable noun & verb*. As a noun this means doubt, suspicion, or a lack of trust: *There was much distrust between the US and the Soviet Union, and every possible means was used by both to spy on the other*. As a verb, **distrust** means to doubt, or fail to trust: *G.B. Shaw distrusted British politics and politicians*.

mistrust *uncountable noun & verb*. As a noun this means suspicion or lack of confidence in someone or something: *The decision left a legacy of suspicion and mistrust to poison relations between the courts and the unions*. As a verb, **mistrust** means to be suspicious of someone or something, or lack confidence in it or them: *Full censorship makes people mistrust the press*.

diurnal, nocturnal, crepuscular

diurnal dī-úrnăl /daɪˈɜːrnəl/ *adjective*, means of or during the day. **Diurnal** is typically used in the natural sciences; however, there is some ambiguity as it can refer to 24 hours or just the daytime. A *diurnal rhythm* usually refers to 24 hours: *Disruption of the diurnal rhythm of melatonin could contribute to the disturbances of the sleep–wake cycle frequently seen in such patients*. However, a *diurnal animal* is one that is active during the daytime and rests during the night.
See **DAY, DAYTIME**.

nocturnal *adjective*, means during the night. **Nocturnal** is typically used in the natural sciences as a contrast to *diurnal* in the sense of daytime activities only. A *nocturnal animal* like the owl is one that is only active during night-time. The term *nocturnal emission* is a medical term for a wet dream.

crepuscular krĕpúskyŏŏlăr /krɪˈpʌskjʊlər/ *adjective*, is a technical, literary and poetic term. When describing an animal it means one that is mainly active during twilight, i.e. at dusk and dawn: *The deer is a typical crepuscular animal*. **Crepuscular** also means resembling or referring to twilight: *Crepuscular rays are the beams of sunlight that appear to radiate from a single point as is often seen at sunrise or sunset*.
Note that the stress is on the second syllable.

divided highway

See **AMERICAN ROAD TYPES**.

dock, berth, wharf

dock *noun*, means an artificially enclosed area of water for loading, unloading or repairing ships, as in the case of a *dry dock*. In AE, **dock** means a wharf or a ship's berth. In BE, people can fall *into* a **dock**; but in AE, they fall *off* one.

berth *noun*, means a place to sleep on a ship or train, or in a holiday home: *I'll sleep in that upper berth*. It also means a mooring for a ship: *He knew the harbour well and quickly found the only empty berth*.
See **HARBOUR (PORT), QUAY (KEY)**.

wharf *noun*, means a flat area next to which ships are berthed to have cargoes loaded or unloaded. The plural is *wharfs* or *wharves*. See **-F, -FE ENDINGS IN NOUNS (WORD FORMATION), QUAY (KEY)**.

Doctor, Dr, Dr.

Doctor *noun*, is a professional title, abbreviated **Dr** in BE and **Dr.** in AE. In Britain, medical practitioners have a degree in medicine and surgery. Specialized surgeons, including dentists, usually call themselves 'Mr', 'Ms' or 'Mrs'. In AE, physicians, surgeons, dentists and vets are called **doctor**. Those who hold doctorates in any field should be formally addressed as 'Dr', not 'Mr', 'Ms', or 'Mrs' in letters, etc. This may sometimes cause confusion with medical doctors.

doctoral degree, PhD

A doctoral dócktŏrăl /'dɒktərəl/ degree or doctorate is the highest degree awarded by a university. The most common type awarded by universities in or based on the UK/US higher education systems is the *Doctor of Philosophy* (abbreviated **PhD** in BE and **Ph.D.** in AE, read as pée aytch dée /'piː eɪtʃ 'diː/). This degree is from any faculty apart from law, medicine and sometimes theology or music. As such degrees are placed after personal names in English, a model to use in writing is: John Smith, PhD. To avoid redundancy, it is better not to use both **Dr** and **PhD** at the same time.

documercial

See ADVERTISEMENT.

dog's breakfast, dog's dinner

See BREAKFAST.

don

See LECTURER.

donate

See ENDOW.

double meaning, double entendre

double meaning *noun*, means a pun or play on words. An example was the Scottish Executive T-shirt campaign designed to encourage women to stop binge drinking. The pink T-shirts carried the logo *Mine's a Double*. The idea was to encourage people to go two days without drinking.

double entendre dooblontóndrĕ /'duːblɒn'tɒndrə/ *noun*, means a double meaning where one of the interpretations has clear sexual overtones: *The England cricket captain was once described as 'standing in the slips with his legs apart, just waiting for a tickle'*.

D

double negatives

In standard English, two negatives in a phrase cancel each other and mean something positive. Sentences like: *Nobody has no skills* are complicated and really mean *'Everybody has some kind of skill'*. The double negative is sometimes used as a rhetorical device to make a statement sound less definite, or to give a cautious confirmation: *It is not impossible to use a double negative*. Equally, in some BE and AE dialects the use of double or even multiple negatives is heard as a way of reinforcing the negative meaning, such as the informal oral expression: *I didn't do nothing*. Generally it is advisable to avoid using the double negative.

An easy trap to fall into is that of using adverbs that have a negative meaning, such as *hardly*, *scarcely* or *rarely*, in a phrase with a second negative: *He rarely said nothing at planning meetings*, which means that this person spoke a lot at meetings. The same warning applies to using a negative like 'not' together with a negative prefix. See NEGATIVE PREFIXES (WORD FORMATION).

'I could not fail to disagree with you less.'
(Politician on 'Have I Got News For You', BBC TV)

dove

See PIDGIN.

download, upload

download *verb*, means to move data from a large computer system to a smaller one: *They spend hours downloading images to their laptops*.

upload *verb*, means to move data from a small computer system to a larger one: *We will upload this on to a central server*.

Down's syndrome

See SYNDROME.

draught, draft

draught *noun*, means a current of air: *The screens were around the bed and the draught from the door set them billowing like sails.* Figuratively the phrase *to feel the draught* means to face problems: *The high street shops will feel the draught most keenly*. **Draught** is also the water depth required under a boat in order for it to float. In a pub, it may also mean the act of drinking – *He took a deep draught of beer* – or the beer served from the barrel, rather than sold in bottles: *What beers have you got on draught?*

draft *noun & verb*. As a noun, this means a preliminary or rough version of something, such as a draft of a report. In banking, it means a payment order: *Pay by bank draft.* In AE, **draft** is the spelling of words spelt *draught* in BE. In AE, another meaning is conscription, i.e. compulsory military service: *The draft has become increasingly unpopular*. Note that this always takes the definite article. As a verb, **draft** means to make a preliminary version of something: *After months of thought, he slowly drafted his letter of resignation*. It can also mean to call a group into service to carry out a specific task: *Extra firefighters were drafted into service.*

draughts, checkers

draughts *noun*, is the name used in BE for a game played on a chessboard with 12 identical pieces for each player. **Draughts** has a final 's' except in a few terms like *draughtboard*, when it is used adjectivally. **Draughts** always takes a singular verb in this sense. Each piece is called a *draught*.

checkers *noun*, in AE is the same game as draughts in BE. Note that **checkers** also takes a singular verb. Each piece is called a *checker*. See AGREEMENT BETWEEN SUBJECT AND VERB (GRAMMAR TIPS).

draughtsman, draughtswoman, draughtsperson

draughtsman *noun*, means the person who makes detailed drawings and technical plans. It also means an artist who is skilled in drawing: *From the collection as a whole there emerges above all a Modigliani who was a most able draughtsman*. In AE, this is spelt *draftsman*.

draughtswoman *noun*, is the female equivalent of a *draughtsman*. In AE, this is spelt *draftswoman*.

draughtsperson *noun*, is the non-gender-specific version of *draughtsman* and is the preferred term to use if one wishes to avoid sexist writing.
See SEXIST LANGUAGE (WRITING SKILLS).

drawing pin, thumb tack, tack

drawing pin *noun*, is a short nail with a flat head that is commonly used in school classrooms for fixing paper on the wall: *The teacher used drawing pins instead of tape for the drawings*.

thumbtack *noun*, is the AE term for *drawing pin*.

tack *verb & noun*. As a verb this means to sail a boat on a zigzag course when heading into the wind. As a noun it is a small nail with a flat head.

drawing room

See SITTING ROOM.

dress codes

Often an invitation to a social event indicates the dress code at the bottom of the invitation. Some of these are listed here:

- *white tie*: The jacket has tails, and both the jacket and trousers are black, worn with a white shirt, white bow-tie and white waistcoat. This is the most formal dress for a man.
- *morning suit*: The coat (not jacket) has swallow tails, black or grey, with a top hat, waistcoat and white tie. This is worn for formal daytime occasions such as weddings.
- *black tie*: The jacket has no tails, but is usually black or white, the shirt white and with a black bow tie and black trousers. The jacket is known in BE as a *dinner jacket*. The American term *tuxedo* is the equivalent.
- *dark suit/evening dress*: For a man, this means a matching jacket and trousers.

When a waistcoat is added, it is called a three-piece suit. It is black, dark grey or navy blue. A tie should be worn. For a woman, this means a long dress.

- *lounge suit/smart dress*: Any suit, regardless of colour, is a lounge suit. A tie should be worn. For a woman, any length of dress or skirt.
- *jacket and tie/trouser suit*: A non-matching jacket and trousers are considered less formal than a suit. A tie needs to be worn. A trouser suit/ trousers for a woman.
- *smart casual*: An open-necked shirt, i.e. with no tie, and lightweight trousers or smart jeans.

See INVITATION.

drier

See DRYER.

drift

See FLOAT.

drinkable, potable

drinkable *adjective*, refers to something that may be drunk, and may be used with positive and negative modifiers. Compare: *The wine was very drinkable, and went well with white meat*; to *The wine was scarcely drinkable. I think it came from a kit.*

potable pṓtăbĕl /'pəʊtəbl̩/ *adjective*, means water that may be drunk, as opposed to being poisonous: *The wells produced evil-looking but supposedly potable water which had a distinctly salty flavour*. Note that **potable** rhymes with 'notable'. See EATABLE.

drizzle

See RAIN.

dryer, drier

dryer *noun*, means a drying device: *A nozzle for concentrated drying is also supplied and the dryer comes with a fitted plug*.

drier *noun & comparative adjective*. As a noun, this is an alternative spelling of *dryer*. As an adjective, **drier** compares the moistness of two things: *This towel is drier than that one*.

dual, duel

dual *adjective*, refers to something that has two parts, either through the duplication of something: *dual nationality*, or by its division into two parts: *dual carriageway*. See BI-.

duel *noun*, is historically a prearranged contest with weapons to settle a dispute between two people: *The duel was to be fought at dawn*. It is used figuratively today to refer to an intellectual contest between two people or groups: *The verbal duel between the two politicians was fascinating*.

duo

See BI-.

duplex

See SEMI-DETACHED HOUSE.

Durex

See ERASER.

Dutch

See NETHERLANDS.

duvet

See QUILT.

dye, die, dice

dye *noun & verb*. As a noun, this means a substance to change the colour of cloth, etc. As a verb, this means to change the colour of something. Note that *dyed, dyes, dyeing* are pronounced the same as *died, dies, dying* which are formed from the verb *to die*.

die *verb & noun*. As a verb, it means to become dead. If a machine *dies* it stops working: *The outboard engine died on me*. As a noun, it means the form used in the shaping of metal. A **die** is also the small cube used in games such as *poker dice* (however, many people use the plural *dice* to refer to a **die**). Note that the expression *the die is cast* means a serious move has been made that is difficult to reverse.

dice *noun*, is now the usual word for the cubes used in games such as *poker dice*. **Dice** is often used for both the singular and the plural: *This dice gives a three and that one a four: the dice are clearly loaded*.

Spelling

defin**i**te	Compare this with *finite*, also ending in -ite
de**s**i**cc**ate	Note single -s-, but double -cc-
develop	Remember that there is no final -e
develo**pm**ent	Note there is no 'e' before -ment
dia**rr**h**oea**	Note -rr-, and -oea at the end
di**ph**theria	Note the -ph- before the -th-
di**ph**thong	Note the -ph- before the -th-
discrep**a**ncy	Note the -a-
di**s**i**ll**usion	Note the single -s- and double -ll-
di**ss**ect	Note the double -ss-
di**ss**olute	Note the double -ss-
di**ss**olve	Note the double -ss-
dum**bb**ell	Note the double -bb-

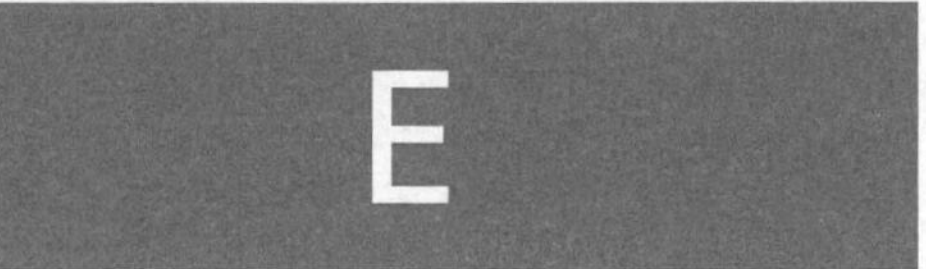

E

each, every, both

each *determiner & pronoun*, means every one of two or more people or things identified and considered separately. As a determiner, **each** is followed by a singular noun and verb: *Each member of staff has a different subject to teach*. As a pronoun, **each** is followed by *of* and a plural noun: *Each of the teachers has a different specialism*. The verb is still singular. When **each** comes after a plural noun, the verb has to be plural: *The teachers each have their own budget*.

every *determiner*, means all of three or more people or things considered together: *Every footballer was paying careful attention to the manager*. Although both *each* and **every** refer to a group of people or things, use *each* when referring to the individual members of the group, one by one: *Each footballer was given new boots*, and use **every** when considering the group as a whole: *Every footballer was given new boots*. Note that **every** takes a singular verb.

both *predeterminer, determiner, pronoun & conjunction*. As a predeterminer, determiner and pronoun, this is used to refer to two people or things taken and identified together: *Both my brothers have red hair*. As a conjunction, **both** is used to emphasize a comparison between two things.

Here the sentence structure needs to be balanced, so write either: *both in Russia and in China* (with 'in' twice) or *in both Russia and China* (with 'in' once). Avoid using **both** with words like equal and equally which already convey the idea of two parts: *He considers the FA Cup and the League to be of equal importance* (not 'both of equal importance'). As **both** always refers to two things, it always takes a plural verb. See TAUTOLOGY.

earlier

See PRECEDING.

earnings, income, revenue

earnings *plural noun*, means the money received in return for work done: *Average earnings in London are about £100 a week higher than in regions outside London*. **Earnings** also means the profit made by companies: *Fewer strikes and smaller wage increases have led to a strengthening of corporate earnings*.

income *noun*, means the money earned from investments, doing work or from business. Individuals, companies, regions and countries have an **income** which implies that a regular amount of money is being received: *This rise in income was long overdue*. The interest on bank accounts or dividends from owning shares in companies is often called *unearned income*.

revenue *noun*, means money or income received by the state, the local authorities or a large company. The tax authorities in Britain are now called *HM Revenue and Customs*. In the US they are called the *Internal Revenue Service* (*IRS*).

earth, ground, soil

earth *noun*, means a number of things. As the name of our planet it is often capitalized especially in a comparative context referring to other planets: *There is good proof that the direction of the Earth's magnetic field has flipped many times during our planet's lifetime*. **Earth** also means *soil*: *That tree needs more earth on its roots*. In electricity, *connect to earth* means inserting a wire in the electrical connection with no current.

ground *noun*, means the solid surface of the Earth. It occurs in the idiomatic phrase: *His* *feet never touched the ground*, referring to an action that happened very quickly. In AE, **ground** also means the same as BE *earth* in the electrical sense. In the plural, *grounds* may mean either a fishing area: *The disputed fishing grounds are off Iceland*; or an area of enclosed land. See **CAMPUS**.

soil *noun*, is the upper layer of earth where plants grow: *Generations have tilled the soil and it is still very fertile*. When used figuratively, **soil** means land as a whole: *He was the first American pilot to land on French soil after the war*.

Earth Science, Natural Science, Life Sciences, Physical Science

Earth Science *noun*, means a science that studies part or the whole of the earth and is made up of a number of sub-fields including geography, geology, geophysics, geochemistry, mineralogy, geomorphology, palaeontology, petrology.

Natural Science *noun*, studies the physical world, and includes physics, chemistry and biology.

Life Sciences *plural noun*, are those that study living organisms and their behaviour and include biology, biochemistry, botany, zoology, sociology, linguistics.

Physical Science *noun*, is concerned with the study of natural phenomena which are not alive, and includes subjects such as physics and chemistry. The term *Physical Sciences* covers more than one such science.

> These terms are commonly used in the plural. Some disciplines may come under more than one of these headings.

east, eastern

east *noun, adjective & adverb*, is the direction of the sunrise. When it refers to a direction, **east** is not usually capitalized: *The wind was blowing from the east*. It is capitalized when it is a regional name: *East Anglia, East End*; a defined region: *He returned East* (eastern region of the USA); part of a continent: *East Africa*; or a country name: *East Timor*. Some geographical areas containing the word **East** reflect the fact that that they are to the east of Europe. Examples: The *Near East* (rarely used nowadays, but comprising Turkey and the whole of the Arab world), *Middle East* (the Arab world including North Africa, and some non-Arab Asian countries such as Israel, Iran and Afghanistan), and *Far East* (China, Japan and South East Asia). See **CAPITAL LETTERS (WRITING SKILLS)**.

eastern *adjective*, is used for the region of a country to the *east*: *There will be rain across eastern England*. **Eastern** is capitalized when it forms part of a proper noun such as: *Central and Eastern Europe*; or when it denotes *The East* (as seen from Europe). *Eastern languages* are the languages of Asia.

eastward, eastwards, easterly, eastbound

eastward *adjective*, means moving towards the east: *The army tried to encircle the enemy by an eastward movement*.

eastwards *adverb*, means towards the east: *Russia expanded eastwards in the nineteenth century*. This is sometimes spelt and pronounced *eastward*, especially in AE.

easterly *adjective & noun*. As an adjective, this means either in a direction *towards* the east: *The annual easterly migration of birds is very late this year*; or describes a wind that is blowing *from* the east: *When they arrived in that part of the Pacific, they used the easterly winds*. Note that **easterly** is normally followed immediately by a noun. As a noun, this is a wind blowing from the east.

eastbound *adjective*, means leading or travelling in an easterly direction: *They patrolled the Central Line trains eastbound from Oxford Circus*. This word is almost always connected with transport or traffic.

easy, easily, facile

easy *adjective & adverb*, means not difficult, obtained or done without great effort. The adjective form is most common: *Easy check-in service on scheduled British Airways flights*. As an adverb, **easy** is only found in fixed idiomatic expressions like: *Easy does it*; *take it easy*; *easy come, easy go*. It cannot be replaced by *easily* here.

easily *adverb*, means without any difficulty or problems: *He easily learned how to waterski*. It cannot be replaced by *easy* here.

facile *adjective*, describes things that are produced without careful thought: *Young girls* *are frequently using facile generalizations*. In another sense it means something with little value as it is obtained too easily: *When he explained this experiment to me I almost laughed at how facile it was*. Note that **facile** is a disapproving word.

eatable, edible

eatable *adjective*, refers to something that can be eaten, although it is not of good quality: *The stew was burnt but still eatable*. The plural noun form *eatables*, which means any food, is only used informally. See UNEATABLE.

edible *adjective*, also refers to something that can be eaten: *He has written a guide to the more common edible fungi with ideas on how to cook them*. The opposite is poisonous. See INEDIBLE (UNEATABLE).

ebb, flood, flow, ebb and flow

ebb *noun & verb*. As a noun, this is the period during which the tide is going out; normally, it is used in the phrase *ebb tide*. Figuratively, **ebb** is found in the phrase *at a low ebb*, which means depressed or disillusioned: *Her spirits were at their lowest ebb*. As a verb, **ebb** means to go out or recede: *The ship was grounded as the tide began to ebb*.

flood *noun & verb*. As a noun, this refers to the incoming tide, and is the opposite of *ebb*. In another sense it means an unusually high water level caused by heavy rain or high winds, putting ground that is normally dry under water: *British holidaymakers told yesterday how they fled for their lives when a killer flood surged through their campsite*. As a verb, **flood** means to cover with water as a result of abnormal weather conditions. As both a noun and a verb, **flood** is often used to refer to something overwhelming, such as an emotion, or a very large number of something: *She felt a flood of joy sweep through her*.

flow *noun & verb*. As a noun, this is the movement of a liquid in a single direction: *The flow tells the engineer how much water has moved where over a period of time*. By analogy, it can also refer to the movement of money from one place to another, to traffic movement, or to the way a piece of music develops, or of anything else that is transferred from one place to another. As a verb, it means to move in a regular way: *The irrigation canals flow from the newly regulated river*.

ebb and flow *noun phrase*, is mainly used figuratively, to refer to something rising and falling: *The ebb and flow of his fortunes were recorded in his diary*. Literally, it refers to the rising and falling of the tide: *In the harbour you got a secondary ebb and flow between the main tides*.

e-business, e-cash

See EMAIL.

eclipse, ellipse, ellipsis

eclipse *noun*, refers to the positioning of the Sun, Moon and Earth. When the Moon is directly between the Sun and the Earth, so that the Sun is hidden for a time, this is a *solar eclipse*. When the Earth is positioned between the Sun and the Moon so that the Earth's shadow stops any of the Sun's light reflecting from the Moon, this is a *lunar eclipse*. In another sense it means the arrival of someone more famous or something more powerful that diminishes the importance of the existing person or thing: *Email has almost led to the eclipse of letter writing*.

ellipse *noun*, is a regular oval shape like a circle that has been stretched evenly on opposite sides, such as the shape of a rugby ball. The plural is *ellipses*, pronounced ĕlípsiz /ɪˈlɪpsɪz/.

ellipsis *noun*, means the omission of a few words in a sentence without changing the meaning. For instance, in a football commentary on TV, the commentator might simply mention the names of the players who have the ball, without saying that one has passed to the other: *Terry . . . Rooney . . . Owen . . . back to Rooney*, which in full would read *Terry passes to Rooney, who passes to Owen, who gives it back to Rooney*. In writing, an **ellipsis** is the three dots (. . .) that show that something has been missed out. If there is a fourth dot this is the full stop at the end of a sentence. The plural is spelt *ellipses*, and pronounced ĕlípseez /ɪˈlɪpsiːz/. See FULL STOP (PUNCTUATION GUIDE).

e-commerce

See EMAIL.

economics, economic, economical, economically, economy

economics *uncountable noun*, means the study of the production and distribution of wealth. Like other academic subjects ending in '-ics', it always takes a singular verb: *Economics is a sound choice at this university*. In other uses, **economics** can take both singular and plural verbs: *The economics of running such services have remained questionable*. See -ICS.

economic *adjective*, refers to the practical distribution of goods and services: *This software measures financial transactions between various economic sectors in a country*. It is also connected with the profitability of a business or other concern.

economical *adjective*, refers to saving money, resources and time. Compare: *Britain's economic performance* (the state of its economy) with *a vehicle's economical performance* (cost savings because of its low fuel consumption). When describing a person, it is more common to use either a positive adjective such as *thrifty* or a negative one such as *mean*. The exception to this is the idiom *economical with the truth*, which implies that a person is lying. See LIE[2].

economically *adverb*, has two meanings. The first is related to the adjective *economic*: *The development of these oil fields is not economically viable*, meaning that it is not profitable to develop them. The second is related to *economical*: *Arms races can give rise to situations that strike the economically minded as wasteful*, meaning that there are better things to spend money on.

economy *noun*, means the relationship between the supply of money and production in a particular region, state or country. The term is often used with 'the': *The economy has had the tonic its doctors ordered*. In another sense it means the avoidance of waste: *This car is for those who are looking for real economy*. In the plural it also means savings: *We shall have to make some economies next year*. See ECONOMY CLASS SYNDROME (SYNDROME)

edible

See EATABLE.

effect, affect

effect ĕfékt /ɪˈfekt/ *verb & noun*. As a verb, this means to do or achieve something: *The plane was grounded until repairs to the engine could be effected*. This is a formal word and done or carried out are alternatives. As a noun, **effect** means a result or consequence: *The loss of habitat worldwide has undoubtedly had a tragic effect on many animals*.

affect ăfékt /əˈfekt/ *verb &* áffekt /ˈæfekt/ *noun*. As a verb, **affect** means to make a difference to or influence something: *If this is the only payment we make, it will not affect your no claim bonus*. As a noun, **affect** (stressed on the first syllable) is a psychological term that means emotion which may influence behaviour.

> Since these words are frequently confused, and misused, a useful rule of thumb is to consider *effect* only as a noun: *the effects of pollution*, and *affect* only as a verb: *Pollution affects us all*.

effective, efficient

effective *adjective*, refers to something that solves a problem or creates a real result: *The measures to halt inflation proved to be effective and prices stabilized*. **Effective** can also refer to the date when a measure is to be implemented: *These measures are effective as of 1 January*. *Cost-effective* describes something that is productive in relation to its cost: *The widespread use of email has proved to be highly cost-effective in most businesses*.

efficient *adjective*, refers to people, machines, organizations or measures that produce results without wasting time or energy: *These car engines are very efficient and consume 30 per cent less petrol*. *Cost-efficient* is another term for *cost-effective*.

effeminate, effete

See WOMANLY.

efficiency apartment

See BEDSIT.

effluent, effluvium

effluent *noun*, means liquid waste, especially sewage or chemical waste: *Effluent in rural* *areas is usually discharged visibly into watercourses.*

effluvium *noun*, means an offensive or harmful smell or discharge. It is usually found in the plural form, *effluvia*: *Every factory must be kept clean and free from effluvia arising from any drain or sanitary convenience*. It is a formal word.

effrontery

See AFFRONT.

e.g., i.e., for example, for instance

e.g. is an abbreviation of *for example* formed from the Latin *exempli gratia*, which is never written out in full or pronounced; nor is it followed by a comma. Avoid home-made abbreviations such as 'f. ex'. Some style guides suggest that *for example* or *for instance* should be used in running text rather than **e.g.** which is best for footnotes, in brackets, and notes. Never use etc. at the end of a phrase beginning with **e.g.**

i.e. means that is to say, and is used to give an interpretation of something, or to repeat an idea in another way. It is an abbreviation for the Latin *id est*, which is never written out in full or pronounced; nor is it followed by a comma. Careful writers always avoid this term in running text and replace it with *that is*, which is followed by a comma: *He demonstrated the HD-ready TV, that is, one that can receive high definition signals*. A typical place where **i.e.** is used correctly is before an interpretation in notes, brackets and footnotes such as the following: *Footnote: John Smith was told that his services were no longer required, i.e. he was fired*. See NAMELY.

for example, for instance are used after exemplification. They are synonymous and normally placed after the example: *There were larger crowds in London and Paris, for example*.

> When exemplifying or illustrating an idea, use *e.g.* When interpreting something, use *i.e.*

egoist, egotist

egoist *noun*, means someone who is self-centred or selfish, often without realizing it: *She called him an egoist who thought only about the next football match he could go to.*

egotist *noun*, means an arrogant, self-centred person who has an inflated opinion of himself or herself: *He's a show-off, an exhibitionist, in fact Mr Know-it-all is a typical egotist*.

eiderdown

See QUILT.

Eire

See IRISH.

either . . . or, neither . . . nor

either . . . or and **neither . . . nor** are used to show a choice between two objects and must only refer to two things.

Either is to be followed by **or**, and **neither** by **nor**: *Either the blue or the black labels can be used; Neither the green nor the white labels are any good*.

Either . . . or, neither . . . nor should be placed together with the part of the sentence they refer to: *The English teacher from Italy is either a genius or a complete idiot*. Note the following points about subject–verb agreement with **either . . . or** and **neither . . . nor**:

- When **either . . . or**, **neither . . . nor** link two singular subjects, the verb is singular: *Either John or Mary is at the door*. When there are plural subjects, the verb is plural: *Either the boys or the girls are here*.
- When **either . . . or**, **neither . . . nor** link a singular subject and a plural subject, in formal English the verb agrees with the last subject: *Either storms or flooding is likely*; *Either flooding or storms are likely*. (In conversation, the plural verb is sometimes used in the first example, when the noun/phrase following 'or' is singular: *Either storms or flooding are likely*. However, most style guides consider this to be informal usage.)
- When **either** or **neither** is the subject of a verb, the verb is singular: *We have contacted Renault and Fiat: neither is interested*.

The words **either** and **neither** have well-established alternative pronunciations: both (n)ī́thĕr /ˈ(n)aɪðər/ and (n)éethĕr /ˈ(n)iːðər/ are generally acceptable in all forms of English.

elapse, lapse

elapse *verb*, means to pass (of time): *Ten months elapsed before he started even looking for a job*.

lapse *verb & noun*. As a verb, this means to be terminated usually because a certain period of time has passed: *The insurance premium was not paid and the policy lapsed*. When **lapse** is used about people it refers to a process that results in negative behaviour: *They lapsed into a lifestyle that destroyed their careers*. As a noun, it means a short period of time when someone fails to do something properly, often due to carelessness or a break in concentration: *A lapse in the goalkeeper's concentration cost them the match*.

elder/eldest, older/oldest

elder/eldest *adjective*, are used to compare the ages of people, especially within a family: *My elder brother is 25* or *My eldest brother is 25*. These words can also be used without a noun: *He is the elder/eldest*. See **ELDERLY (OLD)**.

older/oldest *adjective*, are also used for comparing age, but are used in a broader range of contexts: *This is the oldest church in the country*. It has now become common for **older** and **oldest** to be used instead of *elder* and *eldest*: *She is the oldest of the four sisters*.

> *Elder than* is non-standard. Use *older than*.

election, vote, ballot

election *noun*, strictly speaking means any decision made by an individual choosing between alternatives – he or she *elects* one rather than another. In general terms, an **election** now means the selection of a representative to join a governing body, whether a local council, a parliament, or the board of directors of a company: *The Conservatives will lose those seats at the next election*.

vote *noun & verb*. As a noun, this means either the occasion when a group of people are asked for their opinion in a meeting or at an election: *The matter was put to the vote*; or the total number of people or representatives that support an issue in a meeting or at an election: *The vote was split along party lines with the exception of 15 Democrats who opposed the measure*. It also means the individual choice made by someone at an election: *My vote would always be for the animal rights candidate*. As a verb, **vote** means to make a choice: *The leaders of the party voted not to join the governing coalition*.

ballot *noun*, means either the system of voting using a piece of paper with the names of the candidates on (*ballot paper*): *The election was a farce, as only 22 per cent of voters cast their ballots*; or when a vote is held: *The leader of the party will be selected by the prescribed secret ballot procedure*. In another sense it means the total number of votes in an election: *The new leader secured 70 per cent of the ballot*. See **POLL (POLE)**.

electric, electrical, electronic, electrifying

electric *adjective*, means relating to the direct production of or powered by electricity. Examples include: *electric energy*, *electric clock* and *electric iron*. **Electric** may also be used figuratively, to mean exciting: *It was the way she moved that made her presence so electric*.

electrical *adjective*, refers to things connected with electricity, such as *electrical appliance*, *electrical faults* and *electrical signals*: *This requires skills such as wiring an electrical component*. In some expressions, such as *electric/electrical shock*, either adjective may be used. Note that graduates in *electrical engineering* are called *electrical engineers* and that *electric engineers* could mean those powered by electricity.

electronic *adjective*, refers to appliances and other equipment that are based on computers and microchips. The word is often combined with its applications, such as *electronic banking*, *electronic publishing* or *electronic mail*. See **ELECTRONIC MAILING LIST (CHAT LINE)**, **EMAIL**.

electrifying *adjective*, is mainly used in its figurative sense to describe an exciting or startling performance: *He gave an electrifying speech, and was re-elected*. Literally, it is the present participle of the verb *electrify*, which means to connect an area to an electrical supply: *We will be electrifying the villages in that part of South Africa next month*. The associated noun is *electrification*.

> *'Career as electric engineer.'*
> *(Harper's Magazine)* **!**

elevator

See LIFT.

elicit

See ILLICIT.

eliminate, abolish

eliminate *verb*, means to remove something completely: *This law is designed to eliminate barriers to the free movement of goods and services.* In another sense, it means to defeat a group in a competition: *Man Utd were eliminated from the FA Cup at an early stage.* It can also mean to kill someone who is a threat to the people in power: *The President systematically eliminated the opposition.*

abolish *verb*, means to end or destroy customs, practices and institutions completely: *Slavery was abolished by law throughout the British Empire in the nineteenth century.*

elk

See MOOSE.

ellipse, ellipsis

See ECLIPSE.

El Niño, La Niña

El Niño el née̍n-yō /el ˈniːnjəʊ/ *uncountable noun*, is the pattern of changes in the weather system near the coast of Peru that causes the Pacific Ocean to become warmer. **El Niño** can severely affect global weather patterns.

La Niña laa née̍n-yă /lɑː ˈniːnjə/ *uncountable noun*, is the cooling of the water in the central and eastern Pacific Ocean that also affects global weather patterns.

eloquent

See GRANDILOQUENT.

elucidate

See EXPLAIN.

elucidation

See CLARIFICATION.

elude

See ALLUDE.

emaciated

See THIN.

email, e-business, e-cash, e-commerce, E-number, e-petition

email *noun & verb*. As a noun this refers either to a system for sending electronic messages between registered computer users, or to a message sent over such a system. Most modern BE dictionaries favour the spelling **email** replacing the hyphenated **e-mail**. A formal alternative to **email** is *electronic mail*. Another alternative to **email** is *mail*. As a verb it means to send a message to someone by **email**. In AE *mail* refers both to using **email** and to posting a letter in the postal system. See EMAILS AND LETTERS (WRITING SKILLS).

e-business *noun*, is the abbreviation for *electronic business*. It enables companies to link their internal and external data-processing systems with their partners and suppliers. **E-business** involves strategic decisions that span the entire business chain.

e-cash *noun*, is the abbreviation for *electronic cash*, and is an electronic payment system. A bank card with a chip that supports an electronic wallet is an example of such a system. This is also known as digital cash.

e-commerce *noun*, means *electronic commerce* that consists of buying, selling and marketing goods and products on the Internet.

E-number *noun*, is the code given to food additives. The letter E refers to the fact that the European Union has approved that particular additive for use in foods in the Union. By extension, it is common to use **E-number** informally to mean 'additive': *The processed food was full of E-numbers.*

e-petition *noun*, means a written document on the Internet that is endorsed by a large number of people asking for a change in policy or other action: *The government launched the e-petitions system in November 2006.*

email address, email harvesting

email address. Although the @ sign is called 'at' in English, it is interesting how some other languages have found different names for this sign. The French call it *arobas*, Spaniards *arroba* (an old measure of weight), Italians *chiocciola* (snail). The German name is *Klammeraffe* (monkey), Dutch has *apestaart* (monkey tail), Greek *papaki* (duckling) and Russians call it *sobaka* (dog). In Norwegian it is *krøllalfa* (curly alpha), in Danish *snabel* (elephant's trunk) and in Swedish *snabel-a*. Use the term 'dot' to indicate a full stop on the line in an address and 'underscore' to refer to an underlined letter or space: *andrew_smith@mail.com* is read as 'Andrew underscore space Smith at mail dot com'.

email harvesting or **email address harvesting** means collecting lists of email addresses so that these people can be contacted electronically for some purpose. Methods range from purchasing lists of addresses to using special software: *The party had been email harvesting for years so that they could contact the electorate just before the local election.* See SPAM, WEB SPIDER.

emails and letters

See WRITING SKILLS.

embarrass, harass

embarrass, *verb*, means to make someone feel awkward or ashamed in public: *She had not the heart to embarrass him by refusing a request so diffidently expressed.* See ASHAMED.

harass, *verb*, means to put pressure on someone in order to make them annoyed or worried: *It was not long before the authorities began to harass the unions.*

> Note the difference in spelling between these two words: -rr- in *embarrass*, and -r- in *harass*. *Harass* may be stressed on either syllable, although many speakers prefer first syllable stress: hárrăss /ˈhærəs/ to second (hăráss /həˈræs/).

embassy, consulate, legation

embassy *noun*, is the building that houses the main diplomatic representation of a foreign country, usually in the capital city of a country: *He travelled from the Syrian Embassy back to his rented home in Kingston upon Thames.* **Embassy** also means the personnel who are sent to a foreign country to represent their government: *The King of England sent a small embassy north to Scotland.* See AMBASSADOR.

consulate *noun*, is the office of an embassy that looks after the interests of its country's nationals living in that country: *As we were living far from the capital, we registered our daughter's birth at the British consulate.*

legation *noun*, is the building that houses a diplomatic mission that does not have the status of an embassy, and also the body of personnel that occupies it: *The roofs of every embassy and legation in Rabat are draped with aerials and satellite dishes.* See LEGATE (AMBASSADOR).

embed, imbed

embed *verb*, means to fix something firmly inside another object, such as a nail in a piece of wood: *Before it solidifies embed a few matches into the mixture.* By extension, it also refers to the position of a journalist in a war zone who is attached to a particular fighting unit, giving him or her special access to information and locations with that unit: *Several embedded reporters have been injured in the area.*

imbed is a rare alternative spelling for *embed*.

embodiment

See EPITOME.

embrace

See ENFOLD.

emend

See AMEND.

emigrant, émigré, immigrant, migrant

emigrant *noun & adjective*, refers to movement from a country (think of the 'e' for exit): *The* Titanic *carried many emigrants who departed from Liverpool.* A related noun is *emigration*, and the verb is *emigrate*.

émigré *noun*, means a person who moves from one country to another, usually for political reasons: *Many German-Jewish émigrés became prominent in British academic life.*

immigrant *noun & adjective*, refers to movement into a country (think of the 'i' for into): *Most early twentieth-century American immigrants from Europe were processed at Ellis Island.* A related noun is *immigration*, and the verb is *immigrate*. Note that depending on which side of the Atlantic you are standing, the same person is both an emigrant and an immigrant. Americans will tend to view all migrants as immigrants, whereas Europeans will think of them as emigrants, and this can lead to some odd use of the terms: *My ancestors immigrated from Liverpool in the nineteenth century.* This has to have been written from the arrival point of the ancestors, but the phrase 'from Liverpool' would make *emigrated* a better word in this sentence.

migrant *noun & adjective*, refers to the process whereby people move between countries: *The Turkish migrant workers in Germany have made an important contribution to the economy.* It is also used to describe birds that migrate: *summer migrants* in Britain include swallows and swifts (in South Africa these are *winter migrants*). A related noun is *migration*.

> Note that *emigrants* and *immigrants* move to a new country to settle permanently, but *migrants*, such as workers, stay temporarily to work in another country. Many birds and some other animals tend to *migrate* seasonally.

eminent, imminent

eminent *adjective*, means famous in a positive way, distinguished: *The building was designed by C.J. Phipps, an eminent Victorian architect.*

imminent *adjective*, means on the point of happening: *The recession is over and the start of a recovery is imminent.*

> *'We are pleased to have such an imminent scholar deliver the guest lecture.'* !
> (US university website)

E

eminently, imminently

eminently *adverb*, means clearly, extremely: *This was an eminently reasonable arrangement and nobody could possibly object.*

imminently *adverb*, means in the very near future: *The meetings had been very positive, and minutes were expected imminently.*

emissary

See ENVOY.

emotional, emotive

emotional *adjective*, means either connected with somebody's feelings or connected with strong emotions such as an *emotional outburst*. In this second sense this is disapproving: *She did not need to exhibit such an emotional reaction in the middle of Sainsbury's.*

emotive *adjective*, means causing somebody to feel strong emotions: *Our engagement in that war is a highly emotive issue.*

empathy

See SYMPATHY.

employ, take on

employ *verb*, means either to give someone a job that they will be paid for: *The master craftsman would employ helpers to assist him in the completion of the contract*; or to have someone working for a company for a time: *We employ a freelance team to look after us there.* It can also mean to make use of: *What criteria did the purchasers employ in buying pottery?*

take on *verb*, means to give someone a job: *We have just taken on two temporary members of staff in the computer section.* **Take on** is more informal than *employ*. In AE, this would be *hire*. See HIRE.

empower

See APPROVE.

empty, hollow

empty *adjective & verb*. As an adjective this refers to a building or container that has nothing inside it. In another sense it can mean without meaning: *Life was empty without him*. As a verb it means removing everything from a container, and can refer to things or people: *His first action was to empty his bottle of Southern Comfort*. The object of the verb is always the thing being emptied.

hollow *adjective, noun & verb*. As an adjective this refers to an object that has a large space on its inside. It can also mean insincere: *This was another hollow promise*. As a noun, it means an area whose surface is lower than its surroundings: *Though the house was in a hollow it had a good view of the sea*. As a verb it means to give a flat surface an inward curve: *The waves and currents had hollowed out small pools in the chalk*.

emulate, imitate

emulate *verb*, means to behave like someone else, usually out of admiration: *Watch a film of him and do all you can to emulate his behaviour*. In another sense, a machine can try to **emulate** human behaviour: *The recognition system tries to emulate a 'normal' writing situation such as pen on paper*.

imitate *verb*, means to behave in a similar way to someone – or something – else, often for a humorous effect: *He would often imitate C3PO from 'Star Wars', walking jerkily around the room*.

en, en-[1] (French loan words)

en. There are a number of phrases in English, borrowed in meaning and spelling from French, that start with the word **en**. In all cases, this is pronounced **on** /ɒn/. People who have learned French at school may pronounce it in the French fashion, **aa(ng)** /ɑ̃/.

en bloc	*as a large group*
en croûte	*in a pastry crust (cooking term)*
en masse	*as a whole, all together, in a large number*
en passant	*by the way, incidentally*
en route	*on the way*
en suite	*(of a bathroom) with access direct from a bedroom*

en-. A number of words borrowed from French and beginning with the letters **en-** are pronounced **on-** /ɒn-/. Examples include: *encore, ensemble, entente, entourage, entr'acte, entrecôte, entrée, entrepôt, entrepreneur, envelope* – this last is more usually pronounced as written: **énvĕlōp** /ˈenvələʊp/.

en-[2], em- (verb prefixes)

en- *verb prefix*, means to put into something (e.g. *encase*: put in a case; *endanger*: put into danger), or to make (e.g. *enlarge*: make large).

em- *verb prefix*, is the form of the same prefix used before words beginning with 'b' or 'p', such as *embody* (represent or include), *empower* (put into or give, power).

enclosed please find

See PLEASE FIND ENCLOSED.

endeavour, strive, try

endeavour *noun & verb*. As a noun, this means an attempt to do something difficult: *It is a sincere and honest endeavour to try to inform the government of exactly what is happening*. As a verb, it means to try very hard: *We will endeavour to give you the best possible service*. The AE spelling is *endeavor*.

strive *verb*, also means to try very hard, with the added meaning of struggle: *If he was ever to be an artist, he should strive for more balance*.

try *verb*, means to make an attempt to do something: *Try to break the habit of adding salt at the table, if necessary using a low sodium salt substitute*.

endemic, epidemic, pandemic

endemic *adjective*, refers to anything that is found in one geographical area, or among one group of people, and is often applied to diseases: *Malaria was endemic in these tropical marshes*.

epidemic *noun*, means a widespread short-lived outbreak of a disease: *Many towns in Britain suffered typhoid epidemics during the nineteenth century*.

pandemic *noun*, means an epidemic that covers a whole country or the whole world: *The pandemic of AIDS can alter the course of many societies' social and economic developments*.

endive

See **CHICORY**.

endorse, endorsement

endorse *verb*, means to confirm or approve something: *We have a host of very satisfied customers who would gladly endorse this*. It can also mean to give public support: *That was the virtue of my Right Hon. Friend's remark, which I wholeheartedly endorse*. Originally and literally, **endorse** meant to write on the back of something in order to acknowledge its validity or a change in its status. Nowadays a document may be endorsed on the front as well: *The clerk of the licensing board shall, on payment of the appropriate fee, endorse on the licence a note of the transfer*.

endorsement *noun*, is the act of giving public support to someone or something: *A group of farmers has applied for approval to use the British Standard kite mark as an endorsement of the quality of their beef*. In BE, this term also refers to driving offences, which are recorded on someone's driving licence: *The duplicate will be a copy of the original licence, including any endorsement, and will be valid for the same period*.

endow, donate

endow *verb*, means to give a large sum of money to an organization, such as a school or charity, in order to provide it with an income over a long period: *It is hoped that a private benefactor will be able to endow the chair for a full-time professor*. Figuratively, as a passive verb, *endowed* can also mean having a particular gift or talent: *The bishop was endowed with a powerful voice*.

donate *verb*, means to give money, food or clothes to a good cause, such as a charity. In another sense it means to give blood or a body organ for medical reasons: *Parents are invited to donate blood*.

enemy, enmity

enemy *noun*, means a person or group of people who intensely dislike another, or act or speak against someone: *The enemy attacked us during the night*.

enmity *noun*, means a feeling of hatred towards someone or something: *This was not the first time I had noticed the old enmity towards modern art and architecture*.

enervate, energize

enervate *verb*, means to feel or become weak: *The trip across the Sahara enervated us to the point of collapse*.

energize *verb*, means to give energy to, or to make strong: *After three days in the oasis we were rested and energized and managed the rest of the trip without difficulty*.

enfold, embrace

enfold *verb*, means to surround or cover something completely, or to put one's arms around someone: *His arms reached to enfold her, drawing her against his chest*.

embrace *verb*, means to put one's arms around someone, and by extension, figuratively, to accept a set of beliefs or opinions, or to contain a number of things: *He accepts the need for Labour to embrace the advantages of individualism and market forces*.

engineer, contrive (verbs)

engineer *verb*, means to build or design an object: *It was engineered like no other car in the world*. In another sense it means arranging for an event to take place. This is often considered a negative action as it is done in secret and is advantageous for one party: *On their way to trial in Liverpool, the crowd engineered a riot to secure the escape of the prisoners*.

contrive *verb*, means to find a clever plan that will cause something to happen. This is often used negatively as someone is made to do something he or she did not want to do: *She needed the exercise and whenever my mother had to go shopping I'd contrive to make her walk via the park*. In another sense, **contrive** means to succeed despite difficulties: *Now that they were working different hours it was not so easy for him to contrive to meet her 'accidentally on purpose'*.

England

See **BRITAIN**.

English

See **BRITISH**.

enmity

See **ENEMY**.

enormity, magnitude

enormity *noun*, means the extreme seriousness or cruelty of what someone has done: *The judge told him: 'There must be a severe penalty to punish you for the enormity of your crimes.'* Careful writers should avoid using **enormity** in a quantitative sense to mean great size.

magnitude *noun*, means great size or extent: *The sheer magnitude of public investment should require careful monitoring.* The brightness of stars is measured in magnitudes, with the brightest having the lowest number: *Gamma Cassiopeiæ is usually about magnitude 2.2, but has flared up to 1.6.*

enough, adequate, sufficient

enough *determiner, adverb & pronoun*, means as much or as many as required. As a determiner, **enough** is used before the noun: *Your grandmother had enough money to buy a home.* Note that it sounds dated to place **enough** after the noun: *She had money enough to buy a home.* As an adverb, **enough** follows the adjective it modifies: *The payments were small enough for most pensioners.* In the idiomatic expression *enough is enough*, and in the sentence *there was always enough to eat*, **enough** is used as a pronoun.

adequate *adjective*, usually means satisfactory in quantity or quality: *Everyone has heard about the importance of adequate protein in the diet* (quantity); *We can have an adequate, even advantageous, diet without recourse to flesh* (quality). Like satisfactory, **adequate** can mean only just good enough: *With the original engine, the replacement power plant was no more than adequate.*

sufficient *adjective*, means as much as is needed for a specific purpose: *The fuel would have been sufficient to keep the boat going for only a couple of hours.*

enquire/enquiry, inquire/inquiry

enquire *verb*, means to ask for information: *I must go and enquire if the children had an enjoyable time.* The related noun is **enquiry**. These are the usual spellings in BE.

inquire *verb*, is the usual AE spelling of **enquire**. The related noun **inquiry** is usually pronounced ínkwirri /ˈɪŋkwɪri/ in AE.

> Note that in BE, the spelling *inquiry* is normally used for a formal investigation: *A plan to divert a public footpath over farmland will go to a public inquiry.*

ensure

See **ASSURE**.

-ent

See **-ANT**.

enter

See **KEY IN**.

enterprise

See **BUSINESS**.

enthral

See **ENTRANCE**.

entity, entirety

entity *noun*, is an object with a separate existence or identity: *The future of Britain as an entity could be decided by this election.*

entirety *noun*, is the whole of something. It is often used in the phrase *in its entirety*: *When love is found in its entirety, it represents total bliss.*

entomology, etymology

entomology, *noun*, is the scientific study of the insect world.

etymology, *noun*, is the scientific study of the history and meaning of words, or the description of the history of a particular word.

entrance, enthral, bewitch

entrance *verb*, pronounced ĕntraánss /ɪnˈtrɑːns/, means to fill someone with great pleasure, wonder and delight: *A long-tailed skua glided serenely overhead and I was entranced by its beauty.* Note that the verb is stressed on the second syllable and the noun that means the way into something is stressed on the first syllable, **entrance** éntrănss /ˈentrəns/.

enthral *verb*, means to interest or excite someone so much that they give it their complete attention: *Good theatre can enthral in a way cinema and television rarely does.* This is the BE spelling. The AE spelling is *enthrall*. The past tense and present participle are *enthralled, enthralling* in both BE and AE.

bewitch *verb*, means to put someone under a magic spell, or to bring someone under so much control that he or she can no longer think sensibly: *They were all bewitched by her charm.*

E-number

See EMAIL.

enumerate

See INNUMERATE.

envelop, envelope

envelop ĕnvéllŏp /ɪnˈveləp/ *verb*, means to cover completely: *The shroud of secrecy that envelops matters of state is never lifted more than fractionally.* Note that the stress is on the second syllable, and that there is no final 'e' in the spelling.

envelope énvĕlōp /ˈenvələʊp/ *noun*, is a protective cover for a letter: *A rather special envelope arrived, bearing an engraved card inviting me to be a guest of honour.* The container for gas in a balloon is also called an **envelope**: *The gas was collected through tubes and piped into the envelope of the balloon.* To *push the envelope* means to explore the limit of some activity.

envious, enviable

envious *adjective*, refers to the feeling of wanting something belonging to or enjoyed by another person: *Friends have been teasing her about how much she will earn and are envious that she will be off school for four or five weeks.* The related noun and verb is *envy*.

enviable *adjective*, means being in a position worthy of envy: *He has earned an enviable reputation as one of the best defenders in the modern game.*

environment, milieu, surroundings, setting, background

environment *noun*, means the physical and natural world: *There is no totally 'green' energy source and if we want to help the environment we must be careful with what we use*; as well as social conditions: *Our work environment is conducive to the achievement of excellence.*

milieu *noun*, means the social environment or the people that influence the way one lives and thinks: *I was a complete outsider, out of my milieu, and had none of the social graces.* The plural of **milieu** is either *milieus* or *milieux*.

surroundings *noun*, means the land or conditions around a person or animal: *She will have to move house thereby losing her home, friends and familiar surroundings.*

setting *noun*, means physical surroundings, and is often used in descriptions of holiday resorts: *The hotel had a magnificent setting on a fine white sandy beach.* In another context, **setting** means the scenery, date or location used in literature and films: *The Victorian setting was captured at Ealing studios.*

background *noun*, means the social context and education that shape a person, place or situation: *His academic background in mechanical and electrical engineering gives him a sound grasp of a broad range of scientific disciplines.* In another sense it means something beyond the main focus: *He was the power behind the Prime Minister but always remained a figure in the background.*

envisage, envision

envisage *verb*, means to form a mental picture of a future state of affairs: *He could envisage the beautiful children that her looks would produce.* This word is commonly used in BE.

envision *verb*, means the same as *envisage*, but is mostly used in AE: *Corporate entrepreneurs are people who envision something new and make it work.*

envoy, emissary

envoy *noun*, is a person sent by a government or business organization to give an official message or to negotiate with his or her opposite numbers: *He announced the appointment of a special Middle East envoy.*

emissary *noun*, means a person sent by a government or business organization to deliver an official message or carry out a special task: *His Scottish background, Calvinist convictions and diplomatic skills made him an ideal emissary.*
See AMBASSADOR.

eon

See ERA.

e-petition

See EMAIL.

epidemic

See ENDEMIC.

episode, event, happening, incident, occurrence

episode *noun*, means something that happened or a period of time in a person's life that was memorable for good or bad reasons: *There was no doubt I had emerged from that episode looking like a complete idiot.* It can also mean a single instalment of a TV series: *I was researching a new episode of EastEnders.*

event *noun*, indicates an occasion of significance: *For this unprecedented event some 300,000 people turned out.* This is usually the strongest of the words in this group.

happening *noun*, means a strange event: *She was behaving like she had after the strange happenings on Monument Hill.* In this sense, it is often used in the plural. A **happening** can also be an artistic event, especially one that is unplanned or spontaneous: *An Austrian artist staged a happening involving beef carcasses.*

incident *noun*, means something that happens that is of minor importance: *He sat in the corner, recalling incidents from his childhood in amazing detail.* Any occurrence of a crime is referred to by the police as an **incident**: *Police said they were investigating the incident as a petrol bombing.* In diplomatic terms, an **incident** can be a serious conflict or disagreement that is often violent: *The French ambassador in London risked provoking a diplomatic incident by pushing forward to assert precedence over his Russian colleague.*

occurrence *noun*, means an event, but does not indicate any quality or type of event: *If you can hear next door's music I can assure you it's not a regular occurrence.* This is the most neutral of these words. Note the spelling, which has double -cc- and double -rr-.

epitaph, epithet

epitaph *noun*, is a reminder of a past event, or person, or a short tribute to a dead person, often inscribed on the tombstone or memorial stone: *A sad little grave stood by the side of the church, with some lines by Yeats himself as an epitaph.*

epithet *noun*, is a short phrase, or even just an adjective, that sums up a person's character, for good or evil: *To get your name in here, you need to be master of the easy epithet, king of the cutting adjective.* In AE, this means an offensive phrase that appears in slogans or graffiti: *Racial epithets were to be seen all over the city.*

epitome, embodiment

epitome ĕpíttŏmi /ɪˈpɪtəmi/ *noun*, means the perfect example of something: *James Bond is the epitome of adventure and excitement for many people.*

embodiment *noun*, means a typical example of a quality, idea or characteristic: *The experiment was regarded as the embodiment of that method.*

epoch

See ERA.

equal, more equal

equal *adjective*, means of the same quantity, size or degree: *Attendance is generally around 30, with equal numbers from each group.*
As two things that are **equal** have the same value, the phrase *very equal* is best avoided because there are no degrees in equality. However, things can be *almost equal* or *exactly equal* or even *less than equal*.
See ABSOLUTE ADJECTIVES (GRAMMAR TIPS).

more equal *comparative adjective*, is best avoided in formal writing because there are no degrees in equality. However, the famous quotation from George Orwell: *Some animals are more equal than others* ('Animal Farm', 1945), is a deliberate and ironical use of the phrase.

equations

See STYLE GUIDELINES (WRITING SKILLS).

equinox, solstice

equinox *noun*, is the situation, which occurs twice a year, when day and night are exactly the same length – 12 hours. This usually happens on 21 March and 21 September, although it may be a day earlier or later. At the equator, the sun is vertically overhead at midday on the **equinox**. The related adjective is *equinoctial*. Note that this ends in -ial.

solstice *noun*, is the situation, which occurs twice a year, when the day and night reach their extreme lengths – the longest day and shortest night at the *summer solstice*, and the shortest day and longest night at the *winter solstice*. This happens on or about 21 June and 21 December. In the northern hemisphere, the *summer solstice* is in June, while this is the *winter solstice* in the southern hemisphere. The related adjective is *solstitial*. Note that this ends in -tial.

equitable, fair, just

equitable *adjective*, means reasonable and even-handed, but is used in fairly formal contexts: *The document says that the company intends to formulate a proposal aimed at ensuring equitable treatment between the bondholders and the banks*.

fair *adjective*, refers to equality of treatment: *The function of the judge is to ensure that the accused has a fair trial according to law*. **Fair** also means considerable, when referring to an amount: *At the level of decision-making, it is clear that there is a fair amount of inconsistency*. In the assessment of an examination or piece of work, **fair** means satisfactory, but not especially good. See UNFAIR.

just *adjective*, means reasonable and in accordance with justice: *What was 'just' for the wealthy powerful minority was often unjust for the majority of the nation*. See UNJUST (UNFAIR).

-er, -or, -ee nouns

See WORD FORMATION.

era, epoch, aeon, age

era *noun*, means a period of history that has different characteristics from other periods: *The Victorian era was a period when the sun never set on the British Empire*.

epoch *noun*, means a period of time in history when important events or changes occur: *Marx refers to the dominant ideas of each epoch as 'ruling class ideology'*.

aeon *noun*, means an extremely long period of time. In geology, *aeons* are the major divisions of time. They are divided into *eras* which are divided into periods which are in turn divided into *epochs*: *The Phanerozoic aeon is divided into the Palaeozoic, Mesozoic and Cenozoic eras*. An alternative spelling is *eon*.

age *noun & verb*. As a noun, this means the length of time something has been alive: *She could have been any age between 25 and 40*. It can also mean an indefinitely long time: *The defeated team drifts around deflated for what seems an age*. When capitalized, it can refer to a particular period in history: *The Elizabethan Age will be remembered for its poets and playwrights*. An unspecified period is not capitalized: *It was an age when civilization was becoming more vigorous*. As a verb, **age** means to grow older: *As the owners age, they face considerable mobility problems*. The present participle is spelt *aging* in AE and BE, and may also be spelt *ageing* in BE.

erase, eradicate, delete

erase *verb*, means to remove something completely: *For those who could not laugh, the best remedy might be to try to erase the whole subject from their minds*.

eradicate *verb*, means to destroy something completely: *Efforts to eradicate coca crops in Peru had violated civil rights*.

delete *verb*, means to remove something from a written or printed text, or from a computer file: *It may be a clause that a particular tenant may prefer to delete unless other factors necessitate its inclusion*.

eraser, rubber, Durex

eraser *noun*, means a tool for rubbing out pencil marks, usually made of rubber.

rubber *noun*, means an *eraser* in BE, but in AE means a condom. As an uncountable noun, **rubber** is a liquid extracted from trees that, after it has been processed and made solid, can be stretched or bent, and is used to make balls, boots and vehicle tyres.

Durex *noun*, is a well-known trademark for a type of contraceptive in Britain. In Australia, this is the trademark for a make of sticky tape. Similar tapes are known as Sellotape in Britain and Scotch tape in the US. See CONTRACEPTIVE.

> *A British teacher in California told her class before a maths exam: 'Do not forget your rubbers: anyone can make a mistake.'* !

errant, arrant

errant *adjective*, refers either to doing something wrong or unacceptable conduct (often of a sexual nature): *He had pursued the errant couple from 'The Times' party to Brighton's only Portuguese restaurant*. **Errant** in the original sense of travelling occurs in the noun *knight errant*, a knight who travelled to look for adventure in the Middle Ages.

arrant *adjective*, refers to how misguided someone or something is: *I kicked myself all the way back to the hotel for being an arrant coward*. This term is dated and complete, outright, utter are alternatives.

> Except in the set phrase *knight errant*, these two adjectives usually come before a noun.

error

See FAULT.

-ery

See -ARY.

-es, -s plurals after nouns ending in o

See WORD FORMATION.

eschatological, scatological

eschatological ěskattŏlójjikăl /ɪskætə'lɒdʒɪkl̩/ *adjective*, refers to the part of the study of religion that deals with death and judgment: *The New Testament message was consistently eschatological, having to do with the end of the present order of things*.

scatological skattŏlójjikăl /skætə'lɒdʒɪkl̩/ *adjective*, refers to the waste products of the human body in an unpleasant way: *Many medieval nicknames were of a crude, coarse, scatological kind and have now disappeared*. This is a formal term.

Eskimo

See INUIT.

especial, special, particular

especial *adjective*, means exceptional and to an unusual degree: *All three at Dad's especial wish had spent many hours learning the piano*. This is a formal word, and it can usually be replaced by the more informal *special*: *. . . at Dad's special wish . . .*

special *adjective & noun*. As an adjective, this means specific, made for a specific purpose or a designated reason: *Go to your nearest town occasionally for a special event – a concert, a festival, or a flower show*. As a noun, it means an event or product that is designed or done for a particular occasion: *the election night special on television*. For food, a **special** is usually a lower-priced dish that is not on the regular menu. See SPECIALITY.

> *'Today's special – NO SPECIAL (except the chocolate fondue)'.*
> (Menu – a Marriott hotel, Japan)

particular *adjective*, means individual: *There are colleges but no particular building in*

Cambridge which is the university. It also means specified: *Programmes are booked in advance for a particular room at a particular time*; special: *Begonias are particular favourites of mine*; or extremely exact: *David was very particular in how he arranged his bookshelves*.

especially, specially, particularly

especially *adverb*, means for one reason above all: *I liked him instantly, especially as he was a fitness fanatic*.

specially *adverb*, means for a particular purpose or person: *Try using one of the CDs specially designed to help overcome insomnia*. It also means more than usual: *I hate sports, specially football*. This is informal usage.

particularly *adverb*. The adverb form means especially: *Fresh, live yogurt, without additives, can help all skin types, particularly excessively dry or oily skin*. Note that **particularly** is always preceded by a comma when it is used to introduce parenthetic information, as in the example above. **Particularly** also means specifically: *The blood of animals was sacred, and seen as belonging particularly to the deity*. Remember that **particularly** has two l's, and that both should be pronounced.

essential, vital, imperative

essential *adjective*, means completely necessary, and refers to aspects of anything which cannot be avoided or left out: *An essential precondition for this shift of emphasis lay in peace with France*. However, the noun *essential oil* refers to oils taken from aromatic plants and used in perfumes, shampoos, and in aromatherapy. This does not mean necessary, but made from essences: *The essential oil in citrus fruit is found in the outer rind*.

vital *adjective*, means essential for success: *Photographers were vital to the development and promotion of surfing*. In another sense, **vital** means completely necessary, with an almost life and death urgency implied: *Innovation is seen as vital for the survival of the organization*. When **vital** is applied to a person, it means dynamic and full of energy.

imperative *adjective*, means urgently necessary: *An election miscount necessitates a recount, and it is imperative that the numbers are accurate*.

estate agent, realtor

estate agent *noun*, is the usual BE term for someone who arranges the sale and purchase, or lease of houses and other buildings or land: *The estate agent had found a buyer who was eager to move in as soon as possible*.

realtor *noun*, is an AE term for an *estate agent*, originally a trade name but now in more general use.

estate car, station wagon

estate car *noun*, is the term used in BE for a vehicle that has a rear-opening full-height door and a large area behind the seats for carrying luggage. This is also known as an *estate*. See **SALOON CAR**.

station wagon *noun*, is the AE term for the BE *estate car*.

estate tax

See **INHERITANCE TAX**.

esthete

See **AESTHETE**.

esthetic

See **AESTHETIC**.

estimate, ballpark figure

estimate éstimăt /'estɪmət/ *noun* & éstimayt /'estɪmeɪt/ *verb*. As a noun this means an approximate calculation: *A preliminary estimate suggests a likely ceiling of between 120 and 130 machines*. Note that the final syllable contains a neutral vowel /ə/.
As a verb, **estimate** means to make an approximate calculation of the number, quantity or price of something: *I would estimate that my enjoyment of a play is spoilt on about 25 per cent of occasions*. Note that the final syllable is pronounced 'mate'.

ballpark figure *noun*, is also an *estimate* but this is an informal AE expression that suggests arriving at an estimate, often a price range, that is within certain limits, as exemplified by the boundary of a sports field (*ballpark*): *While there is no official price,*

$400,000 is a ballpark figure that has been bandied about. See **PARAMETER**.

et al., co-worker, colleague

et al. is a Latin abbreviation generally used when referring to three co-authors or more of a text in academic work. Remember always to use plural verbs and pronouns when **et al.** is part of the subject of a sentence: *Jones et al. were challenged and later published a second paper*. Note that **et** is never followed by a stop, as it means 'and'. **Et al.** is an abbreviation of *et alii* (or possibly *et aliae*, if all the authors are female) although the full forms are never used. **Et al.** should be used in the text but not in a reference list as some of the authors will not be cited.

co-worker *noun*, means a person who works with others doing the same kind of work: *The team of co-workers analysed DNA from 14 normal people who did not have cancer*. It is advisable to use a hyphen after 'co' to avoid any confusion with 'cow'.

colleague *noun*, means a person who works with others not necessarily doing the same type of work, especially in a profession, university or business: *He was more than a colleague; he was also a wonderful friend*.

etc., et cetera

etc. is the abbreviation for **et cetera**, and is hardly ever used in its full form. Some tips about how to use **etc.**:

- In formal writing, it is recommended to use **etc.** only in footnotes, brackets, and references.
- *And so on* or *and so forth* are recommended alternatives for **etc.** in reports and other types of formal writing.
- Never pronounce **etc.** as eck-séttĕră /ek'setərə/.
- Use **etc.** for things, not people: *Popular models are Ford, Opel, Toyota, etc.*, but not: *Her boyfriends were Tom, Dick, Harry, etc.*
- As a list ending in **etc.** is not exhaustive, there is no need to write 'and' before the final item (. . . *Opel, Toyota, etc.*, not . . . *Opel and Toyota, etc.*)
- Avoid writing 'and etc.', since 'et' means 'and'.
- The abbreviation **etc.**, is found in most dictionaries. An alternative is the ampersand and 'c': **&c**.
- Never place **etc.** at the end of a list beginning with *e.g.*, *include, including, such as* or *for example*, or other words that already convey the idea of representative examples.

et cetera is occasionally written out in full instead of **etc.** particularly when quoting spoken English. Using the word in this way shows that a list is too uninteresting or extensive to complete: *We've all got to do our duty, pull our weight, et cetera, et cetera*. As a noun, an **et cetera** means something in addition.

ethic, ethics

ethic *noun*, means a system of beliefs: *His parents were keen on the work ethic and equipped him with impeccable manners*.

ethics *uncountable noun*, means the study of morals as a branch of philosophy: *Business ethics is becoming a popular subject in many business schools*. Like other academic subjects ending in '-ics', **ethics** always takes a singular verb.

etymology

See **ENTOMOLOGY**.

euphemism, euphoria

euphemism *noun*, means two things. First, a way of expressing something in a roundabout way in order not to offend the listener or reader: *It has long been argued by feminist critics that 'community care' is merely a euphemism for care by the family – which in turn means care by women*. Second, a way of disguising an unpleasant fact: Pass away, expire, give up the ghost, depart this life, meet one's Maker are just some of the many euphemisms for 'die'.

euphoria *uncountable noun*, means a strong feeling of short-lived excitement and well-being: *The crowd was high on euphoria and drunk with patriotism*.

euphony, cacophony

euphony yo͞ofŏni /'juːfəni/ *noun*, means a sound or word that is pleasant to listen to: *He fell asleep again to the euphony of the dawn chorus*. The related adjective is *euphonious*.

cacophony kăkóffŏni /kəˈkɒfəni/ *noun*, means a mixture of loud and unpleasant sounds: *The children hated the cacophony of the ships' sirens*. The related adjective is *cacophonous*.

Note the difference in spelling of the adjective form endings.

euro, *Euro-*, EUR

euro *noun*, is the single European currency and the EU's official currency, which replaced the national currencies in most EU member states on 1 January 2002. The indefinite article which is used with **euro** is 'a', not 'an'. Officially, this is both the singular and plural form of the currency in English: *1 euro, 10 euro*. The *cent*, formally known as the *eurocent*, is also invariable, so *1 cent* and *10 cent*. Note that **euro** is not capitalized. The *Eurozone* (usually capitalized) means the member states in the European Union that have the **euro** as their currency unit.

Euro- *combining form for nouns & adjectives*, means connected with Europe or the European Union: *He said Euro-policies should now be aimed at creating economic growth and more jobs*. Both *Euro-MP* and *Euro-election* are usually hyphenated. The term *Eurocrat* – a senior official in the European bureaucracy – is often used with disapproval.

EUR is the ISO 4217 code for the euro. When applying for European Commission funding, all budgets must be calculated in EUR.

European plan

See AMERICAN PLAN (PENSION).

evacuate, abandon

evacuate *verb*, means to remove. When it refers to people it can be used in two ways. The object may be the people being moved: *A van, loaded with explosives, blew up outside the bank as police were trying to evacuate hundreds of shoppers*; second, it may be the area or the thing being emptied of people: *The instruction to evacuate the buildings came as a complete surprise*. In technical use, **evacuate** means removing the contents of something: *We evacuated the air from the chamber*.

abandon *verb*, means to give up completely, or to desert: *The islanders have decided to abandon their homes because a volcano is becoming active*. See RELINQUISH (YIELD).

evade

See AVOID.

evasion

See AVOIDANCE.

event

See EPISODE.

even though

See ALTHOUGH.

eventually, eventual, eventuality

eventually *adverb*, means at the end of a period of time, often after a considerable delay or a series of problems: *We engaged a third mechanic, but he turned out to be a troublemaker and we eventually got rid of him*. See PRESENTLY (NOW).

eventual *adjective*, means happening at the end of a process or period of time: *The local council had bought the field for eventual use as a road but had no immediate use for it*.

eventuality *noun*, means something, usually unfortunate, that may happen: *It may be prudent to prepare for the worst eventuality by drawing up contingency plans*. This is a formal term.

every

See EACH.

everyday, *every day*, daily

everyday *adjective*, means commonplace or ordinary: *The smallest denomination coins to be produced in any quantity were too valuable for the everyday needs of retail trade*. There is no stress on 'day'.

every day *adverb*, means each day considered separately: *I drive past there every day on my way to work*. Note that this is written as two words and that both are stressed.

daily *adjective & adverb*, means done or produced every day: *When I mentioned that I bathed daily, she sniffed, making me feel there was something indecent in such luxury*; or on every weekday (i.e. not Sunday): *The group owned national and provincial daily and Sunday papers*.

everyone/everybody, every one, every body

everyone/everybody *pronoun*, means all the people suggested by the context: *This is the film everyone remembers*. **Everyone** and **everybody** are synonyms, but **everybody** is slightly more informal than everyone: *Everybody thinks I know things that I don't*. See ANYONE, NO ONE, SOMEONE.

every one *determiner + pronoun*, written as two words, means each person or object considered separately, and may be used for people or things: *It was difficult to decide which article was best, for every one was superbly written*. Both words are stressed.

every body *determiner + pronoun*, written as two words, means all the corpses: *Every body you saw was a victim of this civil war: there was no real reason for them to die*. Both words are stressed.

> Note that these words always take a singular verb, because they refer to 'every single person, and 'one' or 'body' is the subject.

everything, every thing

everything *pronoun*, means all the things, taken as a whole: *Customs officials and police were insisting on all cases being opened and everything laid out on the floor*.

every thing *determiner + pronoun*, written as two words, means each item in a given situation: *Every single thing in their office was destroyed*. Both words are stressed. As in the example given here, the two words may be separated by an adjective.

> Note that *everything* and *every thing* always take a singular verb, because they refer to 'every single thing', and 'thing' is the subject.

everywhere, everyplace

everywhere *adverb*, means in all places: *The flies got everywhere, into eyes, hair, tents, cups of tea, camera lenses*.

everyplace *adverb*, is only used in AE, and means the same as *everywhere*.

> Note that these words may also be used as pronouns, and then always take a singular verb, because they refer to 'every single place', and 'place' is the subject: *Everywhere/everyplace was home to him.*

evidence, testimony

evidence *uncountable noun*, means a fact or object that demonstrates the truth of a belief or proposal: *There is evidence that links smoking with the risk of contracting lung cancer*. **Evidence** also means the information presented to the court during a legal investigation: *The inquest was adjourned for a month, when Health and Safety officials will give evidence*.

testimony *noun*, is a written or spoken statement by a witness in a court of law: *His testimony at the Crown Court led to the accused being jailed for life for stabbing his victim to death*. See TESTIMONIAL, TURN KING'S/QUEEN'S EVIDENCE (PLEA-BARGAINING).

evocative

See SUGGESTIBLE.

exacerbate

See AGGRAVATE.

exaggeration

See HYPERBOLE.

examination, exam (education)

examination *noun*, means a formal test of a person's knowledge, skill or proficiency in a subject: *These one-year degrees are awarded on the basis of written examinations*. This is a formal term.

exam *noun*, is a short form for *examination* in this sense. It is more common than the longer word, and does not require a full stop after it: *The exam results were posted last Tuesday*.

examine, scrutinize

examine *verb*, means to inspect in detail: *He confirmed that engineers from the Department for Transport would examine the A1(M) and the A66 interchange*. In other senses, **examine** means to test students or consider something in an academic context: *Let us now examine the historical background to this conflict*.

scrutinize *verb*, means to examine something very carefully: *The lawyer closely scrutinized the fine print in the contract*. See PERUSE (READ).

exasperate

See ANNOY.

exceed, surpass

exceed *verb*, means to go beyond what is allowed or stipulated: *The presidential ruling allows power plants to exceed their existing emissions limit*.

surpass *verb*, means to be even better or greater than someone or something else: *The comfort of the journey surpassed what he had expected in a Mini*. Note that **surpass** involves a contrast with someone or something else.

excellent, excellence, Excellency

excellent *adjective*, means outstanding, extremely good: *Plain mixed peppercorns make an excellent flavouring for venison*. Things can be *almost excellent, nearly excellent* or *quite excellent*, but as **excellent** expresses an absolute quality, expressions such as 'more excellent' or 'very excellent' are best avoided in formal contexts. See ABSOLUTE ADJECTIVES (GRAMMAR TIPS).

excellence *uncountable noun*, is the quality of being outstanding, or extremely good: *The three criteria for promotion require the demonstration of excellence in teaching, research and administration*.

Excellency *noun*, is a title given to high officials of a state, particularly ambassadors. Formal letters to such people should be addressed to *His Excellency Hugh Jones* on the envelope, rather than *Mr Jones*.

except

See ACCEPT.

exceptional, extraordinary

exceptional *adjective*, means outstanding or unusually good: *The Frenchman's exceptional talents were rewarded with two goals*. It also means special, when referring to a situation where certain conditions apply: *Appointment over the age of 65 should be regarded as exceptional*; or not typical: *Many contemporary composers write for singers who have an exceptional range and absolute pitch*.

extraordinary *adjective*, means out of the ordinary, or unexpectedly extreme: *He had an extraordinary combination of very black hair and dark blue eyes*. In business, an *Extraordinary General Meeting* is one that takes place in addition to the normal sequence of meetings. See RARE.

excess, excessive

See ACCESS.

exclamation mark (!)

See PUNCTUATION GUIDE.

exclude, bar

exclude *verb*, means to leave something out deliberately or not consider something: *The insurance policies exclude loss or damage caused by insects, birds or domestic pets*. **Exclude** can also mean deny access: *Meetings may exclude the public if confidential information is to be disclosed*.

bar *verb*, means to prevent or ban someone from doing something: *Journalists may be barred from the House of Commons for a period of time*. In another sense, **bar** means to prevent access: *We found the road barred by a rockfall*. Note the double 'rr' in the past tense, and also the present participle: *barring*.

excuse

See PRETEXT.

execute

See IMPLEMENT.

executive, executioner, executor, executant

executive *noun & adjective*. As a noun this means a person either in senior management or in a position that denotes importance: *A* *sales executive with a local company spent his leisure hours coaching local boys in football.* **Executive** can also refer to a group of people who run an organization: *On 13 December the joint meeting of the National Executive and the General Council made a final decision.* The **executive** means the part of an Anglo-European-type government that puts laws into effect: *The executive has the administrative function of conducting government in accordance with the law.* As an adjective, **executive** is only used before a noun, for example, an *executive suite* at a hotel or *executive lounge* in an airport (a lounge reserved for special classes of passengers). *Executive directors* have responsibility for the day-to-day running of a company, while *non-executive directors* have a supervisory role to ensure that all regulations are obeyed, and general standards are maintained. See MANAGING DIRECTOR.

executioner *noun*, means a public official whose job is to carry out the death penalty on convicted criminals: *At the pub where the executioner was once landlord there was a sign on the bar warning: 'No hanging around the bar'.* Note that this word is stressed on the third syllable.

executor ĕgzéckyoŏtŏr /ɪg'zekjʊtər/ *noun*, is a legal term for the person or bank selected by someone making a will to carry out his or her instructions after death: *The bank manager says that I cannot have my inheritance until the executor of the will agrees.* If a woman carries out these duties, she is called an *executrix*. Always remember to put the stress on the second syllable zeck /zek/, to avoid any confusion with *executioner*.

executant ĕgzéckyoŏtănt /ɪg'zekjʊtənt/ *noun*, means a person who carries out an action, or someone who performs a piece of music or drama. It also means a person who creates a work of art. Note that the stress is on the second syllable. This is a formal word.

exhibition

See EXPOSÉ.

expatriate

See PATRIOT.

expect

See ANTICIPATE.

expense, expenditure

expense *noun*, means the cost or the money required for something: *No expense will be spared to entertain the guests on board the Orient Express.* The plural, *expenses*, means money spent by an individual on behalf of an employer or other organization in the course of work: *All these payments were made to cover legitimate club expenses.*

expenditure *noun*, means the amount of money spent: *The total expenditure incurred by the project up to the end of 2008 was £1.4 billion.* This is a formal word that is most commonly used in connection with governments or the national economy, and in business contexts.

experience, experiences

experience *uncountable noun*, means knowledge or skill gained through work or practice and includes the process of acquiring such knowledge: *Work experience is always a good thing to put in your CV as it may help get you a job.* Remember that as this is an uncountable noun, the indefinite article cannot be used before it, and the verb must always be singular.

experiences *countable noun*, means activities or events in life that affect someone: *Life had not been easy and the experiences of childhood had left an indelible mark.* As in this sense *experience* is a countable noun, the indefinite article can be used before it, and the following verb may be either singular or plural: *A good experience leaves a feeling of pleasure.*

experiential, experimental

experiential *adjective*, means based on experience and observation: *Examples of experiential learning methods include role play, structured group exercises and counselling skills exercises.*

experimental *adjective*, means as a result of scientific experiments, or concerned with new ideas or methods: *One must beware of solutions that are presented as if they were based on the results of rigorous experimental tests and bear the stamp of proof.*

expertise, proficiency, skill, competence, competency

expertise *uncountable noun*, means the expert knowledge or skill needed to do a job. It combines an understanding of both theory and practice: *Expertise in nanotechnology is eagerly sought around the world.*

proficiency *uncountable noun*, is a more advanced level of ability than competence or skill in doing something in a particular field: *Aircrew must demonstrate their proficiency in handling this type of navigation equipment before being permitted to land in fog.*

skill *noun*, is the ability to do something well. It is often combined with terms which underline the quality being referred to: *Great skill and accuracy are required to do this job.*

competence *noun*, means the ability to do a task adequately. It does not indicate the quality of skill involved, and so may mean that a person has enough skill to carry out the task without mistakes: *He was without enthusiasm, but showed adequate competence as an office worker*. On the other hand, the work of a researcher with great **competence** demonstrates both quality and skill. **Competence** is generally an uncountable noun, although it can also be used as a countable noun to mean a skill that is required in order to perform a specific professional task. In this sense, it is more common to use the word *competency*.

competency *noun*, is an alternative form for *competence* in the sense of a specific skill required of an employee in order to do a particular job: *He gained an extra competency in librarianship*. **Competency** is a countable noun; the plural form is *competencies*.

explain, elucidate, clarify

explain *verb*, means to make something clear: *He did not bother to explain what he meant by 'their' side.*

elucidate *verb*, means to make something clear by explaining it more fully: *I will try to elucidate the following grammatical problems*. This is a formal word. See ELUCIDATION (CLARIFICATION).

clarify *verb*, means to make something clearer or easier to understand: *The Press asked the President to clarify his position on this aspect of foreign policy*. See CLARIFICATION.

explicit

See IMPLICIT.

exploit

See DEVELOP.

E

exponential, logarithmic, arithmetic

exponential *adjective*, means increasing at a faster and faster rate: *The thickness does not decrease linearly, but follows an exponential curve, with the thickness decreasing much more over the first kilometre than the second, and so on.*

logarithmic *adjective*, means increasing by multiples of a base number: *The Richter scale is logarithmic, so that an earthquake measuring 4 on the Richter scale is twice as powerful as one measuring 3, and not 33 per cent more powerful*. See LOGARITHMIC PROGRESSION (ARITHMETIC PROGRESSION).

arithmetic *noun & adjective*, as a noun is the study of numbers. This is stressed on the second syllable: ărĭthmĕtik /əˈrɪθmətɪk/. As an adjective, **arithmetic** (stressed on the third syllable: arrithméttik /ærɪθˈmetɪk/) means concerned with the study of numbers: *An arithmetic scale is one that goes up in single numbers: 1, 2, 3, 4, etc.* See ARITHMETIC PROGRESSION.

exposé, exposition, exhibition

exposé *noun*, means either a clear statement of facts, or the publication of something that shows the subject in a poor light: *His life became even more complicated when he learnt that his ex-wife was about to publish an exposé of their marriage.*

exposition *noun*, means a statement that explains or interprets certain facts: *This was a clear exposition of the criteria that would be used to assess candidates*. In musical analysis, the **exposition** of a piece of music is the first part of a movement in which the main themes are heard for the first time: *The young pianist's performance of the first movement exposition showed that he had not yet fully mastered the composer's style.*

exhibition *noun*, means a public display of works of art: *The one-man exhibition at the local art gallery consists of drawings, etchings* *and small bronzes*. Note that an **exhibition** is normally of limited duration. The items that are on permanent display are called *exhibits* and form part of a collection. In AE the term *exhibit* means both an **exhibition** and the individual items on display.

expressway

See AMERICAN ROAD TYPES.

extant, extinct

extant *adjective*, means in existence, or still surviving: *The finest Visigothic church that is still extant is near Palencia. It was built in 661*. This is a formal word.

extinct *adjective*, means no longer in existence, or completely dead. This can refer to animals or plants that have died out, or volcanoes that no longer erupt: *Scorpions resemble creatures, now long extinct, called sea scorpions that once terrorized the oceans*. In formal usage, the verb *become* is preferred to *go* in contexts where the process of extinction is being discussed. The British National Corpus records over 10 times as many instances of the phrase *become extinct* as *go extinct*.

extempore, impromptu

extempore eckstémpŏri /eks'tempəri/ *adjective & adverb*, describes something said or performed without notes: *He gave his lectures extempore, walking between the rows of desks as he spoke*.

impromptu *adjective & adverb*, describes something said or performed without preparation: *He hadn't expected to be asked to speak, but gave a five-minute impromptu talk on his work in the rain forest*.

extensive, extended

extensive *adjective*, means covering a large area, either literally or figuratively: *The poetry of China is even more extensive than that of Europe, and only the surface of it has been scratched by the West*.

extended *adjective*, means stretched out, or lengthened: *There was only one benefit in the new contract and that was an extended completion date*. It is frequently used in sociology as part of the term *extended family*, which includes a person's cousins, aunts, uncles, grandparents, etc., and is opposed to the *nuclear family*, which includes only parents and siblings.

exterminate

See MASSACRE.

external student, auditor (education)

external student *noun*, means a student who takes examinations at a university where he or she is not matriculated: *There are several external students taking this subject*. See STUDENT.

auditor *noun*, in the context of higher education is used in AE to refer to a student who attends or audits a course without expecting any formal credit for it: *She audited a few classes before applying for a place at the university*.

extract

See ABSTRACT.

extracurricular, extramural, extension (education)

extracurricular *adjective*, is a general term for activities in a school, college or university that are in addition to teaching: *Extracurricular activities include drama, music and the chess club*. The term also has a second connotation of someone who is having an affair: *Bill is notorious for his extracurricular activities*.

extramural *adjective*. In the context of education, this relates to courses offered to those who study part-time: *Our extramural activities include Internet-based teaching and summer courses*. In a more general context this means outside the walls of a town or city: *He was buried in the extramural cemetery in the fields above the town*.

extension *adjective*. In the context of education, this means either the part of a university or college that offers courses to those who study part-time, or this type of course: *He took a postgraduate extension course at the college*.

extraordinary

See EXCEPTIONAL.

Spelling

easte**r**n	Remember the -r-
ec**s**ta**s**y	Note that -s- occurs twice in this word
ela**bor**ate	Remember there is no 'u' in this word
eleg**ia**c	Note -i- before -a-
emba**rr**a**ss**	Note double -rr- and double -ss
embr**y**o	Note the -y-
enro**l**	Remember the final single -l
en**thus**iasm	Remember there is no 'o' in this word
equat**or**	Note the -or ending
ex**ceed**	See *-cede, -ceed, -sede*
exce**l**	Remember the final single -l
expen**s**e	Note there is an -s-, but no 'c'

E

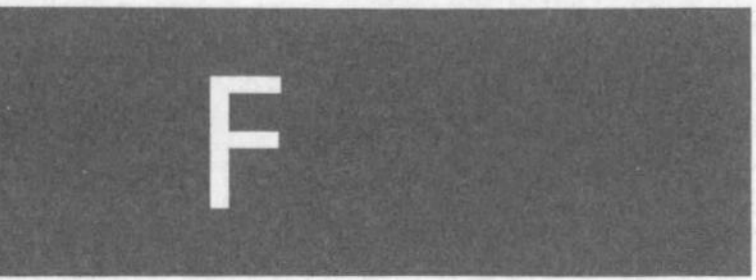

fabricate

See **PRODUCT**.

façade

See **PERSONA**.

facile

See **EASY**.

facility, faculty

facility *noun*, means buildings or equipment provided for a specific purpose: *All companies in the building have access to a staff restaurant facility*. **Facility** can also refer to a feature of a piece of equipment: *Using the freezer facility, I can put all my games on blank DVDs to load faster*. In a formal context it means the ability to do something without difficulty: *With his facility for languages, he could travel widely in Russia*. *The facilities* is an oral expression that is used to mean the toilet, especially in AE.

faculty *noun*, means any of the human senses: *He lost the faculty of hearing at an early age*. It also means the abilities and talents that a person is born with: *A crowd has no critical faculty, and is wide open to influence*. In another sense, a **faculty** is a group of university departments with similar interests and with a single administrative structure: *The Faculty of Music promotes a series of lunchtime concerts*. Note that **faculty** is capitalized when it is part of a title: *Faculty of Arts*. **Faculty** in AE means the teaching staff of a university, college or school. See **SCHOOL**.

fact, in fact, the fact is, as a matter of fact

fact *noun*, is used for a situation that exists without any doubt: *The fact that you have edited the school magazine doesn't make you a writer*. In another sense, **fact** means something that can be proved to be true: *We all die: that is a fact*. The word *true* in the phrase *true fact* is redundant, and is best avoided. See **VERBIAGE**.

in fact is used to add to or correct what has already been said: *We've been together for months now, nine of them, in fact*.

the fact is is used to introduce the truth or the main point: *The fact is they are not interested in peace negotiations*.

as a matter of fact is also used to add to or correct what has already been said: *It has been rumoured that I am a paid official: as a matter of fact, I am not*.

> Note that *in fact* and *as a matter of fact* should not be used in general or introductory statements: *The growth of the Chinese economy has caused a sharp rise in the price of raw materials* (not: *In fact, the growth of the Chinese economy . . .* or *As a matter of fact, the growth of the Chinese economy . . .*).

faculty

See **FACILITY**.

failing, failure

failing *noun*, means a weakness or fault in a person or thing: *The failings of the railway system led to reorganization in the 1990s*.

failure *noun*, means lack of success: *Some campaigns are doomed to failure from the start*. It also means the omission of certain actions: *The authorities' failure to respond to complaints had created a feeling of insecurity*. Note that in this sense, **failure** is followed by the preposition 'to'. **Failure** also refers to something that no longer works as it should: *She suffered kidney failure at a young age*. *Business failure* means the collapse of a business and *crop failure* means that crops have not grown sufficiently to produce an adequate yield.

fair

See **EQUITABLE**, **HAIR COLOUR**.

fairly

See **RATHER**.

fall (season)

See **AUTUMN**.

false friends

Whenever we learn a new language, we have to beware of words which look or sound the same, or almost the same, as words in our native language. For instance, the English word *actual* has an apparent equivalent in most European languages: *actuel* (French), *actual* (Spanish), *atual* (Portuguese), *attuale* (Italian), *aktuell* (German), *actueel* (Dutch), *aktuelan* (Croatian), etc. Unfortunately, the English word rarely, if ever, means the same as it does in any of these languages. The English translation of any one of these is 'current', or 'topical'. This example is a problem for many English-speaking learners of other languages, who need to learn that the English word *actual* cannot be replaced by the words that look or sound the same, and there are many more which may be specific problems in one language or in only a small group of languages. The English word *raisin* means a dried grape, but the French for any grape is *raisin*, while *grappe* is French for a bunch of grapes. The Italian *grappa* meanwhile is a distilled spirit, and the Finnish *greippi* means grapefruit.

familiar, familial

familiar *adjective*, refers to something that is well known: *Polecats are related to the more familiar weasels, stoats and badgers*.

familial *adjective*, means related to or typical of a family. It is most often used in formal medical or genetic contexts: *The profile of the nose was a familial characteristic*. In general use it is more common to use the word *family* as an adjective, as in *a family occasion* or *a family custom*.

family name

See **SURNAME**.

fanatic, fanatical, fanaticism

fanatic *noun*, means either a person who is extremely enthusiastic about something: *Although Bill is a gardening fanatic, he doesn't want a larger garden*; or someone who holds extreme opinions about something: *He was an anti-smoking fanatic*. See **-IC, -ICAL**.

fanatical *adjective*, means extremely enthusiastic: *He was a fanatical fisherman, and knew all the best salmon fishing rivers*. It also refers to a person or ideology considered to hold or promote extreme views: *The wild self-deception led them to embrace the most extreme and fanciful ideologies with fanatical conviction*.

fanaticism *uncountable noun*, means an extreme view or type of behaviour: *The time of fanaticism and non-toleration of the views of others is past*.

F

fanciful

See **IMAGINARY**.

far away, faraway

far away *adverb*, refers to great distance and is spelt as two words: *That is an important country far away across the sea*. Both words are stressed.

faraway *adjective*, also refers to great distance but is spelt as one word: *In that faraway Bengali town there were no European shops*. Only the first syllable is stressed. **Faraway** always comes immediately before the noun it refers to.

farming

See **HUSBANDRY**.

farther/farthest, further/furthest

farther *comparative adjective & adverb*, is the comparative form of *far*, and means at or to a greater physical distance: *I've come from a bit farther than Chelsea tonight*. It also means at the other end of something: *They could not hear as they were at the farther end of the room*. **Farthest** is the superlative adjective form.

further *comparative adjective and adverb, & verb*. As an adjective and adverb, **further** is an alternative to *farther* in the sense of physical distance: *Thousands of pilgrims descended on the shrine from all over the province and even further afield*. **Further** can also mean more or extra: *For further information contact the Information Office*. As an adverb, **further** means to a greater extent: *After the company announced increased losses, the shares slid further*. As a verb, *further one's chances/ambitions* means to make the achievement of an ambition more likely: *'It's shocking what these clubs will do to further their own ends.'* **Furthest** is the superlative adjective form. As an adverb it means at the greatest distance: *Pluto is the planet furthest from the Sun*. It also functions as a noun: *This is the furthest we can go without supplies*.

fashion statement, fashion-forward

fashion statement *noun*, means the wearing or design of something which stands out, to draw attention to the wearer or designer: *For both men and women today earrings are a definite fashion statement*.

fashion-forward *adjective*, means in the forefront of fashion, or even ahead of it: *Today's frames are fashion-forward* according to a newspaper story about fashionable spectacle frames.

fastidious

See **THOROUGH**.

fatal, fateful

fatal *adjective*, means both disastrous: *She wished she could talk about it to her mother, but that would be fatal*; and causing death: *He did not know that he had developed a fatal heart condition*. **Fatal** can only refer to unhappy events. See **DEADLY**.

fateful *adjective*, means far-reaching and decisive. It has nothing to do with death and may refer to happy or unhappy events: *The fateful meeting on that train in Berlin led to a happy marriage*.

fate

See **DESTINY**.

fatherless

See **ORPHAN**.

faucet

See **TAP**.

fault, mistake, error, malfunction

fault *noun & verb*. As a noun, this means a defect in a machine: *If the circuit fails to work, some simple tests should locate the fault*. It can also mean a negative aspect of a person's character: *Being intolerant is one of my worst faults*. As a verb, it means to criticize, and is usually found in the passive: *The referee could not be faulted as the defender cleverly concealed his hands*.

mistake *noun & verb*. As a noun, this is an action or judgement that is wrong or the result of being misguided: *We made a mistake in buying that car*. As a verb, it means either to misunderstand: *He mistook my comments as an insult*; or to recognize someone or something wrongly: *'You can't mistake their car: it's a hideous pink colour.'*

error *noun*, is a more formal word than *mistake* and can be concerned with calculations: *Because of the imprecise data, we allow for an error of 15 per cent in either direction*. **Error** also means misunderstanding or faulty judgement: *If human error is thought to be particularly important then expert advice should be sought*. An *error message* is one that indicates a problem in a computer program.

malfunction *noun & verb*. As a noun, this means a failure in an item of equipment: *The usually reliable pumps had a malfunction and finally broke down*. As a verb it means not to work properly: *He bailed out but his parachute malfunctioned and he was killed*. See **DAMAGE**, **DEFECT**.

> *Error* is the only one of these words that cannot be used as a verb.

> *'All 2001 models are being recalled because of a fault in the nuts behind the wheel.'*
> (major car manufacturer) **!**

faze

See **PHASE**.

feedback, response

feedback *uncountable noun*, means information or advice given to a questioner about the quality of something: *We will ask all our customers for feedback about our new banking service*. **Feedback** is also used in a technical sense to mean the distortion of electrically amplified sound caused by the return of power to a system such as an amplifier: *If the coil windings are loose, feedback from the microphone can occur*.

response *noun*, means either an individual answer: *She always knocked and then walked in without waiting for a response*; or a collective reaction: *This time the stand-up comedian got no response from the audience*. If you just want an answer, reply or **response** are preferable terms to *feedback*. In another sense, **response** is used in the fixed expression *in response to* something meaning as a reaction or reply to something: *Police headquarters provided a statement in response to a number of questions we raised about the case*. See REPLY.

feet

See FOOT.

fellow

See SCHOLAR.

female, feminine

female *adjective & noun*. As an adjective, this refers to the sex of a human or animal capable of producing offspring, or of a plant that can produce fruit: *A woman teacher can become a role model for female students*. It also means related to a woman: *There are few monosyllabic female first names (Ann, Joan, May)*. As a noun, it means either a woman or girl, or in a broader sense, the animal that can bear young or lay eggs, or the plant that produces fruit. See MALE, SEXIST LANGUAGE (WRITING SKILLS).

feminine *adjective*, refers to the qualities traditionally associated with women, such as gracefulness or lack of aggression: *My books were held tightly against my chest in a way which, I was to learn, was feminine and wrong for a man*. **Feminine** is also a grammatical term referring to the gender of a part of speech. In this sense a word with *feminine gender* may refer to a male creature or even an inanimate object. English has a feminine gender only in the personal pronouns, but these are sometimes used affectionately in connection with favourite machines or vehicles, such as ships: *When a sailing ship has a fair wind, the loads in her rigging are moderate*. See MASCULINE (MALE), GENDER (SEX).

fence-mending

See RECONCILE.

ferment, foment

ferment *verb & noun*. As a verb, **ferment** means to change an organic substance chemically by the action of bacteria or yeasts, most commonly used to describe the production of alcohol: *Grapes are crushed and left to ferment in a vat*. Figuratively it refers to ideas that develop, often through anger, over a long period of time: *His plan for revenge had been fermenting in his brain for months*. This is stressed on the second syllable. As a noun **ferment** means a state of excitement or social unrest: *In August to September 1945 Korea was in a ferment of revolutionary upheaval*. The noun is stressed on the first syllable.

foment *verb*, means to encourage trouble or disagreement among people: *The murder was intended to foment open conflict between the two gangs*. Note that it is not the people themselves who are being *fomented*, but the problems between them.

fertile

See FRUITFUL.

fever

See TEMPERATURE.

few, a few, several, many, umpteen

few *determiner & pronoun*, means not many: *Few investors want to sell assets in a falling market*. **Few** emphasizes the small number involved, particularly when combined with *very*. It is used with plural nouns and a plural verb.

a few *determiner & pronoun*, means some or a small number: *Usually it will be only for a few seconds*. **A few** suggests a small number, that is more than *few* without the indefinite article. *Quite a few* means a fairly large number: *I've fallen asleep in the cinema quite a few times*.

several *determiner & pronoun*, means an indefinite small quantity that is more than two but less than many: *She passed several men, but none gave her a second glance*.

many *determiner, pronoun & adjective*, means a large number and is always greater than several: *It was marvellous to see so many young people paying their tribute*. In speech, *a lot (of)* is a more common alternative. As an adjective it refers to the number: *The many types of flowers in the garden*.

umpteen *quantifier*, is an informal expression for a very large indefinite number, and can indicate some annoyance with the number: *After umpteen phone calls to the tax office, I eventually got through to an answering machine!*

fewer, less

fewer *determiner & pronoun*, is the comparative form of few and is used with plural nouns: *Fewer children are in two-parent families today than 50 years ago*.

less *adjective*, is the comparative form of little and is used with uncountable nouns, such as information and damage: *The government has ensured that less information is available*.

fiancé, fiancée

fiancé *noun*, means the man a woman is engaged to be married to: *Her fiancé, the man who was supposed to love her, had not come near her*.

fiancée *noun*, means the woman a man is engaged to be married to: *John plans to marry his fiancée next year*.

These words should be spelled with an acute accent above the first 'e'.

field, area, discipline, subject (education)

field *noun*, is used for a restricted branch of specialized knowledge: *She enjoys the intellectual freedom of her profession, and has published widely in her field of political philosophy*.

area *noun*, means a particular subject or group of related subjects in education. It is an alternative to *field*, but is often combined with *subject*: *The university had a number of multidisciplinary subject areas*. See **AREA (STRETCH)**.

discipline *noun*, means a branch of knowledge or a subject that people study, especially in higher education: *If their assessment of the scientist's standing and contribution to his discipline is favourable, the project goes ahead*. Apart from its academic sense, **discipline** also means obeying rules, keeping order and punishment: *There had been a number of complaints from parents about the increasingly firm discipline in the school*. See **CROSS-DISCIPLINARY**.

subject *noun*, means a branch of knowledge, and as it applies to all educational levels, it is more widely used than **discipline**: *The pupils that take the International Baccalaureat study a broad range of subjects*.

figurative language

We use words figuratively when we extend their meaning to add colour to our speech or writing. For instance, if we say that someone spoke in measured tones, we do not mean that the speaker took out a stopwatch and counted the seconds between the syllables, but that he or she was speaking slowly and deliberately with a lot of thought. Similes and metaphors are two linguistic devices that illustrate figurative speech: *She went as white as a sheet* (simile – meaning that one thing is compared to another) or *He let out a stream of insults* (metaphor – *stream* is used to mean a continuous succession, not a flow of water). Many if not most words can be used figuratively, and in fact many of the common uses of words were originally figurative: *rise*, for instance, was once limited to physical objects going up to a higher level, but is now commonly used figuratively to apply to increases in salary, or to a person or organization gaining influence: *The Labour Party's rise to power in the late 1990s*. Unsurprisingly, given the British obsession with the weather, there are many weather terms used figuratively in English: *thunderous* applause, *snowed* under with work, *showered* with praise, a *hail* of bullets, and a recent one, using a word that many people were not familiar with until the disaster on Boxing Day 2004: *tsunami*. As we were writing this, we came across *the tsunami of hype surrounding the launch of the iPhone* in a daily newspaper. Many style guides warn against the dangers of using two different figures of speech in the same context, when the literal meaning of one does not 'fit' with the meaning of the other – the so-called mixed metaphor. An example would be: *We held out the olive branch of peace, but nothing concrete came of it*. 'The olive branch of peace' is perfectly acceptable, and 'concrete proposals' are fine, but olive branches cannot produce concrete. One or other of them should be replaced. See **CLICHÉ**.

figures

See **STATISTICS, STYLE GUIDELINES (WRITING SKILLS)**.

file, folder, binder (office terms)

file *noun*, means the documentation about business matters held by an organization. **File** may also refer to the physical container of the information, such as a *box file*. A **file** in computing means a collection of information stored under a unique name: *Each entry is stored as a file on the disk system of the computer*.

folder *noun*, means a lightweight cardboard holder for documents: *James looked through the folder once more, then made his decision*. *Files* on PCs are collected in **folders**, as a way of organizing and storing them: *I have just created three new folders so that I can sort out these files*.

binder *noun*, means a stiff cardboard holder for documents: *Every member will be sent an enrolment package in an attractive binder*. *Loose-leaf binders* and *ring binders* are common features in most offices.

Filipina, Filipino

See **PHILIPPINES**.

finance, fund, funding

finance *verb & noun*. As a verb, this means either to provide money for a specific purpose, or to give financial support: *The Treasury decided to finance its budget deficit by selling more short-term securities*. As a noun, **finance** means the money used in order to run a business or other activity, or the management of large amounts of money, by a government or a large enterprise: *He could not raise the additional finance to purchase the bacon-curing business*. **Finance** is an uncountable noun in the above senses. The plural form *finances* is also used in this sense, but in addition can refer to a person's monetary resources: *Weekly payments would let you employ home help without straining your finances*.

fund *verb & noun*. As a verb, this means to provide money for a specific purpose that usually involves public money: *In some cases the housing association will fund the work*. As a noun, a **fund** is a sum of money set aside for a specific purpose: *The broadcast concluded with an appeal for donations to a UN famine relief fund*. Figuratively it may be used for a large amount of anything: *The fund of goodwill which she had brought with her must be almost exhausted*. The plural form *funds* means financial resources in general or money that is available to an organization or person for a particular purpose: *Effective allocation of funds is the basis for free public library services*.

funding *uncountable noun*, means the same as *funds*, but is used with a singular verb: *My research post has been extended, but the funding has not*.

financial, fiscal, monetary

financial *adjective*, refers to matters dealing with money, and can apply to personal finances or corporate or national ones: *We are developing financial services for our members to meet their particular requirements*. People and companies with **financial** problems often try to make matters seem better by using terms such as *being in financial difficulties* or *experiencing financial setbacks*.

fiscal *adjective*, also refers to money matters, but only to public funds, especially taxes: *Keynes was a Treasury man who believed in the value of fiscal control*. It is frequently used with terms such as *policy*. The *fiscal year* means the financial year. See **ECONOMIC**.

monetary *adjective*, means associated with money, particularly with national funds. **Monetary** is frequently used before terms such as policy, union and system: *The USA trade deficit constitutes the other source of instability within the international monetary system*.

find out, ascertain, come out in the wash

find out *verb*, means to discover something: *I took out the map to find out where I was*. The expression to *find someone out* means to discover that a person has not been telling the truth, or has been attempting to hide something: *She would always find him out if he tried to lie or keep wicked secrets from her*.

ascertain assĕrtáyn /æsər'teɪn/ *verb*, means to discover beyond doubt the truth of a situation. It is a more forceful and formal word than *find out*: *Visitors to the area will be* *interviewed to ascertain their expectations*. Note that **ascertain** is stressed on the last syllable. See CERTAIN (SATISFIED).

come out in the wash *verb phrase*, is used to say the truth about a situation will be revealed: *The Minister said 'At the end of the day, the dust will settle and it will all come out in the wash'*; or to find the solution to a problem at some time in the future. As this is an idiomatic expression, its meaning may be unclear to an international audience.

fiord

See LOCH.

fire

See DISMISS.

firm

See BUSINESS.

first name, forename, Christian name, given name

first name *noun*, is the name or names given to a child by its parents at birth. This term is often used on registration cards and other forms requiring personal information: *Write your first name(s) in capital letters*. See SURNAME.

forename *noun*, is an alternative way of expressing *first name*.

Christian name *noun*, was until recently the usual term used for *first name*, but it is no longer in official use since many English-speaking groups are not Christians.

given name *noun*, is in many ways the most preferable of all the terms, as in many languages, for instance Chinese, Korean, Japanese and Hungarian, it is customary to put the family name first, and the given names last: *Mao Zedong*. In most of the English-speaking world, it is usual to address people by their given name(s) followed by their family name: *Stewart Clark*, but in lists, it is normal to put the family name first, followed by a comma: *Pointon, Graham*. However, if a Chinese name, for instance, needs to be included in a list, there is no comma, as the family name naturally comes first. See SURNAME.

firth

See LOCH.

fiscal

See FINANCIAL.

fish, fishes

fish *noun*, means the individual animal or its flesh. **Fish** meaning food is an uncountable noun which takes a singular verb: *The fish is caught fresh every morning*. A plural verb is used only for more than one living **fish**: *The fish have to be caught on lines*.

fishes *plural noun*, is used only when referring to more than one species: *Modern specialists often divide the jawless fishes into two broad groups*; or to make clear that more than one fish is meant: *Some young act as 'cleaners', picking off fungus and animal parasites that infest the skin of the host fishes*.

fjord

See LOCH.

flagrant, fragrant

flagrant *adjective*, means conspicuous or obvious: *The committee decided that there had been a deliberate and flagrant breach of regulations*. This word expresses disapproval. See BLATANT.

fragrant *adjective*, means having a sweet or pleasant smell: *The coffee arrived, strong and fragrant*. See ODOUR, SMELL.

flair, flare

flair *noun*, means skill: *The food is refreshingly simple in concept, but is cooked with originality and flair*; it is also used to mean a natural ability: *Actuaries frequently develop a flair for analysing and solving business problems*. Note that **flair** should not be confused with preference or liking, both of which involve choice.

flare *noun & verb*. As a noun, **flare** means a short-lived blaze of light: *A dull roar and sudden flare announced the explosion of the fuel tank*; or a very bright light used as a signal: *The blue flare of a navigation beacon suddenly shone out*. In the plural, *flares* are trousers which become wider from the knee downwards, also known as *flared trousers*:

Dave the hippy wears big flares – so big they're like vast flapping sails. As a verb, *flare up* either refers to a sudden increase in the height of the flames of a fire: *Many packaging materials contain highly flammable substances that could make a fire suddenly flare up*; or refers to a person's quick temper: *Jamie suffers from a condition that makes his temper flare up uncontrollably*. It can also refer to the rapid appearance of a disease or trouble.

flammable

See INFLAMMABLE.

flea, flee

flea *noun*, is a small jumping insect that feeds on blood: *Rabbits' nests are the breeding ground of the rabbit flea*.

flee *verb*, means to run away: *Rabbits have to learn to flee as soon as they can run*.

Flemish

See NETHERLANDS.

flexible

See INFLEXIBLE (UNBENDING).

float, drift

float *verb*, means to be supported on or close to the surface of a liquid. It is often used for ships and other buoyant objects: *I wonder why some things float and others sink?*

drift *verb*, means to move slowly along: *They drifted through the crowds of shoppers*; or without any special purpose: *Watch your thoughts as they drift like clouds through your mind*.

flood

See EBB.

floor

See GROUND.

flotsam, jetsam

flotsam *uncountable noun*, means the wreckage of goods, parts of boats or rubbish found in the sea or on land: *We went farther up the beach, still finding interesting pieces of flotsam*.

jetsam *uncountable noun*, means things that are thrown away from a ship at sea and are floating or are found ashore: *It was already lost – part of the jetsam of discarded immemorabilia which disappeared astern all the time*. *Flotsam* and **jetsam** are almost always used in combination to mean any discarded odds and ends, or even to refer to people who are lost or destitute: *Better-heeled passengers penned a succession of sad descriptions of the flotsam and jetsam of Europe they encountered*. The original distinction between *flotsam* as wreckage or goods floating in the sea and **jetsam** as wreckage or goods which are washed ashore is not part of modern usage.

F

flounder

See FOUNDER.

flow

See EBB.

fluent, fluid

fluent *adjective*, means having a thorough command of a language, or speaking and writing without hesitation: *Mr Lal's English was even less fluent than my Hindi, so we tried to communicate with a type of sign language*.

fluid *adjective & noun*. As an adjective, **fluid** is often used for gases and liquids that flow: *Basaltic magmas are normally expelled from volcanoes in a very hot and fluid state*; but is more often used figuratively, to mean flowing, or changeable: *The soft-look dashboard design uses fluid, rounded shapes to complement the form of the interior*. As a noun, it means something that can flow – a liquid or gas: *Sodium controls the movement of fluid in and out of body cells*.

fluorescence, phosphorescence

fluorescence *uncountable noun*, means visible or invisible radiation produced by X-rays or ultraviolet light: *A small proportion of the absorbed light will sometimes be re-radiated and it is this that we term the fluorescence*.

phosphorescence *uncountable noun*, means a slight light created by radiation, but in this case no combustion is needed and no detectable heat is created: *The yacht rose on* *a swell which ran down her side in a flowing cascade of phosphorescence.*

flush

See **BLUSH**.

focus, focuses, foci

focus *noun & verb*. As a noun, this means the concentration of action or activity on something: *Our focus remains firmly on the UK because the home market is our largest single market*. This is the singular form. As a verb, it means to concentrate action and activity on something: *The drama must focus on a series of events which create a larger than life situation*. Other verb forms may be spelled with single or double 's': *focuses/focusses, focusing/focussing, focused/focussed*, but most dictionaries give the single form as their first choice.

focuses or **foci** fṓ-sī /'fəʊsaɪ/ are alternative plurals of the noun *focus*. There is no double 's' here. Note that the first syllable of **foci** is pronounced like the word 'foe', and the second like the word 'sigh'.

fog

See **MIST**.

folder

See **FILE**.

folk, folks

folk *noun*, means people in general. In BE, it occurs in the generic terms *menfolk* and *womenfolk*. It is also found in expressions such as *folk dance, folk music, folk song, folklore* and *folk story*. In AE, **folk** means people, which is the term British speakers would use instead: *Louisa's parents were country folk and believed very much in herbal remedies*. See **PEOPLE (PERSON)**.

folks *noun plural*, means a closely related group and conveys the idea of family or mutual friendship. In AE, it also refers to people in general. This is an informal term: *There are not too many folks who think like this*.

foment

See **FERMENT**.

font, character

font *noun*, means the name of the typographical style and size of letters used in printing and computer word processing: *As this text will be used in a PowerPoint presentation, use Arial, which is an easy font to read, and make sure you use 20-point or larger for the font size*.

character *noun*, is a letter, sign or symbol used in printing and word processing: *The size of this box means that you cannot use more than 27 characters including spaces*.

foot, feet

foot *noun*, is a unit of length. **Foot** can be combined with numbers to form a hyphenated adjective: *He is a six-foot goalkeeper*. This means that there is no plural and *a six-feet goalkeeper* is non-standard English.

feet *noun*, means a measured distance, and when the amount follows the verb, in formal usage the number and **feet** are always in the plural and do not form a hyphenated adjective: *The river was 60 feet wide*. In informal or spoken English, *the river was 60 foot wide* is acceptable.

> When combined with *inches*, either 'foot' or 'feet' is correct: *This plank is six feet four inches long*; *How long is it? Six foot four*. It is abbreviated *ft* and the symbol ′ is also used as in *6′4″*. Note that there is no hyphen here. See **INCH, MEASUREMENTS**.

fora

See **FORUM**.

forbid

See **PROHIBIT**.

force

See **STRENGTH**.

forceful

See **AGGRESSIVE**.

forecast

See **PROGNOSIS**.

foreigner

See **STRANGER**.

foreign place names

Country names, capital and other major cities, and some sea and river names, are often spelt and pronounced in English differently from how they appear in their original language. In some cases, the differences are small, but using the English versions may avoid misunderstandings. Here is a selection, English on the left, original on the right:

Athens	Athínai
Baltic Sea	Ostsee (German)
Brussels	Bruxelles (French), Brussel (Dutch)
Bucharest	Bucureşti
Burma	Myanmar
Florence	Firenze
Hanover	Hannover
Nicosia	Lefkosia (Greek)
Paris párriss /'pærɪs/	Paris parreé /paʁi/
Prague	Praha
Rangoon	Yangon
Rhine	Rhein (German), Rhin (French), Rijn (Dutch)
Saragossa	Zaragoza

From time to time, a change may be made, so that a place name acquires a spelling and pronunciation that are closer to the original: in recent years *Peking* has become *Beijing*, *Byelorussia* has become *Belarus*. *Livorno* is a popular tourist destination, but in the nineteenth century it was known in English as *Leghorn*.

Some geographical features keep their original name to the extent that the word for 'mountain' or 'river' is retained: *Rio Grande*, not 'River Grande' or 'Big River'; *Mont Blanc*, not 'Mount White' or 'White Mountain'. Where the name is from a language that is less well known to English speakers than Spanish or French, tautology sometimes occurs: *Sahara* is Arabic for 'desert', but both *The Sahara* and *Sahara Desert* are found in English. See BRITISH PLACE NAMES, NATIONALITY WORDS.

foreign plurals

See WORD FORMATION.

forename

See FIRST NAME.

forest

See WOOD.

foreword, preface

foreword *noun*, refers to the preliminary pages in a technical or academic report. It is written by a distinguished person who is not the author of the work: *'Your book has strong appeal and I would be pleased to consider writing a foreword.'*

preface *noun*, also refers to the preliminary pages in a technical or academic report or book. It is written by the author(s): *The authors state frankly in their preface that the 'treatment of broad themes' is their aim.*

> If a book has both a *foreword* and a *preface*, the *foreword* is always placed first.

for example, for instance

See E.G.

forfeit

See SACRIFICE.

formal English

See WRITING SKILLS.

formally, formerly

formally *adverb*, means officially, or in a formal manner: *Ten days later he was formally charged with manslaughter.*

formerly *adverb*, means at a previous time: *Our oldest member, Ralph, was formerly a bank manager.*

former, latter

former *adjective & noun*. When used as an adjective, **former** means one of any number of predecessors: *He is a former defence secretary and chancellor of the exchequer*. When used as a noun with the definite article, *the former* refers to the first of two, but never more: *He had two ex-wives, Helen and Janet, but only the former had remarried.* (More informally, *the former* could have been replaced here by *Helen*.) If there are more than two use the first (of these) or the first-named.

latter *adjective & noun*. As an adjective, this means towards the end: *Throughout the latter part of the nineteenth century 'citizenship' was part of the civilizing process*. It also means the second of two things, corresponding to the adjective *former*: *In the latter case, buyers must pay 15 per cent commission*. As a noun, it refers to the second or more recently named of two: *The conduct of English and French football supporters was compared; the latter were classified as less fanatical*. If there are more than two use the last (of these) or the last-named.

former student

See ALUMNI.

formula, formulas, formulae

formula *noun*, is the singular form and refers to the letters and symbols that represent a chemical compound: *The formula of a molecular compound shows the number of atoms of each element in one molecule of the compound*; or which indicate a mathematical relationship: *Using historical data, we can derive estimated values for* a *and* b *in the formula*. It also means a method for achieving something: *Can we produce a political formula that will be acceptable to the two communities?* **Formula** may also mean liquid baby food. Here it is an uncountable noun: *The formula provides a perfect blend as well as antibodies and white blood cells which protect against disease*.

formulas *noun*, is the plural of *formula* for use in non-scientific contexts: *Religious rituals have always surrounded the experiences of death and formulas to aid grieving*.

formulae *noun*, is the alternative plural form of *formula* and is frequently used when it refers to mathematical rules and chemical compounds: *The formulae that produce the totals and averages are kept off the worksheet*. It is pronounced fórmyo͝oli /ˈfɔːrmjʊli/. See AE.

forth

See QUARTER.

fortnight, two weeks

fortnight *noun*, means a period of approximately two weeks: *I've got two essays to write in the next fortnight*. This is a BE expression.

two weeks *noun phrase*, is the standard AE expression for *fortnight*. In BE **two weeks** is exactly 14 days: *During the next two weeks you must take this medicine morning and night*.

fortnightly, semi-monthly, bimonthly

fortnightly *adjective, adverb & noun*, means every two weeks. This is only used in BE. See BIWEEKLY (SEMI-WEEKLY).

semi-monthly *adjective, adverb & noun*, means twice a month. Note that the pronunciation semmi- /semi-/ is normal in BE, while semmī- /semaɪ-/ is standard in AE.

bimonthly *adjective, adverb & noun*, means either twice a month or every two months. Because of the ambiguity about its meaning, it is best to avoid this word. Depending on the context, use the less confusing *fortnightly* or *semi-monthly* or every second month. In publishing, however, **bimonthly** always means every two months: *Magazines can be classified by frequency: some are published weekly, others monthly and yet others bimonthly or quarterly*.

> Note the typical positions for these words: before the noun: a *fortnightly* publication (adjective); after the verb: this is published *fortnightly* (adverb); and following an article: this is a *fortnightly* (noun).

fortunate, fortuitous

fortunate *adjective*, means lucky. A **fortunate** coincidence describes something good that happens by chance: *It was a fortunate coincidence that it was his mother who found his lost wallet*.

fortuitous fortéw-itŭss /fɔːrˈtjuːɪtəs/ *adjective*, means happening by chance especially when it give good results: *The winning goal was either a fortuitous ricochet, or some such happy accident*. This is a formal word.

> Note that these two words should be kept apart; *a fortunate meeting* means it was lucky to meet someone, but *a fortuitous meeting* means an accidental meeting that invariably leads to a good result.

forum, forums, fora

forum *noun*, means a place or medium for exchanging views: *The chief lawmaking forum of the Community is the Council of Ministers.* **Forum** is also the word used for a public meeting place in Roman times. This is the singular form.

forums *noun*, is the usual plural form of *forum*: *The political parties were not the only forums in which the idea of citizenship was being debated.*

fora *noun*, the original Latin plural of *forum*, is also an alternative plural form in English, although some usage guides recommend that it should only be used as a reference to ancient Roman marketplaces: *It was laid out on a Roman plan with six fora, theatres, hippodrome, etc.*

founder, flounder

founder *verb*, means to sink. If a boat runs aground, it is also said to have *foundered*: *Two days out the ship foundered in a storm, and sank with everyone aboard.* In a figurative context, **founder** means to fail: *His business had started to founder and his company had gone into insolvent liquidation.*

flounder *verb*, means to struggle in mud or water, etc.: *Hampered by her clothes, her ears, nose and mouth full of foul-tasting water, she floundered.* It can also be used more figuratively to mean struggle in a state of confusion: *The country's fledgling democracy continues to flounder as oppression and censorship are openly employed to silence opponents.*

Both these words indicate failure.

fountain, fount

fountain *noun*, means a machine for sending a flow of water upwards: *There is an excellent swimming complex with pool, waterfall, fountain, wave machine and showers.*

fount *noun*, means a spring of water, or source. Figuratively, it is used to mean the origin of something important: *In the office he was the fount of all knowledge.*

'She has a collection of old photos and is a fountain of knowledge about the area.'

fourth

See QUARTER.

fragrant

See FLAGRANT.

frail, fragile, delicate

frail *adjective*. When referring to people, this means weak and *delicate*: *The doctor said he was saddened by her frail health.* When referring to things, **frail** means easily broken, or not complete: *Some houses remain frail structures of cardboard and plywood.*

fragile *adjective*. When referring to people this means *delicate* and vulnerable, not strong: *The voice from the adjoining bedroom was fragile but it carried clearly*. Things that are **fragile** are easily broken: *Jeremy drew up a chair which looked altogether too fragile for his tall frame.*

delicate *adjective*. When referring to people, this means someone who is prone to illness: *The little boy was in reality a delicate child.* When referring to things, it means something that is fine in texture and colour, *fragile* and beautiful: *There had been jade dragons so delicate that they disintegrated at a puff of breath.*

frame, framework

frame *noun & verb*. As a noun, this means a structure to mount paintings on: *The oil painting is in a gilt frame*. It is also used for the structure that forms the border of doors and windows: *He felt along to a door frame and followed its outline until he found a light switch*. As a verb, **frame** can mean to surround something with an edge to make it more attractive: *They framed the picture with oak beading*; or it can mean to produce false evidence in order to incriminate a person: *He denied the charge and claimed that he was being framed by the police*.

framework *noun*, means a set of ideas or rules such as the scope of a project, proposal or agreement. *We need a better framework for this peace agreement*. In another sense it means the structure of a society or legal or political system: *The proposed reforms were stopped by the traditional and entrenched social framework*. It can also mean the essential supporting structure of a building, vehicle or object.

free, freely

free *adjective & adverb*, means unoccupied. It is used either for people who are not busy: *When would you be free to start?* (in more formal contexts, available should be used here), or for objects that are not in use: *Look: there's a free parking space over there* (in this context, vacant is more formal). In another sense, **free** also means at liberty: *We're going to set him free tomorrow*, and unrestricted: *Every board member is free to question corporate leadership on any matter*. **Free** also means without payment: *While you are pregnant you can get free prescriptions for your medicines*. The expression *to give someone free rein* means to allow them to act however they wish. The phrase *for free* is often seen, but is not recommended in formal writing. As an adverb, **free** means without cost or charge: *Children are allowed in free*.

freely *adverb*, means openly, candidly or without restriction: *He moved out of the country so that he could freely criticize the government*. If something moves *freely* it is without obstruction: *The patient was now breathing freely*. If something is *freely available* it is easy to get, it is not connected to the idea of payment: *That BBC programme is freely available on the Internet*.

freeway

See AMERICAN ROAD TYPES.

freight, goods, cargo

freight *uncountable noun & verb*. As a noun, this means *goods* transported in bulk by any means of transport: *The canal created a shorter route for trade in coal and other freight between the Midlands and London*. **Freight** also means the cost of this transport: *His creditors cannot ascertain whether the freight was paid*. In AE, a *freight train* carries **freight** (*goods* in BE). Also in AE, a passenger train may have some **freight** cars. As a verb, **freight** means to transport goods by sea, rail, road or air: *We guarantee to freight goods anywhere in Europe within three days*. In this sense, **freight** is an alternative to *ship*. See SHIP (BOAT).

goods *plural noun*, is a BE term for objects that are transported: *Goods are carried on all our services*. Although a *goods train* only carries **goods**, a passenger train may have some *goods wagons*. More generally, **goods** means either any product produced for sale: *Consumers have the right to reject faulty goods and demand a refund*; or in the legal phrase *goods and chattels*, someone's personal possessions.

cargo *noun*, means *goods* carried by ship, aircraft or lorry: *It was recently converted from a passenger plane to cargo use*. When the definite or indefinite article is used, **cargo** refers to a particular load that is being transported: *The cargo of salmon was spoiled when the refrigeration plant failed*. The plural is *cargoes*, but note that *cargos* is an alternative spelling in AE.

French

See GAELIC.

freshman, fresher, sophomore, junior, senior (education)

freshman *noun*, means a first-year college or university student: *He won his Blue as a freshman at Cambridge and, in turn, captained his university and country*; or the first year in an American college or university: *She looked forward to her freshman year*. In AE, a **freshman** is a first-year college or university student of either sex, and is also used to mean a student in the first year of the American four-year high school. In AE, **freshman** is also used outside education, such as a *freshman senator*.

fresher *noun*, is a BE alternative to *freshman* in the sense of a first-year college or university student: *Freshers' Week is the first week of the first academic year for undergraduates at this university*.

sophomore *noun*, means either a second-year student in an American college or university or the second year in an American college or university. The term is also used to mean a student in the second year of the American four-year high school.

junior *noun*. In Britain, this means a pupil at junior school. In AE, this means either a third-year student in an American college or high school, or the third year in an American college or high school. See JUNIOR SCHOOL.

senior *noun*. In Britain, this means a pupil at senior school, or an older pupil at any school. In AE, this means either a final-year student in an American college or high school, or the final year in a four-year programme at an American college or high school.

friend

See ACQUAINTANCE.

fringe benefit, perk

fringe benefit *noun*, means an extra given or paid to a worker by the employer: *He exempted employees from tax on the fringe benefit of company nurseries*. This may be shortened to *benefit*.

perk *noun*, is an informal term for *fringe benefit*. This is an abbreviation of the more formal *perquisite* púrkwizit /'pɜːrkwɪzɪt/ which is rarely used in this context: *He announced that the perk of a workplace nursery would no longer be taxable*. Do not confuse *perquisite* with prerequisite. See PREREQUISITE (REQUISITE).

from . . . to

See BETWEEN . . . AND.

frontier

See BORDER.

fruitful, fertile

fruitful *adjective*, describes a tree or plant that produces a large crop. However, this word is most often used in a figurative sense, when it refers to something that produces a lot of useful results: *Annual reports and accounts are a fruitful source of information*.

fertile *adjective*, is used of land or soil that produces a lot of crops or vegetation. A person or animal that is **fertile** is capable of producing offspring. Plants produce fruit if they are **fertile**. In a figurative sense, **fertile** also refers to the capacity to generate ideas: *Her fertile and inventive imagination came to her aid*. Note that in BE the second syllable is pronounced like the word 'tile'; the AE pronunciation of this word rhymes with 'turtle'.

fruitless, hopeless

fruitless *adjective*, refers to a situation that does not bring any useful results: *He's suffering from dehydration because of his fruitless search for water*.

hopeless *adjective*, means with no chance of getting better or succeeding: *Although you're in a seemingly hopeless situation, keep thinking and get your priorities right*.

fruit machine

See VENDING MACHINE.

fry

See ROAST.

fulfil, fulfill

fulfil *verb*, means to achieve an objective or to satisfy a requirement: *They completed the building in time to fulfil the contractual obligations*. This is the BE spelling. The related noun is *fulfilment*.

fulfill *verb*, is an alternative spelling used in AE. When this spelling is used, the related noun should be spelt *fulfillment*.

> Note that the forms *fulfilled* and *fulfilling* have the same spelling in both BE and AE.

full board

See BOARD.

full stop

See **PUNCTUATION GUIDE**.

fulsome, heartfelt

fulsome *adjective*, describes a statement that gives praise but sounds insincere: *The obituary described the politician in such fulsome terms that she wondered whether paradise would be good enough for him*.

heartfelt *adjective*, means strongly felt and sincere: *He said it with such heartfelt force that I believed him*.

fund, funding

See **FINANCE**.

funeral

See **BURIAL**.

funny ha-ha, funny peculiar

funny ha-ha *adjective*, means amusing or comical: *I asked him if he meant funny ha-ha*. See **COMIC**.

funny peculiar *adjective*, means strange: *He replied that no, he meant funny peculiar*. In AE, this is usually called *funny weird* or *funny strange*.

further/furthest

See **FARTHER/FARTHEST**.

further education

See **CONTINUING EDUCATION**.

Spelling

fa**cs**imile	Note the -cs-, despite the abbreviation 'fax'
Feb**r**uary	Remember that there are two r's in this word
for**eig**n	Remember -e- before -i-, and also the -g-
fla**g**on	Remember the single -g-
flo**t**i**ll**a	Note the single -t- and double -ll-
fo**r**est	Note the single -r-
formul**ai**c	Note -a- before -i-
foss**il**	Note the ending: -il
fu**chs**ia	Note the -s- comes after the -ch-, not before
fue**ll**ed	Note the double -ll-

G

gadfly, nuisance

gadfly *noun*, is a bloodsucking fly that attacks and feeds on the blood of cattle and horses, causing them distress. By extension, the word is applied to a person who (usually deliberately) makes provocative comments about people and events in order to obtain a reaction: *Socrates (470–399 BC) was Plato's teacher and the gadfly of Athenian society*.

nuisance *noun*, means something that is objectionable or harmful, such as an uncontrolled rubbish heap, but that can be removed by legal means: *The opencast mining operation has been declared a public nuisance*. A person who is a **nuisance** annoys other people by their persistence in one sort of behaviour or by being in the way: *That child is always a nuisance in the supermarket*.

Gaelic, *Gallic*, French

Gaelic gállik /'gælɪk/ (referring to Scotland) gáylik /'geɪlɪk/ (referring to Ireland), *adjective & noun*, today refers to the Celtic languages: *The word 'whisky' comes from the Gaelic 'uisge beatha' – water of life*.

Gallic *adjective*, refers to something that is considered characteristic of France or the *French*, such as *Gallic humour* or *Gallic behaviour*: *Before long, the famous pouting Gallic shrug may be but a fond memory*.

French *adjective & noun*. As an adjective, this refers to the customs, language and nationality of France. It is used in general contexts such as *French wine* or *French law*. As a noun *the French* means **French** people as a whole, and this form is preferred to the sexist term *Frenchmen*. See NICKNAMES.

gale

See STORM.

gambit

See SACRIFICE.

gamble, gambol

gamble *verb & noun*. As a verb, this means to play games of chance for money. The expression *gamble on* is used for bets and more figurative uses: *He had no money and gambled on being treated to lunch*. As a noun, this means an action that involves risk: *He took a gamble on the train's punctuality, and had another cup of coffee*.

gambol *verb*, means to leap or jump about playfully: *He gambolled about the room with glee*. Note that in AE this has a single 'l' in the past tense and present participle.

Lambs gambling in the fields.

gaol

See JAIL.

gape

See GASP.

garage sale

See CAR BOOT SALE.

garbanzo

See CHICKPEA.

garment

See CLOTHES.

garrulous

See GRANDILOQUENT.

gas, gasoline

See PETROL.

gasp, gape, yawn

gasp *verb & noun*. As a verb, this means to take in a breath rapidly and audibly as a sign of pain or astonishment: *The astonishing question, asked in an ordinary conversational tone, made her gasp*. As a noun, **gasp** is the rapid and audible intake of breath: *She gave a little gasp of surprise*.

gape *verb & noun*. As a verb, this means to stare with open mouth from amazement: *Victorian cities caused our ancestors to gape with awe, admiration or horror*. As a noun, **gape** is a technical term for the widely open mouth of a young bird demanding food from its parents: *A nestling's gape, or wide open beak, provides a stimulus to the parents to feed it*. More generally, it means any wide opening.

yawn *verb & noun*. As a verb, **yawn** means to open your mouth and breathe deeply, in and out, because of tiredness or boredom: *She felt desperately tired but couldn't yawn*. Figuratively, it means to be or become wide open in a frightening way, and is used especially to refer to geographical features: *They stood on the lip of the volcano, and its crater yawned beneath them*. As a noun, **yawn** describes the action of yawning: *The Home Secretary stifled a yawn*. As a noun, **yawn** cannot be used figuratively.

gate

See PLATFORM.

gay, homosexual, lesbian

gay *noun & adjective*, is the word that homosexuals now prefer to use for themselves, especially for homosexual men, and it has become the standard term in general usage. The noun form is generally used in the plural: *This is an area popular with gays*. It is now considered old-fashioned to use the adjective form to mean bright, carefree and happy, but where it means homosexual, it appears in phrases such as *the gay community*, and *a gay bar*.

homosexual *noun & adjective*, refers to both male and female homosexuals, but especially to men. Negative terms for **homosexual** are to be avoided, even if they are used among homosexuals themselves. This term is itself often avoided by using the phrase *lesbians and gay men/gays*. See HOMO-, QUEER.

lesbian *noun & adjective*, refers to female *homosexuals* only: *Lesbian and gay speakers played an important part in the debate*.

geezer

See GEYZER.

gender

See SEX.

genial, congenial

genial *adjective*, means good-tempered or friendly: *I thoroughly enjoyed meeting Stephen. He was an extremely genial host*. This is a formal word.

congenial *adjective*, means pleasant, and is used either to refer to people who share your interests, character and outlook on life: *We enjoyed the congenial company of the locals in that taverna*; or to an environment that makes people feel relaxed and comfortable: *He found the office routine congenial and very professional*. Less formal alternatives to **congenial** are pleasant and friendly.

genitive forms

See GRAMMAR TIPS.

genius, genus

genius *noun*, means in one sense a person who has exceptional talent in an activity or who is highly intelligent: *Salvador Dalí was a genius at self-promotion*. *Geniuses* is the plural of **genius**. See INGENIOUS. In another sense it is the name given to a supernatural spirit in folklore, and has given rise to the more commonly used word *genie* found in the Arabian folk stories: *The genie of the lamp*. The plural of **genius** in this sense is both *genii* and *genies*.

genus jénnŭss, jéenŭss /ˈdʒenəs, ˈdʒiːnəs/ *noun*, is a term used in biology for a group of species that share certain characteristics: *Most ducks belonging to the genus Anas will hybridize in captivity*. The plural is *genera*, pronounced jénnĕră /ˈdʒenərə/.

> Note that the first syllable of *genius* rhymes with 'mean', while the first syllable of *genus* may rhyme with either 'men' or 'mean', but the first syllable of *genera* always rhymes with 'men'.

gentleman

See MAN.

gentleman's agreement

See AGREEMENT.

genuine

See AUTHENTIC.

geometrical progression

See ARITHMETICAL PROGRESSION.

German, Germanic, germane

German *noun & adjective*, means a native or national of Germany: *His two favourite slogans were 'I'm proud to be a German' and 'We want to stay German.'*

Germanic *adjective*, means associated with Germany, or its people, ancient or modern: *This book mainly concerns the Germanic tribes that overthrew the Roman Empire*. German, English, Dutch and Danish are part of the modern **Germanic** language family.

germane jĕrmáyn /dʒər'meɪn/ *adjective*, means relevant. This is a very formal word and often relevant or appropriate may be a better choice: *The articles which are germane to the subject being discussed here are Nos 10 and 11*. Note that the second syllable is stressed.

German measles

See MEASLES.

gesticulate, gesture

gesticulate *verb*, means to make signals with the arms: *He broke off to gesticulate hopelessly with his hands, expressing final despair*. The related noun is *gesticulation*.

gesture *verb & noun*. As a verb, **gesture** means to move the hands or head as a signal: *Bernice could see him raise a bulky suited arm and gesture grandly at the surroundings*. As a noun, it means a movement of the hand or head made in order to express meaning: *'Stop!' she wailed, covering her ears in a childlike gesture*. It is also an action performed in order to express a feeling: *Our train journey was a gesture of support for the railways*.

get, got, gotten

get *verb*, in a basic sense means to receive. However, it has a broad range of meanings, including become, come, experience, go, obtain, receive, succeed, suffer and understand. **Get** is one of the five most frequently used verbs, and is part of many phrasal verbs. It is best to find alternatives in formal English. Compare the informal: *I get your message* with the more formal: *I understand what you mean*.

got *verb*, is the past participle in BE, and the past tense form in both BE and AE of *get*. As a result, **got** has the same range of meanings as *get*: *The impression I got was that they were all coming to dinner*, and should also be avoided in formal English. Note that in addition, **got** is often used with the simple present form of have, in BE. The sentence *I've got a lovely bunch of coconuts* means possessing rather than receiving the coconuts. However, *I've got a new car* means that I've just bought it.

gotten *verb*, is the past participle of *get* in spoken AE, and has the same range of meanings: *He's just gotten a new pick-up*, means he has just acquired it. Possession is indicated by using the verb *have* without *got* or **gotten**: *He has a new pick-up*. Standard written AE uses *got* in this sense: *He got a new car as part of the job package*.

geyser, geezer

geyser *noun*, is a natural hot spring as well as a type of gas-fired water heater.

geezer *noun*, is slang for a man. This often indicates negative or strange characteristics.

> In BE, *geyser* and *geezer* may be pronounced the same, géezĕr /'giːzər/. In AE, and in New Zealand, *geyser* is pronounced gīzĕr /'gaɪzər/.

gibe

See JIBE.

gild, guild

gild *verb*, means to cover with gold. The idiom 'to gild the lily' refers to wasteful actions such as making something that is golden even more golden and spoiling it in the process.

guild *noun,* means an association of people with similar interests or work: *The Ladies' Guild will hold a jumble sale on Tuesday evening*. Historically it is an association of merchants or skilled workers.

gilt, guilt

gilt *uncountable noun & adjective*. As a noun, this means a thin layer of gold. As an adjective, it means covered with gold, and is commonly used in phrases like *gilt-edged securities* which means safe investments. It is related to the verb *gild*.

guilt *noun,* means the fact of having committed a crime or the feeling of having done something wrong which is not necessarily a crime: *He had guilt written all over his face*.

ginger

See HAIR COLOUR.

Gipsy

See GYPSY.

girlfriend

See BOYFRIEND

girlish, girlie, girly

See BOYISH.

given name

See FIRST NAME.

glutton

See GOURMET.

gluttonous, glutinous

gluttonous glúttŏnŭss /ˈglʌtənəs/ *adjective,* means very greedy: *My gluttonous partner went for the chef's selection which featured tasty samples of many delicious desserts*. Note that the first syllable is pronounced like the word 'glut'. See VORACIOUS (VOCIFEROUS).

glutinous glóotinŭss /ˈgluːtɪnəs/ *adjective,* means sticky, like glue: *Glutinous rice is sweet and its sticky texture makes it easy to mould*. Note that the first syllable is pronounced like the word 'glue'.

goal

See AIM.

golden handshake, golden handcuffs, golden hello, golden parachute

golden handshake *noun,* is a large sum of money, shares or other benefits given by a company to an employee leaving the company in return for his or her contribution to its success. It is sometimes given to encourage unwanted employees to resign.

golden handcuffs *noun,* is a large sum of money or other benefits given to an employee to encourage him or her to remain with the company rather than work for another company. This is an informal term.

golden hello *noun,* is a large sum of money or other benefits given by a company to a new employee who has just joined that company. This is an informal term.

golden parachute *noun,* is a long-term arrangement where a company guarantees the financial security of senior employees who are forced to resign, or are dismissed as a result of company reorganization or mergers. This is an informal term.

goodbye, good day

goodbye *exclamation & noun,* is used to express good wishes when parting. This is the BE spelling, and the plural is *goodbyes*: *The drinks party was evaporating slowly as guests said their goodbyes*.

good day *exclamation,* is an informal everyday greeting in AE that is used especially on radio and TV. In BE, this expression is a formal and old-fashioned way to say *hello* or *goodbye*.

goods

See FREIGHT.

gorilla, guerrilla

gorilla *noun,* is a large African ape (*Gorilla gorilla*). In slang, it means a heavily built person, a thug or bodyguard. In this sense it is not a compliment.

guerrilla *noun*, is a member of an independent force fighting against an official army. It may also be spelt *guerilla*: *Many guerrilla movements term themselves freedom fighters*.

gossip

See **RUMOUR**.

got, gotten

See **GET**.

gourmet, gourmand, glutton

gourmet go͝ormay /ˈgʊəmeɪ/ *noun*, is a connoisseur of good food and drink. This is a complimentary word: *Even the most demanding gourmet will be well satisfied with the quality of the food in Sardinia*. Note that the second syllable rhymes with 'bay'.

gourmand go͝ormănd /ˈgʊəmənd/ *noun*, is someone who enjoys eating large amounts of food. It usually expresses disapproval. However, use this word with care, as the original French meaning of **gourmand** is a lover of good food and drink, and sometimes it is used in this way in English too: *He comes across as wonderfully French – a gourmand and an aesthete, an admirer of female beauty*.

glutton *noun*, is someone who eats too much, and is the least complimentary of these three words. However, figuratively, this word is used in a complimentary sense in the phrase *a glutton for punishment*, meaning someone who enjoys taking on difficult tasks.

government, administration

government *noun*. In Britain, the **government** consists of the Prime Minister and other ministers. It may also include MPs and members of the House of Lords who belong to the governing party but hold no office, but does not include the Civil Service, which serves successive *governments*. **Government** is capitalized when it refers to that of a particular Prime Minister or party: *The Blair Government lasted for 10 years*. In the USA, the **government** is usually referred to as the *administration*.

administration *noun*. In politics, this is the nearest American equivalent to the British term *government*, but the *US administration* includes the President of the Republic and elected officials down to the town mayor and town council: *The first and second Bush Administrations*. Outside of politics in BE, **administration** means the managing of a business or process: *The day-to-day administration of the scheme was placed in the hands of organizations already experienced in such work*.

governor, governess

governor *noun*, is a person responsible for the executive control of a geographical territory, such as a state in the USA. When used as a title with a name, this is capitalized: *Governor Mario Cuomo of New York announced his intention to run for a third term*. In BE, **governor** refers to a person in charge of an institution such as a prison or the Bank of England, or a member of a team responsible for running an organization, such as a school: *Although Geoffrey's mother is a school governor she says her son wrote the letter*. A **governor** may be either male or female. In very informal BE, **governor** means the person in charge, usually an employer. This is only used in spoken BE, but in reported dialogue it is often spelt *guv'nor*: *Lenny's the man they call the Guv'nor*. This is sometimes shortened to 'guv' when used as a term of address.

governess *noun*, is a woman employed privately to teach the children of a family, living in their home. This is now mainly a historical term. See **SEXIST LANGUAGE (WRITING SKILLS)**.

gracious, graceful

gracious *adjective*, is often reserved for polite behaviour by the rich and influential that involves kind and generous actions: *The publisher paid £2,000 in compensation as a gracious gesture*. An elegant and comfortable lifestyle is often called *gracious living*.

graceful *adjective*, is used to describe elegant physical movement: *She struggled to find a graceful, even a comfortable, way of carrying her cello*.

grade

See **MARK**.

graduate

See **STUDENT**.

Graeco-

See **GREEK**.

graffiti, writing on the wall

graffiti *uncountable noun*, means the slogans and pictures sprayed, scratched or written on walls, trains, etc. It is a term of disapproval, associated with vandalism, and would not be applied to official notices or advertisements. Originally the word referred to the messages scratched on the walls of what are now classical ruins, such as in Pompeii. Although it is the plural form of the original Italian word, **graffiti** is an uncountable noun and takes a singular verb: *The shelter was covered in graffiti and all its glass had been shattered.*

writing on the wall *noun phrase*, describes a situation when something is likely to fail or become problematical, but is not connected with *graffiti*: *Those miners who saw the writing on the wall started to leave in droves.*

grandiloquent, garrulous, eloquent, loquacious

grandiloquent grandíllŏkwĕnt /græn'dɪləkwənt/ *adjective*, describes speech that uses high-flown or bombastic language: *He sounded a grandiloquent note: 'Who is the master, the logic or I?'*

garrulous gárrŭlŭss /'gærələs/ *adjective*, means talkative, but not necessarily to the point, and perhaps indiscreet: *She learned more from his silences than others did when he was extremely garrulous.*

eloquent éllŏkwĕnt /'eləkwənt/ *adjective*, describes opinions expressed well and persuasively: *The town planner made an eloquent plea for the clear separation of urban and rural.* Used figuratively, **eloquent** describes actions that are meaningful: *He set his teeth and said nothing, but his eyes were eloquent.*

loquacious lŏkwáyshŭss /lə'kweɪʃəs/ *adjective*, describes someone who likes to talk a lot: *Anderson is not consistently loquacious, but he does produce occasionally lengthy utterances.* This is a formal word.

> Apart from *eloquent*, the other words normally imply criticism where *grandiloquent* is the most negative and *loquacious* is the least negative.

grandstand

See **STAND**.

grant

See **SCHOLARSHIP**.

grateful

See **THANKFUL**.

grave

See **SERIOUS**.

gravy, sauce

gravy *noun*, means a thick liquid made from the fat and other juices of meat. In informal AE, **gravy** means money. *The gravy train* means a way to earn money easily. However, the *gravy boat* is just a jug used for serving **gravy** during a meal.

sauce *noun*, means a thick liquid added to food to give moisture or flavour: *This is a classic sauce to serve with fish.*

Great Britain

See **BRITAIN**.

great-grandfather, great grandfather

great-grandfather *noun*, is a direct male ancestor three generations back. Everyone has four *great-grandfathers*. The word *great* used in this way indicates an increase in the number of generations between members of a family. Thus, a *great-uncle* is one generation further away than an uncle. An alternative term for this is *grand-uncle*. *Great* cannot be used for relationships within the nuclear family, such as mother, son or sister. Note that the stress is on 'grand', and that *great* is always connected to the following word by a hyphen.

great grandfather *noun phrase*, means an excellent grandfather who is adored by his grandchildren (they think he is 'great'). Here there is no hyphen and there is stress on *great* as well as *grand*.

> The distinction between these terms applies to other such words including: *great grandmother, great grandson, great aunt.*

Greek, Grecian, Graeco-

Greek *noun & adjective*, means a native or national of Greece or its language or culture: *Greek civilization not only gave rise to philosophy but also produced, in the fifth century* BC, *the first real historians*. The expression *all Greek to me* refers to something that is incomprehensible: *Well, it's all Greek to me, but as long as it keeps him happy. . . .*

Grecian *adjective*, refers to ancient Greece, particularly its architecture and pottery: *Flora wore gold earrings shaped like Grecian urns*.

Graeco- *prefix*, is used in adjectives such as *Graeco-Roman*: *The Corinthian capitals are of Graeco-Roman design*. This is also written without the 'a': *Greco-*. It is pronounced grē´kō- /ˈgriːkəʊ-/.

> *The quality of translations into official EU languages was being discussed and a Greek representative told the European Commission: 'I should not say this, but this translation into my language, is all Greek to me.'*

Green Card

See **RESIDENCY**.

Green Paper

See **WHITE PAPER**.

grey

See **HAIR COLOUR**.

grill, grille, grilling, broil, roasting

grill *verb & noun*. As a verb, this means to cook food under a very strong heat. **Grill** is also used figuratively to mean question someone closely: *A scrawny nationalist tried to grill him about Scottish independence*. As a noun, it is the part of a cooker that is used for grilling.

grille *noun*, is a perforated cover or screen made of metal, used for protection: *The moonlight penetrated the iron grille and made silver stripes across the floor*. This may also be spelt *grill*.

grilling *noun*, means both cooking food in an oven and figuratively confronting someone with a lot of difficult questions: *The Democrat was given a grilling on that talk show last night*.

broil *verb*, is the usual AE term for the BE *grill* in the sense of cooking.

roasting *noun*, is used informally in BE to tell someone in no uncertain terms that you strongly criticize their behaviour: *The manager got a roasting from the fans after the row of defeats and submitted his resignation*. See **ROAST**.

G

grizzly, grisly

grizzly *adjective & noun*. As an adjective this means grey-haired. As a noun it is a short form for *grizzly bear*, a large American bear.

grisly *adjective*, means terrible and frightening: *He met a grisly end by being stabbed to death in a park*. This usually occurs before a noun.

groin, groyne

groin *noun*, is the area between the thigh and where the legs join the front of the body: *The Tyneside star has recovered from a groin injury*. In architecture, it is where two intersecting vaults meet.

groyne *noun*, is a wall built from the shore into the sea for the protection of the shore: *There was considerable erosion on the coast due to the decay of the groyne system*. In AE, this is spelt *groin*.

ground, floor, *storey, story*

ground *noun*, means the natural surface found out of doors: *Below these slopes there are more vineyards planted on flatter ground*. See **GROUND (EARTH), GROUNDS (CAMPUS) GROUNDS (REASON)**.

floor *noun*, means a man-made surface, usually indoors: *He reached down to the floor and folded back the carpet*. Out of doors, **floor** is used only in certain phrases: *forest floor, sea floor, valley floor, cave floor*. **Floor** is also a single level inside a building indicating the activity that takes place there or its use: *Children's wear is on the second floor*. In BE, buildings traditionally have a *ground floor* at ground level, and continue with the first, second, etc. above it. In the American system of numbering, the ground level of a building is the *first floor*, and those above it the second, third, etc. There are signs that the American system is starting to be used in high buildings all over the world.

storey *noun*, is also a single level inside a building but **storey** is used in more structural contexts than *floor*: *The kitchen occupied the lower storey of the dwelling*. **Storey** is the BE spelling and the plural is *storeys*.

story is the AE spelling of *storey*. The AE plural form is spelt *stories*. See **RUMOUR**.

group, holding company, subsidiary, parent company, sister company

group *noun*, means a large industrial enterprise usually comprising a parent company and several subsidiary companies. See **BUSINESS (COMPANY)**.

holding company, *noun phrase*, is a company that controls the shares of other companies, but does not necessarily carry out any business of its own: *The Group Accounts comprise the consolidated accounts of the holding company and all its subsidiaries*.

subsidiary *noun*, means a company that forms part of a group: *RAFA Ads Ltd is a subsidiary company of the Royal Air Forces Association*.

parent company *compound noun*, means the main core company in a group as opposed to the ones that are acquired as the group expands, which are the subsidiary companies.

sister company *compound noun*, means one of the subsidiary companies owned by the same group: *Your holiday flight is planned to be on an aircraft operated by our sister company*.

groupie, hanger-on, stalker

groupie *noun*, is a young person, frequently a young woman, who follows the activities of popular figures such as pop musicians, to try to get to know them: *The groupies had planned numerous tricks to seduce the lead singer*. This is an informal term.

hanger-on *noun*, is a person who associates with others in order to gain benefit: *The Royals and all their hangers-on are often ridiculed in the Press*. The plural form is *hangers-on*. See **HANGER (HANGAR)**.

stalker *noun*, is a person who persistently and obsessively follows someone, giving them unwanted attention, and causing irritation or fear: *A stalker who made threats to a female tennis ace has been arrested*. This is a negative term, with sinister overtones. In another context, a **stalker** is a hunter who follows and tracks animals: *A good stalker only singles out weak animals from a herd*.

group names

The names for people, animals or things in a group have developed in various ways and the following list is just a selection of some common ones:

actors:	*company* or *troupe*
aeroplanes:	*flight* or *squadron*
angels:	*host*
bees:	*hive* or *swarm*
bells:	*peal*
birds:	*flock*
cards:	*pack* or (mainly AE) *deck*
cars:	*fleet*
cattle:	*herd* or *drove*
chickens:	*brood*
concerts:	*series*
cubs:	*litter*
dancers:	*troupe*
deer:	*herd*
dogs:	*kennel* or *pack*
elephants:	*herd*
elk:	*herd*
flies:	*cloud*
flowers:	*bunch* or *bouquet*
fish:	*shoal*
geese:	*gaggle*
goats:	*flock* or *herd*
grapes:	*bunch* or *cluster*
insects:	*flight* or *swarm*
keys:	*bunch*
lions:	*pride*
loaves:	*batch*

monkeys:	*troop*
mosquitoes:	*swarm* or *cloud*
oxen:	*yoke, drove, team,* or *herd*
people:	*audience* (in cinema, concert, theatre), *spectators* (onlookers), *crowd*
pigs:	*herd*
porpoises:	*school*
pups:	*litter*
racehorses:	*string*
sheep:	*flock*
ships:	*fleet* or *squadron* (naval vessels)
stars:	*cluster* or *constellation*
steps:	*flight*
thieves:	*gang*
whales:	*school*
wolves:	*pack*
worshippers:	*congregation*

growing pains

See **TEETHING TROUBLES**.

groyne

See **GROIN**.

guarantee, warranty, guarantor

guarantee *noun & verb*. As a noun, this means a formal, usually written, promise to meet certain conditions: *30-day money back guarantee*. As a verb, **guarantee** means to promise that something will occur: *Money cannot guarantee success in an aerobatic championship*.

warranty *noun*, means a legal written binding guarantee from a company to repair or replace the parts of an object they have supplied: *Three-year manufacturer's warranty*. The phrase *under warranty* refers to the duration of this period: *Under warranty I have had two replacement gearboxes, and a clutch assembly*.

guarantor *noun*, means someone who gives a guarantee to do something, often to be responsible for paying another person's debts: *The mortgage made me personally liable, as guarantor, to pay the £100,000*. An organization can also be a **guarantor**.

guardian, custodian

guardian *noun*, means either a person who guards something: *In Latin mythology, Juno was the guardian of the home*; or one who has the charge of looking after someone else's interests, for instance the interests of a child that has lost its parents, or someone who is absent: *The court must appoint a guardian for the orphaned child*.

custodian *noun*, means a person who is in charge of protecting a building or collection of objects: *He is the custodian of the shrines at which offerings are made to the ancestors*.

G

guerilla

See **GORILLA**.

guild

See **GILD**.

guilt

See **GILT**.

guise

See **DISGUISE**.

guy

See **MATE**.

gybe

See **JIBE**.

Gypsy, Gipsy, Romany

Gypsy *noun*, means a race of travelling people who do seasonal work. Many gypsies prefer to be called *Romany* instead.

Gipsy *noun*, is a variant spelling of *Gypsy*.

Romany *noun*, means a race of originally travelling people who are also known as the *Gypsy people*. The plural is *Romanies*. As an uncountable noun this is the language of the **Romany** people. Alternative spellings are *Roma* for the people and *Romani* for the language.

Spelling

gangr**ene**	Note this ends in -ene, not -een
g**ao**l	Note that when it means 'jail', the -o- follows the -a-
g**au**ge	Note that the -u- follows the -a-
g**au**ze	Note that the -u- follows the -a-
ga**z**e**ll**e	Note the single -z- and double -ll-
ga**z**e**tt**e	Note the single -z- and double -tt-
gene**a**logy	Note this ends in -alogy, not -ology
gi**r**a**ff**e	Note the single -r- and double -ff-
glam**or**ous	Note there is no 'u' before the -r-
gorg**e**ous	Do not forget the -e- following the -g-
gra**ff**i**t**i	Remember the double -ff- but single -t-
gramm**a**r	Note this end in -ar, not -er
gr**ate**ful	Note -ate-, not -eat-
gr**ea**ter	Remember the first -e-

habit, habits, habitat

habit *noun*, means a custom, or form of repeated behaviour: *He had the disconcerting habit of using my name as if he were addressing a butler*. It is also used as a polite word for addiction: *A drug addict will do anything to feed his habit*. A **habit** may also be a sort of uniform dress, particularly in the past a woman's *riding habit* or the robe worn by monks and nuns: *The door was opened by a maid whose uniform was as severe and stiff as the habit of a nun*. In biology, a plant's habit is the typical way in which it grows: *Arrange one or two suitable shrubs that grow with a relaxed, arching habit*.

habits *plural noun*, means customary behaviour in general, rather than a single feature: *In more recent years our dietary habits have changed*.

habitat *noun*, means the usual living area of any creature: *The most significant cause of decline in upland bird species in the UK is the removal of moorland habitat*.

habitable, inhabitable, uninhabitable

habitable *adjective*, means fit for living in: *Experience suggests that following the floods some properties may not be habitable for many months*. Note that this word usually refers to housing. *Unhabitable* is not used today to express the opposite of **habitable**. Use *not habitable*, or *uninhabitable* instead.

inhabitable *adjective*, despite the apparently negative prefix, refers to a place or geographical area that is suitable for living in: *'Inhabitable Earth' is a blog about the effects of climate change*. Note that this word usually refers to larger places than housing.

uninhabitable *adjective*, refers to either housing or a place that cannot be lived in: *The insurance policies will cover the cost of alternative accommodation if your property becomes uninhabitable*.

hail

See RAIN.

hair colour

Many words are used to describe the colour of someone's hair, but only two: *blond* (or *blonde*) and *brunette* (or *brunet* in AE) are used as nouns. Two other compound nouns include a reference to hair colour: *redhead*, and *carrot-top*, although the latter is either facetious or uncomplimentary.

blond(e) *adjective*, refers to a fair-haired person: *He is a blond youth*. Some people distinguish between *blond* for males and *blonde* for females. Both spellings are correct. **Blond** is also used to describe the light brownish colour of wood: *Do you have this in blond oak?*

blonde *noun*, means a fair-haired woman: *He's over there talking to the blonde*. However, this may be regarded as a negative stereotype and can be replaced by *blond* or *fair* as adjectives.

brown *adjective*, is used for both males and females to describe hair which is dark but not black: *He had a magnificent mane of chestnut brown hair*. But as it is the commonest descriptive term for hair, it is the least useful in distinguishing one person from another.

brunette *noun*, is used to describe a woman with dark brown hair: *Before she dyed her hair she was a brunette*. Although not considered as unfavourably as the noun *blonde*, many people prefer to use the adjective phrases *with dark hair* or *dark-haired*. An alternative AE spelling is *brunet*.

fair *adjective*, is often used not only for pale brown or yellowish hair, but also for darker shades of hair if a person's eyes are blue, or pale.

auburn *adjective*, refers to a reddish-brown hair colour.

mousy *adjective*, is an uncomplimentary term for hair that is mid-brown – it covers shades of hair that are neither truly *blonde* nor truly *brunette*.

black *adjective*, is used not only for hair that is intensely black, but also for extremely dark brown hair.

ginger *adjective*, is the description used for reddish or rust-coloured hair. Someone with very bright ginger hair might be described as a redhead or carrot-top (though the latter is facetious or uncomplimentary).

As we age, our hair begins to lose its colour.

grey *adjective*, describes dull silvery hair. Many people associate grey hair colour with general ageing, and the beginnings of old age. However, the *grey pound*, referring to the growing economic power of older people, does not have the negative connotation.

white *adjective*, usually in the compound *white-haired*, is a more positive term for older people.

silver *adjective*, makes a person sound dynamic and elegant, and occurs in the phrase *silver surfer* meaning a retired person who is adept at using the Internet.

hairpin, hairgrip, kirby-grip, bobby pin

hairpin *noun*, is a U-shaped pin that is used to hold long hair in place.

hairgrip *noun*, is a flat hairpin with a spring. This is the BE term.

kirby-grip *noun*, is an alternative name for a sprung hairgrip in BE. This is also spelt *Kirbigrip* (trademarked name).

bobby pin *noun*, is the AE term for a hairpin.

half, halve

half *noun*, means one part of something that has been divided into two. In telling the time, *half past* means 30 minutes after the hour. In AE, the equivalent is *half after two*, etc. Informally, this may be shortened to *half two, half three*, etc. However, note that this short form may confuse Germans, Dutch or Scandinavians, as in all their languages, 'half two' means half past one. A thing that is divided is cut *in half*, whereas several things that are divided are cut into *halves*. See -F, -FE ENDINGS IN NOUNS (WORD FORMATION).

halve *verb*, means either to divide into two equal parts: *Halve the melons and scoop out the seeds*; or to reduce by half: *Giving up smoking after a coronary attack can halve the chance of a recurrence*.

half board

See BOARD.

half-brother, half-sister

See SIBLING.

hall

See ROOM.

halogen

See XENON.

halve

See HALF.

hand

See SIDE.

handicapped

See DISABLED.

handicraft, handiwork, handwork

handicraft *noun*, means work that needs both manual skill and artistic ability, such as sewing, toy-making or fretwork.

handiwork *uncountable noun*, means the products of crafts such as dressmaking and knitting. It also refers to work by a specific person that is considered poor: *These drawings look like the handiwork of a drugged artist*. Although men who do practical jobs are called handymen, the spelling here is **handiwork**.

handwork *noun*, means a manual work as opposed to one produced by a mechanical process: *The Constitution was always represented by conservatives as the handwork of a radical minority*.

handsome, pretty

handsome *adjective*, means good-looking when it is used to refer to a man. **Handsome** can also be used to refer to the appearance of a woman who is attractive with strong, dignified features rather than small, delicate ones. Things such as buildings can be **handsome**. It also means generous: *He received a handsome reward for returning the stolen painting*.

pretty *adjective & adverb*. As an adjective, **pretty** means good-looking and is used to describe babies, young children and girls. When **pretty** is used to describe a woman it suggests someone with small, delicate features. As an adverb, this means to some extent, or almost: *I'll be monitoring her blood-sugar level pretty frequently*. The British love of understatement means that **pretty** is also used to mean very: *You must move pretty fast, though, to avoid the bombs*. This is an informal word, and mostly found in spoken English. See RATHER.

> Care must be taken when combining **pretty** with other adjectives before a noun: *A pretty deaf young woman* may be a good-looking young woman who is deaf, or a young woman who is quite seriously deaf.

hangar, hanger

hangar *noun*, is a large structure for housing aircraft: *An aircraft was in the hangar undergoing engine cylinder pressure checks*.

hanger *noun*, either means something to hang clothes on or a person that hangs things: *He is an expert curtain hanger*. *Hanger-on* is a disapproving term for a fan, follower or groupie. See HANGER-ON (GROUPIE).

hanged, hung

hanged *verb*, is the past tense and past participle of the verb *hang* when it means to kill someone by suspending them from a rope around their neck: *A refugee hanged himself while in detention in Pentonville Prison*.

hung *verb & adjective*, is the past tense and past participle of the verb *hang* in all its other senses. Washing, wallpaper, a door or a painting can all be **hung**, and it can refer to something that droops: *Unable to look into his eyes, she hung her head, whispering, 'I thought I'd never see you again.' Hung* is also the past tense used when we refer to something that remains motionless in the air: *Half a dozen girls sauntered past, and their perfume hung in the still air*. As an adjective, **hung** is used to describe a parliament that has no party with an overall majority, or a jury that cannot reach a verdict.

happening

See EPISODE.

harass

See EMBARRASS.

harbour, harbor

See PORT.

hard

See STRICT.

hardly

See BARELY.

hardship

See DISTRESS.

harmonious, harmonic, harmonize

harmonious *adjective*, as a musical term refers to sounds that are pleasant to listen to when they are combined: *The harmonious sound of the choir drifted out of the church*. By extension, **harmonious** has gained the general meaning of forming a pleasant whole: *Street frontages that were once elegant and harmonious have become ragged and disjointed*. It is also used in this sense when speaking of relationships between people or groups of people, living peacefully together: *Tradition was no guarantee of harmonious relationships in three-generation households*.

harmonic *adjective & noun*. As an adjective, this refers to musical harmony: *His guitar music has just enough harmonic instability to keep the ears alert*. As a noun, a **harmonic** is a component of a sound wave, measured as a multiple of the fundamental frequency.

harmonize verb, means either to combine musical notes to produce chords: *Write a melody first, then harmonize it later*; or to create visually pleasing designs: *No style of building will harmonize so quickly and completely with its surroundings as half-timbering*. In a figurative sense, **harmonize** means to bring about consistency: *The need to harmonize national laws was bound to be frustrated by the Treaty's need for unanimity among all member states*.

harsh

See STRICT.

haughty

See **IMPERIOUS**.

have to

See **SHOULD**.

he, she, they

He (and its 'family' of words) is the regular masculine singular personal pronoun: ***He** looked up; John spoke to **him**; That is **his** book; No, it's **his**; Peter looked at **himself** in the mirror*.

She (and its 'family' of words) is the regular feminine singular personal pronoun: ***She** looked up; John spoke to **her**; That is **her** book; No, it's **hers**; Jane looked at **herself***.

They (and its 'family' of words) is the regular plural personal pronoun: ***They** looked up; John spoke to **them**; That is **their** book; No it's **theirs**; They looked at **themselves***.

If one person is being referred to, and that person's sex is either unknown or irrelevant, several solutions have been suggested:

He or she is good enough if it is only needed once, but becomes heavy if used again and again.

S/he and **(s)he** have been proposed, and may be acceptable in formal contexts such as job adverts: *Wanted: experienced librarian. S/he will be responsible for the Reference Section*; or Internet blogs: *if a doctor recommends a drug, so long as (s)he has followed the principles of prescribing ethically* . . . This causes problems in speech: how should it be pronounced?

They is preferred by most people in speech and informal written contexts: *'I'll put you through to someone who can help you as soon as they're free'*, and this is the form that is used in this book. It is often argued that this must be wrong as **they** is plural. However, examples of **they** being used like this have been found as early as the sixteenth century, and it is recommended by modern BE dictionaries.

See **SEXIST LANGUAGE (WRITING SKILLS), THEY, THEM AND THEIR FOR SINGULAR NOUNS**.

head of state, head of government

head of state *noun*, is the highest official of a country, and is often considered to embody the state. This may be a monarch in a system with hereditary titles, such as the United Kingdom or Luxembourg, or a president in a republic, such as the USA or Germany. In constitutional monarchies and some republican systems, the head of state carries out mostly formal duties, leaving the everyday management of the country's affairs to a prime minister. The plural is *heads of state*.

head of government *noun*, is the person who leads a country. The same person may also be the head of state, as is the case in the USA and France, or may be officially appointed by the head of state following an election, as happens in the United Kingdom and Germany.

The European Union Heads of State and Government meetings are attended mostly by the heads of government, not the heads of state.

heartfelt

See **FULSOME**.

Hebrew

See **ISRAELI**.

height, altitude

height *noun*, indicates a measurement of vertical distance: *The knees must come up as fast as possible to waist height*. **Height** can be used figuratively to refer to an extreme: *The modern historian can use works of reference written while respect for accurate learning was at its height*.

altitude *noun*, means the *height* of an object in relation to sea level: *The land undulates between 200 and 250 feet above sea level, except in the south-east where the altitude nears 300 feet*. The phrase *at altitude* means at a great height above sea level: *At altitude, sunburn can seriously damage your skin*. Note that **altitude** is not used figuratively.

heighten, intensify

heighten *verb*, means to make a feeling stronger: *On a beautiful summer evening we can heighten our awareness of the things around us*.

intensify *verb*, means to increase in strength or degree: *Over the next six months you can intensify your exercise programme to suit your fitness level.*

> Note that *heighten* is more restricted in its use than *intensify* which can usually replace *heighten*, but the opposite is not true. Only things experienced by the brain such as tension or awareness may be *heightened*, but both physical effort and emotions can be *intensified*.

heir, successor, *descendant*, *descendent*

heir *noun*, means a person legally entitled to the estate of another upon the latter's death: *The French recognized him as heir to their throne by a treaty of May 1420.* An **heir** does not have to be related by blood. The *heir apparent* is someone with the legal right to inherit someone's property and who cannot lose this right due to the birth of someone with a stronger claim. An *heir presumptive* is an heir who can lose his or her right to inherit someone's property following the birth of someone with a stronger claim.

successor *noun*, means a person who comes after someone else and takes their place: *Now, with the new movie under his belt, he is proving to be a worthy successor to his father in the business.*

descendant *noun*, means a plant, animal or person that is directly descended from another, such as offspring: *Flyleaf of a 1599 Bible perhaps inscribed by her husband to Shakespeare's last direct descendant.*

descendent *adjective*, means going down or descending. This is a rare word.

hemi-

See SEMI-.

heredity, heritage

See INHERITANCE.

hesitancy, hesitation

hesitancy *uncountable noun*, is a slowness or wavering in thought or action. It shows that there is some unwillingness or doubt: *He was reluctant to begin and his hesitancy made her look questioningly at him.*

hesitation *noun*, is a slowness in response to give time for thought: *When she had asked his name there had been a slight, but noticeable, hesitation before he'd answered.* It is most often used in the negative: *She had no hesitation in breaking the law.*

Hibernian

See IRISH.

hidden agenda

See AGENDA.

high, highly, tall

high *adjective & adverb*. As an adjective, this means elevated above the ground or sea level: *It has a fabulous alpine flora on the high crags.* It is also used to show the exact height of something: *Statuettes come in a range of sizes, from a delicate 600 mm in height, up to 1.8 m high.* **High** also means elevated in terms of quantity or quality: *The effluent contained a very high quantity of zinc which was killing the fish. High summer* is the warmest part of the year. As an adverb, **high** means a long way above the ground: *The plane had to soar high above the thunderstorm.* To *play high* at cards means to put down the most valuable card in a suit. The tide *runs high* when it is combined with a strong current or high waves, and feelings can also *run high* when strong emotions are expressed. Note that *high* as an adverb is usually combined with a verb.

highly *adverb*, means to a great degree: *There are highly qualified instructors on hand to advise you.* In the expressions *speak* or *think highly of*, it indicates a favourable attitude towards a person or thing: *Miss Collins spoke very highly of him, praising his prowess.*

tall *adjective*, is used to refer to the height of people, animals, and narrow objects such as plants or towers: *The tall spire was lost in 1703 but the building remains a good example of a medieval town hall.* A *tall ship* is a square-rigged sailing ship.

high school

See JUNIOR SCHOOL.

hill

See MOUNTAIN.

hinder

See AVERT.

Hinduism, Hindu, Hindi

Hinduism *uncountable noun*, is the main religion in India and Nepal.

Hindu *noun*, is a believer in *Hinduism*. It is a religious term, not a racial one, but most *Hindus* are of Indian nationality or descent.

Hindi *noun*, is one of the official languages of India. As one of the successor languages to Sanskrit, it is an Indo-European language, and is therefore related to English.

hire, rent, lease, let

hire *verb & noun*. As a verb, this means to rent specific objects for a short period: *If you haven't seen the film yet, hire the DVD*. As a noun, **hire** means the amount paid for the short-term use of an object: *As it was early in the season there were plenty of beach huts for hire*. See EMPLOY.

rent *verb & noun*. As a verb, this means to pay for the right to use an object for a specified (often long) period: *How long have they known you were going to rent a caravan?* Note that in AE, **rent** can be used for a short period, and this use is also found in BE. As a noun, this means the amount paid to the owner of a building by its tenant: *For office space this central the rent will be £20,000 a year*.

lease *verb & noun*. As a verb, this means to enter into a contract where one person uses property, land or an object such as a car belonging to another for a specified period and pays a regular rent or fee: *Councils and housing associations will be allowed to lease or buy empty homes*. As a noun, this means the contract for the use of property, a car, etc.: *Instead of the 99-year lease on the land he wanted double – 198 years*.

let *verb & noun*. As a verb, this means to rent out a property: *Other rooms are let out as studios*. As a noun, it means a property rental: *This house is available as a short-term let*. This meaning is more common in BE than in AE.

historic, historical

historic *adjective*, means important or famous, and likely to be remembered. It does not have to refer to a past event: *The elements of a historic bargain are there: our peace for their prosperity*. See -IC.

historical *adjective*, refers to people or things that existed in the past: *There is sometimes a conflict between memory and historical reality. Historical time* is often contrasted with *prehistoric time*, and **historical** is not concerned with the importance of the event described. Contrast *Marx's historic theories* (those that were very important) with *Marx's historical theories* (those about history).

> In standard modern English, the initial 'h' of *historic* and *historical* is pronounced, so the indefinite article 'a' should be used before them in both written and oral contexts. See ARTICLES (GRAMMAR TIPS).

hoard, horde

hoard *noun & verb*. As a noun, this means a treasure or hidden store of something: *A common form of deliberate burial is that of a hoard of objects, such as coins, scrap metal or jewellery*. As a verb, it means to accumulate a store of something: *I know some people who hoard tinned food for years*; often in case of an expected shortage: *In Soviet industry there was a tendency for managers to hoard labour*.

horde *noun*, means a swarm or a shapeless mass of people or animals: *He pointed in the direction of two nuns surrounded by a horde of children*. Originally a **horde** was a nomadic tribe, but once it came to mean specifically the *hordes of Genghis Khan*, it gained an underlying feeling of menace, and this negative association often remains.

> Objects may be *hoarded*, but only living creatures appear as *hordes*.

Hobson's choice

See DILEMMA.

holding company

See GROUP.

holiday

See LEAVE.

Holland

See NETHERLANDS.

hollow

See EMPTY.

home, hone

home *verb*, is used in the phrasal verb *home in on*, meaning to pinpoint or aim at: *Home in on a cause that you can do something about*. See HOUSE.

hone *verb*, means to sharpen or perfect. It is often used in the phrase *hone one's skills* where it refers to developing one's skills and performance over a period of time: *Photographers now take courses where they can hone their skills*.

Boyzone hone in on Blickling.
(BBC Norfolk website, Feb. 2008)

homely, homey

homely *adjective*. When referring to a person (usually female) this means one who is unpretentious, friendly and enjoys her home and family life. When it refers to a place or cooking, it is applied to something one feels comfortable with – just like being at home. Despite **homely** having positive associations in BE, it is a disapproving term in AE when it refers to someone who is unattractive and not good-looking: *She had a homely face, a real plain Jane*.

homey *adjective*, refers to an attractive, comfortable place or surroundings – just like being at home: *a snug, homey atmosphere*. An alternative spelling is *homy*.

homemaker

See HOUSEWIFE.

home page

See WEB PAGE.

homicide

See MURDER.

homo, homo-

homo *noun*, is a Latin word for man. It is the name of the genus to which man belongs, and so occurs in the name of our species, *Homo sapiens*. **Homo** is also found as an abbreviation for *homosexual*, but this implies a negative attitude and is best avoided. See GAY.

homo- *prefix*, is taken from the Greek word meaning 'same'. The way in which words containing it are stressed and pronounced depends on what follows in the word. *Homonym* (stressed on the first syllable) means a word spelt the same as another, but with a different meaning; *homogenized* (stressed on the second syllable) is used for milk and means that it is treated so that the cream does not separate; *homosexual* (stressed on the third syllable) means attracted to the same sex.

Both these terms are often pronounced with a long first 'o': hṓmō /'həʊməʊ/, and some people criticize this on the grounds that in both Latin and Greek the vowel is short. However, English frequently lengthens vowels when they are followed by a single consonant, so such criticism is ill-founded.

homogeneous, homogenous

homogeneous *adjective*, is a formal word used to describe a group of people or things which are of the same type: *An elected body may spring from a multicultural society or a homogeneous one*. Note that this word has five syllables and that the third one is stressed: hommŏjéeni-ŭss /hɒmə'dʒiːnɪəs/.

homogenous *adjective*, is a specialized technical term that means sharing the same structure or evolutionary origin: *Homogenous catalysis occurs when the catalyst and the reactants are in the same phase*. Note that this word has four syllables, and that the second one is stressed: hŏmójjĕnŭss /hə'mɒdʒənəs/.

In well over 90 per cent of cases, the word you need is *homogeneous*, not *homogenous*.

homograph, homonym, homophone

homograph *noun*. **Homographs** are two or more words that are spelt alike, but are pronounced differently: an example is *desert* as a verb and noun: *He was deserted in the midst of the desert*.

homonym *noun*. **Homonyms** are two or more words that are spelt and pronounced alike, but have different meanings. An example is *bank* (slope), *bank* (side of a river) and *bank* (place to deposit money). The verb *bank* has at least four meanings.

homophone *noun*. **Homophones** are two or more words that are pronounced alike, but have different spellings. Examples are *doe* and *dough*, *mail* and *male*, and *their*, *there* and *they're*. As spellcheckers will never indicate this error, it is important to select the correct word.

homosexual

See GAY.

hone

See HOME.

hopefully

See THANKFULLY.

hopeless

See FRUITLESS.

horde

See HOARD.

horizon scanning

See BLUE-SKY.

horoscopes

These are listed under the signs of the Zodiac:

Aries	21 March–19 April
Taurus	20 April–20 May
Gemini	21 May–21 June
Cancer	22 June–22 July
Leo	23 July–22 August
Virgo	23 August–22 September
Libra	23 September–23 October
Scorpio	24 October–21 November
Sagittarius	22 November–21 December
Capricorn	22 December–19 January
Aquarius	20 January–18 February
Pisces	19 February–20 March

horrid, horrible, horrifying, horrendous, horrific

horrid *adjective*, means nasty, unpleasant or unkind: *All home electronics used to be a horrid brown colour*. It is a word that is often used when addressing children.

horrible *adjective*, means dreadful and detestable. It indicates something more intense than *horrid*: *It must be horrible for them when cars crash outside their homes*. This is more commonly used in spoken than in written English.

horrifying *adjective*, means producing a reaction of horror and shock. It is stronger than *horrible*: *Co-opting the top Scottish clubs into a 'British' premier league is still a horrifying prospect to most Scots*.

horrendous and **horrific** *adjectives*, mean extremely shocking or unpleasant and unacceptable: *The journey through Turkey was horrendous*; *This horrific programme should not be seen on TV screens*.

Note that *horrid* and *horrible* should not be used in formal written English.

host, hostess

host *noun & verb*. As a noun, this means someone who entertains others at an event such as a private party: *Nico, our host, serves cool drinks and limited snacks in the bar downstairs till supper time*. A **host** can also be the presenter of a public event such as a television programme: *He is the most famous talk show host in America*. In this second sense, a **host** may be female, although *hostess* is also used. A **host** may also be an organization presenting a special event: *The Oxford Union has played host to prime ministers and American presidents*. As a verb, **host** means to present a television programme, or give a reception or other special event: *A coffee morning hosted by Mrs Andrews raised £100*.

hostess *noun*, is the female equivalent of *host* in the first sense above or may be the wife or partner of a *host* in this sense: *She smiled, like a hostess encouraging a shy dinner guest*. **Hostess** is also used sometimes for a woman who presents a public event: *The 'Generation Game' hostess joins the new BBC1 series this month as presenter*. A **hostess** is also a woman employed to entertain men in a nightclub: *Almost broke, she had worked as a hostess in a Soho club catering for Japanese businessmen*. A female member of the cabin staff on an aircraft is normally called a flight attendant or cabin attendant, not an *air hostess*. See **SEXIST LANGUAGE (WRITING SKILLS)**.

hot

See **WARM**.

hotlink

See **HYPERLINK**.

house, home, building

house howss /haʊs/ *noun* & howz /haʊz/ *verb*. As a noun, it is most usually a dwelling or a structure in which people live: *Kate describes their Victorian home as a 'scruffy, old family house'*. It is more widely used in BE than in AE where *home* is common. As a verb, it either means to provide accommodation for people: *We had to house the refugees in tents at first*; or refers to the building where something is kept or an institution is located: *The Science Centre is housed in the old bank building*. See **SEMI-DETACHED HOUSE**.

home *noun*, is the specific place where a person or family lives and feels secure: *Michael has gone home for a family Christmas to help recover from his injuries*. It can be any kind of dwelling: a flat, a tent or even a hotel, and also a person's native country: *He convinced politicians at home and abroad that he was an eminent doctor*. Estate agents tend to use **home** rather than *house*.
See **HOME (verb)**.

building *noun*, is the normal word for any sort of construction containing a roof and walls. The name of some **buildings** may contain the word *house* or *houses*, e.g. *Houses of Parliament*, but nevertheless, they should be referred to as a **building**, not as a *house* unless a speaker in the Houses of Parliament is referring to the people inside: *This House moves. . . .*

housebreaking

See **BURGLARY**.

house officer

See **JUNIOR DOCTOR**.

housewife, househusband, homemaker

housewife *noun*, means a woman who manages a house and looks after a family, and does not go out to work: *She is to give up being a housewife, put the children in a day-care centre and take paid work*.

househusband *noun*, is the male equivalent of housewife, and reflects the fact that families' domestic arrangements are more flexible than they used to be: *My boyfriend said he would stay at home and be the househusband and look after the children and do the cleaning and cooking if I stayed at work*.

homemaker *noun* has been coined to be a more neutral term than *housewife* and *house husband*. It is used for both women and men. Where *housewife* may imply simply cooking and cleaning, **homemaker** gives the impression of someone who contributes to the comfort and attractive appearance of the home. This is mainly an AE term.

hovercraft

See **HYDROFOIL**.

however, how ever

however *adverb*, means to whatever degree. It can be used to form a contrast with something mentioned previously: *You say affluence; however, do not be deceived, many are living on the verge of poverty*. **However** also means regardless of how: *However they earn their daily bread, they survive*. It is best to place **however** immediately after either a semicolon or a full stop.
See **THOUGH (ALTHOUGH)**.

how ever *adverb*, means in whatever way or manner: *The use of mercury in any process and in whatever quantity, how ever small, requires an official permit*. Spell this in two words when **ever** gives added emphasis to **how**.

human, humane

human *noun & adjective*. As a noun, this means a person as opposed to an animal. An alternative is *human being*. The plural form *humans* may be used as a non-sexist alternative to man or mankind. *Humankind* is an alternative term here. As an adjective, **human** means connected with people, or more specifically having qualities such as kindness and generosity: *The President seemed to me to be genuine, confident, warm and human*. See INHUMAN, SEXIST LANGUAGE (WRITING SKILLS).

humane *adjective*, means compassionate: *Samuel was generally regarded as a humane employer, but even he expected his apprentices to work for 13 hours*. A *humane killer* is a device for killing animals painlessly. See INHUMANE (INHUMAN).

humanism, humanitarian, humanity

humanism *uncountable noun*, is a philosophy that emphasizes the use of reason rather than belief. The fundamental concept is the goodness of human nature: *He found humanism, which adheres to no values outside human beings, very hard to swallow*.

humanitarian *adjective*, means benevolent, concerned with improving the quality of life and easing suffering. It is often used to describe efforts to promote better health and welfare: *The agency is engaged in several humanitarian missions in Africa*.

humanity *uncountable noun*, means people in general: *The crimes that governments commit are an outrage against all humanity*; or the quality of compassion and kindness to people and animals: *They tried to persuade the houseowners to treat the squatters with greater humanity*. See HUMANITIES (ARTS).

humble, modest, demure

humble *adjective*, refers to a person or organization who considers that they are less important than others: *How can City be overshadowed by humble Rovers when it comes to buying players?* **Humble** can refer to low rank or position, or is used ironically to suggest that you are not as important as others even though it is obvious that you are: *In my humble opinion that scene in the office should not be regarded as a resignation matter*.

modest *adjective*, means not talking about your own ability: *Leak your past successes through other people, or disclose them yourself in a suitably modest and reluctant manner, as is the British way*. In another sense, **modest** refers to an unassuming lifestyle that does not involve overspending or living in flamboyant housing: *One by one, his modest properties began to show a satisfactory return*.

demure *adjective*, refers to a female who is serious and avoids attracting attention to herself or her body: *Confidence is not seen as a feminine quality: girls are supposed to be quite demure*.

humility, humiliation

humility *uncountable noun*, means modesty or the quality of not being too proud of oneself: *Respect and tolerance for differences and the humility to accept that a different way may be better are good commonsense guidelines*.

humiliation *noun*, is the state of feeling shame and humbled due to an action where someone is made to feel stupid or weak: *Having to ask his parents for money was a humiliation for someone who was once extremely wealthy*.

humour, humorous

humour *noun*, has many meanings. Usually it refers to an amusing or comic quality: *Her sense of humour is a saving grace, especially when she is not afraid to laugh at herself*. It also means the mood of a person: *The minister seemed to be in very good humour despite the pressure on him*. This is the spelling in BE. The AE spelling is *humor*.

humorous *adjective*, refers to something that causes laughter and amusement: *Sarcasm and ridicule are humorous forms of criticism*. The word is spelt the same way in BE and AE, and there is no 'u' in the second syllable. See -OR, -OUR SPELLINGS.

hundred, hundreds

hundred *number*, can be either an exact number: *A hundred jobs are to go at the building society*; or an approximate amount, when it follows the words *a*, *few* or *several*: *Several hundred workmen were surging round the building baying for the blood of the overseers inside*. In both cases, the main verb must be plural. **Hundred** is followed by a singular verb only when it forms part of a unit of time, distance, money, temperature, etc.: *One hundred centuries takes us back before recorded history*. **Hundred** is also used in speech to express whole hours in the 24 hour clock system: *thirteen hundred hours*. Note that 100th is spelt *hundredth*. See TIME OF DAY.

hundreds *number*, means an unspecified large number ranging from a few *hundred* to many **hundreds**: *In some places the books had not been touched for hundreds of years and could hardly be seen for dust.* **Hundreds** is always followed by *of* when used before a noun. Unlike *hundred*, **hundreds** always takes a plural verb.

hung

See HANGED.

hurdle, hurtle

hurdle *noun & verb*. As a noun, a **hurdle** is an obstacle that has to be overcome: *Scientists are beginning to argue that psychological fitness could be the biggest hurdle to a Mars mission.* As a verb **hurdle** means to leap over objects. A *hurdling race* is a track event in athletics.

hurtle *verb*, means to move quickly. This usually refers to large, heavy objects: *Two ambulances whizzed past and hurtled on towards the scene of the crash.*

'The car was hurdling down the street towards him.'

hurricane, typhoon, tornado, cyclone

hurricane *noun*, is an extreme weather phenomenon that occurs east of the International Date Line: *They stayed like that for hours, hardly daring to move until the noise subsided and the hurricane passed, leaving a trail of devastation in its wake.*

typhoon *noun*, is exactly the same as a *hurricane* except that it occurs west of the International Date Line in the area of the Philippines, the China Sea, or India. They are atmospheric disturbances of about equal intensity: *Most people stay indoors, where they hold typhoon parties, or watch the progress of the storm on the television.* The only difference between a **typhoon** and a *hurricane* is where they occur.

tornado *noun*, is an extremely violent storm which moves in circles often with whirlwinds: *Hundreds were injured when a tornado struck the American Midwest.* The plural forms are *tornadoes* or *tornados*. Twister is an informal AE term for **tornado**.

cyclone *noun*, is a meteorological depression in which the winds blow spirally. This means that **cyclone** is an alternative to both *hurricane* and *typhoon*. See STORM.

husband

See PARTNER.

husbandry, farming

husbandry *noun*, means the care and cultivation of crops and animals, as in *animal husbandry*. It is a positive term that indicates that the farming is being done carefully and well. Another definition of **husbandry** meaning the conservation of resources is considered old-fashioned.

farming *noun*, refers to the business of running, working or managing a farm.

hydrofoil, hovercraft

hydrofoil *noun*, is a device that raises a boat above the water at high speeds. By extension, it is also a vessel that is fitted with such a device, and that travels partly in and partly over the water, as the hull of a **hydrofoil** is almost out of the water at high speed.

hovercraft *noun*, is a vessel that is supported on a cushion of air, and can travel over flat land and water.

hyper-, hypo-

hyper- *prefix*, means above, beyond normal, so that *hyperthermia* means a very high body temperature, and *hypertension* means above average blood pressure. The usual pronunciation is hīpĕr- /haɪpər-/.
See HYPERBOLE.

hypo- *prefix*, means under and means often the opposite of words starting with *hyper-*. As **hypo-** indicates below normal or deficient, *hypothermia* indicates a very low body temperature, and *hypotension* is very low blood pressure. The usual pronunciation is hīpō- /haɪpəʊ-/. See **HYPOCRITICAL**.

hyperbole, exaggeration

hyperbole hīpérbŏli /haɪˈpɜːrbəli/ *noun*, means speech or writing that is done in a vivid manner and conveys more excitement than is warranted: *The hyperbole was out of all proportion compared to the evidence*. Note that the stress is on the second syllable.

exaggeration *noun*, is a description that makes something seem more extreme or important than it really is: *Three years at college has not changed your habit of exaggeration*.

hypercritical, hypocritical

hypercritical *adjective*, means being very critical: *A proud, often sarcastic, hypercritical man, he was handsome and impressive, but he had few close friends*.

hypocritical *adjective*, refers to a person who claims to have higher moral standards than he or she actually has: *Wasn't it hypocritical to pray to a god one didn't believe in?* Note that the first syllable is pronounced hipp- /hɪp-/. A person that is **hypocritical** is a *hypocrite* híppŏkrit /ˈhɪpəkrɪt/, and practises *hypocrisy* hipóckrissi /hɪˈpɒkrɪsi/.

hyperlink, hotlink

hyperlink *noun*, is a place in an electronic document that connects the user to another electronic document via a mouse click: *For more information, click on the hyperlink below*.

hotlink *noun*, is an alternative term for a *hyperlink*.

hypermarket

See **SUPERMARKET**.

hyphenation

See **PUNCTUATION GUIDE**.

hypothesis, hypotheses

hypothesis hīpóthĕssiss /haɪˈpɒθəsɪs/ *noun*, means a theory that still needs to be proved: *For example, a hypothesis might be 'that regular theatregoers are middle class in their family backgrounds'*.

hypotheses *plural noun*, is the plural of *hypothesis*.

> Note that these words are stressed on the second syllable.

hypothetical

See **BLUE-SKY**.

Spelling

ha**r**a**ss**	Remember single -r- but double -ss
h**ei**nous	Unusually, -e- comes before -i-
here**s**y	Note the -s- towards the end of the word
h**ie**roglyph	Remember -i- before -e-
hin**dr**ance	Remember there is no 'e' in the middle of this word
hi**pp**o**p**o**t**amus	Remember double -pp-, then single -p- and single -t-
hume**rus** ('funny bone')	Remember there is no 'o' in this word
hum**or**ous	Note there is no 'u' before the -r-
hundre**d**th	Remember the -d- before the final -th
hya**c**inth	Remember -c- in the middle of this word
hypocri**s**y	Note the -s- towards the end of the word
hypot**e**nuse	Remember -e- between -t- and -n-

I

I, me

I is the first person subject pronoun. When the speaker is carrying out the action of the sentence, this is the correct form to use: *I went shopping*.

Me is the first person object pronoun. When the speaker is the target of the utterance, this is the correct form: *She asked me to do the shopping*.

Is it correct to say 'it is I' or 'it is me'?

Authoritative modern dictionaries agree both are correct, but that *it is I* is best reserved for very formal contexts.

Is it correct to say 'between you and I' or 'between you and me'?

As a preposition such as *between* takes the object case, it is correctly followed by the object pronoun such as *me*. Thus it is correct in standard English to say *between you and me*, and incorrect to say *between you and I*. A test could be to replace the last three words with the subject *we*, or the object pronoun *us*. Obviously 'between we' is incorrect English, while 'between us' is correct.

Is it correct to say 'you and I' or 'you and me'?

When 'you and I/me' is in the subject position, as in *You and I went shopping*, it would be incorrect to write 'You and me went shopping', because **me** is the object pronoun. A good tip is to remove 'You and', and consider whether 'Me went shopping' is acceptable English. Clearly it is not, so *You and I went shopping* is correct.

When 'you and I/me' is in the object position, as in *Mother wants you and me to go shopping*, it would be incorrect to write 'Mother wants you and I to go shopping', because **I** is the subject pronoun. Again, remove 'you and', and consider whether 'Mother wants I to go shopping' is acceptable. See PRONOUNS (GRAMMAR TIPS).

Iberia, Iberian

Iberia *noun*, is the geographical area of Europe to the south-west of the Pyrenees, comprising Spain and Portugal.

Iberian *adjective*, applies to anything concerning Spain and Portugal: *The strategic importance of the Iberian peninsula was evident simply from looking at a map*.

Be careful not to confuse *Iberia* with *Hibernia*. See IRISH.

ibid.

See OP. CIT.

-ible

See -ABLE.

-ic, -ical

The adjectives that end in **-ic** and **-ical** fall into three groups:

- Those with similar meaning in the two forms. Examples are: *arithmetic/arithmetical, cynic/cynical, dynamic/dynamical, fanatic/fanatical, geographic/geographical, geometric/geometrical, periodic/periodical, poetic/poetical* and *strategic/strategical*.
- Those where there is a clear difference in meaning between the two forms. Examples of these are: *classic/classical, comic/comical, economic/economical, electric/electrical, historic/historical, lyric/lyrical* and *politic/political*.
- The final category is the 'survivors', where either **-ic** or **-ical** survives, and the other is outdated, or even does not exist. Examples of **-ic** are: *academic, artistic, domestic, dramatic, linguistic, phonetic, scientific, systematic* and *tragic*; and of **-ical**: *botanical* (*botanic* survives in the phrase 'Botanic Garden'), *identical* and *hypothetical*.

Many of these words are discussed separately in this book.

-ics

Nouns that end in **-ics** and refer to academic disciplines, such as *acoustics, economics, electronics, linguistics, mathematics, phonetics, physics*, or similar words that describe a type of activity, for instance *athletics, gymnastics, hysterics*, are all uncountable nouns. Note that they are singular, despite the final 's': *Mathematics* ***is*** *difficult and some pupils will avoid* ***it*** *if they can*. Certain of these words can also be treated as plural when they are used in a concrete sense rather than in the sense of an academic subject: *The acoustics are poor in that concert hall.*

Other words ending in **-ics** which are not the names of disciplines are plural nouns, and take a plural verb: *The italics are left out*. See LYRICS (LYRIC).

Many of these words are discussed separately in this book.

idle, idol

idle *adjective & verb*. As an adjective, this means inactive and not working: *She was so idle that she never even opened a textbook*. This is a term of criticism that implies that laziness is why someone is **idle**. However, it does not imply criticism when it refers to a large number of people who are **idle** due to unemployment: *One worker in five in this area is idle because of the recession*. A machine that is not in use can also be called **idle**. As a verb, to *idle away* means to spend time doing nothing important: *He idled his life away as a beach bum*. **Idle** also refers to machines that are running slowly but not doing any work: *This device allows the blades to rotate at high speed while the motor is idling or stopped.*

idol *noun*, means an object or person that is loved, admired and worshipped: *Elvis has been dead for a long time, but he is still her idol.*

idolize, venerate, revere

idolize *verb*, means to love, admire or worship a person because you consider that they are perfect and have no faults: *She idolized her boyfriend until they started to live together.*

venerate *verb*, means to have or demonstrate great respect for a person or an object that is considered to be very important or holy: *Temples and shrines were built to his memory, and a cult grew up to venerate him as founder of the empire.*

revere *verb*, means to feel respect or admiration for a person, group or object: *Shakespeare is revered because so many people have found meaning in his writings.*

i.e.

See E.G.

ill, sick

ill *adjective & adverb*. In BE, the adjective **ill** means in poor health: *The crew fell ill with radiation sickness*. It is also commonly used to describe people who have been injured in an accident or by violence: *A woman shot and dumped by the side of the road was critically ill in hospital*. As an adverb, **ill** is most commonly used in compounds to mean badly, or not satisfactorily: *He was ill-equipped for the job of club manager*. Also as an adverb **ill** can be used on its own: *She never speaks ill of him.*

sick *adjective*, usually means vomiting in BE: *I'm going to faint or be sick*. In AE, **sick** means in poor health, but *ill* is also used for more serious illnesses. Some expressions using **sick** for general illness are used in both BE and AE, such as *sick leave* and *sick pay*. In other contexts, **sick** can mean in a bad state: *The economy is sick*. **Sick** can also mean in bad taste or perverted, for example in the term *sick humour*.

illegal

See UNLAWFUL.

illegible, unreadable, illiterate

illegible *adjective*, refers to a piece of writing that cannot be read or deciphered because the letter shapes are difficult to make out: *Unlike machines, human readers can understand many badly formed letters and seemingly illegible words due to information gained from the surrounding context*. See LEGIBLE (READABLE), UNINTELLIGIBLE.

unreadable *adjective*, refers to a piece of writing that is too boring, complicated or difficult to read. A text whose individual words can be clearly made out may still be **unreadable**: *While the Americans go for self-help books, the French buy unreadable books on philosophy*. See READABLE.

illiterate *adjective & noun*. As an adjective, this means unable to read and write. It can also refer to a document whose grammatical structure or style is faulty: *Typing and correcting your misspelt, illiterate, moronic letter gave me a severe headache*. **Illiterate** is also used figuratively to mean ignorant of a subject: *One of the most infuriating habits of the scientifically illiterate is to talk of the 'ice age' as if there had been only one*. As a noun, an **illiterate** is a person who cannot read or write. The related noun is *illiteracy*: the state of being unable to read or write: *Overall illiteracy rates are still 50 per cent, and schooling is not accessible to many children*. See LITERATE.

illegitimate

See UNLAWFUL.

illicit, elicit

illicit *adjective*, means either not allowed by law: *The illicit trade in toxic waste is estimated to be three times larger than the legal trade*; or forbidden by morality or custom: *They both looked forward to these meetings as they were occasions of utter illicit pleasure*.

elicit *verb*, means to succeed in getting information or a response, when this is a difficult process: *The police used an interpreter in order to elicit a statement from the suspect*. This is a formal word.

illuminate

See LIGHT[1].

illusion, allusion, delusion

illusion *noun*, means in one sense a false idea or belief: *The illusion of peace was shaken by the President's decision to invade*. In another sense it means a deceptive appearance: *White bedroom furniture was designed with clean, sharp lines and mirrors to create an illusion of space*.

allusion *noun*, means an indirect reference to something: *The 'day's eye' (daisy), is so-called in allusion to its revealing its yellow disc in the morning and concealing it again in the evening*. See ALLUDE.

delusion *noun*, means a false belief or opinion that is not based on reality: *The American policy-makers were labouring under the delusion that the war would be supported by all Europeans*.

imaginary, imaginative, fanciful

imaginary *adjective*, means existing only in the imagination: *He was eager to meet his imaginary dream woman*.

imaginative *adjective*, means creative or using the imagination: *Menus vary from traditional roasts to imaginative cordon bleu dishes*.

fanciful *adjective*, means not based on fact, or unrealistic: *It is probably fanciful to cast a rock star as Lady Macbeth*. In another sense, it means highly decorative or ornamented: *Picasso was attracted to abstract, fanciful and esoteric sculptures*.

imbalance

See DISCREPANCY.

imbed

See EMBED.

imitate

See EMULATE.

immature

See PREMATURE.

immerse, submerge

immerse *verb*, means to cover completely with liquid: *I held my breath and completely immersed myself under the water*. Figuratively, it means to be completely engrossed in: *Social investigators need to immerse themselves in the social world under study*.

submerge *verb*, means either to put something under water: *Global warming might completely submerge vast expanses of low-lying land*; or to sink: *Some species of whales can submerge for up to an hour and survive on a single breath*. Figuratively, it means to hide or suppress: *In this business it does not pay to submerge your personality*.

immigrant

See **EMIGRANT**.

imminent

See **EMINENT**.

imminently

See **EMINENTLY**.

immobile, immovable, irremovable

immobile *adjective*, means stationary, not moving: *Computer users sit immobile for hours on end, except for rapid and intense finger movements*. This can also apply to objects. See **MOBILE**.

immovable *adjective*, means unable to be moved: *This safe is so heavy it is immovable without a crane*. In an abstract sense it refers to attitudes and opinions that cannot be changed. See **MOVABLE (MOBILE)**.

irremovable *adjective*, means unable to be removed. If someone has tenure at a university, they cannot be removed: *The chair belonged to a professor who was irremovable*. This is a rare word.

immorality, immortality

immorality *noun*, means the lack of moral standards: *Corinth was noted for its immorality – there was a significant part of the population whose god was debauchery*. See **IMMORAL (AMORAL)**.

immortality *noun*, means either indestructibility, everlasting life: *He could not give me immortality; one day I will die*; or the state of never being forgotten: *Dr Johnson found a biographer he could control, and thus secured his immortality*.

immunity, impunity

immunity *noun*, means exemption from an obligation or penalty: *They were guaranteed immunity from any new charges*. **Immunity** also means the body's capacity to protect itself from disease: *Tetanus immunity should be checked for anyone with a cut or deep scratch*.

impunity *uncountable noun*, means freedom from the negative consequences of an action. It is usually found in the phrase *with impunity*: *In our dreams we can do with impunity things we would like to do in real life*.

immunize

See **VACCINATE**.

impact

See **INFLUENCE**.

impediment, impedimenta

impediment *noun*, means either an obstacle that stops movement or a physical problem: *She stuttered and had suffered from a speech impediment from an early age*.

impedimenta *plural noun*, means the baggage and equipment taken on a trip. *As there is usually too much handling the impedimenta become a problem*. This is a formal or humorous word.

impel

See **COMPEL**.

imperative

See **ESSENTIAL**.

imperious, arrogant, haughty

imperious *adjective*, means dictatorial, domineering: *As she said 'Go!', she flung up her right hand in an imperious gesture*.

arrogant *adjective*, means conceited and self-important: *He was an arrogant man who thought he had only to crook his finger and she would come running*.

haughty *adjective*, means proud and contemptuous, and is used about a person who thinks that they are better than other people: *The painter replied with a haughty laugh: his inspiration had not come from the Impressionists*.

impertinent

See **IMPUDENT**.

implement, carry out, execute

implement *verb*, means to put into practice an agreed decision, plan or course of action:

Britain has been slow to implement a nationwide recycling programme.

carry out *verb*, means to perform an action: *She knew he would carry out his threat and have her dismissed.*

execute *verb*, means either to complete an action: *They oversee safety and execute numerous welfare and cultural responsibilities*; or to carry out instructions: *I am confident that the management team will continue to successfully execute our strategy.* **Execute** also means to kill a prisoner, either legally following a guilty verdict in a trial by the state: *Moves to execute juvenile offenders are contrary to international human rights standards*; or illegally, if it is carried out by a self-styled authority: *They were believed to have been executed by the rebels or the death squads.* See EXECUTIVE.

implication, inference

implication *noun*, means the underlying and unspoken consequence of a statement: if A is true, then B is the result; or the consequence of a previous action: *Research has shown women are more conscious of the environmental implication of the products they buy than men.* Both these meanings derive from the verb *imply*. A separate, unrelated meaning, derived from the verb *implicate*, is involvement: *The personal implication of the narrator in the story could not be more clearly signalled.*

inference ínfĕrĕnss /'ɪnfərəns/ *noun*, means a conclusion drawn from evidence or a statement: *There are invariably more mature female goats around than males, and the inference is that the males are more likely to die during the winter.* See CONNOTATION.

> One quotation that sums up the difference between these two terms is: *Implication is an indirect way of conveying one's own meaning; inference is a process of discovering a fact outside oneself.* (*Learning the Law.* Williams, G., 1982)

implicit, explicit

implicit *adjective*, has two meanings. First, it refers to something that is understood without being stated directly: *The Press picked up the minister's implicit criticism of the ongoing research in the pharmaceutical industry.* Second, **implicit** means absolute or unquestioning: *He had implicit trust in the righteousness of the people's liberation movement.*

explicit *adjective*, refers to something stated very clearly: *The minister said that his statement was not explicit criticism of research in the pharmaceutical industry.* A person who is **explicit**, says or does things in a very direct manner and leaves little to the imagination: *We need to be able to show that being explicit about sex is not inherently harmful or damaging.* The mass media use the term **explicit** to refer to material containing obscene language, violence or sex scenes: *The film has some very explicit language and is unsuitable for minors.*

imply, infer

imply *verb*, means to suggest or hint something without saying it directly: *Even if some form of family is natural or inevitable, that does not imply that any particular form is optimal.*

infer *verb*, means to draw a conclusion from evidence or a previous statement: *First babies tend to cry more than subsequent ones; doctors infer from this that the mother's inexperience is an important factor.*

> *Imply* and *infer* are often confused, but they maintain a useful distinction, and it may help to remember that *a speaker implies*, while *a listener infers*.

important

See MAJOR.

impossible, improbable

impossible *adjective*, refers to something that cannot be true, cannot exist or cannot happen: *Continuous rain had made it impossible to keep a fire burning.* **Impossible** also refers to a person or situation that is very difficult to deal with: *His former secretary described him as 'amusing, utterly impossible, kind, and a bully'.* See ABSOLUTE ADJECTIVES (GRAMMAR TIPS).

improbable *adjective*, means unlikely to be true, to exist or to happen: *The new James Bond gives a smooth, suave performance in this wildly improbable story.* **Improbable** also means strange and unexpected: *He speaks English in a curious way, that improbable Dutch-accent tongue slapping down hard on the vowels.*

impotent, infertile

impotent ímpŏtĕnt /ˈɪmpətənt/ *adjective*, means powerless: *Ordinary people are impotent in the face of a centralized, powerful state*. It also means unable to have sexual intercourse: *He was generally impotent the first time he slept with women of his own class, though matters improved later*.

infertile *adjective*, means not capable of producing young: *She did not use contraception because she believed she was infertile*. It is also used of land that is not productive: *Deforestation results in the already poor soil becoming virtually infertile, due to loss of topsoil.*

> A man who is *infertile* may not be *impotent*, and there is no reason to think that an *impotent* man must be *infertile*.

impractical, impracticable

impractical *adjective*, means not practical, realistic or sensible: *Trying out all the different permutations of routes is clearly impractical: there are 3,628,800 different ways of making a journey between 10 towns*. **Impractical** also refers to a person who is not very good at making or doing things with their hands: *She was the ideal partner for such an unworldly and impractical scholar, taking all the burdens of daily living off his shoulders*. **Impractical** is sometimes used to mean *impracticable*, especially in AE. If a clear distinction needs to be made, **impractical** can be replaced by useless, unrealistic or not sensible.

impracticable *adjective*, means not feasible, or impossible to carry out: *He explained that the amount of paperwork involved made running a company impracticable*.

improbable

See IMPOSSIBLE.

impromptu

See EXTEMPORE.

impudent, impertinent

impudent *adjective*, means rude and disrespectful: *She stood in line with the multitude to endure the emptying of pockets and the impudent fumblings of security*. This is a formal word.

impertinent *adjective*, means disrespectful to someone who has higher status or is older: *As it seems impertinent to invite you to sit down in your own laboratory, I won't*.

impulsive

See COMPELLING.

impunity

See IMMUNITY.

impute, attribute

impute *verb*, means to accuse someone of being responsible for something, or of believing something, often unfairly: *The defence imputed the damage to the person who owned the car*. This is a formal word.

attribute ătríbbewt /əˈtrɪbjuːt/ *verb &* áttribewt /ˈætrɪbjuːt/ *noun*. As a verb, this means to assign: *A summary of the cost accounts, which attribute costs to particular committees, is set out below*. As a noun, **attribute** means a characteristic: *If the dwelling was without some necessary attribute such as a damp course or a roof, then it would be unfit for habitation*.

inability, unable

inability *uncountable noun*, means the lack of power to do something, even though there may be no physical or mental disability in the way: *The manager's inability to delegate responsibilities or to communicate to those lower down led to his dismissal*.

unable *adjective*, means lacking the skill, means or opportunity to do something: *Norman could hear but was unable to move a muscle*. This is the only adjective related to *inability*.

inapt

See INEPT.

inch, inches

inch *noun*, is a unit of measurement (equivalent to 2.54 cm), 12 of which make one foot. When **inch** is used adjectivally in compounds, it behaves like all other adjectives, and has no plural form: *a four-inch nail* (note the hyphen in *four-inch*). The abbreviation is *in.* and the symbol ″ is used to denote inches: *a 4″ nail*.

inches *noun*, is the plural of inch: *I measured that nail: it is four inches long*. With height or other measurements over a foot, **inches** is often omitted, as in: *He is only five foot six*. Note that singular verbs are often used with units of measurement when the total measurement is considered as a single entity: *Twelve inches equals one foot*. But when the unit is being counted individually, it takes a plural: *Eleven inches make almost one foot*. See FOOT, MEASUREMENTS.

incident

See EPISODE.

incite

See INSIGHT.

income

See EARNINGS.

incomprehensible

See UNINTELLIGIBLE.

incredible, incredulous

incredible *adjective*, means unbelievable: *It is incredible that he made that misstatement about Ohio*. It is also used in a colloquial sense, to mean amazing: *Dave and Julie have got this incredible new kitchen*. See CREDIBLE.

incredulous *adjective*, means sceptical, unwilling to believe something: *The officials were so incredulous they twice remeasured the width of the goal*. See CREDULOUS (CREDIBLE).

indefinite article

See ARTICLES (GRAMMAR TIPS).

indent

See REQUISITION.

independent

See DEPENDANT.

index, indexes, indices

index *noun*, means both an alphabetic listing of topics dealt with in a report or textbook, usually placed at the end, and a scale used for measuring changes in prices, etc. The *index finger* is the one nearest the thumb, used for pointing. A *card index* is an alphabetical arrangement of information kept on cards.

indexes *noun plural*, is one of the plurals of *index*. It refers to alphabetical lists: *The book has comprehensive author and subject indexes*; and stock market **indexes**: *The London Stock Exchange operates several indexes of share prices*.

indices *noun plural*, is the other plural of *index*. It is used in mathematics for the small superscript number in formulae: *A billion means* 10^9 (read as 'ten to the ninth'). In other sciences it means indicators: *We have reliable physiological indices of when dreams are likely to occur*. See PLURAL NOUNS (WORD FORMATION).

indigenous

See NATIVE.

industry, industrial, industrious

industry *noun*. When used as an uncountable noun, **industry** means economic activity related to the development of raw materials into finished goods in factories and plants: *Safety authorities in Britain are under growing pressure to warn of the dangers of a common inert gas used widely in industry*. (Note that the definite article cannot be used before **industry** in this sense.) **Industry** as a countable noun refers to a specific sector of commercial activity: *Traditionally, labour in the construction industry has been employed on a casual basis*. (Here the definite article is used.) See BUSINESS, UNCOUNTABLE NOUNS (GRAMMAR TIPS).

industrial *adjective*, means relating to industry: *Iron deposits changed Corby into one of the chief industrial centres of the East Midlands*.

industrious *adjective*, means diligent and hard-working: *The islanders are industrious; they are either out at work or working at home*.

inedible

See UNEATABLE.

inept, inapt, unapt

inept *adjective*, means awkward or unskilled: *The general was criticized for his inept handling of the attack that killed 150 civilians.* Alternative terms are foolish or bungling. The related noun is *ineptitude*.

inapt *adjective*, means unsuitable: *The general's comment about collateral damage was most inapt considering the casualties.* This is a formal word. The related noun is *inaptitude*.

unapt *adjective*, means unfitted, not appropriate in the circumstances, embarrassing: *As the waiter had just dropped a pile of plates, it was unapt to mention a circus clown in his hearing.* The related noun is *unaptness*.

These words are all very close in usage but *inept* is used mostly to describe behaviour and *inapt* usually refers to phrases and comments. *Unapt* is a rare word and does not appear in the British National Corpus.

inequality, inequity, iniquity, injustice

inequality *noun*, means difference in size, degree or circumstances between two things. Most commonly it is used to mean an unfair difference between two groups of people or two sets of circumstances: *Economic relationships create inequality as one class dominates and exploits the other.*

inequity *noun*, is a formal word that means a lack of fairness: *The bluntness and social inequity of the community charge – or 'poll tax' – helped fuel a considerable popular protest in the early 1990s.*
See INEQUITABLE (UNFAIR).

iniquity *noun*, is a formal word that means wickedness or sinfulness: *Experience clearly showed that virtue, not numbers, triumphed over the iniquity of the enemy.* In another sense it means unfairness: *The report highlighted the iniquity of per capita payments in rural areas.*

injustice *noun*, means a failure to practise fairness or justice: *You do the teacher in question a terrible injustice by saying these things about him without a shred of evidence.*

'It was transformed from a den of inequity into a restaurant and bar.'
('Harlem's Vanguard')

inequitable

See UNFAIR.

inexpensive

See CHEAP.

inexplicable, unfathomable

inexplicable *adjective*, means unable to be explained: *Though for some totally inexplicable reason, that seems to be the truth.* See INCOMPREHENSIBLE (UNINTELLIGIBLE).

unfathomable *adjective*, refers to things that are too strange and mysterious to be understood: *What happened in the next few hours or days has remained one of the mountain's unfathomable secrets.* This is a literary term that may puzzle international audiences.

in fact

See FACT.

infamous, notorious

infamous *adjective*, means famous for being evil: *The Massacre of Glencoe is probably the most infamous event in Scottish history.* Note that this word is stressed on the first syllable, not the second: ínfămŭss /ˈɪnfəməs/. The related noun is *infamy*, also stressed on the first syllable: ínfămi /ˈɪnfəmi/.

notorious *adjective*, means famous for having a poor reputation: *He inherited the property after his elder brother (a notorious spendthrift) was disinherited.* It is often interchangeable with *infamous*, but as an adverb, *notoriously* is applied to something with an extremely bad reputation: *This software is notoriously difficult to use.* *Notoriously* is used more often than *infamously*. The related noun is *notoriety*, stressed on the letter i, pronounced 'eye': nōtŏrī́-ĕti /nəʊtəˈraɪəti/.

infectious

See CONTAGIOUS.

infer

See IMPLY.

inference

See IMPLICATION.

infertile

See IMPOTENT.

inflammable, flammable, non-flammable

inflammable *adjective*, means easily set on fire and means, the same as *flammable*, not the opposite: *Because raw cotton is an inflammable material, mills had to be made fireproof*. These two words have caused confusion and injury, as goods can be labelled **inflammable** or *flammable* according to the place of origin. **Inflammable** can be used figuratively to mean aggressively emotional: *The regime has cast its fury in the inflammable language of a Holy War*.

flammable *adjective*, means easily set on fire: *The internal combustion engine will run on almost anything that is flammable*. The British Standards Institution has ruled that **flammable** and its opposite, *non-flammable*, are to be used for substances and materials, rather than *inflammable* and its opposite, *non-inflammable*.

non-flammable *adjective*, means difficult or impossible to set fire to: *Although CFCs are non-flammable and cheap to make they are now banned*.

> Despite *inflammable* having what seems to be a negative suffix, it means the same as *flammable*. The prefix here means *into*.

inflexible

See UNBENDING.

inflict, afflict

inflict *verb*, means to impose a punishment: *The teacher's authority to inflict punishment on a pupil is widely criticized today*. In another sense it means to cause suffering: *The industrial action inflicted serious damage on the entire sector*.

afflict *verb*, means to hurt, or cause to suffer: *A diet rich in vitamin C can help to prevent the development of cataracts, which frequently afflict the over-65s*.

inflow, influx

inflow *noun*, means the movement of people or things from one place to somewhere else: *These losses roughly equalled the total inflow into the Mediterranean before the dam was built*.

influx *noun*, is the result of a movement of people from one place to another: *At ten o'clock the gates were shut to prevent a sudden influx of new voters*.

I

influence, impact

influence *noun*, means the unobtrusive effect that a person or thing has on another: *Mao Zedong's wife could always be counted on to use her influence and support the most extreme policies*. It can also mean the capacity to have an effect: *This equipment will have a positive influence on in-car safety*.

impact *noun*, means a great impression or strong effect: *A housing slump would have a major impact on removal firms*. **Impact** literally means the effect of a collision between two bodies: *The flasks used for transporting spent fuel must be designed to survive the impact of a 9 m fall – equivalent to an impact of 30 mph*.

informant, informer, whistle-blower

informant *noun*, is either a person who passes information to the police or other authority: *The name of the informant must not be disclosed*; or in the social sciences, a person who assists researchers by providing information: . . . *the classic use of an anthropological informant is hardly necessary*.

informer *noun*, means a person who passes information about others to the police or other authority: *Mr Grass had the perfect name for an informer*.

whistle-blower *noun*, means an informer who passes on evidence of wrongdoing in the organization they work for.

information, news

information *uncountable noun*, means facts based on evidence or data. It never has a plural form and always takes a singular verb: *It is worth taking a look at the various ways in which information is currently being produced. A piece of information* (formal) or *a bit of information* (informal) are ways of saying that there is just one item of **information**. *A good deal of/much information* expresses the idea that there is a lot of **information**.

news *uncountable noun*, means recent *information* about current events: *Eyes down for our weekly quiz about the news of the last seven days*. In radio and TV stations that run continuous news broadcasts, the phrase *breaking news* refers to events as they are happening. Note that **news** always takes a singular verb.

infotainment

See ADVERTISEMENT.

infuriate

See ANNOY.

ingenious, ingenuous, ingénue

ingenious *adjective*, means inventive, skilful, original and resourceful: *As the Victorian age got under way, ever more ingenious technologies aided the steady advance of drainage*. Note that the second syllable rhymes with 'mean'.
See GENIAL (GENIUS).

ingenuous *adjective*, means unsophisticated, naive and unsuspecting: *It is ingenuous to suppose that peace process brokers do not have their strategic interests first and foremost in mind*. Note that the second syllable rhymes with 'men'.

ingénue ánzhaynew /ˈænʒeɪnjuː/ *noun*, means an innocent young female, usually in a theatre play or film: *In this production, Rose is no vulnerable young ingénue*. Although rare, the masculine form *ingénu* does exist for the male equivalent. Those who speak French may prefer a more French-like pronunciation: á(ng)zhaynü /ɛ̃ʒeny/.

inhabitable

See HABITABLE.

inhabitant

See RESIDENT.

inherent, intrinsic

inherent *adjective*, means innate and inseparable: *Does a nurse have the duty to inform the patient about inherent risks?*

intrinsic *adjective*, means genuine or essential: *Grants have been given to churches for their intrinsic architectural importance*.

inheritance, heritage, heredity

inheritance *noun*, means what is received from a deceased person. This may be belongings or an estate: *The advent of mass owner occupation has meant that inheritance of house property has become increasingly common*; or it may mean characteristics passed on by genetic features or status: *The inheritance of acquired characteristics is a means of adapting organisms to changes in their environment*. **Inheritance** is also used in a limited number of expressions, such as *cultural inheritance* and *artistic inheritance*, where it has a similar meaning to *heritage*.

heritage *noun*, means a set of shared cultural traditions and qualities. This is a formal word: *This is a building of historic interest and deserves to be preserved as part of the town's heritage*.

heredity *uncountable noun*, means the characteristics, looks and diseases passed from generation to generation: *DNA is the stuff of which genes are made: the basic units of heredity which determine what kind of creatures develop*.

inheritance tax (BE), estate tax (AE)

inheritance tax *noun*, is the name used in BE for the tax to be paid on a person's estate after his or her death.

estate tax *noun*, is the AE name for the BE *inheritance tax*.

inhibit

See AVERT.

inhuman, inhumane

inhuman *adjective*, means having no human feelings, brutal: *Many people still live under governments that use torture and other cruel, inhuman and degrading treatment against them*. It also means not human, either in character or form: *The City and industry are* *joined by a network of computers, forming a remorseless inhuman environment.*

inhumane inhewmáyn /ɪnhjʊˈmeɪn/ *adjective*, means without compassion for suffering: *This is not the only country which detains mentally ill people under inhumane conditions.* Note that the last syllable is pronounced mayn /meɪn/ and stressed. See **HUMANE (HUMAN)**.

> If the intention is to focus on something that is an animal rather than a human, use the prefix 'non-' with *human*: *There were only non-human tracks in the snow.*

iniquity

See **INEQUALITY**.

injure

See **WOUND**.

injustice

See **INEQUALITY**.

in-law, in-laws

in-law *suffix*, indicates relation by marriage to a husband's or wife's parents and siblings, or to a child's or sibling's spouse: *After his marriage, William gave up his employment to manage his father-in-law's estate.* Note that the plural s is added to the headword: *mothers-in-law, fathers-in-law, brothers-in-law, sisters-in-law*, etc.: *He had aunts in Bombay and sisters-in-law in Australia.*

in-laws *noun*, is the generic term for the relations-in-law: *I had to meet my son's future in-laws on my own last week.* Do not confuse **in-laws** (plural) with the genitive forms *in-law's* and *in-laws'*: *She was at her brother-in-law's* (genitive singular), meaning at his house; *He was pictured beaming over his in-laws' garden gate* (genitive plural).

in name only

See **SO-CALLED**.

innovation, invention, discovery

innovation *noun*, means a new product, system or idea: *Traditional industries such as steelmaking and clothing are in desperate need of innovation.* The phrase 'new innovation' is to be avoided, unless it is necessary to show a contrast with a previously mentioned innovation, since all innovations are new by definition. See **TAUTOLOGY**.

invention *noun*, means a creation or design that has not existed before, or the act of creating: *The invention of printing in the fifteenth century resulted in a rapid spread of literacy.*

discovery *noun*, means the act of finding out something that already exists, such as a comet or a scientific law: *A new discovery might require a long series of observations like Kepler's laws of planetary motion.*

innovative, new

innovative ínnŏvaytiv /ˈɪnəveɪtɪv/ *adjective*, means having features that are advanced and original: *In the post-war new towns circumstances permitted experimentation with all manner of innovative layouts.* Note that the stress is on the first syllable. Do not combine 'new' with **innovative**.

new *adjective*, means either not existing before or unused and unworn. In AE, the pronunciation is often 'noo'.

innuendo, insinuation

innuendo *noun*, means a comment that suggests an unpleasant, particularly sexual meaning, without stating it clearly: *Political campaigns often contain lies, half-truths, gossip and innuendo.*

insinuation *noun*, means a comment that suggests an unpleasant meaning, but without the sexual overtones: *He winced at the insinuation about his poor computer skills.*

innumerable, numerous

innumerable *adjective*, means too many to be counted, but as this is rarely literally correct it usually means many: *Very quickly the greatest fortune tends to be dissipated among innumerable descendants.*

numerous *adjective*, means consisting of a large number: *What was left of the fortune was subjected to numerous forms of taxation over the years.*

innumerate, enumerate

innumerate inéwmĕrăt /ɪˈnjuːmərət/ *adjective*, refers to a person without basic mathematical or arithmetical skill: *These figures are a mixture of fractions and decimals and this means that those who are innumerate will not make head or tail of them.* The related noun is *innumeracy*.

enumerate ĕnéwmĕrayt /ɪˈnjuːməreɪt/ *verb*, means to make a list of: *The number of possibilities is very large and it would be tedious to enumerate all of them.* This is a formal word.

> *The literacy levels in the company involved so many problems that they could not innumerate them.* **!**

inoculate

See VACCINATE.

inquire, inquiry

See ENQUIRE.

in regard to

See REGARDING.

insane, mad, neurotic, paranoid

insane *adjective*, is used in the technical sense of having a serious mental illness: *We cannot punish people for crimes if they are found to be insane.* **Insane** can also be used to mean irrational: *She had an insane desire to speak, but for once she managed to keep a check on her tongue.* Informally, it can also mean unable to think properly: *Please put me in touch with some other mums before I go totally insane!* See LEARNING DIFFICULTY.

mad *adjective*, means foolish or ill-advised: *Reason tells him he is mad to want to continue farming.* **Mad** can also mean angry: *He slapped Liam across the face and got mad at me when I complained*; or to have a passionate interest in something: *He is mad about jacket potatoes with lots of butter, but no cheese.* As **mad** is no longer used to mean *insane* in psychiatry, it is only used informally.

neurotic *adjective*, in its technical sense refers to someone suffering from a neurosis – a mental disturbance involving acute anxiety: *He did not believe that neurotic symptoms all had a sexual cause.* Informally, it is applied to anyone who is obsessive about something, or oversensitive: *We may feel that we are being neurotic if we have a poor self-image.*

paranoid *adjective*, is a technical medical term for a very serious form of mental illness in which sufferers believe that the whole world is conspiring against them. It is now informally used to describe anyone who feels hard done by: *He has always been paranoid about his personal security.* **Paranoid** is best avoided in formal writing unless it is to be used in the strict medical sense.

insecure

See SECURE (SAFE).

insensible, insensitive

See SENSIBLE.

insight, incite

insight *noun*, means either a deep understanding of something: *His fine grasp of language in no way hinders his poetic insight*; or an improved knowledge of something: *Our invited speaker gave us a fascinating insight into the operation of the light rail system.* Note that the stress is on the first syllable.

incite *verb*, means to provoke someone to behave in a particular, often violent, way: *The spirit of rebellion was exploited to incite peasant risings.* Note that the stress is on the second syllable.

insinuation

See INNUENDO.

insoluble

See SOLUBLE.

instability

See UNSTABLE.

instance

See CASE.

institute, institution, institutionalize

institute *noun & verb*. As a noun, this is an organization that has a particular purpose, especially connected with education or a particular profession: *Institute of Fiscal Studies; Massachusetts Institute of Technology.* As a verb, **institute** means to introduce or put something into effect: *The prison authorities instituted a hunt to recover their prisoners.*

institution *noun*, means a large organization that has a particular purpose: *Institution of Mechanical Engineers; Royal National Lifeboat Institution*. Colloquially, an **institution** can be a residential home for elderly or mentally unstable people, or a penal establishment: *About 5 per cent of the population aged 65+ is resident in some form of institution*. It can also refer to an established custom such as marriage or the monarchy. **Institution** is also used in the sense of introducing or putting something into effect: *The most striking feature of the reforms was the institution of 'metropolitan counties' for heavily urbanized areas of the country*.

institutionalize *verb*, means to make something part of the permanent organization of society: *Apartheid tried to institutionalize differences where nature offers only subtleties and complexities*. Another meaning is to make someone accustomed to institutions: *The nationwide childcare strategy aims to institutionalize more children at a younger age*; to put someone into an institution: *Schizophrenics are often institutionalized for their own safety*; or to cause someone who has lived too long in an institution to be unable to cope outside one: *After five years in prison, he had become institutionalized and found it difficult to cook and shop for himself*.

instruction, instructions

instruction *noun*, means the process of teaching a particular skill or of education in general: *He delegated elementary instruction to an assistant, while he took the advanced students*. In these senses, **instruction** is an uncountable noun. As a countable noun, an **instruction** is either an order to do something: *I will inform the bank in writing if I wish to cancel this instruction*; or a piece of information about how to do something: *There will usually be an instruction which tells you to either press, or cover with a damp cloth*. See TEACH.

instructions *plural noun*, means detailed information about how to complete an operation: *The documentation on disk with this program comes with full instructions and details of installing and loading*.

insulate, isolate

insulate *verb*, means to prevent the transmission of heat or sound: *The purpose of a sleeping bag is to insulate the body from the cold and prevent heat from escaping*. **Insulate** also means to protect something from direct contact with electricity: *Connect the two wires to the plug and then use tape to insulate the visible parts of the leads*. If a group of people is *insulated* from an unpleasant influence, it is protected from it, but not completely cut off: *Try to insulate children from arguments and rows*.

isolate *verb*, means to separate someone or something: *Should the youth workers have tried to integrate these boys into 'the community', or to isolate them from it?* *To feel isolated* means to experience a sense of being alone: *Professionally I feel rather isolated at the moment*.

insurance

See ASSURANCE.

insure

See ASSURE.

intelligent, intellectual

intelligent *adjective*, refers either to a person or animal that has highly developed mental abilities: *These dogs are very intelligent and relatively easy to train*; or to a computer that can develop its own solutions to problems: *If the user receives a document containing a font that is not already installed, the intelligent software will be able to construct a close match*.

intellectual *adjective & noun*. As an adjective, this refers to thinking philosophically about life and to a logical sense of reasoning: *Alcohol depresses the nervous system, and taken in excess impairs intellectual functioning*. As a noun, an **intellectual** means a person who thinks deeply and philosophically about their life and the serious things in life such as art, science and literature: *Johnson was voicing an intellectual's fashionable enquiry into the lastingness of common interest*.

> Note that *intelligent* does not necessarily imply academic ability but *intellectual* does.

intense, intensive

intense *adjective*, means extreme or very strong: *Intense competition in the insurance market has kept premiums low.*

intensive *adjective*, means highly concentrated: *The intensive use of highly automated equipment has reduced the workforce.*

intensify

See **HEIGHTEN**.

inter, intern

inter *verb*, means to bury a dead person: *Her ashes were interred in the church's garden of remembrance.* See **BURY**.

intern *verb & noun*. As a verb, this means to imprison without trial, either for political reasons, or for security in time of war: *He was arrested on allegations of anti-American activities and interned on Ellis Island.* As a noun, it is used in AE as the equivalent of BE house officer in a hospital, and also means a person, usually a student, gaining work experience through a temporary job. See **INTERNSHIP (WORK EXPERIENCE)**.

inter-, intra-

inter- *prefix*, means between or among: *international* (between nations), *interdisciplinary* (involving two or more academic subjects). It also means mutual, as in *interaction* (the way in which two or more things act on each other): *Science must be viewed as an interaction between scientists and society.*

intra- *prefix*, means within or inside: *intranational* (within a nation), *intravenous* (within, or into, a vein)

> *Internet* is a blend word derived from *international network*, but by analogy, an *Intranet* is a local computer network based on World Wide Web technology, but restricted in access to the staff in a single organization. See **BLEND WORDS (WORD FORMATION)**.

interdisciplinary

See **CROSS-DISCIPLINARY**.

interface, connection

interface *noun & verb*. As a noun in technical usage this means the surface between two types of matter: *the air/liquid interface*. In computing, the term means much more than a boundary and means either the connection between two items of hardware such as the *printer – laptop interface* or even the way in which information is presented to users: *the Windows user interface*. Thus the term involves the design and layout of icons and menus on the screen. As a verb, **interface** can mean to combine and cooperate: *The project team will interface with customers on a regular basis*. Overuse of **interface** means that boundary, connection and layout may be more exact terms for the noun and contact, link, connect and join are all alternatives to the verb.

connection *noun*, means either the point at which two units in an electrical or mechanical system are connected, or the link between two factors or ideas. In this sense **connection** focuses on two things. The spelling *connexion* is sometimes seen as an alternative in BE. See **CONNECTIONS**.

interfere

See **MEDDLE**.

interment, internment

interment *noun*, means the act of burying a corpse or a person's ashes: *Her life excited such admiration that after her death the interment had to be delayed for some days.* This is a clinical and legal term and is not suitable in general contexts. Note that the stress is on the second syllable: intérmĕnt /ɪnˈtɜːrmənt/. See **BURIAL**.

internment *noun*, means imprisonment without trial, usually of enemy nationals during wartime: *When war broke out he had to endure four months' internment as an enemy alien.*

intermission, interval

intermission *noun*, means a break, particularly in a theatre performance or concert: *Let's order drinks for the intermission now, so we won't have to queue then.*

The internment will be in the parish burial ground immediately after the service. (British order of service for a funeral)

interval *noun*, means a gap or a length of time, in particular the break in a theatre performance between acts or between sessions of play in sports: *City added a fourth just before the interval*. In music an **interval** is the amount of pitch difference between two notes: *An octave interval means a doubling of the wave frequency from the lower to the upper note*. In the sense of a break in a theatrical performance, **interval** is an alternative to *intermission* in BE, but not in AE.

intern

See INTER.

internment

See INTERMENT.

internship

See WORK EXPERIENCE.

interpret

See TRANSLATE.

interstate, intestate

interstate *noun & adjective*, means between states. The numbers of two-lane highways for fast trans-state travel in the USA are preceded by **Interstate** or *I*: *The Pentagon is surrounded by Interstate 395 and Washington Boulevard*. Note the word is capitalized here. See AMERICAN ROAD TYPES.

intestate intéstayt /ɪn'testeɪt/ adjective, means that a person dies without making a will: *He died intestate and administration of his estate was granted to his son John*.

> *. . . the circumstances surrounding the investment made by this client who died interstate . . .*
> (Nigerian scam email) **!**

interval

See INTERMISSION.

into, in to

into *preposition*, means movement from outside to inside something: *The hotel operates a bus service into the village for a small charge*. In this sense, **into** is written as one word.

in to *adverb + preposition*. When **in** forms part of a phrasal verb such as *give in*, and is followed by **to**, this is always written as two words: *The President has given in to the nationalists over the question of property restitution*. This is also the case when **in** is used as an adverb followed by **to**: *Alice went in to join the others around the table*.

intolerable, intolerant

intolerable *adjective*, refers to someone or something that cannot be endured: *Caring for her two elderly parents and her own three children was an intolerable burden*.

intolerant *adjective*, refers to someone who is not able to accept or agree with people whose ideas or behaviour are different from their own: *Her father was grumpy, without any sense of humour, and was intolerant of those who believed in equal rights*.

intoxicate

See POISON.

intra-

See INTER-.

intrinsic

See INHERENT.

introduction

See STYLE GUIDELINES (WRITING SKILLS).

Inuit, Eskimo

Inuit *noun plural*, are the indigenous people living in northern Canada, parts of Alaska and Greenland. The singular form is *Inuk*. *Inuktitut* is the name of their language.

Eskimo *noun*, are the indigenous people in Siberia and south and west Alaska. Although this is the only common term to describe the entire *Inuit*/**Eskimo** people, some prefer to be called *Inuit* and regard **Eskimo** as offensive.

inundate, overwhelm

inundate *verb*. To be inundated means to have problems keeping up with a lot of incoming work or requests. When you are inundated this is usually a temporary state of affairs: *The spam filter did not work and we were all inundated with spam emails last week*. A piece of land can be inundated by water in flood conditions. In this sense **inundate** is a formal word and flood is an alternative.

overwhelm *verb*, means to be overcome by force or to be inundated: *The demonstrators were overwhelmed by the police in a matter of hours*. In another context, it means to be overcome by emotion: *She was overwhelmed by the amount of messages of support that she received*.

invalid

See DISABLED.

invalidate

See ANNUL.

invaluable

See VALUABLE.

invasive, non-invasive

invasive *adjective*, refers to surgical operations that involve introducing instruments into the body, either by cutting open the skin, or by instruments penetrating any of the body's orifices: *Minimal invasive surgery involves executing the maximum amount of work through the smallest incision*. **Invasive** is also used to describe illnesses such as cancer which spread through the body: *Invasive cells spread into the tissues surrounding the primary tumour*; and plants which spread easily and are difficult to control: *Mint is extremely invasive, sending out new shoots everywhere from its creeping underground stems*.

non-invasive *adjective*, describes medical procedures that do not involve inserting instruments into the body, such as X-rays, ultrasound, or blood pressure measurement: *A reliable non-invasive diagnostic technique would represent a considerable advance*. Illnesses which remain in one place and do not spread are also called **non-invasive**: *Unlike melanomas, basal cell carcinomas are slow growing and non-invasive and are readily curable if treated early*. **Non-invasive** also applies to plants which do not spread: *This imported plant has long-lived flowers, and is non-invasive*.

invention

See INNOVATION.

inverse

See REVERSE.

inverted commas

See PUNCTUATION GUIDE.

invitation, invite

invitation *noun*, is a spoken or written request to attend an event: *The other day I sent you the invitation to the assembly here in June*; or to do something: *Gordon Brown accepted the Queen's invitation to form a government*. In formal English, *invitations* are *extended* and are either *accepted* or *declined*. Informally, an **invitation** is *offered*, and in the case of rejection this can be *turned down*. If a formal invitation ends with the abbreviation *RSVP* (*Répondez s'il vous plaît* – French for 'please reply') this means you are expected to let the hosts know whether you will attend or not. See DRESS CODES.

invite ínvīt /'ɪnvaɪt/ *noun* & invīt /ɪn'vaɪt/ *verb*. As a noun this is an informal word to mean an invitation: *We're going to a party on Saturday night – it's my friend's birthday party, I'll see if I can get you an invite*. As a verb, **invite** means to ask someone to attend an event: *We will invite some of the neighbours over*. In another context a contribution is politely requested: *You are invited to submit an article of 3,000 words*.

ionic, Ionic

ionic ī-ónnik /aɪˈɒnɪk/ *adjective*, means related to ions. This is not capitalized unless it is the first word in a sentence. See **ION (IRON)**.

Ionic *adjective*, is the style of ancient Greek architecture associated with Ionia: *an Ionic column*. In this sense, **Ionic** is always capitalized.

Iran, Iranian

Iran *noun*, is the name of the country bordering Iraq in the west, and Afghanistan in the east, pronounced ira̋an /ɪˈrɑːn/. It was formerly known as Persia.

Iranian *adjective & noun*, means the people of *Iran*, their culture and languages. Note that the second syllable is pronounced 'rain': iráyni-ăn /ɪˈreɪniən/.

Iraq, Iraqi

Iraq *noun*, is the name of the country bordering Iran in the east, and Saudi Arabia in the South, pronounced ira̋ak /ɪˈrɑːk/.

Iraqi *adjective & noun*, means the people of *Iraq* and their culture. It is pronounced ira̋aki /ɪˈrɑːki/. The plural is *Iraqis*. Note that there is no 'u' in this word.

Irish, Eire, Hibernian

Irish *adjective & noun*, means related to Ireland, its people or the Celtic language spoken there. See **GAELIC**.

Eire áirĕ /ˈeərə/ *noun*, is the Celtic name for the Republic of Ireland. Note that this is pronounced as two syllables.

Hibernian *adjective*, means of or related to Ireland and is now only used in names of institutions and clubs. It originates from the Latin *Hibernia*. Note that the Edinburgh football club of this name is pronounced hibbérni-ăn /hɪˈbɜːrniən/, and abbreviated to 'Hibs'.

iron, ion

iron *noun & verb*. As a noun, **iron** has several meanings. First, it is the name of the metal with the chemical symbol Fe. Like all elements, **iron** is an uncountable noun and always takes a singular verb: *Wrought iron rusts much more slowly than steel*. Second, an **iron** is a type of golf club: *At the 13th he hit the green with a perfectly struck long iron for his four*. Third, it is an appliance for pressing clothes in order to eliminate creases in the fabric: *I use a fairly hot iron over the neck area*. In these last two senses, **iron** is a countable noun. As a verb, **iron** means to press clothes: *We recommend that you iron the tablecloth on the reverse side while still damp*. Note that in southern BE the 'r' is silent in **iron**.

ion *noun*, is a technical term in physics meaning an electrically charged particle. A positively charged **ion** is called a *cation*, pronounced kátt-ī-ŏn /ˈkætaɪən/, and a negatively charged **ion** is an *anion*, pronounced ánn-ī-ŏn /ˈænaɪən/.

irregardless

See **REGARDLESS**.

irreligious, non-religious, sacrilegious

irreligious *adjective*, refers to a person or organization that is hostile to or against religion: *The Pharisees and Scribes would not eat with the ordinary people as they considered them to be irreligious*.

non-religious *adjective*, means not religious but has no connotations of hostility to religion: *Many religious people are as worried as non-religious people about the abuse of religion*.

sacrilegious *adjective*, means disregarding the holy nature of a religious object: *I felt it was rather sacrilegious to mention Jesus's name aloud where we were*. In a sense extended from this, **sacrilegious** means treating something without respect: *There is something vaguely sacrilegious about disturbing the wildlife in the woods at night*.

> Note that although *irreligious* and *non-religious* are related to the word *religion*, *sacrilegious* is not, and is spelt '-rileg-' in the middle.

irremovable

See **IMMOBILE**.

irreparable, unrepairable

irreparable irréppărăbĕl /ɪˈrepərəbl̩/ *adjective*, refers to damage or loss that cannot be made good: *Peat-cutting operations are causing irreparable damage to the fragile habitat of lowland peat-bogs*. It can also refer to reputations that cannot be repaired: *The newspaper article caused irreparable damage to the author's reputation*. The opposite adjective is *reparable*, pronounced réppărăbĕl /ˈrepərəbl̩/. See **REPARABLE (REPAIRABLE)**.

unrepairable unrĕpaírăbĕl /ʌnrɪˈpeərəbl̩/ *adjective*, refers to material objects that cannot be repaired: *They broke four legs off a bed making it unrepairable*. The opposite adjective is *repairable*, pronounced rĕpaírăbĕl /rɪˈpeərəbl̩/. See **REPAIRABLE**.

irrespective

See **RESPECTIVE**.

-ise

This book has followed the style of the *Longman Dictionary of Contemporary English* and used the *-ize* spelling for verbs when this is one of the alternatives. However, some verbs derived from nouns may *only* be spelt **-ise** in both BE and AE. Here the 'parent' nouns will usually have either an 's' or a 'c' in the spelling. Examples:

advertise; advise; apprise; arise; chastise; circumcise; comprise; compromise; despise; devise; disenfranchise; disfranchise; disguise; enfranchise; excise; exercise; franchise; improvise; incise; merchandise; revise; supervise; surmise; surprise; televise.

-ise is also the only correct spelling in both BE and AE when the ending of the word is pronounced 'ice' īs /aɪs/, 'iss' iss /ɪs/ or 'ease' eez /iːz/ as in *precise*, *practise* and *expertise*. Also note the pronunciation izz /ɪz/ that is spelt **-ise** in *premise* and *promise*.

-ise is also the only correct spelling in both BE and AE when a noun has an ending pronounced 'eyes' īz /aɪz/: *demise*; *enterprise*. See **-IZE (-IZATION)**.

Islam, Muslim, Muhammadan, Islamism, Islamist

Islam *uncountable noun*, is the religion of those who follow the teaching of Mohammed. The two main branches of **Islam** are Sunni and Shia. Note that the first syllable of **Islam** is stressed and the second syllable rhymes with 'calm': ísslaam /ˈɪslɑːm/. A related adjective is *Islamic* which is used in phrases such as the *Islamic movement*. Note that the second syllable is stressed and rhymes with 'cam': isslámmik /ɪsˈlæmɪk/.

Muslim *noun & adjective*, is a follower of the religion of **Islam**. Most modern English dictionaries list this spelling for the religion and organizations such as the *Muslim Brotherhood*. Note that in the correct pronunciation, the first syllable rhymes with 'puss' and not with 'buzz': mŏ́osslim /ˈmʊslɪm/. *Moslem* is an older variant spelling.

Muhammadan *noun & adjective*, is an archaic term for *Muslim* that is disliked by *Muslims*. *Muhammadanism* is also an offensive term for *Islam* and should be avoided. When referring to the prophet Muhammad, use a capital M. Mohammad and Mohammed are alternative spellings.

Islamism ísslămizm /ˈɪsləmɪzm̩/ *uncountable noun*, is a controversial term often used, by Muslims and non-Muslims alike, to mean the promotion of the values of *Islam* and Sharia law throughout the world, and not just in traditionally *Muslim* countries. At one extreme, it may simply be a synonym for *Islam*, and at the other it is used as a convenient shorthand in the Western media for *Islamic extremism*.

Islamist ísslămist /ˈɪsləmɪst/ *noun*, is often used in the Western media to mean an advocate of the extension of Islamic beliefs and practices to all countries, or an Islamic extremist. It can also be a synonym for *Muslim*. As it may have negative connotations, this word should be used with care.

isle, aisle

isle *noun*, means an island. It is generally used only in literary contexts or in proper names such as the *Isle of Wight* or the *British Isles*.

aisle *noun*, means a passageway between rows of seats in a building, a plane or train: *Susan and I sauntered down the aisle and took seats a few rows back*. *To walk down the aisle* means to get married, but *rolling in the aisles* means constantly laughing: *The* *stand-up comedian had the audience rolling in the aisles.*

ISO is a word

Many people have noticed the lack of correspondence between the full title of the *International Organization for Standardization* and the short form, **ISO**, which is a word, not an abbreviation or acronym. Neither of the official full names – *International Organization for Standardization* in English and *Organisation internationale de normalisation* in French – can be shortened to ISO. The term is derived from the Greek *isos*, meaning equal, which is the root of the prefix *iso-* in numerous terms, such as *isobar* (line on a map connecting points of equal air pressure), *isocline* (line on a map connecting points of equal gradient), and *isometric* (having equal dimensions). Note that the pronunciation of the prefix with such words is íssō /ˈaɪsəʊ/. The normal English pronunciation of ISO is either éssō /ˈiːsəʊ/, which is the more usual one, or íssō /ˈaɪsəʊ/. (For more on ISO, see http://www.iso.ch/iso/en/aboutiso/introduction/index.html)

isolate

See INSULATE.

Israeli, Israelite, Jew, Jewish, Judaism, Hebrew

Israeli *noun & adjective*. As a noun, this means a native of Israel. The plural is *Israelis*: *Israelis are pleased with the change in US regulations*. As an adjective, it means of or relating to the modern state of Israel: *An Israeli diplomat visited Vietnam in early February*.

Israelite *noun*, is a term for the ancient Hebrew nation and is only used in biblical and historical contexts. It is often regarded as an offensive term if used for a *Jew* today.

Jew *noun*, is a member of the people and cultural community that claims descent from the biblical children of Israel: *Spinoza was a Dutch Jew of Portuguese descent*. The feminine form *Jewess* is often offensive and can be replaced by *a Jewish woman/Jewish girl*.

Jewish *adjective*, means associated with *Jews* or *Judaism*. This is the correct adjective form: *Jewish laws on hygiene are among the most stringent in the world*. There is no language called **Jewish**.

Judaism *noun*, is the religion of the *Jews*. Note that this word has three syllables and the second one is pronounced 'day': jóoday-izm /ˈdʒuːdeɪɪzm̩/.

Hebrew *noun*, is the national language of Israel. In modern times, **Hebrew** refers only to the language: *Courses in Hebrew language and literature are provided by the Faculty of Arts*, although in biblical usage, the **Hebrews** were the children of Israel. Nowadays it may be offensive to refer to a person as **Hebrew**.

issue

See TOPIC.

italics, italic, italicize

italics *noun*, is the name of the sloping typeface used in this book for parts of speech and examples of usage. It takes a plural verb: *Italics are often used for emphasis*.

italic *adjective*, refers to a sloping typeface such as that used in this book for the part of speech of each headword. When capitalized, **Italic** is a technical term in linguistics which refers to the group of ancient Indo-European languages to which Latin, Oscan and Umbrian belonged.

italicize *verb*, means to write something in *italics*: *Make sure you italicize all the command words in this document*.

itinerary

See ROUTE.

its, it's

its *pronoun*, means something belonging to a thing or animal: *Every society needs its flawed heroes*. Note that none of the possessive pronouns (*his, hers, ours, yours* and *theirs*) includes an apostrophe. See APOSTROPHE (PUNCTUATION GUIDE).

it's is the contraction for *it is* or *it has*: *It's a sign of growing up; It's got windows on all sides*. **It's** is correct in spoken and informal written English, but note that *it is* and *it has* are correct in formal writing. See **CONTRACTIONS**.

> *'Use our full-text international translation – known for it's accuracy and readability.'*
> (Web advert)

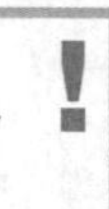

Ivy League

See **OXBRIDGE**.

-ization, -isation, -ize, -ise

-ization, -isation

-ization and **-isation** are alternative spellings in BE. Only the **-ization** spelling is used in AE. As a result, all UN organizations, ISO – *the International Organization for Standardization*, and most of the international business community use the **-ization** spelling. However, much of British industry and some European institutions use the **-isation** spelling. The most important rule is to be consistent: do not mix the spellings in the same document.

-ize, -ise

In BE, **-ize** is becoming established as the ending of many verbs and many recent BE dictionaries have used the **-ize** spelling throughout and noted **-ise** only as an alternative. This book favours the **-ize** spelling wherever it reflects the root of the word. Note that after -y, BE consistently uses *-yse*. In AE, the **-ize** spelling applies to most verbs and after 'y' only the *-yze* spelling is used: *analyze, electrolyze, paralyze*. See **-YSE**.

Note that **-ise** is always the correct spelling in both BE and AE for certain verbs. Examples include: *advertise, advise, comprise, exercise, practise, supervise*. See **-ISE**.

Adding **-ize** to create new verbs is standard and stresses an activity or change of state: *characterize, finalize, hospitalize, prioritize* and *randomize*. All are accepted in BE. Some of these verbs are struggling to become accepted, and *tailored solutions* are better than *customized* ones in formal BE. It is best to use such new verbs with care, as *slim down* is preferred to *slenderize* and *burgle* is preferred to *burglarize*.

Those who use British English and the **-ise/-isation** spellings (as used by the British press) may inadvertently make readers feel that their research paper, brochure, report or document is written exclusively for the British market. If your work is aimed at the international market, it is worth following the trend in the latest BE dictionaries and using the **-ize/-ization** alternatives, which for once agree with American spelling.

It is incorrect to consider these spellings as the respective forms of AE and BE verb endings. Although AE has always used the **-ize** form with a few exceptions, the spelling in BE was **-ize** from the sixteenth century (from Greek or Latin stems) and it was the influence of French that brought **-ise** into more general use in BE.

Spelling

iceb**e**rg	Note this is -berg, not -burg
ic**i**cle	Note -i- as the second vowel
idi**osy**ncra**sy**	Note the -osy- and final -sy
ignom**in**ious	Remember the -in-
impl**e**ment	Note the -e- in the second syllable
impu**g**n	Note the -g-
imp**un**ity	Note there is no -g-
inaug**u**ral	Note the second -u-
independ**ent**	Note the -ent at the end
indi**ct**	Note the -c- (which is not pronounced)
infall**i**ble	Note -ible, not -able
i**n**oculate	Note that there is only a single -n-
i**nn**ocuous	Note that there is a double -nn- in this word
int**eg**rate	Note there is no 'r' before the -g-
inter**cede**	See *-cede, -ceed, -sede*
irre**par**able	Note the single -p- and no 'i' following the first -a-
i**rr**esist**ible**	Note the -rr-, and -ible at the end

J

jail, gaol

jail *noun*, means a prison. This is the usual spelling in BE and the only spelling in AE: *Los Angeles police handcuffed him and hauled him off to jail.* A *jailbird* is someone who has often been in prison.

gaol *noun*, is an alternative BE spelling of *jail*: *For his pains the House of Commons put him in gaol.* The pronunciation remains the same.

jargon

Jargon means technical language used by any group for communication within that group. Specialized work on a particular subject, such as the law, linguistics, computer science, medicine or chemistry, will be full of terminology that the general reader could not be expected to understand. For instance, this quotation from *GUT: Journal of Gastroenterology and Hepatology*: 'The staining of the epithelial cells is cytoplasmic, involving the basolateral and, to a lesser extent, the apical surfaces of the cells.' The meaning of this is likely to be obvious among gastroenterologists, and there is probably no other way to say the same thing so clearly for that audience. However, in everyday speech, the use of 'epithelial', 'cytoplasmic', 'basolateral' and even 'apical' would be unacceptable, and doctors explaining a diagnosis to their patient would be well advised to find more everyday words to describe their findings.

Because some specialists find it difficult to put themselves in the position of non-specialists, the word **jargon** is often used in a critical way to dismiss this sort of language as incomprehensible and meaningless. The language used by computer specialists has come in for a great deal of criticism because the people who work in this field seem unable or unwilling to avoid technical terms when speaking to non-specialists. See **SLANG**.

jetsam

See **FLOTSAM**.

Jew, Jewish

See **ISRAELI**.

jibe, gybe

jibe *noun & verb*. As a noun this means an insulting or mocking remark about someone or something: *The SNP has now taken to calling Labour 'Tartan Tories', a jibe once more fairly directed at them.* As a verb it means to make such a remark: *'After all those hamburgers, you're far too heavy to be a jockey,' Nevil jibed.* In BE this is also spelt *gibe*. In AE, this verb also means to match: *His claim to speak Spanish doesn't jibe with all the errors he makes.*

gybe *noun & verb*. This is a variant AE spelling of *jibe*.

job

See **POSITION**.

jobless

See **REDUNDANT**.

journal, periodical

journal *noun*, means a newspaper or magazine. Many specialist academic journals and scientific journals have the word **journal** in their titles: *Wall Street Journal*; *British Medical Journal*. In another sense **journal** means a written record of things that are done usually in the context of an expedition or journey: *They kept a journal of their voyage up the Amazon.*

periodical *noun & adjective*. As a noun, this means a magazine that is published at specified intervals. Many periodicals concentrate on specialist subjects or are academic journals: *This periodical is published weekly and has a circulation of 40,000.* As an adjective, it can mean occurring or appearing at intervals: *On his journey, he endured hot summers and periodical earthquakes.*

journey

See **TRAVEL**.

Judaism

See **ISRAELI**.

judge

See **REFEREE**.

judgement, judgment

judgement *noun*, means the ability to make considered decisions: *This is a sound judgement of the school curriculum: it has to be related to the child's needs*. It is usually spelt with both e's in BE.

judgment *noun*, is standard AE spelling and also the spelling used in BE in legal contexts: *The law courts in the Strand pronounce a terrible judgment on the visitor as soon as he enters*.

judicial, judicious

judicial *adjective*, refers to legal matters and courts of law: *The courts are taking a very restricted attitude to their powers of judicial review in these cases*.

judicious *adjective*, refers to good judgement: *The British aristocracy has managed to preserve its wealth through judicious marriage arrangements*. This word has nothing to do with legal matters. It is a formal word.

juggernaut

See **LORRY**.

junction, juncture

junction *noun*, is a point where two or more things join: *At the next junction take the left path signed Webbers Post*.

juncture *noun*, means a particular point in time: *At this juncture the Chair suggested a vote was taken*. It is often used by politicians or business people to refer to a delicate stage in a crisis or during negotiations: *The changes to his report seem bound to weaken his position at an important juncture in the country's political life*. **Juncture** is also a technical term used in linguistics to mark the boundaries of two utterances or the transition between two elements of an utterance. This is a formal word.

junior

See **FRESHMAN**.

junior doctor, house officer

junior doctor *noun*, means a person in postgraduate medical training starting at graduation with a medical degree and culminating in a post as consultant or general practitioner. The term **junior doctor** may be misleading as it refers to a training process lasting for several years.

house officer *noun*, is the title used for the first two years for a junior doctor working in a hospital. The full title of the position is *Foundation House Officer* in the UK. The title of this post was formerly *houseman*. In other parts of the world this stage is called an internship. See **INTERN (INTER)**.

Both these terms are BE usage.

junior school, junior high school, high school, junior college

junior school *compound noun*, is part of the compulsory education system in England and Wales and is typically for pupils aged between 7 and 11.

junior high school *compound noun*, is part of the compulsory education system in the USA and Canada and is for pupils in the seventh to ninth grades (aged 12 to 14). See **SCHOOL**.

high school *compound noun*, is a secondary school in the USA for pupils aged 14 to 18. In Britain this is not a type of secondary school but is used in the names of some schools with pupils aged 11 to 18 (e.g. *Wycombe High School*).

junior college *compound noun*, is part of the higher education system in the USA. Education at **junior college** starts after high school and offers either a complete two-year course or preparation for full degree education.

juror, jurist

juror *noun*, means a member of a jury: *A juror's duty is to make an assessment on evidence available at the time*.

jurist *noun*, means an expert on the law, particularly someone who writes on legal subjects: *He was a keen jurist and in legal matters he had the respect of the majority in the National Assembly*. In AE, a **jurist** may also mean a lawyer or judge.

just

See EQUITABLE.

juvenile, puerile

juvenile *adjective & noun*. As an adjective, **juvenile** means not adult or fully grown and is used for people or animals: *The influx of 17-year-olds has doubled the number of juvenile offenders coming before magistrates*. As a term of disapproval, **juvenile** means childish: *Laura chided herself for having over-reacted in such a feeble, juvenile way*. As a noun, **juvenile** means a person or animal that is not fully mature: *She had several convictions for theft although she was only a juvenile*. An actor who plays the parts of young people is also known as a **juvenile**: *The new romantic juvenile looked the part but could not act*.

puerile *adjective*, means silly, childish. It is almost always used in a critical or disapproving way: *One can scan a whole evening's TV programmes and find only puerile junk on every channel*.
See CHILDISH (CHILDLIKE).

Spelling

j**ea**lousy	Remember the -ea- in the first syllable
j**eo**pardy	Note the -eo- in the first syllable
jocul**ar**	Note the ending: -ar
judi**c**ial	Note the ending: -cial

Kashmir

See CASHMERE.

kerb

See CURB.

kerosene, kérosine

See PARAFFIN.

ketchup, catsup

ketchup *noun*, is a type of spicy tomato sauce. This is the usual BE spelling.

catsup is the usual AE spelling and pronunciation of *ketchup*.

key, quay

key *noun, adjective & verb*. As a noun, a **key** is the instrument used to open or close a lock. Figuratively the **key** is the element that guarantees success: *Industrialization was seen as the key to international strength*. The **keys** on a PC keyboard are the buttons that are pressed to enter information. In music a **key** is both one of the black and white blocks that are pressed down to create the sounds on a keyboard, and the names of the scales, according to the note they begin on: *The minuet movement is in the key of C minor*. In addition, a reef or low island such as those off the coast of Florida is known as a **key** (also written *cay*). As an adjective **key** means essential: *A national communication policy will be a key element in future planning*. As a verb, see KEY IN.

quay *noun*, is a landing stage built alongside water or projecting into it for ships to moor at: *The weather-worn fishing fleet was moored in tidy rows against the quay*. Note that **quay** is pronounced **kee** /kiː/. See DOCK.

key in, type in, enter, overwrite

key in *phrasal verb*, means to enter data on a computer system by means of the keyboard or rows of buttons, as in a cash machine: *Whenever you want to make a withdrawal, just key in the amount at any cash machine*. Note that **key in** is used for short commands.

type in *phrasal verb*, originally meant to type characters on a typewriter and is now used for writing something on a keyboard: *This brings up a dialogue box, where you type in the necessary alterations*.

enter *verb*, means to write information into a computer, especially on a form or dialogue box: *Enter the name of the source you wish to update*.

overwrite *verb*, means to replace data that has already been entered in a file or on the screen of a computer: *In the overwrite mode you erase existing text to the right of the cursor and replace it automatically with your alteration*.

kickback, kick-off

kickback *noun*. In business this is an informal term of disapproval for a secret payment to someone who facilitated a transaction: *A 10 per cent kickback – or bung – to the football agent is the norm*. **Kickback** also means the recoil from a gun: *The kickback from the rifle hurt his shoulder*. In this sense, **kickback** is an uncountable noun. See BUNG (BRIBE).

kick-off *noun*. This is an informal word for the start of something: *This weekend is the start of Golden Week, the traditional kick-off for Japan's holiday season*. This is borrowed from the football term meaning the point at which the game starts or is restarted after a goal: *Rangers lost the ball from the kick-off, and stood and stared as their opponents cut through their defence*.

kilo-

See MIL..

kind of/sort of, type of

kind of/sort of *noun phrase*, means the common characteristic of a group of people or things: *He has this image in his head of the kind of/sort of person he'd like to be*. Note that **kind of/sort of** should be treated as a singular, and *kinds of/sorts of* should be treated as a plural. Some usage guides and dictionaries consider 'these kind/sort of' ungrammatical, but it has been recorded since the fourteenth century. In AE, **kind of/sort of** (written and pronounced 'kinda'/'sorta') is widely used in informal speech as a way of making something sound less harsh: *'You'll like it here; it's kinda/sorta fun.'* This informal usage is becoming more common in BE as well.

type of *noun phrase*, also means a group of people or things with a common feature. Although **type of** is sometimes interchangeable with *kind of* or *sort of*, it can refer to a more precise means of classification. Compare *This is the kind/sort of chocolate I like*, (plain rather than milk) with *This is the type of chocolate I like* (one brand rather than another).

> These noun phrases indicate means of classifying people or things. Note that they can all be used in singular or plural forms: *This type/kind/sort of book is interesting* and *These types/kinds/sorts of books are not sold here*. Careful writers avoid mixing the singular and plural. Phrases such as *these type/kind/sort of books are not sold here* should be avoided.

kink, kinky

kink *noun*, means a twist in a rope: *If a loop in the cable is overlooked, it becomes a small kink*; a short deviation from a straight line: *There was a very obvious kink where the avenue made a bend to avoid some particularly valuable eighteenth-century houses*; a problem to be solved: *There are still some kinks in this software*; or (informally) someone with unusual sexual preferences: *He is a kink and is building up a cult where sexual abuse is advocated*. The last of these senses is the least common.

kinky *adjective*, refers to unusual sexual behaviour or preferences: *His partners did not like his kinky habits in bed*. Although **kinky** can mean twisted or curly, as in *kinky hair*, its most usual meaning refers to sexual perversion, so this word needs to be used with care. See PERVERSE.

kirby-grip, Kirbigrip

See HAIRPIN.

knell, knoll

knell *noun*, is the sound of a bell ringing slowly to signal a death. It often appears figuratively in the phrase *death knell*: *This row signalled the death knell of their marriage*. This is a literary term.

knoll nōl /nəʊl/ *noun*, means a low rounded hill: *The hill, or knoll, was almost completely surrounded by suburbs*.

knifes, knives

knifes *verb*, is the third person singular present form of the verb *to knife*, meaning to attack with a *knife*. It is an informal word, and most often found in newspaper headlines: *Father knifes son, 10, police say*.

knives *plural noun*, is the plural form of the noun *knife*.

knot, miles per hour, metres per second

knot *noun*, is a unit of speed that means one nautical mile per hour. As **knot** is a speed, not a distance, 'knots per hour' is incorrect and should be avoided. The **knot** is used to measure the speed of the wind over the sea for ships or at high altitude for aircraft: *With a 26 to 30 knot wind 30 degrees off the runway at Santander we had a rough landing*. The phrase *a good rate of knots* means a reasonably high speed.

miles per hour *noun phrase*, is also a measure of speed. *Per hour* must be included as a *mile* is a distance, not a speed. This measure of speed is used for the wind at ground level over land, and for the speed of anything else on land. The normal abbreviation is mph: *The cheetah can attain speeds of 60 mph for about 20 seconds*.

metres per second *noun phrase*, is used to measure wind speeds in many parts of the world: *Winds in the Alps will reach 35 metres*

> *With a name like Kinki Nippon Tourist Company you are asking for it in the English-speaking world and Japan's second-largest tourist agency was mystified when it received repeated requests for unusual sex tours. Instead of obliging, Kinki Nippon changed its name.*

per second today. The standard scientific abbreviation is m/s but the abbreviation m/sec is also used. A rough conversion to mph is to multiply metres per second by two.

> If something is travelling at 50 mph, this is equivalent to 43 knots or 22 m/s (metres per second).

knowledge, wisdom

knowledge *uncountable noun*, means the understanding and skills acquired through education or life experience: *You must continually assimilate new information into the context of your earlier knowledge*. In another sense, it means awareness of a particular situation: *I don't do things like this without the full knowledge and approval of the Royal Family*. The derived adjective *knowledgeable* is written with three e's.

wisdom *uncountable noun*, means the application of knowledge in order to make sensible decisions and to offer sound advice: *She was an old friend, and the experience of a long life gave us the benefit of her words of wisdom*.

kudos

See PRESTIGE.

K

Spelling

kal**ei**doscope	Note the -ei-
knapsack	Note the initial k-
knowledg**e**able	Remember the -e- following the -g-

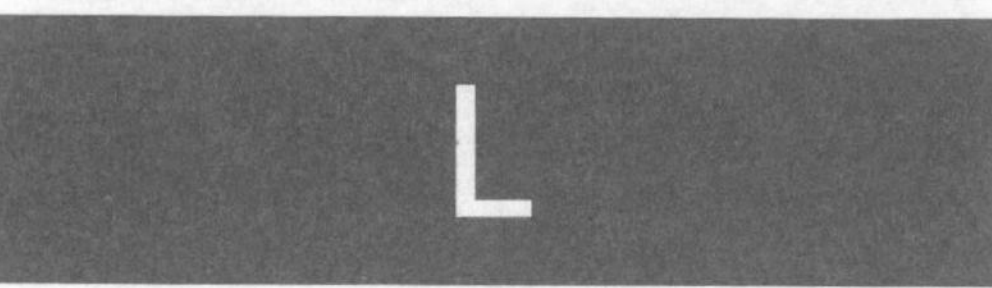

L

labor union

See TRADE UNION.

lady, Madam, ma'am, madame, mesdames

lady *noun*, is a rather formal way to refer to a woman: *We stepped back as the elderly lady began to pick up her bag*. It is the correct title to give to the wife of a lord or knight, and also appears as part of some job titles: *tea lady*. In the House of Commons, a female member of another party is called the Hon. Lady: *I am grateful to the Hon. Lady for her support*. When addressing a mixed group in a formal situation the standard initial phrase is: *Ladies and Gentlemen*.

(Cocktail lounge notice)

Madam *noun*, is a polite way of addressing a woman at the start of a formal letter or email: *Dear Madam*, and is thus the female equivalent of *Dear Sir*. In speech, it is used before a title to address a female: *Madam President, Madam Mayor*. Otherwise its only use is to refer respectfully to a female customer in shops or restaurants: *Would Madam like a seat by the window?* In all these senses, **Madam** has an initial capital letter. Without a capital letter, a *madam* is the woman in charge of a brothel, or a bossy or cheeky girl.

ma'am *noun*. In spoken AE, **ma'am** is used as a polite way to address any woman: *Pleased to meet you, ma'am*. In BE, this is used as the equivalent of 'sir' when addressing a superior female military or police officer, pronounced maam /mɑːm/, and in addressing female royalty, when it is pronounced mamm /mæm/ to rhyme with 'jam', and written with a capital M.

madame *noun*, is the French word for lady, and is used in English as a title for women in certain areas of the arts such as ballet, or for fortune tellers.

mesdames *noun*, is the plural of *madame*.

lager

See BEER.

laid

See LIE[1].

lama

See LLAMA.

landscape

See SCENERY.

landward, landwards

landward *adjective*, means facing towards land: *You will get a better view of the island from the landward side of the boat*. Note that this is only used before a noun.

landwards *adverb*, is the corresponding adverb, and describes a movement towards land: *After three hours, the ship sailed landwards*. *Landward* is an alternative form, especially in AE.

lane, carriageway (roads)

lane *noun*, means a division of a road marked by painted lines to separate the lines of traffic: *Extensive bus lane and priority traffic signalling has been approved for the city centre*. Three-lane motorways are divided into the *inside lane*, *middle lane* and *outside lane*. The *inside lane* is also called the *slow lane* and the *outside lane* (*passing lane* in AE) is also called the *fast lane*. Figuratively *life in* *the fast lane* means a life full of excitement, danger and expense. **Lane** also means a road in a town or city where it sometimes occurs in road names like *Park Lane*. It can also be a small narrow street between buildings in a town and a narrow road, often in the countryside. See STREET.

carriageway *noun*, means one of the two sides of a large road or motorway for traffic moving in the same direction: *The northbound carriageway on the M25 is blocked*. This is a BE term that is often combined with 'dual' as in *dual carriageway* (this is called a 'divided highway' in AE). See AMERICAN ROAD TYPES.

La Niña

See EL NIÑO.

lapse

See ELAPSE.

large, substantial, considerable, big

large *adjective*, refers to size, quantity or extent: *a large hole, a large retail chain, a large population centre*. It is found in several set expressions, including *at large, as large as life* and *by and large*.

substantial *adjective*, means extensive in size, amount, form or significance: *If you have followed through all the exercises in this book, you have done a substantial amount of work*.

considerable *adjective*, also means extensive in size, amount or significance, but usually less than substantial: *Teaching machines had considerable appeal to the military and to large-scale industry*.

big *adjective*, means extensive in terms of size and importance: *Your wedding should be the biggest day of your life*. In the sentence *He was a big man*, **big** may mean either important or tall. In such cases, it is better to choose a less ambiguous adjective. **Big** has a variety of informal meanings, including enthusiastic: *He's a big Stones fan*. In formal writing, **big** is often a poor choice and it is better to use a more precise word such as *large, great, substantial* or *considerable*.

last, latest

See RECENT.

last name

See SURNAME.

Latin abbreviations in English

Many of the abbreviations used in formal written English are the short forms of Latin words. See entries for: **ca**, **cf.**, **e.g.**, **etc.**, **et al.**, **ibid.**, **i.e.**, **op. cit.**, **viz.** for some tips about how to use some of the most common ones.

Latin America

See AMERICA.

latitude, longitude

latitude *noun*, means the distance of a geographical position from the equator, expressed in degrees, minutes and seconds. The North Pole is 90° N (= ninety degrees north), and the South Pole is 90° S (= ninety degrees south): *San Francisco is situated at 37°46′45.48″ N*.

longitude lónjitewd /ˈlɒndʒɪtjuːd/ *noun*, means the distance of a geographical position east or west of an arbitrary meridian, expressed in degrees, minutes and seconds. The universal prime meridian, 0° of longitude, was fixed in 1884 as Greenwich. Places are shown as a number of degrees east or west of Greenwich. The maximum distance from Greenwich is thus 180° (half the circumference of the earth): *San Francisco is situated at 122°25′9.12″ W*.

Degrees, like hours, are divided into 60 minutes, and the minutes in turn are divided into 60 seconds.

latter

See FORMER.

laudable, laudatory

laudable *adjective*, means admirable, or worthy of praise, even if not totally successful: *The winter Olympic plans were laudable, the result – no gold medals – is sadly not*. See CREDITABLE.

laudatory láwdătŏri /ˈlɔːdətəri/ *adjective*, means expressing praise: *The new manifesto included a laudatory front-page endorsement* *from two national daily newspapers*. This is a formal word.

> Note that *laudable* and *laudatory* should never be interchanged.

lawful

See **LEGAL**.

lawyer

See **SOLICITOR**.

lay

See **LIE**[1].

lb

See **POUND**.

lead, led

lead[1] *noun*, is a soft metal, with the chemical symbol Pb: *From the late 1980s, lead was gradually eliminated from petrol*. **Lead** rhymes with 'fed'. *Lead pencils* actually contain graphite.

lead[2] *noun*, means the front of a group of moving people or animals: *As the procession reached the corner, we could see the school band in the lead*; or the advantage of one person or team in a competition: *The home team took the lead from a fifth-minute penalty*. Note that **lead** in this sense rhymes with 'feed'.

lead *verb*, means to be in charge of something: *Last year's captain will continue to lead the club this season*; or to be at the front: *The Irish horse was leading as they came to the last furlong marker*. *Lead to* can also mean to cause: *Excess stress on the body can ultimately lead to prolonged illness and possible death*. In another sense, **lead** means to experience: *She wanted to live in a flat, lead an ordinary life, and wait*. Note that **lead** in this sense also rhymes with 'feed'.

led *verb*, is the past tense and past participle of the verb *lead*: *Ahead of me was a glass-panelled oak door which led out to the sun terrace*.

> Never confuse the spellings of *lead* (metal) and *led* (past tense of the verb *to lead*), although they are pronounced the same.

leak, leek

leak *noun & verb*, refers to the accidental loss of gas or liquid from a pipe or container: *A gas leak at Bhopal, India, killed 2,500 people*. Figuratively, **leak** refers to the disclosure of confidential information: *The leader denied that any member of the party was connected with the leak; I can't carry on employing staff who might have been able to leak sensitive information*.

leek *noun*, is a vegetable related to the onion. It is also the Welsh national emblem: *The soup of the day is leek and cauliflower served with a crusty roll*.

lean

See **THIN**.

learned, learnt

learned[1] *adjective*, means scholarly, or refers to a person with much knowledge: *a learned author*. It can also be applied to publications: *In Britain, a learned journal about the impact of global warming has just been launched*. Note that with this meaning, the word is always pronounced as two syllables: lérnid /ˈlɜːrnɪd/.

learned[2] *adjective*, refers to knowledge that has been acquired: *Affirmative assessment must go beyond seeing anxiety, anger, guilt and sadness as simply newly learned reactions*. With this meaning, the word is pronounced as one syllable: lernd /lɜːrnd/.

learned *verb*, is the past tense and past participle of the verb *to learn* in BE and AE. In AE, **learned** is the only past participle form. *Learn* means to acquire knowledge through study or experience: *I learned a great deal from Fred*. When used as a past tense or past participle, **learned** is pronounced as one syllable: lernd /lɜːrnd/.

learnt *verb*, is an alternative form of the past tense and past participle of *to learn* but as the past participle is only used in BE: *I never went to drama school, but have learnt my craft the hard way*. See **LEARN (TEACH)**.

learning difficulty, mental handicap

learning difficulty *noun*, means a mental problem that may affect how well a person can learn something: *Dyslexia is a common* *learning difficulty, but one that is hard to define*. This can also be termed a *learning disability*. This is regarded as a positive term and is an accepted alternative to the negative term *mental handicap*. See **BACKWARD**.

mental handicap *noun*, is a term formerly used in Britain for a learning difficulty. It is now considered discriminatory by many people, as it focuses on the cause of the problem, not its effect. The phrases *mentally handicapped*, *mentally retarded* and *mentally defective* should also be avoided.
See **DISABLED**.

lease

See **HIRE**.

leave, holiday, vacation, recess

leave *uncountable noun*, means time spent away from work for an approved reason, for example a holiday or illness. It is usual to differentiate between types of leave, such as *compassionate leave* (following a bereavement, or to look after a sick relative, for instance); *sick leave* (when the person on leave is ill; or *maternity/paternity leave*). Otherwise, **leave** is understood to mean the normal holiday entitlement of someone in the armed forces or public service: *We took three weeks' leave and had a fantastic time in Italy*.

holiday *noun*, is the standard BE term for a period of time spent away from work or school, and often from home as well: *A fifth of British animal lovers refuse to take a holiday if the pet cannot come too*. See **PUBLIC HOLIDAY**.

vacation *noun*, is a standard AE term for holiday: *They are on vacation in Hawaii at the moment*. It is also used in BE for the interval between terms at university: *While I was an undergraduate, I worked in a factory on a vacation research project*.

recess *noun*, is used in BE and AE for the time when Parliament or Congress is not sitting: *The Bill will be published before the Commons rises for the Christmas recess*. **Recess** is also used in AE to mean a break during the school day, which in BE is termed break(time) or playtime. Note that in this sense the word is stressed on the second syllable in BE: rĕsséss /rɪ'ses/, but in AE it is stressed on the first syllable: réessess /'riːses/.

lecture

See **TALK**.

lecturer, senior lecturer, don

lecturer *noun*. In the UK this refers to the holder of a permanent position in a university which involves both teaching and research.

senior lecturer *noun*. This is the level above lecturer in the UK university hierarchy. In some of the newer universities in the UK, a third rank has been established – principal lecturer. See **PROFESSOR**.

don *noun*, is either a general term for a university teacher, especially at Oxford or Cambridge, or it refers to a tutor or fellow at an Oxbridge college. In AE, **don** means among other things the head of a family in the Mafia. See **SCHOLAR, FELLOW**.

led

See **LEAD**.

leek

See **LEAK**.

left, left-hand, left-handed

left *noun, adjective, adverb & verb*. As a noun, adjective or adverb this refers to the side of a person or thing which is facing west when that object or person is looking north. As a noun, it means the **left** side or direction: *The wind was gusting, swirling, coming at you from the left*. It can also refer to socialist groups or parties: *The President, addressing the Supreme Council, warned of a creeping coup from the left*. The adjective form means on, towards or connected with the **left** side of something or someone: *She was very afraid of taking the weight on her left leg*. As an adverb, **left** means on or to the **left** side: *After 600 yards turn left at the fork (signposted)*. **Left** is also the past tense and past participle of the verb *leave*: *We want to find out what time it left Euston*.

left-hand *adjective*, only means on or towards the *left*. Note that **left-hand** as an adjective is hyphenated: *The breakthrough came after an excellent left-hand catch by Smith at short leg*. It can only come before a noun.

left-handed *adjective*, refers to people who use their **left** hand more naturally than their right: *This was the third century in 10 Tests for the left-handed opener*. This form can also occur when it follows the verb: *You will find it easier to reverse the positioning of your hands if you are left-handed*.
See BACK-HANDED COMPLIMENT.

left bank

See BANK.

legal, lawful, legitimate

legal *adjective*, means related to the law: *Legal principles are laid down by the decisions of judges over time, or proclaimed in legislation*. In this sense it must precede the noun. **Legal** also means permitted by law: *A roadside breath test showed he was two and a half times over the legal alcohol limit*.
See ILLEGAL (UNLAWFUL).

lawful *adjective*, also means permitted by law, or rightful, but its use is mostly limited to technical contexts, such as the wording in a court judgment or Act of Parliament: *The correct lawful fare for the journey was in the region of £10.50*. See UNLAWFUL.

legitimate *adjective*, means correct and acceptable according to the law: *The will of the people, all democrats agree, is the legitimate basis of political order*. **Legitimate** can also mean justifiable: *He accepted that the local archaeological society had legitimate cause for concern*. Children born to parents legally married to each other are also called **legitimate**. See ILLEGITIMATE (UNLAWFUL).

legate

See AMBASSADOR.

legation

See EMBASSY.

legible

See READABLE.

legislation, legislature, legislative

legislation *uncountable noun*, means laws made by a parliament or a collection of laws: *Legislation had to be brought in to control 'houses in multiple occupation'*.

legislature *noun*, is a lawmaking body, such as Parliament in Britain or Congress in the US: *Only through the legislature of the nation can the battle for common justice be effectively fought*.

legislative *adjective*, means lawmaking, or having the power to make laws: *The doctrine of the legislative supremacy of Parliament is often referred to as 'Parliamentary Sovereignty'*.

legitimate

See LEGAL.

lend

See BORROW.

lesbian

See GAY.

less

See FEWER.

let

See HIRE.

lethal

See DEADLY.

letters and emails

See WRITING SKILLS.

levee, levy

levee *noun*, means an embankment to stop a river from overflowing: *Various flood damage mitigation options need to be investigated, such as property height raising, levee construction and flood proofing*.

levy *noun & verb*. As a noun, this means a tax: *Each training board was financed by a levy on the relevant industry*. As a verb, **levy** means to make a charge: *Inheritance tax is levied on the value of a deceased's estate on the date of death*.

liable

See APT.

libel, slander

libel *noun & verb*. As a noun, this refers to a written, broadcast or published statement:

Libel is a defamatory statement made in writing, or – in the case of films and videotapes – at least in some permanent form. When it is used as a verb, the past tense and past and present participles all have double 'll' in BE, but a single 'l' in AE. The related adjective is *libellous* in BE but *libelous* in AE.

slander *noun & verb*, refers to a spoken statement or even a gesture that is considered offensive: *I consider your defamatory comment is slander, sir.* The related adjective is *slanderous*.

> Both terms are the act of damaging a person's reputation by a false statement. As *libel* is written and *slander* is spoken, one easy way to remember the difference is that *slander* is spoken.

liberal arts

See **ARTS**.

licence, license

licence *noun*. As an uncountable noun, **licence** means freedom: *Some politicians think that they should have greater licence in law when dealing with terrorists.* As a countable noun, **licence** refers to a specific permit such as a *driving licence*, or *television licence*. This spelling is used only in BE.

license *verb & noun*. As a verb, this means to give permission. This is the correct spelling of the verb form in both BE and AE: *Some firms license the use of the results of their own research out to their competitors.* **License** is also the correct spelling of the noun form in AE. The process of obtaining a *licence* is called *licensing*. Cars in the US have *license plates*. These are called number plates in the UK. See **REGISTRATION (RECORD)**.

> The verb is spelt *license* in BE and AE, the noun is spelt *licence* in BE and *license* in AE.

licorice

See **LIQUORICE**.

lie[1], lay, laid

lie[1] *verb*, means to be in a horizontal position: *For a few moments the clouds open and we lie in the heat of a hazy sun.* In standard English it is incorrect to say *We are laying in the sun*. This should be *We are lying in the sun*. Note that **lie** is an intransitive verb, i.e. it does not take an object and is followed by a preposition before a noun. The past tense of **lie**[1] is *lay*, and the past participle is *lain*.

lay *verb*, means to set someone or something down or in place: *Instructions: Lay paper under the hole, and mark the edges with a very sharp pencil.* It is always followed immediately by a noun or pronoun. An animal or insect is said to **lay** eggs, when eggs are produced from its body and deposited: *The females lay their huge eggs in the same nest.* Note that **lay** is also the past tense of the verb *lie*[1].

laid is the past tense and past participle of the verb *lay*: *She went back into the kitchen and laid a cloth on the table.* The statement '*She was hoping to get laid*' is an explicit informal sexual comment.

> Note that the past tenses of *lie* and *lay* are a source of confusion.

lie[2], economical with the truth, window dressing

lie[2] *verb & noun*. As a verb, this means to write or say something that is untrue: *I could lie, I could bluff, but what I told you is the truth.* This verb, which has a different origin from both *lay* and *lie*[1], has the past tense and past participle form *lied*: *The police said: 'He lied and took us on a wild goose chase.'* As a noun this means that something that is written or said is untrue. *Although he was photographed in the bank waving a pistol, he told the police a barefaced lie.* In AE this is termed *a bald-faced lie*.

economical with the truth *adjectival phrase*, is a euphemistic way to say someone is lying or deliberately not telling all the facts: *The UN's press officer was often economical with the truth – a failing common to such people around the world.*

window dressing *noun*, means literally the skill or job of making the display in thc glazed frontage of a shop: *Effective window dressing and attractive in-store displays are an important form of advertising*, but it is also a term used figuratively for doing or saying something in a way that hides the true

L

situation: *This was more to do with window dressing and the government's need to be seen to be doing something, rather than a serious attempt to tackle the problems.*

lieutenant

See **SERGEANT**.

lifelong learning

See **CONTINUING EDUCATION**.

Life Sciences

See **EARTH SCIENCE**.

lift, elevator

lift, *noun*. This is the BE name for the machine that moves people vertically between floors of a building: *Leaving the lift at the third floor, instead of the fourth, he stood listening.*

elevator *noun*, in its most common meaning, is the American equivalent of the BE *lift*: *We entered an elevator and went down.* It has two other meanings, which are more specialized. First, by extension, in AE a *grain elevator* is a place for storing large quantities of grain – in BE this is called a silo: *The grain elevator and the stock pens reflect the whole life of the community and its local region.* Second, it is the name given to the hinged flap on an aircraft's tailplane that controls pitching: *Gliders today have a fixed tailplane and a normal elevator.*

light[1], illuminate

light[1] *noun & verb*. As a noun, this means the electromagnetic radiation from the sun or another source that makes it possible to see things: *We tidied the tent as the light started to fade.* In this use, **light** is an uncountable noun. In another sense, **light** means an object such as a lamp: *They've switched the Christmas tree lights off.* In this use, **light** is a countable noun. As a verb, **light** means either to start to burn, or to make something brighter: *The hotel neon sign lights up our faces.*

illuminate *verb*, means either to light something up: *He switched off the light, letting the moon illuminate the room*; or, in formal use, to make a matter easier to understand: *The purpose of learning about geology is to illuminate people's understanding of the environment.*

light[2], *lite*

light[2] *adjective*, means not heavy: *The binoculars were light enough to be hand-held without awkward shake.*

lite *adjective*, means calorie-reduced (for food). It occurs in the name of the beer *Miller Lite*, but in both AE and BE, most brands that sell a less calorific version alongside the original use the word *diet* instead: *Diet Coke, Diet Pepsi*. **Lite** is an informal spelling and is restricted to the names of the same brands sold in non-English-speaking countries: *Coca Lite, Pepsi Lite*. It may also be used to make a critical comment on someone's character, or the quality of their work, by comparing it with a good example: *Many inferior late eighteenth century composers may be considered as 'Mozart lite'.* A simplified version of something may also be described as **lite**, as in this headline from 'The Times': *The rise of imperialism lite is prolonging the Iraqi horror.*

lightning, lightening

lightning *uncountable noun*, is a high-intensity, natural discharge of electricity: *The thunder and lightning seemed to have moved away.* This word has only two syllables: lī́t-ning /ˈlaɪtnɪŋ/.

lightening *verb*, means either making something lighter in weight: *Fennel makes a delightfully feathery green addition, lightening other, heavier and denser blocks of foliage*; or becoming less dark: *If you've been lightening your hair for years, this is the time to rethink your shade.* This word is the present participle of the verb *lighten*. Note that it has three syllables: lī́tĕning /ˈlaɪtənɪŋ/.

light year

See **MILE**.

like

See **SIMILAR**.

likeable, likable

likeable *adjective*, means pleasant and friendly: *He is an extremely likeable type of person.*

likable is an alternative spelling of *likeable* which is commonly used in AE.

limit, delimit

limit *verb & noun*. As a verb, this means to restrict the amount of something: *Candidates were asked to limit their replies to three or four minutes*. As a noun, **limit** means boundary, an extreme point that may not be crossed: *Of these adverts, 88.5 per cent mentioned an age limit of 40*.

delimit *verb*, means to determine or fix boundaries or limits: *We must first delimit the area we are to consider*. This is a formal word.

linage, lineage

linage *uncountable noun*, is the number of lines of printed or written matter: *The cost depends on the linage*. It is pronounced as two syllables: lī́n-ij /ˈlaɪnɪʤ/.

lineage *noun*, means descent from an ancestor: *She was an orphan of noble lineage with no immediate family*. It is pronounced as three syllables: línni-ij /ˈlɪniɪʤ/. This is a formal word and ancestry is a less formal alternative.

linguistic, linguistics

linguistic *adjective*, means related to language or linguistics: *Perhaps the most dramatic opportunity being developed for linguistic studies is the British National Corpus*.

linguistics *uncountable noun*, is the scientific study of language and its structure. Like other academic subjects ending in '-ics', it always takes a singular verb: *Linguistics is becoming very popular among advanced students*.

link words

See WRITING SKILLS.

liqueur

See ALCOHOL.

liquid, liquidate, liquidize

liquid *noun & adjective*. As a noun, this means a substance that flows, such as oil or water. It is also one of the three most familiar states of matter: gas, **liquid**, solid. These can be changed from one to another by variations in temperature or pressure: *The hottest parts of a liquid are also the least dense*. As an adjective, as well as referring to physical matter, **liquid** also has a financial sense, when it means easily convertible into cash: *In most countries the supply of liquid assets is directly controlled by the central bank*.

liquidate *verb*, as a business term usually means to sell assets to raise money: *With commercial property companies crying out to liquidate their assets these are boom days for auctioneers*. **Liquidate** also means to kill by violent means: *His followers had tried to liquidate the guerrilla movement in the south but had failed*. See EXTERMINATE (MASSACRE).

liquidize *verb*, means to make *liquid*: *Liquidize a large, raw carrot to a smooth paste*. The machine that **liquidizes** substances is called either a *liquidizer* or *blender*.

L

liquor

See ALCOHOL.

liquorice, licorice

liquorice *noun*, is a chewy, black sweet made from the root of a plant. The root itself can be chewed, and it has certain medicinal properties. This is the BE spelling. It is pronounced either líckĕriss /ˈlɪkərɪs/ or líckĕrish /ˈlɪkərɪʃ/.

licorice is the AE spelling of *liquorice*.

lists

See WRITING SKILLS.

lite

See LIGHT[2].

liter

See LITRE.

literally, verbatim, *literal, littoral*

literally *adverb*, means in a literal sense, or exactly: *This year's plum harvest is so good that some trees literally can't take the strain*. It is not advisable to use **literally** as an intensifier without a lot of thought; otherwise nonsense appears: *This record is literally aglow with vibes*.

verbatim verbáytim /vɜːr'beɪtɪm/ *adverb & adjective*, means word for word, exactly as something has been said or written on an earlier occasion: *He repeated the famous Gettysburg address verbatim* (adverb). *The transcript was a verbatim account of our phone conversation* (adjective).

literal *adjective*, refers to the basic meaning of a word, not a figurative or metaphorical meaning: *'Eat or be eaten' is a phrase with literal meaning in the animal kingdom and a metaphorical one in the human*; or it refers to a translation which represents the exact words of the original text: *A literal translation might turn out to be very stilted, and not the way most people would use the language*.

littoral *noun*, means a geographical area near to the coast: *The states of the Baltic littoral have formed a regional council*. These countries are the ones that have a coastline on the Baltic Sea. It is a technical word.

literate, numerate, computerate

literate *adjective*, means able to read and write: *Written records of the past, for example, will by definition have been written by the literate*. By extension, it means competent in some field of knowledge: *Many children are becoming literate in the ways of the countryside*. Note that the related noun is *literacy*. See ILLITERATE (ILLEGIBLE).

numerate *adjective*, means able to manipulate numbers and do simple mathematical calculations: *A key skill for students in accountancy is being numerate*. Note that the related noun is *numeracy*. See INNUMERATE.

computerate *adjective*, is a blend word formed from *computer* and *literate*, meaning knowledgeable about and able to use computers: *All students on this programme will acquire extensive computerate skills*. See BLEND WORDS.

litre, liter

litre *noun*, is a measurement of volume, equivalent to about 1.75 pints. This is the BE spelling.

liter is the AE spelling of *litre*.

little, small

little *adjective & adverb*. As an adjective, **little** means not large in size, quantity or degree: *Most commuters have little leisure time*. When **little** is used without an article, as in the above example, it means a smaller amount than if the indefinite article is included: *Some commuters have a little leisure time* (meaning some spare time). **Little** is sometimes used to express a sneering dislike: *I bought a couple of magazines from a seedy little newsagent*; or an approving attitude: *It's a lovely little cottage and the owner has a sweet little border collie*. As an adverb, **little** means not much, or not at all: *He was fully occupied at home, and came to London as little as possible*.

small *adjective*, means not large in size, quantity or degree: *Our village has a small junction station on the local railway system*. **Small** is less colloquial than *little*, and so in technical or official contexts, it is often a better choice: *Another thousand pounds would perhaps be sufficient for the building of a small laboratory*.

littoral

See LITERALLY.

live-in, live together

See COHABIT.

livid, lurid

livid *adjective*, means extremely angry: *One farmer was livid that he could not go into his local National Park and chop wood for his barbecue*. In another sense, when it refers to bruises or other discolorations of the skin, it means dark-coloured: *The wound was swollen and livid: the colours of bruising were showing already*. However, in literary use, a *livid face* means a pale one.

lurid *adjective*, means deliberately shocking and explicit: *People used to tell their lurid dreams when we were in the locker rooms*. In another sense it means overly brightly coloured: *They repainted the car in a lurid purple colour*.

living room

See SITTING ROOM.

llama, lama

llama *noun*, is a member of the camel family found in South America.

lama *noun*, is the name given to a priest in Tibetan Buddhism. The *Dalai Lama* is the spiritual leader of Tibetan Buddhism.

'Nancy Pelosi made one of the highest-ranking US official visits ever to the home of the Tibetan spiritual leader, the Dalai Llama, today.'
(ABC News, March 2008)

loan

See BORROW.

loath, loathe

loath *adjective*, means reluctant and unwilling: *She paused, loath to voice the dreadful rumour*. This word is mostly used in formal English. It has an alternative spelling, *loth*, and is pronounced to rhyme with 'both'.

loathe *verb*, means to detest someone or something: *I hate him, I loathe him; he never says anything nice to me*.

As these words are frequently confused, it may be better to use one of their close synonyms: reluctant for *loath* or detest for *loathe*.

local, locale

local *adjective & noun*. As an adjective, this describes someone or something which belongs to, or inhabits, the immediate neighbourhood: *If you are not already an active supporter, contact your local branch to find out what is being organized in your area*. As a noun, it means an inhabitant of a particular community and can be used instead of terms like *local inhabitant* or *local resident*: *The Tourist Office has revamped certain traditional festivals so they will appeal more to both tourists and locals*. In BE, *the local* can mean a neighbourhood pub. *The local* in AE means a branch of a union. See INHABITANT.

locale lōka̍al /ləʊˈkɑːl/ *noun*, is a place connected with a specific event or type of event: *There is a small group that sees the countryside as a locale for recreation*. It can also be a venue, or setting, the place where something happens: *The locale is described as a university in the north of England: it could be anywhere from Nottingham to Newcastle*. Note that the stress is on the second syllable.

local authority, local council

local authority *noun*, is a body that administers local government: *The local authority is going to have a tough time getting these measures accepted*. This is more commonly used in BE than in AE.

local council *noun*, refers to the elected officials in local government, and may also be used as a synonym for *local authority*: *The local council elections in May appeared to be a watershed in the party's fortunes*. See COUNCILLOR.

locality, location

locality *noun*, means the area being spoken of, usually referred to as *the locality*: *The 'village community' can also mean the pattern of social relationships which exist in the locality*. It also means a specific site: *The main Sussex wintering locality for this species is Rye Bay*.

location *noun*, is a particular position or site: *The Safari Beach is in a stunning location in 12 acres of tropical gardens*. **Location** as in the phrase *on location* refers to the process of making a film outside the studio.

loch, lough, firth, fjord

loch *noun*, is the Scottish word for what is usually called a lake in England, or a *lough* in Ireland: *The whole Loch Tay area has a fascinating and rich history*. It is usual for the word **loch** to come before the specific name: *Loch Lomond*, but there are exceptions: *Duddingston Loch* in the Queen's Park in Edinburgh, for example. The Scottish pronunciation of the final *-ch* uses the same sound as the German 'achlaut': lo<u>ch</u> /lɒx/ although many English people say 'lock'.

lough lo<u>ch</u>, lock /lɒx, lɒk/ *noun*, means a lake. This is the Irish spelling of *loch*: *Below Enniskillen, the lough kept appearing and reappearing, interrupted by birch woodlands.*

firth *noun*, is a Scottish word for an estuary: *While approaching the Firth of Forth the ship took on a lot of water*; or an inlet of the sea, when it may also be called a *sea loch*: *Our loch is a sea loch, but that isn't the same as the sea – it's much tamer*. In names, **firth** may appear first or last, but for each individual **firth**, its place is fixed: *Firth of Forth*, but *Solway Firth*, for instance. The word has the same root as *fjord*.

fjord fi-órd /fiˈɔːrd/ or fée-ord /ˈfiɔːrd/ *noun*, means a long, usually narrow inlet from the sea with high cliffs or mountains on each side, and is usually restricted to Scandinavian contexts. When referring to a specific **fjord**, it is advisable to spell it as two words, both capitalized: *Hardanger Fjord*. **Fjord** can also be spelt *fiord* in English.

log

See BLOG.

logarithmic

See EXPONENTIAL.

longitude

See LATITUDE.

loose, loosen, lose

loose *verb & adjective*. As a verb, this means to detach, set free or release: *As the sail whipped free of the masthead, he leaped back into the cockpit to loose the spinnaker sheets*. More common alternatives are *set loose*, *cut loose* or *loosen*. **Loose** is usually an adjective, when it means not firmly fixed: *A loose valve seat usually falls out totally and damages the engine very quickly*; or not confined: *Emily took her hat off and shook her hair loose*.

loosen *verb*, means make something less tight: *If your waistband is too tight, loosen it*.

lose *verb*, means to be deprived of something: *We lose some of the sense of taste as we get older*; or, as the newspaper headline below should have said: *Use it or lose it*. It also means to cease to have: *There are parents who lose control of their children for reasons that are entirely understandable*; or to fail to win: *Arsenal won their first five matches and did not lose until the tenth*.

Lose is the only English word ending in the spelling '-ose' that is pronounced ooz /uːz/. The only English word that ends in '-oose' and pronounced ooz /uːz/ is *choose*. All other words that end in -oose are pronounced ooss /uːs/ (*goose*, *loose*, *moose*).

'Use it or loose it.'
(Newspaper review of book that encouraged the elderly to have an active sex life)
!

lopsided

See ONE-SIDED.

loquacious

See GRANDILOQUENT.

lorry, truck, juggernaut

lorry *noun*, means a large vehicle for goods transported by road. This is a BE term. *Lorry drivers* are known as *truckers* in AE. An *articulated lorry* is a lorry with a flexible joint that allows its two sections to turn corners easily.

truck *noun*, means, in BE, a small *lorry*, or an open wagon for goods on the railway. In AE, **truck** is the normal term for what in BE is called *lorry*. *Trailer-truck* is the AE term for an *articulated lorry*.

juggernaut *noun*, is a large articulated lorry. This is a disapproving term. Figuratively it can mean any action that is carried out despite opposition and that seems to be unstoppable: *The truth is that public spending is a juggernaut that is almost out of control*.

lose

See LOOSE.

loud, loudly, aloud, out loud

loud *adjective & adverb*, means making a lot of noise: *Her laugh was so loud it attracted glances from the people in the room*. It can also be used for clashing or extreme colours: *She wears rather wonderful, loud print dresses*. As an adverb, it has the same meanings: *She taught me how to sing loud or sing softly*.

loudly *adverb*, means noisily: *This was shouted so loudly that passers-by reacted*. It is also used figuratively to mean garishly: *He was dressed loudly in a bright red shirt, and yellow check trousers*.

aloud *adverb*, means reading or saying something so that others can hear: *They all looked at her questioningly and she explained: 'I was just thinking aloud.'* **Aloud** can also mean in a loud voice: *Privacy was not a word in our vocabulary, and postcards and diaries were mercilessly read aloud*.

out loud *adverb*, means speaking aloud, especially so that others can hear: *We couldn't help laughing out loud*. It is less formal than *aloud*.

lough

See LOCH.

lounge

See SITTING ROOM.

Low Countries

See NETHERLANDS.

Ltd

See PLC.

lumber

See TIMBER.

lurid

See LIVID.

luxuriant, luxurious

luxuriant *adjective*, means rich and profuse in growth: *The heavy rains have brought luxuriant green vegetation to these normally arid islands*. Hair, beards and moustaches may also be described as **luxuriant**.

luxurious *adjective*, means characterized by luxury, extravagant: *This magnificent hotel is undoubtedly one of the most luxurious and well equipped in the Middle East*.

lyric, lyrics, lyrical

lyric *adjective & noun*. As an adjective, this refers to a type of poetry that expresses strong personal emotions: *The ideas of the lyric poet are projections of himself*. As a noun it means the words of a song: *He only knew one word in three of the lyric he'd chosen*. It is less common in this sense than the plural form *lyrics*.

lyrics *plural noun*, means the words of a song, particularly a popular song: *I sang the first 16 bars in a soft velvet voice, and let the sad lyrics speak for themselves*. See -ICS.

lyrical *adjective*, means beautifully expressed and full of emotion: *It was an extremely lyrical account of his youth*. This does not need to have anything to do with poetry and is often used in the expression *to wax lyrical*: *Some people still wax lyrical about arcane grammatical rules*. When it is used to describe music, **lyrical** often means tuneful and romantic: *The music for the two lovers is predominantly lyrical, rather than heroic*.

L

Spelling

laborat**ory**	Note -ory at the end
la**cq**u**er**	Note the -cq- and the -er ending
la**t**i**t**ude	Note the single -t- each time
le**agu**e	Remember the -a- and the -u-
le**a**rner	Remember the -a-
legi**tim**ate	Note -tim-
l**ei**sure	Note -e- before -i-
len**g**th	Remember the -g-
leni**e**nt	Note the -ent ending
l**eop**ard	Remember the -o-, and the single -p-
lett**uce**	Note the ending -uce

l**iai**son	Note the second -i-
licen**s**ed	Remember this word has an -s-
l**ieu**tenant	Note the three vowels together: -ieu-
lightning (*noun*)	Note there is no 'e' in this word
liqu**e**fy	Note the -e- in the middle of this word
liqu**eur**	Note there is no 'c' in this word, and that it ends in -eur
liqu**or**	Note there is no 'c' in this word, and that it ends in -or
li**z**ard	Note there is only one -z- in this word
lon**git**ude	Note there is only one -t- in this word
l**o**sing	Note there is only one -o- in this word
lux**ury**	Note this word ends in -ury

M

macho

See MALE.

mad

See INSANE.

Madam, ma'am, madame, mesdames

See LADY.

Mademoiselle, Mesdemoiselles, Mlle(s)

Mademoiselle madĕmwăzéll /mædəmwəˈzel/ *noun*, is the French equivalent of Miss, and was used in the past in English for a French governess of young children.

Mesdemoiselles maydĕmwăzéll /meɪdəmwəˈzel/ *noun*, is the plural of *Mademoiselle*.

Mlle(s) is the abbreviation of *Mademoiselle* and *Mesdemoiselles*.

magnitude

See ENORMITY.

maid, au pair

maid *noun*, is a domestic helper. The term is disliked in BE, but not in AE. Hotels use the term *chambermaid*.

au pair ō pái̇r /əʊ ˈpeər/ *noun*, means a young foreign person, often a girl, who is given board and often pocket money by a family in return for helping to look after the house and the children.

mail

See POST[2].

maize

See CORN.

major, important, significant

major *adjective*, means much greater in value than might be expected in the average case: *These paintings form a major contribution to modern British art.* **Major** also has special uses in the context of music and education, where *major key* and *major subject* contrast with minor ones. See MINOR.

important *adjective*, means having great value: *The important discoveries in genetics by Mendel became widely known in the mid-nineteenth century*.

significant *adjective*, means noticeable in a meaningful way: *The availability of milk represents a significant nutritional advance for poor families.*

majority, plurality

majority *noun*, means the number of votes by which a person or political party wins an election. In American politics, in order for a **majority** to be achieved, more than half the total number of votes cast must have been for one candidate or one side in a contest or dispute. In BE this is called an *absolute majority* or *overall majority*: *A second round of voting was necessary as no candidate had succeeded in obtaining the necessary first-round overall majority*. In British use, a candidate gains a **majority** by receiving more votes than any of the other candidates, even if he/she receives fewer than half of all the votes cast. This is also called a *simple majority*. The phrase *the majority of* takes a plural verb: *The majority of the votes have been counted*. But in BE **majority** without 'of', being a collective noun, may take either a singular or plural verb. See COLLECTIVE NOUNS (GRAMMAR TIPS).

plurality *noun*, in American politics means the largest number of votes cast for a single candidate, but less than half the total number cast: *85 per cent voted to reject the simple plurality single member system (first-past-the-post) currently in use*. This term is equivalent to the BE use of *majority*. In AE, **plurality** must be followed by a singular verb.

male, masculine, macho

male *adjective*, refers to the biological sex of plants, animals or people: *The male animal is usually larger than the female*. **Male** is used when there is a contrast with female. See **FEMALE, SEXIST LANGUAGE (WRITING SKILLS)**.

masculine *adjective*, refers to characteristics that are generally accepted as being typical of men as opposed to women: *'I'm sorry,' he said in a voice that was more masculine than his appearance*. **Masculine** is not used to refer to the sex of animals or as a means of contrasting the male and female sexes in humans. In grammar, **masculine** is frequently the name of one of the gender classifications for many languages: *Learning that the masculine gender in French does not always apply to a male creature is often a problem for English schoolchildren*. See **FEMININE (FEMALE)**.

macho mátchō /ˈmætʃəʊ/ *adjective*, refers to a male who takes pride in his masculinity in an aggressive manner: *Social inequalities underlie much of the aggressive macho behaviour in men*. **Macho** is usually a disapproving term. Note that the -ch- is pronounced as in 'church'.

malfunction

See **FAULT**.

mall

See **SUPERMARKET**.

man, gentleman

man *noun*, is the general term used to refer to a male human. In another sense it means a person of either sex (many people object to this use on the grounds that it is sexist): *All men are equal in terms of the law*. **Man** or the alternative *mankind* can also refer to people as a group: *Eradicating this disease will be a giant step for man*. In slang, **man** is used more in AE than in BE, for example in the colloquial form of address to another male: *Hey man!* See **SEXIST LANGUAGE (WRITING SKILLS)**.

gentleman *noun*, means a well-educated male who is polite and well behaved. It is commonly used in expressions like: *Ladies and Gentlemen* (used to open a speech, or a formal business letter in AE), or when there is some degree of politeness involved: *It was just lucky for me this gentleman was passing*. Staff in hotels and restaurants often use the term **gentleman** to refer to their male guests: *Show the gentleman to his table*. Members of the House of Commons use **gentleman** when referring to male MPs belonging to another party: *I am grateful to the Honourable Gentleman for his remarks*. (Note that members of the same party are called *my Honourable Friend*.)

manager, management, supervisor

manager *noun*, means a person who is in charge of organizing the work of other people, or of looking after accounts. A **manager** can run a shop, an entire organization or just part of an organization. A typical small or medium-sized manufacturing company might have a *production manager*, a *financial manager* and a *personnel manager*, all reporting to the managing director. In a large organization, a person with the title of **manager** is typically in a middle management position. Thus a *bank manager* runs one branch of a bank and a *hotel manager* runs one hotel, but a bank director is at the corporate level and the hotel director helps to run the chain of hotels. In sports such as soccer, the **manager** is the person in charge of training, team selection and organization: *The Italian team had three managers last season*, meaning three in succession.

management *noun*, means the people who run and control a business. Large organizations distinguish between *senior management* – those who make decisions that influence the whole organization; *middle management* – those who are responsible for a section or department of the organization; and *junior management* – those who have very limited responsibility or who are *management trainees*. Only the members of the *senior management* are likely to have the individual titles of director.

supervisor *noun*, in the business world means a person in charge of an operation or part of a work process at the operational level: *Sometimes one wants to delegate a task to a supervisor, who is responsible to a line manager*. University students have a **supervisor** who is a member of the academic staff who provides support and guidance for their research project or dissertation. At undergraduate level, students have a personal tutor, who can offer more general support.

managing director, CEO, president

managing director *noun*, means the person in charge of the day-to-day management of a business: *He was the managing director of a large commercial organization*. In some companies, the **managing director** is a member of the board. On business cards or conference programmes, it is normal to place such titles after a person's name and to capitalize them. In running text they are not usually capitalized and can be placed before the name: *our managing director, John H. Jones*. The abbreviation for **managing director** is *MD*. This term is the usual title in BE for a person at this level of management.

CEO *noun*, is an abbreviation for *Chief Executive Officer* and means the person with the highest rank in the day-to-day management of a business. In some companies, the **CEO** is a member of the board. If the **CEO** position is held by someone who is both a board member and in charge of daily management, the title *Managing Director and CEO* is often used. (In AE, this person would have the title *President and CEO*.)

president *noun*. In the context of the words in this group, **president** is the AE equivalent to the BE term *chairman* or, in smaller companies, *managing director*. In a wider context, it is used in AE to refer to the person in charge of any commercial organization: *The company president was in Japan last week explaining corporate policy to Japanese shareholders*. On business cards or conference programmes, it is normal to place such titles after a person's name and to capitalize them. In running text they are not usually capitalized: *our corporate president John H. Jones*. See EXECUTIVE.

mandatory

See COMPULSORY.

mania, phobia

mania *noun*, is extreme enthusiasm or a craze: *Football mania brought the entire country to a halt during the World Cup*. As an uncountable noun it means a serious mental illness that causes an obsession about something with the result that sufferers become very anxious, violent or confused.

phobia *noun*, is an extreme, unreasonable fear or dislike of something: *She came to consult me because she suffered from a phobia about birds*. Specific phobias are all uncountable nouns. There are many types, which include:

- *acrophobia*, a fear of heights.
- *arachnophobia*, a fear of spiders.
- *xenophobia*, a strong feeling of fear and dislike towards foreigners. It is pronounced zénnŏfṓbiă /zenə'fəʊbɪə/.

See CLAUSTROPHOBIA.

manifest

See APPARENT.

manner, manor

manner *noun*, means the way in which an action is carried out: *He waved the hammer around in a manner that threatened to do someone a serious injury*. It may also be the way in which a person behaves: *His manner towards me was as cold as ice*.

manor *noun*, historically means an area of land in the English countryside belonging to the local nobleman, and administered as a unit, but now refers mainly to the large house that he lived in: *This is an exceptionally fine manor house surrounded by parkland*. Informally it is used by the police in BE to refer to the area that a group are responsible for: *There are no villains in this manor any more*.

manpower

See WORKFORCE.

manslaughter

See MURDER.

mantel, mantle

mantel *noun*, is a shortened form of the words *mantelpiece* or especially in AE, *mantelshelf*. It means the ornamental shelf above a fireplace, or *manteltree*: the arch of a fireplace. It also appears in the phrase *mantel clock*: a clock that sits on a *mantelpiece*. It may also be spelled *mantle*.

mantle *noun*, is the part of the structure of the earth that lies immediately below the crust: *The mantle is mainly solid and contains*

M

minerals of high density. In a literary sense, it means a covering: *A mantle of snow covered the lawn*. The phrase *to don the mantle* means to take over an important role or duty from another person or organization: *The move was to prevent the USSR from donning the mantle of world leadership through its sudden concern for smaller nations*.

many

See FEW.

map, chart

map *noun*, is a representation in two or more dimensions of a geographical area, showing the relative positions of various features, such as towns, rivers, mountains. The phrase to *put someone* or *something on the map* means to make them or it famous: *He aimed to put his own business on the map by deeply undercutting any competition*.

chart *noun*, means a diagram showing information, lists of figures or the presentation of a situation such as on a weather chart: *This bar chart shows our monthly sales figures and the pie chart gives the sales volume by product for last year*. It can also mean a detailed map, especially of an area of the sea or stars: *Hipparchus was the Greek astronomer who drew the first accurate star chart*.

marginal, marginally, slight, slightly

marginal *adjective*, refers to a small change that is of minor importance. **Marginal** also refers to something related to or located at the edge of something: *These are areas where there is marginal agricultural land, almost nothing will grow here*. In economic terminology it describes a small change in one factor: *At best this will only produce a marginal profit or perhaps we will just break even*. A *marginal constituency* is one in which the voting pattern would have to change very little to bring about a change in party representation.

marginally *adverb*, means not very much: *Prices rose only marginally last year*.

slight *adjective*, means small in degree: *Did she imagine the slight hardening of his expression?* A person who is small and thin can have a *slight figure*.

slightly *adverb*, means a little: *By raising our prices slightly we get a certain sort of customer*. A *slightly built* person means someone who is small and thin.

> *Marginally* can always be replaced by *slightly*, but *slightly* cannot always be replaced by *marginally*, e.g. 'a slightly built person' cannot be 'a marginally built person'.

marine, maritime

marine *adjective*, means relating to the sea: *They ran a broadly based marine business but specialized in marine cargo insurance*. In another sense it refers to living in the sea: *The noise would have caused enormous damage to the sensitive hearing of marine mammals*.

maritime *adjective*, means connected to the sea especially when referring to commercial activities: *The whale's jawbone arch across the River Esk is a reminder of the town's maritime history*. In another sense it refers to being near the sea: *The maritime Antarctic region has numerous types of penguins*.

marital, nuptial

marital *adjective*, refers to marriage, or relations between husband and wife: *He has been evasive in answering questions about his marital status*. The term *extramarital* nearly always refers to a sexual relationship with a partner who is not the husband or wife.

nuptial núpshăl /ˈnʌpʃl̩/ *adjective*, refers either to marriage or to the wedding ceremony: *Ten years later their nuptial bliss still blossomed*. This is a formal word. The related plural noun *nuptials* only refers to the wedding: *The early morning ceremony appears to be an essential part of the nuptials*. Note the spelling of this word, with final -ial, not -ual.

mark, grade (education)

mark *noun*, is a BE term for an assessment in school or university on a numerical or letter scale: *They want you to use the graph and that's what they're giving the marks for*.

grade *noun*, means assessment, often according to an A, B, C, D scale, or other non-numerical types: *For students entering the A-level stream, grade C or better is normally required*. **Grade** is the normal AE equivalent of BE *mark*. The elementary level of education in AE is referred to as *grade school*. In AE, **grade** also means the class level or form: *My daughter is in the fifth grade*. The term *grading system* is used in BE and AE for an assessment system that gives marks or grades.

mark, marque

mark *noun*, is used with a number to specify a particular model in a series of cars, aircraft or other vehicle: *The Spitfire fighter plane was produced in many models, the Mark V being the most common*.

marque *noun*, means a make of car or other vehicle, not a specific model: *Meetings were held of MG enthusiasts determined not to let the marque die*.

martial, marshal

martial *adjective*, refers to war and fighting: *The military were planning to declare martial law*.

marshal *noun*, is an officer of the highest rank in the army or air force in some countries: *In September, the field marshal visited the town to inspect the troops camped there*. It is capitalized in connection with a name or specific rank (Marshal of the Royal Air Force). It can also be a person who controls crowds or in AE, a federal police officer: *US Marshals are the nation's primary fugitive hunters*.

> *'It is not easy to declare marshal law because of the basic setup of the US Government.'*
> (One of 4,000 such confusions found by Google) !

masculine

See **MALE**.

massacre, decimate, exterminate

massacre *noun & verb*. As a noun, this means the indiscriminate killing of a group of people, particularly if cruelty is involved: *An enquiry into the Glencoe massacre declared the deaths of the Macdonalds to be murders*. Figuratively it is used when one sports team beats its opponent by a very large margin: *Playing against Brazil would be a massacre for our team*. Note that **massacre** is spelt *-re* in both BE and AE. As a verb it is used in the same senses as the noun.

decimate *verb*, nowadays means to kill a large proportion of a group: *Battalion after battalion decimated solely by the bombardment would be replaced in the line by others*. Originally, **decimate** meant to kill one in ten as a form of execution. This use is generally classified as historical and most people now use **decimate** in the sense of killing a large number. There is no necessary implication of cruelty or deliberate killing involved in the modern meaning of this word: *Plague decimated the population of Europe in the fourteenth century*. **Decimate** is also used informally today to mean cause severe damage: *Local industry has been decimated by job cuts*.

exterminate *verb*, means to kill everyone in a group by a planned process, or to make a group of animals extinct: *Other groups of reptiles were not exterminated at this time, even though their fossils may be found*.

masterly, masterful

masterly *adjective*, means performed very skilfully: *The complex decoration was restored with masterly skill*. **Masterly** should not be used to describe someone who is domineering.

masterful *adjective*, has two meanings. First, to refer to something that is performed very skilfully: *He writes with masterful ease, and succeeds in making his subject accessible*. Second, it means powerful and authoritative: *It was a kind face, but it had a rather masterful look about it*. It is sometimes difficult to decide which of the two meanings is intended: *The opening batsman scored a masterful 109* – was the performance skilful, or powerful?

mate, guy

mate *noun*, is an informal word for a good friend in BE, especially between male youths or men: *Look, mate, we're never going to have this amount of money and time again*. This may cause confusion, as **mate** can also mean the sexual partner of a person, bird or other animal: *The animal may need bright colours for social reasons – to attract a mate, for* *instance*. **Mate** is also used together with another noun to show the social relationship between two people: *flatmate, room-mate, classmate*. There are no sexual connotations in such terms. See **FRIEND, PARTNER**.

guy *noun*, is an informal word for a man, and occurs in phrases such as *wise guy* (clever), *tough guy* (brutal) and *bad guy* (criminal). In AE especially, the plural form can be used to refer to a group of people of either sex: *I saw you guys splashing around in the surf*. It originated as the name of *Guy Fawkes*, who tried to blow up the Houses of Parliament in 1605.

material, matériel

material *noun*, means the stuff of which something is made, including cloth for clothing: *She bought five yards of material to make a dress*; and text used in a book or orally: *Publicity material should make clear when staff will be available*. In the plural, *materials* also means equipment for carrying out a task: *If education is supposed to be free, then educational materials should also be free*.

matériel mǎteeri-éll /mətɪəri'el/ *noun*, borrowed from French, means the equipment and munitions used by an army: *The government announced that it had authorized the use of its airport for the transit of matériel, troops and casualties*. This is contrasted with personnel, which means the people who make up the army. Note the acute accent over the first e, and that it is stressed on the last syllable.

mathematics, maths, math

mathematics *noun*, is an academic subject dealing with number, quantity and space. Like other academic subjects ending with '-ics', **mathematics** takes a singular verb when it means the discipline: *'I don't want to get too technical because mathematics does get very difficult.'* When it means operations involved in a calculation, **mathematics** is often treated as a plural: *The mathematics were simple; save £10 a week over 30 years, add the interest and you have a tidy nest egg*. See **-ICS**.

maths *noun*, is the common BE abbreviation of *mathematics*. It takes either a singular or a plural verb, in the same way as *mathematics*.

math *uncountable noun*, is the AE abbreviation of *mathematics* in the sense of academic subject: *What did you get on your math test, Tommy?* As this is treated as an uncountable noun in AE, it always takes a singular verb.

matrix, matrices

matrix máytricks /'meɪtrɪks/ *noun*, means a situation or environment where something can grow and develop: *At that time, Trinity College was the matrix for scientific breakthroughs*. It can also mean a mould in which something is shaped, for instance type for printing, or vinyl for making LPs; or the material that holds something else: *These exquisitely preserved gastropods are largely free of the enclosing matrix, and look now much as they would have done 60 million years ago*. As a mathematical term, a **matrix** is an arrangement of numbers or other data in columns and rows that is considered as a single entity. In management, a *matrix organization* allows managerial control across functional boundaries, whilst retaining the line management.

matrices máytrisseez /'meɪtrɪsiːz/ *plural noun*, is the plural of *matrix*: *To reissue a vinyl LP in digital form, it is essential to include not only details of the original matrices but also reasonably accurate dates for the recordings*. An alternative plural of *matrix* is *matrixes*.

maximum, minimum, maximal, minimal

maximum *adjective & noun*. As an adjective, this means as great, as high or as intense as possible: *The maximum investment per child is £1,000*. Note that a *maximum decrease* reduces something to the smallest amount possible: the *minimum*. **Maximum** as an adjective is only used before a noun and is often contrasted with *minimum*. In its noun form, when it means the greatest extent possible, the plural is *maxima* or *maximums*.

minimum *adjective & noun*. As an adjective, this means the smallest possible: *The minimum investment is £5,000*. Note that a *minimum decrease* means almost no decrease at all. **Minimum** as an adjective always comes before a noun. In its noun form, when it means the smallest amount possible, the plural is *minima*.

maximal *adjective*, has a very similar meaning to *maximum* – the greatest possible:

The big question in sport is that the effects of maximal exercise are unknown. **Maximal** usually comes before a noun. This word is often contrasted with *minimal*.

minimal *adjective*, has a very similar meaning to *minimum*. It also means negligible: *The law has traditionally played a minimal role in controlling the use of sanctions at school.* Note that unlike *maximal*, **minimal** can be placed after the verb.

may

See CAN[1].

may be, maybe, perhaps

may be *verb phrase*, means a possibility: *I may be visiting Paris next year* (i.e. this may or may not happen). **May be** consists of *may + be* (both words are stressed) and is always followed by the present or past participle: *I may be gone for a long time.*

maybe *adverb*, conveys uncertainty: *Maybe she'd been wrong to accept this job.* It can also be used to give additional information for someone to consider: *A little homesick, for your roots, maybe?*

perhaps *adverb*, is a fairly formal word that expresses uncertainty. This is a useful word in a written text to avoid being too definite: *A 5 per cent pay rise is perhaps going to be possible for the staff next year.* **Perhaps** can always replace *maybe* without any change in meaning: *Maybe I'll visit Paris next year.* In formal English, **perhaps** is preferable to *maybe*.

maze

See CORN.

mean

See AVERAGE.

means (singular and plural)

means *noun*, is another word for method or methods: *Incentive schemes were accepted as a means of increasing productivity.* It may be used as a singular or plural: *this means of travelling* or *these means of travelling.*

means *plural noun*, indicates financial resources: *It is in everyone's interest that those who live on modest means can have a decent life.* Someone who has insufficient money may be said to have *limited means*.

meantime, meanwhile

meantime *noun & adverb*. As a noun, this is used in the adverbial phrase *in the meantime* to indicate the interval between one event and another: *I'll see you again next week, but if you need anything in the meantime give me a ring, will you?* As an adverb, **meantime** is used in the same way as *meanwhile*.

meanwhile *adverb*, also refers to the interval between one event and another: *The plane is refuelling. Meanwhile undo your safety belts.* **Meanwhile** can also refer to a period of time when something else is happening: *Leave the pizza in the oven. Meanwhile prepare a green salad.* It can also be used to contrast two elements that are different. Thus it is similar in meaning to whereas or on the other hand: *Jogging can cause damage to joints and muscles. Swimming, meanwhile, is an excellent form of exercise.*

> Note that although these words appear to be made up of *mean* and *time* or *mean* and *while*, they should never be written as two words.

M

measles, German measles, mumps

measles *uncountable noun*, is an infectious disease characterized by a fever and eruptions of small red spots on the skin.

German measles *uncountable noun*, is now more usually known as rubella. Like *measles*, it is an infectious disease showing as a pink rash. It is milder than *measles*, but can be dangerous for the foetus if caught by a pregnant woman.

mumps *uncountable noun*, is an infectious disease which shows as a painful swelling of the glands in the neck. If caught by an adult male, it can lead to sterility.

> All three diseases end in 's' but always take singular verbs.

measurements

When referring to metric units such as *kilo, metre* and *tonne*, use decimals: *2.2 kg* (read as *two point two kilos*). If the amount is less than one, e.g. 0.72, this is read as *nought point seven two* (BE), or *zero point seven two* (AE). Note that all digits following the decimal point should be read separately: never pronounce them as a number higher than 9.

Where the imperial system of measurements is used, it is normal to use fractions: *one and a half miles, two and three-quarter gallons*. Simple fractions like $^1/_2$, $^3/_4$ are read as *one-third* and *three-quarters* (BE) or *three-fourths* (AE). Complex fractions such as 251/625 should be read using the term 'over': *two hundred and fifty-one over six hundred and twenty-five*.

When a person's height is being given, 'tall' is often omitted: *She is five foot four*; but other measurements need an extra word, such as 'deep', 'wide' or 'across' to clarify their meaning: *The swimming pool is six feet deep; The road is twenty feet wide; The Atlantic Ocean is 3,000 miles across*.

When the dimensions of an object such as a piece of furniture are being given, they are written *2 × 3 × 4 metres*, but read as *2 by 3 by 4 metres*.

Units of measurement are hyphenated when they are placed before the noun they refer to: *a 5,000-kilometre journey, a ten-pound sack of rice*. Here the hyphenated unit of measurement combines with numbers to form a hyphenated adjective and is invariable – so it does not have a plural 's'. There is no hyphenation if the noun comes first: *a journey of 5,000 kilometres*. Here the unit of measurement is a noun and can be singular or plural.

See FOOT, MILE, NUMBERS, TONNE.

mechanical

See AUTOMATIC.

meddle, interfere

meddle *verb*, means to deliberately get involved in and try to influence a situation that you do not understand and does not concern you: *The teacher had no right to meddle in the student's love life*. To *meddle with* something means to carelessly touch something that you do not know how to use or does not belong to you: *He asked who had been meddling with the settings on his mobile*. This is a disapproving term.

interfere *verb*, means to deliberately get involved in and try to influence a situation where you are not needed so that it annoys other people or groups: *The police are very unwilling to interfere in family matters*. The phrasal verb *interfere with* can refer to touching a child in a sexual way (where it is typical of BE usage) and also prevent something from happening as it was planned often using illegal methods or bribery.

Note that *interfere* does not have a double 'rr' in the past tense or present participle. Google has over 200,000 hits for misspellings of what should be either *interfered* or *interfering*.

'National says minister interferred with the Accident Compensation Corporation.'
(Online TV3 News, New Zealand)

media, medium

media *noun*, means mass communications. Like family, **media** is often treated as a collective noun and takes a singular verb: *The media is free to publish and be damned, so long as damnation comes after, and not before, the word gets out*. Careful writers still prefer a plural verb here. A useful distinction is to use the plural verb for different types of **media**: *Traditionally, the media are considered to consist of TV, radio and the press*, and a singular verb if the **media** is treated as one group: *If green shoots are now appearing in the economy, the media is entitled to claim some credit for watering them*. Although it is now acceptable to write *the media is*, never write 'a media'. Also, as **media** is the plural of *medium*, 'medias' is non-standard.

medium *noun*, is the singular of *media*: *Radio had only recently developed into a mass medium for news and entertainment*. **Medium** also means either a way of expressing ideas: *The blog is a medium for expression*; or a language such as the *medium of instruction*. A person who claims to communicate with the dead, by acting as an intermediary between the dead and the living, is called a **medium**. In this sense, the plural is *mediums*: *Clairvoyants and mediums are* *often rechristened mind-readers, especially by those who do not believe in a spirit world.*

median

See **AVERAGE, CENTRAL RESERVATION.**

medical, medicinal

medical *adjective*, refers to the treatment of illness or injury, or to medicine: *Severe sunburn needs urgent medical attention.*

medicinal *adjective*, describes something used for the treatment of illness: *Plants are the principal source of medicinal drugs for all the world's civilizations.*

medieval, middle age, Middle Ages

medieval *adjective*, means of or related to the Middle Ages: *Ely is an ancient market town famous for its magnificent medieval cathedral.* In another sense, **medieval** means primitive and old-fashioned usually in a negative way: *I despise them for the medieval certainty of their beliefs.* An alternative spelling is *mediaeval.*

middle age *noun*, is the period of life from about 45 to 60, although this is rather subjective: *As the actor approaches middle age, his weight has increased to some 15 stones.* Note that the adjective form *middle-aged* is written with a hyphen: *A middle-aged woman had a lucky escape when a 40 ft tree crashed down on to an open-top bus.*

Middle Ages *noun*, refers to a period of history. Note that this is capitalized and used in the plural. The **Middle Ages** is often narrowly defined as the period from about 1000 to 1450: *York Minster archives contain much material from the Middle Ages to the present (1150 onwards).*

> *'Separation of church and state started in middle aged Europe and now is a part of our US Constitution.'* !
> (Student essay)

mediocre, middle-of-the-road, second-rate

mediocre *adjective*, means of moderate quality, generally in a negative sense: *However mediocre they may sound, these melodies are our own.* As things are either **mediocre** or not, phrases like 'more mediocre' and 'most mediocre' should be avoided. This is the spelling in both BE and AE.

middle-of-the-road *adjective*, means average or unexciting, particularly when describing the sort of music used as background in shops and lifts: *Their last record was alright but it is very middle-of-the-road material.* In this sense it is a disapproving term. **Middle-of-the-road** political opinions are ones that are not extreme: *The President's choice of a middle-of-the-road candidate for the Supreme Court received considerable bipartisan approval.*

second-rate *adjective*, means of insufficiently good quality: *Consumed with guilt, she felt like a character in a second-rate detective film.*

M

medium

See **MEDIA.**

meeting, rendezvous, appointment

meeting *noun*, is an arranged gathering, which can be on a personal level or an arrangement such as an athletics event. It stresses the activity and the place, not the time: *She had shopping to get, a visit to make, a meeting to attend.*

rendezvous róndivoo /ˈrɒndɪvuː/ *noun*, means a meeting place and time, stressing the place where a meeting will be held. The word is typically used for a meeting between two people: *This elegant building is a fine setting for a summer rendezvous.* It is also used in a military sense for a meeting place and time for troops, vehicles, etc. The plural form is also **rendezvous** but pronounced róndivooz /ˈrɒndɪvuːz/. The derived verb form *rendezvousing* is pronounced róndivoo-ing /ˈrɒndɪvuːɪŋ/, and the past tense and participle are *rendezvoused*, pronounced róndivood /ˈrɒndɪvuːd/.

appointment *noun*, means a meeting of a more personal nature: *I had an extremely important appointment in town and I couldn't find a parking space anywhere.*

melt

See **DISSOLVE.**

melted

See MOLTEN.

membership fee

See SUBSCRIPTION.

memo, memorandum

See NOTE.

memory

See REMEMBRANCE.

mend fences

See RECONCILE.

mental handicap

See LEARNING DIFFICULTY.

menu bar, pull-down menu

menu bar *noun*, is a series of words or icons shown as a column or row along the edge of a computer screen. It typically contains words such as *File, Edit, View, Insert, Help* or icons showing representations of a floppy disk (meaning 'save'), a printer, a pair of scissors ('cut'), etc.

pull-down menu *noun*, is a list of computer functions that appears when an item on the menu bar is clicked on with the left mouse button (or mouse equivalent on a laptop computer). A particular item on such a list may then be selected by left-clicking again.

merge

See MORPH.

meritorious, meretricious

meritorious *adjective*, means deserving praise or honour: *A case of wine is awarded to individuals who have done something which seems particularly meritorious*.

meretricious *adjective*, means gaudy, or showily attractive: *He surveyed the room: the prints, the meretricious chandelier and the knick-knacks accumulated from various holidays*.

These are both very formal words.

message

See NOTE.

metal, mettle

metal *noun*, means any one of a number of substances that are generally shiny and good conductors of heat and electricity. Examples are iron, sodium and mercury: *The vehicle contains a high proportion of recycled metal (steel and aluminium)*.

mettle *noun*, means determination and the ability to do something difficult: *She showed her mettle as a dancer and won the hearts of the audience*. The phrase *on one's mettle* means prepared to demonstrate one's ability in difficult circumstances.

method, methodology, Methodist

method *noun*, is a general word for a systematic procedure or particular way of achieving something: *The method of preparing an ore affects the amount of impurities in the metal produced*.

methodology *noun*, is the system of methods used in a particular field or area of study. **Methodology** is normally used in connection with academic work and research: *The methodology draws on a combination of statistical sources plus an intensive programme of interviews and information gathering*.

Methodist *noun*, is a member of a Protestant Christian Church that was founded in the eighteenth century.

meticulous

See THOROUGH.

metre, meter

metre *noun*, is a unit of measurement in the metric scale. This is the spelling in BE of **metre** and all its combinations, e.g. *centimetre* and *kilometre*. Compounds of the word are stressed on the first syllable. The only exception is *kilometre*, which is also pronounced kilómmĕtĕr /kɪˈlɒmɪtər/.

meter *noun*, means a measuring instrument, e.g. *electricity meter, thermometer* and *speedometer*. Compounds of the word are stressed on the syllable before *-meter*, e.g. speedómmĕtĕr /spiːˈdɒmɪtər/. This is the spelling in both BE and AE. The words in the metric scale spelt *metre* in BE, are spelt **meter** in AE, e.g. *centimeter, kilometer*.

metres per second

See KNOT.

mettle

See METAL.

micrometer, micrometre

micrometer mīkrómmĕtĕr /maɪˈkrɒmɪtər/ *noun*, is an instrument for measuring very small distances.

micrometre mī́krōmeetĕr /ˈmaɪkrəʊmiːtər/ *noun*, is one-millionth part of a metre. This is the BE spelling. In AE, it is spelt *micrometer*.

Be careful to distinguish the pronunciations of these two words.

mid- *prefix*, means either in the middle of something: *mid-twentieth-century politics*, or halfway between two extremes: *The angler stood midstream*. **Mid-** is either hyphenated to the following word, or written as part of a combined word without a hyphen. It is best to consult an authoritative dictionary for individual examples.

Here are some common words with **mid-**:

mid-air; mid-Atlantic; mid-June; mid-morning; mid-off (fielding position in cricket); *mid-on* (fielding position in cricket); *mid-sentence; mid-sixties*

midday; midfield; midlife; midnight; midpoint; midriff; midstream; midsummer; midway; midweek; midwicket (fielding position in cricket); *midwinter*

middle

See CENTRE.

middle age, Middle Ages

See MEDIEVAL.

middle of the road

See MEDIOCRE.

might

See CAN[1].

migrant

See EMIGRANT.

mil., milli-, kilo-

mil. *noun*, is the abbreviation for *millimetre*, or *millilitre*, i.e. a thousandth of a metre or a litre.

milli- *prefix*, means either thousand, as in the invertebrate animal *millipede*, literally a thousand feet, or, in units of measurement, a thousandth part: *There was a tiny gap of only 2 millimetres*.

kilo- *prefix*, means thousand in the metric system. In financial jargon, the abbreviation *k* or sometimes *K* is often used to mean thousand: *London allowance, company car and salary of 35k*. Combining k with the ISO currency codes may be confusing. It is better to use the ISO currency code and write the figure in full: *EUR 200,000*, not 'EUR 200K'.

mile, light year

mile *noun*, is a unit of distance used in the UK and US. A **mile** on land is 1,760 yards, or approximately 1.6 km and a *nautical mile* is approximately 2,025 yards, or 1.852 km. As with other units of distance, use the singular form when **mile** is combined with numbers to form a hyphenated adjective, such as: *A 400-mile pipeline* (not 'miles'). Note that the phrase is hyphenated. The plural is used if **mile** occurs as a noun: *The pipeline is 400 miles long*.

light year *noun*, is a unit of astronomical distance that represents the distance light travels in one year, which is about 6 trillion miles (6×10^{12}). As **light year** is a distance, never use it with expressions that show time: *six light years away* (not *ago*).

Informally, ideas that are a long way ahead of the competition can be described as being *miles ahead* or if even further ahead, *light years ahead*.

milieu

See ENVIRONMENT.

miles per hour

See **KNOT**.

militate

See **MITIGATE**.

millennium, millenary, millinery

millennium *noun*, means a period of 1,000 years: *The second half of the third millennium* BC *saw the introduction of the first metalworking into Britain*. The year 2000 was often referred to as *the millennium* even though it only marked a change in the first figure of the year number: *The increase in earnings from tourism came in the year after the millennium*. Note that **millennium** and the corresponding adjective *millennial* are spelt with two 'l's and two 'n's. The plural is either *millennia* or *millenniums*.

millenary milénnări /mɪ'lenəri/ *noun*, means a period of 1,000 years or a thousandth anniversary. Note that **millenary** is spelt with a single 'n', and is stressed on the second syllable.

millinery míllinĕri /'mɪlɪnəri/ *noun*, means hats in general, and the manufacture of hats: *He had little interest in the millinery world, for he hardly ever wore a hat*.

million, millions

million *number*, means a thousand thousands (10^6). There is no final *s* when an exact number, or one of the words *a*, *few* or *several* comes before it: *3 million people, a few million litres, several million tonnes*. When **million** is used to show an amount of time, distance, money or temperature, it takes a singular verb: *Five million dollars is a lot of money*. Otherwise, a plural verb is used: *10 million smokers have succeeded in kicking the habit*. The standard abbreviation is *m*.

millions *number*, is the plural of *million* and refers to an inexact very large number. Often it has 'tens of' or 'hundreds of' immediately before it. Thus **millions** can range from a few million to many million: *Millions of tourists visit this country every year*. **Millions** is sometimes followed by 'of' when, informally, it means very many: *'Seventeen-year-old Asian girl interested in having fun needs millions of friends'*. Note that **millions** is always followed by a plural verb.

miner, minor

miner *noun*, is someone who works in a mine: *Compare the working conditions experienced by an office clerk with those experienced by a coal miner*.

minor *noun & adjective*. As a noun this is someone who is not legally termed an adult. As an adjective, **minor** means of less importance: *Many girls came down with minor ailments, such as skin rashes and tonsillitis*. **Minor** also has special uses in the context of music and education, where *minor key* and *minor subject* contrast with major ones. See **MAJOR**.

minimum, minimal

See **MAXIMUM**.

minister, secretary (political)

minister *noun*, is the usual word to use for any of the members of the British government who belong to either the House of Commons or the House of Lords, including the department heads: *the Health Minister*. Technically, a **minister** is not the head of a department: that post is held by a *Secretary of State*. It is very rare, and nowadays almost impossible, for a member of the government in the UK not to be also a member of one of the Houses of Parliament. See **CLERGY**.

secretary *noun*, is the title given to the head of a British or American government department, who, in Britain, may have several **ministers** reporting to him or her, such as: *the Home Secretary*. Thus, in the UK there are a number of *Secretaries of State*. In the USA, however, there is only one *Secretary of State*, and this title is equivalent to the Minister of Foreign Affairs in other countries. The other members of the US government are also termed **Secretary**, and their deputies are *Under Secretaries*. In the USA, the **Secretaries** and their *Under Secretaries* are selected by the President, and are not allowed to be members of Congress.

minute, minutes

minute[1] mīnéwt /maɪ'njuːt/ *adjective*, means very small: *The pollen is so minute that it can get up your nose and give you hay fever*. Note that the stress is on the second syllable.

minute[2] mínnit /'mɪnɪt/ *noun*, relates to time and geographical position. When referring to time, note that adjectival expressions containing **minute**, such as *ten-minute break*, are hyphenated. The symbol ′ is used immediately after the number of *minutes* when giving a geographical position: 10° 35′ W (read as ′ ten degrees, thirty-five minutes west').

minutes *plural noun*, is the plural of *minute* referring to time and geographical position. In another sense it is the written record of what is said and decided at a meeting: *The company secretary would have to keep records, set the agenda for board meetings and take the minutes*. This is always used in the plural. The related verb is *minute*: *Please do not minute that comment* (i.e. 'do not record it in the minutes').

miscarriage

See ABORT.

misprint

See TYPO.

mist, fog, smog

mist *noun*, means a thin cloud of water droplets at ground level that reduces visibility: *It was still quite early, and banks of mist lay between the mountain peaks*.

fog *noun*, means a thick cloud of water droplets in the air at ground level that reduces visibility. It is sometimes defined as visibility that is less than 1 km: *Ghostly shapes loomed out of the fog and then disappeared*. Figuratively, **fog** is used to mean confusion or uncertainty: *The origins of local government in Britain are lost not so much in the mists of time as in a fog of detail*.

smog *noun*, is a blend of *smoke* and *fog*. This is a pollution problem that occurs in some industrialized areas: *London's long-standing reputation for 'fog' was based on smoke-filled fog, or 'smog', in which thousands of people choked to death*. See BLEND WORDS (WORD FORMATION).

M

mistake

See FAULT.

mistrust

See DISTRUST.

misuse

See ABUSE.

mitigate, militate

mitigate *verb*, means to lessen the effect of something: *The rainforest is held to be useful to us because it will help to mitigate the worst impacts of global warming*. See ALLEVIATE.

militate *verb*, means to have an important effect, or when used as a phrasal verb it means to make something more difficult. In this case it is almost always followed by the word 'against': *Institutional structures and political realities militate against the poor, especially the rural poor*.

mobile[1], cellphone

mobile[1] *noun*, is used as a short form for a *mobile phone*: *I will call her mobile*. In another sense, a **mobile** is a toy suspended above a child's cot, or from the ceiling, which rotates with the movement of the air.

cellphone *noun*, is the usual AE term for a *mobile* (phone) in BE. This is often shortened to *cell*.

mobile², movable, moving

mobile² *adjective*, refers either to something that is easy to move; or to something that can move by itself: *A mobile library visits the village once a fortnight*. The opposite, *immobile*, refers to an object, person or group that cannot or will not move. See **IMMOBILE**.

movable *adjective*, refers to things that may be moved, but only with some effort. A wooden shed which can be taken down and re-erected elsewhere is **movable** (i.e. can be moved by lorry). *Moveable* is an alternative spelling. The opposite, *immovable*, refers to objects that cannot physically be moved, or attitudes or opinions that cannot be changed. See **IMMOVABLE (IMMOBILE)**.

moving *adjective*, refers to something that changes place or position: *Make sure that you keep your fingers clear of the moving parts on that machine*. It can also mean something sad that affects a person deeply: *The celebration was a very enjoyable and moving occasion*. The opposite, *unmoving*, refers to a person who is still, or to something that does not cause any emotion.

mobile home

See **CARAVAN**.

moderate

See **MEDIOCRE**.

modest

See **HUMBLE**.

molten, melted

molten *adjective*, refers to metal or rock that becomes liquid when heated at very high temperatures: *Molten lava erupts and builds the ocean crust along the mid-ocean ridge system*.

melted *verb*, is the past tense and past participle of the verb to *melt* and refers to things that become soft or liquid at moderate temperatures: *Heat together the butter and olive oil in a large pan or casserole dish, until the butter has melted*. Figuratively it can refer to something that disappears such as anger. See **MELT (DISSOLVE)**.

moment, momentary, momentarily

moment *noun*, means a brief period of time: *Just wait a moment and I will fix the lamp*. Although *at this moment in time* is a standard expression, *at the moment* is usually enough to convey the message.

momentary *adjective*, means lasting for a very short time: *After only a momentary hesitation she nodded*.

momentarily mṓmĕntărili /ˈməʊməntərɪli/ *adverb*. In BE this means lasting for a very short time: *The bird closed its wings momentarily revealing the delicate moss green mottling*. In AE, **momentarily**, pronounced mōmĕntérrili /məʊmənˈterɪli/, means at any moment, or very soon: *We will be landing at JFK momentarily*. Thus this word can cause some confusion. See **SOON**.

monetary

See **FINANCIAL**.

monologue, soliloquy

monologue *noun*, is a long speech by an actor in a play when others are present on stage. In a more everyday situation, a **monologue** means a long boring speech: *No one wants a rambling, spur of the minute monologue at the end of the day*.

soliloquy sŏlíllŏkwi /səˈlɪləkwi/ *noun*, is particularly used for a speech in a play when an actor talks to himself – is thinking out loud

– with no one else present on stage: *He jutted his jaw and delivered the 'Is this a dagger which I see before me' soliloquy with fiery passion.*

moonlight, moonlit, moonshine

moonlight *noun & verb*. As a noun, this is quite literally the light of the moon at night: *The clouds clear and the moonlight sparkles on the snow*. Informally *to do a moonlight flit* means to vacate a flat or house in the middle of the night to avoid paying money that is owed. This is a BE expression. As a verb it means to have a second job. This is often one that is kept secret from the tax authorities, etc: *Every employee must moonlight in second, even third jobs simply to subsist.*

moonlit *adjective*, is the visual effect of light from the moon: *It was a bright moonlit night and frost glistened on the rooftops.*

moonshine *noun*, is illegally made alcoholic spirits. In another sense in BE it means a very foolish statement: *He dismissed the man-in-a-pub story as moonshine*. This is an informal word.

> *'Special Ride Evening Moonshine Trips.'*
> (Tourist information, Gütersloh, Germany) **!**

moose, mousse, elk

moose *noun*, is the largest species of the deer family, *Alces alces*. The plural form is also **moose**. This word is particularly used in AE.

mousse *noun*, is a culinary term for a soft whipped dish. This is pronounced the same as *moose* but the plural is *mousses*, pronounced mo͝ossiz /'muːsɪz/.

elk *noun*, is the largest species of the deer family, *Alces alces* and is a BE term for *moose*. When considered as a target for hunters, the plural is **elk**: *The elk are moving this way*, but in other contexts, *elks* may be used as the plural form. This word is particularly used in BE.

moot

See MUTE.

moral, morals, morale

moral *adjective & noun*. As an adjective, this refers to the principle of right and wrong behaviour: *Civil rights is not a political issue but a moral issue*. As a noun, a **moral** is a lesson to be drawn from a story or an experience: *Writers should be shy about forcing a particular moral down the throat of their readers.*

morals *noun*, are standards of conduct and behaviour especially in matters connected to sex: *The publishers were convicted on charges of conspiring to corrupt public morals.*

morale mŏra̍al /mə'rɑːl/ *noun*, means the enthusiasm and confidence of a person or group: *Despite its promises, the government failed to boost the morale of most teachers.* Note that the stress is on the second syllable.

M

moratorium

See AMNESTY.

more equal

See EQUAL.

more than perfect

See PERFECT.

morph, merge

morph *verb*, means to use a special effect in animated films and motion pictures to change one image seamlessly into another. Modern morphing software can be used on most PCs: *Our morphing techniques can generate compelling 2D transitions between images.*

merge *verb*, means to amalgamate two or more objects: *The Prime Minister decided to merge parts of ministries into the newly created Department for Business, Enterprise and Regulatory Reform.*

mortal

See DEADLY.

mortar

See PLASTER.

Moslem

See ISLAM.

most of, all of

most of *determiner & pronoun*, means nearly all, or the majority of: *Most of the work was done*; *Most of the votes were counted*. Note it is the noun following **most of** that determines whether the verb will be singular or plural. *To make the most out of* something means to take full advantage of it.

all of *pronoun*, means the whole quantity or amount. **All of** can be followed by a singular or plural noun, and it is the noun that determines whether the verb is going to be singular or plural: *All of the work was done*; *All of the votes were counted*. However, unlike *most of*, the word 'of' can be omitted in **all of**: *All (of) my friends are coming to the party*.

motherless

See ORPHAN.

motif, motive

motif mōtéef /məʊ'tiːf/ *noun*, is a distinctive feature, idea or image that is often repeated in a work of music or literature: *Composers have sometimes used a recurring motif or melodic phrase to establish the atmosphere of a piece*. In another sense it means a pattern: *Choose an appropriate motif and use it on the base of the pot*. Note that the stress is on the second syllable.

motive *noun & adjective*. As a noun, this means a reason for doing something, especially when it is hidden: *His motive in studying agriculture was to improve the lot of the labouring poor*. As an adjective it describes the power or driving force for a machine: *They patented the engine which provided the motive power for the Waterjet*.

mountain, hill

mountain *noun*, means a steep and elevated area of land that rises over the surrounding countryside. A land mass has to be 1,000 feet above the surrounding area to be classified as a **mountain** in the UK.

hill *noun*, is a rising area of land not high enough to be classified as a mountain. Steep slopes on roads are often called *hills*.

mousse

See MOOSE.

mousy

See HAIR COLOUR.

movable, moving

See MOBILE[2].

movies

See THEATRE.

Mr, Ms, Mrs

Mr is the BE spelling for the abbreviation of the title *Mister* used before a surname or full name of a male adult: *Mr Smith* or *Mr George Smith*. It is normal to use **Mr** for someone else, not for yourself. Note that in AE spelling, **Mr.** (with a stop) is normal. In AE, **Mr.** is used in combinations such as *Mr. President* and *Mr. Ambassador*. Whether abbreviated or spelt in full, **Mr** and *Mister* are always capitalized. *Messrs* méssĕrz /'mesərz/ is the plural of **Mr**: *Messrs Brown and Smith*. This is the abbreviation of the French word *Messieurs*. It is used formally or in business English for the names of companies, but not elsewhere. See SEXIST LANGUAGE (WRITING SKILLS).

Ms is a salutation in letters and emails; or when formally introducing or addressing a woman whose marital status is either not known, or not indicated. **Ms** is recommended for use as a neutral alternative to *Mrs* or *Miss*. It is becoming the standard in many companies and organizations around the world. **Ms.** is the AE spelling (with a stop).

Mrs is nowadays used with a married woman's surname: *Mrs Smith* or full name: *Mrs Mary Smith*. Traditionally, this was the style for a divorced or widowed woman but many married women prefer this to **Mrs** with her husband's name, i.e. *Mrs John Smith*. In business, many women prefer *Ms Mary Smith*. Similarly *Mr and Mrs John Smith* is now mostly used for ceremonial and formal occasions and the format *Mary and John Smith* is an alternative. **Mrs** is not used with other titles, so that a woman doctor is Dr Jones and a woman mayor may be Madam Mayor. **Mrs.** is the AE spelling (with a stop).

Muhammadan

See ISLAM.

multidisciplinary

See **CROSS-DISCIPLINARY**.

multilateral

See **UNILATERAL**.

mumps

See **MEASLES**.

mundane

See **WORLDLY**.

murder, manslaughter, homicide

murder *noun & verb*. As a noun, this means an unlawful, planned, killing: *A man and a woman are being questioned by detectives investigating the murder of a man whose body was found at a sewage works.* **Murder** is sometimes used figuratively to mean terrible: *The traffic in London is sheer murder.* As a verb, **murder** can also be used informally to mean perform badly: *They murdered that Elvis classic.* In oral BE it is an informal way to state that someone is desperate for something to eat, drink or smoke: *'I could murder a lager and a slice of pizza.'*

manslaughter *noun*, means a killing which is neither planned nor done with evil intent: *A person who kills while driving carelessly may be guilty of reckless manslaughter.*

homicide *noun*, is another term for the killing of one person by another. In AE, *Homicide* (with a capital letter) is the name of the police department that deals with such crimes.

Muslim

See **ISLAM**.

must

See **SHOULD**.

mute, moot

mute mewt /mjuːt/ *adjective & verb*. As an adjective this means unable to speak, or silent: *A fragment of plastic ribbon fluttered from a low branch, a mute reminder of the recent tragedy.* As a verb, it means to silence, or to muffle the sound (of a musical instrument): *You should then lightly strum these muted strings as indicated.* Note that this word rhymes with 'newt'.

moot moot /muːt/ *adjective & verb*. As an adjective this means arguable. It is most often found in the phrase *a moot point*, meaning one that is not certain and may be discussed. As a verb, **moot** means to put forward a point for discussion: *The Channel Tunnel project had first been seriously mooted at the start of the nineteenth century.* Note that this word rhymes with 'boot'.

mutual, reciprocal

mutual *adjective*, can refer to actions or feelings that are experienced equally by two or more people or organizations for each other: *Mutual cooperation between banks and their larger customers is rooted in their common interests.* **Mutual** also refers to something that is shared by two or more people: *A well-known angler boasted of my record catch to a mutual friend.*

reciprocal *adjective*, is used for something done or felt in return for something similar done by another person. An act that is **reciprocal** involves repayment: *Agreement on reciprocal most-favoured-nation status was reached, to be finalized when the condition of free emigration was met.*

> These words both involve two or more people or organizations.

mysterious, mystical, mystique

mysterious *adjective*, means puzzling, secretive or impossible to understand: *All the speed cameras in the area developed mysterious malfunctions.* **Mysterious** can also mean strange and fascinating: *I will always puzzle over the mysterious footprints in the snow.*

mystical *adjective*, means something difficult to understand that is related to spiritual and non-material feelings: *Love has inspired more mystical utterances than any other human emotion.*

mystique *noun*, means fascination and awe for people or things which are regarded extremely highly: *The tiger has a mystique, majesty and power that man has always respected.*

Spelling

ma**c**a**r**oni	Note the single -c- and single -r-
m**a**h**o**g**a**ny	Note the order of the vowels: -a-, -o-, -a-, and the single -g-
main**ten**ance	Note the -ten- in the middle
man**oeu**vre	Note the -oeu- in the middle
me**d**a**ll**ion	Note the single -d- but double -ll-
me**m**ory	Note the single -m- in the middle
meta**ll**urgy	Note the double -ll-
mi**ll**e**n**ary	Note the double -ll- but single -n-
mi**ll**e**nn**ial	Note the double -ll- and -nn- in this word
mi**ll**e**nn**ium	Note the double -ll- and -nn- in this word
miner**a**logy	Note this ends in -alogy, not -ology
min**u**scule	Note the -u- in both the second and third syllables
mischie**vo**us	Note there is no 'i' before the final -ous
mi**ss**pell	Remember the double -ss-
mist**le**toe	Note the -le-
mnemonic	Remember the initial m- (which is not pronounced)
mor**t**gage	Do not forget the -t-
murm**ur**	Note the ending: -ur

N

nadir

See **ZENITH**.

naked, nude, bare

naked *adjective*, refers to a person not wearing clothes: *The boy was drying his wet, naked brown body in the sun*, or, less commonly, to a part of the body that is unclothed: *The sun beat down mercilessly on his naked head*. It can also refer to something that is not enclosed by a cover such as a *naked light* or *naked flame*. **Naked** can be used to refer to truth or aggression that is open for all to see: *The invasion of the island was an act of naked aggression*.
See **ALTOGETHER (ALL TOGETHER)**.

nude *adjective & noun*. As an adjective, this means wearing no clothes, and is used especially to describe a *naked* human form in art or photography: *The paintings were executed with the nude model directly in front of the artist*. It can also refer to something being done by people who are not wearing clothes such as a *nude scene* in a film. As a noun, **nude** means a *naked* human form in a work of art. The expression *in the nude*, used after the verb, describes a person who is wearing no clothes.
See **NATURIST (NATURALIST)**.

bare *adjective & verb*. As an adjective, this means not covered by clothes, and is frequently used to refer to a part of the body: *Her red hair flowed over bare white shoulders*. However, the informal expression *bare-arsed* means completely *naked*. **Bare** can also mean not decorated or empty: *He was standing in the bare, empty front room of his own house*. As a verb, **bare** means to uncover: *There were people lined up on both sides of the street, bared heads bowed as we passed*.

> Note that *naked* and *nude* refer to being without any clothes, but *bare* usually means that only a part of the body is uncovered.

namely, viz., videlicet

namely *adverb*, means that is to say, and is used to mention the names of those referred to: *Two players were outstanding, namely Gerrard and Torres*. It can also identify or specify something mentioned immediately before: *Special tools should be used, namely the block brush and the block scraper*.

viz. *adverb*, is the abbreviation for *videlicet*, and means *namely*. It is best used in formal written English, especially BE, to give an explanation rather than to name people: *Several such telescopes are in use, viz. the facilities in San Diego, New Mexico and Hawaii*. Although in informal English this is often pronounced vizz /vɪz/, in formal spoken contexts most people would read it as 'in other words' or 'namely'. The use of 'z' in the abbreviation is explained by 'z' being a medieval symbol for 'et'.

videlicet vidéllisset /vɪˈdelɪset/ *adverb*, means namely and is a more formal term for *viz*.

nationality words

There are no easy rules to learn for the derivation of nationality words from country names. In many cases, the adjective and language name have the same form, and often the noun describing a national of the country is also the same. Here are some examples:

1. Many adjectives end in ***-(i)an***: *German, Ghanaian, Indian, Italian, Norwegian*. All South American nationality adjectives end in ***-an*** or ***-ian***, but note *Argentinian* (alternative *Argentine*), *Brazilian, Ecuadoran, Peruvian* and *Venezuelan*. In other words, the way the country name ends does not determine the form of the nationality ending. The noun to describe nationals of almost all these countries is the same as the adjective form.
2. A smaller group has adjectives ending in ***-ese***: *Burmese, Chinese, Congolese, Portuguese*. There is no noun for these nationalities, and a person from one of these countries has to be described as 'a person from . . .' or 'a . . . ese man/woman'.

3. Many Asian nationality words end in **-*i***: *Bangladeshi, Iraqi, Omani, Pakistani, Qatari*.
4. Some mainly north-western European nationalities end in **-(*i*)*sh***: *English, Irish, Welsh, Danish, Swedish, Turkish. French* and *Dutch* may also be included here. In this group the noun form is always different: either add -man/woman to the -(i)sh form, or in some cases use a different word: *Dane, Swede, Turk. Scottish, Scots, Scotch* have particularly specialized uses. See SCOTS.
5. Some country names ending in **-*land*** form the adjective by adding **-*ic***: *Greenlandic, Icelandic*, and the nationality noun by adding **-*er*** (*New Zealander* follows this pattern for the noun). Although it is not a nationality, *New Englander* follows the same pattern.
6. Exceptions: *Arab/Arabian/Arabic, Greek* and *Filipino*. See ARAB, GREEK, PHILIPPINES (FILIPINO).
7. Nationality words are capitalized, and this also applies in fixed phrases where there is a clear connection with the country: *Russian roulette, French fries, Danish pastry*.

There are some combining forms which are used in hyphenated words to indicate bilateral relations between states: *Anglo-* (which in effect also means 'British'), *Dano-, Euro-, Franco-, Hispano-* (Spanish), *Indo-, Luso-* (Portuguese), *Russo-, Sino-* (Chinese): 'Dano-Norwegian language'; 'Hispano-Suiza cars'; 'Indo-European languages'; 'Sino-Soviet pact'. Note that both parts are capitalized. See CAPITAL LETTERS, FOREIGN PLACE NAMES.

native, indigenous

native *adjective & noun*. As an adjective, this refers to someone's birthplace: *After some time in London he returned to his native Ayrshire*. When **native** refers to plants or animals, it means originating or existing naturally: *The bird garden operates a breed and release scheme for native owls*. As a noun, **native** means someone who is born in a certain place: *I am a native of Stoke on Trent, although I haven't lived there for many years*. The word **native** was formerly used by Europeans for the inhabitants of countries that they were colonizing. This is now considered offensive, although the plural form is sometimes used humorously in colloquial BE to mean the local residents of a town or village: *You really must visit us here. The village is lovely and the natives are friendly*.

indigenous *adjective*, is a formal equivalent to native, in the sense of originating or occurring naturally in a place. It can refer to people, plants or animals: *In the 1950s, the colonial powers in Africa started to hand over government to the indigenous populations*.

When these words are followed by 'to', the area or habitat follows: *Tea is the leaf from the plant Camellia sinensis which is native to Assam, China and Japan; This bird is indigenous to all parts of Canada*.

Native American, American Indian, Red Indian, redskin

Native American *noun*, is the politically correct term used officially today for the American Indians in the USA. Canadians use the terms *Native Peoples* or *Natives* in official contexts. See BLACK. Alaskan native peoples are sometimes included in the term **Native American**. See INUIT.

American Indian *noun*, is the preferred term for *Native Americans* used by the **American Indians** themselves and is a widely accepted term. An alternative is to refer to the specific people, for instance the Cherokee or Apache. Note that an Indian American is an American with ancestry from India.

Red Indian and **redskin** *nouns*, are offensive terms for *Native Americans* and are to be avoided except in historical references.

naturalist, naturist

naturalist *noun*, is an expert in or student of natural history, especially one who works out of doors rather than in a laboratory. *Local naturalists are to play an important role in the world's first global bird conservation organization*. In art or literature, a **naturalist** is someone who depicts natural life realistically.

naturist *noun*, is a term that is used especially in BE for someone who enjoys the opportunity to wear no clothes because they consider this practice to be more healthy and natural: *During the Second World War a nudist village for evacuee naturists was established near here*. An alternative term is *nudist*. See NAKED.

Sally is both a naturist and naturalist.

Natural Science

See EARTH SCIENCE.

nature reserve, national park, reservation

nature reserve *noun*, is an area of land set aside for the protection of wildlife and the landscape. This may also be known as a wildlife sanctuary or simply a reserve. See RESERVE (CONSERVE).

national park *noun*, is an area of countryside designated by the state for the public to use and also for the welfare of the wildlife.

reservation *noun*, is an area of land kept for a specific purpose. Lands assigned to Native American tribes in the US or Australian Aborigines in Australia are called *reservations*. See CENTRAL RESERVATION.

naught

See ZERO.

nauseous, nauseated

nauseous *adjective*, means feeling sick, as if about to vomit: *She suddenly felt nauseous, and went to the sink and heaved uncontrollably*. It also refers to something that makes a person feel sick: *The smell in the village was nauseous: we were walking ankle-deep in slops*.

nauseated *adjective*, means either disgusted: *The crude pornography made my broad-minded friend feel nauseated and he left*; or affected by nausea: *She felt nauseated most of the time during her pregnancy*.

naval, navel

naval *adjective*, refers to the navy: *In 1982, a naval task force was despatched to the Falkland Islands*.

navel *noun*, is the round depression in a person's belly caused by the cutting of the umbilical cord: *He disapproved of shaving and had grown a beard down to his navel*. **Navel** is also a type of orange.

> *'Alfred von Tirpitz – 1849–1930, German Navel officer responsible for submarine warfare.'*
> *(Web article on Famous Freemasons)* **!**

nay

See YEA.

NB, sic

NB is used in writing to make a reader take special notice of something: *NB The Welding Regulations 1970 are fictitious*. It is an abbreviation of *nota bene* but is read as énn bée /ˈen ˈbiː/. It may be punctuated as: *N.B.* Do not use an exclamation mark after **NB**.

sic *adverb*, means as written, and is used in square brackets immediately after a typo or strange word to show that a quoted word or passage is what was written in the original and is not the present writer's mistake: *The Chenin Blanc conferes [sic] this wine a touch of sofistication [sic], combining a sour taste and fruty [sic again] flavour*. This is not an abbreviation, and thus should not be followed by a stop.

near, nearby

See CLOSE.

negative

See POSITIVE.

negative prefixes

See WORD FORMATION.

negligible, negligent

negligible *adjective*, means too slight or unimportant to have an effect: *The amount of lead is so small that it represents a negligible hazard to health*.

N

negligent *adjective*, means inattentive, or careless, leading to serious consequences: *Due to John's negligent driving the car crashed and Brian was injured.*

Negro

See BLACK.

neighbourhood, vicinity

neighbourhood *noun*, means the locality or district where someone lives: *There has been an increase in violent attacks in the neighbourhood.* The term 'the whole neighbourhood' can refer either to the location or its residents. In another context it means approximately: *The work in the kitchen will cost in the neighbourhood of £10,000.* In the region of something has the same meaning.

vicinity *noun*, means the area around a particular place: *The gang was said to operate in the immediate vicinity of the station.* In another sense it means close to an amount or measurement: *Each of these paintings will fetch in the vicinity of £500,000.*

neither . . . nor

See EITHER . . . OR.

nervous, nervy

See ANXIOUS.

Netherlands, Holland, Low Countries, Dutch, Flemish

Netherlands *noun plural*, is the official English name for the European country. Its name goes back to the times when they were literally 'the nether (i.e. low) lands'. The definite article is no longer part of the name. However, *The Netherlands* is still found in a few dictionaries. As with other countries with a plural form 'the' (with lower case 't') is normally used in running text: *A chemical fire caused toxic materials to be transported as far as the Netherlands.* See ARTICLES (GRAMMAR TIPS).

Holland *noun*, is often used as a synonym for the Netherlands. This should be avoided as the name **Holland** refers only to the western provinces of the Netherlands.

Low Countries *noun plural*, is the historical name for the area covered by the present-day Netherlands, Belgium and Luxembourg. This is sometimes referred to by the acronym Benelux.

Dutch *adjective & noun*, means the people of the Netherlands or their language. **Dutch** is a Germanic language that is spoken by over 20 million people mainly in the Netherlands, parts of Belgium and in former Dutch colonies. Some common expressions with **Dutch** include *going Dutch* which means sharing the cost of a meal in a restaurant equally among those eating it; a *Dutch auction* which means a public sale where the price of the item goes down until someone bids for it; a *Dutch uncle* who is a person who gives friendly but firm advice (mainly an AE expression); and *Dutch courage* which means the false confidence that a person may get from drinking alcohol (mainly a BE expression); *double Dutch* is an informal expression meaning badly expressed spoken or written language that is difficult to understand.

Flemish *adjective & noun*, refers to the people and culture of Flanders, an area of north-eastern France, Belgium and the Netherlands. As an uncountable noun, **Flemish** is a variant of standard *Dutch* spoken in parts of Belgium. The local Germanic language spoken there is called *Dutch* by some and **Flemish** by others.

netiquette

Netiquette means an Internet code of behaviour. Some have taken this to apply just to email etiquette. However **netiquette** is more. It covers email, chat groups, mailing lists, voice messaging, in fact the whole range of communications using the World Wide Web. There is no one authoritative source that defines **netiquette**. A search on the web reveals that there is a host of useful suggestions. Some differentiate between guidelines for users and those for administrators. Most suggestions boil down to using common sense, accountability, stating your sources and remembering that email and other web media are open to others and that there is no such thing as a private conversation in such a medium. A confession, suspicion, hoax, gossip or just a hunch can be on the desks of competitors, news media, the authorities and people you have never met half way around the world in seconds. Now that courts have started to admit emails as evidence in some countries this is a reminder of how careful one must be when sending mails from a corporate email system. The impact of an email has proved to be just as powerful as that of a letter.

neurotic

See INSANE.

new

See INNOVATIVE.

news

See INFORMATION.

nice, delightful

nice *adjective*, is a word with a broad range of meanings, including pleasant, delightful, agreeable, pretty and satisfactory: *We'll find a nice dress for you to wear.* Since **nice** has such a variety of meanings, it is often used without careful thought. Therefore, it may be more appropriate to use other adjectives such as beautiful or lovely when expressing an opinion informally: *Look. What a beautiful sunset!* Note that **nice** is not generally used in formal writing, except in the older sense, not found in informal English, of a very small, but important, distinction: *There is a nice distinction in management between giving advice to employees and interfering in their work.*

A British politician in California told a colleague, 'That was the 21st today. I'll murder the next person who tells me to have a nice day.'

delightful *adjective*, means very pleasant, agreeable and satisfactory and can often replace *nice*, especially in formal English: *The programme you laid on was full of delightful music.*

niceness, nicety

niceness *noun*, means pleasantness or basic goodness: *The politician was perplexed that his niceness was considered an electoral disadvantage.* It is often combined with the word *essential* to mean that this is a deep-seated characteristic: *Some people still pretend to believe in the essential niceness of the human race.*

nicety *noun*, means a small detail, particularly of behaviour: *This is no semantic nicety: the distinction reveals their political differences.* It is more commonly found in the plural: *The leader's faith in legal niceties was only a gesture.* The phrase *to a nicety* means exactly: *The egg was perfectly boiled: he had timed it to a nicety.*

nicknames, sobriquets

nicknames may be formed by a play on the surname or appearance of a person, as in *Chalky* for *White* and *Lofty* for someone who is tall or (ironically) very short. However, most nicknames are pet names for people formed by making a short form of their first name such as:

Ed, Ned, Teddy for *Edward* or *Edwin*

Rick, Dick for *Richard*

Jen, Jenny for *Jennifer*

Kate, Katie for *Katherine*

Liz, Lizzie, Bet, Betty for *Elizabeth*

Moll, Polly for *Mary*

Nowadays these names may be used on birth certificates, in which case they are not nicknames.

A **sobriquet** is a type of nickname that is formed because of characteristics associated with a person or thing and is just as much used as the correct name. Examples include:

Alma mater for *your university*

Auntie, Beeb for the *BBC*

Big Apple for *New York*

Buck House for *Buckingham Palace*

Frogs for *the French* (derogatory)

Kiwis for *New Zealanders*

Pommie, Pom for *the British* (Australian, New Zealand term)

Stars and Stripes for the *US flag*

Uncle Sam for *the USA*

N

nil

See ZERO.

no

See AYE.

nobody

See NO ONE.

nocturnal

See DIURNAL.

Noel

See XMAS.

no-go area, dead zone

no-go area *noun*, means an area – part of a city, for instance – to which normal access is denied, either because of the violence likely to be suffered by intruders, or by means of barricades to keep people out: *People in the area blame vandals and troublesome youngsters for making it a nightly no-go area.*

dead zone *noun*, can mean the same as *no-go area*, but its more usual meanings are first a place where nothing interesting ever happens: *They were happy to live in the dead zone between the High Street and the Leisure Centre*; and second an area where there is no signal for mobile phones.

noise

See SOUND.

non-availability, non-existence

non-availability *noun*, means a temporary situation where a given product or service cannot be supplied at that particular moment: *Their work was halted because of the non-availability of medical supplies.*

non-existence *noun*, means something that is unreal and has never existed or does not yet exist: *These swamps were impassable in the nineteenth century because of the non-existence of hovercraft.*

> Note that both *non-availability* and *non-existence* usually have 'the' before them or a linked adjective such as 'total'.

non-flammable

See INFLAMMABLE.

non-invasive

See INVASIVE.

non-religious

See IRRELIGIOUS.

no one, none, nobody, nonentity

no one *pronoun*, means no person: *The owner is accountable to no one in the running of his business*. Note that **no one** always takes a singular verb, because it refers to 'no single one', and 'one' is the subject: *'Supper is a family gathering and no one leaves the table till it's over!'*

none *pronoun*, means not one or not any: *Don't use any more hot water, or there'll be none left for me*. When *none of* is followed by a plural noun it means not one of three or more things and can take a singular or plural verb: *None of these questions has a satisfactory answer; None of the girls complain, because they are afraid.*

nobody *pronoun & noun*. As a pronoun, **nobody** means *no one*, and is mainly used in less formal contexts than *no one*. As a noun, a **nobody** is a person who is unknown or unimportant: *The captain of the England football team was a nobody until the age of 19*. **Nobody** takes a singular verb.

nonentity *noun*, means a person without any special abilities or achievements, although he or she may enjoy high status: *According to one historian, 'George III went mad, George IV was a playboy and William IV was a nonentity.'* This is a term of disapproval.

> *None* is the only one of these words that can take a singular or plural verb, depending on the context.

nor, or

nor *conjunction*, is used with 'neither' to form the second part of a negative alternative: *She looked neither older nor younger than her age*. It may also be used on its own: *Her ambition never faltered, nor did the belief of her parents.*

or *conjunction*, is used with 'either' to form the second part of a positive alternative: *The eight-cylinder engine could be either* *supercharged or non-supercharged*. It is also used on its own to offer an alternative: *He looked like a traditional elderly headmaster, or an obscure peer of the realm*. See EITHER . . . OR.

If both nouns that are linked by *nor/or* are singular, the verb will be singular: *Either the conductor or the orchestra* ***has*** *to go*. If these nouns are plural, the verb will also be plural: *Neither the violins nor the other strings* ***were*** *impressive*. If there is a singular and a plural noun involved, the verb agrees with the nearest noun. *Neither the violins nor the conductor* ***was*** *satisfied. Neither the conductor nor the violins* ***were*** *satisfied*.

Nordic countries

See SCANDINAVIA.

normal

See COMMON.

north, northern

north *adverb, adjective & noun*, is the direction of the North Pole. When it refers to a direction, **north** is not usually capitalized: *To the north of the village there is extensive meadowland*. It is capitalized when it is part of a continent, country or region: *Passenger traffic through North American airports increased every year*.
See CAPITAL LETTERS (WRITING SKILLS).

northern *adjective*, means located in the north or connected with the north in some way: *Somehow he had been persuaded to leave the northern frontier*. **Northern** is only capitalized when it is part of a proper noun: *Northern Ireland* or *Northern Territory*.

North America

See AMERICA.

northerly, northward, northwards, northbound

northerly *adjective*, means either in the north: *Caithness is mainland Scotland's most northerly county*; or in a direction towards the north: *The boat drifted while we repaired the sail, then we reassumed our northerly course*. It also means a wind that is blowing from the north: *Nearly all harbours on the south coast of England are problematic in a northerly wind*. Note that **northerly** is normally immediately followed by a noun.

northward *adjective & adverb*, means moving in a northerly direction: *Soon we were off, heading northward, along the coastal road*.

northwards *adverb*, means towards the north: *The birds migrated northwards*. This can only be used with verbs.

northbound *adjective*, means travelling towards the north: *The northbound lanes of the M6 were blocked at junction 33*.

notable, noteworthy, noticeable, prominent

notable *adjective*, means deserving attention: *The students have made a notable improvement, and should be congratulated*. This is a formal word.

noteworthy *adjective*, means deserving attention or to be noticed as the person, object or fact referred to is unusual or important: *It is noteworthy that over 200 students were registered for the course but fewer than 40 sat the examination*.

noticeable *adjective*, means clear and definite: *The students made a noticeable improvement, but they can still do better*.

prominent *adjective*, means well known and important: *He was one of a number of prominent Labour figures*. It also means easily seen, noticeable or sticking out: *Other natural sites acting as terminal points are prominent rock outcrops and springs*.

note, notice, message, memo, memorandum

note *verb & noun*. As a verb, this means to pay particular attention: *As you go up the stone steps, note the view over the city*. The phrasal verb *note down* means to record something briefly in writing, for future reference: *Note down clearly what he says*. As a noun, **note** means a few words written down, for example as a reminder: *It might help to make a note of your doctor's answers as a reminder of what is said*. If someone or something is *of note* this means especially interesting or important: *The launch of a new type of electric car is an event that is worthy of note*. See BANKNOTE.

notice *verb & noun*. As a verb, this means to be aware of something: *They were too busy* *shouting at one another to notice that she had disappeared*. As an uncountable noun, **notice** means attention: *Green issues are important and everyone should take notice of the problems*. It can also mean a warning that something is going to happen: *A committee member may resign by giving notice in writing*. As a countable noun, it means an announcement in a newspaper or on a sheet of paper: *A formal notice of the decision reached will appear in the next available issue of 'Banker's Monthly'*. See FIRE.

message *noun*, means any sort of communication that is spoken or written, sent to, or left for, another person: *On the black paint of the door was chalked a message: eleven o'clock*. Even the most formal communications by email are called messages, rather than letters.

memo *noun*, means a written message, and is most often used in a professional context: *I refer to my earlier memo in connection with the above*. It is an abbreviation of *memorandum*. See CLIPPED WORDS (WORD FORMATION).

memorandum *noun*, means a note, but can formally mean a document which records agreed terms, for instance a company's *memorandum* of association: *This memorandum was a formal, public document, evidently intended by the parties to be binding upon them*. Both *memoranda* and *memorandums* are acceptable plural forms.

nothing, nothing but

nothing *pronoun*, means not a single thing: *'You've said nothing about getting married.'* As the subject of a verb, **nothing** always takes a singular verb: *Nothing was learned from the experiments*.

nothing but *pronoun + preposition*, is an emphatic expression which means only: *What I said to you was nothing but the truth*. This also takes a singular verb.

> *'The mess food is aptly named and leaves you nothing to hope for.'*
> (Warning to recruits) **!**

noticeable

See NOTABLE.

notorious

See INFAMOUS.

nought

See ZERO.

Nowell

See XMAS.

no-win

See WIN–WIN.

noxious

See OBNOXIOUS.

nude

See NAKED.

nuisance

See GADFLY.

a number of, the number of, amount

a number of *noun phrase*, means several or some. It is followed by a plural countable noun, and takes a plural verb: *A number of people **are** undecided*.

the number of *noun phrase*, means the size of the total. It is followed by a plural noun, but always takes a singular verb: *The number of people outside **is** increasing*.

amount *noun*, means a quantity. In the phrase *an amount of/the amount of* . . . it is followed by an uncountable noun, and the verb is always singular: *An unknown amount of money has gone missing*.

> One way to remember whether to use a plural or singular verb with *number* is the codeword **PAST**. This stands for **P**lural with **A** number, **S**ingular with **T**he number.

numbers

numbers in digits

101 – means a basic level course in a specific subject at university: *Composition 101 is a mandatory course at this university*. This is mainly an AE term.

20/20 – means perfect eyesight not needing either glasses or contact lenses: *The doctor said I still had 20/20 vision*. This is read 'twenty twenty'.

24/7 – means 24 hours and 7 days a week, and refers to shops that never close: *There's a garage just down the road that's open 24/7*. This is read 'twenty-four seven'.

4 × 4 – means a vehicle with four-wheel drive: *Sales of 4 × 4 vehicles have continued to boom despite tax increases*. This is read 'four by four'.

2.2 – is an example of a decimal number and is read as 'two point two'. See **MEASUREMENTS**.

Digits are used in various ways for expressing time, dates, and telephone numbers. See **DATES, TELEPHONE NUMBERS, TIME OF DAY**.

ordinal and cardinal numbers

Ordinal numbers are those that indicate the order things are grouped in: 1st, 2nd, 3rd, and 4th, etc., or first, second, third, fourth, etc. These are used either to indicate rank: *He is second in command at the moment*; or the order of events: *The team managed to equalize in the 47th minute*. Ordinal numbers are also used in music to indicate the size of an interval between two notes: *major third, minor sixth*.

Cardinal numbers are absolute, and say nothing about ordering: 1, 2, 3 and 4, etc., or one, two, three, four, etc. These are used when expressing size or quantity. See **DATES**.

numbers in words

decade *noun*, is the normal word for a period of 10 years: *This has been around for a decade or more*. A decade expressed in numerals should be *1990s* without any apostrophe before the 's'. If two or more decades are referred to, it is best to add the plural to each part: *In the 1970s and 1980s*. The decades in the present millennium are being increasingly referred to in speech as the 'twenty-twenties', etc. rather than the 'two thousand and twenties', etc.

ten years *noun*, means the same as *decade* but most people use 'ten years' in informal English: *They have been here for about ten years*. When the number ten is important, the more specific 'ten years' must be used: *The money was paid over a period of nine or ten years*.

teens *noun* means the period of a person's life between 13 and 19 years old. The span can be narrowed by adding early or late to teens: *Even in their late teens they still enjoyed holidays with their parents*. The related adjectives are *teenage* and *teenaged*.

twenties, thirties, forties, fifties, etc. All describe temperature, age, decades and sometimes banknotes or coins. For temperature, words like 'low', 'mid' and 'high' are added to show what part of the range is referred to: *The temperature in summer is always in the mid-twenties*. With age, words like 'early', 'mid' and 'late' can be added: *Several of the teachers were in their early sixties*. See **NUMBERS IN NUMERALS OR WORDS (WRITING SKILLS), NUMERALS – ARABIC OR ROMAN (WRITING SKILLS)**.

dates For years up to 1999 inclusive, pronounce in two 'halves' – 'nineteen ninety-nine', or for the century year, 1900 'nineteen hundred'. 2000 is always 'two thousand', but 2001–2009 may be pronounced either 'two thousand and one . . .' (the more usual way), or 'twenty oh one . . .' (much less common). For 2010 onwards, most people have started to say 'twenty ten . . .' rather than 'two thousand and ten . . .'.

zero or **nil** can be expressed in several ways depending on the context. See **INDEFINITE ARTICLE (GRAMMAR TIPS), ZERO**.

numbers given by prefixes

It is often possible to work out what an unusual word means by looking at its prefix: For example, the word 'quinquennial', which means lasting for five years or recurring every five years, starts with 'quin' – the number five. Here are some examples of prefixes that indicate a number, and words that are formed in this way:

uni- (one)	*unilateral negotiations* – one-sided
mono- (one)	*monolingual* – speaking only one language

N

bi- (two)	*bilateral negotiations* – two parties involved
duo- (two)	*duologue* – a dialogue between two actors
tri- (three)	*a triangle* – a three-sided plane figure
quad- (four)	*quadruplets* – four babies in one birth
tetra- (four)	*tetrasyllable* – a word with four syllables
quin- (five)	*quincentenary* – a five-hundredth anniversary
penta- (five)	*pentagon* – a five-sided plane figure
sex- (six)	*sextet* – six musicians in a group
hex(a)- (six)	*hexapod* – a six-footed animal (e.g. an insect)
sept- (seven)	*September* – originally the seventh month in the Roman year
hepta- (seven)	*heptathlon* – a seven-event athletics contest
oct- (eight)	*octopus* – an animal with eight tentacles
nona- (nine)	*nonagon* – a nine-sided plane figure
deci- (ten)	*decimal* – the ten-numeral system
deca- (ten)	*decathlon* – a ten-event athletics contest

numerate

See LITERATE.

numerator, denominator

numerator *noun*, is the part above the line in a fraction, so in ¾, the numerator is 3.

denominator *noun*, is the part below the line in a fraction, so in ¾, the denominator is 4.

numerous

See INNUMERABLE.

nuptial

See MARITAL.

nutritionist, dietitian

nutritionist *noun*, means someone who is an expert on the relationship between food and health: *The sports nutritionist states that regular exercise reduces tension and improves the ability to cope with stress.*

dietitian *noun*, means someone whose job is advising people on the kind of food they should eat to stay healthy or build up their health: *All patients received advice from a dietitian at the hospital on diet and food supplements.* This is also spelt *dietician*.

nutritious, nutritional

nutritious *adjective*, refers to food ingredients that are full of things that are good for the body: *You should get all the main vitamins and minerals by eating a balanced, nutritious diet.*

nutritional *adjective*, refers to the efficiency with which the body processes the nutrients in food: *Green, leafy vegetables and yellow and orange fruits are of especial nutritional value to good health.* Note that food cannot be described as **nutritional**, but it can be *nutritious*.

Spelling

ne**c**e**ss**ary	Remember: single -c-, double -ss-
n**ie**ce	Remember -i- before -e-
nigg**ar**dly	Remember -ar-
nin**e**t**ie**th	Note the -e- before the -t-, and the -ie-
no**nd**escript	Note there is no 'e' before the -d-
nostr**il**	Note the ending: -il
notic**ea**ble	Do not forget the -ea-
num**e**rous	Remember the -e-, but no 'b' in this word
nupt**i**al	Note that this word ends in -ial, not -ual

O

obdurate

See OBSTINATE.

objective

See AIM.

oblivious

See UNAWARE.

obnoxious, noxious

obnoxious *adjective*, means extremely unpleasant or offensive and is only used about people and their behaviour and the effect this has on others: *This is the most evil, obnoxious, bad-tempered thug I have ever encountered.*

noxious *adjective*, usually means poisonous and is a technical term: *Two teachers were treated in hospital after being overcome by noxious fumes in a classroom.* It is occasionally used figuratively to mean very unpleasant: *They spent the other half of their time engaging in noxious nostalgia about their youth.* Here its meaning comes close to *obnoxious* which shares the same root.

obsequious

See SERVILE.

observation, observance

observation *noun*, means the act of watching someone or something carefully: *Only prescribe such medication for patients who have been under observation.* **Observation** can also mean a remark or statement: *He had the following observations to make after reading the students' essays.*

observance *uncountable noun*, means the practice of obeying a ceremony, rule or law: *Peace can only be founded on the observance of, and respect for, human rights.* It is a formal word.

obsolescent, obsolete

obsolescent *adjective*, means in the process of becoming outdated or no longer useful: *He did not know whether the fridge had been manufactured to last or to become obsolescent quickly.* This is a formal word. The related noun is *obsolescence.*

obsolete *adjective*, means outdated or no longer useful: *New anti-tank missiles, particularly when used from helicopters, are making battles between tanks obsolete.* Note that **obsolete** is the stage in the existence of something that follows *obsolescence.*

obstinate, obdurate, stubborn, determined

obstinate *adjective*, means refusing to change one's way of behaving or thinking: *Only one bugbear remains: the members' obstinate refusal to grant full rights to women subscribers.* This is a term of disapproval.

obdurate *adjective*, means refusing to change one's opinions or behaviour in a way that others think is unreasonable: *I argued this point with him, but he was obdurate in the matter.* This is a very formal word.

stubborn *adjective*, means either obstinate, when it is usually a disapproving term: *You'll be locked in here until you decide not to be so stubborn*; or persistent, when it means long-lasting: *Britain's javelin maestro is struggling with a stubborn injury to his throwing shoulder.*

determined *adjective*, means decided and resolute. This does not have the disapproving associations of *obstinate* and *stubborn*: *It took determined effort to regain his place in the national squad.* See DECIDE (DETERMINE).

obverse

See REVERSE.

obvious

See BLATANT.

occupy, preoccupy

occupy *verb*, means, among many other things, to keep busy and active: *Many police officers find themselves increasingly occupied with routine paperwork.*

preoccupy *verb*, means to take up someone's attention to the exclusion of everything else: *The question for politicians of all parties must be: what is likely to preoccupy voters most?*

occurrence

See **EPISODE**.

ocean

See **SEA**.

ochre, ocher

ochre *noun*, is a rich yellowish colour. This is the BE spelling.

ocher *noun*, is the AE spelling of *ochre*.

octopus, octopuses

octopus *noun*, is an eight-armed mollusc.

octopuses *noun*, is the usual plural of *octopus*. Most BE dictionaries consider the plural 'octopi' to be non-standard. However, both plurals are used. 'Octopi' is based on the misunderstanding that *octopus* is derived from Latin. In fact, it is a word of Greek origin.

odd

See **QUEER**.

odorous, odious

odorous *adjective*, means having or emitting a smell that may be strong and unpleasant: *When such toxic substances are odorous, their odour can effectively warn us of their presence*.

odious *adjective*, means extremely unpleasant, repulsive: *I held the view that shooting foxes was always both odious and wrong*. Note that this word has nothing to do with smell.

odour, odor

odour *noun*, is a distinctive smell that is usually unpleasant: *The fetid odour of damp refuse filled the air and the soldier pulled a disgusted face*. **Odour** is the BE spelling, but most words formed from it, such as *odorous* and *deodorize*, have no 'u'. An exception is *odourless*. See **-OR, -OUR SPELLINGS (WORD FORMATION), SMELL**.

odor is the AE spelling of **odour**.

offence, offense

offence *noun*, means either a crime or illegal action: *It is an offence for companies to recruit a non-disabled worker when they are below the quota*. It also means the feeling of being offended and distressed: *Domestic broadcasters decided to ban any songs or plays that could cause offence*.

offense *noun*, is the AE spelling of *offence*. One way to remember the correct spelling is to think of offen<u>s</u>e and the United <u>S</u>tates.

> Note that the related noun and adjective *offensive* is spelt with an 's' in both BE and AE.

offensive

See **AGGRESSIVE**.

office staff

See **CLERK**.

official, officious

official *adjective*, means related to an authority or public body and its duty or position: *You will need official permission before that lab can be opened to students*. It also means authorized, such as an *official policy*, or an *official representative*.

officious *adjective*, means eagerly asserting authority in a domineering way: *He felt humiliated by the officious treatment he received from the pompous men at Immigration*. This is a term of disapproval.

oh

See **ZERO**.

old, aged, elderly

old *adjective & noun*. As an adjective, this means having lived or existed for a long time, or describes a person or thing that is no longer young. It may also mean former: *When war broke out, Leslie wanted to rejoin his old regiment*. **Old** can also be used informally for people where affection, not age, is indicated: *'Take care of her, old man', he said*. Compound adjectives indicating age are hyphenated: *12-year-old boys*. As a collective noun, **old** can mean the *aged*: *This procedure is unsafe for the* *old and frail*. **Old** as a noun is used in combinations like *12 year olds*. Note there is no hyphenation and the plural 's' is added to 'old', not 'year'. See **HYPHENATION (PUNCTUATION GUIDE), YEAR, OLDER/OLDEST (ELDER/ELDEST)**.

aged *verb & adjective, noun*. As the past tense of the verb *age*, this refers either to people getting older: *He had aged noticeably, but he was still alert mentally*; or food or drink developing in flavour over time: *This wine has body: it must have been aged in oak barrels*. As an adjective, it means at the age of: *His father died in 1982, aged 77*. Note that as a verb or adjective in this sense, **aged** is pronounced as one syllable. When **aged** means very old, and is used before a noun or after the verb to be, it is pronounced as two syllables: áyjid /ˈeɪdʒɪd/. As a collective noun, **aged** is also pronounced as two syllables and means old people collectively: *A team of actors, under medical guidance, will try to simulate the behaviour of the aged and infirm*. Note that this is used with the definite article.

elderly *adjective & noun*. This means people who are *old*: *The use of drugs for elderly people should be closely monitored*. It is a more polite term than calling people *old*. As a collective noun, **elderly** is used with the definite article: *It is important for the elderly to have heating in their bedroom*. See **ELDER/ELDEST**.

on behalf of . . . /on someone's behalf, on the part of . . . /on someone's part

on behalf of . . . /on someone's behalf means behaving in someone else's interests, or as their representative: *He accepted the gift on behalf of his mother/on his mother's behalf*. Both forms mean the same thing, and are interchangeable.

on the part of/on someone's part implies responsibility by the person mentioned: *Utter exhaustion on the part of the gunners reduced both the rapidity and accuracy of their fire*. The two forms are interchangeable.

on, upon

on *preposition*, refers to place: *The office is on the third floor*. For time, **on** refers to days and dates: *It happened on Friday; I will be back on 25 July*. See **AT**.

upon *preposition*, is the formal version of *on* (especially in BE): *The emphasis was rather upon providing children with basic skills*. It is used in phrases such as *once upon a time* or when referring to a great amount of something: *There were still miles upon miles of desert to cross*.

one

See **PRONOUNS (GRAMMAR TIPS)**.

ones, one's

ones *noun*, is the plural of *one*, meaning specific people or things: *I've put the white and green curtains in your room instead of the beige ones*.

one's *pronoun*, is either the genitive: *To do one's best*; or the contracted form of *one is* and *one has*: *We have three balloons: one's blue, one's red, and one's got a hole in it*. See **CONTRACTIONS**.

one-sided, lopsided

one-sided *adjective*, means unfair and showing only one aspect of an issue: *The press began to be accused of being one-sided and not giving a balanced picture*. In sport, **one-sided** refers to an event that has opposing players or teams of unequal abilities: *Even the one-sided 6–4, 6–0 scoreline didn't reflect the German's supreme domination of the match*.

lopsided *adjective*, means leaning to one side, or unbalanced: *He smiled a funny little lopsided grin*.

onlookers

See **PUBLIC**.

on to, onto

on to *adverb + preposition*. Here *on* means further, and is written separately from 'to' when it forms part of a phrasal verb: *It was the kind of thing a man might pass on to his son some day*. This is both the BE and AE spelling in this sense.

onto *preposition*, means movement from one surface or level to another: *He pointed to the French windows that led out onto the terrace*. This is the standard AE spelling, in one word. *On to* is an alternative BE spelling in this sense.

onward, onwards

onward *adjective*, means going further in a journey or in time: *From Schiphol airport, onward travel is by rail or coach to The Hague*.

onwards *adverb*, means beginning at a particular time and continuing after that: *This course offers students a wide choice of units of study, with emphasis on literature from the Renaissance onwards*. The phrase *onwards and upwards* means that developments will continue. This is the BE spelling. *Onward* is an alternative form, especially in AE.

op. cit., ibid.

op. cit. *abbreviation*, means in the book or work already cited. In Latin, *opus citatum* or *opere citato* are the full forms but only the abbreviation **op. cit.** is used in English: . . . *as Hector says (op. cit.), 'By 1600 it was being written* . . .'. This is a formal term.

ibid. *adverb*, means in the book or paper that was just mentioned or was cited before. **Ibid.** is an abbreviation of the Latin *ibidem* and means in the same place. It always refers to the work last quoted: *Table 4.2, adapted and added to the original (ibid.: 246) indicates the techniques*. In modern style, **ibid.**, and an alternative abbreviation *ib.*, are often replaced by the author's name, a date and page number: (*Jones, 1992, pp. 11–14*). In technical writing, either the name-and-year reference: (*Jones, 1992*), or just a reference number is used. See REFERENCES (WRITING SKILLS).

> These are both formal terms and are mainly used in academic writing.

opening

See VACANCY.

opera

See OPUS.

opinion, view, point of view

opinion *noun*, means a judgement or personal estimation about something by a speaker, or by people in general: *We want the magistrates to see the full picture, to hear the full range of local opinion*. An **opinion** is more considered and formal than a *view* particularly when it refers to the beliefs or views of a group of people or specialists in the legal or medical profession. Here it is treated as an uncountable noun with a singular verb: *A second opinion is going to be needed before we can operate*.

view *noun*, means both what can be seen from a particular place and a way of understanding existing circumstances: *Bus services can be run quite cheaply to large towns in view of marginal pricing*.

point of view *noun*, means a specific attitude about something: *As a mother, she says she sees the parents' point of view*. In another sense it is a way of judging a situation: *From the point of view of the authorities, revitalizing the universities was a policy fraught with danger*.

opportunity, possibility, chance

opportunity *noun*, means the circumstances or a situation when it is easy to do something. A person is given or gets an **opportunity**: *A pedestrian zone gives you the opportunity to wander through the wide selection of shops*. In another sense it means the chance to do something that may result in improving the present situation: *She has always worked for equal opportunities*.

possibility *noun*, means something that may happen or be true. A **possibility** is just a potential likelihood: *The possibility of a new wing to house the college library is under discussion*. Note that **possibility** is often used with *of* or *that*: *This raises the distinct possibility that global warming may be a contributing factor*.

chance *noun*, means both the *opportunity* to achieve something if fortune is favourable, and the *possibility* of something happening: *He would go for a walk and give her a chance to calm down*. **Chance** corresponds to both *possibility* and *opportunity*, but is a more informal and less precise word.

optic, optics

optic *adjective*, describes the eye and sight. It is common in anatomical connections such as the *optic nerve*, and is also used in compounds such as *fibre-optic sensor*.

optics *uncountable noun*, means the science that deals with visible and invisible light and also vision. Like other academic subjects ending in '-ics', it always takes a singular verb: *Optics provides a superb meeting point between art and science because optical problems are integral to both science and art.* When **optics** refers to the lenses, prisms and mirrors found in an optical instrument, it is a plural noun and a plural verb is required: *Fibre optics are built into the thermal panels.* See -ICS.

optician, optical

optician *noun*, means someone trained to test people's eyes and sell glasses or contact lenses in BE (also called an *ophthalmic optician* or in AE an optometrist). In AE, an **optician** is someone who makes the lenses for glasses or contact lenses.

optical *adjective*, means making use of the science or the principles of optics: *Optical character recognition is a problem that puzzled scientists for many years.* It also relates to the eye and vision, such as *an optical illusion.* An *optical specialist* could mean someone working and researching in optics, or an *optician*: *Holographic edge filters are now available from your laser and optical specialists.*

optional, voluntary

optional *adjective*, means not compulsory: *Laboratory instruction was an optional extra, to be paid for if taken.* When a product has *optional extras* these are things that can be chosen from a fixed selection, but that can be left out if preferred. In education, **optional** may have the more restricted meaning of a forced choice from among a group: *Four courses are to be taken – the three marked X are compulsory, the two marked Y are optional.*

voluntary *adjective*, refers to something done willingly, not because you are forced to make a choice: *This course is not compulsory, attendance is voluntary.*

opus, opera

opus *noun*, means an artistic work, especially on a large scale: *Many composers' works are given opus numbers.* It is usually abbreviated to *Op.* when followed by a number: *Beethoven's Fifth Symphony is his Op. 67.* The plural is usually *opuses*, but *opera* is an alternative. Because of the possible confusion with the usual meaning of *opera*, this is not used as the plural when referring to musical works in English.

opera *noun*, is a stage work for singers and an orchestra. A *soap opera* is a long-running sentimental or melodramatic serial on radio or television, so-called because the first ones in the US were often sponsored by soap manufacturers. The plural form is *operas*. See PLURAL NOUNS (WORD FORMATION).

or

See NOR.

-or, -our spellings

-or spellings are found in both BE and AE for nouns that indicate a condition, such as *error, pallor, tremor, horror, terror*. Words that indicate a comparison also end in **-or** in BE and AE: *major, minor, senior, junior*. AE also spells many other words with final **-or**, such as *color, humor, neighbor, vapor* and *vigor*, where BE has *-our*.

-our spellings are used in BE in nouns such as *colour, humour, neighbour, vapour, vigour*. However, even in BE, the 'u' is omitted in words derived from these that end in *-ate, -ize* and *-ous*: *invigorate, vaporize, humorous*.

oral

See VERBAL.

ordinal number

See NUMBERS.

ordinance, ordnance

ordinance órdinănss /'ɔːrdɪnəns/ *noun*, means an order or instruction issued by a national government: *The Ministry of Fisheries issued an ordinance limiting the length of drift nets.* In AE it is also used for a local decision that restricts people's behaviour: *An old county ordinance forbids the riding of cows along the public highway.* Note that this word has three syllables.

ordnance órdnănss /'ɔːrdnəns/ *uncountable noun*, means the weapons, ammunition and vehicles used in war: *Several tons of ordnance were moved up so that the attack could take place.* Note that this word has two syllables.

ordinary

See **COMMON**.

orient, oriental

orient áwri-ĕnt /ˈɔːriənt/ *noun*, áwri-ent /ˈɔːrient/ *verb*. As a noun, when capitalized, this is an old-fashioned term for what is now called the East or the Far East: *The cultures of the Orient and Polynesia blend with the sophistication of the Western world.* As a verb, it means to give a lot of attention to something: *The university is very oriented towards internationalization*. It can also mean to find where you are or to find a direction by looking at a map. As a verb, **orient** is not capitalized. *Orientate* is an alternative form for the verb **orient**. See **EAST**.

oriental *adjective*, means characteristic of the Far East: *Oriental rugs are partly defined by the manner in which they are made*. It is offensive to use this term for a person from that region. It is recommended to use Asian or their nationality instead. See **ASIAN**.

orphan, fatherless, motherless

orphan *noun*, means a child whose parents have both died: *She was an orphan, and the uncle and aunt she lived with were not well off*. This word should not be used for a child who has lost one parent.

fatherless, motherless *adjectives*, refer to a child who for some reason lacks a parent: *The chances are great that he was brought up in a fatherless household*. Often, *lost his father/mother* is used when it is clear that the death of the parent has occurred: *It was a routine call on the bereaved woman who had lost her father*.

-ory

See **-ARY**.

ostensible, ostensive

ostensible *adjective*, means seeming to be the reason or purpose for something when the real reason or purpose is hidden: *The ostensible reason for the meeting was the location of the new car park*. **Ostensible** implies the deliberate intention to conceal something. This is a formal word. See **APPARENT**.

ostensive *adjective*, refers to a way of explaining a definition by direct demonstration: *The teacher picked up a valve and gave an ostensive explanation of components in the electrical circuit*. This is a formal word and also a technical term used in linguistics.

ought to

See **SHOULD**.

ounce, oz.

ounce *noun*, means a unit of weight in the imperial system (1 ounce equals about 28 g). It is used figuratively to mean the last bit: *We pushed the car and used every ounce of strength*.

oz. *abbreviation*, is an abbreviation of *ounce* but is read as 'ounce'. The 'z' is explained by its origin, *onza* (Italian).

outcome

See **RESULT**.

outdoor, outdoors

outdoor *adjective*, means in the open air as in: *It's open late, and has a massive outdoor cinema screen*. An alternative form is *out-of-door*. Both forms may only be used before a noun.

outdoors *adverb*, also means in the open air: *People who work outdoors all the time are more at risk of skin cancers*. The phrase *out of doors* has a similar meaning: *I decided to fetch a book and read out of doors*.

out loud

See **LOUD**.

outstanding, unpaid

outstanding *adjective*, means exceptionally good: *He gave an outstanding performance in his comeback match*. In another sense it means very obvious or important: *One outstanding feature of that war was how few civilian casualties there were*. In a third sense, **outstanding** means unpaid: *They had many bills outstanding at the end of the month*. See **EXCELLENCE**.

unpaid *adjective*, refers either to an outstanding debt, or to working without pay:

She was fed up with hour upon hour of unpaid work in the home.

outward, outwards

outward *adjective*, means in a direction going away from home. This is used before a noun as in: *The outward journey to France included a rough Channel crossing*. It also refers to what the external appearance of a person or situation seems to be rather than what it really is: *The banker's nervous twitch was the only outward sign of his worry.*

outwards *adverb*, means in a direction to the outside or from the centre of something: *The effects of hypocrisy in Macbeth spread outwards from the king's murder. Outward* is an alternative form, especially in AE.

overestimate, underestimate

overestimate *verb*, means to consider something more important or at a higher level than it really is: *Even adults sometimes overestimate their driving skills on icy roads.*

underestimate *verb*, means to consider something less important or valuable than it really is: *It would be dangerous to underestimate the seriousness of those talks.*

These words are often used in contexts where they express the opposite of what the writer intended, as in this example, from the British National Corpus: *It is hard to underestimate the impact of the monasteries, especially in the twelfth and thirteenth centuries.* Although the writer means that the impact of the monasteries is very great, the phrasing says 'the monasteries had so little impact that it is difficult to say how little'. The writer should have written: 'It is hard to *overestimate* the impact . . .'

overflow, overfly

overflow *verb & noun*. As a verb, this refers to something that is too full and thus goes beyond its limits. The subject may be water in a lake or river: *A 25-mile stretch of the River Severn overflowed*; or used about people: *It was a popular event and the guests overflowed into the garden*. It is also used figuratively to mean ideas: *His head overflowed with bright ideas*. It has the past tense and past participle *overflowed.*

As a noun, an **overflow** is a pipe fixed in a tank to prevent it becoming too full: *At Eastwood House he found the overflow dripping*. As a verb, **overflow** is stressed on the third syllable, but as a noun, it is stressed on the first syllable.

overfly *verb*, refers to aircraft or birds flying over something: *It is a mystery why starlings choose to overfly suitable roost sites closer to daytime feeding grounds*. It has the past tense *overflew* and the past participle *overflown*: *A Peruvian helicopter gunship has just overflown Ecuadoran territory.*

overhead

See TRANSPARENCY.

overlook, oversee, oversight, overview

overlook *verb*, means to fail to notice something or not to see its importance: *We should not overlook the fact that six students on the same course have admitted plagiarism.* In another sense it means to choose to ignore: *I'm prepared to overlook your behaviour just this once*. It can also mean to see something from a building or high point: *A couple of bedrooms overlook Loch Ness*. See VANTAGE POINT (BIRD'S-EYE VIEW).

oversee *verb*, means to supervise a person or a task: *The pollution inspectorate is expected to oversee the clean-up process.* This is a formal term.

oversight *noun*, means an unintentional failure to notice something: *By some oversight the full 'Oxford English Dictionary' never recognized the existence of the term 'addictive'*. It also means the supervision of a person or task: *Only four local authority services are subject to oversight by inspectors.*

overview *noun*, means a general summary or review of a topic: *This chapter gives a broad overview of accounting practices in the UK.*

overtone, undertone

overtone *noun*, means a sign of an emotion or attitude that is not expressed directly: *There were clear racial overtones in the way the police presented their evidence in court.* Note that in this sense the word is usually plural.

O

undertone *noun*, means a feeling or quality that is recognized but not expressed directly: *This undertone of political symbolism is much more prominent in his more recent paintings*. Note that in this sense the word is usually plural: *I was writing a comedy with sinister undertones*. In another sense, it means a subdued sound or colour: *Simon mumbled for the third or fourth time in an aggressive undertone*.

overwhelm

See INUNDATE.

overwrite

See KEY IN.

Oxbridge, Ivy League

Oxbridge *noun*, means the English universities of Oxford and Cambridge. There is no such physical place, being simply a blend of the two words. See BLEND WORDS (WORD FORMATION). Note that graduates of Oxford University write *Oxon* after their degrees: 'J. Smith, BA Oxon' Similarly, graduates of Cambridge University write *Cantab* after their degrees: 'M. Smith, BA Cantab'. See CANTAB, REDBRICK UNIVERSITY.

Ivy League *noun*, means the group of eight long-established universities in the eastern United States. The group consists of Harvard, Yale, Princeton, Pennsylvania, Brown, Columbia, Dartmouth and Cornell. The name may come from the ivy that traditionally grows on the walls of these institutions.

Oxon

See CANTAB.

oxymoron

An **oxymoron** ocksimáwron /ɒksɪ'mɔːrɒn/ is a combination of two words that seem to mean the opposite of each other. Occasionally one word with contrasting elements such as *firewater* is termed an **oxymoron**. Terms like *previous breaking news* are used without us thinking about what we are really saying. A double classic is *fresh frozen jumbo shrimp*, where apart from its dubious freshness we have the problem of size when 'jumbo' implies very large, and 'shrimp' means both a shellfish and also something very small. Appropriately, the term **oxymoron** is itself oxymoronic because it is formed from two Greek roots with opposite meanings (*oxus* 'pointed' and *moros* 'foolish', the same root as the word 'moron'). **Oxymoron** is the singular form and both *oxymorons* and *oxymora* ocksimáwră /ɒksɪ'mɔːrə/ are used as the plural.

Oxymorons are not necessarily mistakes or errors in speech or writing. They make effective titles and phrases as in Shakespeare's 'parting is such sweet sorrow' and the journalist Malcolm Muggeridge's comment that 'Good taste and humour are a contradiction in terms, like a chaste whore'.

Oxymorons are the basis of clichés like: *half naked, small fortune, open secret, working holiday* and *living dead*. Even some foreign loan words are oxymoronic such as *sophomore* (wise fool).

Perhaps the greatest problem with *oxymorons* is avoiding them. Here are some prize specimens from trade names and elsewhere:

dry Martini	*elevated subway*
new classic	*plastic glass*
silent scream	*exact estimate*
tight slacks	*slack tights*

Journalists often relish satirical *oxymorons* such as 'the Senator's popularity soared like a lead balloon'. Here are some choice examples from the 'Financial Times' database:

English cuisine	*pleasant villain*
colourful accountant	*poor bookmaker*
vegetarian haggis	*French queue*

Note that these are only effective for people who share the cultural background of native English speakers and overusing such terms is likely to prevent other people understanding the message.

Spelling

obedi**e**nce	Note that this word ends in -ence.
obli**g**e	Note there is no 'd' in this word
observ**a**nce	Note that this word ends in -ance.
o**cc**asion	Note the -cc-
o**cc**u**rr**ence	Note the double -cc- and double -rr-
od**o**rous	There is no 'u' before the -r-
offe**r**ed	Note the single -r-
o**m**inous	Remember there is only one -m-
o**m**ission	Remember there is only one -m-
o**m**it	Remember there is only one -m-
o**m**i**tt**ed	Remember the single -m- and double -tt-
one**'**s	Remember the apostrophe when this is possessive
o**ph**thalmic	Remember the -ph before the -th-
o**pp**o**nent**	Remember the double -pp-, single -n- and -ent ending
ostr**ich**	Note the ending -ich, not -itch
ours	Remember – no apostrophe
outrag**eous**	Note the ending -eous

O

P

p., pp. (pages)

p. This abbreviation is used in two ways. First, for a page number in reports and references, when it is written before the number: *p. 116*. Second, to indicate how many pages there are in a book cited on a reference list, when it is written after the number of pages: *75p*. See **PENCE**.

pp. This is the plural form of *p.* in its first use only. Write *pp. 11–16*. See **P.P.**

pace

See **TEMPO**.

package, packet, pack

package *noun*, means something wrapped in paper and posted or delivered to an address. This is also called a parcel.
It also means the paper or plastic wrapped around food in AE: *a package of potato chips*, equivalent to *a packet of crisps* in BE. In another sense, a **package** is a set of proposals or collection of benefits or incentives: *The government has a package of measures for combating inflation*.

packet *noun*, means a paper, cardboard or plastic container or box that things such as envelopes, cornflakes or cigarettes are sold in. In AE, a **packet** is the same as a sachet in BE, i.e. a small flat paper or plastic container with individual portions of such things as sugar or ketchup.

pack *noun & verb*. As a noun, this means a small container that goods are sold in, such as rice or frozen vegetables. In BE, a *pack of cards* means a complete set of playing cards. This is called a deck of cards in AE. A *six-pack* is six bottles or cans of beer packaged together. As a verb, to **pack** means to put objects into a container, especially neatly and tightly. See **BACKPACK (RUCKSACK)**.

> A *packet* of biscuits in BE is a *package* of cookies in AE.

paediatrician, paedophile

See **PEDERAST**.

pair, pairs, couple, brace

pair *noun*, means either two similar things such as *a pair of shotguns*, or one thing that has two parts joined, such as *a pair of jeans . . . scissors . . . pliers . . . glasses*, or comes in two parts, such as gloves, socks, shoes. As **pair** is the headword, these phrases are all treated as singular: *A pair of glasses* ***was*** *perched on the end of his nose* . . . However, in further references, it is best to ignore *a pair of*, and treat the item as plural: . . . *and he kept pushing* ***them*** *up so that he could see her better*. Note that if two people are described as a **pair**, this may mean either two people who live together or are emotionally involved, or simply two people who are associated in a particular activity: *The pair turned on him after he spotted them breaking into the car*. See **SCISSORS**.

pairs *noun*, is the normal plural of *pair*: *two pairs of socks*. Use **pairs** when you refer to a plural: *Policemen had walked in pairs there in the old days*. (Note that *pair* as a plural is non-standard in BE.)

couple *noun*. When it refers to people, **couple** can mean two individuals who have something in common: *Before he could do any more harm a couple of bystanders restrained him*. **Couple** can also mean people who are married, or otherwise emotionally involved: *They weren't just Maggie and Neville any more, but a couple*. Note that in BE, **couple** usually takes a plural verb, although it is possible to use a singular verb when the **couple** is considered as one unit. In AE, **couple** always takes a singular verb. **Couple** otherwise means two or, informally, a small number, as in: *Alex threw a couple of logs on to the glowing embers*. See **COLLECTIVE NOUNS (GRAMMAR TIPS), FEW**.

brace *noun*, means a pair, and is often used by hunters in the specialized sense of two birds or animals that have been shot: *Between them they killed 20 brace of partridges with 40 shots*. It can also mean something to support or stiffen a structure or part of the body such as a *neck brace*. The metal device that children have inside the mouth to help their teeth grow straight is called either a **brace** or **braces** in BE (but only **braces** in AE).

Braces are also used to hold up trousers. These are called *suspenders* in AE.

palate, palette, pallet

palate *noun*, is the roof of the mouth, or the ability to distinguish between different flavours: *The wines tasted very curious to my inexpert palate.*

palette *noun*, means a board on which an artist mixes paint: *The trolley with his brushes, tubes of paint, and palette was beside the easel.* It also means the range of colours that a particular artist uses: *My palette is changing and I am introducing more colours.*

pallet *noun*, is a portable platform for storing things or moving them, often by means of a forklift truck: *Straight onto a pallet, wrap it, forklift it, stack it three high.* A **pallet** also means a rough cloth bag filled with straw that was used in the past as a mattress: *She got no pay and slept on a straw pallet in the lower scullery.*

pampas

See PRAIRIE.

pandemic

See ENDEMIC.

paradigm shift, step change

paradigm shift *compound noun*, means a fundamental change in the way that something is done or thought about: *The new geophysical evidence supporting plate tectonics led to a rapid paradigm shift in the earth sciences.*

step change *compound noun*, means a significant change in the way that something is done in an organization or society: *The introduction of email brought a step change in the way people communicate in writing.*

paradox

See DICHOTOMY.

paraffin, kerosene

paraffin *noun*, is a light fuel oil for heating and for use in lamps: *There was no electricity – only candles and paraffin.*

kerosene *noun*, is the AE term for *paraffin*. It is also the standard term in all forms of English for a type of fuel oil in a technical sense: *Where particularly high-energy fuels are a necessity – for example in aircraft – the only practical fuel is kerosene. Kerosine* is an alternative spelling.

parameter, perimeter

parameter *noun*, means a numerical or other measurable characteristic that determines operational conditions: *Targets will be set for all parameters that can be measured, such as project cost and project performance.* **Parameter** is also used in the plural as a more formal alternative to limits or guidelines: *The meeting should only set broad parameters for the worker.* See ESTIMATE (BALLPARK FIGURE).

perimeter *noun*, means the boundary of an enclosed area. It is only used in this physical sense: *While trying to get through the perimeter they were discovered by a patrol.*

paramount, supreme

paramount *adjective*, is used in connection with overall power in a culture or society: *The title of the constitutional head of state of Malaysia, Yang di-Pertuan Agong, is often translated as 'Paramount ruler'.*

supreme *adjective*, refers to the highest person or body in an organization or structure: *supreme commander; supreme court.*

> These terms do not refer to *an* important factor or person, but to the *most* important one. When they refer to general things rather than to specific things as in the above examples, there is little difference between these terms: *These factors are of paramount/supreme significance.* Avoid combining these words with 'more' or 'most'.

paranoid

See INSANE.

parent company

See GROUP.

parentheses

See BRACKETS.

part[1] (adverb), partial, partially, partly

part *adverb*, means to some extent and is commonly used in phrases as part of a contrast: *To its discoverers, the duck-billed platypus appeared to be part mammal and part bird.*

partial *adjective*, means in part, or not complete: *Climbing shrubs and vines formed a partial canopy to keep out the fierce sun.* **Partial** also means one-sided: *The reporter's account of the attack was extremely biased and partial.* To be *partial to* something means to be fond of it: *If you are partial to Californian wine, you could be in luck.*

partially *adverb*, means to some degree: *His parachute failed to open, and he was partially paralysed by the fall.* This is a formal term.

partly *adverb*, means to some extent or not completely. **Partly**, not *partially*, is used for material things: *The project was partly funded by the Erasmus programme.* **Partly** is used to explain the reason for things. Here *because of* or *due to* are added: *Every bride looks beautiful – partly because of what she is wearing.*

part[2] (noun), portion, share

part *noun*, has numerous meanings. As an uncountable noun it either refers to some but not all of a thing: *Part of the information was misleading*; or a person or thing belonging to a group. As a countable noun it means a section: *Parts of the voyage were highly dangerous*; a region or a piece of a machine or a body: *He covered his private parts.* See ON BEHALF OF.

portion *noun*, is a piece of something or part of a whole. When it refers to food it is usually qualified by words like small or generous: *He took a generous portion of chicken.* When it means a share of something, **portion** refers to a part shared with others: *Her portion of the money was deposited in her account.* **Portion** is more restricted in its use than *part*.

share *noun*, means part of a divided amount or part of an event involving several people: *He accepted his share of the criticism.* It also refers to an acceptable portion of things such as fortune, happiness and luck: *She had had more than her share of unhappiness in life.* In business it refers to stock in a company. *His shares were worth almost a million.*

particular

See ESPECIAL.

particularly

See ESPECIALLY.

partner, spouse, husband, wife

partner *noun*, can refer to a personal relationship when it means one of two people who are married or otherwise have a sexual relationship. Using the word **partner** avoids delving too much into people's marital affairs and sexual preferences: *Many firms pay for an employee and his or her partner to visit the new office area.* **Partner** can also refer to someone sharing a common interest, such as sport: '*If you ever need a tennis partner, you know where to find me.*' In the business sense, **partner** means one of the owners of certain types of companies: *Each partner is entitled to share in the profits of the business.*

spouse *noun*, means a husband or wife when considered in relation to their partner: *Many firms pay for an employee (and spouse) to visit the new office area.* This is a formal or legal term. In everyday language, people tend to use the word *husband* or *wife* instead. See SEXIST LANGUAGE (WRITING SKILLS).

husband, wife *noun*, are common alternatives to *spouse* in less formal or non-legal contexts.

party, side (in agreements, conflicts)

party *noun*, means a single person, or a group, in legal contexts: *third-party insurance* means insurance against harming someone other than the insurer or the insured person (who are the *first* and *second parties*). This is a formal term.

side *noun*, means a person or group opposing others in a conflict, dispute, sporting event, business deal or in politics: *The Tigers were at full strength with a side full of internationals.*

pass, past, send

pass *verb*, means to go alongside, by the side of, or through something: *She did not pass through the normal arrivals lounge.* **Pass** also means to transfer something to someone: *Can you pass me the salt, please?* **Pass** can also mean to approve: *To change the rules, the Club will have to pass a resolution*. The phrase to *pass water* means to urinate. The past tense and past participle is *passed*: *They passed close by Kidderminster*.

past *adjective, adverb, noun & preposition*. As an adjective, this refers to time that has gone by: *She hadn't dreamt about Tony for the past three nights*. As an adverb, it means travelling from one side to the other: *The bungalow showed no sign of life when they drove past*. As a noun, **past** means a period of time that has gone: *It feels most comfortable if the present merely repeats the past*. As a preposition, it means beyond: *Thousands of shoppers walked past the tree*. In BE, **past** is used when telling the time: *ten past three*. The AE equivalent is often *after*: *ten after three*. See TIME OF DAY.

send *verb*, means to be taken to a place or cause to move: *The peacekeeping force was sent to Somalia*. **Send** also refers to messages or objects transmitted by post, radio or email: *The DVD was faulty so we sent it back to the manufacturer*.

> *'Not one single bottle gets the label until the brew has been tasted and passed by a panel of German beer experts.'* (Beer advert) **!**

passer-by, passers-by

passer-by *noun*, means someone who happens to go past something on foot: *A passer-by alerted detectives after he noticed a window had been forced*.

passers-by *noun*, is the plural form of *passer-by*. As with other such hyphenated compounds, the plural 's' is added to the noun in the compound: *His eyes were on the street, scanning the few passers-by*. See PLURAL NOUNS (WORD FORMATION).

password

See USER ID.

pastoral, pastorale

pastoral pa̋astŏrăl /'pɑːstərəl/ *adjective*, as a literary term refers to rural life and the countryside: *They pictured a pastoral place where streams trickled through lush meadows*. *Pastoral farming* means the raising of sheep or cattle. In religious and educational contexts, **pastoral** refers to advice given by priests or tutors on personal matters, not those connected with religious doctrine or education.

pastorale pastŏra̋al, pastŏra̋alay /pæstə'rɑːl, pæstə'rɑːleɪ/ *noun*, is a slow instrumental composition. The plural is *pastorales*.

patch

See BADGE.

patent, patently

patent[1] páttĕnt /'pætənt/ *noun & verb*. As a noun, this means the official sole right given to an individual or company to exploit an invention or to use a title, for a limited time: *Having secured the patent for the fax machine, Bain never actually made one*. As a verb, it means to obtain the sole right to exploit an invention or to use a title. Note that the first syllable rhymes with 'bat'.

P

patent[2] páytĕnt /'peɪtənt/ *adjective*, means protected by a *patent*, and is also used to mean blatant: *The convoy cut through the traffic with patent disregard for everyone*. **Patent** is also used in other contexts, like *patent leather*, or *patent medicines*. Note that the first syllable rhymes with 'bait'. See BLATANT.

patently páytĕntli /'peɪtəntli/ *adverb*, means without doubt and emphasizes the negative quality of something: *This cannot be a proper trial because the evidence is patently unfair*. **Patently** is often used in the phrase *patently obvious*. Note that the first syllable rhymes with 'bait'. This is a formal term.

path

See TRACK.

pathetic, bathetic

pathetic *adjective*, means creating feelings of pity or sadness: *The wet dog was a pathetic sight*. Informally, **pathetic** is used to mean useless or unsuccessful: *He was a pathetic liar and no one believed him*.

bathetic *adjective*, means ordinary, uninspired: *The words were bathetic but behind them there was despair*. This is a literary term derived from *bathos*.

pathfinder

See **TRAILBLAZER**.

pathos, bathos

pathos, *uncountable noun*, is a quality that inspires pity or compassion in the reader, listener or observer: *There is an acute sense of the pathos of the situation of the individual, inherently lonely and undefended against the blows of fate*.

bathos, *uncountable noun*, is a term used in literary criticism to mean a change in mood from the highly serious to the trivial, that is not usually intended on the part of the writer: *Such titles and ornamentation can create the effect of bathos, or comic undermining of what you do achieve*.

> Note that both *pathos* and *bathos* take singular verbs.

patience, *patients*, patient

patience *noun*, means the quality of waiting for a long time without becoming angry or upset: *He tested everyone's patience with his boasting*. **Patience** is also a card game for a single player. This is called *solitaire* in AE.

patients *noun*, are people undergoing medical treatment in a doctor's care or admitted to hospital: *These patients were withdrawn from the drug trial and treated in other ways*. The singular form is *patient*.

patient *adjective*, means being able to wait for a long time without irritation: *He was extremely patient considering he was a London cab driver*.

patriot, compatriot, expatriate

patriot páttri-ŏt /'pætriət/ (BE), páytri-ŏt /'peɪtriət/ (AE, also BE) *noun*, is a person who is proud of his or her country, and supports its actions: *It is the land of my birth and I feel I know it well, but only as a student, not as a patriot*.

compatriot kŏmpáttri-ŏt /kəm'pætriət/ (BE), kŏmpáytri-ŏt /kəm'peɪtriət/ (AE, also BE) *noun*, is a person who shares the nationality of another person: *When Arsenal played Barcelona, Cesc Fábregas was pleased to meet his compatriots again*.

expatriate ekspáttri-ŏt /eks'pætriət/ (BE), ekspáytri-ŏt /eks'peɪtriət/ (AE, also BE) *noun*, is a person living away from his or her native country: *She's an American expatriate living in Paris*. This is often shortened to *expat*. Note that the spelling 'expatriot' is not given in authoritative dictionaries. If it were, it would mean a person who is no longer a supporter of his or her country.

patron

See **CLIENT**.

pavement, sidewalk

pavement *noun*, in BE means a paved or asphalt area for pedestrians or a path beside a road: *Hundreds of people sit at cafés on the pavement on either side of the road*. **Pavement** in technical contexts and in AE generally means the hard surface of a road or airport runway: *The pavement was good, even in the Rockies*. Historically, a **pavement** can be a Roman mosaic floor: *The tessellated pavement of the villa corridor was excavated*. See **KERB**.

sidewalk *noun*, is the AE term for the BE *pavement*: *They stood on the sidewalk waiting for a streetcar*.

pay, salary, wage

pay *uncountable noun & verb*. As a noun this is a general term for money received for doing regular work and is always followed by a singular verb: *Directors gave themselves an average 5 per cent pay rise in the past year* (AE = *pay raise*). **Pay** is often combined with other terms like *pay claim, holiday pay* and *pay cheque* (AE = *pay check*), *payroll* and *rates of pay*. As a verb it means to give someone money that has been earned during work or for services and goods received: *We will pay your travel costs to get there*. Note the past tense and past participle are spelt *paid* in these contexts. In another sense, **pay** means to let out a greater length of rope: *The kite has a hundred metres of the line payed out*. Note that the spelling of the past tense and participle is *payed*.

salary *noun*, means a fixed regular payment by an employer to employees. It is usually made on a monthly basis but is referred to by its annual total: *The new Chairman saw his salary rise from £233,000 to £425,000 last year*. In the UK, ads often refer to *Salary 35k* (pronounced '35 **kay** /keɪ/') meaning £35,000. **Salary** is the term used for pay for professional people and white-collar workers such as staff in offices in the service or private sectors.

wage *noun & verb*. As a noun, this is often used in the plural *wages* and means a regular fixed payment on a daily or weekly basis by employers to employees such as manual and unskilled workers: *The labour shortage served to drive wages up*. *Wages* is a term associated with blue-collar workers, such as those doing physical work in industry. Use *wages* for payment for work, and **wage** before nouns in phrases such as *wage earner* and *wage packet*. As a verb, **wage** means to carry on a war or campaign: *He was a conscientious teacher, who was concerned to wage war on sloppy language and sloppy thinking*.
See EARNINGS.

As *pay* means both *salary* and *wage* it is a useful term for avoiding the social distinctions between these two words.

payment, repayment, remittance, settlement

payment *noun*, means the act or process of paying money or settling an account or debt: *Directors normally expect payment for their services*. **Payment** can be in instalments, *part payment*, or in full: *The payment was due on 1 April*. The plural form is used for a series of financial transactions: *They made themselves homeless by defaulting on the mortgage payments*. Economists use the term *balance of payments* to mean the difference between the amount paid for imports and received from exports in a given period: *A higher pound makes exports dearer and imports cheaper, so that the balance of payments deteriorates*.

repayment *noun*, means the paying back of an amount that has been lent, in full or in instalments: *Banks and bondholders are being asked to wait for repayment of nearly £1 billion*. The plural form is used for a series of such repayments: *Monthly repayments are fixed throughout the term of the loan*.

remittance *noun*, refers to money that is sent especially, but not only, by post: *Remittance may be made by Access/Visa, postal order or cheque*. **Remittance** is a formal word that is usually only used in this commercial sense; *payment* is a more general term.

settlement *noun*, in the financial sense means the act or process of paying the full amount outstanding on an account. If someone is slow in paying, you can request **settlement**: *Early settlement of your account would be appreciated*. **Settlement** is a formal word in this sense; *payment* is a more general term. See VILLAGE.

peace, piece

peace *uncountable noun*, means freedom from disturbance or conflict, quiet: *May this be a year of peace and happiness for all!* If people ask to be *left in peace*, it means that they do not want to be disturbed. *Peace of mind* is a lack of worry.

piece *noun*, means a portion of something: *a piece of paper*. **Piece** also refers to the parts into which something divides: *all the pieces in the jigsaw puzzle*. **Piece** in other contexts refers to a written or musical composition and a coin. In BE usage, **piece** is the normal term to use with coins up to and including 50p: *I picked up his 10p piece*. *Piece of* is a useful phrase to use when referring to uncountable nouns such as advice, information or news: *An interesting piece of news has just been broadcast*.
See BANKNOTE (COIN).

!

'This hotel is renowned for its piece and solitude. In fact, crowds from all over the world flock here to enjoy its solitude.'
(Hotel brochure)

peaceful, peaceable

peaceful *adjective*, refers to a time or place that is quiet and calm: *A tree-lined lane descends to this peaceful village*. It also refers to a situation that is free from disturbance or violence: *We welcome the peaceful way in which the elections were conducted*.

peaceable *adjective*, means avoiding conflict and is used for people or their intentions: *'I'm a peaceable man but I'll murder them if*

P

they come up here with their bulldozers!' A *peaceable situation* means one that is calm without violence: *They are working towards a peaceable solution during these talks*.

peak

See PEEK.

peal, peel

peal *noun & verb*. As a noun, this means a succession of loud sounds, especially pleasant-sounding ones: *He gave a great peal of laughter with lots of teeth flashing*. Less pleasantly, it can describe thunder: *There was another great peal of thunder, then more lightning*. As a verb, it means to ring (of bells): *The bells pealed out to celebrate their wedding*.

peel *noun & verb*. As a noun, this means the skin of a fruit or vegetable, and as a verb, the act of removing it: *Fetch the potatoes, peel them, then cut them in pieces*. By extension, as a verb **peel** is used for removing the top layer of anything, from a coat of paint to sunburnt skin: *Simply peel off the cover, and pop the plastic pack in the microwave*. To *peel something off* means to remove clothing, especially wet or damp clothing: *She peeled off her wet swimsuit and began to towel her body*.

pebble

See ROCK.

pedal, peddle

pedal *noun & verb*. As a noun, this is a flat bar that each foot presses against to propel a vehicle such as a bicycle, or a foot lever for drums, keyboards, etc.: *The effect of the sustaining pedal must always be taken into consideration*. As a verb, **pedal** means to use the feet to propel a bicycle: *He seized his bike and pedalled furiously away from the fire*.

peddle *verb*, means to sell goods from house to house. It also means to sell something illegal such as drugs, and in another context propagate and spread harmful or untrue ideas or theories: *We should discover the facts before we peddle half-baked and unscientific ideas*.

pedlar, peddler

pedlar *noun*, is a person who travels around selling small objects. This is the BE spelling, and is found mostly in historical contexts.

peddler *noun*, is the AE spelling for *pedlar*, and is both the AE and BE spelling for someone who sells illegal drugs: *For years the cocaine peddlers seemed to control Colombia*.

pederast, paedophile, paediatrician

pederast péddĕrast /ˈpedəræst/ *noun*, means a man involved in sexual activity with a boy: *The police notified the school that a notorious pederast had moved into the area*. Note that the first syllable rhymes with 'led'.

paedophile peédŏfīl /ˈpiːdəfaɪl/ *noun*, means a person who is sexually attracted to children of both sexes: *The paedophile ring on the Internet was discovered by accident*. The AE spelling is *pedophile*. Note that the first syllable is pronounced like the word 'pea'.

paediatrician peedi-ătríshăn /piːdiəˈtrɪʃn̩/ *noun*, means a doctor who studies the diseases of children: *The paediatrician has been wrongly accused of being a paedophile*. The AE spelling is *pediatrician*. Note that the first syllable is pronounced like the word 'pea'. The branch of medicine connected with children's diseases is called *paediatrics* peedi-áttricks /piːdiˈætrɪks/ (AE *pediatrics*).

pedestrian, unimaginative

pedestrian *noun & adjective*. As a noun, this means a person who is on foot, as opposed to one travelling by vehicle. It is often combined in phrases such as *pedestrian crossing, pedestrian precinct*, or found on notices, such as: *No cars, pedestrians only*. As an adjective, it means uninspired, ordinary: *Too often the curriculum is narrow and pedestrian rather than promoting the full development of individuals*.

unimaginative *adjective*, means lacking in thought, dull: *Deaf workers find their careers blocked by unimaginative employers*.

pedestrian crossing, zebra crossing, pelican crossing, crosswalk

pedestrian crossing *noun*, is a specially marked place for people to walk across a road. This is a BE expression.

zebra crossing *noun*, means a *pedestrian crossing* marked by beacons and bands on the road. This is a BE expression.

pelican crossing *noun*, means a *pedestrian crossing* with traffic lights that are controlled by people who want to cross the road, and is marked by bands on the road. This is a BE expression.

crosswalk *noun*, is an AE term for a *pedestrian crossing*.

peek, peak

peek *verb & noun*. As a verb, this means to have a quick look at something, often something that you should not be looking at: *He was not supposed to even peek behind the curtains. Peek out* can also be used figuratively to mean become partly visible: *His thumb peeked out through the hole in his glove*. It is also a noun, with the same meaning: *Gloria gave Dot a hug and said, 'Take a peek at that'*.

peak *verb & noun*. As a verb, this means to reach a maximum level: *They can retain the world title, provided they peak again on Saturday*. As a noun, this means the highest point, the summit of a mountain, or an achievement: *After that year it never again neared the peak of 470,000*.

peel

See PEAL.

peeping Tom

See VOYEUR.

peer, pier

peer *noun & verb*. As a noun, this means an equal in age or social status: *He has now become an outstanding goalkeeper without peer in Britain*. Sociologists use the term *peer group* to mean a group of people with something in common (interests, age, social status, for example): *The power of the peer group to control a deviant is known and used by both sides of industry*. The phrase *peer of the realm* refers to a person of noble rank in the UK: *'You can never tell quite how the Lords will vote', says a nervous peer*. As a verb, **peer** means to look at something that cannot be seen clearly: *She put her glasses on to peer at the smear of mascara*.

pier *noun*, means a wharf, a support for a bridge, or a jetty. A **pier** in an English seaside resort is for recreational use, and may hold shops, stalls or even a funfair. A **pier** can also function as a breakwater, holding back the sea to protect the shore from the action of the waves. See DOCK.

peer review, peer pressure

peer review *noun*, means the evaluation of scientific or academic work by others working in the same field: *A peer review is likely to reveal errors, omissions, ambiguities and weaknesses in style*.

peer pressure *uncountable noun*, means the influence of a peer group on an individual to behave in the same way as its other members, for example by wearing the same clothes or doing the same things: *It is peer pressure which has the greatest weight when it comes to children deciding which toys they most want*.

peer-to-peer, client-server

peer-to-peer *adjective*, is a computing term that refers to networks that allow all the machines on them to share all their functions, each acting as a server to all the others, rather than using dedicated machines to provide all of these facilities centrally.

client-server *adjective*, is a computing term that refers to networks that have one central provider of functions (the server), attached to many terminals that access files and applications from the server.

P

peerage

There are two main types of peers in the UK: hereditary, whose titles are passed down through the generations, and life peers, who have a personal title which is not hereditary.

Ranks of the peerage in descending order:

Male	*Female*	*Estate*
duke	duchess	duchy, dukedom
marquess	marchioness	marquessate
earl	countess	earldom
viscount	viscountess	viscountcy
baron	baroness	barony

See TITLES (WRITING SKILLS).

pelican crossing

See **PEDESTRIAN CROSSING**.

penny, pence

penny *noun*, is the smallest unit in the British monetary system. It also refers to the individual coin: *He dropped a penny*. **Penny** has two plurals, *pence* for the price of something and *pennies* for the coins: *She looked in her purse and found only pennies*. In AE, **penny** is used informally to refer to a one-cent coin. The BE expression *the penny dropped* usually means that someone has grasped an idea: *Then the penny dropped, and her eyes widened in horrified shock*. If someone is *penniless*, this means that he or she is very poor: *Many people die virtually penniless*. See **BANKNOTE (COIN)**.

pence *noun*, is the plural of the smallest unit in the British monetary system: *There are 100 pence to a pound*. When referring to the price of something both *20 pence* and *20p* (pronounced like the word 'pea' – informal) are used: *The newspaper costs 80p on Sunday*.

pendant, pendent

pendant *noun*, is a hanging ornament worn around the neck: *A jade-green pendant on a chain was hanging around her neck*.

pendent *adjective*, means either hanging: *The pendent branches on the willows reached the grass*; or undecided: *The matter is among our pendent claims*.

pending, back burner

pending *adjective*, means waiting to be decided. This is a common term for business or official matters that are not processed: *The pending election may cause unrest in many French suburbs*. The term *patents pending* is frequently seen on the labelling of new products. **Pending** can also refer to something that will happen soon: *Because proceedings are now pending, I cannot comment any further*.

back burner *noun*, is used in the phrase *put something on the back burner*, which means to postpone a decision or action until a later date: *'I've put it on the back burner, but haven't given up the long-term goal of sailing round the world.'*

peninsula, peninsular

peninsula *noun*, means an area of land surrounded by water on three sides. The land mass of Spain and Portugal is referred to as the *Iberian peninsula*.

peninsular *adjective*, refers to something that happens on or is connected with a peninsula. Note this has a final 'r'. The two forms should not be confused, even though they are usually pronounced the same: *The French were defeated in the Peninsular War*.

pension, board, American plan

pension pénshŏn /ˈpenʃn̩/ *noun*, means a regular payment made by an employer or the state to people above retirement age: *The basic state pension is not a universal benefit, but is based on the level of payment*. **Pension** also means the rate or terms offered by a hotel or guest house. It is used in expressions like *full pension* or *half pension*, although this is now more often referred to as *full* or *half board*. The term **pension** (which may also be pronounced paá(ng)ss-yō(ng) /ˈpɑ̃sjɔ̃/), means a small, inexpensive hotel, usually outside Britain.

board *noun*, also means the rate or terms offered by a hotel or guest house. If all meals are provided, this is called *full board*. If only breakfast and an evening meal are provided, this is called *half board*. Note that in the context of hotel rates, **board** is always used with a singular verb: *Half board is also available with meals taken at the nearby Gasthof*.

American plan *noun*, means *full board*. This can be contrasted with *European plan* which means *half board*. This is an AE term.

pensioner, senior citizen

pensioner *noun*, means someone who receives a regular payment from the state, through a former employer, or from an insurance company. This is used particularly for those who receive an old-age pension: *An 85-year-old Wigan pensioner is now looked after by her daughter*. But this often has negative associations, implying incapacity of some sort, and should be avoided. People in the UK who cannot work through injury or other disability receive benefits, not *pensions*, and so should not be referred to as *pensioners*, but are 'on benefit'.

senior citizen *noun*, means a person of retirement age or older but is sometimes used as a more positive term than *pensioner*: *The pool caters for all age groups from the toddler to the senior citizen*. In AE this may be shortened to *senior*.

Pentecost

See WHITSUN.

people, peoples

See PERSON.

people of colour

See BLACK.

per, pr.

per *preposition*, means for each. It is not an abbreviation, so it should not be followed by a stop. **Per** may be abbreviated to 'p.' in phrases such as *per annum* (*p.a.*). **Per** can also be combined with non-Latin words in phrases such as *per hour*, and *per room per night*.

pr. is a common abbreviation for *pair*, not for *per*.

per annum, per capita, per diem

per annum *adverb*, means each year and is abbreviated *p.a.*: *The original grant of £500 per annum has been steadily increased*. Recommended alternatives are 'a year' or 'annually', but *per year* is not recommended in formal writing.

per capita *adjective & adverb*, means for each person: *They contrasted the per capita income for the six member states* (adjective). *They also measured spending per capita* (adverb). **Per capita** can be abbreviated *p.c.*, but this abbreviation is generally avoided due to possible confusion with PC meaning personal computer, police constable and politically correct. The alternative 'a head' is sometimes possible, but *per head* is not recommended in formal writing.

per diem *noun, adjective & adverb*. As a noun and adjective this refers to the daily allowance paid by an employer to an employee when travelling to cover hotel expenses and subsistence costs. This is often referred to as the travel allowance: *They receive a per diem of £150 for every day they are away* (noun). It also means the daily salary rate: *He calculated his fee based on his per diem rate* (adjective). As an adverb it means on or for each day: *These drivers are paid per diem*.

per cent, percentage

per cent *adverb, adjective & noun*, means a specified amount in every hundred: *The doctors had their salaries increased by 50 per cent, while the teachers were granted a 20 per cent rise*. In formal writing, the words **per cent** are preferred to the % sign. **Per cent** is normally written as two words in BE, but as one word in AE.

percentage *noun*, is a rate for an amount that is so much in a hundred. **Percentage** may be followed by a singular or plural verb depending on the noun that follows: *Only a low percentage of his income* ***is*** *used for rent; A high percentage of the houses* ***are*** *to be redecorated*, although some writers prefer to use a singular verb in all contexts. It is best not to use **percentage** on its own to mean some or a lot. Use: *a small* or *a low percentage*, or *a large* or *high percentage*. However, when the amount is implied by the context of the sentence, **percentage** may be used without a qualifying adjective: *The percentage of false negatives generated by a cancer test was of great concern*. Note that **percentage** is written as one word in both BE and AE.

perennial

See ANNUAL.

perfect, more than perfect

perfect *adjective*, means as good as something can be, and consequently 'less perfect', 'least perfect', 'more perfect' or 'most perfect' should be avoided. An interesting departure from this rule is found in the US Constitution which refers to a 'more perfect union': *We, the People of the United States, in order to form a more perfect union . . . establish this Constitution for the United States of America*. Recommended phrases to express near perfection include 'almost . . .', 'nearly . . .', and 'practically perfect': *His English was almost perfect*.

more than perfect is, illogically, used from time to time, but is not recommended in

P

formal writing. See **ABSOLUTE ADJECTIVES (GRAMMAR TIPS)**.

perhaps

See **MAY BE**.

perimeter

See **PARAMETER**.

periodical

See **JOURNAL**.

perk

See **FRINGE BENEFIT**.

permissible, permission, permissive

permissible *adjective*, means allowed by the rules or by law: *Divorce is a permissible solution to marital difficulties*. This is a formal word that may be replaced by allowed or permitted. See **PERMIT (ALLOW)**.

permission *noun*, means consent to do something: *Permission to park at the house may be obtained at the Visitor Centre*. In more formal English you may *seek permission*, and it may be granted.

permissive *adjective*, means not strict and allowing freedom of behaviour: *The Act is permissive: a licence should be granted unless good cause is shown justifying refusal*. **Permissive** is often used to describe behaviour that some people would disapprove of: *In that country's permissive atmosphere people use guns, not lawyers, to settle disputes*.

perpendicular, vertical

perpendicular *adjective*, means at 90 degrees to a given line, plane or surface: *Looking over his left shoulder, he raises his arms perpendicular to his sides*.

vertical *adjective*, means at 90 degrees to the horizon: *In the windless valley, the rain dropped from the sky in vertical sheets*.

There can be a 90 degree difference between these positions if a mountaineer climbing a *vertical* rock face leans on the ropes and stands *perpendicular* to the rock face. See **ABSOLUTE ADJECTIVES (GRAMMAR TIPS)**.

perpetuate, perpetrate

perpetuate verb, means to make a belief or unfortunate situation persist, usually for a long time: *The regime had perpetuated the oppression of minorities for over a decade*.

perpetrate *verb*, means to carry out an illegal action or crime: *The kidnap was apparently perpetrated by a cell of international terrorists*. See **COMMITTED**.

> *'. . . the person who was alleged to have perpetuated the crime was a member of two gun clubs' – Parliament of Victoria, Australia. Hansard, 2003.*
> (One of 4,000 hits from Google)
> **!**

perquisite

See **FRINGE BENEFIT**.

persecute, prosecute

persecute *verb*, means to treat somebody or a group cruelly and unfairly: *In seventeenth-century England, both Catholics and Nonconformists were persecuted by the state*. **Persecute** can also mean to harass or persistently annoy a person in order to make their life miserable: *It is quite wrong to persecute one man for using the law to his advantage*. The related noun is *persecution*.

prosecute *verb*, means to start legal action and charge an organization or a person with a crime in a court of law: *One local council says it will prosecute traders who break the law*. The related noun is *prosecution*.

persistent vegetative state

See **VEGETABLE**.

person, people, peoples

person *noun*, means an individual: *It is hardly a question a sane person can answer*; or someone unknown: *Even after some months not one person had come further than the front door*. Although the plural of **person** is usually *people*, in AE, the plural form *persons* is used for public notices or in legal English as in BE: *Foul play perpetrated by a person or persons unknown*. The phrase 'on or about your person' means something in your clothes or on your body: *Airport security* *found a knife about his person*. This is a formal expression.

people *noun*, is the usual plural of *person* in BE: *Many people practise relaxation techniques, or read in bed*. Here, **people** takes a plural verb. However, when **people** means a group united by race, religion or nationality it is considered a single unit and has a singular determiner and verb: *This peace-loving people is being driven off its land*. See FOLK.

peoples *noun*, refers to populations of different ethnic tribes, groups or nationalities: *This book calls itself a history of the European peoples*.

persona, façade

persona *noun*, means the way someone behaves in public that gives an insight into their character: *On TV he has an amusing persona, but he is very different when you meet him face to face*. The plural is *personas* or *personae*.

façade *noun*, means a way of behaving that hides your real feelings: *This implies that somehow the truth is being hidden behind her glossy, false façade*. In other contexts it refers to the front of a building.

personal, personnel

personal *adjective*, means belonging to an individual rather than other people, such as a personal identification number. It can also relate to your private life: *She had some personal tax problems*. It can also describe coarse comments or criticism: *He made some very personal remarks*. In a broader sense, **personal** can mean designed for individual use: *A personal computer*.

personnel *noun*, means either the staff employed in an organization, in which case it takes a plural verb: *Many personnel were wearing T-shirts with the new company logo*; or the part of an organization concerned with staff matters (recruitment, discipline, welfare, etc.). Here it takes a singular verb, and no determiner: *I went over to Personnel and said, 'What about my son-in-law?'* In the first sense, **personnel** is a rather formal term, and may be replaced by *staff* or *employees*, and occasionally *team*. Many organizations are now abandoning the term *personnel department* in favour of 'human resources department'.

perspective, prospective

perspective *noun*, means a viewpoint or way of thinking about something: *The year in India gave him a new perspective on life*. Figuratively it means aspect or relationship: *There is undoubtedly truth in this argument but it must be placed in perspective*. It also means the way solid objects in space are represented on a flat surface: *In the drawing, distance is achieved through the use of colour and aerial perspective*.

prospective *adjective*, means likely to happen or expected: *Most estate agents regularly circulate details of new projects to prospective purchasers*.

perspire

See SWEAT.

persuade

See CONVINCE.

P

peruse

See READ.

perverse, pervert

perverse *adjective*, refers to actions that are deliberate and obstinate and carried out in a way that most people find unreasonable or unacceptable: *Hitler was driven by a political vision, albeit a perverse one*.

pervert *noun & verb*. As a noun, this means a person with sexual behaviour that is abnormal and unacceptable: *She might be a rare type of pervert – vociferously condemning all the vices she actually practises*. Note that the stress is on the first syllable: pérvert /ˈpɜːrvɜːrt/. As a verb, **pervert** means to change something such as a system or behaviour so that the result is immoral or completely unacceptable: *There will always be unscrupulous people who attempt to pervert the rules for their own gains*. Note that the stress is on the second syllable: pĕrvért /pərˈvɜːrt/. The legal phrase *pervert the course of justice* means not to tell the truth thus making it difficult for the police to investigate a crime: *A solicitor's clerk has appeared in court accused of conspiring to pervert the course of justice*. See KINKY.

petite, *petit*, *petty*

petite pĕteét /pə'tiːt/ *adjective*, means small and is used to refer to a woman who is small and slight: *She was petite and lively*. **Petite** is also used for a clothing size for small women.

petit pétti /'peti/ *adjective*, also means small and is used in the names of *petit four*, which is a small fancy cake, or *petit beurre*, a type of biscuit. Among other things, the *petit bourgeois* (also spelt 'petty bourgeois') means a lower social class or those who pay too much attention to their possessions or social position. Note that **petit** is pronounced like the word 'petty'.

petty *adjective*, means small and unimportant: *His petty objections were quickly dismissed by the committee*.

petrol, gas, gasoline

petrol *noun*, is the BE term for refined petroleum used as fuel for cars: *He ended one weekend on the moors, where he ran out of petrol*.

gas *noun & verb*. As a noun, this is any air-like fluid substance. **Gas** is a substance that can be used for cooking or heating. In AE, **gas** is the usual word for the liquid fuel used in cars. The plural is *gases*. As a verb, this means to harm or kill with **gas**: *The policy of gassing badger populations has been and gone*. Note the doubling of the 's' in the forms *gassing* and *gassed*.

gasoline *noun*, is the AE term for *petrol* and has the abbreviation *gas* in AE. The AE equivalent of petrol station is *gas station*.

> ! *The petrol-station attendant near Manchester was astonished when the American tourists wanted him to fill the car up with gas.*

phase, faze

phase *noun & verb*. As a noun this means either a changed situation such as 'a new phase of life' or a stage in a process: *Molecules of both A and B have a greater tendency to escape from the liquid phase into the vapour phase*. The shape of the moon and characteristics of electronic signals can be described in **phases**. As a verb it means to do something in stages over a period of time: *More than a decade was to pass before conscription was phased out*. See STEP.

faze *verb*, means to make a person disconcerted so that they are confused or upset and are unsure of what to do: *You couldn't help liking her; nothing fazed Rosie*.

PhD

See DOCTORAL DEGREE.

phenomenon, phenomena

phenomenon *noun*, means a fact or situation that occurs or exists: *Compulsory state education for all is, in the historical sense, a recent phenomenon*.

phenomena *noun*, is the plural of *phenomenon*. Always write and say ***these** phenomena **are** . . .*, not ***this** phenomena **is**. . . .* 'Phenomenons' is not an acceptable plural of *phenomenon*. See PLURAL NOUNS (WORD FORMATION).

Philippines, Filipino, Filipina

Philippines *noun*, is an island republic in the Pacific Ocean. Its official name in English is *Republic of the Philippines*. Note the spelling with initial 'Ph-', and that the final syllable rhymes with 'beans'.

Filipino *noun & adjective*. As a noun, this is either a native of the *Philippines*: *Measures have been initiated to improve the employment situation among Filipinos*; or the name of the national language: *Do you speak Filipino?*

Filipina *noun & adjective*, is an alternative form for a female native of the *Philippines*: *The Filipina singer was a great success*.

> Note that this nationality noun and adjective can distinguish between the sexes and that they are spelt with initial 'F'.

phishing, computer fraud

phishing *noun*, means the sending of email or text messages with the intention of getting the recipient to reveal confidential material so that a fraud can take place: *After their phishing expedition, the crooks managed to defraud bank customers of several million pounds*. See SPAM.

computer fraud *noun*, is fraud committed by accessing other people's computer systems and stealing information, or fraud carried out as a result of tricking people into revealing confidential information by means of fake messages.

phobia

See **MANIA**.

phone, call, ring

phone *noun & verb*. As a noun, this is now the standard short form of *telephone*, and should not be spelt with an apostrophe: *Cramer used the phone in the garage to make the call*. When giving a *phone number* in writing, the abbreviation 'tel.' is often placed before it. As a verb, **phone** means to speak to someone on the **phone**: *'I'll phone the hotel to check the time of Garry's arrival,' he said*. Note that using the full form *telephone* as a verb is formal and is used mainly in BE. See **TELEPHONE NUMBERS**.

call *noun & verb*. As a noun, this means a phone conversation: *When she arrived at the airport she made a phone call to Amsterdam*. As a verb, **call** means to speak to someone on the phone: *For a catalogue, call our sales office*.

ring[1] *noun & verb*. As a noun this means a phone call in informal BE: *Tell John that I will give him a ring tonight*. As a verb, it means to make a bell produce a sound, or (especially in BE), to make a phone call: *She remembered to use his phone to ring the hospital*. It can also refer to the object making the sound: *The phone/alarm clock is ringing*. The past tense is *rang*: *He rang the bell*; and the past participle is *rung*: *I have rung the bell*.

ring[2] *noun & verb*. As a noun, this means a circle, or something formed into a circle: *She had a wedding ring on her finger*. As a verb, **ring**[2] means to encircle or surround: *Please ring the correct answer on the exam paper*. It would be more common to say *put a circle around* in this sense. This verb has the past tense and past participle forms *ringed*: *The field was ringed by security guards*.

> When used as verbs in the context of telephones, *phone*, *call* and *ring* mean the same thing, but *ring* is rare in AE.

phone-in

See **CHAT SHOW**.

phoney, phony

phoney *adjective*, means false or not genuine: *The burglar was surprised by the police, but managed a phoney smile*. This is an informal word. This is the usual BE spelling.

phony *adjective*, is an alternative BE spelling and the usual spelling in AE.

> There are two plurals: *phoneys* and *phonies*, depending on the choice of spelling for the singular.

phosphorescence

See **FLUORESCENCE**.

phosphorus, phosphorous

phosphorus *noun*, is a chemical element, with the symbol P: *Red phosphorus is used for making matches*. See **PHOSPHORESCENT (FLUORESCENT)**.

phosphorous *adjective*, means related to *phosphorus*: *The flask contained phosphorous acid* (H_3PO_3).

> Avoid confusing *phosphorus* with the adjective form *phosphorous*, as the two words sound the same. In almost all cases, the noun, ending *-rus*, will be the word required.

photocopy

See **XEROX**.

phrasal verbs

See **GRAMMAR TIPS**.

Physical Science

See **EARTH SCIENCE**.

physician, physicist

physician *noun*, is the normal term in AE for a medical doctor who does not carry out surgery. In BE the term is used in the names of institutions such as the *Royal College of Physicians*, but otherwise it is dated and doctor or GP (general practitioner) are the normal terms. See **DOCTOR**.

P

physicist *noun*, means a scientist with expertise in physics: *According to one physicist, CO_2 should be pumped into underground storage.*

physics, physique

physics *uncountable noun*, is one of the physical sciences that studies the nature and properties of matter and energy, particularly phenomena such as heat, light, sound and electricity. Like other academic subjects ending with -ics, **physics** takes a singular verb when it means the discipline: *He said that physics is usually divorced from a consideration of moral issues.*
See -ICS.

physique *noun*, is the size and appearance of a person's body: *Even in physique they were very much alike, both being thick in the shoulders.*

picaresque, picturesque

picaresque *adjective*, describes an epic style in literature that presents the adventures of a dishonest but likeable hero: *'The Adventures of Tom Jones' and 'Tristram Shandy' are two eighteenth-century examples of English picaresque novels.*

picturesque *adjective*, means visually attractive and charming: *Fine coastal walks and lovely gardens complete this picturesque resort.* Language can also be termed **picturesque** if it is vivid and unusual.

pick

See CHOOSE.

pidgin, pigeon, dove

pidgin *noun*, is a simplified form of language, such as English mixed with elements of local languages, which helps Asians and English-speaking traders to communicate. It is reputedly derived from a Chinese alteration of the word 'business'.

pigeon *noun*, is a family of birds including the doves: *All that was left was one fat old pigeon sitting on the lawn.*

dove *noun*, is a group of species within the pigeon family. **Dove** is preferred to pigeon in symbolic contexts. 'The white pigeon' does not have the same appeal as 'the white dove of peace' even though they may be members of the same family. **Dove** is used in the names of certain species of the pigeon family, such as the *turtledove* or *rock dove*.

> *'My volcabulary is getting better, why thank you me old son which is more than can be said about your pidgeon English'.*
> (Reader's comment to *Watford Observer* – online) **!**

piece

See PEACE.

pier

See PEER.

pigeon

See PIDGIN.

pigeonhole

See SHELF.

PIN, chip and PIN

PIN *noun*, is an abbreviation of *personal identification number* which means the number allocated to someone in order to validate electronic transactions or to gain access to a building. The expression *PIN number* is commonly used: *A gang of youths forced her to reveal her PIN number*, but as the N in **PIN** stands for *number*, many organizations use the expression *PIN code*.
See TAUTOLOGY.

chip and PIN *noun*, is a system of paying for something with a credit card that has a microchip with information stored on it: *When you enter your PIN it proves that you have the right to use the card.*

pincers, pliers

pincers *noun*, are tools for grasping things. They have sharp rounded jaws with a circular space between them: *A pair of pincers is useful for removing floorboard nails.*

pliers *noun*, are also tools for grasping things but they have long and somewhat tapering jaws to bend or cut wire: *The valve can be operated by gripping the stub in a pair of pliers.*

As both these terms refer to things that are made up of two parts, they always take a plural verb.

Pinyin

See **CHINESE**[2].

pitiful, pitiable, piteous

pitiful *adjective*, means either shameful and deserving pity: *The firm paid pitiful wages*; or not worthy of respect: *It was a pitiful performance and the people had little time for their president*.

pitiable *adjective*, means shameful or badly paid. It also means in poor condition and worthy of compassion: *The general election reduced the Lib Dems to a pitiable number of MPs*.

piteous *adjective*, means deserving pity. This nearly always refers to people in a dire state: *His face, between heaves, was piteous and terrified*.

place, put

place *verb*, means to position something carefully or exactly in a particular situation: *She drew off her fine kid gloves and placed them on the table*. **Place** can be used figuratively: *This placed the government in a difficult situation*. Here **place** is typically used in written English. Many of the informal AE adverbs that include 'place' such as *anyplace, no place*, have 'where' in BE: *anywhere, nowhere*.

put *verb*, means almost the same as *place*, but *putting something in position* implies less care and neatness than placing it there. **Put** can be used figuratively: *This put the minister in a difficult position*. **Put** is less formal than *place*, and is the basis of many phrasal verbs, such as *put in*, which can mean place inside or publish: *They put her letter in the newspaper*. If the letter was *placed in the newspaper* it would sound like a conspiracy plot to mislead the newspaper readers, but one can *place an ad* in a newspaper, without any sinister connotations.

placement

See **WORK EXPERIENCE**.

plagiarism, reverse engineering

plagiarism *noun*, means the copying of someone else's work in order to pass it off as one's own: *Either rewrite thoroughly or quote exactly: if not, you are in danger of plagiarism*. See **COLLUDE (COOPERATE)**.

reverse engineering *compound noun*, means the close examination of a product, in order to discover how it is made and how it works, so that it can be copied: *Reverse engineering for the purpose of copying or duplicating programs may constitute a copyright violation*.

plaid

See **TARTAN**.

plain, plane

plain *noun & adjective*. As a noun, this means a large area of flat country like the Great Plains in the USA. As an adjective, **plain** describes things that are easy to understand or obvious: *It was quite plain that she had not forgiven or forgotten*. It also means uncomplicated, not fancy: *plain country food*, as well as without a pattern: *Use plain paper*. See **COMMON, USUAL (TYPICAL)**.

plane *noun*, means a level surface. In a figurative sense, it means a different level: *Light that actually comes out will be vibrating in specific planes*. Both *aeroplane* (BE) and *airplane* (AE) are abbreviated to **plane**. See **AIRCRAFT**.

plan, planning

plan *noun*, means intention: *We have some plans to reduce unemployment*; or a detailed proposal about how to achieve something: *We drew up a five-year plan to attract more jobs to this area*. It can also be a technical drawing.

planning *noun*, is the process of making plans: *The candidate was never comfortable with the planning or the preparation for the campaign*. See **BLUEPRINT**.

Both *plan* and *planning* may lead to tautology as plans must refer to the future. Thus *future plans* or *future planning* should only be contrasted with *present plans* or *earlier plans*. See **TAUTOLOGY**.

P

plaster, cement, concrete, mortar

plaster *noun & verb*. As a noun, this is a material used for coating walls and ceilings to give a smooth surface: *There were places where the plaster had chipped and no repairs had been done*. **Plaster** is also the material used to encase broken limbs to hold them rigid: *The next day he had both arms in plaster*. In these senses, it is an uncountable noun. When **plaster** means a flexible covering for a cut or small area of skin damage, it is a countable noun: *When the blister burst, he put a plaster over it*. As a verb, it means either to cover a wall with **plaster** or to cover any surface with objects. Expressions such as *plastering posters all over town* imply disapproval of this action. 'Putting up posters' would be a neutral alternative.

cement *uncountable noun & verb*. As a noun, this is a grey lime-based powder that can be mixed with sand and water either to make bricks stick together (another name for this mixture is *mortar*); or to make durable floors: *We picked our way across the cement which had just hardened*. As a verb, **cement** also means to join people, organizations, countries and the like together: *To cement the deal, IBM has bought an equity stake in the firm*.

concrete *uncountable noun & adjective*. As a noun, this is a building material made by mixing cement with sand or small stones. **Concrete** can be used to make numerous building elements and can also be reinforced with steel or iron rods: *The bridge is mainly concrete and has one of the longest spans in the world*. As an adjective, it can refer either to things that are built of **concrete** such as a *concrete bridge*, or in a wider sense to things that are based on real, tangible facts, not ideas: *As no one is able to offer concrete proof, I must write what I believe to be true*.

mortar *uncountable noun*, is used for finishing walls, or for plastering, and when laying bricks. **Mortar** is made from *cement*. The expression *bricks and mortar* means the cost of a building or its value: *In terms of bricks and mortar, the school cost £20 million. Then we need furniture and equipment*.

plateglass university

See REDBRICK UNIVERSITY.

platform, bay, gate (transport)

platform *noun*, means the raised area in a railway station where trains can be boarded: *The train now approaching Platform 5 is the 12.10 to Birmingham*. In AE, the track that the train travels along is announced, rather than the **platform** that the passengers are standing on: *The train for Delaware will leave from Track 6*.

bay *noun*, means the place in a terminus where the different coaches or long-distance buses depart from: *The service to Oxford departs from Bay 12*.

gate *noun*, is used in an airport to show where planes depart from: *The delayed flight to Paris Charles de Gaulle is now boarding from Gate 16*.

plc, Ltd

plc, Plc and **PLC** *abbreviations*, are BE abbreviations for **p**ublic **l**imited **c**ompany. A British company which is eligible for listing on the London Stock Exchange always has **plc** after its name. It is written without full stops, and may be written in upper case, lower case, or with just the 'P' in upper case.
See COMPANY (BUSINESS).

Ltd *abbreviation*, is short for ***limited*** and is used by companies which are not listed on the Stock Exchange. A limited company is one in which the share-owners' liabilities are restricted to the amount of money they have invested. In AE, **Ltd** is pronounced **éll tee dée** /'el tiː 'diː/, but in BE it is pronounced as the full word: límmitĕd /'lɪmɪtɪd/.

plea-bargaining, turn King's/Queen's evidence

plea-bargaining *uncountable noun*, is an arrangement in court where the accused admits that a lesser crime was committed if the charge for a more serious crime is dropped: *Plea-bargaining is a clear feature of the system's operation under traditional rape laws*. Informally, this is known in its verbal form as *cop a plea*. See PLEA (APPEAL), TESTIMONY (EVIDENCE).

turn King's/Queen's evidence *phrase*, is a BE term that means to provide information to the authorities against other criminals in order to receive a lower sentence. The word *King* or *Queen* is used depending on the sex of the monarch at any given time. In the USA, the equivalent is *to turn state's evidence*.

please find enclosed . . . , enclosed please find

please find enclosed *phrase*, is a dated business expression used as an opening phrase in a letter or email. It is better to use: 'I enclose' or 'We enclose' with letters and 'I attach' or 'We attach' with emails.

enclosed please find *phrase*, is another dated business expression. It is better to use: 'I enclose' or 'We enclose' with letters and 'I attach' or 'We attach' with emails.

pleonasm

See TAUTOLOGY.

plethora, plenty

plethora pléthŏră /'pleθərə/ *noun*, means a larger amount than is necessary or can be used. This is generally used as a disapproving term: *The eurobond market has seen a plethora of subsidiary innovations, many of which have been one-off or flourished only for a time*. 'An abundance of' or 'plenty of' are often good alternatives to 'a plethora of'.

plenty *noun & adjective*. As a noun this means a situation where there is abundance: *With land prices set to fall further, the opportunities will be there in plenty*. As an adjective this is commonly used in the phrase 'plenty of': *I am always punctual and on the platform in plenty of time*.

pliers

See PINCERS.

plough, plow

plough *noun*, is a piece of farming equipment for digging and turning over soil prior to sowing seeds. This is the BE spelling. When capitalized, *The Plough* refers to a group of stars that is visible in the northern hemisphere. This is called *The Big Dipper* in AE.

plow *noun*, is the AE spelling of *plough*.

plural nouns

See WORD FORMATION.

plurality

See MAJORITY.

point of view

See OPINION.

poison, intoxicate

poison *verb*, means to use a substance that will harm or kill a person, animal or plant: *It is wrong to poison the sea with substances that are difficult to control*. In a figurative sense, **poison** also means to have a negative effect on something: *I hope we can reach agreement and it will not poison our relationship right across the board*.

intoxicate *verb*, means to make drunk: *The police suspected the driver of being intoxicated*. **Intoxicate** can also be used in a figurative sense meaning to feel very excited: *The three young students were intoxicated by the thought of easy money*.

pole, poll

pole *noun*, is either a thin straight piece of metal or wood used as a support: *tent pole, telegraph pole, barge pole*, or the two points at the opposite ends of the earth: *North Pole* and *South Pole*. In physics, the opposite ends of a magnet are also called *poles*. When capitalized, it also means a Polish person.

poll *noun*, apart from meaning a survey of public opinion (*opinion poll*), this term means the process of voting at an election: *The polls open tomorrow for elections to county councils*; the process of counting the votes, or the total number of votes in an election: *Labour got 44 per cent of the poll*. Two related terms are *straw poll* – informally asking a number of people who they would vote for in an election; and *exit poll* – asking voters who they voted for immediately after an election in order to predict the result. See ELECTION.

> ! *The idea of speed controls on Autobahns should not be touched with a barge poll.*
> (*The Independent* October 2007)

politic, body politic

politic *adjective*, means wise and well judged and prudent: *As the soldiers arrived, he found it politic to depart*. See -IC.

body politic *noun*, means everyone in a nation involved in political activities: *It comprises the entire body politic with all its citizens*.

political, politics, policy

political *adjective*, describes matters relating to the state or public affairs: *This government is formed by the political party with majority support in the House of Commons*. When used about a person, **political** means interested in politics: *He became very political after 20 years in business*.

politics *noun*, means the art or science of government, or the debate about how to manage a country or relations between states: *Politics is a process of competition, bargaining and compromise between the different interest groups*. Use a singular verb here. However a plural verb is used when referring to a person's or a group's political sympathies: *Green politics are based on the belief that the resources of the planet are finite*. See -ICS.

policy *noun*, means a plan of action agreed or chosen by a political party, a business or a government: *It is vital that we have a clear policy on environmental issues*. In another sense it means an insurance contract.

political correctness

Political correctness (abbreviated PC) means avoiding certain attitudes, actions and forms of expression which are likely to be offensive. A general rule is to avoid references to a person's age, race, colour, sexual preference or physical disability when this has no relevance to the situation. In working life, racist or sexual harassment are not allowed. A major concern of political correctness has been to avoid racist or sexist language or jokes that will offend particular groups.

In the USA, the terms 'African American' instead of 'Black' and 'Native American' instead of 'Indian' are examples of PC. Elsewhere, 'Saami' has replaced 'Lapp' and 'Inuit' has replaced 'Eskimo'. See INUIT.

PC is also about avoiding sexist language and 'Ms', for example, has been used for a long time as a title for women who do not wish to identify themselves as being either married 'Mrs' or single 'Miss'. Other PC phrases, such as 'chair' or 'chairperson' (replacing 'chairman') are also common. See SEXIST LANGUAGE (WRITING SKILLS).

In the area of physical disability there is less agreement about the terms to use. However 'blind' is often replaced by 'visually impaired' and 'deaf' by 'hearing impaired' or 'people with a visual/hearing impairment'. Describing people who are short as 'vertically challenged' and 'fat' as 'differently sized' have won little general acceptance.

poll

See POLE.

pollute, contaminate

pollute *verb*, means to make something impure, and is most often used to refer to air or water resources: *Chemicals used on golf courses can pollute local water supplies*.

contaminate *verb*, means to make something impure or dirty: *Rats are a worry because they are so dangerous and can contaminate food*.

popular, trendy

popular *adjective*, means liked or enjoyed by many people: *popular music*. When **popular** refers to ideas, beliefs and opinions, or the average people in a country, it is used before a noun: *Many commentators have dubbed the Corolla as 'the world's most popular car'*. Otherwise, **popular** can be used independently: *Television has made some sports incredibly popular*.

trendy *adjective & noun*. As an adjective this describes something that is in fashion: *It's very trendy to be a Native American these days*. As a noun it means a person who is fashionable: *More trendies from the college in their trendy clothes, hair and lifestyle*. This is usually disapproving.

populous, populace, population

populous *adjective*, describes a place that is heavily populated: *Los Angeles is the most populous county in America; it has more people than 42 states*. Note that only areas are **populous**.

populace *uncountable noun*, means all the ordinary people living in a country or an area. It means the general public not the inhabitants: *He saw the new world in the people's eyes; and if the populace wanted change, then there could be no return to what had been*. Note that the definite article is normally used with **populace**. See RESIDENT.

population *noun*, means all the citizens of a country or area, regardless of their social status: *The rural population has been declining for many years*.

> *'. . . and it is in students' hands that the populous must place their trust'.*
> (UK Student Essay competition 2005 – winning entry)
> !

pore, pour

pore *noun & verb*. As a noun, this means a minute opening in a surface, commonly the skin. As a verb, it means to study with great attention: *She pored over nineteenth-century French texts*.

pour *verb*, means to cause a liquid or other substance to flow rapidly: *The mine flooded, and cadmium and other toxic heavy metals poured into the river*.

'In the study the Vicar poured over his books.'
(Project Gutenberg)

port, *harbour, harbor*

port *noun*, means a place where ships travel to and load or discharge cargo: *We arrived at the Port of London*. **Ports** have harbours as well as quays and docks. See DOCK.

harbour *noun*, means a place where ships can moor either to get shelter or as a part of a port. A **harbour** may be natural or can be protected from the sea by man-made jetties. This is the BE spelling.

harbor *noun*, is the AE spelling of *harbour*.

portable, transportable

portable *adjective & noun*. As an adjective this describes an object that is light enough to be picked up and easily carried: *a portable battery pack*. As a noun it means a small type of machine that is easy to carry such as a laptop computer.

transportable *adjective*, describes something that can be moved or transported from place to place, usually by a vehicle: *We will need a transportable power unit here if we are going to avoid power cuts*. In computer science, it means software that can be applied on other platforms: *The programs will also be fully transportable for immediate implementation on any large machine*.

portentous

See PRETENTIOUS.

portion

See PART[2].

position, post[1], job (occupations)

position *noun*, means employment and is mainly used for academic, managerial or professional occupations: *He held a senior position with a large company*.

post[1] *noun*, also means employment and is usually reserved for professional, military or diplomatic work: *The search is on for someone to fill a top post in the UN*. See POST[2].

job *noun*, means any form of work. It may be unpaid: *I can't come for a drink tonight, I have too many jobs to do around the house*; but is usually paid: *I have a job with this pizza delivery service*. In this sense it is used informally for any occupation: *I've packed my job in at the Transport Department*. **Job** also means responsibility: *In difficult times the chief's job is to vanish*; function: *The bridge looks somewhat minimalistic, considering the job it has to do*; or piece of work: *This was a*

P

specialist civil engineering job. It is used in many combinations such as: *job cuts, job description, job evaluation, job losses, job offer, job opportunities, job satisfaction, job security* and *job (re)training*. The phrase *on the job* means while working: *They urged more efforts to recruit women – unqualified if need be, to be trained on the job*. **Job** is the most informal of these three words.

positive, negative

positive *adjective*, means either confident and encouraged: *The experiment is working well and feedback is very positive*; or certain to produce a successful result: *They sounded very positive about the chances of peace in the region*. In a scientific sense, a test which is **positive** shows that some substance is found to be present: *The race official confirmed that the rider had tested positive*.

negative *adjective*, either describes something that is harmful: *The teacher's racist jokes had a negative influence on the children*; or means not being hopeful and lacking enthusiasm: *Unemployed people tend to describe their time in very negative ways, as being empty and as having nothing to do*. In a scientific sense, a test which is **negative** shows that some substance is not found or present: *The pregnancy test was negative*.

> *The doctor received a punch on the nose after telling the young boy that he had tested negative.* **!**

possibility

See OPPORTUNITY.

post[1]

See POSITION.

post[2], mail

post[2] *uncountable noun & verb*. As a noun, this is a BE term to refer to a postal service, such as the Royal Mail – the state-run UK postal service provider. As a verb, **post** means to hand something into the postal service for delivery, either personally at a *Post Office* desk in a shop or by putting it into a letter box. This is normal BE usage.

mail *uncountable noun & verb*. As a noun, this has the same meaning as *post*, but mail is normal AE usage. **Mail** also means *email*. As a verb, this is the only word used in AE to mean send something through the postal service. Note that although both **mail** and *electronic mail* are uncountable nouns and may only be used in the singular, the abbreviated form *email* can be plural: *When he returned from holiday 20 spam emails were waiting for him*. See EMAIL.

> The differences between BE and AE in the usage of *post* and *mail* can be found in other related terms, such as *postbox* (BE) / *mailbox* (AE) and *postal worker* (BE) / *mail carrier* (AE).

postcode

See ZIP CODE.

postgraduate

See STUDENT.

postpone

See ADJOURN.

potable

See DRINKABLE.

potent, strong

potent *adjective*, refers to something that has a powerful effect or influence, and when it is restricted to contexts such as medicine, drink and argument, it focuses on the effect on a person's body or mind. In another context it means effective: *A good company pension scheme remains a potent weapon when it comes to attracting and keeping staff*.

strong *adjective*, refers to the power to move heavy objects or do hard physical work. It also refers to a person or object that can withstand pressure or wear and is not easily injured or damaged: *He bought four strong brass padlocks*. It is commonly used figuratively to mean *great*: *There had been a strong improvement in business last year*.

> When a drink is described as *potent*, this focuses on its effect. When it is *strong*, the focus is on its intense flavour or the concentrated volume of alcohol.

pound

See **BATTER**.

pound, lb

pound *noun*, is a unit of weight (about 0.45 kg) or a unit of currency used in the UK and some other countries. The £ symbol is used in a number of countries and one way to ensure that people know that you are referring to pound sterling is to use the ISO currency code 'GBP'. The term *pound sign* is used in BE to mean £. In AE, a *pound sign* is # which is the usual way of referring to that button or key on a telephone (in BE, # is called the hash sign and the hash button or hash key on the phone). See **TELEPHONE KEYS (TELEPHONE NUMBERS)**.

lb *noun*, is the abbreviation for pound weight: *She put on 5 lb during the summer on the farm.* Both **lb** and the # sign are used in some parts of the world to mean pound weight. The origin is the Latin *libra* (pound). It is read as 'pound'.

pour

See **PORE**.

power

See **STRENGTH**.

power breakfast

See **BREAKFAST**.

p.p., signed by

p.p. is the abbreviation for the Latin *per pro* or *per procurationem*, which are never used. When someone signs a letter by authority or proxy because his or her superior is not available the usual format is:

Yours sincerely,

John Jones, p.p. Charles Baker.

In a holiday brochure, the prices are often indicated using the abbreviation **p.p.** which stands for *per person*. See **P.**.

signed by . . . in the absence of . . . is common in AE and is the equivalent of **p.p.**

PPS

See **PS**.

pr.

See **PER**.

practical, practicable

practical *adjective*, means useful or sensible, as opposed to theoretical. Things which are **practical** are connected with real situations, not ideas: *How to protect yourself and others – practical advice on how to avoid infection. A practical solution to air pollution* takes into account the conditions that exist, such as available funding. **Practical** has two negative forms, *impractical* and *unpractical*.

practicable *adjective*, means feasible and capable of being put into practice. It can also mean easy to use: *He had to certify that restoration was both practicable and in the public interest.* Consequently a plan, method, or suggestion may be both *practical* and **practicable**, so that the two words are interchangeable in some contexts. On the other hand, an idea can be **practicable** and not *practical* – meaning it is possible, but would be too costly, or not be useful. The negative form of **practicable** is *impracticable*.

P

practice, practise, practitioner

practice *noun*, means the use of an idea or method: *The sheep were penned in the yard, a usual practice at clipping time.* **Practice** is the spelling of the noun in BE and AE. But in AE, **practice** is also the common spelling of the verb. See **BEST PRACTICE**.

practise *verb*, usually means to repeat actions in order to become more skilled: *Unless you practise, there in only one way to go – down.* Fully qualified professionals doing their job are also said to **practise**, as doctors or lawyers, for instance. This spelling with an 's' only occurs in BE.

practitioner *noun*, means a person who works in a profession such as law, medicine or dentistry. The expression *general practitioner* (GP) in BE means a medical doctor who works in a locality and treats people for all sorts of minor ailments or chronic conditions.

prairie, pampas, savanna(h), steppe, veld(t)

prairie *noun*, is a large open area of grassland in North America: *He wanted to* *study the grasslands of the prairie before they were completely destroyed by the plough.*

pampas *noun*, are the large treeless plains in South America: *We lived in a small town lost in the southern pampas of Argentina.* Note that **pampas** can take a singular or plural verb.

savanna(h) săvánnă /sə'vænə/ *noun*, is tropical grassland anywhere, but this term is particularly used in Africa: *The common zebra is widely distributed over the grassland savannah in eastern and southern Africa.* The spellings with and without final 'h' are both used.

steppe *noun*, is flat unforested grassland in south-east Europe and Siberia: *The climate could become much warmer and drier, and large areas of steppe could turn to desert.*

veld(t) felt /felt/ *noun*, is grassland or uncultivated land in southern Africa: *He grows tomatoes on the low veld of the north-east Transvaal.* The spellings with and without final 't' are both used.

> The main difference between these terms is geographical. As landscape, they are almost identical.

praiseworthy

See CREDITABLE.

precede

See PROCEED.

precedence, precedent

precedence préssĕdĕnss /'presɪdəns/ *noun*, means something that has a greater importance than something else and will be dealt with first: *Your wishes do not always take precedence over other people's.* Note that this involves ranking: *Because of limited space, full-time students will be given precedence on this course.* This is a formal word.

precedent préssĕdĕnt /'presɪdənt/ *noun*, is an earlier event or decision that may serve as an example or rule for a later one such as setting a *legal precedent*: *The precedent for this approach is the work done earlier.* If you break with **precedent** you do things in a new way. This is also a formal word.

preceding, earlier

preceding prĕssééding /prɪ'siːdɪŋ/ *adjective*, describes what comes immediately before: *Only do light training on the two days preceding the match.* **Preceding** is a formal word, and phrases such as 'the preceding day' or 'the preceding section' may be replaced by the day before or the last section respectively. Note that the indefinite article cannot be used before **preceding**. Never confuse **preceding** with *proceeding*. See PROCEEDING.

earlier *adverb*, means before. However this word is not as precise as *preceding*, as it does not give the exact context in time. Compare 'an earlier section of this report' with 'the preceding section'.

precipitate, precipitous

precipitate prĕssíppităt /prɪ'sɪpɪtət/ *adjective*, prĕssíppitayt /prɪ'sɪpɪteɪt/ *verb & noun*. As an adjective this means quick and sudden. It often implies that more care or thought should have been given before acting: *That was somewhat precipitate.* As a verb it means to lead to something or make something happen where the outcome is usually negative: *This might precipitate the collapse of the banking system.* As a noun, it means a solid that is separated from a liquid in a chemical process: *The precipitate counted on a gammacounter.* Note the different pronunciation of the final syllable in the adjective and verb forms.

precipitous *adjective*, means very steep and implies a sharp descent or fall: *I rode the board down that precipitous slope like a man tobogganing down a glacier.*

precipitation

See RAINFALL.

precise, accurate

precise *adjective*, means exact, clear and correct: *Applicants are to give precise details of their previous education.* Here the focus is on exactness.

accurate *adjective*, means correct in every detail: *Applicants are to give accurate details of their previous education.* Here the focus is on things that can be checked and verified. These examples show that there are two aspects to the term correct: *precise* = exact and *accurate* = verifiable.

> Note that when these words are used after verbs they can mean different things: If the Minister's explanation was *not very precise* it may be correct but lacks details. If the explanation was *not very accurate* some of the details are incorrect.

precision, accuracy

precision *uncountable noun*, means the quality of being correct and exact: *A robot can play darts with incredible precision*.

accuracy *uncountable noun*, means the quality of being correct and true. It also means being able to do something without making mistakes: *Andrew was an excellent darts player and had incredible accuracy*.

> These examples show that the robot can group the darts exactly in a small area which may or may not be near the bullseye. However Andrew can land his darts wherever he wants on the darts board. This means that something with *precision* does not have to be accurate, but something with *accuracy* can have *precision*.

precondition

See REQUISITE.

predicament

See DILEMMA.

prediction

See PROGNOSIS.

preface

See FOREWORD.

prefix

See WORD FORMATION.

premature, immature

premature *adjective*, describes something that occurs before it is scheduled to: *Premature death from heart disease outweighs all other causes of death*. It also describes something that happens before it is considered advisable: *It would be premature to make a statement before the report has been published*. A *premature baby* is one which arrives three or more weeks early.

immature *adjective*. When it refers to plants or animals, this means undeveloped or not fully grown: *Immature predators digest prey more thoroughly than do adults*. When referring to humans, **immature** often implies restricted emotional or intellectual development: *She played in an immature manner and was very understimulated*.

premier, premiere

premier prémmi-ĕr /ˈpremɪər/ (BE), prĕmeér /prɪˈmɪər/ (AE) *noun & adjective*. As a noun, this means the First Minister, or Prime Minister. As an adjective it means foremost: *The museum is deemed a premier destination for philanthropic largesse*. Avoid using **premier** to mean something sought after. Alternatives are *desirable, superior* or *attractive*.

premiere prémmi-air /ˈpremieər/ *noun*, means a first public performance: *There was a scandal at the premiere in Paris last year*. **Premiere** is not spelt with an accent in modern English (formerly *première*).

premise, premises

premise *noun*, means the statement or idea that you accept as true is used as the basis for an argument: *I'm working on the premise that this person is innocent*. This is a formal word and assumption is a less formal alternative. An alternative spelling is *premiss*.

premises *plural noun*, means both the plural of *premise* and also a house, site, block of offices, or building occupied or owned by a person or company. *Licensed premises* means a pub.

preoccupy

See OCCUPY.

prepositions

See GRAMMAR TIPS.

prerequisite

See REQUISITE.

prescribe, proscribe

prescribe *verb*, means to give instructions to a pharmacist to make up a certain remedy: *Some GPs prescribe tranquillizers and anti-depressants for insomnia and irritability*. It also means to lay down rules for correct procedures: *'I'm not going to prescribe the exact way teachers should teach children.'*

proscribe *verb*, means to prohibit or ban: *The Act proscribes discrimination on the grounds of sex or marital status*. This is a formal word.

prescription, proscription

prescription *noun*, means a written order from a medical doctor to a chemist regarding medicine that is only to be taken under medical supervision: *The over-prescription of penicillin is becoming a problem*.

proscription *noun*, means the banning of people, or conventions: *'And' at the beginning of a sentence should not be an absolute proscription: some careful writers of English place 'and' there*. This is a formal word and matters are often proscribed on legal grounds.

presently

See SOON.

preservation

See CONSERVATION.

preserve

See CONSERVE.

president

See MANAGING DIRECTOR.

pressure, stress

pressure *noun*, means force, or the act of putting under strain: *You should never apply pressure to the spine itself*. This can be physical or mental: *Local authorities have come under increasing pressure to control costs*.

stress *noun, adjective & verb*. As an uncountable noun, this means mental or physical pressure. This normally applies to people: *Vitamin C helps to combat stress from worry*. *Physical stress* also relates to pressure or tension on objects such as buildings or bridges. In this sense, **stress** can be a countable noun: *There are a number of stresses that affect trees, including climate, frost and unnatural air pollution*. The adjective forms are *stressful* and *stressed*: *A stressful situation can make a person feel stressed* (informally *stressed out*). As a verb, **stress** means to place emphasis on something that is said or written: *'We must stress the importance of saving energy', said the minister*.

prestige, kudos

prestige *noun*, means widespread respect for achievement or quality. Thus it can be used before a person has achieved anything: *Authority can cover up ignorance with prestige*.

kudos kéwdoss /ˈkjuːdɒs/ *noun*, means praise and honour for something that has been achieved. This word is singular and always takes a singular verb: *A lot of kudos was bestowed on the peacemakers*.

presume

See ASSUME.

pretentious, portentous

pretentious *adjective*, refers to something or someone who pretends to be grand or makes excessive claims: *He is a pretentious phoney who claims to understand Greek drama*. This usually implies that a person is being pompous.

portentous *adjective*, means either foreshadowing a coming and ominous event: *The ravens were a portentous omen*; or pompous and weighty: *The portentous decor in the House of Lords amazed the tourists*. This is a formal word.

> When these words mean pompous, they signal a disapproving attitude.

pretext, excuse

pretext *noun*, means a false reason that is given for doing something: *He invented some pretext for coming to see Peter and Mary*. See CAUSE (REASON).

excuse *noun*, means a true or invented reason for doing something: *She made a feeble excuse to avoid the meeting*. In another sense it means a true or invented reason for not doing something: *They are using this scientific research as an excuse for taking no action.*

pretty

See **HANDSOME**.

prevaricate, procrastinate

prevaricate *verb*, means to avoid telling the truth by not answering directly: *Asked if he had broken the window, he prevaricated by saying he was not the only one playing cricket.*

procrastinate *verb*, means to put off a difficult or unpleasant decision or action that you should do because you do not want to do it: *Often people procrastinate because they are afraid of failure.*

These are both formal terms.

prevent

See **AVERT**.

price, cost

price *noun*, means the amount of money that has to be paid for something in order to buy it: *The price includes dinner (or lunch), bed and breakfast.*

cost *noun*, also means the amount of money needed to pay for an object but in addition it refers to the price of services and processes: the *cost of living*, *cost of rail services*, and *production costs*. **Cost** in a broader sense can mean the effort or loss included in doing something: *This represents an enormous cost to industry*.

priceless

See **VALUABLE**.

priest

See **CLERGY**.

primeval, primitive

primeval *adjective*, refers to the earliest time in the history of the earth: *The idea of a primeval golden age can be traced back to the Sumerians*.

primitive *adjective*, refers to a simple way of life that existed in the past or things that are simple and without modern refinements: *Primitive technology has no part to play in the safety systems used in nuclear power stations.*

principle, principal

principle *noun*, means the basic idea that a plan or system is based on: *The underlying principle is the need for measures to achieve equal opportunities*. In another sense it means a belief, or moral standard: *Napoleon established principles of justice in his legal code*.

principal *noun & adjective*. As a noun, this means someone in authority, such as *the college principal*, in AE (the head teacher, or head, in BE). As an adjective, it means the main or most important: *the principal islands in the area*.

prise

See **PRIZE**.

private school, public school

private school *compound noun*, means a school that is not supported by government funds and charges fees for education. Often some or all of the pupils board at the school, and 'boarding school' is an alternative name if this is the case. Another name for **private school** is 'independent school', as opposed to 'state school', which is one funded out of taxes.

public school *compound noun*. In England and Wales, this is a *private school* or independent school that is mainly funded by fees paid by parents. In the USA and Scotland, a **public school** is a free local school paid for by the state out of taxes. There are about 200 **public schools** in England and Wales and traditionally many of the male leaders and public figures in Britain were pupils or 'old boys' of **public schools** such as Eton and Harrow. The name seems contradictory, but originally, **public schools** were intended for the education of poor scholars who would not have to pay.

prize, prise

prize *noun & verb*. As a noun, this means an award for winning a contest or competition, or for eminence in some field: *Marie Curie won the Nobel Prizes for both physics and chemistry*. It can also mean outstanding, as with *prize bull*. Note that *a prize idiot* means a complete idiot. As a verb, it means to value something highly: *Recent generations have prized freedom and individualism above order and the common good*.

prise *verb*, means to use force to open something with difficulty: *He was strong enough to prise open the bars with his bare hands*; or to obtain with force: *Use the crowbar to prise the frame from the wall*. In AE this is spelt *prize*.

pro, con

pro *noun*, means the arguments for.

con *noun*, means the arguments against and is an abbreviation of *contra*.

> These Latin words are used together in English in the idiomatic expression the *pros and cons*, which means the arguments both for and against a proposal.

proceed, precede

proceed *verb*, means to pursue a course of action: *The decision to proceed with the hydropower project has been taken*. In another sense, it means to move forward, or advance: *From the town centre proceed down Windmill Road*. In this second sense, **proceed** is a fairly formal word.

precede *verb*, means to be in front of someone or something: *The escort should precede the guest into the room*. In another sense, **precede** means go ahead of: *Agricultural development must precede industrial development*.

proceeding, proceedings

proceeding *noun*, means either a course of conduct: *They had no idea of the danger of such a proceeding*; or a legal action: *In any proceeding the judge may ask the parties to appear before him*.

proceedings *noun*, means events in a series: *The proceedings in the House of Commons were televised*, or the minutes or written record of a formal meeting. In conferences, the **proceedings** are the written record that includes the papers and presentations given. In a legal sense, **proceedings** means the use of a court of law to settle a dispute: *She is taking legal proceedings against her bank*.

procrastinate

See PREVARICATE.

prodigy, progeny

prodigy *noun*, means an exceptionally skilled person, usually a child or adolescent: *Mozart's father recognized that his son was an infant prodigy*. This is a formal word.

progeny *noun*, means offspring or descendants and may take either a singular or plural verb: *She looked upon her progeny simply as reproductions of herself*. This is also a formal word.

product, produce, fabricate

product *noun*, is something grown for sale such as *farm products*, or manufactured, such as *industrial products*. It is also used about people to mean the outcome of a process: *He was a typical product of a middle-class upbringing*. Secondary products of a reaction or industrial process are called *by-products*.

produce próddewss /ˈprɒdjuːs/ *noun &* prŏdéwss /prəˈdjuːs/ *verb*. As a noun, this means things made or grown in large quantities. **Produce** is usually associated with farming: *A lot of dairy produce is being imported*. Note that the noun is stressed on the first syllable. As a verb, **produce** means to grow something or to manufacture it: *The factory produced all kinds of furniture*. Note that the verb is stressed on the second syllable.

fabricate *verb*, means to manufacture an industrial product from prepared components: *The factory will be fitted out to fabricate the new computer chips*. In another sense, **fabricate** means to invent something with deliberate intent to deceive: *The police fabricated the evidence that led to a false conviction*.

professor, chair

professor *noun*, in BE is a university academic with the highest rank. In AE and in some parts of the EU, **professor** alone or in combinations like *assistant professor* (lecturer) and *associate professor* (senior lecturer) are widely used for various categories of university teachers. **Prof.** is an informal abbreviation of **professor** and should be avoided by careful writers and speakers. See LECTURER.

chair *noun*, is the position held by a professor; this may also be termed a *professorship*. See CHAIR.

proficiency

See EXPERTISE.

profit & loss account, balance sheet

profit & loss account *noun*, is a part of the accounts of a business that lists the income and expenditure, and the total profit or loss during a particular period.

balance sheet *noun*, is a written statement showing the total assets and liabilities that a company has on the final day of its financial year. The assets and liabilities must equal each other (i.e. 'balance') so that the accounts describe how the earnings have been allocated.

progeny

See PRODIGY.

prognosis, prediction, forecast

prognosis *noun*, means an opinion about how a medical problem is likely to develop: *International medical experience with this disease is so limited that we cannot make a reliable prognosis*. **Prognosis** is also used in other contexts to refer to a judgement about how a situation is likely to develop: *Our prognosis for the consequences of global warming in this area will be presented next year*. This is a formal word. Note that the plural is *prognoses* prog-nṓsseez /prɒg'nəʊsiːz/ with the final syllable pronounced like the word 'seas'.

prediction *noun*, means a statement or estimate that something will happen in the future: *The first two parts of her prediction have come true*.

forecast *noun & verb*. As a noun, this is a prediction or estimate about a future incident or trend: *Planning should begin with an analysis of the present position and a forecast of future developments*. *Forecasts* are based on factual records and are used for the weather: *The Meteorological Office now has reliable five-day forecasts*. When it is used as a verb, **forecast** is more frequent as the past tense and past participle than the alternative *forecasted*.

> While a *forecast* is based on factual information, a *prediction* is often based on assumptions.

programme, program

programme *noun & verb*. As a noun, this means a plan, a course of study, a list of events or a TV/radio performance: *The programme for the visit will include a meeting with the minister*. As a verb, it means to plan, cause action or give instructions: *The committee will programme its research work*. This is the BE spelling. The AE spelling of both the noun and verb is *program*.

program *noun & verb*. As a noun, this means computer software. As a verb, it means to write software: *To program a computer*; or to prepare an electronic machine to carry out certain actions at a future time. Note that the person doing the computer programming is spelt *programmer*, and that both *programming* and *programmer* have two 'm's.

prohibit, forbid

prohibit *verb*, means to say that an action is illegal or not allowed: *Since 1 July 2007, smoking in enclosed spaces has been prohibited in England*. It also refers to a situation that makes something impossible: *The high cost of land prohibits the building of a new golf course*. The related adjective and noun forms are *prohibitive* and *prohibition*.

forbid *verb*, means to say something is not allowed. This usually relates to actions that are stopped by exercising personal authority, not a law: *After the fire it was forbidden to smoke in the house*.

prominent

See NOTABLE.

prone, supine

prone *adjective*, means lying facing downwards: *When the shooting started he lay in a prone position pressing his stomach to the ground*. It also means likely to do something badly, or to suffer from something: *Flowers are prone to rot in wet weather*.
See LIABLE (APT), PROSTRATE.

> *Two tourists driving through Wales arrived at 'Llanfairpwllgwyngyllgogerychwyrndrobwllllantysiliogogogoch' and were unsure about how to pronounce the name of the village. They stopped for lunch at a fast food restaurant and asked the waitress 'Could you please pronounce the name of this place . . . very slowly?' The girl leaned over and said slowly and clearly 'Burrrrrrrrgerrrrrrr Kiiiiing'.* !

supine *adjective*, means lying on the back: *Images were obtained from all patients lying supine in the MR scanner*. It also means lazy or negligent: *An almost entirely supine parliamentary opposition has stagnated to the point of inertia*.

pronounce, pronunciation

pronounce prŏnównss /prəˈnaʊns/ *verb*, means to make the sound of a letter or word: *Knowing how to pronounce a word doesn't necessarily mean you know how to spell it*. A second meaning is to make a formal public declaration: *The Commission is demanding greater powers to pronounce on merger policy*, and in this case, the related noun is *pronouncement*.

pronunciation prŏnunssi-áyshŏn /prəˌnʌnsiˈeɪʃn̩/ *noun*, is the way sounds or words are spoken: *I cannot give the correct pronunciation of the Gaelic names of the mountains*.

> Note the differences in spelling, pronunciation and stress of these two words.

pronunciation and accent

In this book, we have added pronunciation guidance to some words, either because the word itself is often mispronounced, or because it may be pronounced in two ways, showing a change of meaning or function. We have chosen to use a respelling system for this, as well as the alphabet of the International Phonetic Association that is found in many dictionaries, so that readers can interpret the guidance in their own accent. *Accent* and *pronunciation* are related, but different: we all speak with an accent that gives away the part of the world that we come from, or says something about the sort of education and upbringing that we have had. We can speak Standard English using any accent we choose, but Standard English includes what is called the 'accepted pronunciation' of individual words, which is not dependent on accent. For instance, English is divided into two large groups of accents: speakers of one pronounce the letter 'r' wherever it appears in the spelling (these accents are technically called 'rhotic'). Speakers of these accents distinguish between the words 'father' and 'farther' by pronouncing the 'r' in the first syllable of 'farther' (they also always pronounce the 'r' at the end of both words). Speakers of the other group of accents (called 'non-rhotic') pronounce 'r' only when it is immediately followed by a vowel, so they pronounce 'father' and 'farther' alike (and they only pronounce the final 'r' if the next word begins with a vowel). The two pronunciations of 'father' are equally acceptable in Standard English within the terms of their respective accents. There is another pronunciation of 'father', which we may represent by the respelling 'fáythĕr', that is used in some dialects. This is not acceptable in Standard English. The respellings given in this book are to be spoken in the reader's usual accent.

pronouns

See **GRAMMAR TIPS**.

propaganda, publicity

propaganda *uncountable noun*, means the organized spreading of information to form public opinion by false or misleading news. **Propaganda** always takes a singular verb: *He made the mistake of believing his own propaganda*. See **SPIN**.

publicity *uncountable noun*, means the organized spread of information, but has no negative or positive connotations. Like **propaganda**, it takes a singular verb: *She thrived on the publicity she professed to loathe*.

propel

See COMPEL.

propellant, propellent

propellant *noun*, means something that propels: *This spray can does not use environmentally harmful propellants.*

propellent *adjective*, describes the means of driving or moving something: *This spray may contain propellent gases.*

Note the spelling difference in these soundalikes.

prophecy, prophesy

prophecy próffĕssi /ˈprɒfəsi/ *noun*, means the prediction of what will happen in future, often in connection with religion or magic: *His prophecy was now coming true, sooner than he had dreamed.*

prophesy próffĕssī /ˈprɒfəsaɪ/ *verb*, means to say what will happen in the future: *As Mark Twain said: 'Never prophesy, especially about the future.'*

Note the spelling and pronunciation differences between these two words.

prophet, seer

prophet *noun*, means a person sent by God whose mission is to lead and teach people their religious beliefs. Prophets are found in the Christian, Jewish and Muslim religions. The Prophet means Muhammad, the founder of Islam. **Prophet** is always capitalized here. In a non-religious sense, a **prophet** is someone who teaches a new idea: *There is a distinction between the one who is a prophet and those who from time to time prophesy.*

seer *noun*, means a person with supernatural powers who can see visions of the future: *The Seer's visions are always ideal and beyond human senses.* This is a literary term.

prophylactic

See CONTRACEPTIVE.

proposal, proposition

proposal *noun*, means a plan or suggestion that is made formally to an official group or body: *They put forward a proposal to increase the use of electric cars in the city centre.* A **proposal** is also an offer of marriage: *His proposal came on the anniversary of their first date.*

proposition *noun*, means a statement based on considered opinion: *The proposition will reduce greenhouse gas emissions.* It also means a suggestion or scheme to be considered, particularly in business and investment: *When a favourable opportunity presented itself, he would submit his proposition again.*

proscribe

See PRESCRIBE.

proscription

See PRESCRIPTION.

prosecute

See PERSECUTE.

prosecution

See DEFENCE.

prospective

See PERSPECTIVE.

prostrate, prostate

prostrate próstrayt /ˈprɒstreɪt/ *adjective &* prŏstráyt /prəˈstreɪt/ *verb*. As an adjective, this means lying down, but often has the added meaning of feeling weak through shock or illness: *The severe attack of pneumonia left him prostrate for a month.* As a verb, this is used if someone is lying down in order to express adoration or submission: *He prostrated himself before the paramount chief.* Note that the position of the stress changes between the adjective and verb. See PRONE.

prostate *noun*, is the name of a gland found in a male's body. It produces a liquid in which sperm are carried. It is also called the prostate gland: *A simple blood test has been available over the last four years which can detect the likely presence of prostate cancer.*

Note that the name of the gland has no 'r' in the second syllable.

P

proved, proven

proved *past participle*, is the usual form of the past participle of *prove* in BE: *Can it be conclusively proved that he stole the money?* It is also the only form of the past tense.

proven *past participle & adjective*, is used as a past participle and for the Scottish legal verdict *not proven*. In BE, only **proven** is used as an adjective: *He has a proven sales record.* (Note that *proved* cannot be used here.)

> These are the two past participles of *to prove* which means to demonstrate the truth of something.

provide

See SUPPLY.

providence

See DESTINY.

provision

See SUPPLY.

prudent

See CAREFUL.

PS, PPS

PS is the abbreviation for *postscript* that is placed before additional text at the end of a letter after the signature and capitalized: *PS. This letter will take ages to get to you. Do you have email?*

PPS is a second or subsequent *postscript*.

public, audience, congregation, spectators, onlookers

public *noun & adjective*. As a noun, this means people as a whole and is always used with 'the': *Shops must sell what the public wants to buy*. **Public** can also refer to people with a common interest in a specific activity: *The theatregoing public still enjoy Shakespeare*. Note that **public** can take both singular and plural verbs. As an adjective, **public** means available to everybody: *If public transport is improved, fewer people will use their own cars*; or belonging to everybody through the state: *Public spending peaked at over 49 per cent of the gross national product*. It also means known about by many people: *There was a furious row over the negotiations which were soon made public*. See COLLECTIVE NOUNS (GRAMMAR TIPS).

audience *noun*, means a group of people who watch or listen to a performance either together (at a theatre, show, cinema, concert, etc.): *A composer should write music that compels an audience's attention*; or individually at home (in the case of the readers of a book: *She is a novelist with a wide audience*; or listeners or viewers for a radio or TV programme: *The BBC's highlights programme had an audience of 5.8 million*). The **audience** is nearly always indoors: *The audience in the TV studio had to be told when to clap*. Note that **audience** can take either a singular or a plural verb. See COLLECTIVE NOUNS (GRAMMAR TIPS), VIEWER.

congregation *noun*, only refers to the gathering at a religious service: *Despite the snow a huge congregation turned up in Corpus Christi Church*. Note that **congregation** can take either a singular or a plural verb. See COLLECTIVE NOUNS (GRAMMAR TIPS).

spectators *noun*, means a group of people at a sporting event or a show who intend to watch the event: *Terracing opposite the stand was enlarged to hold 24,000 spectators*.

onlookers *noun*, means people who watch something but do not get involved as an *audience* or *spectators* do: *As usual there was a crowd of onlookers waiting outside Buckingham Palace*.

public convenience

See TOILET.

public holiday, bank holiday

public holiday *compound noun*, means any national holiday (New Year's Day, Christmas Day) which may be on any day of the week. In AE this is simply called a *holiday*.

bank holiday *compound noun*, in the UK means a holiday on a weekday, generally a Monday, when banks, public offices and many other businesses are officially closed: *Bank Holiday Monday is a popular time for taking a long weekend break*. In AE, a **bank holiday** is a weekday when banks are closed, usually on special instructions from the Federal Administration. In AE these are also called a *public holiday* or *federal holiday*.

publicity

See PROPAGANDA.

public school

See PRIVATE SCHOOL.

puerile

See JUVENILE.

pull back

See RETIRE.

pull-down menu

See MENU BAR.

pummel

See BATTER.

punctual, punctilious

punctual *adjective*, means doing something or meeting at the agreed time: *He is so punctual that you can set your watch by him.*

punctilious *adjective*, means exact, paying careful attention to detail: *He was punctilious about working out the precise sum owed.* This is a formal word.

pungent

See ACID.

pupil

See STUDENT.

purposely, purposefully

purposely *adverb*, means on purpose, deliberately: *The outhouses were purposely designed so that they could also be used as stables.*

purposefully *adverb*, means either resolutely: *He went into the kitchen for solitude, and began purposefully to wash the dishes*; or with a specific end in view: *People on early shift were heading purposefully to work.*

put

See PLACE.

P

Spelling

pa**r**a**ff**in	Note single -r-, but double -ff-
para**ll**e**l**	Note where the double -ll- and single -l- come
pa**r**ish	Note the single -r-
par**lia**ment	Note the -i- following the -l-
peculi**ar**	Note the ending -ar
peninsul**a** (noun)	Note that there is no 'r' in this word
peninsul**ar** (adjective)	Note that this word ends in -ar
per**su**ade	Note this is spelt -su-, not -sw-
phar**ao**h	Note -ao- in the second syllable, not -oa-
phosph**o**r**ou**s (adjective)	Note there is only one -u- in this word
phosph**o**r**u**s (noun)	Note there is only one -u- in this word, and no 'o' before it
p**ie**rce	Note this is -i- before -e-
plag**ia**rism	Note the -ia-
pon**ies**	Note this ends in -ies
pre**cede**	See *-cede, -ceed, -sede* words
privi**lege**	Note that there is no 'd' in this word
pro**ced**ure	Note the single -e- in this word
pro**ceed**	See *-cede, -ceed, -sede* words
pro**f**e**ss**or	Note: one -f-, but double -ss-
pro**nun**ciation	Note that there is no 'o' in the second syllable
prop**a**ganda	Remember the -a- in the second syllable
p**u**rsue	Note the first vowel is -u-

quality assurance, quality control

quality assurance *uncountable noun*, means the management of the way goods are manufactured or services delivered in order to ensure high standards: *Many companies attribute their success to extensive use of quality assurance*. The standard abbreviation is *QA*.

quality control *uncountable noun*, is a system for checking products as they are being manufactured to ensure they maintain a high standard: *In science as in manufacturing, quality control pinpoints inferior procedures*. The standard abbreviation is *QC*. See **CONTROL**.

quandary

See **DILEMMA**.

quarter, *fourth*, *forth*

quarter *noun*, usually means 25 per cent of something. When followed by *of* and a noun, it is the noun which determines whether a singular or plural verb should be used: *A quarter of the flock* **was** *killed; A quarter of the hens* **were** *killed*. **Quarter** is also used in AE to refer to the 25c coin. In music a *quarter note* in AE is called a crotchet in BE. It also means a part of a town or city with a special character: *the Latin Quarter of Paris*. See **BLOC, MEASUREMENTS, TERM**.

fourth *number*, is the ordinal number: *Meetings will be held in the community hall on every fourth Sunday*. Note that AE speakers tend to use **fourth** as a noun when describing 25 per cent of something: *A fourth of the voters supported that candidate*. See **NUMBERS**.

forth *adverb*, refers to movement onwards or out of something. The term is almost archaic, and semi-humorous: *After several cups of coffee, the golfers set forth on to the links*. However, it is also used in a number of common fixed expressions, including *so on and so forth* and *back and forth*.

quash, squash

quash *verb*, means to cancel or overturn a decision: *The appeal court decided to quash the prison sentence and impose a severe fine*. It also means to crush something such as a rebellion, and to stop rumours or speculation.

squash *verb*, means to crush or squeeze, especially something soft: *He liked to squash flies with a rolled-up newspaper*.

quasi, *quasi-*

quasi kwáyzī /'kweɪzaɪ/ or kwa̋azi /'kwɑːzi/ *adjective & adverb*. As an adjective, this means resembling or having a resemblance to something: *It was a fraud that was disguised in a quasi contract*. As an adverb, it has the same meaning: *The Manpower Services Commission is a quasi autonomous public body which operates under the surveillance of the Ministry*. This is sometimes hyphenated and is mainly used in technical contexts.

quasi- kwáyzī /'kweɪzaɪ/ or kwa̋azi /'kwɑːzi/ *prefix*, means apparently, but not really: *The quasi-scientific descriptions given in 'The Da Vinci Code' have persuaded many people that the book is factual*.

quay

See **KEY**.

queer, strange, odd

queer *noun & adjective*. As a noun, this refers in a negative sense to homosexuals. Though **queer** is offensive when used by heterosexuals about people understood to be homosexual, it is used by the homosexual community in a positive sense about themselves: *queer rights*. As an adjective, **queer** means strange and odd: *Her hands were full of queer yellow mushroom things*. This usage is now considered old-fashioned and *strange* is a better choice. See **GAY**.

strange *adjective*, means unusual, eccentric or odd so that it is difficult for others to understand: *Even his family considered his behaviour was strange*.

odd *adjective*, usually means strange or unusual: *The ideas outlined here may seem a bit odd, cranky even, and certainly impractical.* **Odd** can also mean occasional: *I go to the odd fitness class now and again.* Another use of the word is to indicate an indefinite number by hyphenating it to another number: *He wrote 50-odd songs* (meaning just over 50 of them) in contrast to *He wrote 50 odd songs*, sometimes . . . *50 rather odd songs* or . . . *50 very odd songs* (meaning 50 strange ones).

quilt, eiderdown, duvet

quilt and **eiderdown** *nouns*, are alternative names for bedclothing placed on the top of a bed over the other bedclothes: *There was a narrow iron bed, covered by a patched quilt; Dragging the eiderdown from her bed, she wrapped it round her shoulders.* The two names reflect different aspects of their manufacture: *quilting* is the method of retaining any insulating material between two layers of cloth by sewing sections separately, while **eiderdown** refers to the down (soft inner feathers) of the eider duck originally used in the best quality *quilts*.

duvet *noun*, is a type of quilt with a removable cover, and replaces the top sheet, blankets and eiderdown on a bed: *A duvet is more practical than sheets, blankets and eiderdown.*

quite, quiet

quite *predeterminer & adverb*, means either to some degree: *He knew the person he was speaking to quite well*; or to the greatest possible degree or absolutely: *The castle probably looks quite different in the sunlight.* In the first sense, **quite** is used before *a* or *an* when it modifies a phrase: *A team with quite an extraordinary group of players . . .* but in the second sense, when **quite** is only modifying an adjective, the indefinite article comes first: *A quite extraordinary group of players were in the team.* See FAIRLY (RATHER).

quiet *adjective & noun*. As an adjective, this means making or having little or no noise: *He lives on a quiet residential street in Eastbourne.* It can also mean that there is no activity, or business is slack. As an uncountable noun, it means the state of being calm and peaceful: *I've had a terrible day. I just want some peace and quiet.* The informal phrase *doing something on the quiet*, meaning in secret, is a typical BE expression and may not be understood internationally.

> *'Excellent property for those in need of peace and quite.'*
> (Estate agent's advert)
> **!**

quotation marks

See PUNCTUATION GUIDE.

quotation, quote, quota

quotation *noun*, means an exact extract from a printed work or from a speech: *A quotation from a recently published document makes the position clear.* It is also the price calculated for a piece of work or a service and given to the potential customer for them to consider: *A written quotation is available on request from any of our branches.* **Quotation** is used on the stock exchange for the prices of shares: *There may be difficulties with becoming a public company and obtaining a Stock Exchange quotation.*

quote *noun & verb*. As a noun, this is an informal abbreviation for *quotation marks* and *quotation* in all its senses: *The quote taken out of context trivializes the dreadful crime.* A related term is *air quotes*, which means a hand gesture to indicate that a speaker is putting a word or phrase in inverted commas or *quotes*. As a verb, to **quote** means either to repeat someone else's words, often from poetry or drama: *I will quote what Hamlet said in the identical situation*; or to give the price of something, particularly on the stock exchange and for betting odds: *The agent was able to offer a ticket and quoted a fare of £153.* See CITE.

quota *noun*, means the amount of something that is officially allowed. It may mean a maximum amount: *If the quota is exceeded, growers could be forced to stop planting*; or a minimum: *Two-thirds of companies fail to employ their quota of registered disabled*; or a share of something that has been allocated: *The research councils may allocate a quota of awards to individual university subjects or departments.*

Spelling

Qatar	Note that there is no 'u' in this name
quand**a**ry	Note that this word ends in -ary
quatercentenary	Note that there is no 'r' after the first -a-
questio**nn**ai**r**e	Note that there is a double -nn-, but a single -r-

R

racist language

It is not easy to use words for skin colour and certain religious or ethnic groups without being accused of linguistic racism. Collections of synonyms must be used with care in this tricky area. See ABORIGINE, BLACK, COLOUR WORDS, NATIVE AMERICAN.

racket, racquet

racket *noun*, means a loud, unpleasant noise: *What is that terrible racket?* **Racket** is also an illegal scheme for obtaining money: *The police managed to uncover the protection racket*. See SOUND.

racquet *noun*, is the name given to the piece of equipment used to hit the ball in tennis, squash and badminton. An alternative spelling is *racket*.

radio, wireless

radio *noun & verb*. As a noun, this is the usual word nowadays for the device used for receiving sound broadcasts or the service for transmitting them: *Someone claimed to have heard him on the radio*. The plural is *radios*. As a verb, **radio** is used with the meaning of transmitting sound: *Lawrence picked up the handset and radioed into headquarters*.

wireless *adjective & noun*. As an adjective this refers to a network or computer peripheral that sends and receives instructions by means of infrared signals or radio waves rather than by electrical impulses through wires: *Guests can obtain a password from Reception to access our wireless network*. As a noun, this is a now old-fashioned term for *radio*: *The wireless crackled for a few moments until the voice of Mr Chamberlain became clear*.

radius, radii

radius *noun*, is the distance from the centre of a circle to its edge. This is its mathematical meaning, but **radius** is often used generally to mean an area within a certain distance from a central point: *The cordless phone can be operated within a 300-metre radius of the house*. This is the singular.

radii ráydi-ī /ˈreɪdiaɪ/ *noun*, is the plural of *radius*. An alternative plural is *radiuses*.

railway, railways, railroad

railway *noun & adjective*. As a noun, this means a track with rails used by trains: *This railway has not been used for years*. As an adjective, **railway** is used to describe specific parts of the system for the transport of passengers and goods: *railway station* (called a *train station* in AE), *railway worker*, *railway line*. Sometimes train-operating companies have **railway** as part of their name: *Great Western Railway*.

railways *plural noun*, means the entire system required to operate train services – the tracks, staff, organization and the trains themselves: *My father worked on the railways all his life*.

railroad *noun & verb*, is the main AE term for both *railway* and *railways*. The term is only used in BE as a verb. This means to force someone or something to decide or act quickly without allowing time for thought: *A government seeking to minimize awkward questions will try to railroad a Bill through Parliament*.

rain, drizzle, hail

rain *uncountable noun & verb*, is the general word for water droplets falling from the clouds: *Then the rain stopped and the skies cleared*. As **rain** is an uncountable noun the indefinite article can never appear immediately before it unless it forms part of a compound such as *rainstorm* or *raincoat*. The plural form *rains* refers to the season of heavy **rain** in tropical regions: *Thousands have escaped the grip of hunger thanks to the rains that ended a severe drought*. As a verb, **rain** refers either to the droplets that fall from clouds, or to objects that fall in large quantities: *Bullets rained down on the houses from the gunship*. When an event such as a football match is *rained off*, this is termed *rained out* in AE. See RAIN CHECK, SLUSH (SNOW).

drizzle *uncountable noun & verb*. As a noun, this means persistent fine light rain: *The men ahead of him were hunched against the drizzle*. As a verb, **drizzle** means to rain persistently with very small droplets, and it is also used to mean pour a liquid slowly over food: *Toast the bread and, while still warm, drizzle a little olive oil over it*.

hail *uncountable noun & verb*. As a noun this means showers of small drops of ice: *The hail stung our faces*. While *rain* evaporates, **hail** melts: *The hail on the grass melted slowly*. The indefinite article can be used before compounds such as *hailstone* or *hailstorm*. **Hail** is used figuratively to mean a bombardment of missiles: *He nearly died in a hail of bullets*. Or it can refer to abuse: *The hail of derision that followed our latest defeat should be put in perspective*. As a verb, **hail** means to make a gesture to stop a taxi or bus. In another sense, it means to praise someone or something for success, a brave action, or similar: *All the critics hailed the play as a masterpiece*.

> *Hail* is used less frequently as a verb than either *rain* or *drizzle*.

rain check, defer

rain check *noun phrase*, means an offer or suggestion that might be accepted at some future time: *'Do you want a coffee?' 'I'll take a rain check, thanks.'* It is an informal term that is used a lot in business when it is difficult to give an answer on the spot. This expression originated in AE as the term for a new ticket issued for a rescheduled baseball or American football match stopped because of rain or bad weather conditions. See **POSTPONE (ADJOURN), RAIN**.

defer *verb*, means put off or delay: *You can defer your retirement for up to five years*. Note that *defer to something* or *somebody* means to agree to accept what another person or body has decided: *Parts of Europe continued to defer to the leadership of the United States*. This is a formal term.

rainfall, precipitation

rainfall *uncountable noun*, is the total amount of rain that falls in a specific area during a defined period of time: *Of the annual rainfall of 975 mm, more than two-thirds occurs between October and March*.

precipitation *uncountable noun*, in this context is the technical term that covers all types of moisture that falls to the ground. **Precipitation** is also used to express the amount over a period: *Recorded annual precipitation ranges from just over 1,000 mm to over 2,400 mm on some of the higher summits*. See **SNOW**.

> The term *precipitation*, rather than *rainfall*, is recommended when giving annual totals because in some areas of the world *rainfall* is only part of the total *precipitation* (snow and hail are also *precipitation*).

raise

See **RISE**.

ranch house

See **BUNGALOW**.

rapport

See **REPORT**.

rapt, wrapped

rapt *adjective*, means paying very careful attention, engrossed: *Hamish gazed with a rapt expression at the almost static panorama outside the window*.

wrapped *past participle*, is from the verb *wrap*: *A pair of locked chests were wrapped with leather strapping*. Note that to be *wrapped up in* refers to both an object that is contained within paper or soft material: *There was a hot-water bottle in the bed, wrapped up in an old blanket*; and a person who is engrossed in something: *'I used to get very wrapped up in myself when I was pregnant.'*

rare, rarely, seldom

rare *adjective*, means extremely uncommon: *Many species of animals that were common before the war now became rare*. **Rare** can also mean not often: *'I applaud this rare instance of Tories supporting the rights of the worker.'*

rarely *adverb*, means not very often: *His colleagues were astonished, as he rarely praised the Tories*.

seldom *adverb*, means not very often, and is equivalent to the adverb *rarely*: *I knew we had* *visitors, for Carl seldom played the violin otherwise*. See **SCARCITY**.

Seldom is a more formal term than *rarely*, and 'not very often' is a less formal alternative.

rather, fairly

rather *adverb*, means to a fairly large extent: *This lapse of memory made him rather thoughtful*. **Rather** is often used to modify adjectives which express criticism: *He hung about like a good-natured but rather sleepy St Bernard dog*. However, when used before a verb, **rather** makes a sentence sound less forceful: *She rather dreaded the prospect*. In another sense, **rather** is used to mean 'more precisely': *I should have informed the police when she was fit for visitors, or rather the hospital should have*; and it can also mean on the contrary: *All contributions will be judged not as predictions for the future, but rather as analyses of the current situation*. The expression *rather than* means instead of: *The legislation set the number of constituencies at 430, rather than 377 as had been proposed*. See **QUITE**.

fairly *adverb*, means in a just and reasonable manner: *Competition must be conducted fairly and openly*. When used before an adjective, **fairly** means to some extent, but no more than average: *There are over 180 km of marked walks, some of which are fairly strenuous*. See **FAIR (EQUITABLE), QUITE, PRETTY (HANDSOME)**.

Although both terms can mean to some extent, *rather* usually means to a greater degree than *fairly*. Compare *a rather strenuous trip* with *a fairly strenuous trip*.

ravage, ravish

ravage *verb*, means to devastate and destroy: *He completed the restoration of the chapel, which was ravaged by death-watch beetle*.

ravish *verb*, is a literary word meaning to rape: *She feared he would come back in a drunken stupor and ravish her*. **Ravish** in poetry and in literary prose means to enchant, and this has given us the everyday word *ravishing* used to describe a person or object that is very attractive: *She wore a ravishing dress of white tulle with a red velvet scarf*.

raw material, commodity

raw material *noun*, means the basic material from which a product is made. This can either be an industrial commodity: *The chemical industry expanded quickly with the use of oil both as raw material and as fuel*; or something more intangible: *The primary raw material of dictionary work today is electronic databases or corpora of modern usage*. **Raw material** can also be used figuratively: *Switzerland is famously 'a country whose only raw material is brains'*.

commodity *noun*, means a product that can be bought and sold: *Most of these retailers deal in only one commodity – e.g. shoes, clothes or wine*. *Raw materials* such as copper and primary agricultural products, like coffee, are traded in bulk, and referred to as *commodities*: *In one year alone, primary commodity prices fell sharply by an average of 9 per cent*. The London International Financial Futures and Options Exchange is a major world market for *commodity trading*. In another context, **commodity** also means something that is useful and valuable: *Luck is a rare commodity but the harder a manager works the more he has of it*.

raze

See **RISE**.

re, re-

re *preposition*, is used in business correspondence to introduce the subject of the letter or email: *Re: Account no. 24783/2*. **Re** is a shortened form of the Latin phrase *in re*, which means 'on the subject of' or 'regarding'. **Re** is sometimes used in running text to mean regarding, but this should be avoided in formal English. **Re** is pronounced ree /riː/. See **CF**.

re-[1] *prefix*. Many verbs, and nouns derived from these verbs, begin with the prefix **re-**, meaning to do something again: *re-cover, re-elect/re-election*. It is necessary to include a hyphen when there is a risk of confusion with a similarly spelt word (e.g. *re-sign*, compared to *resign*), or (in BE) when the verb being prefixed begins with 'e': *re-elect*. AE does not use a hyphen here. In all other cases, there is no need for a hyphen: *redevelop, reopen, retouch*. With this meaning, **re-** is pronounced ree /riː/, and stressed. See HYPHENATION (PUNCTUATION GUIDE).

re-[2] *prefix*. Other verbs (and their associated nouns) starting with **re-** do not mean to do something again. In these cases, there is never a hyphen, the prefix is not usually stressed, and its pronunciation depends on the stress pattern of the whole word: *repair* (ripaír /rɪˈpeə*r*/), *represent* (reprĕzént /reprɪˈzent/), *reprimand* (réprimaand /ˈreprɪmɑːnd/ *noun*, reprimaáand /reprɪˈmɑːnd/ *verb*).

There are two cases where *re-* is used with a hyphen:

1. When the main verb starts with 'e'. Examples: *re-elect, re-enter, re-examine*. This is standard in BE, but AE does not have hyphenation here. See HYPHENATION (PUNCTUATION GUIDE).
2. When a hyphen is necessary to distinguish between two verbs with the same spelling but different meanings. See RECOVER, REFORM, RESIGN, RESORT. A few nouns also have the **re-** prefix. See RECREATION.

read, skim, study, peruse

read *verb*, means to understand a written text or musical notation, and to speak the words aloud or sing the music or play it on a musical instrument: *Many singers did not read music – as the accompanying orchestras had to remember*. In BE, to **read** a subject at a university, means to study it: *In his youth Lee had read mathematics at Cambridge*. This is not used in AE. People who *lip-read* interpret the movements of someone's lips to understand what they are saying. Computers are also said to **read** files when they can retrieve data from a storage device: *A desktop publishing package should be able to read files from a wide range of word processors, databases, spreadsheets and graphics packages in their native format*.

skim *verb*, means to read something quickly and superficially: *You can skim, which involves just reading the first sentence of every paragraph and anything prominent or highlighted*.

study *noun & verb*. As a noun, this means an examination of something to understand it: *In their study, they interviewed women in depth about the violent experiences they had suffered*. As a verb, **study** means to look at carefully and draw conclusions: *He studied her face to see if she had been crying*.

peruse *verb*, means read carefully and thoroughly: *The Law Society will peruse the bill and documents and certify that the sum charged is fair and reasonable*. Many people misunderstand this formal term. **Peruse** should not be used to mean glance at a text or skim through it. See SCRUTINIZE (EXAMINE).

> *'I have quickly perused the Official Report.'* **!**
> (Deputy Minister in the Scottish Parliament)

readable, legible

readable *adjective*, refers to the quality of a text. It means that something is interesting to read and not boring or too difficult to understand: *The papers presented are highly readable and accessible to the general reader*. Note that documents that are scanned by modern technology are termed *machine-readable*. See UNREADABLE (ILLEGIBLE).

legible *adjective*, means that something is clear and can be read: *There was more writing beneath this, but it was printed too small to be legible*. See ILLEGIBLE.

real, really, true, truly

real *adjective*, means actually existing and not imaginary: *One wonders which was real and which was only a reflection*. **Real** can also mean genuine: *Our prehistory tells us that this is not a dream but a real possibility*. In informal AE, **real** is used as an adverb in phrases like 'real good', 'real soon', 'real sorry', to mean 'very good', 'very soon', 'very sorry'.

really *adverb*, means authentically or genuinely: *Excess sugar really does cause many problems for lots of people*. When it modifies an adjective, **really** can also mean extremely or very thoroughly: *Take the trouble to rinse your hair really thoroughly, especially round the hairline*. In another sense, **really** is used to emphasize something: *'It's quite simple really', the headmaster assured me*.

true *adjective*, means correct, connected with facts and not invented: *'They say bad luck* *comes in threes, but I hope this time that's not true.'* In this sense, **true** can be placed before a noun, or (more commonly) after the verb as its complement as in the example above. Both **true** and *real* can be used to describe the quality of something that is genuine and proper: *He was a true gentleman who believed in true love.* In this sense, **true** always comes before its noun.

truly *adverb*, means genuinely and is used to emphasize the sincerity or correctness of something: *A truly revolutionary approach to Shakespeare would be to dismiss him as irrelevant.* Formal letters in AE use *Yours truly* as an ending. See EMAILS AND LETTERS (WRITING SKILLS).

reality, realty

reality *noun*, means things that are real: *After 48 hours without sleep, she lost her sense of reality.*

realty *noun*, means real estate. It is mainly a legal term and retains the original meaning of the word *real* which meant property (ultimately from Latin *res* 'thing').

really unique

See UNIQUE.

realtor

See ESTATE AGENT.

rearward, rearwards

rearward *adjective*, means directed towards the back. In modern English, this is only used in the adjective form: *The legroom in the car is generous because of the rearward seat adjustment.* See BACKWARD.

rearwards *adverb*, means towards the back: *This system not only sends power rearwards when needed, but also to each rear wheel separately.* This typically comes after the verb. In AE, *rearward* could be used here. See BACKWARDS.

reason, grounds, cause

reason *noun*, is the explanation for something that happens: *The reason they succeed or fail is management.* **Reason** is used here in phrases like *the reason for* (+ noun phrase or verb): *The reason for hospital admission was severe pains in the neck*; or *the reason why* (+ verb): *The reason why they succeed or fail is management.* Note that many careful writers will consider 'why' redundant in this construction, and omit it. See EXCUSE (PRETEXT).

grounds *noun*, means the reason for doing, saying or believing something: *The grounds for working-class discontent struck even the least sympathetic observer.* **Grounds** usually takes a plural verb. See also GROUNDS (CAMPUS).

cause *noun*, means the source or person that makes something happen: *The root cause of the aircraft disasters was a rivet hole an eighth of an inch in diameter.* The focus is on the basic causative factor. See CAUSE (BANDWAGON).

rebate

See DISCOUNT.

rebellion

See REVOLT.

rebound, redound

rebound *verb & noun*. As a verb, this means to bounce back: *The ball rebounded to the striker, who put it in the back of the net.* It is also used figuratively, especially in financial terms, to mean increase again after a fall: *The FTSE rebounded yesterday after early falls.* This means that share prices rose again. As a noun, **rebound** is used figuratively in the phrase *on the rebound* to describe a person who is vulnerable because their relationship has just ended: *On the rebound from Andrew she took up with the first boy that said she was cute*; also to describe something that has reversed its direction: *By 2004 the Stock Market was on the rebound.* It is also used literally: *He caught the ball on the rebound.*

redound *verb*, means to improve people's opinion of someone: *He hoped his diplomatic efforts would redound to his credit.* This is a formal word.

> Both these verbs means to return something to an earlier state, but in none of these example sentences can one word be substituted for the other.

recall

See REMEMBER.

receipt, receipts

receipt *noun*, means a piece of paper that proves that you have received something or paid for it: *'Could I have a receipt for that?' he asked*. The phrase *on receipt of* is mostly used in business to refer to a future action, and means 'when we have received'.

receipts *plural noun*, means money earned in a given period by a business, government or organization: *Leave popular players out of your side and gate receipts could drop*.

recent, last, latest

recent *adjective*, refers to something that happened or started only a short time ago: *The message of recent opinion polls has clearly got through*. The time referred to can cover a longer period: *In recent hot summers, red spider mite has become a severe problem in some gardens*.

last *determiner & adjective*, means either final as in *famous last words*, or the most recent of a series that is considered complete such as *last year*. When it is an adjective it modifies a noun: *He was the last person I expected to meet in a disco in Paris*.

latest *adjective*, means either of recent date, or the newest in a series that is expected to continue: *The latest available figures show satisfactory output*.

recess

See LEAVE.

reciprocal

See MUTUAL.

recollect

See REMEMBER.

recollection

See REMEMBRANCE.

reconcile, mend fences

reconcile *verb*, means to find a compromise between two points of view: *The new code of practice is designed to reconcile the interests of conservation and tourism*; it also means to persuade two people who have disagreed to become friendly again: *The lawyer said the father of four was now reconciled with his wife*. A third meaning of **reconcile** is to accept something, although unwillingly: *The directors' hostility meant that he could never hope to reconcile them to his ownership of the club*.

mend fences *verb*, means to repair a relationship that has broken down: *Stephen wants to mend fences with the council, not build obstacles*. The noun *fence-mending* means an attempt to improve relations between two groups that are in disagreement.

record, register, registration, registry

record réckord /ˈrekɔːrd/ *noun &* rĕkórd /rɪˈkɔːrd/ *verb*. As a noun, **record** can mean a written account or information that is stored on a computer or database: *Online records are now available for public inspection and copying*. **Record** also means a newly established extreme standard: *The price of copper has risen to nearly $7,000 a tonne, which is a record*. In this sense, **record** should only be combined with 'new' if it is clear that there is a contrast to an old or earlier **record**: if it is a **record**, it must be a new one. As a verb, **record** means to set down information for permanent retention: *Books of Remembrance record the names of over 125,000 men and women who gave their lives in the Service*. Note that the noun is stressed on the first syllable, and the verb on the second.

register *noun & verb*. As a noun, this means an official list of names and records: *Inside this ancient church is the parish register with the entry for 3 November 1728*. The place where births, marriages and deaths are recorded in the UK is known as the *register office*. As a verb, it means to record data on an official list: *People register as unemployed in order to draw unemployment and other benefits*. In terms of recording measured data over time, **register** means to display a reading automatically: *The tiny voltmeters at each porthole all register the voltage for their porthole*. As a verb with no object, **register** means to reach someone's consciousness: *He must have heard about the new law but it must have failed to register*. See REGISTER OFFICE.

registration *noun*, is the act of making an official record of something: *The statutory* *system governing the registration of British fishing vessels has been radically altered*. In BE, a motor vehicle has *registration plates* or number plates containing a *registration number* (license plates in AE). See **LICENSE (LICENCE)**.

registry *noun*, means a place where official records or information is kept. *Registry office* is an informal alternative to *register office*.

recount, retell

recount[1] rĕkównt /rɪˈkaʊnt/ *verb*, means to tell someone about a personal experience: *Get him to recount his experiences and suggestions*. It is stressed on the second syllable.

recount[2] reé-kównt /ˈriːˈkaʊnt/ *verb &* reékownt /ˈriːkaʊnt/ *noun*. As a verb, this means to count something two or more times, particularly votes in an election, but it can also be used in general contexts: *A child may be able to count five ducks but may have to recount if they are moved round to form a different pattern*. There is no hyphenation in modern BE, but the first syllable is pronounced with a long vowel, and both syllables are stressed. **Recount** may also be used as a noun in this sense: *A miscount necessitates a recount, and it is imperative that the numbers are accurate*. Note that the stress is placed on the *first* syllable only.

retell *verb*, means to tell a story once more. This can be something that has not been experienced personally: *I intend to retell the story from the perspective of a Roman emperor*. **Retell** is pronounced with a long first vowel, and both syllables are stressed.

> Note that there are two verbs spelt *recount*, with different meanings and pronunciations.

recover, re-cover

recover *verb*, means to get better after an illness, accident or shock: *His daughter is still finding it difficult to recover from her traumatic assault in New York*. A second meaning is to find or regain possession of something: *Proceedings to recover the debt were started in the county court*. It is pronounced with a short first vowel.

re-cover *verb*, means to cover something again or put on a new cover: *We have received an estimate for £244.50 to re-cover the snooker table*. This is hyphenated. The first syllable is pronounced with a long vowel, and both halves of the word are stressed.

recreation, recreate

recreation[1] *noun*, means leisure activity, something done in one's own time, for enjoyment: *He lived a quiet life, with country pursuits his main recreation*. The first syllable is pronounced like the word 'wreck'.

recreation[2] *noun*, means the process of creating something again: *As historical recreation or biography, these films were interesting*. The first syllable is pronounced ree /riː/, and both halves of the word are stressed.

recreate *verb*, means to make something again from the beginning: *Explore junk shops and markets for costume jewellery to recreate this expensive look*. The first syllable is pronounced ree /riː/, and both halves of the word are stressed.

> Note that there are two nouns spelt *recreation*, with different meanings and pronunciations.

R

recto

See **VERSO**.

redbrick university, plateglass university

redbrick university *noun*, refers to one of the large civic universities such as Birmingham, Manchester and Liverpool founded in Britain in the late nineteenth and early twentieth centuries. Since then the term has been extended to include other universities founded up to the mid twentieth century. The term refers to the building material and contrasts with the stone used in Oxbridge colleges. See **OXBRIDGE**.

plateglass university *noun*, refers to one of the several universities such as East Anglia, Sussex and Warwick founded in Britain from the 1960s onwards. The term has been extended to refer to about 10 newer universities. The term reflects the architectural design of that time, which uses plate glass extensively.

redecorate, restore, refurbish, renovate, rehabilitate

redecorate *verb*, means to change the way a room looks by repainting it, hanging new curtains or putting new wallpaper up: *She'll be pondering some new colour schemes for a room that she wants to redecorate*.

restore *verb*, means to make something return to a previous state or condition. Buildings, works of art and pieces of furniture are typical objects that are **restored**: *One coach only needs a small amount of work to restore it to its original condition*. The phrase *restore to its former glory* means to make something as beautiful as it was previously: *The orchard has been restored to its former glory*. **Restore** is also used more widely than simply to refer to objects. The health, confidence and faith of people can all be **restored**: *The group managed to restore peace before the police arrived*.

refurbish *verb*, means to redecorate, repair and modernize a building: *I wanted to refurbish the waiting room and surgery and install new furniture and equipment*. It is typically used in BE.

renovate *verb*, means to repair and restore an old building to a good condition. Note that to **renovate** a building involves more extensive work than to *refurbish* it, such as new windows or roof tiles: *We renovate derelict inner-city sites, sometimes preserving buildings of architectural interest*.

rehabilitate *verb*, means restore an area of buildings or land to a better standard or a good state, and can refer to whole urban areas including industrial sites: *The government intends to ask for assistance to rehabilitate the polluted areas around the mines*. It is also used for people who are disabled, who have been imprisoned, or who have lost privileges and are being helped to get a job, or back into their former status: *We require prisons that rehabilitate offenders rather than create career criminals*.

Red Indian, redskin

See NATIVE AMERICAN.

redound

See REBOUND.

reduction

See DISCOUNT.

redundancy

See TAUTOLOGY.

redundant, jobless, unemployed

redundant *adjective*, means superfluous, no longer needed or useful. In BE, *to make someone redundant* means to dismiss an employee and abolish the position because it is no longer required: *The 12 staff employed in European offices have been made redundant*. This does not reflect on the employee, but on the circumstances of the employer. *Redundant information* means unnecessary information: *This software will delete redundant information or duplicate commands*. See DISMISS, RETIRE.

jobless *adjective & noun*. This refers to the status of a person who does not have a job: *The area is among the worst jobless blackspots with unemployment at 36 per cent*. It is also used as a noun by journalists – *the jobless*. This is an informal term.

unemployed *adjective & noun*. This also refers to the status of a person who does not have a job: *unemployed workers* (adjective); *There were 300 jobs for the unemployed in the town* (noun). This is a more formal term than *jobless*.

referee, umpire, judge

referee *noun*, means someone who ensures that the rules of a game are observed and also settles any disputes. *Referees* are found in American football, basketball, billiards, boxing, hockey, rugby, snooker, soccer and wrestling. *The ref* is used in this sense as an informal abbreviation: *The ref called me over and gave me my marching orders*. Outside sport, a **referee** is a person who is willing to make a statement about the character or ability of someone who is applying for a job: *Is there anyone who would act as a referee or recommend me for the job?* See REF. (CF.).

umpire *noun*, means a referee in certain sports. **Umpires** are found in American football, badminton, baseball, bowls, cricket, hockey, polo, table tennis, tennis and volleyball: *They all abided by the umpire's decision, whichever way it went*. When there is both a *referee* and an **umpire**, as in American football, the *referee* is in charge of the game and the **umpire** controls the behaviour of the players. In hockey, both terms are used. Outside sport, an **umpire** is used to arbitrate between two parties in dispute and try to bring them to an agreeable decision.

judge *noun*, is a public officer appointed to pass sentence on persons found guilty in a law court: *The judge imposed concurrent periods of three years' imprisonment on each of the charges*. A **judge** can also be someone who decides the result of a competition, or (as *line judge*) if a ball is in or out in tennis: *I disliked watching the world's no. 1 player rant at a line judge recently*.

references, referencing electronic documents

See STYLE GUIDELINES (WRITING SKILLS).

referendum, referendums, referenda

referendum *noun*, is a choice given to voters about whether to adopt or reject a proposal – not a person. In 2005, the voters of France and the Netherlands chose in a referendum to reject the proposed European constitution. In another sense, the **referendum** is also the question asked on the voting form: *A group of politicians . . . began collecting signatures in favour of the referendum*. **Referendum** has two plurals, and careful writers distinguish them.

referendums means the vote being held: *The 11,000 island voters have rejected the treaty in six referendums since 1983*.

referenda is the other plural of *referendum*, and means the questions to be decided: *One of the referenda urges that abortion should be permitted in cases where the life of a mother-to-be is considered at risk*.

reform, re-form

reform *verb & noun*. As a verb, this means to make a change for the better: *If the aim of the prison system is to reform the individual, the method is education*. The first syllable has a short vowel. As a noun, it means a change to a system in order to improve it: *There are some far-reaching reforms necessary in state education*.

re-form *verb*, means to form again: *An employee group hopes to re-form as a software and parallel systems integration firm*. This is hyphenated. The first syllable is pronounced with a long vowel, and both syllables are stressed.

refurbish

See REDECORATE.

refuse, decline, deny, refute

refuse *verb*, means either to be unwilling to do something or to deny someone what they ask for: *Occasionally it will be necessary to refuse or delay access to certain items of information*.

decline *verb*, can mean to *refuse*, in a formal and polite way: *I quickly declined his offer by shaking my head*. **Decline** in another sense means to decrease gradually, especially in quantity or value: *The period 1945–90 saw the number of morning papers decline, with total sales fluctuating*.

deny *verb*, can mean to say that something is not true: *Both men deny causing the deaths by reckless driving*. It can also mean to disallow, especially permission, opportunity or access: *The goalie saved brilliantly to deny Drogba a certain goal*.

refute *verb*, means to prove that an idea or statement is not correct: *Sometimes to refute a single sentence it is necessary to tell a life story*. A second meaning is to strongly deny or reject something: *I would refute the idea that hard times have wrecked the business lunch*. This usage is not accepted by many people and is best avoided in formal contexts: use *deny* instead. **Refute** is only used in formal English. See DISPROVE.

regarding, in regard to/with regard to

regarding *preposition*, means about or concerning something: *Section 3.0 of these notes contains instructions regarding the use of such support*. Alternatives are *concerning* and *respecting*.

in regard to/with regard to *prepositional phrase*, means as concerns, or in respect of something: *A submission of no case to answer was also made in regard to the second charge*. These expressions are more formal than *regarding*, but are normal in some business contexts: *I write with regard to the letter from*

R

Mrs Madeley in your January issue. Note that it would be unsuitable to use *regarding* here.

regardless, irregardless

regardless *adverb*, means nevertheless or without caring about the results: *'You know I don't like you to play games without me, but you went ahead regardless.'* **Regardless** is often combined with *of*: *They paid a pension, regardless of the length of service*.

irregardless *adverb*, means without regard, and is a blend of the two words *irrespective* and *regardless*. Although it is listed in some recently published dictionaries, many usage guides deny that this is an acceptable word. There are only two examples of it to be found in the British National Corpus. Use *irrespective* or *regardless* instead. See **IRRESPECTIVE (RESPECTIVE)**.

register office, registry

register office *noun*, is the official name for the local government office in the UK where civil marriages, births and deaths are registered: *The happy couple decided to marry at the Ipswich Register Office*. See **RECORD**.

registry *noun*, means the place where records are kept, such as the *Land Registry*, and the *Trade Marks Registry* in the UK. *Registry office* is also commonly used although it is officially called a *register office*. See **RECORD**.

registration

See **RECORD**.

regretful, regrettable

regretful *adjective*, means feeling disappointed or sad for something you have or have not done: *He was staring at the lake, regretful perhaps that he'd said too much*. This is a formal word.

regrettable *adjective*, refers to an unpleasant situation that has occurred: *'If Ruth is unwell, that's very regrettable, but there is nothing we can do for her.'*

regulations

See **RULES**.

rehabilitate

See **REDECORATE**.

reign, rein

reign *noun & verb*. As a noun, this means the period during which a king or queen holds the position of Head of State: *They lived comfortably in a house built in King Edward's reign*. Figuratively, a **reign** can also be a period when someone or something is most important or powerful: *This team had a four-year reign as ice hockey champions*. As a verb, it means to be on the throne or to be in control: *Until recently the philosophy of 'wetland is wasteland' reigned*.

rein *noun*, is a strap attached to the bit that controls a horse: *As the horse responds, lighten the rein and ride forward again*. To be given *free* (or *full*) *rein*, means to be given complete freedom: *In this book I ask you to allow your curiosity full rein*. In figurative use, the verb *rein in* means to start to control an activity more closely: *There was an awkward silence when Ruth managed to rein in her silly chatter*.

Do not confuse these soundalikes.

'General Suharto carefully set about grasping the reigns of power.' (http://news.bbc.co.uk)

reiterate

See **REPEAT**.

relaid, relayed

relaid *verb*, is the past tense and past participle of the verb **relay** when it means lay again: *Eight years ago my driveway was relaid with paving slabs*. Note that the first syllable is pronounced **ree** /riː/, and that both syllables are stressed.

relayed *verb*, is the past tense and past participle of the verb **relay** when it means retransmit, or pass on: *The crematorium chapel was full and the service was relayed to crowds outside*. The first syllable is not stressed, and contains a short vowel.

relations

See CONNECTIONS.

relinquish

See YIELD.

relocate

See TRANSFER.

remains, remainder, remnant, relic

remains *noun*, means the parts left over after something has been eaten or used: *Laura put the remains of her gin and tonic down by her canvas chair*. **Remains** also means historical relics: *Remains of a number of fortified buildings exist*. In another sense **remains** means a dead animal or corpse: *Human remains have been discovered on the site*.

remainder *noun*, means the part of a whole that has not yet been mentioned, obtained or used: *The remainder of the book is taken up with a detailed study; The remainder of the buildings are of eighteenth- and nineteenth-century construction*. Note that it is the noun that **remainder** refers to that determines whether a singular or plural verb should be used. Unlike *remains*, the word **remainder** implies nothing about the quality of what is left.

remnant *noun*, means a small remaining part of a whole with the same quality as the rest: *The Jewel Tower is a remnant of the medieval Palace of Westminster*. In the plural, **remnants** means what is left over but with inferior quality: *William was wearing gumboots and the jaunty remnants of a straw hat*.

relic *noun*, means an interesting survival, something left over from the past: *The mines have long been closed but a relic survives in a blacksmith's forge behind the crumbled walls*. **Relic** is often used in a religious sense to mean a revered fragment of a holy person's body, or of an item connected with a religious event: *They showed the sacred relic of the blood of Christ*.

remember, recollect, recall, remind

remember *verb*, means to bring something to mind with little conscious effort: *I remember the war and my travels around the world*. To *remember to* means not to forget: *Remember to check the plants daily for any pests*.

recollect reckŏlékt /rekə'lekt/ *verb*, is to remember something especially by making an effort: *He could not recollect anything similar having happened to him*. It is a formal word. Note that the first syllable rhymes with 'wreck'. Occasionally **recollect** also means to collect again, and in this sense the verb is pronounced reé-kŏlékt /ˈriːkə'lekt/, with two stresses.

recall *verb & noun*. As a verb, this means to bring a memory or event back to mind. It is often used when someone is telling others about something: *Immigrants are being asked to recall how they successfully adapted to British life*. **Recall** also means to order someone or something to be returned: *Despite the country's mounting problems, the Prime Minister arrogantly rejected demands to recall Parliament*. As a noun, **recall** may also be stressed on the first syllable: reékawl /'riːkɔːl/, and means the act of bringing something back to mind, or the demand for a return of something: *Recall is what fails to happen when you are stumped by an examination question*.

remind *verb*, means to generate a memory and help someone to remember something important: *Now, suddenly I had to remind myself of the truth*.

R

> *Recall* is the only word in this group that may be used as both a verb and a noun.

remembrance, memory, reminiscence, recollection

remembrance *noun*, means when people remember or recall an event or a solemn occasion, particularly involving death: *They held a service in remembrance of the dead*. The related verb is *remember*.

memory *noun*, means the ability to remember things: *Scenes such as this remained most vividly in my memory*. In this sense, **memory** is an uncountable noun. As a countable noun, a **memory** is an individual thing remembered from the past: *That day you gave us a memory we'll never forget*. A computer's **memory** is the capacity for storing data in it. The related verb is *memorize* which means to learn something perfectly.

reminiscence *noun*, means a pleasant memory of the past: *These three volumes of anecdote and reminiscence are a useful source* *for biographers*. This is most often used in the plural: *The interview opened with reminiscences of the first film he made in Paris*. The related verb is *reminisce*.

recollection *noun*, means something remembered or called to mind, often only with some effort: *Whatever it was, she still had no recollection of it at all*. The related verb is *recollect*.

remittance

See PAYMENT.

remnant

See REMAINS.

rendezvous

See MEETING.

renounce

See ABJURE.

renovate

See REDECORATE.

rent

See HIRE.

repairable, reparable

repairable rĕpaírăbĕl /rɪˈpeərəbl̩/ *adjective*, means capable of being mended: *Claims for articles damaged but repairable are paid on the basis of the repair cost*. This word is used for physical things that have been damaged. See UNREPAIRABLE (IRREPARABLE).

reparable réppărăbĕl /ˈrepərəbl̩/ *adjective*, also means capable of being mended, but refers especially to reputations, or other non-physical attributes: *As he controlled the media, the reputation of the President was always reparable*. See IRREPARABLE.

> Note the difference in pronunciation and stress pattern between these two words. Also the opposites are different: *unrepairable* and *irreparable*.

repayment

See PAYMENT.

repeat, reiterate, repetitive

repeat *verb, adjective & noun*. As a verb, this means to say or write something again, often in the same words: *They were asked to repeat their lectures a few days later*. As an adjective, it describes an action that is carried out more than once: *Five repeat performances were staged in one day*. As a noun, it means a radio or television programme that has already been broadcast: *The show was a repeat, so they didn't bother to watch it*. In music, a **repeat** is either a sign that tells the performers to play a passage again, or the passage itself: *Let's not bother with the repeats this morning*.

reiterate *verb*, means to repeat something a number of times for emphasis or to make things clear: *It is necessary to reiterate the point made at the beginning of this chapter*. This is a more formal word than *repeat*, and can only be used for the repetition of non-physical actions.

repetitive *adjective*, means saying or doing the same thing many times. When referring to speech it means using an unnecessary number of words: *The speech was an ordeal, extremely repetitive and lasted for three hours*. For an action it refers to something carried out many times: *Regular inspection is required even if it is extremely repetitive*. This is usually a negative word.

repel, repulse

repel *verb*, means to suffer something unpleasant that causes disgust: *'You're all so smug you repel me.'* In another sense it means to defend oneself against attackers and drive them away: *The city was fortified and was able to repel raids by pirates*. As a scientific term in electromagnetism, **repel** is the opposite of attract: *Like poles repel, but unlike poles attract each other*.

repulse *verb*, means to feel disgust or strong dislike: *Audiences at early screenings were repulsed by the brutality*. It also means to drive back an attack or repel it: *The government claimed that its troops had repulsed an attack on the city*. **Repulse** is a more formal word than *repel*.

repellent, repulsive

repellent *adjective & noun*. As an adjective, this means distasteful: *'I loathed all sport to* *the point of finding its ethics repellent.'* Fabrics that repel moisture are called *water repellent*. As a noun, it means something that drives back or repels: *Diluted TCP makes an excellent fly repellent*.

repulsive *adjective*, means disgusting and causing extreme distaste: *Bernice thought the woman's eating habits were repulsive, and turned away*. **Repulsive** is a stronger word than *repellent*.

repetition of words

See WRITING SKILLS.

replace

See SUBSTITUTE.

replica, replicate

replica *noun*, means an exact copy of an object such as a building, museum exhibit or work of art: *The centrepiece was an exact replica of a Portuguese explorer's helmet*.

replicate *verb*, means to do a study using another scientist's methods or trying to get the same results: *This appendix is a valuable resource for anyone aiming to replicate this important work*. When something *replicates*, it produces exact copies of itself: *The virus replicates itself, and each new copy goes on to carry out the task for which the virus was designed*.

reply, answer

reply *noun & verb*. As a noun, this means a response to someone or to a specific issue: *She could not wait for a reply, but spelt out the answer herself*. As a verb, **reply** means to give a reaction: *'I would like to reply to two letters published in the November issue.'* As both noun and verb, **reply** may be followed by *to*. See RESPONSE (FEEDBACK).

answer *noun & verb*. As a noun, this means a response to a specific issue: *I do not always know the answers to the questions*. It may also mean the solution to a problem: As a noun, **answer** is followed by *to*. As a verb, **answer** means to *reply*: *You have not answered our last letter*. Note that as a verb, **answer** is not followed by *to*.

report, rapport

report *noun & verb*. As a noun, this means a written or spoken presentation of a situation, event or research findings: *Contained in the report are a cash flow statement and balance sheet*. As a verb, it means to give information: *He left it to Peter to report any snippet of information he managed to get*.

rapport rappór /ræ'pɔːr/ *noun*, means a close and harmonious relationship: *There was an immediate rapport, as if we'd been friends for years*. **Rapport** is a formal word and alternatives like relationship and working relationship are less formal. Note that the final 't' is silent, and the second syllable is stressed and pronounced like the word 'pore'.

reprobate, degenerate

reprobate *noun*, means someone who behaves in an immoral way: *Even the designers had trouble in making an elegant photographic portrait of the old reprobate*. Note that the last syllable rhymes with 'eight'.

degenerate dijénnĕrăt /di'dʒenərət/ *noun, adjective &* dijénnĕrayt /di'dʒenəreɪt/ *verb*. As a noun, this means someone who behaves in a morally unacceptable way: *He was publicly humiliated in the press as a degenerate and a womanizer*. As an adjective, it means morally unacceptable: *The exhibition of degenerate art has some paintings which were criticized as total madness*. As a verb, it means to become worse: *The battle degenerated into several vicious internal conflicts*. Note that while the noun and adjective end in a neutral vowel, the last syllable of the verb rhymes with 'eight'.

> Although *reprobate* is often used humorously, *degenerate* as a noun is not.

repulsive

See REPELLENT.

requisite, prerequisite, precondition, requirement

requisite réckwizit /'rekwɪzɪt/ *noun & adjective*. As a noun, this means a qualification, or something necessary to meet a specific purpose: *For those with the requisite classical music training this will be a delightful holiday venue*. Physical objects are sometimes termed *requisites*: *Why not call a spade a spade instead of a garden requisite?* As an

R

adjective, it means necessary: *Training will be given in the requisite biochemical analysis*. This is a formal word.

prerequisite *noun & adjective*. As a noun, this means a prior condition or something necessary prior to a specific event or purpose: *A general education in the sciences is a prerequisite of professional medical training*. As an adjective, it means required beforehand: *The student must have the prerequisite knowledge and skills to begin learning the task*. This is also a formal word. See **PERQUISITE (FRINGE BENEFIT)**.

precondition *noun*, means something that must exist before something else can be achieved: *A precondition of peace is no violence*.

requirement *noun*, means a demand that must be met: *An important requirement is to specify the source of the data*.

requisition, indent

requisition *verb & noun*. As a verb, this means to demand or confiscate goods or services. It is most often used in a military context: *The government assumed powers to requisition at fixed prices all cereal products*. As a noun, it means the demand for or confiscation of goods or services: *There was a row about the requisition for scrap of his wrought-iron gates*.

indent indént /ɪn'dent/ *verb &* índent /'ɪndent/ *noun*. As a verb, this means to order goods or services, and is used within companies and the military: *We indented for a new printer/copier and 50 reams of paper*. In word processing **indent** means to move a line or lines of text inwards from the margin: *Press the Tab key to indent*. As a noun, in word processing, **indent** is the amount a line or lines of text is moved inwards from the margin of the page: *An indent for the first line of the paragraph can be set by pressing the Tab key*. **Indent** also means an order for goods or services: *'It seems that our line manager has refused to approve the indent,' he said*.

rescind

See **ANNUL**.

reservation

See **NATURE RESERVE**.

reserve

See **CONSERVE, NATURE RESERVE**.

resettle

See **TRANSFER**.

residence, residency

residence *noun*, is a formal word meaning a house that gives the impression of grandeur: *This eighteenth-century building was once a private residence of the famed Medici family*. The phrase *take up residence* is a formal way of saying that someone is moving into an area: *He can always take up residence at his college again*. See **HOUSE**.

residency *noun*, is another formal word that means a building where a government official lives, especially abroad: *Before leaving the Ministry Owen rang the Consul-General's Residency*. Students often have to follow special regulations about how much time is to be spent at university. These are called *residency requirements*. A period spent by an artist, author or musician at a college or institution, and in AE the time a doctor spends in hospital undergoing advanced medical training, is also called a **residency**. As an uncountable noun, it is the right to live in a country or area: *Do you have a US passport or residency permit (commonly known as a 'Green Card')?*

resident, inhabitant, citizen, subject

resident *noun*, means someone who lives in a place that is their permanent home: *The less isolated new residents feel, the faster they settle down*. **Resident** can also mean a person staying in a hotel.

inhabitant *noun*, means any person who lives in a town or country, and is not connected with citizenship or permanent settlement: *He felt privileged to be an inhabitant of a town such as Richmond*. **Inhabitant** is a rather impersonal term, and is used in contexts where the word *person* or *people* might be considered misleading or too informal. **Inhabitant** can also be used in a figurative way: *It is hard to believe that an inhabitant of the political jungle can be pleasant*.

citizen *noun*, is someone who was born in a particular state or has acquired citizenship of it by naturalization: *Each adult citizen may have one vote*.

subject *noun*, is used in some monarchies as an alternative to citizen: *James Joyce never settled in England, though he chose to live and die a British subject*. In English law the two terms are not synonymous: British passports state that while British *citizens* have the right of abode in the United Kingdom, British *subjects* do not necessarily have that right. See **SUBJECT (FIELD)**.

resign, re-sign

resign *verb*, means to announce one's decision to leave a job or position, often as a way of resolving a difficult situation: *A spokesman said: 'His offer to resign will be accepted.'* To *resign oneself to fate* means to accept being in a position that cannot be changed. See **DISMISS**, **REDUNDANT**, **RETIRE**.

re-sign *verb*, means to sign a document again. In the world of sport, a player or coach who **re-signs** enters into a new contract with his or her employer: *A spokesman said: 'I persuaded him to re-sign.'* Note the hyphenation.

resolve

See **DECIDE**.

resort, re-sort

resort *noun & verb*. As a noun, this means a holiday destination: *Catering for the sports enthusiasts has become a top priority for the resort*. The phrase *as a last resort* means if everything else fails: *This treatment should only be used as a last resort*. As a verb, it means to do something extreme as there is no other possible course of action: *The protesters will resort to any methods to get international attention*.

re-sort *verb*, means to sort something once more: *Children often find endless pleasure in sorting and re-sorting boxes of buttons*. Note that this is hyphenated, that the first syllable is pronounced with a long vowel, and that both syllables are stressed.

respectable, respectful, disrespectful

respectable *adjective*, means behaving in an acceptable and proper way: *The building society movement made borrowing respectable*. **Respectable** also means of adequate quality: *Overall performance falls in the middle bracket and is respectable for a normally powered car*.

respectful *adjective*, means demonstrating or feeling respect: *The undertaker was an expert in the art of respectful silence*.

disrespectful *adjective*, means having or showing no respect for someone: *At times, the press has been extremely disrespectful to the monarchy*.

respective, respectively, irrespective

respective *adjective*, means belonging or referring to two or more people or things mentioned separately: *Both clubs showed their return to form by winning their respective leagues last season*. Note that the noun following **respective** is always plural.

respectively *adverb*, means separately and in the order already referred to. It is used when referring to a list of items: *Telephone and postal rates went up by 58 per cent and 81 per cent respectively*. Note that **respectively** focuses on the order mentioned and normally comes at the end of a sentence.

irrespective *adverb*, describes something that has no effect on the situation: *The health service provides excellent treatment irrespective of income*. See **REGARDLESS**.

response

See **FEEDBACK**.

responsible, accountable

responsible *adjective*, means having a job, an obligation to do something, or being reliable: *He is very responsible and mature for such a young boy*. A person can be *responsible for* other people, actions or things in his or her care: *Students are responsible for their own progress and the achievement and monitoring of their goals*. *Responsible for* is also used to refer to a person who is the cause of something unpleasant or criminal: *Do you know who was responsible for breaking this window?* If a person is *responsible to* someone or something, this indicates a line of command: *They work in accordance with the instructions of ministers and they are responsible to ministers*. See **LIABLE (APT)**.

accountable *adjective*, means personally answerable and required or expected to justify actions or decisions: *Someone must be held accountable for this security failure. Accountable to* means having to report or justify one's actions to authority: *At a general election, politicians are accountable to the voters.*

People may be *accountable* or *responsible*, but inanimate objects can only be *responsible* for a consequence. For instance, floods may be *responsible* for damage, but cannot be *accountable* for it.

restaurant, café, diner

restaurant *noun*, means a place where people can buy and eat meals: *In the restaurant guests are offered traditional cuisine.* The owner of a **restaurant** is formally called a *restaurateur*. Note that this word has no 'n'.

café káffay /ˈkæfeɪ/ (BE), kaffáy /kæˈfeɪ/ (AE) *noun*, means a place to buy light meals and snacks: *To sit down in a café you had to buy a cup of tea.* Note that the spelling *cafe* without the acute accent is given as an alternative in modern dictionaries.

diner dīnĕr /ˈdaɪnər/ *noun*, means a customer in a restaurant: *A diner called the waiter over to complain about his food.* In the USA it also means either a small inexpensive restaurant: *Nathan and Yvonne stopped for coffee and doughnuts in a diner on the highway*; or a dining car on a train. A *kitchen-diner* is a room in a house that combines the functions of kitchen and dining-room. See BUFFET.

restive, restless

restive *adjective*, means bored and impatient: *Some of the crowd had been waiting for several hours and they were becoming restive.*

restless *adjective*, means either unable to keep still: *She was too restless to stay still for even a moment*; or without real rest or sleep: *It was too stuffy and hot in the tent and Andrew had another restless night.*

restore

See REDECORATE.

result, outcome

result *noun*, means the consequence of a previous event: *If water penetrates window sills, doors or their frames, the result is wet rot.* As a plural noun, *results* means the final number of votes or points at the end of a competition: *Here are the football results.* Examination marks are often called *examination results*. In AE, these would be termed examination grades. In business, the *results* are the financial accounts for a specified period: *The half-year results showed an increase in profits.*

outcome *noun*, means the result of a series of events: *The outcome of the dispute was hailed by the parents as a victory.* This is especially used when it is uncertain what the conclusion will be: *Bookmakers are finding it impossible to predict the outcome of the Boat Race this year.*

résumé, resume

See CURRICULUM VITAE.

retell

See RECOUNT.

retire, retreat, withdraw, pull back

retire *verb*, means to cease working because of age or poor health: *'Now at least I can retire with some money', said Alex, after working for 46 years.* In formal English, to *retire for the night* means to go to bed. In a military context, if soldiers **retire** in the face of the enemy, this means they make a planned and orderly withdrawal. See REDUNDANT, RESIGN.

retreat *verb*, means to move away from someone or something when faced with a difficult situation: *We either move forward or retreat into isolationism.* In a military context, **retreat** means to move away from the enemy because of the risk of defeat.

withdraw *verb*, means to move troops back from an area of land and stop them taking part in an armed conflict. This is the usual meaning. **Withdraw** also means to take something back: *Will the Hon. Member withdraw that allegation?* It can also mean leave a contest: *He withdrew from the elections.*

pull back *verb*. In a military sense, this means to *withdraw* soldiers. In a sporting context, **pull back** means to improve the situation after falling behind: *'You'll never pull back a 6–0 deficit', said one spectator*.

retronym

See WORD FORMATION.

revenge

See AVENGE.

revenue

See EARNINGS.

revere

See IDOLIZE.

reverent, reverend

reverent *adjective*, means feeling admiration or showing deep respect: *They spoke in the specially reverent voice reserved for times of bereavement*.

reverend *noun*, refers to a person to be revered. It is used as a title for the clergy and is capitalized. The correct form of address in BE is *Reverend John Smith* or *the Reverend J. Smith*. In AE, the Christian name is omitted: *Reverend Smith*. The abbreviation is *Rev*. or sometimes *Revd* (in AE this has a stop: *Revd.*) which is always capitalized. Note that the final letter and sound of the word is 'd'. See CLERGY.

Both *reverent* and *reverend* are formal words.

reversal, reversion

reversal *noun*, means a change to the opposite direction or way of doing something: *The total reversal in educational ideology affected all the schoolchildren in the country*.

reversion *noun*, means a return to a previous state or condition: *There are signs of a reversion to a more primitive level of superstition*. In law, **reversion** means either the transfer of property back to its previous owner: *Discussions are in progress to permit the reversion of Northern Cyprus to the Republic of Cyprus*; or the right of succession to an office on the death of the present holder. This is a formal word.

reverse, inverse, obverse

reverse *noun, adjective & verb*. As a noun, this means the other side of an object: *The reverse of the fabric has stripes of two rows of each of the colours being used*. As an adjective, it means opposite: *At the end of the ceremony, the procession leaves the hall in reverse order*. As a verb, **reverse** can mean to overturn a previous decision: *It may be a difficult political task to reverse these defeats on the floor of the House*; to go backwards: *I jumped into the car and started to reverse*; exchange two things: *The father reversed the traditional roles in the home*; or move in the opposite direction.

inverse *adjective*, means opposite or contrary in position, direction or order: *There has always been an inverse relationship between the power of a tool and its ease of operation*. **Inverse** is often linked to terms such as ratio and relationship, particularly in mathematics and statistics.

obverse *noun*, is a technical term that means the side of a coin carrying the main inscription and design. In formal contexts, the **obverse** is the opposite of a fact or truth.

R

Reverse is a more general term than *inverse* and *obverse*. Note that a coin has its secondary design on the *reverse* side. See BACK (BACKSIDE).

reverse engineering

See PLAGIARISM.

review, revue

review *noun & verb*. As a noun, this means a careful examination of a situation or process: *The specialist social worker undertook a review to examine resources for children*. A **review** can also be a critique of literary or artistic work: *The competition invited young people to write a short review of one of the films*. As a verb, **review** means to examine something to see if changes are necessary: *This plan will enable us to review the main effects of the reform*. See PEER REVIEW.

revue *noun*, means a theatrical entertainment with songs and sketches: *After some years in theatrical revue he became a successful Broadway director*.

revolt, rebellion, riot, uprising

revolt *noun & verb*. As a noun, this means a violent action by people against their rulers: *Joan of Arc stirred up patriotism and led a revolt against the reign of King Henry VI*. As a verb, **revolt** has two meanings: first to take violent action against rulers usually in order to take power away from them, and second, to disgust. Sentences such as *The students are revolting* may cause amusement, and it is better to use *rebellious* or *disgusting* instead.

rebellion *noun*, means opposition to established power. The seriousness of the opposition depends on which word **rebellion** is combined with. At one end of the scale it can mean armed revolution: *For nearly three years, the elected Spanish government held out against Franco's fascist rebellion*; and at the other end, mild opposition to a teacher or parent: *People talk about rock 'n' roll as the music of rebellion*.

riot *noun*, means a localized outbreak of violent and uncontrolled behaviour sparked by protest against something: *Urban France has had a succession of riots and disorder in recent years*.

uprising *noun*, means a widespread armed protest against authority, a rebellion: *He tried to encourage an uprising of extremists in the south-western lowlands*.

revolve around

See **CENTRE IN**.

rich, affluent, wealthy

rich *adjective*, means having a lot of money: *The town had no rich merchants to build fine houses round the marketplace*; or full of interesting things, colours or sounds: *The decoration here is very rich in figures and picture carving*. It also means having plentiful resources: *We have land rich in minerals*; or refers to food having a high content of fat, sugar or fruit.

affluent *adjective*, means having plenty of money and a high standard of living: *Bentley customers are younger but no less affluent than typical Rolls-Royce buyers*. In another sense, **affluent** is often used to describe societies with a high standard of living: *The term 'The Affluent Society' was defined by John Kenneth Galbraith in his book of that title in 1958*.

wealthy *adjective*, means having a lot of money or possessions: *There have always been a minority of wealthy older people and a majority struggling to survive in poverty*.

> *Rich* is the least formal of these terms, and is more widely used than *affluent* and *wealthy* which are generally restricted to economic contexts.

Richter scale

See **BEAUFORT SCALE**.

right, rightly, correct, right-hand, right-handed

right *adjective, adverb & noun*. As an adjective, this refers to action in a morally justified, correct and accepted way: *They feel this is the right course of action to take*. It can also refer to a part of a body: *My right ankle makes cracking noises*; or the side of something like a football pitch or a vehicle: *The right wing hit the ground; the plane flipped over and then exploded*. In politics, the *right wing* of a party is considered reactionary and traditionalist. As an adverb, **right** means without mistakes: *'If I do it right, can I go home, please?'* **Right** also means exactly: *Right on target*; straight: *Keep right ahead*; and immediately: *Do this right away*. It can also point in a direction: *At the end of the street, turn right*. **Right** as a noun can mean the direction: *As they fled north, he pointed to the right: 'Look', he said. 'The sun is rising'*; and also what one is entitled to: *He was told he had the right to remain silent*. See **WRITE**.

rightly *adverb*, means correctly or for a good reason: *They rightly insist on being treated as individuals*. Note that **rightly** means correctly when it is placed just before a verb or an adjective.

correct *adjective*, means without mistakes: *Make sure that your GP has your correct address, especially if you have moved house recently*. In another sense it describes the approved way: *It would be more correct to raise the matter in debate*. The term *politically correct* means selecting terms that will not cause offence to specific groups of people. See POLITICAL CORRECTNESS.

right-hand *adjective*, only means on the right side, and this is the usual way of expressing this except for referring to parts of the body or vehicles. Note that **right-hand** as an adjective is hyphenated: *Against the right-hand wall was a row of old machines*; and can only come before a noun.

right-handed *adjective*, refers to people who use their right hand more naturally than their left: *Right-handed males who are very susceptible to hypnosis also seem to show a preference for using the right hemisphere of the brain*; or to the way a screw is bored or a machine rotates: *A screw that goes in as you turn it clockwise is called right-handed*.

right bank

See BANK.

rightward, rightwards

rightward *adjective*, refers to movement or curvature to the right: *The wall above is climbed via a shallow, rightward-curving crack*. Note that this is usually placed before a noun.

rightwards *adverb*, also refers to movement or curvature to the right: *The Main Face includes all the cliff stretching rightwards from here*. Note that this usually occurs after a verb. This is sometimes spelt and pronounced *rightward*.

rigid

See UNBENDING.

rigorous

See STRICT.

rigour, rigor

rigour *noun*, means care and thoroughness to ensure something is correct: *This dissertation is unsatisfactory because of a lack of academic rigour*. In this sense it is a formal word, and an uncountable noun. In the plural, *rigours* means harshness and austerity: *The players were all exhausted after the rigours of the World Cup*. See RIGOROUS (STRICT).

rigor ríggŏr /ˈrɪgər/ *noun*, means muscular stiffness as in *rigor mortis*, or uncontrollable shaking caused by the onset of a disease. In BE this may also be pronounced ríٖgŏr /ˈraɪgər/, especially by people in the medical profession. In AE, **rigor** is the spelling of *rigour*.

> The related adjective is spelt *rigorous* in both BE and AE. See -OR, -OUR SPELLINGS.

ring

See PHONE.

riot

See REVOLT.

rise, *raise*, *raze*

rise *noun & verb*. As a noun, this means an upward movement or an increase in number, amount or value: *More than 20 million households are facing another rise in their insurance premiums*. In another sense a **rise** can mean an increase in power or importance: *The industrial revolution spawned the rise and expansion of the middle class*. Note that **rise** in BE can mean an increase in pay. This is called a *raise* in AE. As a verb, **rise** has the past tense *rose* and the past participle *risen*. **Rise** never has an object: *The sun rises*. See ASCENT.

raise *verb*, means to lift something: *I was waiting for Mum to raise her hand, but she did not move*; to bring to someone's attention: *I did not raise the topics of the previous evening*; or to gather money for a specific purpose: *We must raise £1,200 per day to continue our vital work*. Note in these examples how **raise**

R

always takes an object (her hand . . . ; the topics . . . ; £1,200). **Raise** has the past tense and past participle *raised*. In AE, **raise** can mean to rear children and animals. In BE, **raise** in this sense is informal and *bring up* (for children) and *breed* (for animals) are standard.

raze *verb*, means to destroy something completely so that no trace remains: *I'd like to raze it and plough over the site like the Romans did with Carthage*.

rite

See WRITE.

road

See STREET.

road reflectors

See CATSEYES.

roast, fry

roast *verb, adjective & noun*. As a verb, this usually means to cook food such as meat or vegetables in an oven or over a fire: *We can have a coke brazier to roast some chestnuts*. Coffee beans are also *roasted*. Although the past tense and past participle are *roasted*, the adjective, unusually, is **roast**: *The dish of the day proved to be roast beef and Yorkshire pudding*. As a noun, **roast** means a joint of roast beef or other meat. Figuratively, a *roasting* is used informally in the sense of criticizing severely or very intensively: *The Prime Minister submitted his resignation after more than a week of public roasting*.
See ROASTING (GRILL).

fry *verb*, means to cook food in oil or fat in a pan: *Add the oil and deep fry the pork*. In the plural, *fries* is used especially in AE to mean potato chips. These are also called *French fries*. In AE slang, **fry** means to execute by means of the electric chair.

rob

See BURGLE.

rock, stone, pebble

rock *noun*, means the main solid surface of the earth: *The river eroded 150 feet of solid rock*. In this sense, **rock** is an uncountable noun. In the plural, *rocks* means an outcrop of **rock**: *Looking down he could watch the sea crashing against the rocks*. As a countable noun, a **rock** is a very large stone that may be too heavy for one person to lift. This is the normal usage in BE. In AE, **rock** also refers to small stones, thus British speakers may be surprised that Americans are strong enough to throw *rocks* at crows. However, this 'light' use of **rock** is now starting to appear in BE.
See BOULDER (BOLDER).

stone *noun*, means a piece of rocky mineral that can be found lying on the ground: *He crossed the river on the stepping stones*. In this sense it is a countable noun. As an uncountable noun, **stone** means the hard mineral that can be used as a building material: *It was a large house, made of old stone*.

pebble *noun*, means a small smooth stone that is found in or near water: *I picked up a pebble and flung it out to sea*.

> A *pebble* is smaller than a *stone*, which is smaller than a *rock*. Buildings are made of *stone*, which is hewn from *rock*.

rock bottom

See BOTTOM LINE.

rocket science, brain surgery

rocket science *uncountable noun*, is a phrase used to indicate how easy something is: *Changing the wheel on a car is hardly rocket science*.

brain surgery *uncountable noun*, is also a phrase used to show that something was easy to do: *Putting those shelves up wasn't exactly brain surgery*.

> Both these phrases are informal and imply a negative attitude in these contexts.

rode, rowed

rode *verb*, is the past tense of the verb to *ride*: *They rode for 10 miles* (on horses or two-wheeled vehicles). The past participle is *ridden*.

rowed *verb*, is the past tense of the verb to *row*: *They rowed for 10 miles* (in a rowing boat). The past participle is also **rowed**.

role, roll

role *noun*, means the character played by an actor in a play or film, or an activity or purpose involved in a particular job: *The club captain said his role might change under the new manager*.

roll *noun & verb*. As a noun, this means an official list of names: *The largest school taking part had 1,432 pupils on the roll*. It can also mean a small round individual loaf of bread, or a piece of paper made into the shape of a tube. As a verb, **roll** means to turn like a wheel or ball: *The children rolled down the hill*; or to wrap: *Roll one rasher of bacon around each sausage*.

Romany

See GYPSY.

room, hall, chamber

room *noun*, means part of the interior of a building with its own walls, floor and ceiling: *I saw him go into the room where the telephone is*. As an uncountable noun, **room** means space for a particular thing or activity: *She thanked him and made room for Tommy by her side*. This can include appetite: *He always had room for another burger*.

hall *noun*, is the entrance area just inside the front door of a building: *She ushered Melissa out of the room into a small entrance hall*. It is also a building or large room for public events: *One of our neighbours rang to say she'd booked the village hall*.

chamber *noun*, is a room in a public building: *They all sit together in the same circular chamber*. **Chamber** also means a legislature or other official organization: *This was done through the Council and the Chamber of Commerce*.

rouble, ruble, rubble

rouble *noun*, is the main currency unit in Russia. This is the preferred BE spelling. The first syllable is pronounced roo /ruː/.

ruble *noun*, is the AE spelling of rouble.

rubble *noun*, means waste fragments of stone, brick or concrete usually following demolition: *The rubble from the bombed buildings filled the street*.

round

See ABOUT.

round-the-clock

See DAY.

rouse

See ARISE.

route, itinerary, service

route *noun*, means the path taken to get from one place to another: *As always, he had mapped his route before setting out*. Figuratively, it can be a way of arriving at a particular result: *This economic policy is a certain route to disaster*.

itinerary *noun*, means a plan that lists the places passed through on a journey. This is often worked out for a single trip: *Included in the itinerary was a stopover on the way back in Bangkok*. Note that both 'r's in the word should be pronounced.

service *noun*, means an official system for providing regular travel by bus, coach, train, air or coastal routes: *Only one ferry company now offers a service between Dover and Boulogne*. See SERVICE (SERVE).

rowed

See RODE.

row house

See TOWN HOUSE.

rowing boat, rowboat

rowing boat *noun*, is a small boat propelled by oars. This is the BE spelling.

rowboat *noun*, is the AE form of rowing boat.

R

rubber

See **ERASER**.

rubble, ruble

See **ROUBLE**.

rubella

See **(MEASLES)**.

rucksack, backpack

rucksack *noun*, means a bag for carrying clothes or other supplies on the back especially when taking a long walk: *She had some T-shirts and two cuddly toys in her rucksack*. This is particularly a BE term.

backpack *noun*, is a bag carried on the back to leave the arms free. A *backpacker* is a person who is travelling for pleasure by economical means with all their possessions in a backpack: *He has been a backpacker for over 25 years*.
See **PACK (PACKAGE)**.

rules, regulations, stipulations

rules *noun*, are the principles by which something is governed or operated: *They accepted or doled out punishments according to the rules of the game*.

regulations *noun*, are rules that have the force of law: *Failure to comply with the regulations can result in a £2,000 fine or six-month prison sentence*.

stipulations *noun*, are conditions laid down in a contract: *You must follow the stipulations of the law in force at that time*.

rumour, gossip

rumour *noun*, means a story passed from one person to another, which may or may not be true: *Rumours of the death of the leader were proved wrong when a videotape showed him holding a recent newspaper*. It is also used as an uncountable noun: *The stock exchange was rife with rumour*.

gossip *noun & verb*. As a noun, this means news or information about people passed on informally, and often either unkind or untrue: *She grinned as if she was about to reveal an amazing piece of gossip*. A **gossip** is a person who likes commenting on others and spreading rumours. This is a disapproving term. As a verb, **gossip** means to exchange stories about people: *Daisy and Rose were gossiping in the pantry*.

run (for office)

See **STAND (FOR OFFICE)**.

rural area, countryside

rural area *noun phrase*, means a part of the country that is mostly farmland, with no settlements larger than villages.

countryside *uncountable noun*, means land outside towns. It includes farmland, woodland and land for grazing: *He built up a detailed knowledge of the countryside of Herefordshire*. Note that the term *the country* can be used to mean the same as **countryside**, but country without the definite article has numerous other meanings. See **COUNTRY**.

rutabaga

See **TURNIP**.

Spelling

rar**e**fied	-r**e**f-, not -r**i**f-
rec**ede**	See *-cede, -ceed, -sede*
rec**ei**ve	-**ei**-, not -**ie**-
re**c**o**mm**end	-**c**- and -**mm**-, not -**cc**- and -**m**-
rel**ie**f	-**ie**-, not -**ei**-
rel**ie**ve	-**ie**-, not -**ei**-
respons**i**ble	-**i**ble, not -**a**ble
restaur**at**eur	Note that there is no 'n' in this word
r**h**yt**h**m	Note that -h- occurs twice in this word
rig**o**rous	Note that there is only one -u- in this word

S

sack, sac

sack *noun*, means a large bag without handles. In AE, **sack** has the informal meaning of being in or going to bed: *I will hit the sack*. In BE, *to be given the sack* means to be fired. See **SACK (DISMISS)**.

sac *noun*, means a hollow flexible structure like a bag inside plants or animals: *This snake has venom in its sac*.

sacrifice, gambit, forfeit

sacrifice *noun & verb*. As a noun this means an offering of something valuable in order to gain something more valuable: *His parents made many sacrifices so that he could take a university education*. A **sacrifice** is also the slaughter of an animal or person for religious purposes. As a verb it means to give something that is important or valuable in order to gain something that is more important: *He suddenly sacrificed two pieces to expose his opponent's king*.

gambit *noun*, is technically an opening move in chess that involves a sacrifice: *He used his favourite castle gambit*. Avoid using the term *opening gambit* in chess, as all gambits are first moves. The word is also used to mean a particular tactic: *His gambit of looking pointedly at his watch made the latecomers uneasy*. Note that the idea of sacrifice is lost, but it still means something that is a calculated move.

forfeit *noun & verb*. As a noun, this means the penalty of having something taken away because of breaking a rule, of a game, for instance: *I'll happily pay my forfeit and sit here by the fire while you carry on playing*. As a verb, it means to lose something, because regulations have been broken: *On moving to Switzerland, he had forfeited his German citizenship*.

sacrilegious

See **IRRELIGIOUS**.

SAD

See **SEASONAL AFFECTIVE DISORDER**.

safe, secure

safe *adjective*, means being protected from harm or danger: *He devoted his life to making the village safe for children*. In another sense, it means unlikely to lead to physical harm: *When driving, always keep a safe distance from the car in front*.

secure *adjective & verb*. As an adjective, this means safe: *I like to feel secure at work*. **Secure** can also mean firmly fastened: *Check that posts are secure and there are no gaps in hedges*. The opposite of **secure** as an adjective is *insecure*. As a verb, it means to obtain something, especially as a result of effort: *We can secure the release of refugees if we can find them somewhere to live*; or to make certain of something: *His goal secured them a place in the Cup Final*. It can also mean to fasten something firmly: *Drill guide holes in the corner of the mitre and hammer home some pins to secure the joint while the glue sets*. The opposite in the sense of something that is not fastened or tied on firmly is *not secured*: *The part of the load that was not secured fell off the back of the lorry*.

safety, security

safety *uncountable noun*, means the condition of being protected from harm or the risk of injury: *A fire escape should be built to improve safety at the home*. **Safety** is also the state of not being dangerous: *car safety measures*.

security *uncountable noun*, means measures that are taken to keep a person, organization or country safe from a danger or threat: *An alarm should be fitted to improve security at the home*. **Security** is also protection against espionage, terrorism and theft: *Security awareness must be part of the company culture*. In another sense as a countable noun, **security** means an item of value used as a guarantee for a loan. In the plural, *securities* means stocks and bonds: *But other securities such as government bonds have their yields quoted before income tax*.

salary

See **PAY**.

saleable, salable

saleable *adjective*, means able to be sold: *There is considerable illegal trade in saleable antiquities*. This is the usual BE spelling, and an alternative spelling in AE.

salable *adjective*, is the usual AE spelling of *saleable*, and an alternative spelling in BE.

sales clerk

See SHOP ASSISTANT.

saline, salty

saline *adjective*, is a technical term that means containing salt: *Biopsy specimens were washed in a saline solution*. The related noun is *salinity*.

salty *adjective*, refers to a substance that contains or tastes of salt: *The soup was ruined – it was just too salty*. The related noun is *saltiness*.

salon, saloon

salon sálonn /'sælɒn/ *noun*, means a business that specializes in hairdressing (*hairdressing salon*), or beauty treatments (*beauty salon*): *This top London salon will work out a personalized hairdressing programme*. The first syllable is stressed and the second syllable is pronounced like the word 'on'.

saloon sălóon /sə'luːn/ *noun*, means a public room on a ship, or a bar where alcoholic drinks are sold: *They moved into the saloon bar*. This is a BE term. In AE this is a historical term for a bar. The second syllable is stressed, and rhymes with 'moon'.

saloon car, sedan

saloon car *noun*, means a five-seater family car that has a boot: It is also called a *saloon*. This term is mainly used when there is a contrast with other types of car, such as a hatchback or 4 × 4. See ESTATE CAR.

sedan *noun*, is the AE term for a *saloon car*.

saltwater, salt water

saltwater *adjective*, usually refers to plants or animals that live in salty water or the sea: *The secretary is also a keen saltwater angler*. This term is used as a contrast to *freshwater*.

salt water *noun*, is the phrase used to refer to seawater: *The largest proportion is in the oceans, which hold roughly 1,370,000,000 (1.37 billion) cubic kilometres of salt water*.

> Note that the adjective is written as a single word and the noun is written as two words. They are both stressed on the first syllable.

salty

See SALINE.

salutations

See WRITING SKILLS.

same-sex marriage, civil partnership

same-sex marriage *noun*, means a marital agreement governing a relationship between people of the same sex. This is legally recognized as a *civil partnership* in the UK.

civil partnership *noun*, means an official relationship between two people of the same sex that gives them the same legal rights as two people who are married: *The Civil Partnership Act 2004 came into operation on 5 December 2005 and enables a same-sex couple to register as civil partners of each other*.

sanction, sanctions

sanction *noun & verb*. As a noun, this means official permission or approval: *The ambassador started these negotiations without the official sanction of his government*. As a verb, **sanction** means to officially accept or allow something: *The measures were sanctioned by the General Assembly*. On the other hand, **sanction** also means the opposite – to impose a penalty: *The Security Council agreed to sanction Iran*.

sanctions *noun*, means the measures that one state or body takes to try to force another state or body to behave in accordance with international law: *Economic sanctions were imposed as a last resort*.

satisfactory, satisfying

satisfactory *adjective*, refers to something that is acceptable and good enough for a particular purpose: *The essay was satisfactory but not outstanding*.

satisfying *adjective*, means giving fulfilment or pleasure: *Cooking the traditional Sunday lunch gave him a warm, satisfying feeling*.

satisfied, certain

satisfied *adjective*, means pleased because something has developed in the way intended, or happy because a desired event has occurred. In another sense **satisfied** means being sure or convinced of something. Thus it is necessary to use **satisfied** with caution in an ambiguous context: *The pilot said that he was satisfied that the rocket hit the house*. This raises the question whether he was pleased that he had hit the target, or was convinced that he had.

certain *adjective*, means being sure and confident of something without any doubts: *He was certain that the rocket had not hit the house*. In another sense, when it is preceded by *a*, it means that the speaker cannot be more precise: *There was a certain air of worry about him*.

sauce

See GRAVY.

savanna(h)

See PRAIRIE.

sawn-off shotgun, sawed-off shotgun

sawn-off shotgun *noun*, means a shotgun with part of its barrel cut off. This is a BE term.

sawed-off shotgun *noun*, means a *sawn-off shotgun*. This is the AE term.

scales

See BALANCE.

Scandinavia, Nordic countries

Scandinavia *proper noun*, has both geographical and cultural definitions:

- The countries of Norway, Sweden and Denmark (geographical).
- The countries of Norway, Sweden, Denmark, Iceland, Finland and often the Faroe Islands (cultural).

Nordic countries *noun*, means Norway, Sweden, Denmark, Iceland, Finland and the Faeroe Islands. This is also known as the Nordic region.

scapegoat, stalking horse

scapegoat *noun*, means someone who gets the blame for an action done by someone else, or for a failure: *The British egg industry was made a scapegoat for food poisoning by the government*. In AE this is called the 'fall guy'.

stalking horse *noun*, means someone or something that is used to conceal the true purpose of an action. In politics the **stalking horse** challenges a political leader, but does not have any real aspiration to leadership: *The stalking horse would bring serious challengers into the leadership race*.

scarcely

See BARELY.

scarcity, shortage

scarcity *noun*, means a situation where there is an insufficient amount of common resources such as food and money: *The scarcity of local currency precipitated a dramatic rise in its value against the US dollar*.

shortage *noun*, means a situation where something that is needed is not available, or there is not enough of a key resource: *The storm damage resulted in a shortage of oil-refining capacity*.

> A *scarcity* may be created deliberately in order to maintain the value of something, such as prestige fashion items, while a *shortage* means there is just not enough of something.

S

scatological

See ESCHATOLOGICAL.

scenery, landscape

scenery *uncountable noun*, means the natural features of a particular region or place, particularly when they are attractive to look at: *The place has always attracted writers and artists and lovers of strange and dramatic scenery*. **Scenery** can also mean the painted hangings or movable set on the stage of a theatre.

landscape *noun*, means all the features of an area of land that are visible, and usually refers to a rural environment: *We turned course southwards to a queer featureless* *world, flat and muddy, with a shifting landscape*. In art, a **landscape** is a painting of the countryside.

> *Scenery* implies an attractive vista but *landscape* is simply descriptive of what the land looks like.

sceptic, sceptical

See **CYNIC**.

sceptre, scepter

sceptre *noun*, means an ornamental staff carried by rulers during formal ceremonies. This is the spelling in BE.

scepter *noun*, is the AE spelling of *sceptre*.

> Note that the 'c' is silent.

schedule, timetable

schedule shéddewl /ˈʃedjuːl/ (BE) skéddewl /ˈskedjuːl/ (AE and BE) *noun*, means a plan with the dates and activities for the future: *The professor had a full schedule for the next term*. See **DIARY**.

timetable *noun*, means a list of times of planned events, for instance arrival and departure times of public transport or planned teaching in school: *He had the winter timetable for the local bus service*.

> In the context of travel times and routes in AE, *schedule* is the equivalent of *timetable* in BE, e.g. *train schedule* in AE; *train timetable* in BE.

scheme

See **BLUEPRINT**.

scholar, scholarly, fellow (academic)

scholar *noun*, means a learned person, teacher or researcher in the classics, arts and humanities, or other non-scientific disciplines: *She was a Latin scholar*. It can also mean the holder of a scholarship such as *a Rhodes Scholar*. See **ACADEMIC, LECTURER**.

scholarly *adjective*, refers to serious academic study: *a scholarly paper*. This is used only in a positive sense. **Scholarly** can also be used to describe a person who is studious, learned or engaged in university research.

fellow *noun*, has different meanings in BE and AE. In BE it is a member of a prestigious academic body such as *Fellow of the Royal Society* or a very senior member of a university or college: *a Fellow of King's*. **Fellow** in this sense is often capitalized. In AE, it means a graduate student of either sex receiving a fellowship to support study at master's or doctoral levels: *He was a Fulbright Fellow*.

scholarship, grant, bursary, stipend

scholarship *noun*. As a countable noun, this means the financial support granted to a student usually related to paying the fees for a place to study: *He won a scholarship to the LSE*. As an uncountable noun, **scholarship** means the achievements of a scholar: *Admirers of his scholarship dedicated a statue in his honour*. In another sense it means a body of academic knowledge: *the scholarship of the ancient Greeks*. In this sense, it is also an uncountable noun.

grant *noun*, means financial support, which may come from different bodies: a *government grant* means financial support for a university or organization. Individuals may receive a *travel grant* or a *research grant*.

bursary *noun*, means financial support for an individual so that they can study at a college or university. This is a BE term: *Afterwards a bursary from the school enabled him to continue his studies at the university*.

stipend *noun*, in BE, means a sum of money (in effect a salary) regularly paid to a member of the clergy: *Most of the stipend at Durham came from the canonry*. **Stipend** in AE means a sum of money such as a scholarship paid to any category of student.

school, college

school *noun*, generally covers institutions for compulsory education. In most of Britain a school is pre-university level, but in AE it can mean any level including post-compulsory and even university. A **school** can be a vocational training establishment such as a *secretarial school*. In AE, parts of universities are usually known as **schools**. This is equivalent to the faculty in many European universities. This is occasionally used in UK higher education for the name of a specialized part of a university, such as the *School of Oriental and African Studies*. See **FACULTY (FACILITY)**.

college *noun*, can refer to an independent secondary school, such as Eton College. It can also refer to adult education and higher education institutions such as *art college*; and non-specialized units within a university – *Trinity College, Dublin*; *Imperial College, London*. Some professional bodies in the UK also use the term **college**: *Royal College of Surgeons*. In AE, **college** is used for institutions in adult education and higher education, and usually refers to vocational training institutions, or specialized units within a university. *College of Engineering* in AE may be the equivalent to the Faculty of Engineering at many European universities. See **HIGH SCHOOL**, **UNIVERSITY**.

scientist

See **ACADEMIC**.

Scots/Scottish, Scot, Scotch

Scots/Scottish *adjectives*, means people from Scotland, who are generally described as **Scots** or **Scottish**. **Scots** is used particularly for *Scots pine*, and *Scots accent*, while **Scottish** is the more general term. As a noun, **Scots** is used to refer to the distinctive Germanic language of Scotland, which has many grammatical as well as lexical differences from the English used in England. See **GAELIC**.

Scot *noun*, means a person who comes from Scotland. This is the only one of this group of words that can be used as a noun in this way: *It was a great triumph for a Scot who learnt his rowing at Oxford*.

Scotch *adjective & noun*, is used mostly for whisky. Calling the people of Scotland *the Scotch* is likely to insult both drinkers and teetotal *Scotsmen* and *Scotswomen* alike, although in former times, it was common for Scots to refer to themselves as 'Scotch'. The word **Scotch** is used in a few expressions such as *Scotch broth* and *Scotch egg*. Note that there is at least one brand of **scotch** which includes 'Scots' in its name. See **FERMENT**.

scrutinize

See **EXAMINE**.

scull

See **SKULL**.

sea, seas, ocean

sea *noun*, means the large areas of salty water that cover most of the earth's surface, or a defined area covered by salt water such as the Caspian Sea, North Sea or the Mediterranean Sea: *The challenges of getting oil from the North Sea are solved and now we face deeper waters*.

seas *noun*, either means the plural of *sea* or it means waves, particularly large waves: *They were rocked by the heavy seas*. The phrase *the seven seas* is a poetic way of referring to all the earth's oceans.

ocean *noun*, means very large expanses of *sea* that cover most of the earth's surface. There are five *oceans*: Atlantic, Pacific, Indian, Arctic and Antarctic: *The Barents Sea borders the Arctic Ocean*.

> When describing a large expanse of salt water in general terms, BE uses *sea* and AE often uses *ocean*.

seabed, sea floor

S

seabed *noun*, means the ground under the sea: *The pipeline followed the contours of the seabed*.

sea floor *noun & adjective*. As a noun, this is an alternative name for the *seabed*: *This creature lives half-buried in the sand of the sea floor*. As an adjective, **sea floor** is hyphenated: *With this discovery the concept of sea-floor spreading was almost universally accepted*. Geologists often distinguish between the **sea floor** and the *seabed*, the **sea floor** being the layer below the seabed.

seasonal, seasonable, seasoned

seasonal *adjective*, means happening or required during a particular season: *He also weeds the existing beds, prunes the roses and, as well as all the other seasonal jobs, cuts the lawns and hedges*. In another sense it means typical of a particular season: *This year our seasonal fare is orange-date, pumpkin and Christmas muffins*. The phrases *season's greetings* or *seasonal greetings* are often used by large organizations on Christmas cards to avoid using Christian terminology like 'Merry Christmas'. See **CHRISTMAS**.

seasonable *adjective*, means usual or suited to a particular time of year: *All the children on board will have the opportunity to meet Santa, receive a gift from him and enjoy the seasonable atmosphere*.

seasoned *adjective*, means either containing spices: *He was renowned for his well-seasoned curry*; or someone who is experienced in a specific job or activity: *The club finally signed a seasoned goalie*.

seasonal affective disorder, SAD

seasonal affective disorder *uncountable noun*, is a medical condition which makes somebody feel tired and depressed due to the lack of sunlight. This is typical of the late autumn and winter: *The specialist believes that anyone suffering from excessive sleepiness only during the winter months may suffer from seasonal affective disorder*.

SAD *acronym*, means seasonal affective disorder. **SAD** must be a perfect acronym, as it is read as 'sad'.

seasons, terms used

In some parts of the world the seasons are described as *dry* or *rainy*. In other parts, *summer* or *winter* seasons are sufficient. In Europe, there are four seasons: *spring*, *summer*, *autumn* and *winter*. In AE, *fall* is used instead of *autumn*. See **AUTUMN**.

second a motion

See **TABLE A MOTION**.

secondment, second (work)

secondment *noun*, means a period of temporary duty doing a different job usually in another sector: *He is a banker who previously spent two years on secondment to the Department of Industry*.

second *verb*, means to send a member of staff to another office or sector to do different work for a temporary period: *I was seconded to a public relations unit, run by a delightful and eccentric colonel*.

Note that the pronunciation of these two words is sěkóndměnt /sɪˈkɒndmənt/ and sěkónd /sɪˈkɒnd/, with stress on the second syllable.

second-rate

See **MEDIOCRE**.

secretary

See **MINISTER**.

secular, sectarian

secular *adjective*, means non-religious: *Chantrell's secular buildings were in the Greek Revival manner, notably the South Market at Leeds*. Note that if clergy are termed **secular**, this refers to the members of the Church who reside among ordinary people, not within a religious community: *Much Catholic power lies with secular clergy*. In economics, it refers to the persistence of a trend over a long period: *This is mainly the result of the secular fall in interest rates*.

sectarian *adjective*, means related to the differences found between groups often with different religions or denominations: *He went on to stress the likelihood of sectarian clashes had the procession followed the original route*. As **sectarian** literally means belonging to a sect, it can be used in non-religious contexts where it may signal a disapproving attitude towards the group.

secure

See **SAFE**.

security

See **SAFETY**.

sedan

See **SALOON CAR**.

-sede

See **-CEDE**.

seer

See **PROPHET**.

seldom

See **RARE**.

select

See CHOOSE.

sell-by date, use-by date, shelf life

sell-by date *noun*, is the date printed on perishable goods after which they may not be sold. It is also used in an extended sense: *This government is well past its sell-by date.* In AE this is called the 'pull date'.

use-by date *noun*, is the date on perishable goods that shows that they may be unsafe to eat after this date. Many products include the words 'best before' on their packaging.

shelf life *noun*, means the length of time perishable goods can be kept on the shelves in shops, before they reach the *sell-by date*. This is often used figuratively when talking about professions where updating and retraining are required: *Bill believes that the shelf life of an engineer is only about five years.*

semester

See TERM.

semi-, demi-, hemi-

semi- means exactly half as in *semicircle*, or partly, as in *semiconscious*. Unlike *demi-* and *hemi-*, below, **semi-** is used for making new words. Examples include: *semi-automatic, semicolon, semiconductor, semi-final* (consult a dictionary to check if there is hyphenation or not). The pronunciation sémmi- /'semi-/ is normal in BE, while semmī- /'semaɪ-/ is standard in AE.

demi- means half or partly. It is generally used in connection with words of French origin such as *demi-pension* and *demi-sec*.

hemi- means half and is used in connection with terms of Greek origin such as *hemisphere*.

> These three words that all mean half illustrate the richness of English: *semi-* comes from Latin, *demi-* comes from French and *hemi-* comes from Greek.

semicolon (;)

See PUNCTUATION GUIDE.

semi-detached house, duplex

semi-detached house *noun*, means a house joined to another house on one side. This is also informally known as a *semi*.
See DETACHED HOUSE.

duplex *noun*, is the AE term for a *semi-detached house*, as well as for a residential building divided into two flats. In AE and BE, a *duplex apartment/flat* means a unit with two floors.

semi-monthly

See FORTNIGHTLY.

seminar

See CONGRESS.

semi-weekly, biweekly

semi-weekly *adjective*, means twice a week. Note that the pronunciation sémmi- /'semi-/ is normal in BE, while sémmī- /'semaɪ-/ is standard in AE.

biweekly *adjective & noun*, means either twice a week or every two weeks. Avoid this ambiguous word and use either *twice weekly* or *fortnightly*. See FORTNIGHTLY.

send

See PASS.

senior

See FRESHMAN, SENIOR CITIZEN (PENSIONER).

senior citizen

See PENSIONER.

senior lecturer

See LECTURER.

sensible, sensitive, insensible, insensitive

sensible *adjective*, refers to the ability to be reasonable and practical and to show good judgement: *For once, those who commanded the armed forces made a sensible decision.* Practical furniture and clothing are termed **sensible** if they are comfortable and hard-wearing rather than trendy. If one is *sensible* *of* something, this is a formal term that means being aware of it: *They were sensible of the fact that maths is not a popular subject among children in general*.

sensitive *adjective*, means quick to react to changes: *Further developments include more sensitive hydrocarbon sensors, so that oil pollution can be spotted more quickly*. **Sensitive** also means easily upset: *He was sensitive about his baldness*. It can also refer to a person's skin that can easily be bruised or damaged. The word also refers to objects that can be harmed or damaged: *The environment here is too sensitive to allow mass tourism*. Companies often term their commercial secrets, *sensitive information*.

insensible *adjective*, means without feeling or unconscious: *He'd locked himself in their room and drunk himself insensible*. Note that even though it has the prefix 'in', this word is not the opposite of *sensible* in most contexts, and silly, stupid, ridiculous, impractical are used to express the opposite of *sensible* when referring to judgements, furniture and clothing. However, when *sensible* is used formally, one can use **insensible** to express someone's lack of awareness: *He was not insensible to the ideal of the aristocratic amateur in the arts*. (Note that this word is frequently used as part of a double negative.)

insensitive *adjective*, means not influenced by adverse criticism or not caring how someone feels: *She learnt how to be insensitive and ignore the reporters*. **Insensitive** can also mean bodily reactions to pain: *His feet were so cold that they were totally insensitive to pain*.

sensor

See **CENSOR**.

sensual, sensuous

sensual *adjective*, refers to bodily rather than mental feelings, especially physical pleasure connected particularly with sex: *sensual lips*, *sensual desire* and *sensual appearance*.

sensuous *adjective*, means related to the senses, not the intellect. Thus it can suggest that someone is interested in sexual pleasure: *Katherine gazed at the girl's openly sensuous movements*.

> As *sensual* and *sensuous* are closely related to sexual pleasure, words such as stimulating and enjoyable may be used to describe non-sexual pleasure.

septic

See **CYNIC**.

sequence of events

See **STRING (OF)**.

sequestration

See **STOCKPILE**.

serendipity, serendipitous

serendipity *noun*, means the accidental occurrence and development of an event, an accidental discovery: *Post-it is based on a glue that failed, a case of serendipity for the manufacturers*.

serendipitous *adjective*, refers to discoveries that are fortunate as well as accidental.

serf

See **SURF**.

sergeant, lieutenant

sergeant *noun*, is a non-commissioned rank in the army or air force. In Britain, a **sergeant** is the rank between constable and inspector in the police force. In the US, a **sergeant** is a police officer below the rank of lieutenant.

lieutenant *noun*, lefténnănt /lef'tenənt/ (BE Army), lŏŏténnănt /lʊ'tenənt/ (BE Navy and AE) is a middle-rank officer in the army and navy below captain. When used in compounds, it means an officer just below the rank mentioned, thus a *lieutenant colonel* is the rank just below colonel. In the US, it is the police officer rank above sergeant.

> Two spelling tips: *serge* + *ant* and *lieu* + *tenant*.

series, *serial*, *cereal*

series *noun*, means several events of a similar type or events that occur one after the other but not necessarily close in time: *The series of lectures on computer science started last year*. A TV or radio **series** is a regular programme that is broadcast one or more times a week: *'Star Trek' is a TV series that has been running for decades*. **Series** does not change from the singular to plural: *This series is . . . ; These series are. . . .*

serial *noun & adjective*. As a noun, this is a book, radio or TV programme that is published or broadcast in instalments: *'Lord of the Rings' was broadcast as a 26-part radio serial*. As an adjective, **serial** describes a phenomenon that happens repeatedly and in the same way, such as a *serial killer*. The verb *serialize* and its derivative noun *serialization* are used to describe the publication of extracts from a book in successive issues of a newspaper or magazine. A book published in sections is known as a 'part work'.

cereal *noun*, is a general term for grain. In this context, it is often used in the plural: *The price of cereals is going up*. It also means a type of breakfast food, made mainly from grain, and in this context it may be used in the singular: *This cereal is an old favourite*.

The difference between a *series* and a *serial* is that each episode of a *series* is self-contained, whereas a *serial* has a single ongoing story.

serious, grave

serious *adjective*, means important: *The university has 50,000 students, and parking is a serious business*; as well as sincere: *Our discussions were serious and well informed*; not joking: *Rose was serious when she said she was leaving*; and significant: *A more serious complication of diabetes is damage to the retina*. **Serious** is also used informally to mean a large quantity: *He earns a serious amount of money*.

grave *adjective & noun*. As an adjective, this means very worrying: *The economic and financial crisis is grave and growing graver by the hour*. **Grave** can also mean solemn: *My doctor's manner was so grave as to imply danger to my life*. As a noun, **grave** means a hole in the ground used as a place of burial.

serve, service

serve *verb*, means to give somebody food or drink, usually in a restaurant: *Serve these customers the dessert immediately*. **Serve** also means to help customers in a shop or meet the needs of something: *The road is totally unsuitable to serve a further housing development*. It can also mean to be useful or suitable: *How well does the government serve the interests of the business community?* In formal contexts, **serve** means to work for a company, organization or country: *He was not the first of his family to serve the English crown*.

service *verb*, is a less general verb than *serve*. It means to examine a vehicle or machine, repairing it if necessary: *Maintenance crews soon learned how to service the plane*. In business English, the expression to *service a debt* means to pay interest on money borrowed: *These African countries have been unable to service their debts*. It can also mean provide support to another group: *They service the regional telecommunications industry*. See SERVICE (ROUTE).

session

See CESSION.

settee

See SOFA.

setting

See ENVIRONMENT.

S

settlement

See PAYMENT, VILLAGE.

several

See FEW.

severe

See STRICT.

sew, sow

sew *verb*, means to use a needle and thread to make stitches in order to repair clothes or fasten a button to clothing. The past tense of **sew** is *sewed*, and the past participle either *sewn* or *sewed*: *She sewed her wedding gown herself*. Informally as a phrasal verb with 'up' **sew** can mean to arrange things in a satisfactory way: *Unix sewed up a deal last week with IBM*. A related noun is *sewer*, sṓ-ĕr /ˈsəʊər/, meaning a seamstress sémstrĕss /ˈsemstrəs/ (for a female) or a person who sews clothes. This rhymes with 'lower' and must not be confused with sewer, séw-ĕr or sóo-ĕr /ˈsjuːər/ See SEWER (SEWAGE).

sow *verb*, means to plant or scatter seeds on an area of ground: *Sow the grass seed thinly*. The past tense is *sowed*, and the past participle is either *sowed* or *sown*. A figurative meaning of **sow** occurs in the idiom to *sow the seeds of something*, meaning to try to spread ideas or feelings that may have a widespread effect: *The school hosted a symposium on medical education which sowed the seeds of curriculum reform in the minds of many of the staff*.

> Note that *sew, sewn* and *sewed* are pronounced the same as *sow, sown* and *sowed*.

sewage, sewer, sewerage

sewage séw-ij or sóo-ij /ˈsjuːɪdʒ/ *uncountable noun*, means a mixture of waste water and excrement that is transported away from housing in underground pipelines: *Raw sewage was pumped and mixed with treated sewage*. A *sewage farm* is a processing plant and a *sewage works* is usually designed for recycling **sewage**: *Septic tanks are more like miniature sewage works and rely on the action of bacteria to break down the sewage into harmless liquid and sludge*.

sewer séw-ĕr or sóo-ĕr /ˈsjuːər/ *noun*, is the underground pipe through which *sewage* is removed: *The term 'drain' refers to a single house, whereas 'sewer' refers to a collective system serving more than one property*. Do not confuse this with 'sewer', sṓ-ĕr /ˈsəʊər/, which means a seamstress sémstrĕss /ˈsemstrəs/ (for a female) or a person who sews clothes. See SEW.

sewerage *uncountable noun*, means the system that carries waste material in *sewers* as well as the treatment and processing of *sewage*: *Severn Trent provides water and sewerage services to 8 million customers*.

sex, gender

sex *noun*, means the set of characteristics that make up the biological differences between males and females: *In blackbirds, the sexes are clearly different*. It also means the act of copulation: *Sex is a natural way of expressing human feelings but sometimes there are risks*. Otherwise **sex** combines with many other nouns to form terms like: *sex discrimination, safe sex, sex typing, sex worker* which have carefully defined meanings. It is always best to consult an authoritative dictionary before using such terms.

gender *noun*, means the fact of being male or female. It emphasizes the social and cultural aspects of being a male or female. Thus *gender gap, gender roles, gender models* are phrases that stress culture, not biology. **Gender** is also a grammatical term used to name classes of nouns. In some languages, like French, other parts of speech, such as pronouns, take the **gender** of the noun they refer to. In English, pronouns agree only with the *sex* of the noun they stand for, and **gender** has no relevance: male creatures are 'he', female ones are 'she', and all inanimate objects are 'it', with the rare exception of ships, and occasionally favourite land or air vehicles, which may be referred to as 'she'. But even this is dying out. Living creatures whose sex is either irrelevant or unknown may be called 'they', in order to avoid attaching a sex label to them.

> As someone once said, tongue in cheek: 'Remember that words have gender, plants and animals have sex.'

sexist language

See WRITING SKILLS.

sexually transmitted disease, venereal disease

sexually transmitted disease *noun*, means a disease that is spread through sexual intercourse, such as syphilis. The modern abbreviation is *STD*: *The frequency of sexually transmitted diseases among young teenagers is worrying*.

venereal disease *noun*, means a disease spread through sexual intercourse. This is an older term than the equivalent *sexually transmitted disease* and is abbreviated to *VD*.

shade, shadow

shade *noun & verb*. As a noun this means a place of relative darkness and coolness sheltered from the sun: *I chose the deep shade of the palm grove*. **Shade** is also used to distinguish how light or dark a colour is: *many rich shades of purple*. It is also used for objects that reduce the intensity of light such as *lampshade* and informally *shades* (sunglasses). As a verb it means to stop direct light from the sun or a lamp by means of a screen, a parasol or vegetation: *The trees shaded the courtyard*. See TONE.

shadow *noun, verb & adjective*. As a noun, this means either a dark area or a clear sharply defined shape made by the shade of someone or something. As a verb, **shadow** means either to be covered by a shadow: *But will its pre-eminence be shadowed by the reunification of Germany?* or to follow: *No matter how fast he covered the ground, his every move was shadowed*. As an adjective, it is used to refer to politicians in the UK who are in the opposition and are ready to be government ministers if their party comes into power: *The Shadow Cabinet were all in a meeting*.

shall, will

shall *verb*. **Shall** is often used with a first-person pronoun when asking questions or making offers and requests: *Shall I get you a coffee?* or *Shall we dance?* Otherwise, it is becoming less common in modern English than it was a couple of generations ago. It often feels old-fashioned to use **shall**, almost like a command. In legal texts or regulations **shall** is often used to show that there is no doubt: *Suppliers shall be liable for the VAT charge*. In general, **shall** is used less in AE than in BE.

will *verb*, means going to, and is the usual way to express the future: *I will have to walk home*. As *shall* is often considered old-fashioned today, **will** is the common replacement. This is partly explained by the contracted use of the *'ll* form, as in *I'll open the door* which could be either *shall* or *will*. See CONTRACTIONS.

> *Shall* and *will* distinguish the meaning in some contexts: *Shall we get a drink?* (Would you like one with me?) and *Will we get a drink?* (Do you know whether they will give us one?)

share

See PART[2].

sharp, sharply

sharp *adjective & adverb*. As an adjective, this means having a thin edge or point that can cut things easily such as a *sharp knife*; or a sudden rise or fall: *a sharp rise in share prices*. If someone is **sharp**, they are either quick on the uptake: *the child's razor-sharp intelligence*; or they can be angry: *Her mother was always sharp to me*. As an adverb **sharp** means abruptly: *Turn sharp right*; or to be punctual: *Be there at 9 sharp*.

sharply *adverb*, means either harshly: *Speak sharply to those children*; suddenly or rapidly: *The stock market fell sharply last week*. It is also used with verbs like stand out and contrast.

she

See HE.

shear, sheer

shear *verb*, means either to cut the wool off sheep, or to deform and break a metal, as a result of structural strain: *The wing sheared off the plane*. The past tense form of both uses is *sheared*, but the past participle forms are *shorn* and *sheared* respectively.

sheer *adjective & verb*. As an adjective, this is used to emphasize the size of something: *He concluded that the 'Oxford English*

Dictionary' was the most suitable due to its sheer size. **Sheer** also means utter or complete: *Buying that house was sheer extravagance.* As a verb, **sheer** means to swerve or change course quickly: *The car suddenly sheered off the road.*

> *'The proper season for sheering sheep . . .'*
> (from an essay on sheep sheering (sic.) from www.njcu.edu)
> **!**

shelf, shelve, pigeonhole

shelf *noun*, means a narrow flat board attached to a wall or in a cupboard for placing books or ornaments on. The only plural is *shelves*. If something is *off the shelf* that means it is standard: *Off-the-shelf software*. If a person is *on the shelf* this is an informal expression that means too old or no longer useful for a specific purpose. See SHELF LIFE (SELL-BY DATE).

shelve *verb*, means to place books on a shelf. By extension it means to decide not to continue with a plan or to put things aside: *We have been forced to shelve our plans to hire new staff*. If the ground *shelves*, it slopes gently downwards. See TABLE.

pigeonhole *verb*, means to put something aside: *Plans for the new bypass have been pigeonholed*. It also means to place someone or something in a category which may not be accurate: *Companies love to pigeonhole their customers according to the goods they buy*. This comes from the small boxes on a wall used for putting letters and messages inside.

ship

See BOAT.

shop assistant, sales clerk

shop assistant *noun*, means someone whose job is to help customers in a shop.

sales clerk *noun*, means *shop assistant*. This is an AE term. *Clerk* is pronounced **klurk** /klɜːrk/ in AE, but **klark** /klɑːrk/ in BE. See CLERK.

shopping centre

See SUPERMARKET.

short, shortly

short *adjective & adverb*. As an adjective, this refers to a limited distance, measurement or duration. A person who is **short** may be below average height. If you are **short** with someone this means being rude and unfriendly towards them: *He was extremely short on the phone*. As an adverb, **short** means that there is not enough of something. This may be distance: *The rocket stopped short of its target*; or time: *He was cut short in the middle of the speech*.

shortly *adverb*, means soon when referring to the future: *I'll be ready shortly*. It also means in a short time, which can be either in the past or the future: *He arrived shortly after dinner*. **Shortly** also means sharply: *'It may take longer than that', he said rather shortly*.

short form

See CONTRACTIONS, FORMAL ENGLISH (WRITING SKILLS).

shortage

See SCARCITY.

should, ought to, must, have to

should *verb*, is used to say what is the right and sensible thing to do. It also means to give advice or to say which action is best and appropriate: *I think that we should stop this farce, here and now*. **Should** can also be used to give instructions politely: *You should always use safety glasses when operating this machine*. Note that **should** is followed by the infinitive without *to*: *You should see that film*. **Should** can be used to talk about something that is expected to happen: *He should be home by 6*.

ought to *verb*, is used to say what is the right thing to do, to give advice or to say which action is best: *In a common curriculum, everyone ought to study English*. Note that **ought** is infinitive without *to*. **Ought to** is used to talk about something that is expected to happen or it is hoped will happen: *He ought to be home by 6*.

must *verb*, is used to say that something is necessary or very important (often referring to a rule or a law): *To qualify for this support you must be responsible for one or more children aged under 16*. It is also used to give advice, especially when speaking persuasively and enthusiastically about something: *You must read these books, they are fantastic*. Note that **must** is only used in the present tense, and it is followed by the infinitive without *to*.

have to *verb*, is used to emphasize that something must be done: *To qualify for this support you have to document that you are responsible for one or more children aged under 16*. It is also used to give advice or make a recommendation: *All students have to read the following books*. Note that **have** is followed by *to*. As *must* is only used in the present, use **have to** if you want to express obligation in the past or future tenses.

sibling, stepbrother, stepsister, half-brother, half-sister

sibling *noun*, means a brother or sister or two or more children with a common parent. The term is usually restricted to academic writing and can be used where the sex of the child referred to is irrelevant: *Her parents had been very aware of the problems of sibling rivalry when the younger child was born*.

stepbrother, stepsister *noun*, is the son or daughter of a step-parent, i.e. not the biological parent.

half-brother *noun*, means a brother with whom you share one parent.

half-sister *noun*, means a sister with whom you share one parent.

sic

See NB.

sick

See ILL.

sick building syndrome

See SYNDROME.

side, hand

(On one) side *prepositional phrase*, usually means a specific position, such as *the sun shone on one side of the valley*. If you want to contrast this with something else, use 'the other side' for the second object: *The other side of the valley was in the shadow of the mountain*. See PARTY.

(On the one) hand *prepositional phrase*, is used to introduce different points of view or ideas, particularly when they are opposites: *On the one hand there was the central government and its economic and taxation strategy; on the other hand was the club*. Often the second 'hand' is omitted. *They removed the artificial distinction between universities on the one hand and polytechnics and colleges on the other*.

sidewalk

See PAVEMENT.

sight

See SITE.

sign, signal

sign *noun*, means an event or action that indicates that something is happening or is true: *These flowers are the first distinct sign of spring*. This is commonly used as a negative: *little sign of, no sign of*, etc. It also gives information on a piece of paper or metal such as *a road sign*.

signal *noun*, means a sound or action that is made to tell another person what to do: *When he started clearing the table it was a clear signal that it was time to go*. It can also give a *sign* of something: *In the rest of Europe, what you wear on your feet is seen as a crystal-clear signal of your professional status*. Here, *sign* and **signal** overlap in use. However a **signal** can give a warning.

> Note that if there is no reaction to a *sign*, a positive reaction to a *signal* is expected: *After he drove past the stop sign, the police made a clear signal that he had to pull over*.

signed by

See P.P..

significant

See MAJOR.

silicon, silicone

silicon síllikŏn /ˈsɪlɪkən/ *uncountable noun*, is a non-metallic chemical element (chemical symbol Si), that exists as a solid or powder. It can be used to make glass and computer chips: *Silicon Valley produces computers and electronic products, not silicon*.

silicone síllikōn /ˈsɪlɪkəʊn/ *uncountable noun*, is a chemical containing silicon. There are several types and products range from paints to flexible plastics for, among other things, human breast implants.

silk, silky

silk *noun*, means the thread made from the fibre produced by silkworms: *She wore a delicate silk dress*.

silky *adjective*, is used for things that are soft, smooth and shiny like silk: *the cat's silky fur*. A person's voice can be termed **silky** if it is smooth and gentle.

silver

See HAIR COLOUR.

similar, like, alike, as if

similar *adjective*, means almost the same or having a resemblance to a thing or person without being identical: *The weather was similar to the severe smog episodes in Los Angeles*. Note that **similar** is often used together with *to* and is more formal than *like*.

like *preposition & conjunction*. As a preposition, this means having the same characteristics or qualities as some other person or thing: *To the interviewer, the victim looks like a frightened rabbit*. (Note that *similar* could not be used here.) It can also indicate an example: *Food like eggs and cheese should be avoided for the next week*; or something that is typical: *It is just like the Italians to arrive late*. As a conjunction, **like** is used in informal contexts such as: *He acts like he owns the world*. In a more formal context, replace **like** with *as if*.

alike *adjective & adverb*. As an adjective, this indicates that two or more people, animals or things are similar: *They became really good friends because they were very alike*. As an adverb it is used to add the idea of 'both' or 'equally' to the groups of people referred to: *He was adored by the whole camp, men and women alike*.

as if *conjunction*, indicates a comparison or makes a suggestion about something: *He acts as if he owns the world*. There must always be a clause containing a verb after **as if**.

simple, simplistic

simple *adjective*, means not difficult, easily understood, plain and uncomplicated: *KISS stands for 'keep it short and simple'*.

simplistic *adjective*, means less difficult in appearance than in reality: *'Your views are too simplistic for me', said the young politician loftily*. **Simplistic** is a disapproving term that conveys the idea of being naïve and unsophisticated which are alternative terms.

simulation

See STIMULATION.

sink, submerged, sunken

sink *verb*, means to go below the surface of water or move towards the bottom. This has the past form *sank* and the past participle is *sunk*.

submerged *adjective*, means being below the surface of water or a liquid. Figuratively it can mean hidden: *Questions that had been submerged have now surfaced and have been rephrased*. See IMMERSE.

sunken *adjective*, means fallen to the bottom or being submerged in water or at a lower level than the surrounding area: *We are in an orchard with a sunken road leading into it from the main road*. When referring to facial characteristics, **sunken** means hollow: *He had grey skin, red-rimmed eyes and sunken cheeks*.

sir, *Sir*, Dame

sir *noun* (not capitalized), is used as a polite way to address a man in a position of authority, an officer of higher rank or a male guest in a hotel or restaurant, or even a shop or hairdresser's: *How are you feeling today, sir?* Both 'ma'am' and 'madam' are the female equivalents.

Sir *noun* (capitalized), is the title given to a man who has received one of the highest British honours. A man who has been knighted is formally addressed as 'Sir' followed by his first name and surname: *Sir Alex Ferguson*; or just **Sir** with the first name: *Sir Alex*. Do not omit the first name: *Sir Ferguson* is incorrect. The wife or widow of a knight is called 'Lady'. In formal business correspondence (including emails), *Dear Sir* is used as a salutation (note, **Sir** is capitalized here). The female equivalent is 'Dear Madam'. See EMAILS AND LETTERS (WRITING SKILLS), LADY.

Dame is the title given to a woman who has received the British female honour equivalent to the rank of 'Sir'. Like 'Sir', **Dame** is placed before the first name: *Dame Mary*, or before the first name and surname:

Dame Mary Smith. Do not omit the first name: *Dame Smith* is incorrect.

sister company

See **GROUP**.

site, sight, cite

site *noun & verb*. As a noun, this means the area of ground where something happened (such as the **site** of a battle) or where a building or object is to be located: *This is the site for the new laboratory*. It also means an enclosed location used for a specific purpose: *The caravan site covered the whole hillside*. As a verb, it means to locate: *This is where they have planned to site the new office*.

sight *noun*, refers to vision or the physical ability to see something: *The boat was just in sight near the harbour wall*. **Sight** is often used figuratively: *The end of the course was in sight*. *A sight for sore eyes* refers to a very surprising but welcome appearance.

cite *verb*, means to refer to or quote: *He cited a famous passage from 'Hamlet'*. When a word or phrase is *cited* in running text, it should be distinguished by means of inverted commas or the use of italics – but not both. **Cite** is frequently used in legal contexts in order to mention something that supports an idea or principle: *The defence cited Brown et al. v. the Board of Education of Topeka*. For the use of **cite** in electronic referencing, see **REFERENCING ELECTRONIC DOCUMENTS (WRITING SKILLS)**.

> *'He was a site for sore eyes.'*
> (Student essay) **!**

sitting room, living room, lounge, drawing room

sitting room *noun*, is used in BE to refer to the main room used for relaxation when there is a separate room for eating (dining room or breakfast room): *Let's go in the sitting room and sit down, and you tell me all about it*. Small hotels or guest houses may call their lounge a sitting room to make it sound more homely: *The sitting room has a TV, games, and maps to help guests plan their activities*.

living room *noun*, is the usual term for the main room in a house that is used for relaxation: *There was carpet in the living room, lino elsewhere*. This is the usual word if it is the only room without a special function: kitchen, bathroom, bedroom, etc.

lounge *noun*, means a space for sitting and relaxing in a public place: *Hotel lounge; Airport lounge*. In BE it also means a *living room*.

drawing room *noun*, is another term used in BE for sitting room. Like *lounge*, it may be thought too formal and old-fashioned for many people: *You will find your aunt in the drawing room*.

situation, state of affairs

situation *noun*, means a set of circumstances as they exist at a specific place and time. It can refer to a range of circumstances: *Given the present financial/social/political situation . . . and puts the government in an awkward/embarrassing situation*. It is old-fashioned to use **situation** for a job: position is more common. However it is still used in newspapers as a general heading for job advertisements: *Situations Vacant*.

state of affairs *noun*, also means the current circumstances, but emphasizes their quality. It is used with adjectives such as *happy*, *unfortunate*, *present* and *current*: *Are there any measures that will rectify this unhappy state of affairs?* See **STATE OF PLAY (BALL GAME)**.

S

size, sized, sizeable

size *noun*, means how large or small something is. When talking about shoes or clothes, **size** is one of a range of standard measurements. Avoid using *large in size* or *large-sized*, 'large' is enough. See **TAUTOLOGY**.

size and **sized** are used as a part of compound adjectives. One or the other may be normal in particular combinations: *outsize dress*, *life-size painting* or *life-sized painting*, *large-sized house*.

sizeable *adjective*, means fairly large: *We have a sizeable programme of help for every sector of the industry*. This word can be spelt either with or without 'e' before the 'a'. The British National Corpus has five times as many hits for *sizeable* as for *sizable*.

ski (noun and verb), skiing

ski *noun*, means both the long flat objects that are fastened to the feet in order to travel across snow or water (when pulled by a motorboat) and the runners on an aircraft or vehicle for operating on snow. *Skis* is the plural of **ski**.

ski *verb*, means to travel over snow or water on *skis*. A person who *skis* is a *skier*. The verb forms are *skiing*, *skied* and *skied* (past tense and participle): *We skied down the icy slope without falling over*.

skiing *uncountable noun*. This refers to the activity or sport: *downhill skiing* and *cross-country skiing*.

skilful, *skillful*, skilled

skilful *adjective*, means being good at doing something, especially something that needs ability or special training both practically and theoretically: *The director made skilful use of the lighting in the outdoor theatre*. This is the BE spelling.

skillful *adjective*, is the AE spelling of *skilful*.

skilled *adjective*, suggests an accomplished capable person with knowledge, ability and training in a craft. This can apply to professional as well as manual work: *He was a highly skilled lawyer*.

skill

See EXPERTISE.

skim

See READ.

skinny

See THIN.

skull, *scull*

skull *noun*, means the bones of the head: *Fossilized human skulls are still being discovered in East Africa*. Informally, **skull** may include the brains: *Get that into your skull* (indicating lack of brains).

scull *noun*, means a kind of oar, or a light racing boat: *The team easily won the double sculls*.

> *An application to Brussels to fund 'a skulls development project' was almost rejected until they realized there was a typo in 'skills development.'* **!**
> (See TYPO.)

slack, slacken

slack *adjective*, means loose: *You simply clip the sail on and leave it slack*; or it refers to a low level of business: *There has been a slack demand all season*. In a third sense **slack** means lazy: *Try to curb your impatience with those who are slack in their work*.

slacken *verb*, means to become less intense: *The rain slackened off after 30 minutes*. It also means to make something less tight: *Slacken the rope*. In another sense it means to become slower: *After a two-hour march, he finally slackened the pace*. In business, the phrase *slacken off* means to become less active or stop growing.

slander

See LIBEL.

slang

Slang is informal language, irreverent, often insulting or even obscene, and is constantly changing. Many social groups have their own brand of slang that sets them apart from other groups. The slang of one group is often condemned by outsiders, who do not realize that they in turn have their own slang. Slang is different from jargon, which is at the other end of the formality scale. Some words that are now firmly embedded in the standard language started life as slang – *mob* and *blurb* are two well-known examples, but most slang is short-lived as new terms replace the previous generation's favourites.

There is nothing so old-fashioned as last year's slang. In the mid-twentieth century, 'cool' was used to mean excellent: *The Beatles are cool*, but at the time of writing, its use has been extended by young people to be a slang term of approval: *I'm cool with that*; or agreement: *'See you tomorrow morning, then', 'Cool!'* Perhaps, in 10 years' time, *cool* may have yet another meaning. Slang should not be confused with dialect, which has a whole system of grammar and phonology as well as vocabulary that is different from the standard language, nor with accent, which involves the sounds used in speech, but not vocabulary.
See DIALECT, JARGON.

slate, slated

slate *noun*, means a type of rock that splits easily into thin flat layers. It is used for roof tiles and as a stone for writing on, and from this use, in BE slang it means a place for noting a debt in a pub: *Put it on the slate*. In AE, it means the list of candidates in an election: *a slate of candidates*.

slated *verb participle*, means censured and criticized: *The environmentalists have been slated for not being active enough in helping create measures to reduce diesel vehicle emissions*. In AE it can mean nominated, scheduled or planned: *He is slated for President*. A newspaper story with the headline 'Peace talks slated' is thus likely to be interpreted differently on the two sides of the Atlantic.

sledge, toboggan, sleigh

sledge *noun & verb*. As a noun, this means a vehicle on runners for transporting people or goods over ice and snow: *He pulled the children across the lake on a sledge*. As a verb, it means to travel on a **sledge**. An alternative form of the word is *sled*. *Sledging* is also an informal term used to describe insulting remarks made on the cricket field to shake the confidence and concentration of an opposing player.

toboggan *noun & verb*. As a noun this means a light vehicle on runners that one sits astride. Used as a verb, it means to sit on a **toboggan** and run down a snowy or icy slope: *We are going tobogganing*.

sleigh *noun*, is a common name for a large sledge, which has seats and is pulled by a horse or reindeer: *The children enjoyed the sleigh ride in Finland*.

sleet

See SNOW.

slide

See TRANSPARENCY.

slight, slightly

See MARGINAL.

slim

See THIN.

sliver, slither

sliver *noun*, means a thin piece of brittle material broken off or cut from a larger piece: *Digital watches work because a small sliver of quartz inside them pulses at a rhythmic and unchanging frequency*. Figuratively it can mean a thin piece: *a sliver of Parmesan cheese*; or an area of something: *A narrow sliver of light showed that the door was not closed*.

slither *verb*, means either to move close to the ground in a smooth manner: *A green snake slithered silently across the wet patch*; or to move anywhere without much control: *Five minutes later he had slithered down the sandy cliffs*.

> *'Hazards . . . resulting in breakage and perhaps the release of a fragment or slither of glass.'*
> (Safety at Glass Cutting Machines, Health and Safety Executive, 2001) **!**

slot machine

See VENDING MACHINE.

slow, slowly

slow *adjective & adverb*. As an adjective, this means not moving or being done or happening quickly: *They were stuck on the motorway in the slow lane*. If a person is **slow**, this may refer to speed of movement or mean that the person is not regarded as being clever. As an adverb, **slow** is often used with go, as in *go slow* meaning doing something at a slow tempo.

slowly *adverb*, means not fast or not quickly: *The bellows were operated by a handle that had to be turned slowly*. **Slowly** is commonly used with verbs such as walk, drive and speak.

> Note that only *slowly* can be placed before a verb: *I then slowly walked along Fulham Broadway in complete darkness.*

slush

See SNOW.

small

See LITTLE.

smart, clever

smart *adjective*, means either clean, neat and fashionable: *He dressed in smart suits and stayed in smart hotels*; or intelligent and cunning: *He made his fortune after some smart deals*. This is the standard AE term for being clever in this sense.

clever *adjective*, means skilled, intelligent and bright. **Clever** is not only used for people, an object can also be described as **clever** if it has a good design or functions well: *Some clever software means the pen-based computers are starting to become available at a realistic price*. If a person is *too clever by half*, he or she is annoying or causes suspicion about the origin of their wisdom. This word has negative connotations in AE.

> Both words can signal disapproval by others. A *smart alec* or *smart ass* (AE) refers to a person who shows off. A *clever Dick* or *clever clogs* (both BE) means a person who is always right and irritates others by showing off. The expression *Don't get clever with me* shows irritation with someone who is being disrespectful and makes snappy answers.
>
> These are all informal phrases.

smash

See **WRECK**.

smell, stink, stench

smell *noun & verb*. As a noun this means an odour or scent. **Smells** can be pleasant or unpleasant: *People with a good sense of smell can describe it as pleasant, unpleasant, faint, strong, bland, pungent or rancid*. As a verb, **smell** means to detect a **smell**: *Whenever I smell roasted chestnuts, I remember my childhood*; or to have an odour: *This fish smells off to me*. The past tense and past participle forms in BE are either *smelt* or *smelled*. In AE, *smelled* is more common for both. See **FRAGRANT (FLAGRANT), ODOUR**.

stink *noun & verb*. As a noun this means a very unpleasant smell: *All around, the rich stink of sweat, urine, spilled ale, even a trace of potpourri*. Figuratively, *to cause a stink* means to cause trouble: *They'll just cause a stink and then the truth will come out in the press*. As a verb, if 'something stinks' it is very bad or dishonest.

stench *noun*, means a strong, very unpleasant smell: *It was nothing but the stench of dead, rotting rats and of bats' dung*. Figuratively, it means something extremely unpleasant: *The odour of that gossip, the stench of that incomprehensible malice, seems to fill the room*.

smog

See **MIST**.

snow, sleet, slush

snow *uncountable noun*, means either the soft white flakes of frozen water that fall from clouds or the covering from such flakes on the ground: *According to one linguist it is an urban myth that the Inuit have more words for snow than speakers of English*. Skiers may be familiar with terms like *coarse-grained snow* and *fine, powdery snow*. Figuratively, **snow** is either an indicator of purity: *Her conscience was white as snow*; or coldness, illness or shock: *Susan's face was as white as snow and she was shaking with cold*. Informally in AE it refers to deception – *a snow job* means the covering up of something which is true.

sleet *uncountable noun*, means half-frozen rain falling from the clouds. Once **sleet** freezes it turns into ice. See **RAIN**.

slush *uncountable noun*, means partly melted snow and ice on the ground. **Slush** is usually dirty: *the people slipping and sliding on the pavements, spattered with slush by the passing traffic*. If a film or book is described as **slush** this is a disapproving way to say it is of little value or silly. The term *slush fund* refers to an amount of money kept to finance illegal activities, especially in politics.

soar

See **SORE**.

sobriquet

See **NICKNAMES**.

so-called, in name only

so-called *adjective*, means described inappropriately: *His so-called expertise in football management was questioned*. Avoid overusing **so-called**, as it expresses a personal opinion that others may disagree with. The term that is **so-called** is sometimes enclosed by quotation marks: *The so-called 'permissive society' was not protecting women from being treated as sex objects.*

in name only *phrase*, means generally recognized, but not genuinely valid. This is a more formal way of implying the same idea as *so-called*: *Commenting afterwards on this unfriendly aspect to a friendly, the coach explained: 'Games like this are friendly in name only.'*

sociable, social, societal

sociable *adjective*, refers to people who are friendly and enjoy spending time with others or to an occasion for social interaction: *Participation in this tutorial will offer an opportunity for sociable learning.* This is a positive word that is often combined with *very*: *Before her illness, Pearl was a very sociable person enjoying a full life.*

social *adjective*, refers to things that are connected with society as in *social class* and *social reform*: *Every one of these stories should create a picture of the social life of the time.* **Social** can also mean *sociable*.

societal *adjective*, refers to something connected with society and its organization: *The very beginnings of societal structures reveal the desire to have secret organizations.*

social science, social studies

social science *noun*, is the study of people in society, and the *social sciences* include academic subjects such as sociology, political science and economics: *There is a touching tendency for each social science to assume that it is the Queen of the Sciences.*

social studies *uncountable noun*, is the study of people in society. This is more broadly based than *social science* and is the name of a subject taught in secondary school and in higher education: *The examination is set and marked in such a way that it excludes from Science and Social Studies papers any questions based on the local environment.* Note that this is a plural form that is combined with a singular verb.

social security, social security number

social security *uncountable noun*, means government payments to support people who are on benefit due to unemployment, illness or old age.

social security number *noun*, is an identity number. In the USA it is a nine-digit number issued to citizens, permanent residents and temporary residents who work. It is used as identification for bank cheques and driving licences and elsewhere. Both children and adults must have a social security number. The abbreviation is SSN. Some other countries have similar systems to the USA for the identification of their citizens. This is not the case with the national insurance numbers in the UK, which are not proof of identity.

social worker, caseworker

social worker *noun*, means a person whose job is to give help and advice to residents in an area who have financial or family problems: *Regular visits from a social worker can be of immense value to old people living alone.* This is a BE term.

caseworker *noun*, means a *social worker* and is used mainly in AE.

societal

See SOCIABLE.

sodium nitrate, sodium nitrite

sodium nitrate *noun*, is a white solid ($NaNO_3$) that is used in fertilizers and explosives as well as in glass and pottery enamel. It is also a food preservative.

sodium nitrite *noun*, is a solid ($NaNO_2$) that is used in photography to fix colour and as a preservative in fish and meat. In meat it is used to induce a pinkish colour: *The doctor advised a reduction in preservatives such as sodium nitrite.*

sofa, settee, couch, chesterfield, davenport

sofa *noun*, is a seat with a back and two arms for more than one person.

settee *noun*, is a type of sofa that usually has arms.

couch *noun*, is a type of sofa typically with an armrest on either side. Some types just have a raised end: *He lay on the doctor's couch.*

chesterfield *noun*, is a padded leather sofa.

davenport *noun*, means a large, upholstered sofa. This is an AE term. In BE a **davenport** is a type of ornamental writing desk with drawers.

soil

See EARTH.

solicitor, lawyer, attorney, barrister, counsel

solicitor *noun*, means a person who is trained in the law and qualified to advise clients and draw up legal documents. A **solicitor** can represent a client in the lower courts. In AE, a **solicitor** is the most senior legal officer in a town, city or government department.

lawyer *noun*, means a person who is trained in the law and qualified to advise clients, draw up legal documents, and brief barristers: *A suspect may be accompanied by a lawyer when brought before the prosecutor*.

attorney ătúrni /ə'tɜːrni/ *noun*, is the general AE term for a lawyer, particularly if he or she appears in court: *The bank was charged with global banking fraud, following a two-year inquiry by the Manhattan district attorney*. In Britain, the word is used in *power of attorney* (a legal document allowing one person to act on behalf of another who is unable to manage his own affairs) and the title *Attorney General*, who is the government's chief law officer.

barrister *noun*, means a lawyer who can argue cases in the higher courts. This is a BE term.

counsel *noun & verb*. As a noun, this means a barrister (in BE) or attorney (in AE) or a group of legal advisers that represents an individual or organization in court: *Counsel for the defence was asked to approach the bench*. This is also a formal word that means advice. In this sense it is an uncountable noun. As a verb, it means to give advice: *He was counselled by the Pentagon that civil war was likely in that region*.

soliloquy

See MONOLOGUE.

solstice

See EQUINOX.

soluble, solvable, solution

soluble *adjective*, refers to something that can be dissolved in a liquid: *Salt is soluble in water*. **Soluble** also refers to things that can be solved such as problems and challenges. The opposite in both senses is *insoluble*. See DISSOLVE.

solvable *adjective*, refers to problems or mysteries that can be solved: *This has the attraction that poverty is a solvable problem, unlike viewing the bottom 10 per cent as perpetually being in poverty*. The opposite is *unsolvable*.

solution *noun*, means a way of solving a problem or dealing with a dispute: *The time has come to find a solution to prevent Britain becoming an enormous, dangerous rubbish tip*. It also means a liquid in which a solid is dissolved: *Filters were rinsed several times at room temperature in a solution containing sodium dodecyl sulphate*.

some

See ANY.

somebody

See ANYONE.

someday, some day

someday *adverb*, means at a future, but not specified time: *He'll be back someday*. This is sometimes spelt *some day*.

some day *determiner + noun*, means a specific day: *Let's meet some day next month*.

someone

See ANYONE.

sometime, some time, sometimes

sometime *adverb & adjective*. As an adverb this means at some unspecified time: *I was awakened sometime in the small hours with a snorting and snuffling*. *Some time* is an alternative spelling. As an adjective, **sometime** is only used before a noun, and in BE refers to what somebody used to be: *Leon was a stockbroker, a sometime LibDem MP*. This is a formal word. In AE, it means an occasional contributor to something: *'He is a sometime guest on my talk show.'*

some time *determiner + noun*, also means that a job may require many hours or days: *Reading that report will take some time*. Note that both words are equally stressed.

sometimes *adverb*, means on some occasions but not always: *Sometimes, sadly, even a bad deal is better than no deal at all*.

somewhere, someplace

somewhere *adverb*, means in or to an unspecified place: *The plane was lost somewhere between England and Iceland*; or an unspecified amount of money or a range of time, distance: *We have somewhere between £20,000 and £40,000 in the bank*. Note that **somewhere** is used in positive sentences or questions where the expected answer is 'yes'. See ANYWHERE.

someplace *adverb*, means *somewhere* and is used more in AE than in BE. It is an informal word that is mainly used in spoken English: *He's a professor of art someplace*.

soon, presently, at present

soon *adverb*, means within a short time: *He had left soon after two o'clock*. See MOMENTARILY (MOMENT), SHORTLY (SHORT).

presently *adverb*, in BE refers to something that happens after a short time: *For a few minutes she knelt by the grave, and was presently joined by Maria*. Note that this is a formal word. As this usage is typical of written English and is becoming old-fashioned in the spoken language, phrases like *'That's a legal matter, it will all be arranged presently'* could be rephrased so that **presently** is replaced by *soon*, in a moment or in a minute. In AE, **presently** means now or currently: *The plane is presently landing*. This may confuse BE speakers, who consider that the plane will be on the ground in a short time, not now.

at present *adverb*, means at the moment or currently and is the usual expression to be found at the beginning of a sentence: *At present its budget is a modest billion pounds*, although it is also found elsewhere: *Mr Riley is at present engaged on a history of the parish*. Never confuse **at present** with *presently* in the sense of *soon*. See EVENTUALLY.

sophomore

See FRESHMAN.

sore, soar

sore *adjective & noun*. As an adjective this means painful and inflamed: *Her feet were sore after the long walk*. **Sore** is also used figuratively in the expression *a sore point*. The phrase *stick out like a sore thumb* refers to a person or thing that is unpleasantly noticeable. As a noun, it refers to a wound or infection somewhere on one's body.

soar *verb*, means to increase, or reach a high level quickly: *Oil prices soared dramatically as soon as the war started*. **Soar** also means maintain a high level; this can be a bird or the volume of music. Figuratively if someone's *spirits soar*, this means that he or she is happy and pleased with something.

'Your nipples are soar?'
(Wiki.answers.com)

sort of

See KIND OF.

sound, noise

sound *noun*, is generally used for things that are heard: *the unmistakable buzzing sound of the alarm clock*. In this sense, it is a countable noun. However, **sound** is uncountable when it refers to the controls on a TV set and the vibrations though air or water in technical terms such as *sound waves*.

noise *noun*, is a sudden and unpleasant sound that is unwanted and may cause discomfort. In technical use, **noise** is an unwanted signal: *This TV set just puts out white noise*. **Noise** is often used together with adjectives that are negative, such as *horrible* or *dreadful*. The phrase *making a lot of noise* can be literal or can refer to talk about something that might happen: *A lot of noise was made about a supposed crisis in British art*.

south, southern

south *noun & adjective*. As a noun this means the direction to a person's right when facing the rising sun. When it refers to a direction, **south** is not usually capitalized: *The wind was blowing from the south*. It is capitalized when it is part of a country or continent name: South Korea; South America; or the name of a defined region: *She sold her villa in the South of France and returned to the South* (SE part of the USA). As an adjective it means in or towards the south and occurs before a noun: *We had a holiday on the south coast*. See CAPITAL LETTERS (WRITING SKILLS).

southern *adjective*, means located in, or connected with, the *south*: *There will be warm weather across the whole of southern England*. **Southern** is only capitalized when it forms part of a proper noun such as the Southern Alps or Southern Cross.

South America

See AMERICA.

southward, southwards, southerly, southbound

southward *adjective*, means in a southerly direction: *We studied the southward drift of the population*. **Southward** typically comes before a noun.

southwards *adverb*, means towards the south: *The birds migrated southwards*. It typically comes after the verb. This is sometimes spelt and pronounced *southward*.

southerly *adjective*, means either in a direction *towards* the south: *According to the map we were supposed to leave the road and take a southerly path about here*; or a wind that is blowing *from* the south: *A mild southerly wind warmed us although it was midwinter*. Note that **southerly** is normally followed immediately by a noun.

southbound *adjective*, means travelling towards the south: *The southbound lanes of the M1 were blocked at junction 20*.

sow

See SEW.

spam, unsolicited bulk email (UBE)

spam or **email spam** means identical or nearly identical email messages or advertising sent to numerous recipients. **Spam** is usually unwanted, commercial and sent by automated means: *At present about 90 billion spam messages are sent a day and often 80 per cent of the incoming email is in this category*. The most common products advertised by *spammers* are pornography websites, prescription drugs, sexual enhancement products, notification of lottery wins, fake brand name goods, mortgage offers, and fake diplomas from non-accredited universities. See DIPLOMA MILL, PHISHING.

unsolicited bulk email (UBE) is a technical term for spam.

spatial, spacial

spatial *adjective*, means relating to space and the position of things in it: *Railway lines, with stations, signal boxes, tunnels, bridges, and long or short trains lead to more ideas of spatial awareness*.

spacial *adjective*, is an alternative spelling to *spatial*.

> The British National Corpus has over 1,200 examples of the spelling *spatial*, but only 13 of *spacial*. Google reveals that the *spatial* spelling is 30 times more frequent than *spacial*.

special

See ESPECIAL.

speciality, specialty, specialism

speciality *noun*, means a type of product or food that is characteristic of a company, person, region or restaurant: *Game pie is a speciality in this restaurant*. Someone who has a specific skill or is an expert also has a speciality: *He is good on the wing, but corner kicks are his speciality*. See ESPECIAL, ESPECIALLY.

specialty *noun*, is an AE alternative to *speciality*. It is also used in BE in the medical profession: *Public health medicine is a goal-driven medical specialty*.

specialism *noun*, means an area of study or work that someone has specialized in: *The movement towards subject specialism within the primary school has already begun*.

specially

See ESPECIALLY.

species, variety

species *noun*, means a group of animals or plants whose members are similar and can breed to produce young animals or plants. Note it is unchanged in the singular and plural forms: *This species* ***is*** *rare; those species* ***are*** *rarer*.

variety *noun*, means a type or stock of plant or animal developed by breeding: *They successfully marketed a new variety of rice in South East Asia*.

spectators

See PUBLIC.

spectra, *spectre, specter*

spectra *noun plural*, means ranges of sound waves or bands of colour as in a rainbow. This term is widely used in science: *Figure 1 shows the power spectra stacked in order of mean count rate for the observation*. Its singular *spectrum* can be used in non-scientific contexts to refer to related qualities or ideas: *The House represented most views from across the political spectrum*. As a *spectrum* is a continuum, often range and variety may be better alternatives.

spectre *noun*, means an unpleasant future threat that causes anxiety and despair: *He said that the spectre of famine threatened many parts of Africa*. In literary contexts a **spectre** is a ghost: *Thought to be the spectre of a horseman who once drowned nearby, Hob is condemned to plague other travellers*.

specter *noun*, is the AE spelling of *spectre*.

> *'We can offer a broad spectre of concerts, and something for every musical taste.'* (visitnorway.com) **!**

speech

See TALK.

speed, sped, speeded

speed *noun & verb*. As a noun, this is the rate of progress and is either given as a number such as: *They were travelling at a speed of 50 mph*; or by words that refer to a scale such as 'high' or 'low': *His speed was too high for such narrow roads*. It also means rapidity: *Real time processing is possible due to the speed of modern computers*. As a verb, **speed** means to hurry, to drive too fast, above the speed limit, or to make something go fast or happen faster.

sped *verb*, is the past tense and past participle of to *speed* in the sense of hurry: *The woman was pushed to the ground before her attackers sped off in her Ford*.

speeded *verb*, is the past tense and past participle of to *speed* in the sense of go too fast: *They speeded all the way home* (broke the speed limit); or to go faster: *In the film about time travellers in the future, the whole story is speeded up and rerun in about two minutes*.

spell, spelt, spelled

spell *noun & verb*. As a noun, this means a period of time: *I did a spell in the army*. Weather is typically described in terms of *spells*: *There were some heavy spells of thunder and lightning*. A **spell** can also be a piece of magic, or the words used to carry out the magic, as in fairy stories. As a verb, **spell** means to form a word by putting the letters in the correct order. *To spell out* something means to explain it in detail: *They had to spell out all the details in the contract*.

spelt *verb*, is the past tense and past participle of the verb *to spell*. **Spelt** is the BE form: *He spelt too many words wrong*. It is also used to indicate something bad or unfortunate: *He said that a peace settlement spelt danger for Jordan*.

spelled *verb*, is an alternative spelling for the past tense and past participle of *to spell* and is the preferred AE form. This is used in AE when two people share a watch and take it in turns to be awake. *I spelled him until midnight*.

spellcheck, spellchecker

spellcheck *verb*, means to use a computer program to check the spelling of a document: *Please spellcheck this form before we photocopy it*.

spellchecker *noun*, is a computer program which checks the spelling of words in a document.

> *I have a spelling checker*
> *I disk covered four my PC.*
> *It plane lee marks four my revue*
> *Miss steaks aye can knot see.*
> *Eye ran this poem threw it.*
> *Your sure lee glad two no.*
> *Its very polished in its weigh,*
> *My checker tolled me sew.*
> ('An Ode to a Spell Checker', author unknown)

spill, spilt, spilled

spill *noun & verb*. As a noun, this means a liquid coming out of a pipeline or tank: *Miles of coastline were polluted by the oil spill*. As a verb, it means to flow over the edge of a container by accident: *The children keep spilling milk on the table*.

spilt *verb*, is the past tense and past participle of the verb *to spill*. This is the BE form. The phrase *He spilt the beans* means he revealed something secret to a third party.

spilled *verb*, is an alternative spelling for the past tense and past participle of *to spill* and is the preferred AE form.

spin, spin doctor (news)

spin *noun*, in this context means the presentation of information in a way that puts a favourable bias or angle on one particular standpoint: *The President's advisers put a favourable spin on this accident*. This is mainly used as a term of disapproval or contempt. Journalists often refer to the room in which government press conferences take place as the *spin room*.

spin doctor *noun*, means a spokesperson who is skilled in presenting information to the media that favours one organization or group: *As the image-maker or spin doctor, he is credited with transforming the Party's fading image*. See PROPAGANDA.

spire, steeple, tower

spire *noun*, is a tapering structure on top of a building, often on top of a tower: *The dreaming spires had etched themselves deeply on my imagination*.

steeple *noun*, means spire, but it can also mean both the tower and the spire in a church: *They walked up the steeple stairs*. This is probably impossible in a spire.

tower *noun*, is a tall, relatively narrow building, often part of a castle or church: *The Tower of London is one of the oldest buildings in the capital*.

spiritual, spirited

spiritual *adjective*, refers to non-material things that affect the spirit or soul: *Man will seek spiritual satisfaction elsewhere if Christianity does not provide it*. In the House of Lords, the Lords spiritual are the bishops and the other members are called the Lords temporal. See TEMPORAL (TEMPORARY).

spirited *adjective & verb form*. As an adjective this refers to someone or something that is full of energy, enthusiastic and determined: *It was not easy for a spirited young woman to be the wife of a country vicar*. A person who is *public-spirited* is someone who helps others in their community. As a verb, **spirited** is usually linked to *away* and means quickly and secretly removed: *The gleaming casket containing Dennis's mortal remains was spirited away to the nether regions of the crematorium*.

split infinitives

split infinitives are verb forms in which a word has been inserted between the infinitive marker and the verb stem, such as between 'to' and 'make', as in 'to really make'. Splitting the infinitive has often been regarded by purists as one of the deadly sins in English. However, most modern authoritative books about English usage point out that this is misguided and based on the argument that as Latin could not split infinitives therefore English should follow suit. If this is something you heard in school, it is best to forget it.

Inserting a word, usually an adverb, between 'to' and the following infinitive may result in greater precision such as: *His only wish was to really sleep* (sleep very well and undisturbed). Compare this with: *His only wish really was to sleep* (means just to sleep and says nothing about the quality of sleep). This example of an adverb splitting an infinitive is natural in many cases. *I wish to **flatly*** *forbid* sounds more natural than *I wish to forbid* ***flatly*** or *I wish* ***flatly*** *to forbid*. *Always, finally, fully, nearly, really* and *simply* are typical adverbs that naturally split infinitives today. On the other hand, a lengthy gap between 'to' and the following infinite is not recommended and *He wanted* **to** *completely and comprehensively* ***redesign*** *the training programme*, should be rephrased.

The splitting of infinitives is a natural part of modern English and there is nothing wrong in writing 'to always use' or 'to really remember'.

spouse

See PARTNER.

sprain, strain

sprain *noun & verb*. As a noun this means a twisted ligament. As a verb, it refers to twisting the ligaments particularly of the ankles and wrists: *He fell on the ice and sprained his wrist badly*.

strain *noun & verb*. As a noun, this means worry or mental pressure because there is much to do or there are difficulties dealing with problems. This normally applies to people: *The strain of repaying the debt caused his nervous breakdown*. Physical **strain** is the pressure on objects such as a rope or cable under tension: *If you clear them from the surface regularly, the net will not break under the strain of a large catch*. As a verb, **strain** means to injure a part of one's body such as a muscle: *The footballer strained a muscle in his leg*.

Spraining something is more serious than *straining* it.

squash

See QUASH.

stadium

See STAND.

staff

See WORKFORCE.

stage

See STEP.

stairs

See STEPS.

stalagmite, stalactite

stalagmite *noun*, means a piece of rock containing calcium salts that protrudes upwards from the floor of a cave. It grows as water containing lime drips off the roof.

stalactite *noun*, means a long pointed rock containing calcium salts that hangs like an icicle from the roof of a cave. It grows as water containing lime drips off the roof.

A way of remembering the difference between these terms is that mites grow up and tights come down.

stalker

See GROUPIE.

stalking-horse

See SCAPEGOAT.

stamp, stomp

stamp *verb*, means to put one's feet down heavily and noisily. This can be caused by anger: *She stamped her foot in the classroom*; or because of cold weather. Figuratively you can *stamp your authority* or return to your *stamping grounds*, your favourite haunts.

stomp *verb*, means to walk noisily with heavy steps: *The boys stomped out of the room*. The phrase *stomping grounds* is an AE variant for *stamping grounds*.

stanch

See STAUNCH.

stand (for office), run (for office)

stand for office *verb*, means to be a candidate in an election for a public position. This is a BE term: *George is standing for office at the next by-election*.

run for office *verb*, is the AE term for stand for office. The presidential elections in the USA are usually between pairs of main candidates. The main candidate has a *running mate* who will get the less important job if they win.

stand, grandstand, stadium, arena

stand *noun*, means a tiered construction in a stadium for spectators to sit in and watch football matches and similar sporting events. The name reflects the time when people stood and watched soccer. A **stand** is also a raised platform.

grandstand *noun*, is a large structure with rows of seats at a sports stadium or racetrack. A *grandstand view* means the best view possible.

stadium *noun*, means a building for public events with a sports field surrounded by rows of seating: *It was a small rally that started at the Olympic Stadium*. The plural is *stadiums*. The alternative plural, *stadia*, refers to the site of Roman chariot races.

arena *noun*, means a building which is flat in the centre and has seats around it, that is used for people to watch a sporting event or entertainment: *The local fire brigade refused to issue a safety licence for the arena*. **Arena** can also be used figuratively to mean an area of activity, particularly one involving disputes between different groups or countries: *It was a measure of how much the green political arena had changed*.

starlight, starlit

starlight *noun*, means light from the stars: *We could find our way across the snowy mountains, thanks to the starlight*.

starlit *adjective*, means that the sky is lit up with stars and the total visual effect is referred to: *The starlit sky was incredible last night*.

state

See COUNTRY.

state of affairs

See SITUATION.

state of play

See BALL GAME.

state of the art, cutting edge

state of the art *noun & adjective*. As a noun, this means the newest ideas, most up-to-date features or the most recent stage in product development: *This new BMW is the state of the art*. Note that there are no hyphens. As an adjective, **state-of-the-art** is used before a noun: *This Peugeot has state-of-the-art design*. Note that this is hyphenated.

cutting edge *noun & adjective*. As a noun, this means the latest or most advanced stage of development. It can also be used for pioneering and/or innovative research: *This work is at the cutting edge of subsea robotics*. As an adjective, **cutting edge** requires a hyphen when it is used before a noun: *This is cutting-edge technology*.

> Both phrases describe leading developments or leading research work. The difference is that many can claim to have reached the *state of the art* in their field, but only a few are at the leading edge or *cutting edge* of developments.

stationary, stationery

stationary *adjective*, means standing still with no movement or change in condition: *The car was completely stationary*. As a *stationary office* can only be compared with a *mobile office*, it is surprising that there about 400,000 hits on the Internet for *stationary office*.

stationery *noun*, means writing paper and envelopes. *Office supplies* is a more general term that includes staplers, ring binders, paper clips and tape dispensers: *We went to the stationery office to collect some office supplies*.

> *'Extracted from British Admiralty Charts with the permission of the Controller HM Stationary Office.'*
> (www.thecrownestate.co.uk)

station wagon

See ESTATE CAR.

statistics, stats, figures (information)

statistics *noun*. As a countable noun, this means a collection of information that is presented in numerical form: *The number of new jobs is rising. These statistics are due to be released at the end of November*. Note that

statistics is used as a plural in this sense. It is also possible to have a *statistic*: *The percentage rise in Brent oil is a vital statistic to watch*. If a person feels dehumanized, he or she may complain: *I want to be treated as a person not as a statistic*. As an uncountable noun, **statistics** is an academic subject: *Statistics is an essential part of the training for an academic historian*. Note that like other academic subjects ending in -ics, **statistics** is used as a singular in this sense. See **-ICS**.

stats *noun*, is an informal abbreviation for *statistics*: *The match stats made interesting reading*. Note that **stats** is used as a plural.

figures *noun*, means a number that represents a specific amount usually presented in official or published information: *The figure of £1,000 a head is taken from a new survey by 'The Guardian'*. Informally *figures* can mean arithmetic: *I don't have a head for figures*.

statue, statute

statue *noun*, means a sculpture of a person or animal that is made in stone, metal, wood, etc. that is often life-size or larger: *The monument comprises a statue of the great man on a plinth of red granite*. A related word is *statuette*, meaning a small statue.

statute *noun*, means a law passed by a parliament, council, etc. and formally written down: *The Inner Urban Areas Act reached the statute book before the Conservatives took office*. It also means the written and formal rules of an association or company: *The statutes of the club were changed to admit female members*.

> *'He remains a convicted murderer in Nigeria's statue books.'*
> (www.guardian.co.uk) **!**

staunch, stanch

staunch *adjective & verb*. As an adjective this refers to someone who is loyal in their opinion and attitude: *As a staunch feminist, she grew alarmed as all the positions of power were taken by men*. As a verb it means to stop the flow of a leakage, especially blood: *She worked quickly to staunch the flow of blood*.

stanch *verb*, is an AE variant spelling of *staunch*.

stay, visit

stay *verb & noun*, means to spend a period of time as a guest in a hotel or in someone else's home: *So you can eat out or stay in the inn itself*. It can also mean to remain in one place: *Are you going to stay in London after you've retired?* This meaning of where to live as a permanent resident is common in Scottish, Indian and South African English; so for such speakers the question: *Where do you stay?* does not mean *Which hotel are you staying at*?

visit *verb & noun*, means to go to see someone or to stay somewhere for a short time: *He had only visited Russia once before*. It may be an invitation to click on a website: *For further information, visit our website*. In BE one visits people; in AE one visits *with* them. As a noun, a **visit** means a short stay: *Mark Twain wrote an account of his visit to the Holy Land*; or an official call: *The Pope made a three-day visit to Ireland*.

steal

See **BURGLE**.

steeple

See **SPIRE**.

stench

See **SMELL**.

step, stage

step *noun & verb*. As a noun this means a position on a scale or one of a series of events in a process: *The first step to fame and fortune came at the age of 12*. The phrase *a step in the right direction* means a positive move. As a verb it means to lift your foot and move it. Figuratively it means to move into another era: *The oak beams (some of which are 1,000 years old) give one the impression of stepping back in time*. See **PHASE**.

stage *noun & verb*. As a noun this means a particular time or state passed through when something grows or develops: *She has reached the stage where she feels much more inclined to strike out to underline her independence*. A **stage** can also be a distinct part of a predetermined process: *The insect* *was in its larval stage*; or a raised area in a theatre for actors to perform on. *To go on the stage* means to become a professional performer: *He went on the stage at the age of 16*. As a verb **stage** means to organize a play or an event: *Who is staging the next Olympics?*

stepbrother, stepsister

See SIBLING.

step change

See PARADIGM SHIFT.

steppe

See PRAIRIE.

steps, stairs

steps *noun*, means a series of flat narrow pieces of wood or stone especially outside a building, and an alternative term is a *flight of steps*: *At the rear, steps led down to a canal*. **Steps** is also a truncated form for *stepladder*.

stairs *noun*, means a set of *steps* inside a building or structure that is used for going from one level to another: *He led the way along the hall and up a winding flight of stairs*. An alternative term is *staircase*. As **stairs** are inside something, this means that in a large aircraft, passengers can be asked to take the *staircase* and go *upstairs* or *downstairs*. However, when a plane is on the ground it may be boarded by going up the *steps* outside.

stereotype

See ARCHETYPE.

stile

See STYLE.

stimulus, stimulant

stimulus *noun*, is something that helps a process to develop more quickly or produces a reaction in a person, plant or animal: *Hunger, caused by lack of food, is the most obvious and indeed the most powerful stimulus*. A **stimulus** can also be a means of helping development or an incentive: *The clarification of such issues could well provide the stimulus for a school language policy*. The plural of **stimulus** is *stimuli*.

stimulant *noun*, means a drug or substance that quickens bodily action or a mental process: *Coffee is a good stimulant early in the morning*.

> A *stimulus* usually lasts for a long time, but a *stimulant* is short-lived.

stimulation, simulation

stimulation *uncountable noun*, means the process or state that encourages or helps an activity to begin: *Children require stimulation and security*. Note that **stimulation** is a more general term than stimulus or stimulant.

simulation *noun*, means the activity of producing an artificially created condition which represents a real-life situation for study or experimentation: *Computer simulation has been used in the design of artificial limbs or hips*. In another sense, it can mean action or behaviour through which someone tries to deceive others.

stink

See SMELL.

stipend

See SCHOLARSHIP.

stipulations

See RULES.

stockpile, storage, sequestration

stockpile *noun & verb*. As a noun, this means a large supply of food, oil, materials or weapons that is kept ready for future use: *The growing stockpile of used tyres is a worldwide problem*. As a verb, **stockpile** means to build up and maintain a large supply: *Managers stockpile raw materials to guard against future shortages*.

storage *uncountable noun*, means the process of putting or keeping something in a special place while it is not being used: *The furniture was put in storage*. In computing, **storage** means the way information is stored so that it can be retrieved: *We need an external hard disk for storage*.

sequestration *noun*, in the chemical sense of the word, means the formation of a stable compound so that further reactions are prevented: *The sequestration of CO_2 in suitable reservoir rock is preferable to allowing it to build up in the atmosphere*. Whereas *storage* means the retention of something for use at a later time, **sequestration** is like locking something up and throwing the key away. The word has a completely different meaning in legal contexts. See ISOLATE.

stomp

See STAMP.

stone

See ROCK.

storage

See STOCKPILE.

store card

See BANK CARD.

storey

See GROUND.

storm, gale

storm *noun*, means a period of extreme weather that can include rain or snow, strong winds and often lightning. **Storm** is often combined with nouns such as *sand, snow* and *thunder*: *Because of a sandstorm, the pilot failed to find the landing lights and belly-flopped in the desert*. In figurative use, **storm** means a display of strong feeling: *The Lord Justice faced a storm of controversy and provoked sustained public outcry*.

gale *noun*, means a very strong wind: *The March gale hurled itself against our windows*. **Gale** is a measurement of wind speed on the Beaufort scale. See BEAUFORT SCALE, HURRICANE.

story

See GROUND, RUMOUR.

straight, strait

straight *adjective & adverb*. As an adjective, this means in a line, or direct: *The shortest distance between two points is a straight line*. A sports team can have three *straight wins* (consecutive wins). As an adverb it means immediately, or without deviation: *Now you just drive straight there and back*.

strait *noun*, means a narrow passage of water, often one that connects two seas and passes between two land areas: *They sailed through the strait*. In some proper names the plural form is used as in: *The Straits of Gibraltar*. To be in *dire straits* means to be in serious difficulty.

strain

See SPRAIN.

strand

See WIRE.

strange

See QUEER.

stranger, foreigner, alien

stranger *noun*, is a person who is not known. The expressions *perfect stranger* and *total stranger* emphasize the fact that the person is completely unknown. A **stranger** is also a person who is in a place that they have not been in before. The phrase *no stranger to something* means that someone has experienced something many times before: *He is no stranger to scandal and was photographed in the hotel corridor in his striped pyjamas yesterday*.

foreigner *noun*, is a person of a different country. Informally **foreigner** may refer to someone of the same nationality but who is an outsider, or a *stranger* to a particular group: *Although I was from Worcestershire, I was considered a foreigner by people from Gloucestershire for at least 25 years*.

alien *adjective & noun*. As an adjective, this means something very different from what is familiar: *Middle-class ideals of playing the game have always been alien to rough working-class culture*. In another sense, it means distasteful and frightening: *Both ideas were culturally alien to Mrs Singh*. As a noun, it is a technical word used by the authorities in various countries to mean *foreigner* (in AE, non-citizen). In other contexts it can mean a creature from another planet – an extraterrestrial.

strategy, tactic

strategy *noun*, means either a planned series of actions to achieve a particular objective or skilful planning in general: *The firm has confirmed its strategy of disengagement from the US and has sold most of the assets*.

tactic *noun*, is the method or detailed procedure involved in achieving something or carrying out a *strategy*. This word is usually plural: *Such delaying tactics can have a serious impact on the supplier's working capital cycle*. A **tactic** refers to a single action: *The Welsh and Scots adopted a different tactic*.

> A *strategist* is a person who is skilled in devising *strategies*. A *tactician* is a person who is skilled in working out *tactics*.

stratum, strata

stratum *noun*, means a layer of rock: *We are drilling through a sandstone stratum*. In another context, **stratum** means a level of society.

strata *noun*, is the plural of *stratum*. **Strata** should always take a plural verb: *These strata were formerly buried to depths and temperatures sufficient to generate oil*.

> These nouns are respectively singular and plural in English as in Latin but Google records over 25,000 hits for *this strata* which is non-standard.

street, road, avenue, boulevard, alley

street *noun*, is a road in a town or city that has buildings on either side: *Regent Street*. *High Street* means the main shopping **street** in towns in the UK, and is often its official name. The AE equivalent is *Main Street*.

road *noun*, means a highway that connects places and is sometimes named after the place it goes to: *London Road*. There are many exceptions to this basic distinction between **road** and *street*, such as *King's Road* in Chelsea. See MOTORWAY.

avenue *noun*, originally meant a wide, tree-lined street but has come to be used generally in street names: *He parked his car off Warwick Avenue and began his search*. **Avenue** is also used in cities in the USA for the names of the major roads in a grid pattern of highways: *Fifth Avenue*; and in BE and AE outside urban areas to mean a tree-lined road: *The main road enters Dentdale through an avenue of trees*.

boulevard *noun*, means a broad avenue such as *Sunset Boulevard* in Hollywood.

alley *noun*, means a narrow passageway in a town between or behind buildings: *A policeman directed her to Manette Street, a narrow alley between two tall buildings*. See LANE (FILE[2]).

> Note that names of all highways carry stress on both parts of the name, except for those in which the second part is *street*, which is never stressed:
>
> *Oxford Road*: ócksfŏrd rṓd /ˈɒksfərd ˈrəʊd/
> *Oxford Street*: ócksfŏrd street /ˈɒksfərd striːt/

strength, power, force

strength *noun*. As an uncountable noun this means the quality of being physically or mentally strong. *We do not have the strength for this*. Here only the context will indicate if this is physical or mental **strength**. It can also mean opinion and influence: *We must negotiate from a position of strength*. As a countable noun it means the quality of something or someone that gives them an advantage: *Any sport is about playing to your strengths and playing on your opponents' weaknesses*.

power *noun*. As an uncountable noun this means the strength in a part of the body. In a machine the power is the energy that enables it to work: *This electric car may not have the power to get up that steep hill*. When applied to people or groups it means the state or condition of having authority: *the balance of power*. As a countable noun it means a country with influence: *one of the major powers*; or the particular ability of someone: *His powers of persuasion are fascinating*. The related adjectives are *powerful* and *potent*. See POTENT.

force *noun*. As an uncountable noun this means violent action: *Military force settled the issue*; or the physical strength or energy that is used to do something: *The force of its descent has created a natural jacuzzi in the head pool*. It can also mean the authority of something: *The Act confers the force of* *law on the Budget*. As a countable noun it means a person or thing with great power or influence: *Market forces are in action again*. It can also mean a group organized for a specific purpose: *So far the force of the carefully selected 300,000 union staff has not been used*. **Force** is used to describe the application of physical strength, action or power, whereas both *strength* and *power* are qualities that do not have to be used. **Force** is often combined with terms such as centrifugal, driving or magnetic. The related adjective is *forceful*. See VIGOUR.

stress

See PRESSURE.

stretch, tract, area

stretch *noun*, means a long and narrow area that is either land or water, but not both: *It was a difficult stretch of road/the river/ the coast*.

tract *noun*, means a large area of land: *Vast tracts of savannah cover most of eastern Africa*.

area *noun*, means part of a country, region, town or a geographical location. It can also mean the surroundings: *Forest fires swept the following local areas*. See AREA (FIELD).

> *Area* is the most general of these words.

strict, hard, harsh, rigorous, severe, tough

strict *adjective*, means expecting others to obey rules or do as you say. It also describes something that must be obeyed: *He is under strict orders not to get involved in domestic politics in India*.

hard *adjective & adverb*. As an adjective **hard** means difficult: *It's hard to believe that he started painting so long ago*; solid and firm and not easily broken: *The wall was flat and hard and followed the river bank*. When people are called **hard**, this means that they are physically and mentally strong without fear: *They like to be seen as hard men or macho men*. It can also mean strong or intense, as in *hard liquor*. As an adverb, this means strenuously: *If they try hard enough, they will always find someone to do their dirty work*; or severely: *The judge came down hard on the terrorists*.

harsh *adjective*, means unpleasant and bright to see, as in the *harsh light of dawn*; an unpleasant voice can also be **harsh**. It also means cruel: *Science students were particularly harsh about the 'uselessness' of the arts*; as well as unkind: *This would be harsh punishment, but fitting*. **Harsh** is also used about a climate that is hostile.

rigorous *adjective*, means careful, exact and thorough: *The company has started to make a profit following a rigorous restructuring programme*. Note that the spelling of the noun is *rigour*. See -OR, -OUR SPELLINGS, RIGOUR.

severe *adjective*, means either very serious: *They all suffered severe injuries*; or extreme: *Problems were compounded by severe food shortages*. **Severe** also means unkind: *The teacher always had a very severe expression*; and receiving *harsh* punishment: *The sentence was the most severe on any of the eight convicted defendants*.

tough *adjective*, means difficult to do or deal with: *Unless those tariffs are removed our textile industry will have a tough time*. **Tough** also means firm in order to ensure rules are followed: *Inspectors are instructed to take tough enforcement action*.

S

strike, stricken

strike *verb*, means to hit or fall against a surface with force. The past tense and past participle is **struck**: *A struggle ensued, during which many blows were struck*.

stricken *adjective*, means very badly affected by trouble, illness or ill fortune: *The countryside lay half-deserted and stricken by famine*. This is a formal word.

string (of), succession (of), sequence of events, train of events

string (of) *noun*, means either a series of similar items: *A string of Sunday newspapers lined up to call for the Managing Director to go*; or similar events that occur soon after one another: *She had had a string of unhappy love affairs*. Note that **string (of)** stresses both the similarity and closeness in time or place. This is a less formal word than the others in this group.

succession (of) *noun*, means a number of people or things that follow in time or place: *Since then, the property has had a succession of owners*. Note that a **succession of** something may have a negative connotation of there being too many: *The referee's assistants became rather flag happy with a succession of offside decisions which infuriated players and crowd alike*.

sequence of events *noun*, means a series of related events that occurs in a particular order, which may be planned: *Rarely is there a neat sequence of events from the recognition of a problem to the implementation of the solution*.

train of events *noun*, means a series of events where each action causes the next to occur without its being planned: *You may well be setting in motion a train of events which will cause harm and destruction*.

strive

See ENDEAVOUR.

strong

See POTENT.

structure

See STYLE GUIDELINES (WRITING SKILLS).

stubborn

See OBSTINATE.

student, undergraduate, graduate, postgraduate, pupil

student *noun*, means someone studying in secondary or higher education. In formal contexts a **student** is usually someone taking college or university education in BE. The term *university student* is often used to add precision. See EXTERNAL STUDENT.

undergraduate *noun*, means a university student taking a first degree (BA, BSc or equivalent). This is sometimes abbreviated informally to *undergrad*. See ALUMNI.

graduate *noun & verb*. As a noun, this means a university student who has passed a first degree. Although the term **graduate** is often used alone: *Sam Jones is an Oxford graduate*, AE uses *graduate student* to mean someone who continues to study after a first degree: *She is a graduate student from Yale*. As a verb, **graduate** means to be awarded a university degree. In AE this has a wider use, meaning to successfully leave senior high school or college, or to be awarded a university degree. Note the difference in pronunciation between the noun (gráddyoŏ-ăt /ˈgrædjʊət/) and verb (gráddyoŏ-ayt /ˈgrædjʊeɪt/).

postgraduate *noun*, means a university student who holds a first degree and is doing advanced study. This is the equivalent to a graduate student in AE. This is sometimes abbreviated informally to *postgrad*. See DOCTORAL DEGREE.

pupil *noun*, means a schoolchild. However this usage is becoming old-fashioned and *student* is increasing used for those in secondary education. A person of any age being directly instructed by a barrister, musician or painter can also be termed a **pupil**: *Several of her singing pupils were over 30*.

studio

See BEDSIT.

study

See READ.

style, stile

style *noun*, means the way of doing or expressing something. It can also mean an attractive or impressive way of doing something: *After a year in Rome, she dressed with style*.

stile *noun*, is a step or steps for climbing over a wall or a fence.

subject

See FIELD, RESIDENT.

submerge

See IMMERSE.

submerged

See SINK.

subnormal

See ABNORMAL.

subscription, membership fee

subscription *noun*, means something you pay in advance in order to get a service, such as a **subscription** to a magazine or newspaper: *Because it was difficult to buy in Germany, they took out a subscription to 'The Economist'*. It can also mean an annual fee paid to belong to a club.

membership fee *noun*, means an amount of money paid on a regular basis to an association by its members: *The membership fee for the tennis club is becoming too expensive*. Note that in BE, one pays a fee for membership *of* a club. In AE, the fee is for membership *in* a club.

subsidiary company

See GROUP.

subsistence, subsidence, subsidy

subsistence *noun*, means livelihood and in the context of agriculture, *subsistence farming* means the bare minimum needed to support life: *As the peasant moves from subsistence agriculture to the production of cash crops, he loses a basic food supply*. In a business context, it covers compensation for food and accommodation: *He put in a claim for his travel and subsistence costs*.

subsidence súbssidĕnss /'sʌbsɪdəns/, sŭb-sīdĕnss /səb'saɪdəns/ *noun*, means the process by which an area of land sinks below the surrounding land: *The last few years have seen widespread damage to homes through subsidence caused by drought*. The second pronunciation, where the second syllable is pronounced like the word 'side', is recommended so there is no danger of this word being confused with *subsidy* or *subsistence*.

subsidy *noun*, is money granted by the government or an organization to help reduce production costs in agriculture or industry: *The telecommunications sector may soon need a government subsidy*. See SCHOLARSHIP.

> *'Policy exclusions: If your home is in an area which suffers from severe flooding or subsistence.'*
> (Excite.co.uk website) **!**

substantial

See LARGE.

substitute, replace

substitute *noun & verb*. As a noun, this means the replacement of one person or thing by another: *Wealth was not a substitute for happiness*. As a verb, the participle *substituted* without a preposition may not make it clear who is the **substitute** and who is being *substituted*. In a football match, it is not enough to say that *David is substituted*. But *John is substituted for David* has a clear meaning. The preposition *for* clarifies that it is David who is going off the field. *Replaced by* or the nouns *substitution* and *replacement* could also be used instead.

replace *verb*, also means to remove one thing or person in favour of another: *John replaced David in the second half*. This could be rephrased as *David was replaced by John in the second half*. Note how the subject and the preposition *by* make it clear who is leaving the field.

succession of

See STRING OF.

successor

See HEIR.

sufficient

See ENOUGH.

suffix

See WORD FORMATION.

suggestible, suggestive, evocative

suggestible *adjective*, means easily influenced by others: *It can be dangerous to hypnotize those who are highly suggestible*.

suggestive *adjective*, means similar to something or bringing something to mind: *The wine expert claimed the taste of the latest vintage was suggestive of blackberries*. Remarks and behaviour that are **suggestive** have sexual connotations.

evocative *adjective*, means bringing an image or feeling to mind in a pleasant way: *Her palette of evocative earth and sea tones also seemed to link her to an English landscape tradition*.

suit, suite

suit *noun*, means a set of clothes made of the same material such as a jacket and trousers for a man or a skirt and jacket for a woman. For a woman a suit can also be a *trouser suit* (BE) or *pantsuit* (AE). In other contexts, **suit** is also used for one of the four 'sets' in a pack of playing cards, or for a *lawsuit*. See CLOTHES, DRESS CODES.

suite *noun*, means a set of rooms, a group of furniture, or even a set of pieces of music intended to be performed together. An *en suite bathroom* is one that can only be accessed from the bedroom to which it is connected. Note that this is pronounced like the word 'sweet'.

sulphur, sulfur

sulphur *uncountable noun*, is a chemical element (symbol S) that is a light-yellow, non-metallic solid that occurs in volcanic deposits.

sulfur *uncountable noun*, is the AE spelling of *sulphur*.

> There are many words that begin with *sulph-* in BE and with *sulf-* in AE. Examples of the BE spelling: *sulphate*, *sulphide* and *sulphuric acid*.

sum, total

sum *noun*, means an amount of money: *For this reason, we have been forced to increase our minimum sum insured to £17,500.* It also means an elementary mathematical problem usually of addition: *The company got its sums wrong*; or the total arrived at by adding numbers together: *The sum of 21 and 7 is 28.* Note that a singular verb is used here. The expressions *sum total* or *princely sum* are often used ironically to mean insignificant: *It had been increased only twice and now stood at the princely sum of £30.*

total *noun & adjective*. As a noun, this means the final amount after adding a series of numbers, people or things together: *A total of 1,500 academics teaching subjects no longer in demand were offered generous compensation to retire early.* As one should avoid starting a sentence with digits, the phrase *a total of* is often useful in front of a number at the beginning of a sentence to avoid writing long numbers in words. As an adjective, **total** refers to the amount arrived at when several figures are added together: *Total revenue will be £442,000 and total profit will be £102,000.* **Total** also means complete, and is used in phrases such as *total darkness* and *total eclipse*. See ABSOLUTE ADJECTIVES (GRAMMAR TIPS), COMPLETE, NUMBERS IN NUMERALS OR WORDS (WRITING SKILLS).

sunken

See SINK.

super-, supra-

super- *prefix*, means more, such as: *super-fit*; to a greater extent, such as *superhuman*; or having great influence, such as *superpower*.

supra- *prefix*, means above in the sense of going beyond, as in *supranational law* meaning law that has international validity.

supermarket, hypermarket, shopping centre, mall

supermarket *noun*, means a large self-service shop that sells food and drink as well as items that households need regularly.

hypermarket *noun*, is a very large *supermarket* on the outskirts of a town or city that sells a wide range of consumer goods. This is typically a BE term.

shopping centre *noun*, is a large facility built for shopping that contains a lot of different shops that may be either in the centre of a town or city or outside the centre: *The nearest shopping centre is several miles out of town.*

mall *noun*, is a large facility built for shopping that contains a lot of different shops and is outside a town or city centre. It is a typical AE term for a *shopping centre* but is used internationally. The pronunciation mawl /mɔːl/, which rhymes with 'all', originated in AE but is commonly heard in BE in this sense. Otherwise the pronunciation is mal /mæl/ (rhyming with 'pal') in AE and BE.

supervisor

See **MANAGER**.

supine

See **PRONE**.

supply, provide, provision, deliver

supply *verb & noun*. As a verb, this means to provide people with something that is needed, especially regularly and over a longer period of time: *The pipeline supplies 25 per cent of the gas to this part of the country*. As a noun, **supply** means the quantities available for use: *Another problem is the supply of wood for shelters and fuel.* Note that *supplies* (only plural noun) refers to food, medicine, etc. required by expeditions and troops.

provide *verb*, means to give something, or make it available for somebody to use: *We provided food to the refugees*. Note that *supply* and **provide** refer to similar activities, the difference being in the scale and size of the operation.

provision *noun*. As a plural noun, this means the supply of food, particularly to the armed forces or expeditions: *They were exhausted and provisions were running low when they saw the rescue helicopter*. However *to make provision* means to supply or distribute services, benefits or even money: *They made provision for the education of the village children*.

deliver *verb*, means to take goods or other objects to a particular place or person or to many people from time to time. **Deliver** focuses on the handing over of something: *The food for the refugees was delivered to the wrong village*.

supreme

See **PARAMOUNT**.

surf, serf

surf *noun & verb*. As a noun, this means a line of breaking waves: *Ahead of them, Trent could hear the surf smashing on the reef*; and as a verb it means to ride the breaking waves as a sport: *He swam up to her and said, 'If you want to surf like a man you're going to be treated like a man.'* By extension, **surf** is now the usual expression used to mean search the Internet. A *surfer* can mean either someone who rides the waves or someone who spends time moving from site to site on the Internet or channel surfing on TV.

serf *noun*, means an agricultural labourer bound to his land and landlord (this is now a historical term only).

surname, family name, last name

surname *noun*, means the name a person shares with his or her parents, in contrast to given name(s), first name(s) or Christian name(s). See **FIRST NAME**.

family name *noun*, is an alternative to *surname* and is sometimes used on printed forms to make sure that everyone understands which name is required.

last name *noun*, also means a *surname* but is a term to avoid as it may not be understood. This is because some cultures and languages reverse the order of the given name and *surname* (e.g. Hungarian, Korean, Chinese, Japanese).

surpass

See **EXCEED**.

surrender

See **YIELD**.

surroundings

See **ENVIRONMENT**.

suspect, suspicious

suspect súspekt /'sʌspekt/ *noun, adjective &* sŭspékt /səs'pekt/ *verb*. As a noun, this means a person or thing that is thought to be guilty of a crime: *A suspect may be accompanied by a lawyer when he is brought before the prosecutor*. As an adjective, it refers to something that cannot be relied upon or is dishonest: *The minister's son was involved in some suspect business dealings in Asia*. It can also mean illegal and dangerous: *The police removed the suspect package, which was later found to be harmless*. As a verb it means either to feel that something is wrong: *The* *blue smoke from the car made him suspect that he had an oil leak*; or to be distrustful about somebody without being able to prove anything: *He strongly suspected her motives in taking another trip to Paris*. Note that the noun and adjective are stressed on the first syllable, but the verb is stressed on the second syllable.

suspicious *adjective*, means thinking that someone is guilty or doing something dishonest: *They were suspicious that he had such an extremely expensive car*. It also means feeling distrust: *She was also suspicious of his motives in taking a month's business trip to Rome*. In another sense it means arousing suspicion: *I thought it was a bit suspicious that he didn't tell us where he was going*.

sweat, perspire

sweat *noun & verb*. As a noun, this means the drops of salty liquid that come through someone's skin caused by heat, fear or illness: *Sweat was running down Rufus's back, between his shoulder blades*. In this sense, **sweat** is less formal than perspiration. Informally, **sweat** can also mean hard work. The informal expression *no sweat* means that everything is under control: *Mike just said, 'No sweat: I'll get the report finished.'* As a verb, **sweat** means either to produce drops of liquid on the skin or informally to work very hard: *John was sweating blood to get his part of the report finished*.

perspire *verb*, means to *sweat*: *The dancers were perspiring after the performance*. **Perspire** is a formal word.

A traditional hint about how these words are used is the saying that horses *sweat*, men *perspire* and ladies *glow*.

'Sweat from the trolley.'
(Dessert menu)
!

swede

See **TURNIP**.

sweetcorn

See **CORN**.

swelled, swollen

swelled *verb participle*, this is one of the past participles of *swell*. **Swelled** is used if the increase in numbers or size has no positive or negative connotations: *The graduate entry scheme has swelled the numbers entering the profession*. Figuratively this refers to emotions: *We had all swelled with pride*.

swollen *verb participle*, is the other past participle of *swell*. **Swollen** is used if there is a dangerous increase that may cause damage: *Her abdomen had swollen alarmingly*. Figuratively this means excessive: *The public-sector deficit has swollen to more than 10 per cent of GDP*.

Both these words can function as the past participle of *swell*, but only *swelled* can be used for the past tense, and *swollen* is much more common as an adjective.

syllabus

See **CURRICULUM**.

symbols on the Internet and elsewhere – Latin alphabet only

Symbol	*Read as*
é	e-acute accent – René
è	e-grave accent – Molière
R&D	and (the sign is called ampersand* – see below)
's	apostrophe
*	asterisk
@	at
\	backslash (not used in Internet addresses)
3–45	dash
11.5	decimal point in mathematics
stewart.clark	dot (in emails and web addresses)
//	double slash or double forward slash
–	en dash

—	em dash
/	forward slash
re-cover	hyphen
ï	i-diaeresis[†] – naïve (see also ü below)
abc	lower case
%	per cent (spelt percent in AE)
‰	per thousand
‘ ’	quotation marks
ñ	n-tilde – señora
ü	u-umlaut[†] – Zürich (see also ï above)
s	underscore s
ABC	upper case

*__ampersand__ *noun*, is the symbol **&**. This is used either informally to replace **and** in short notes and in set phrases like *R&D* (research and development); or formally in the names of companies: ‘Procter & Gamble’; ‘Johnson & Johnson’. Note that unless specific reference is being made to the **&** symbol, **ampersand** is always read as ‘and’.

†**diaeresis** (pronounced dī-ēerĕssiss /daɪˈɪərɪsɪs/) or **umlaut** (ŏomlowt /ˈʊmlaʊt/) *noun*, are alternative names for the two dots placed above some vowels to show that they are separately pronounced, as in *naïve*, or *Noël*. The AE spelling is *dieresis*, and the respective plurals are *diaereses* (BE) and *diereses* (AE). This word is borrowed from Greek, while **umlaut**, for the same symbol, is borrowed from German.

sympathy, empathy

sympathy *uncountable noun*, means the understanding and compassion someone feels for another person: *He found it hard to express sympathy and, in any case, he was more interested in legal matters*. In another context **sympathy** is the act of supporting or approving a cause or action: *The sailors came out early in the strike in sympathy with the dockers*. In a formal context, the phrase *deepest sympathy* is often used: *On behalf of the House we offer our deepest sympathy to those who were injured*.

empathy *uncountable noun*, means the ability to understand how another person feels because you can put yourself in their place: *It is also to do with using your own past experiences to show empathy and understanding when others need it*.

symposium

See CONGRESS.

syndrome

A syndrome is a collection of symptoms that characterize an illness, which taken separately might not be enough for a diagnosis of that disease.

Acquired immune deficiency syndrome (AIDS): is a result of being infected with the human immunodeficiency virus (HIV). It may be diagnosed as a result of one of a number of separate medical conditions.

Asperger's syndrome: is a variant of autism. See AUTISM.

Down's syndrome: is a genetic condition caused by the occurrence of an extra chromosome in the body that stops normal mental and physical development. It may be referred to simply as *Down's*.

Economy class syndrome: is the development of deep vein thrombosis in the legs of long-distance air travellers. It is caused by dehydration and lack of exercise in flight.

Sick building syndrome: is used to describe symptoms suffered by people who work in a particular building, the inference being that it is some feature of the building that has caused the problems.

Tourette's syndrome: is a neurological disorder in which patients suffer from involuntary repetitive acts such as uncontrolled speech, or jerky movements (tics); or are obsessed with a particular form of behaviour, such as hand washing caused by worry about dirt. It may be referred to simply as *Tourette's*.

synthetic

See ARTIFICIAL.

Spelling

sacr**a**ment	Note the -a- in the second syllable
sacr**i**l**eg**e	Note -i- in the second syllable, -e- in the third, and no 'd'
sacr**i**l**e**gious	Note -i- in the second syllable, -e- in the third
Scand**i**navia	Note the -i- in the second syllable, not 'a'!
s**c**ien**c**e	Remember the two 'c's
sec**r**et**a**ry	Remember the first -r-
s**ei**ze	Note -e- before -i- contrary to the normal rule
sep**a**rate	Note there are two 'a's and two 'e's in this word
s**e**rg**e**ant	Note there are two 'e's and an 'a' in this word
ski**l**fu**l**	Note that -l- is single twice in BE
s**o**briquet	Note -o- in first syllable, not -ou-
straitjacket	Note there is no 'gh' in this word
straitlaced	Note there is no 'gh' in this word
suc**ceed**	See *-cede, -ceed, -sede*
super**sede**	See *-cede, -ceed, -sede*
su**r**prise	Remember the first -r-
su**spic**ious	Note that this word ends in -ious

T

table a motion, second a motion

table a motion *verb phrase*, means in BE to put forward a formal proposal for discussion in a meeting: *The motion was tabled and carried by four votes to three*. In AE, the same phrase means to forget the matter or put it aside indefinitely. As these different uses are a source of transatlantic misunderstanding, this phrase must be used with care. See SHELVE.

second a motion *verb phrase*, means to support a proposal: *I wish to propose the following motion. Will anyone second it?* See SECOND (SECONDMENT).

These words can also be combined with other nouns including *bill* and *proposal*; *table a bill, second a proposal*.

tables

See STYLE GUIDELINES (WRITING SKILLS).

tack

See DRAWING PIN.

tactic

See STRATEGY.

take

See BRING.

take a rain check

See ADJOURN.

take on

See EMPLOY.

tale, story

tale *noun*, means an imaginative story or an exciting description which may or may not be true: *She wondered how any of them had survived to tell the tale*. Note that to *tell tales* means to inform someone in authority about another person's wrongdoing. This is commonly used by children. The informer can be called a *telltale* (*tattletale* in AE).

story *noun*, means a description of events by a writer or speaker. In some contexts as in a newspaper's *exclusive story* or *lead story*, this may be accurate and true. In other contexts, such as a *children's story*, or a *hard luck story*, many elements are invented. The word **story** should be handled with care: if someone tells the **story** of their life, it may be completely true, but if someone is *telling stories* they are probably untrue; and a *tall story* is utter fantasy. See GROUND.

These two words can be used interchangeably in idioms such as *to tell a different tale/story* meaning to give some information that is different from what you expect or have been told, and *to tell its own tale/story* meaning to explain itself, without needing any further comment or clarification: *The expression on the doctor's face told its own story.*

talisman, amulet, charm

talisman *noun*, means an object that is considered to be magic and that will bring good luck: *Melanie folded the letter and kept it, as a kind of talisman, to remind her the past was real*. The plural is *talismans*.

amulet *noun*, means a piece of jewellery that is worn because it is considered that it will bring protection from illness or bad luck: *She felt no fear as she entered, but briefly touched the jet amulet round her neck for luck*.

charm *noun*, means a small object worn usually hooked on a bracelet, that is believed to bring good luck: *The small horseshoe was her lucky charm*.

talk, speech, lecture, address

talk *noun*, means an oral presentation that is usually prepared: *We went to a talk on alternative medicine*. When **talk** is used as an uncountable noun it means the process of communication: *It used to be said in the Second World War that careless talk costs lives*. See TALKS.

speech *noun*, is a presentation that is carefully prepared and designed to gain support or present an argument: *The Foreign Secretary gave a major speech on relations with France*. An *after-dinner speech* is supposed to be prepared and entertaining. When **speech** is used as an uncountable noun it means the ability to speak: *The doctors helped him recover the faculty of speech.*

'Here speeching American.'
(Continental shop sign)

lecture *noun*, is a prepared presentation for teaching purposes: *This lecture will be transmitted to students on three campuses.*

address *noun & verb*. As a noun, **address** means a formal oral presentation. *He gave an address at Washington University on 'American Language and American Literature'.* In BE the second syllable is stressed in both the noun and the verb, but in AE the first syllable is stressed when **address** is used as a noun: áddress /'ædres/.

All these words may be combined with the verbs give and deliver.

talks, discussion

talks *plural noun*, means serious formal discussions between governments: *Britain and China ended their third round of talks about environmental issues yesterday*. In a domestic setting, **talks** between unions and management may decide about levels of pay and conditions. See TALK.

discussion *noun*, means a meeting that considers different ideas or opinions on a particular subject: *Discussions between the two leaders are now taking place in Cairo.* See CONVERSATION.

tall

See HIGH.

tap, faucet

tap *noun & verb*. As a noun, this is a device to control the flow of liquid from a pipe or container: *The most likely reason the waste pipes have frozen is that you have a dripping tap*. In electronics, **tap** also means a device for listening in to phone calls: *a wire tap*. As a verb, it can mean to make use of a resource: *He tapped into the expertise of his colleagues.* It can also mean to listen secretly to phone calls or electronic communications.

faucet *noun*, means a water tap and is the usual AE term. This is a French word for the device used to draw a liquid from a cask.

target

See AIM.

tartan, plaid

tartan *noun*, is a chequered woven woollen cloth in a Scottish textile design. Each design is associated with a particular Scottish clan: *The tartan cloth was made into a kilt.*

plaid pladd /plæd/ *noun*, is a length of tartan fabric worn over the shoulder as part of Scottish Highland dress: *He looked magnificent in his plaid and kilt.*

Plaid is often confused with *tartan* outside Scotland.

tasteful, tasty, delicious

tasteful *adjective*, refers to something that is made or selected with good taste. This especially applies to clothing and decor: *We were all very surprised to see the modern bathrooms and tasteful surroundings.*

tasty *adjective*, generally refers to food with a pleasant taste: *Mussels make a very tasty pasta sauce*. However, *a tasty bit of news* means gossip.

delicious *adjective*, means very pleasant to the taste or smell: *What a delicious aroma coming from the kitchen – roast beef and Yorkshire pudding.*

tasteless, unsavoury

tasteless *adjective*, is the opposite of tasty when referring to food. As it is also the opposite of tasteful it can refer to a lack of tact, or something that is offensive and inappropriate: *But if the sculpture seemed tasteless, vulgar and dumb, its power was undeniable.*

unsavoury *adjective*, means unpleasant to taste, smell or look at. It is frequently used figuratively to refer to offensive actions that are morally unacceptable: *His disclosures have already caused several deaths, and every time he talks it reminds the world of his unsavoury past.*

taught, taut

taught *verb*, is the past tense and past participle of to teach: *'I don't want my child taught by that teacher!'* See TEACH.

taut *adjective*, means stretched tight. This can apply to ropes and sails or to skin and muscles: *He began rubbing his taut muscular shoulders*. People can also be **taut** if they are anxious or tense: *Charles's nerves were so taut: he jumped when the cork popped*.
See TIGHT.

tautology

Tautology means the unnecessary repetition of the same idea, in the same phrase, often using synonymous words or expressions, where just one is sufficient. Here are some examples that careful writers should try to avoid:

bisect in two	*sad misfortune*
future plans	*past history*
large in size	*red in colour*

Tautology also appears in expressions like:

6 a.m. in the morning

They stood in a line, one behind the other

He was ambidextrous and could use both hands equally well

Sometimes, **tautology** occurs because writers do not remember what the last letters in acronyms and abbreviations stand for. Common examples include: *LCD display* (liquid crystal display – use just *LCD*), *HIV virus* (human immunodeficiency virus – use just *HIV*), *PIN number* (personal identification number – use *PIN* or *PIN code*) and *OPEC countries* (Organization of Petroleum Exporting Countries – use *OPEC member(s)*, or *member(s) of OPEC*). Reports often contain tautology caused by combining 'such as', 'like' and 'examples include' with 'etc.' or 'and so on' at the end. Example: *Traffic such as: lorries, trucks and vans, etc*. Combining foreign words with English sometimes leads to **tautology**. Examples: 'and etc.', 'salsa sauce' ('salsa' means sauce) and 'RSVP, please reply'.

taxi (noun and verb)

taxi *noun*, means a vehicle with a driver that can be hired for transport.

taxi *verb*, is used of aircraft, and means to move slowly along the ground (or water, if a seaplane) before take-off or after landing: *He had already done his instrument checks as he was taxiing*. Note the double 'i' spelling in *taxiing*. The past tense is spelt *taxied*.

teach, train, learn

teach *verb*, means to give instruction in a subject in an educational setting or on an informal basis. One can also teach people to act or think differently: *You can teach a young dog old tricks, but not an old dog new tricks*. In AE the expression *to teach school* means to teach in a school. See INSTRUCTION, TAUGHT.

train *verb*, means to instruct a person or an animal in the skills necessary for a particular job or activity: *A choke chain is used to train dogs like these to walk properly on the leash*. **Train** also means to devote a lot of time for exercise to prepare for a particular sport or activity.

learn *verb*, means to receive instruction or gather experience by hands-on practice over a period of time: *We learned how to use that new program yesterday; Jane began learning French at the age of 6*. See LEARNED.

T

One way to distinguish between *teach* and *learn* is to consider the direction of the instruction: *I taught French last week, but the pupils learned very little*.

team

See TEEM.

technician, technologist, techie, technocrat

technician *noun*, means either someone whose job is keep machinery functioning or equipment in good condition or a very skilled person in some technical aspects of a sport or science: *A surgical technician of great standing will head the operation*.

technologist *noun*, means an expert in technology.

techie *noun*, means a technologist or someone who is enthusiastic about technology, especially computers. It is also spelt *techy*. This is an informal term.

technocrat *noun*, means someone with great scientific expertise, often one who is a member of a scientific elite in politics. The related term *technocracy* means a society controlled by technocrats.

technical, technique, technology

technical *adjective*, means relating to practical use of machinery or methods in science and industry. It can also refer to a subject, such as technical terminology, or the skill required for doing a particular task: *Technical skill is a fundamental basis for most, if not all, great art.*

technique *noun*, means the way of doing something, especially involving the learning of special skills. It can also refer to one practical skill: *Karajan, it seems, always had a superb baton technique.* An AE spelling of **technique** is *technic* which is pronounced técknik /ˈteknɪk/ or teckneék /tekˈniːk/.

technology *noun*, means the application of the most recent scientific knowledge to design new systems: *Information and communication technology is one of the leading areas of research here.*

technical drawing

See DIAGRAM.

teem, team

teem *verb*, means either be full of something: *Morton drifted into the grand salon, which was teeming with people*; or pour, rain hard: *By the time the game was due to start it was teeming with rain.*

team *noun & verb*. As a noun, this is a group of people who cooperate in playing a game or work together on a particular job: *The sales team is having a meeting for the rest of the day.* As a verb, *to team up* means to join a group or a colleague for a specific activity: *Why not team up with another couple and get a reduction on the sightseeing trip?*

> *'Paphos is positively teaming with history.'*
> (www.cyprusisland.com) !

teething troubles/problems, growing pains

teething troubles/problems *plural noun*, means the minor difficulties with a product launch or after starting up a company: *There were an awful lot of teething troubles in the first year or so, but it is working very well.* Note how these phrases are mainly used in the plural.

growing pains *plural noun*, means problems experienced by a company as it starts to expand: *Its goals of supporting advanced features will inflict costs in reliability while it experiences its share of growing pains.*

> Both these terms refer to short-term problems experienced by young companies, just as they are by babies and young people.

telephone numbers

reading telephone numbers

When giving someone a telephone number it helps to group them in two or three digits at a time. There is also a tendency to use a rising intonation and pause at the end of each group, and for the intonation to drop at the end.

+44 20 7437 4514 (or, within the UK, 020 . . .)

+4′4 2′0 7′4 3′7 4′5 1‵4

+4′4 2′2 3′4 6′6 9‵6

When using English to non-native speakers it will help if all the digits are in the range of 0 to 9. Thus 34 is three–four, not thirty-four.

0 is normally pronounced 'oh' in BE and usually 'zero' in AE.

telephone keys *noun*, on most phones there is a [✳] star button or star key and a [#] hash button or hash key. In AE, this is called the pound button or pound key.

writing telephone numbers

According to international standards, telephone numbers are written in pairs, without hyphens between digits:

+32 16 23 90 96

the + sign means the international code, which is usually 00 today.

In Britain, telephone numbers are usually divided into two or three parts, the first is the area code (e.g. 01279), and the second is the local number, which may be six, seven or eight digits. If it has six digits, they are written together, e.g. 579579. If there are seven or eight digits, the last four are written apart from the first three or four, e.g. 020 7765 4305, or 0131 554 1923.

In informal English, *telephone numbers* can mean large sums of money.

(This expression often refers to high numbers, not just long ones.)

teller

See **CASHIER**.

temerity

See **TIMIDITY**.

temperature, fever

temperature *noun*, means the measurement of how hot or cold a person, object or place is. This can be in general terms like high and low, rising and falling, or expressed in exact terms by degrees indicated by a number: *It is 25 degrees Celsius today*. The phrase *to have a temperature* means that a person has a higher temperature than normal. This may be a symptom of an illness. See **CELSIUS**.

fever *noun*, means an illness or medical condition where the patient has an abnormally high body temperature: *The girl had not regained consciousness and she had a very high fever*. **Fever** can also mean nervous excitement: *World Cup fever comes to Trinidad and Tobago*.

tempo, pace

tempo *noun*. In music, this means the speed or rhythm of a piece. Here the plural is *tempi*. In other contexts it means the speed of action or movement: *The tempo of speech differs depending on the urgency (rapid) or deliberation (slow) of the speech*. The plural here is *tempos*.

pace *noun and verb*. As a noun, this means the speed at which something happens. **Pace** refers to something which is fast or slow: *Children can work at their own pace*. As a verb, it means to walk in a restricted area many times as a sign of nervousness or anxiety: *He began to pace silently along the bridge*; or to measure a distance by the number of steps it takes to cover it: *The referee paced out the ten yards and told the players to stay there*.

These words can sometimes overlap: *We can increase or decrease the tempo and pace of life*. But something can only gather *pace* or move at a walking *pace*.

T

temporary, temporal

temporary *adjective*, refers to something that lasts for a short time and is not permanent: *Temporary work seems to have an important role to play in the transition from unemployment to employment*.

temporal *adjective*, refers to the physical world, as opposed to religious affairs. The division between spiritual and **temporal** is often used: *Almost all Bills in Parliament are discussed by the Lords Spiritual and Temporal, and the Commons*. See **SPIRITUAL**.

temporary solution, band-aid solution

temporary solution *noun phrase*, means something that is not permanent: *This is only a temporary solution. Get the car to the garage as soon as you can*.

band-aid solution *noun phrase*, means a temporary solution that does not satisfy a long-term need: *Sending tinned food to the earthquake zone is just a Band-Aid solution.* This is an expression which comes from **Band-Aid**, an American trademark for an adhesive bandage similar to Elastoplast in the UK.

tender, bid

tender *noun & verb*. As a noun, this means a formal statement of the price charged for doing work or supplying goods or services. Someone who submits a **tender** is called a *tenderer*. As a verb, it means to submit a **tender**: *Next week we will issue an invitation to tender*. This is a formal BE term.

bid *noun & verb*. As a noun, this means either *tender*, which is commonly used in AE, or an attempt to win something: *He was within a few inches of Olympic disaster last night in his bid for the 110 metres hurdles crown*. As a verb, **bid** means to make an offer to buy something, especially at auction, and the past tense of the verb is **bid**: *She decided to bid for the painting*.

> In the context of tendering, in BE *tender* is used as the noun and verb, while in AE only the noun form of *bid* is used.

tenure, term[1]

tenure *uncountable noun*, means the period of time when a person holds an important position. In politics this is limited by the constitution or practice. It can also refer to the right to live somewhere. In universities, getting tenure or security of tenure means that a lecturer or professor has the right to stay permanently in their job.

term[1] *noun*, means the period of time something lasts. In politics it can be the US President's term of office (four years). It also means the period that money is loaned for: *The term of the loan is 15 years*. Note that both *short-term* and *long-term* contain hyphens.

term[2], semester, trimester, quarter (university terms)

term[2] *noun*, means one of the three periods in the academic year. This is a typical BE term: *We have teaching in the autumn, spring and summer terms*. Some universities have other names for their terms: Oxford has *Michaelmas, Hilary* and *Trinity*, Cambridge has *Michaelmas, Lent* and *Easter*.

semester *noun*, means one of the two periods in the academic year. This is typically used in universities in North America, parts of Europe and also in a few universities in Britain such as Bath and Edinburgh. **Semesters** usually last for four months: *Spring* and *Fall semesters* (AE) or *Spring* and *Autumn semesters* (Europe), though the word literally means six months.

trimester *noun*, means one of the three periods in the academic year. This is a typically AE word, and spring, fall and winter are common names for *trimesters*: *We would like to congratulate all the students who have achieved Dean's List status during the Fall trimester*. Note that the first syllable rhymes with 'try'.

quarter *noun*, means one of the four periods in the academic year. This is a typically AE word: *Spring Quarter '08 began on March 31*.

terminable, terminate

terminable *adjective*, describes something that can be ended: *Both have contracts with the company terminable at three years' notice*.

terminate *verb*, means to stop or end something such as an agreement, pregnancy or a journey: *This contract terminates at the end of January*.

terminal, terminus

terminal *noun & adjective*. As a noun, this means a large building for passengers at an airport, or a place where journeys by sea, rail or road begin or end: *The fifth terminal at Heathrow caused a lot of trouble in its first week*. In computing, a **terminal** is usually a keyboard and screen connected to a central computer system: *The terminals are now replaced by PCs*. As an adjective, it refers to a fatal illness that has reached its final stages such as *terminal cancer*.

terminus *noun*, is the station or stop at the end of a bus or train line, such as a *railway terminus*. The plural is either *termini* or *terminuses*.

terraced house

See TOWN HOUSE.

testify

See WITNESS.

testimonial, testament

testimonial *noun*, means a tribute to someone. If it is in writing, it is usually a formal statement or reference about a person's abilities and character: *She was given an excellent testimonial*. In sport, it is usually a game arranged in honour of a player who receives a share of the profit: *The testimonial at Elland Road brought him over £100,000*. See TESTIMONY (EVIDENCE).

testament *noun*, means either a section of the Bible, when it is capitalized; or a will: *But here in her last will and testament she revealed some of the disappointments in her life*.

thankful, grateful

thankful *adjective*, is used either to express pleasure and gratitude about something: *Not for the first time, I was thankful that she was such a good barrister*; or to express relief that the outcome of something was better than feared: *The car was written off but we are thankful that no one was injured*.

grateful *adjective*, describes a wish to thank a person, group of people or organization that has been helpful to you: *I am grateful to the following people for the assistance they have given me in writing this report*.

> The spelling 'greatful' is wrong. Even so Google picks up almost 100,000 hits for the phrase 'I am greatful' on the Web.

thankfully, hopefully

thankfully *adverb*, means with thanks: *He accepted the new boots thankfully*. When it modifies a sentence, it means fortunately: *Thankfully, leather mountain boots are reasserting themselves*. As **thankfully** can be misunderstood, it should be used with care. The sentence *Thankfully, he moved out*, opens up the question whether he was pleased to be going, or whether she was pleased that he was leaving.

hopefully *adverb*, means either in a hopeful way: *He waited for her phone call hopefully*, or when it modifies a sentence, it means it is hoped that: *Hopefully, he would wait for her phone call before he left for Spain*.

> The use of both these words to modify a sentence has been criticized, but most linguists find no grounds for this criticism and as about 80 per cent of the entries in the British National Corpus show they are widely used as sentence modifiers, *hopefully, people will stop criticizing this usage*.

that, who and which (in clauses)

that and **who** are used interchangeably to refer to *people* in clauses like *The student that/who rang yesterday is on the phone now*. The information in the clause *that/who rang yesterday* identifies which student and is essential to understand the meaning of a sentence. Clauses like this are not marked off by commas and are called *restrictive relative clauses*. Though both these relative pronouns are correct in a clause like this, **who** is more formal than **that**. If you refer to a noun that represents a group of people, use **that** not **who**: *The students that you met yesterday are arriving now*.

Both **that** and **which** can be used in *restrictive relative clauses* to refer to *things*: *We stayed at the hotel that/which you told us about*. In informal English, the relative pronoun is often omitted: *We stayed at the hotel you told us about*.

who is used to refer to a *person* in clauses that add extra information like *Mary, who is a real chatterbox, is on the phone now*. Clauses like this add extra information (which can be omitted without changing the meaning of the sentence) and are marked off by commas. These are called *non-restrictive relative clauses*. Dashes and brackets (like the 'which' clause used two sentences earlier) can also be used to mark off such a clause. See COMMA (PUNCTUATION GUIDE).

which is used to refer to *things* in *non-restrictive relative clauses*. As these clauses add extra information, remember the commas: *My folding bike, which has eight gears, saves me using the car*. It is non-

T

standard to use **that** here instead of **which**. A simple rule of thumb is to use **that** in *restrictive relative* clauses (those without commas) and **who** or **which** in *non-restrictive relative* clauses (those with commas).

the

See **ARTICLES (GRAMMAR TIPS)**.

theatre, theater, movies

theatre *noun*, is a place where people are entertained, or where they are operated on in a hospital. Note that in a hospital the BE *operating theatre* is called operating room in AE. In another sense, **theatre** can also mean a lecture hall. This is the BE spelling.

theater *noun*, is the AE spelling. Note that a **theater** can be a cinema in AE where it is usually called *movie theater*.

movies *noun*, is either an abbreviation of *movie theatre* or usually in the singular a film: *All she wants is a star role in that movie*. When it is used as the plural in this sense it means films in general: *This was the sort of thing that only happened in the movies*. This word is typically used in AE.

there, their, they're

there *adverb & pronoun*. As an adverb, this can mean in that place or position and contrasts with *here*. As a pronoun, it acts as a 'temporary' or 'dummy' subject to allow the real subject of a sentence to follow the verb: *There is still a lot of furniture to move*.

their *possessive determiner*, means belonging to or connected with people or things that have already been mentioned: *The Irish are renowned for their folk music traditions*.

they're *verb*, is the contraction of *they are* or *they were*: *He looked down the road and said 'they're coming'*. See **CONTRACTIONS**.

thereafter, thereby, therein, thereof, thereon, thereto, thereunder, thereupon, therewith

Apart from **thereby** which means as a result of a move or measure: *He got to his feet, thereby prompting a steadily growing cheer*; all these adverbs are common in legal English, but can seem very formal or archaic and are best replaced by *afterwards*; *in there* or *of it*; *of there*; *on there*; *to there*; *under there*; *on there*; *with the thing mentioned*.

Here can also be prefixed to the same prepositions and the resulting words are equally formal.

therefore, therefor

therefore *adverb*, means for that reason or consequently: *I was late and therefore I was very agitated, I'm sorry*.

therefor *adverb*, means for that purpose. It is a very formal word and is classified in modern dictionaries as an archaic piece of legal terminology to replace 'for'.

thesis, dissertation

thesis *noun*, means a long piece of work that is part of an advanced university degree in British universities. In many American universities, a **thesis** is a piece of work submitted for a lower or master's degree: *She finally submitted her thesis*. The plural of **thesis** is *theses*. The second syllable of the plural is pronounced like the word 'seas'.

dissertation *noun*. In most British universities this means a lengthy piece of work that is written as part of a degree: *He was delighted when the completed dissertation could be presented*. In most American universities, a **dissertation** is work at doctoral level: *A dissertation for the degree of Ph.D. should contain at least five chapters*.

In other parts of the English-speaking world, both terms are used for doctoral work.

the writing on the wall

See **GRAFFITI**.

they, them, their and themself for singular nouns

It is often argued that if a noun is singular, any following reference to it by means of a pronoun should also be singular, i.e. by using *he/him/his*, *she/her/hers* or *it/its*. Logic, as applied to mathematical formulae, would demand this, but language does not always follow the rules of mathematical logic. Examples of the third person plural pronouns being used to refer to a singular noun have been found in writing dating back 400 years, including in the King James translation of the Bible (1611) – a translation often held up as a model of English style. For instance, in Deuteronomy 17:5, we read *Then shalt thou bring forth that man or that woman . . . and shalt stone them with stones.*

An alternative to using a pronoun is to repeat the noun in full, but this often results in unwieldy phrases. The Canadian Department of Justice has published guidelines that illustrate this, and contrasts:

> *Every person who is qualified as an elector is entitled to have the person's name included in the list of electors.*

with

> *Every person who is qualified as an elector is entitled to have* ***their*** *name included in the list of electors.*

The first phrase is heavy as well as ambiguous: does *every person* and *the person* refer to the same person? The second with *their* is immediately understandable and unambiguous.

Informally, the reflexive pronoun *themself* has started to appear for cases where the sex of the individual is unknown or not relevant. Many dictionaries still consider this form to be incorrect, and Word will not allow it – it is automatically corrected to *themselves*, but the British National Corpus has 26 examples of its use, including: *Paula asked her 'how could someone hang themself?'* and *You won't be the first or last man or woman who gets themself involved in a holiday romance.* These are both examples of colloquial speech, and it is best to avoid using the word in any contexts except very informal English.

There are cases when it is advisable to use *he, she* or *it* to refer to a singular noun but the relevant plural pronoun *they, them, their,* is an alternative that is recommended by modern BE dictionaries and therefore used in this book. See HE, SHE, THEY.

they're

See THERE.

thieve

See BURGLE.

thin, lean, slim, skinny, emaciated

thin *adjective*, is a general word to describe a person who has little fat on their body. It is often disapproving and may suggest weakness: *She was thin, with a bony face and bulging, frightened eyes.*

lean *adjective*, means thin in a healthy way that implies fitness: *He was a lean and athletic high jumper.*

slim *adjective & verb*. As an adjective, this refers to someone who is attractively thin: *She looked at the young, slim beauty of his body, the clear, healthy eyes, the shining hair.* As a verb, to **slim**, or to *slim down*, means to lose weight by eating differently or taking more exercise. If a company downsizes, the process can be called *slimming down*.

skinny *adjective*, means very thin, unattractive and also implies weakness: *In a race on Sports Day, his skinny, uncoordinated limbs flung out in all directions.*

emaciated *adjective*, refers to an animal or person who is thin and weak, usually because of illness or lack of food: *I noticed a girl at our local swimming pool, painfully emaciated, like something out of a concentration camp.*

T

thing

thing is a word careful writers try to avoid as it means anything and everything. Instead of writing 'an important thing about English is its rich vocabulary', note how *an important attribute of/characteristic of/feature of/English is its rich vocabulary* lifts the level of your language.

thorough, meticulous, fastidious

thorough *adjective*, means complete in all details: *The doctor reappeared and began to administer the most thorough medical check-up I have ever experienced.* Informally it can emphasize how annoying something is: *This will make a thorough mess of the local ecosystem.*

meticulous *adjective*, means paying careful attention to every detail: *It was a dedicated task for meticulous and logical individuals with a mathematical bent*.

fastidious *adjective*, means caring about details and wanting everything to be correct: *My fastidious fiancée gave me a comprehensive briefing on ironing strategy*. In another sense it means disliking things that are untidy or dirty: *He was extremely fastidious about his appearance and personal hygiene*.

though

See ALTHOUGH.

thousand, thousands

thousand *number*, means an exact number. When **thousand** follows a number like: *five thousand*, or the words *a, a couple, a few, several,* or *many*: *three thousand people, a few thousand soldiers, several thousand litres*: *Fifty thousand people were watching the football match*, a plural verb is used. However, when **thousand** is used in a unit of time, distance, money, temperature, or such like, it takes a singular verb: *Fifty thousand pounds is required by next week*. This is often abbreviated to 'k' for kilo in job advertisements: *25k plus car*.

thousands *number*, means an inexact number. **Thousands** may be preceded by *several* or *many* but it should not have an exact number before it: *Several thousands of pounds were wasted on that project*. Note that **thousands** takes a plural verb.

thread, cotton

thread *noun*, means a long thin strand of cotton, nylon, silk or other fibres, but not metal: *The thread was loose and the button fell off*. **Thread** is also used figuratively for a connection or theme: *A common thread was their interest in soccer*.

cotton *noun*, means thread spun from the cotton plant that is used for sewing: *You must use a doubled piece of red cotton with this button*.

through, thru

through *preposition & adverb*, describes movement from one side of something to the other. In AE, expressions of duration like *Monday through Friday* include both Monday and Friday as well as the days in between.

thru *preposition & adverb*, is an informal abbreviation for *through*. This is used in SMS messages but should not be used in formal writing unless it is the name of a highway in the USA: *The New York State Thruway (officially the Governor Thomas E. Dewey Thruway)*.

throughway, thruway

See AMERICAN ROAD TYPES.

thumb tack

See DRAWING PIN.

tidbit

See TITBIT.

tight, tightly

tight *adjective & adverb*. As an adjective, this means close fitting: *Her dress was too tight*; or strictly controlled: *They kept a tight grip on fiscal policy*. **Tight** also indicates a lack of time: *a tight schedule*. As an adverb, **tight** means very firmly: *Ma came and picked her up, holding her so tight she could hardly breathe*.

tightly *adverb*, means very firmly and closely: *She held the baby tightly in her arms*.

In many cases, either form may be used as the adverb, but *tight* often follows the past participle: *The case was packed tight*, while *tightly* often comes before it: *The case was tightly packed*. However some adjective phrases reverse this order, such as *tight-lipped* and *tight-fisted*.

till

See UNTIL.

timber, timbre, lumber

timber *noun*, means wood prepared for building and carpentry: *There were massive timber beams in the house*.

timbre *noun*, is the characteristic quality of a musical instrument or a voice: *A man's voice answered, husky, with a pleasant timbre*. Note that **timbre** is pronounced 'tamber'.

lumber *noun*, in BE is an old-fashioned word for furniture or other large objects that are unused and being stored. In AE, **lumber** means timber, and is commonly used in the term *lumberjack*: *One of the best remembered songs on 'Monty Python's Flying Circus' is the Lumberjack Song*.

time of day

There are three systems to choose from when presenting the time of day. They should not be mixed. The **o'clock** and **a.m./p.m.** systems are both based on the 12-hour clock, and there is also the **24-hour** system.

o'clock

In formal writing, use o'clock with words, not digits: *six o'clock*, not '6 o'clock'. Do not use o'clock with a.m. or p.m. It is incorrect to write 'nine o'clock a.m.', use 'in the morning/afternoon/evening' or 'at night' after o'clock: *nine o'clock in the morning* and *ten o'clock at night*. Note that o'clock is only used for whole hours. O'clock comes from the days of the town crier: 'three of the clock', thus it is important to remember the apostrophe after 'o'.

a.m./p.m.

When writing the a.m./p.m. system for hours or fractions of an hour, use digits, not words: *8 a.m.* or *9.15 p.m.*, not *eight a.m.* The abbreviation a.m. means 'before noon' (Latin: *ante meridiem*) and is the period from midnight to noon; p.m. means 'after noon' (Latin: *post meridiem*) and is the period from noon to midnight. An easy way to remember this is that a.m. comes before p.m. alphabetically. As there is confusion between '12 a.m.' which is midnight, and '12 p.m.' which is noon, 'midnight' or '12 midnight' and 'noon' or '12 noon' can be used instead. With this system, write and say: *8.35 a.m.* and *4.20 p.m.* In AE, a colon is used instead of a stop between the hour and the minutes. The system is commonly used in schedules and programmes and if it is obvious when the events take place, a.m./p.m. can be omitted: *9.15 Opening, 10.30 Coffee, 1.00 Lunch, 5.15 Closing Session*. A careless error is combining *in the morning/afternoon/evening* and *at night* with a.m. or p.m., as in: '8.30 a.m. in the morning'. See TAUTOLOGY.

The 24-hour clock system

This is common in transport timetables and military use. Only four-digit numbers are used in this system and there is no combination with o'clock or a.m./p.m. The time can be written with or without a stop between the hour and minutes: *13.25* or *1325*. Note that *12.00* means 12 noon and *24.00* is 12 midnight.

When discussing the time of a meeting with Germans, Scandinavians or Dutch people it is best to use the form 'eight thirty', 'nine thirty', 'ten thirty', etc. rather than 'half eight', 'half nine' or 'half ten'. This is because in all these Germanic languages the half + time phrase means 30 minutes before the hour referred to. So the Swedish 'halv tio' (literally half ten) means 'half before ten' or 9.30.

> *'Nobody calls me stupid: meet me outside when the little hand points down, and the big hand points up.'*

timetable

See SCHEDULE.

timidity, temerity

timidity *noun*, means a lack of confidence, shyness or fearfulness: *She had seen his timidity, his ignorance of housekeeping, his lack of authority as a man*.

temerity *noun*, means daring or contempt for danger. This is a formal word and an informal equivalent is *cheek*: *The master of the hunt brandished his whip at the protesters for having the temerity to stand in his way*.

Note that these two words have opposite meanings.

tin

See CAN[2].

time zones with abbreviations

Note that the plus and minus signs in these selected time zones indicate the number of hours ahead or behind UTC (which stands for Coordinated Universal Time) which is the same as GMT (Greenwich Mean Time).

Abbreviation	*Full name*	*Location*	*Time zone*
BST	British Summer Time	Europe	UTC + 1 hour
CEDT	Central European Daylight Time	Europe	UTC + 2 hours
CEST	Central European Summer Time	Europe	UTC + 2 hours
CET	Central European Time	Europe	UTC + 1 hour
CST	Central Standard Time	North America	UTC – 6 hours
EEDT	Eastern European Daylight Time	Europe	UTC + 3 hours
EEST	Eastern European Summer Time	Europe	UTC + 3 hours
EET	Eastern European Time	Europe	UTC + 2 hours
EST	Eastern Standard Time	North America	UTC – 5 hours
GMT	Greenwich Mean Time	Europe	UTC
PST	Pacific Standard Time	North America	UTC – 8 hours
UTC*	Coordinated Universal Time	Europe	UTC

* UTC is used as the abbreviation because the International Telecommunication Union wanted a single form for all languages. Since the English speakers and the French in this international advisory group could not agree, the compromise UTC was arrived at.

tinge, tint

See TONE.

tire

See TYRE.

titbit, tidbit

titbit *noun*, means a morsel or small selected piece of food: *When the puppy comes to your calling its name, reward it with a titbit*. If it refers to gossip it means a small but interesting snippet: *The papers might as well be handed that titbit in tomorrow's press statement*.

tidbit *noun*, is the AE form of *titbit*.

titillate, titivate

titillate *verb*, means to excite or stimulate, especially in a sexual way: *But they are paid, like the tabloids in England, to titillate their public*. This is a disapproving term.

titivate *verb*, means to improve the appearance by making small changes that smarten up something or someone: *Is there any way he can titivate that flat?*

titles: use in writing and meetings

See WRITING SKILLS.

toboggan

See SLEDGE.

today, tomorrow

today *adverb & noun*, means on this day or in the present period. The spelling *to-day* is old-fashioned.

tomorrow *adverb & noun*, means on the day after today or in the future. The spelling *to-morrow* is old-fashioned.

toilet, toilette, WC, bathroom, public convenience

toilet *noun*, is both the room and the WC. In AE, the term *bathroom* is common and **toilet** is rarely used. In a meeting the term 'comfort break' is used to see if anyone wants to go to the **toilet**/bathroom. The expression *toilet water* refers to a kind of mild perfume.

toilette twaalétt /twɑːˈlet/ *noun*, is an old-fashioned term that means washing, dressing and attending to one's hair: *This painting shows some scantily clad maidens at their toilette.*

WC *noun*, is an abbreviation for *water closet*, which is a dated term, although **WC** is used on maps and signs, and in other places to save space.

bathroom *noun*, means a room with a bath or shower, a washbasin and sometimes a toilet. In AE, it means a room in which there must be a toilet. Thus, the AE expression *I need to go to the bathroom* means 'I want to use the toilet'.

public convenience *noun*, means a toilet in a public place.

> *In Italy, Schweppes Tonic Water was translated as 'Schweppes Toilet Water'.* **!**

tomorrow

See TODAY.

tone, tint, tinge

tone *noun*, means a shade of a colour: *Rich Plum is mid brown with purple tones*. See SHADE.

tint *noun*, means a shade or small amount of a specific colour: *He wears sunglasses that have a fading inbuilt, pinky-orange tint*. See SHADE.

tinge *noun*, means a small amount of a colour: *The light had a cold bluish tinge and the air was cooler too.*

> Although *tone* and *tint* are often found in the plural, *tinge* is rarely used as a plural. This word should not be confused with its near soundalike *twinge*.

> *'My back might be showing signs of strain . . . the little tinges of pain confirm I have done a lot of heavy lifting.'* (Editor, *Sea Angler*) **!**

tonne, ton

tonne *noun*, means 1,000 kg. This may be referred to as the *metric ton* or alternatively, *metric tonne*. The plural is **tonne** or *tonnes*.

ton *noun*, as a measurement of weight needs to be specified carefully as it means the *metric ton* (1,000 kg), the *short ton* which is the American system (2,000 lb or 907.19 kg) and is used a lot in the oil industry, or the *long ton* in the imperial system (2,240 lb or 1,016.5 kg) which is used in parts of the English-speaking world.

topic, issue

topic *noun*, means a subject that is to be talked about, written or learnt: *With a talk, the topic is specified in advance and you will be expected to keep to your brief.*

issue *noun & verb*. As a noun, this means an important topic for discussion, or it can also mean a problem: *The Canadian Court turned to an analysis of the game of ice hockey to address this issue*. In another sense, an **issue** is a particular edition of a periodical publication, such as a newspaper or magazine: *'The Bookseller' is publishing a special feature in its issue of 4 June*. Informally, **issue** means problem and is used in phrases such as *to have issues with somebody*: *The website specializes in helping those who have had issues with credit card companies*. As a verb, **issue** means to publish: *I issue regular catalogues about every 3–4 months*. This is also used in a formal or official context: *The opposition issued a press release accusing the government of inconsistency*.

> When referring to subjects for discussion, a *topic* is more up to date than an *issue*.

tornado

See HURRICANE.

tortuous, torturous

tortuous *adjective*, refers to something that is winding like a steep mountain path. In another sense it refers to things that are complicated and difficult to understand: *You knew the law with all its tortuous language and convoluted clauses*. In its second meaning this is often a disapproving term.

torturous *adjective*, refers to something that involves torture, pain or suffering: *his former teammates undergo a torturous five days of fitness testing abroad*.

> As *tortuous* means complicated and lengthy it can overlap with *torturous* when one is referring to something like a carefully scheduled fitness programme.

total

See SUM.

touch upon

See BRING UP.

tough

See STRICT.

tour

See TRAVEL.

Tourette's syndrome

See SYNDROME.

tournament

See CHAMPIONSHIP.

towards, toward

towards *preposition*, means in the direction of something. A plane may fly **towards** a direction: *Flying towards the east*; but *to*, not **towards**, its destination: *We are now flying to Beijing*. In another sense it means close to a point in time: *It happened towards the end of our holiday*. Also it can mean in relation to someone or something: *Our attitude towards pollution has changed*. This is the BE spelling.

toward *preposition*, is the AE form of *towards*.

tower

See SPIRE.

town, city

town *noun*, means an urban settlement that is smaller than a city. Sometimes part of a city is called a **town**, as in the *old town*. If one goes *up to Town* (capitalized), in the UK this means London. *Small-town* refers both to small towns in general and to narrow-minded values. See VILLAGE.

city *noun*, usually means more than just a large *town*. In Britain and the USA, *civic status* is an honour conferred on a community officially by the monarch or the state, respectively. Most *cities* have a cathedral and/or a university. Size is usually, but not always, important. The *City of London*, for example, has over a million people working there, but has an area of only one square mile and a resident population of about 6,000. When **city** is used to mean the *City of London*, it is capitalized and requires the definite article: *He is something in the City*. There are also quite small *cities* in the American West. In other parts of the English-speaking world, many large *towns* are called **city** without any legal rights or royal charter.

town house, terraced house, row house, brownstone

town house *noun*, means a multi-storey urban house, that can be attached or detached. It is typically built close to the street and scaled similarly to surrounding houses. **Town houses** are usually tall and narrow and are often built to be slightly different from neighbouring houses. In AE, it is usually spelt as one word: *townhouse*.

terraced house *noun*, means one of a row of attached houses, usually in the same style as other parts of the same development. The row itself is called a *terrace*. This is typically a BE term.

row house *noun*, is the AE term for a terraced house, all the houses in a row usually being in the same style.

brownstone *noun*, is the AE term for a townhouse or row house that has a brown sandstone façade.

toxic, toxics, toxin

toxic *adjective*, refers to something that is poisonous: *Public health groups are worried about toxic discharges from paper mills that use chlorine bleach*. The related noun is *toxicity*.

toxics *plural noun*, means poisonous substances: *Some dangerous toxics were stolen from the laboratory*.

toxin *noun*, means a poisonous substance produced by living cells or organisms that causes disease: *Most countries joined the Biological and Toxin Weapons Convention of 1972*.

track, trail, path

track *noun & verb*. As a noun, this means a rough road such as a cart track through the scrub. It can also mean the marks or signs left by the passage of a person, animal or vehicle: *He had been tempted to use the President's Land-Rover but the tracks would have shown*. This is normally used in the plural. As a verb, it means to use strenuous efforts to locate an object, animal or person that is difficult to find: *Underground networks try to track down women and girls who have run away from their families*.

trail *noun & verb*. As a noun, this means a narrow track in the countryside: *From here the trail enters forest land taking paths leading to many lovely reed-fringed lakes*. It also means the marks or signs left by someone or something. As a verb, it means to follow behind someone or something: *Wales were convincing winners even though they trailed 15–6 with half an hour to go*.

path *noun*, means a narrow track that is either built, or made by people walking: *A path takes you through a delightful forest, past an incredible waterfall, and up to the ridge*. The word *footpath* shows that this track is reserved for walking.

tract

See STRETCH.

trade union, labor union

trade union *noun*, means an organization in a particular trade or profession that represents workers. This is a BE term. An alternative is *trades union*: *Trades Union Congress (TUC)*.

labor union *noun*, is the equivalent term to *trade union* in AE: *The Coalition of Labor Union Women supports the rights of working women and families*.

In BE, the phrase *trade union* is stressed on 'union', while in AE, *labor union* is stressed on the word 'labor'.

trademark, brand name, brand

trademark *noun & verb*. As a noun, this means the special sign, word or name that is found on a product to characterize a product sold by a company. A **trademark** cannot legally be used by another company. Some *trademarks*, such as Xerox or Polaroid, have become generic for the type of product. Upper case is usual for the **trademark** such as Frisbee when referring to the company owning the **trademark**. In another sense, a **trademark** also means a characteristic way of dressing or behaving: *She was instantly recognizable with her trademark pink hair and pink hat*. As a verb, lower case is used for *trademarks* such as to hoover (vacuum clean) and to xerox (photocopy). See XEROX.

brand name *noun*, means the name given by a manufacturer to one of its products: *The advertising agency came up with the brand name 'Corny', but it was rejected by the company*.

brand *noun*, means the type of product made by a company with its particular name or design: or refers to a range of products: *This brand of toothpaste comes in four different flavours and three tube sizes*.

trail

See TRACK.

T

trailblazer, pathfinder

trailblazer *noun*, originally meant a person who found a new track through unknown country. This is often used today to refer figuratively to an innovator: *He was a trailblazer in this important area of genome research*.

pathfinder *noun*, originally meant a person or a group that found their way over unknown land. This is often used today for an innovative way of doing something. The term was formerly used for pathfinder aircraft that mark targets for bombers, but more recently NASA and others have used the term for space missions and innovative software.

trailer

See CARAVAN.

train

See TEACH.

train of events

See STRING (OF).

traitor

See TREACHERY.

tranquil

See CALM.

transcribe, transliterate

transcribe *verb*, means to transfer thoughts, notes, data or often recordings into full text: *I'll transcribe the tape more or less verbatim and then work in the other material*.

transliterate *verb*, means to write or print words or letters from one alphabet to another using corresponding letters: *If you transliterate the Danish word sjørøver into English it will be sjoeroever*. *If you translate it, it means 'pirate'*. See TRANSLATE.

transcript, academic record

transcript *noun*, means a written version of material noted in another medium: *a complete transcript of the video dialogue*. In an academic context, a **transcript** is an academic record. This term is common in AE and is used in many universities around the world.

academic record *noun*, means the official record of a student's work with courses they have taken and the marks/grades achieved: *You can obtain a copy of your academic record from the Student Services Centre or Student Registry Services*.

transfer, relocate, resettle

transfer *verb*, means to move from one organization or job to another, or to make someone else move within the same organization: *At the end of the year, the development team will be transferred to our Glasgow office*. Money, property, skills and phone calls are all transferred from one person to another. When travelling, **transfer** means to change to a new flight or take a bus to your hotel.

relocate *verb*, means to move to a different place: *The tax incentives are very attractive for businesses that relocate to Northern Ireland*. People can also be *relocated: Six families had to be relocated when the new bypass was built*.

resettle *verb*, means to go to live in a new country or new area, or to help people do this: *Syria secretly offered to resettle 300,000 refugees as part of a comprehensive settlement*. This word also means to settle again, and refers to people returning to an area that was formerly settled.

translate, interpret

translate *verb*, means to express the meaning of something that is in one language by means of another. This includes written as well as spoken language. The word is often used figuratively to mean convert: *Anyone who sought to translate their feelings into political activity soon found themselves in jail*.

interpret *verb*, means to *translate* a speech or discussion from one language to another orally as it is going on. In another sense it means to explain the meaning of something in simpler or more understandable terms: *People find it easier to interpret and take in pictures than words*. In a figurative sense it means to obtain meaning and understanding from something: *These early experiments were sometimes difficult to interpret*.

transliterate

See TRANSCRIBE.

translucent

See TRANSPARENT.

transmit, broadcast

transmit *verb*, means to send electrical signals containing messages or information. Although emails are *transmitted*, most people use the more informal term *send*. **Transmit** has a variety of other meanings connected with passing one thing on to another. These can be diseases or feelings such as fear or anxiety: *The survivors of the crash transmitted their joy at being rescued to the people watching on television*.

broadcast *verb*, means to transmit radio or TV programmes: *During the week the BBC took the opportunity to broadcast part of another pre-recorded interview*. The past tense, past participle and present tense are all spelt **broadcast**.

transparency, slide, overhead

transparency *noun*, means three things beside the quality of being transparent (see next entry). First, a sheet of plastic through which light can be shone to throw an image on to a large screen. Second, a transparent photograph that is printed on glass or plastic and can be viewed using a device such as a slide projector: *Avoid too many transparencies and talk to the audience, not to the screen*. Third, as an uncountable noun, it means the quality of being honest and easy to understand, especially when explaining an idea or policy: *The system will allow greater transparency and make clear how the extra funding will be spent*.

slide *noun*, in the context of photography means a mounted transparency that can be placed in a projector and viewed on a screen: *The whole family suffered two hours of John's holiday slides of Tenerife*.

overhead *noun*, means a transparency designed for use with an *overhead projector*. The term **overhead** often refers to the projector as well: *Let me use a couple of overheads, I will just find out how to turn the overhead on*. Some people use the term *overhead transparency* when referring to sheets of plastic film: *I have this presentation both on PowerPoint and overhead transparencies*.

Technology is overtaking these terms and most of the items referred to are now only found in digital form on a laptop. Even so, we refer to *transparencies, slides* and *overheads*.

transparent, translucent

transparent *adjective*, refers to something such as clear window glass that allows light through and the objects on the other side to be seen clearly: *The tiny eel was almost transparent, except for the jet black, pinprick eyes*. **Transparent** is also used figuratively to mean clear and understandable: *Our government will lay out a series of transparent measures*.

translucent *adjective*, refers to something that lets light pass through, such as frosted glass where the light can be seen, but no clear objects can be seen on the other side: *At this thickness most rock-forming silicate minerals are translucent*. It can also mean very pale and delicate as in *her translucent skin*.

transport, transportation

transport *noun & verb*. As a noun, this means the system or means of conveying people and goods from place to place: *Cycling is a totally sustainable form of transport: it creates no pollution, and minimal congestion*. As a verb, **transport** means to convey things. Note the stress in the verb is on the second syllable.

transportation *noun*, means the system or means of transport for people and goods: *It would mean that British Gas would put a mileage rate on the transportation of gas*. This word also has a historical meaning: the act of sending convicts out of England to settle new territories: *The transportation of convicts to the colonies ended in 1868*. In AE, **transportation** corresponds to the BE use of *transport*.

transportable

See PORTABLE.

travel, journey, trip, tour, voyage

travel *noun & verb*. As a noun, this means the activity of travelling especially over long distances. As an uncountable noun, **travel** refers to types of movement like *air travel, business travel*, never to a specific trip. As a plural noun, *travels* means journeys to places far away, usually for pleasure: *'Travels with my Aunt'* (Graham Greene novel). As a verb, it means to make a long journey, especially abroad. Note that in BE, the verb forms are spelt *travelled* and *travelling*. In AE, the equivalent forms are spelt *traveled* and *traveling*.

journey *noun & verb*. As a noun, this means the act of travelling from one place to another especially when they are far apart: *We have a long journey in front of us through mountains and deserts*. A **journey** may also be short, if it is done regularly: *He only had a 15-minute journey to work*. In AE, *trip* is an alternative in this sense. As a verb, to **journey** means to *travel*. This is a literary word.

trip *noun*, means a *journey* to a specific destination, particularly for pleasure: *We only had time for day trips last summer*. As this term may be associated with pleasure, it is

T

common to use *business trip* to indicate a *journey* where pleasure was not the objective. Such trips are collectively called *business travel*.

tour *noun & verb*. As a noun, this means either a journey for pleasure where several places are visited; a thematic trip: *a tour of Shakespeare's England*; or a conducted visit to a tourist attraction: *The guided tour of Stratford-upon-Avon starts at 6 p.m.* **Tour** also has the idea of visiting and performing (for music) or playing (for sports) in several different places: *the All Blacks' tour of England*.

voyage *noun*, means a long journey in a spacecraft or ship: *The Greek-registered ship left Singapore on a voyage advertised as a 'cruise to nowhere'*. **Voyage** is a word typically used in writing, and *trip* is more usual in other contexts.

Note that *travel* puts the emphasis on general movement from place to place. *Journey* puts the emphasis on the activity of travelling, and *trip* puts the emphasis on where you are going or why you are going there.

treachery, treacherous, traitor, treason

treachery *noun*, means betrayal of a trust: *Selling the computer code was an act of treachery*.

treacherous *adjective*, refers to someone or something that is untrustworthy or dangerous: *Black ice is a treacherous road surface*.

traitor *noun*, means a person who betrays another person, a cause or a principle: *He was denounced as a traitor*. The related adjective *traitorous* is a formal word.

treason *noun*, is the legal term for the offence of betraying one's country: *It was a clear act of treason*. This is commonly termed *high treason*. The related adjectives are *treasonable* for an act or offence and *treasonous* for a person.

treaty, accord

treaty *noun*, means a formal written agreement between two or more governments or states: *NATO stands for the 'North Atlantic Treaty Organization'*. See AGREEMENT.

accord *noun*, often means a formal agreement between countries or groups, that is less formal than a treaty: *The general Peace Accord ended the country's 16-year civil war*.

treble, triple

treble *verb, adjective & noun*. As a verb, this means to become three times as large in size or number: *Land prices in some areas have trebled in a year*. As an adjective, it means consisting of three parts: *He bought a new treble-pronged fish hook*. As a noun it has various meanings in sport such as *Chelsea are heading for the treble* (meaning success in three competitions), and it means the relatively high pitch in music: *Turning down the treble helps to control fuzziness in the violin sound*. In music, a **treble** is a child with a high voice (especially a boy), and the **treble** is the top line of music sung by the child.

triple *verb, adjective & noun*. As a verb, this means to increase by three times as much: *We have tripled our production*. As an adjective, **triple** means three times as much: *Average earnings there are triple those in Britain*; or being in three parts: *a triple-glazed window*; *a triple rhyme* means a rhyme using three syllables. *Triple time*, in music, means having three beats in a bar. As a noun, **triple** refers to a set of three things, such as a betting system demanding that the first three horses in a race be placed in the specified order.

The verb forms overlap but the use of *triple* is more common in AE and many BE speakers would use the verb *treble*: *We have trebled our production*. Note how *treble* and *triple* have very different meanings in music.

trendy

See POPULAR.

trilateral

See UNILATERAL.

trillion

See BILLION.

trimester

See TERM.

trip

See TRAVEL.

triple

See TREBLE.

troop, troupe

troop *noun*, means a group of soldiers or more generally people or animals: *UN peacekeeping troops are deployed in the region*.

troupe *noun*, is a group of touring actors or dancers: *The Chippendales troupe is currently on tour in Europe*.

trooper, trouper

trooper *noun*, means a soldier in the cavalry: *The mounted troopers filed past the visiting president*. In AE, a **trooper** can mean a police officer.

trouper *noun*, means a professional actor or entertainer with long experience. Informally it also means a dependable person: *Frank was a real trouper*.

truck

See LORRY.

true, truly

See REAL.

truth, truthfulness, veracity

truth *uncountable noun*, means the state or quality of being true, based on fact and not imagined: *The truth is, I look upon both candidates in the same light*. **Truth** is also a countable noun with a plural, but this usage is less common: *We hold these truths to be self-evident . . .* (US Declaration of Independence).

truthfulness *uncountable noun*, means the honesty of a person: *You can always rely on the truthfulness of his answers*. It can also mean the facts about something in a statement: *No one could question the truthfulness of the statement he made in court*.

veracity *uncountable noun*, means the accuracy and truth of something: *The reporter checked the veracity of the claim made by the opposition*. This is a formal word.

try

See ENDEAVOUR.

tumour, tumor

tumour *noun*, means a swelling caused by abnormal growth of cells in or on a part of the body where they should not be. This is the BE spelling.

tumor *noun*, is the AE spelling of *tumour*.

turnip, swede, rutabaga

turnip *noun*, is a general term for a group of root vegetables. In some parts of Britain, it contrasts with *swede*, a large vegetable (*Brassica rutabaga*) with yellowish flesh. The **turnip** (*Brassica rapa*) is smaller, about the size of an onion, with white flesh. In other parts of Britain, **turnip** means both *Brassica rutabaga* and *Brassica rapa*.

swede *noun*, is a large round root vegetable: *The vegetarian diet of swede, potatoes and beans provided some healthy meals*. This is called a *turnip* in some parts of Britain.

rutabaga rootăbáygă /ruːtəˈbeɪgə/ *noun*, is the AE term for a *swede*.

turn King's/Queen's evidence

See PLEA BARGAINING.

turnpike

See AMERICAN ROAD TYPES.

tuxedo

See DINNER JACKET.

two weeks

See FORTNIGHT.

type in

See KEY IN.

type of

See KIND OF.

typhoon

See HURRICANE.

typical, characteristic, usual, customary

typical *adjective*, refers to something distinctive about a particular type of person or thing: *It* *was as we hoped for – a typical English Sunday lunch.* **Typical** also refers to things that are normal: *Table 4 is an example of a typical day's food intake.* See DISTINCTIVE (DISTINCT).

characteristic *adjective & noun.* As an adjective, this means typical of a particular person, group, place or thing: *A refusal to linger is often characteristic of the true professional.* As a noun, it means a feature of someone or something that is typical and easily recognizable. It is often used in the plural: *The distinguishing characteristics of this car were its doors that opened upwards.*

usual *adjective,* means normal or typical regarding what is habitual or occurs frequently: *The British got there in their usual resourceful way.* The phrase *business as usual* implies carrying on as if no difficulties had occurred, such as after a fire.

customary *adjective,* refers to things that are usual and typical of specific social groups or situations: *He was beginning to feel unaccountably cheerful despite the disappointment of missing his customary pint of beer.* **Customary** is more formal than *usual.*

These words are very close in meaning but *typical* is something normal and *characteristic* can refer to an attribute or quality.

typo, misprint

typo *noun,* means a typographical error caused by a slip of the hand when typing, but does not extend to a mistake caused by the ignorance of the writer. Examples include poor word division between lines of type, such as 'legends' split into 'leg-ends', and using the wrong font or case. The word **typo** is used informally and often too broadly to include mistakes in books which do not come from the printers.

misprint *noun,* means a mistake in spelling when a document or book is printed. One **misprint** to avoid is misspelling *misspell* as *mispell.*

To indicate that the mistake in a text you are quoting was in the original, it is common practice to write [*sic*] after it. See SIC (N.B.).

'Ms Gray is Head of Department Six, and not as reported in our June Newsletter, Department Sex.'
(Staff magazine)

!

tyre, tire

tyre *noun,* means a rubber covering around a wheel. This is the spelling in BE: *Snow tyres may have studs fitted in parts of the world where there is a long icy season.*

tire *noun,* is the AE spelling of *tyre.* Note that the verb *to tire* means to become weary. This is the only spelling in BE and AE.

Spelling

ta**<u>riff</u>**	Note single -r- and double -ff
temp**<u>o</u>**ral	Note the -o-
temp**<u>or</u>**ary	Note the -o- and that -r- comes twice
thei**<u>rs</u>**	No apostrophe
therefor**<u>e</u>**	Note the final -e
th**<u>ie</u>**f	-i- before -e-
thre**<u>sh</u>**old	Note that there is only one -h- in the middle of this word
tin**<u>sel</u>**	Note the ending: -sel
tomat**<u>oes</u>**	Note the ending with -e-
tra**<u>d</u>**itional	Note the single -d-
tranqui**<u>ll</u>**ity	Note the -ll- in British English
tr**<u>u</u>**ly	There is no 'e' in this word
ty**<u>r</u>**a**<u>nn</u>**y	Note the single -r- but double-nn-

U

UK

See **BRITAIN, UNITED KINGDOM**.

ultrasound

See **X-RAY**.

umlaut

See **SYMBOLS**.

umpire

See **REFEREE**.

umpteen

See **FEW**.

unable

See **INABILITY**.

unapt

See **INEPT**.

unaware, oblivious

unaware *adjective*, means not realizing or understanding that something is the case: *She was unaware of her own prettiness*. In another sense it means not realizing what is happening: *He was unaware of the police car behind him*.

oblivious *adjective*, means taking no notice of something: *Club professionals appear oblivious to the needs of left-handed golfers*. **Oblivious** in this sense may be followed by either *of* or *to*. **Oblivious** can also mean unmindful, and is then often followed by *of*: *A young soldier and his girlfriend sat on the balustrade, oblivious of anyone else*.

unbalanced, biased

unbalanced *adjective*, refers to a lack of balance in someone or something. For a person this is a way of saying that he or she is suffering from a mental illness. In a report or presentation of something it means being one-sided and inaccurate: *Editors often cut a vital sentence, too, and made the whole thing unbalanced*.

biased *adjective*, means unfair to one group at the expense of another because of prejudice or special interest: *They have tried to influence the editorial policy of the BBC and have complained of biased reporting*.

unbending, inflexible, rigid

unbending *adjective & verb*. As an adjective this means unwilling to change decisions or opinions: *He was so tough, so unbending and uncompromising, and I don't think he's changed*. As a verb, to *unbend* means almost the opposite – to behave in an unreserved way: *You should have seen our chief accountant unbending after a few drinks*.

inflexible *adjective*, means unwilling or unable to change: *The vast majority of the public maintain stubborn and inflexible attitudes to the subject of mental handicap, especially if the problems intrude into their lives*. This word usually conveys a disapproving attitude, so when referring to this quality in a material or object, it is preferable to use a different word, such as *rigid*. People or things with the opposite characteristic are *flexible*.

rigid *adjective*, refers to rules, regulations and attitudes that are very strict: *This time, however, employers' resistance was rigid and the strike soon lost momentum*. A **rigid** object is one that is stiff and difficult to move.

All these adjectives can convey a disapproving attitude to someone or something.

underestimate

See **OVERESTIMATE**.

undergraduate

See **STUDENT**.

underneath, under, below

underneath *preposition & adverb*, means directly below something, or covered by something: *He shouted for help from underneath the rubble*. **Underneath** also refers to a lower surface: *The pizza was* *burnt underneath*. In another context it refers to someone's real feelings, not just how they act: *Underneath his veneer of self-confidence, Luke was very shy*.

under *preposition*, means directly beneath something: *The child was hiding under the bed*. **Under** can also be used with amounts of money, periods of time or age: *It cost under £10; They were waiting for under two hours; Under 18s will not be served*. It also refers to control as in *under martial law*, or in the course of: *under construction, under difficult conditions*.

below *preposition & adverb*, means at a lower level than something else: *Most of this part of the country is below sea level* (preposition); *Mist lay in the valley below* (adverb). **Below** can also mean lower on a scale: *They are below us in the rankings*. For another sense, see BELOW (ABOVE).

Note that *under* and *underneath* mean directly beneath something: *The ship was moored underneath London Bridge*; *the ship was sailing under London Bridge*; whereas *below* means on the seaward side or lower down the river: *The ship was below London Bridge*. Thus it follows that 'above London Bridge' refers both to a vertical position in the air and upstream from London Bridge.

undershirt

See VEST.

understandable

See COMPREHENSIVE.

undertaking

See BUSINESS.

undertone

See OVERTONE.

underwear

Underwear refers to clothing worn next to the skin, or usually hidden by some other clothing. Some terms are used differently in BE and AE, referring to underwear in the one, and outerwear in the other. Likewise, some terms are specific to male clothing, others to female clothing, while others may be used for both.

When the headword given below ends in '-s', the word is plural, and must be followed by a plural verb. It may be made singular by using the phrase *a pair of . . .*, which takes a singular verb. The other words are singular, with the exceptions of **lingerie** and **pantihose**.

boxers are loose-fitting male **underpants**. This is an abbreviation of *boxer shorts*, so-called because of their resemblance to the clothing worn by boxers.

bra originally an abbreviation of the French word *brassière*, still seen sometimes, is the item of clothing that covers and supports a woman's breasts.

corset is a tight-fitting women's garment intended to make the body look slimmer. The same word is used for a medically prescribed garment which supports a weak back, and which may be worn by either sex.

garter in BE is a band used to support a sock (for men) or stocking (for women), some of whom wear them decoratively. In AE **garter** is used for BE **suspender**.

knickers in BE is a general term for the female garment which covers the buttocks and genitals. In AE **knickers** are trousers for either sex that end just below the knee. The informal BE expression *Don't get your knickers in a twist* means don't get excited and worried about something.

lingerie la᷄anzhĕri /lɑːnʒəri/ is a general term used to describe women's underwear. It is almost always the word used by department stores. Like *underwear*, it is an uncountable noun and therefore always takes a singular verb.

long johns are a close-fitting item of underwear for the lower half of the body.

panties is the usual AE term for the BE **knickers**.

pantihose is the usual AE term for the BE **tights**. This takes a plural verb.

pants in BE may be used either for male **underpants** or female **knickers**. In AE this is the usual equivalent for BE *trousers*. Informally, if something is *pants*, this means very bad: *That show was pants*. This is a BE oral expression.

petticoat is a female loose-fitting garment hanging either from the shoulders or the waist, and worn under a dress or skirt.

shorts is the usual AE word for male BE **underpants**. In BE **shorts** are short trousers.

slip is an alternative word for a **petticoat**.

suspenders is used in BE to refer to the belt from which clips hang to support a woman's stockings. A man may also wear *sock suspenders*, which are attached to each leg just below the knee, although this is now rare. In AE **suspenders** are also the straps hanging from the shoulders which hold up a man's trousers (called *braces* in BE).

thong is a piece of underwear or the bottom half of a bikini with a string instead of the back part. In AE, **thongs** also refer to a shoe with a strap between the toes. These are called *flip-flops* in BE.

tights is the BE term for the tight-fitting leg covering worn by women, which stretches from waist to toe.

underpants is the general BE term for the male garment which covers the buttocks and genitals.

undershirt is the usual AE term for the BE **vest**.

underskirt is an alternative term for **petticoat** or **slip**.

vest in BE is a garment for either sex which hangs from the shoulders and covers the trunk. It may be sleeveless or have short or long sleeves. In AE a **vest** is a sleeveless overgarment worn over a shirt and that has buttons on the front. In BE this is called a *waistcoat*.

Y-fronts is the BE term for **underpants** with a front opening, shaped like an upturned Y. It is a trade mark, but widely used for any **underpants** with a front opening.

(Bangkok dry cleaner's shop)

uneatable, inedible

uneatable *adjective*, refers to things that are not fit for consumption: *Hunting is a sport once described as the unspeakable in pursuit of the uneatable*. See EATABLE.

inedible *adjective*, also means not good enough to eat but this is either because it is of poor quality or poisonous: *He says that he only takes pike because eels have become inedible due to pollution*. See EDIBLE (EATABLE).

unemployed

See REDUNDANT.

U

unexceptionable, unexceptional

unexceptionable *adjective*, refers to something that is satisfactory and does not give any reason for criticism but often has no special qualities: *The food was bland and unexceptionable, but plentiful enough*. This is a formal word.

unexceptional *adjective*, refers to something that is commonplace and not especially good: *My destination was unexceptional, simply a footbridge over the tracks, a row of villas, a couple of trees*.

unfair, inequitable, unjust

unfair *adjective*, means not right or fair according to given principles, or not treating people equally: *The award is intended to compensate for financial loss resulting from the unfair dismissal*. **Unfair** is mostly used when referring to personal relationships. *He was unfair to his female staff.*

inequitable *adjective*, means unfair because of unequal treatment: *The scheme has operated on the inequitable basis of paying different amounts of compensation for the same injury*. This is a formal word. See INEQUITY (INEQUALITY).

unjust *adjective*, means unfair and not deserved. An *unjust law* is considered to be morally incorrect. *The rich are more inclined to say that they would break an unjust law than the poor*. **Unjust** often applies to social structures. See JUST.

unfathomable

See INEXPLICABLE.

unilateral, bilateral, trilateral, multilateral

unilateral *adjective*, refers to an action by one group, person or country without the agreement of the anyone else: *Unilateral action by the United Kingdom to stop defence sales did not stop the arms trade.*

bilateral *adjective*, refers to an action or agreement that involves two groups or countries: *A bilateral cooperation agreement covering trade and education was signed.*

trilateral *adjective*, refers to an action or agreement that involves three groups or countries.

multilateral *adjective*, refers to an action or agreement that affects three or more groups or countries: *A multilateral treaty may be broken down into a series of annual phases.*

unimaginative

See PEDESTRIAN.

uninhabitable

See HABITABLE.

unintelligible, incomprehensible

unintelligible *adjective*, refers to spoken or written language that is impossible to understand: *We reserve the right to edit all letters so that all the nasty, unintelligible bits get taken out*. See ILLEGIBLE.

incomprehensible *adjective*, refers to actions, behaviour or texts that cannot be understood: *What we want is down-to-earth accountability, not lots of incomprehensible grand ideas*. See INEXPLICABLE.

Although both these words refer to difficulty in understanding language, *incomprehensible* also covers actions while *unintelligible* refers only to communication problems.

uninterested

See DISINTERESTED.

unique, really unique

unique *adjective*, refers to an item that is the only one of its kind. Careful writers will therefore avoid using comparatives like *more* and *most* together with **unique**. However informally **unique** also means very special, and then comparatives like *more, most, totally* and *absolutely* are sometimes used with it: *I look for artists of exceptional talent, artists who are totally unique, irrespective of genre*. In general it is best not to overuse **unique**, and alternative adjectives such as *exceptional, rare, exclusive, sole, distinctive* or *unusual* may be considered instead.

really unique means remarkable or extremely unusual. This is best kept for informal English: *Looking for a really unique birthday gift?* See ABSOLUTE ADJECTIVES (GRAMMAR TIPS).

As *unique* has a consonant sound at the beginning, the indefinite article before unique is always 'a', never 'an', in writing as well as in speech.

Although New Orleans often uses the slogan 'the most unique city in America', a quick Google for this phrase reveals that New York, Las Vegas, San Antonio and Miami all make similar claims.

United Kingdom, United States of America, United Nations, UK, USA, UN

United Kingdom, United States of America, United Nations *proper nouns*. Countries and organizations using the same format as these always have a definite article before them (without a capital) in running text unless they are being used as modifiers: *Only United Nations peacekeepers will be given visas*. Also, as they are seen as one unit, the verb is singular: *Since 1946, the United Nations has been located in New York*. See BRITAIN.

UK, USA, UN *abbreviations*. These abbreviations refer to the country or organization and are written without stops. In running text, UK, USA, UN, etc. always have a definite article before them (without a capital) unless they are being used as modifiers. The **USA** refers to the country but the abbreviation US is often used for its people, soldiers, armed forces, business, etc.: *US business reports predict a fall on Wall Street*.

> Note that when these words are not the subject of a sentence, the following verb may be plural: *Wage levels in the United Kingdom are often too low*. Here the subject is wage levels not the United Kingdom.

university, uni, varsity

university *noun*, means an educational institution where students can study for a degree and where academic research is done. The standard abbreviation is Univ. See GRADUATE, SCHOOL.

uni *noun*, is an informal BE term for a university. This may not be understood outside Britain or Australia.

varsity *noun*, is an old-fashioned word for *university* in BE. A *varsity match* is a sporting fixture between two rival universities. The *Varsity Match* is the annual rugby match between Oxford and Cambridge universities. In AE, **varsity** means the main university or college sports team. The word **varsity** may also have local meanings at specific universities.

unjust

See UNFAIR.

unlawful, illegal, illegitimate

unlawful *adjective*, means forbidden by law, or not conforming to the law: *A verdict of death by unlawful killing was recorded by the coroner*. **Unlawful** is a formal word, often used in legal documents, that focuses on how the law is put into effect. See LAWFUL (LEGAL).

illegal *adjective*, means forbidden by law: *A cartel is illegal because it is trying to impose a monopoly on the market*. **Illegal** is used in some expressions such as: *illegal alien*, *illegal drugs* and *illegal exports*. See LEGAL.

illegitimate *adjective*, means not allowed by law or by a set of accepted standards: *It is important to distinguish between legitimate and illegitimate share trading*. In another sense, **illegitimate** means born to unmarried parents: *A person who is illegitimate may very well resent being called a bastard, although it happens literally to be true*. See LEGITIMATE (LEGAL).

unpaid

See OUTSTANDING.

unreadable

See ILLEGIBLE.

unrepairable

See IRREPARABLE.

unsatisfied, dissatisfied

unsatisfied *adjective*, refers to a demand or need that is not being met. For a person it means not having had enough of something: *In middle age, his emotional needs unsatisfied, his political career was finished by a scandal*.

dissatisfied *adjective*, means unhappy and disappointed by things such as poor service: *The last thing he wants to be bothered with is having to deal with complaints from dissatisfied guests*.

> Note that only *unsatisfied* can refer to states or situations, while both terms can refer to people.

U

unsavoury

See TASTELESS.

unsocial, unsociable

See ANTISOCIAL.

unsolicited bulk email (UBE)

See SPAM.

unsolvable

See SOLVABLE (SOLUBLE).

unstable, instability

unstable *adjective*, refers to things that are likely to change, fail or give way. Governments, currencies, bridges and the ground can all be described as **unstable**. When a person is described as **unstable** this usually refers to the state of their mental health: *He had very unstable health and his mood was liable to change very quickly*.

instability *noun*, means a situation or state where there is a lack of stability: *Rising prices and falling incomes are likely to cause political and economic instability*. **Instability** may also refer to a person's mental condition where there are likely to be sudden changes.

until, till

until *conjunction & preposition*, means happening or occurring up to a point in time, and then stopping: *until death do us part*; or continuing up to a particular place: *Stay on this road until you reach Oxford*. **Until** is the correct word to use at the beginning of a sentence. **Until** is sometimes shortened to *till*, *til* or *'til* but this is only in informal contexts.

till *conjunction & preposition*, means until. In many cases these words are interchangeable, but **till** is used in spoken contexts to refer to a specific time: *He did not fall asleep till 5*. It is best to avoid **till** at the beginning of a sentence.

> *Until* is used more frequently than *till*, especially in writing. However, *till* is regarded as more informal than *until*.

upload

See DOWNLOAD.

upon

See ON.

uprising

See REVOLT.

urban, urbane

urban *adjective*, means characteristic of or relating to towns and cities: *Most of these areas were urban centres on the coast or their immediate rural hinterlands*. Note that **urban** is usually placed before a noun. It is often contrasted with *rural*. In another sense, **urban** relates to music and culture such as rap and reggae that originates in black communities.

urbane *adjective*, usually refers to a person who has confidence and knows what to say and how to behave socially: *He was capable of being urbane, relaxed and downright frivolous*.

US, USA

See UNITED KINGDOM.

usable, useable

usable *adjective*, means available or in good enough condition to be used: *Once you are satisfied that the flue is in a usable condition, you can turn your attention to the fireplace itself*.

useable *adjective*, is an alternative spelling of *usable* in BE and AE.

> The British National Corpus gives about 20 times more hits for *usable* than the alternative *useable*. As *usable* starts with a consonant sound, it is preceded by the indefinite article 'a'.

usb, usb port

usb *abbreviation* for *universal serial bus*, is an interface device for connecting a printer, storage device or other peripheral to a computer.

usb port *noun*, means the place on a computer where a cable for connecting a printer, storage device or other peripheral to a computer is attached.

use, utilize, usage

use *noun & verb*. As a noun, this means the fact of serving a purpose or the purpose it was designed for: *The use of vacuum cleaners for removing dried leaves is not recommended*. Note that *use of* takes a singular verb. *To have the use of* something means that one has the right, permission or ability to use something: *It took three months before the injured footballer regained the use of his legs*. In linguistics, it means the way a word is spelt, written or used. As a verb, **use** means to employ a tool or method for a specific purpose: *Have you used a lawnmower like this before?* In another sense, it means to consume goods or services: *Cars like that use too much petrol*. It also means to treat people badly: *He was just using me*. In another sense it means to take drugs regularly. Note that the noun rhymes with 'loose' and the verb rhymes with 'lose'.

utilize *verb*, means to put something to effective and practical use: *We are trying to utilize solar energy to convert seawater to fresh water*. Some people use **utilize** too much, and *use* may often be a better choice. See DEVELOP.

usage *noun*, means the amount of use something undergoes: *Therefore, to increase the train usage rate for non-business travellers, some special price arrangements are needed to encourage people to leave their cars at home*. In linguistics, **usage** means the way words and phrases are employed: *Many details about English are explained in reference books on usage*.

use-by date

See SELL-BY DATE.

user ID, username, password

user ID *noun*, means the name that someone uses when operating a computer program or system: *If further abuse occurs, you will be removed from the list and your site informed about the abuse carried out by this user ID*.

username *noun*, means the name that identifies a person and permits access to a computer or computer system: *You can change this username if you wish*.

password *noun*, means a series of letters and/or numbers that are typed into a computer to enable it or a particular program to be used: *A password must be entered to start the system up again*.

used to, be used to

used to yo͞ost tŏ /'juːst tə/ *verb*, refers to situations or events that occurred regularly in the past, but which do not happen now: *He used to go down to Cardiff from London for big games, rarely missing an international*. In questions, use *Did he use to go to Cardiff?* rather than *Did he used to go to Cardiff?* This second version is clearly non-standard. The same applies to negatives: *He didn't use to play football* is recommended usage, but *He didn't used to play football* is non-standard. Note that the alternative *He used not to play football on Sundays* is correct usage but too formal for most contexts.

be used to *verb*, means to become familiar with something that was once unfamiliar or strange and which now happens every day: *The undernourished children are now used to three meals a day*. With this sense, the pronunciation of *used* is yo͞ost /'juːst/. In another sense, it means to be employed for some purpose: *Rumour can be used to support or destroy a career*. Here the pronunciation of *used* is yo͞ozd /'juːzd/. Note the 'zd' ending here.

U

usual

See TYPICAL.

utilize

See USE.

Spelling

un**c**le	Note the -c- (cf *ankle* with -k-)
unti**l**	Note the single -l
us**a**ge	Note there is no 'e' before the -a-
us**ur**p	Note the -ur-

V

vacancy, opening

vacancy *noun*, means an employment position that is waiting for applicants: *The vacancy must be filled within three days*.

opening *noun*, means a *vacancy* but this is often at one remove, rather than a specific position that is available now: *We will have an opening within the next three months.* This word is often used in the plural in this context: *The previous two sections have reviewed briefly some of the career openings and the training possibilities*.

vacant, available

vacant *adjective*, refers to an employment position, an unoccupied hotel room or a seat on public transport that is not being used. It is also used to show that a public toilet is not in use, and contrasted with 'engaged' in this sense. *Situations vacant* is a common heading for job adverts in newspapers. The noun phrase *flat with vacant possession* means that the previous occupant has left, and the new one may move in immediately. A *vacant expression* means a look on someone's face which indicates they are not thinking about anything at all.

available *adjective*, refers to things that are obtainable or can be purchased: *We have six seats available in the west grandstand*. When something is not available it does not exist or cannot be obtained: *When oil is no longer available, the use of hydrogen has been suggested as one of the answers to future transport fuel needs*. A person who is **available** is able to meet and talk to someone: *I will give him your message as soon as he is available*.

> When seats are *vacant*, they are not being used. When seats are *available* they can be booked or places bought.

vacation

See LEAVE.

vaccinate, inoculate, immunize

vaccinate *verb*, means to protect a person or an animal against a disease by means of a vaccine, usually, but not always, given in the form of an injection.

inoculate *verb*, means to protect a person or animal against a disease by injecting a weak form of it, encouraging the body to develop resistance.

immunize *verb*, means to protect a person or animal permanently against a disease by means of a vaccine.

> Technically, *vaccinate* and *inoculate* mean the same thing, but *vaccinate* is often used in the context of smallpox, while *inoculate* is used more generally. While a person who is *immunized* should never suffer from the disease afterwards, it may be necessary to be *vaccinated* or *inoculated* more than once to maintain protection.

valuable, invaluable, priceless

valuable *adjective*, means worth a lot of money and also refers to advice or information that is very useful or important: *I would like to thank all staff for their continuing valuable contribution in another extremely difficult year*.

invaluable *adjective*, means very precious or extremely useful: *Here the minister made an invaluable contribution through the creation of a new national curriculum*. Note that the opposite of *valuable* is never **invaluable**, even though **invaluable** begins with the prefix *in-*.

priceless *adjective*, means extremely valuable or valued so much that it is difficult to estimate a price: *He faces selling his priceless collection of Ferraris to pay off creditors*. It is also used figuratively: *History is a priceless preparation for citizenship, work and leisure*. Informally, something that is **priceless** is extremely amusing.

> Note that *valuable* is the least valuable of these three words.

valueless, worthless

valueless *adjective*, means having no value, worth or importance. This is a formal word and the opposite of *valuable*: *He was an important businessman, but his opinion was valueless when the negotiations started.*

worthless *adjective*, means without any practical or financial value. This word is more informal than *valueless*: *The cheque had been stolen and was worthless.* When referring to a person who has no good qualities or useful skills, **worthless** is the term to use, not *valueless*: *Who else do you know who thinks the old so-and-so is a worthless layabout?*

value creation, wealth generation, added value

value creation *noun*, is a term used in economics to mean the development of profitable activities for a company or other organization, often as a result of applied research: *The closer the target bank is to the acquirer, the better the chance of value creation, because expense control is more easily managed.*

wealth generation *noun*, means the accumulation of capital for private individuals: *Wealth generation and the creation of employment opportunities lie at the very heart of economic development.* An alternative term for this is *wealth creation*: *His success at wealth creation meant that he could provide practical help to those that need it.*

added value *noun*, means the additional value gained by a product at each stage of production or refinement: *The attractive packaging gave the product an added value of 20 per cent.* A related term is value added tax (VAT).

vantage point

See BIRD'S-EYE VIEW.

vapour, vaporize

vapour *noun*, means a mass of minute drops of liquid in the air: *The human body produces something like two litres of water vapour in an average night.* This is the spelling in BE. *Vapor* is the AE spelling of **vapour**.

vaporize *verb*, means to turn into gas: *About −80 °C, antifreeze turns to pink ice and gasoline (petrol) fails to vaporize or ignite.* Note that there is no 'u' in the second syllable. See -OR, -OUR SPELLINGS.

variety

See SPECIES.

various

See DIFFERENT.

varsity

See UNIVERSITY.

vegetable, cabbage, persistent vegetative state

vegetable *noun*. Apart from meaning an edible plant, **vegetable** is also an offensive term for someone who is severely physically and mentally disabled and can do nothing unaided. *Severely mentally disabled* is a recommended alternative. See DISABLED.

cabbage *noun*, as well as being a green vegetable, **cabbage** is also an offensive term for a person who cannot move or speak due to brain damage. It is mostly used in BE. *Severely mentally disabled* is a recommended alternative.

persistent vegetative state *noun*, is a medical term that describes someone in a coma and unable to move or help themselves because of brain damage. This is not an offensive term.

veld(t)

See PRAIRIE.

venal, venial, venereal

venal *adjective*, refers to something that is corrupt or a person who is capable of being bribed: *The law courts are venal and can take decades to decide a case.* This is a formal word.

venial *adjective*, refers to a sin or mistake, which is not as serious as a mortal sin and thus may be forgiven: *He had compounded a number of venial failings with the mortal sin of adultery.*

venereal *adjective*, refers to diseases that are transmitted through sexual contact. See SEXUALLY TRANSMITTED DISEASE.

vending machine, slot machine, fruit machine

vending machine *noun*, is a machine where food, drink, sweets and other items can be bought when coins are inserted.

slot machine *noun*, means a gambling machine where winnings depend on getting the right combination of symbols. In BE, a **slot machine** also means a vending machine where people can buy food or drink.

fruit machine *noun*, means a gambling machine originally with a handle that made reels with fruit symbols spin. An alternative term is one-armed bandit.

vendor, vender

vendor *noun*, means either a supplier that sells a particular product, or a person offering something for sale, especially a street trader such as a *newspaper vendor*. In property sales, the selling party is legally termed the **vendor**. However, Clarity (the lawyers' campaign for the use of plain English) approves the replacement of **vendor** by seller.

vender *noun*, is an alternative spelling of *vendor* used in AE.

venerate

See IDOLIZE.

venereal disease

See SEXUALLY TRANSMITTED DISEASE.

vengeance

See AVENGE.

venial

See VENAL.

veracity

See TRUTH.

verbal, *oral*, *aural*, written

verbal *adjective & noun*. As an adjective, this means related to words. It generally means spoken words in contrast to written words: *An initial warning is often verbal, even if it is logged in writing for the record*. A person who suffers from *verbal diarrhoea* talks too much. This is a disapproving term. As a noun it has the grammatical meaning of a word formed from a verb. But as an uncountable noun it is an informal term to mean critical or abusive language: *The crowd started giving the ref. a lot of verbal*. It is mainly used in BE in this sense.

oral *adjective*, refers to speech and the mouth: In an *oral examination*, which can be in any subject, students are tested on their ability to demonstrate their knowledge in discussion with the examiners. A dentist is concerned with *oral hygiene*. An *oral contraceptive* is one that is swallowed.

aural *adjective*, refers to ears and hearing. Tests designed to assess a student's listening comprehension skills are often called *aural comprehension tests*, as distinct from *oral tests*, which usually refer to an evaluation of a student's proficiency in speaking a foreign language. Note that *oral* and **aural** are pronounced the same.

written *adjective*, refers to words that are in writing, not spoken or oral: *Every student hates the ordeal of long written examinations*.

verbatim

See LITERALLY.

verbiage, verbosity

verbiage *uncountable noun*, means either the use of too many words, or of words that are unnecessarily difficult when presenting an idea.

verbosity *uncountable noun*, means the use of too many words: *The speaker was an exponent of the art of verbosity: He called a spade 'an implement for cultivation by hand'. I would have called it 'a spade'*. The related adjective is *verbose*.

> These terms and the related adjective *verbose* are all disapproving.

> ### verbiage
>
> Some examples of verbiage, with some suggested alternatives:
>
> *all of* – except with pronouns, *of* is unnecessary.
>
> *as to whether, whether or not* – *whether* is usually sufficient.

at an earlier date – use *before, previously*.

at this moment in time – use *at the moment*.

in character – this is often redundant, as in 'the work was demanding in character'.

due to the fact that/in view of the fact that – use *because* or *since*.

end result – use *result*, unless there has been a *preliminary result*.

fact – all facts are true and actual, so it is redundant to say *actual fact* or *true fact*.

first of all – this is redundant, omit.

in order to – simply use *to*.

in some cases – use *sometimes, often*.

in the final analysis – use *finally*, or omit.

in view of the fact that – use *because*.

knots per hour – per hour is redundant; a knot means 1 nautical mile (1,852 m) per hour.

nature – this is often redundant in phrases like *work of an experimental nature*.

-speaking – this is redundant in expressions such as *experimentally speaking* (how do experiments speak?)

revert back – simply use *revert*.

subsequent to – use *after*.

unique – means without equal, the only one of its kind. As this is rarely the case, it may be better to find another term. See ABSOLUTE ADJECTIVES (GRAMMAR TIPS).

utilize – *use* is often a good alternative.

very – do not overuse; *important* is often stronger than *very important*.

-wise – not recommended as a home-made ending; *clockwise* is standard; *costwise* is not.

verso, recto

verso *noun*, means the left-hand page of a book or the back of a printed page.

recto *noun*, means the right-hand page of a book or the front of a printed page.

vertex

See VORTEX.

vertical

See PERPENDICULAR.

vest, undershirt, waistcoat

vest *noun*, means a sleeveless undergarment in BE. Sometimes a **vest** can be worn as outerwear: *He was dressed in a plain white vest rather than one of his multicoloured T-shirts*. See UNDERWEAR.

undershirt *noun*, is the AE term for the undergarment called a *vest* in BE.

waistcoat *noun*, means a close-fitting, sleeveless, buttoned garment, worn under a jacket: *He wore a velvet waistcoat, a flamboyant bow tie and bright yellow jeans*. In AE this is called a *vest*.

vet, veterinary surgeon, veterinarian

vet *noun*, is the standard abbreviation of *veterinary surgeon*: *We'll have to call out the local vet*. In AE it is also short for *veteran*, meaning a US soldier who has served in a battle.

veterinary surgeon *noun*, is someone qualified to treat diseased or injured animals: *She'd been a practising veterinary surgeon for over 10 years, and was highly recommended*. This is the BE term. This is one of the few English words in which the standard pronunciation omits a written 'r' in all accents: véttinări /ˈvetɪnəri/.

veterinarian *noun*, is the AE term for a *veterinary surgeon*. The usual AE pronunciation is vettĕrináiri-ăn /vetərɪˈneərɪən/.

via, by means of

via *preposition*, means by way of and is used either for routes: *We travelled from Paris to Madrid via Lyon*; or for a method of electronic communication: *The message came via the Internet*. **Via** is also used to indicate the person who conveys a message: *I heard this via George*.

by means of *prepositional phrase*, refers to the methods used to achieve something: *Oil is brought ashore by means of a pipeline*. **By means of** is often replaced by *through* (for a person) or *by* (for the method of transport): *This sort of cargo is normally sent by air*.

vicar

See CLERGY.

vice, vise

vice *noun*, can mean criminal activities involving sex or drugs: *The fight against vice is never over*. It can also mean a bad habit: *Biting my fingernails is my only vice*. When it refers to rank, **vice** means next in seniority to or a deputy of: *vice president, vice-admiral, vice-chairman* and *vice-chancellor* (dictionaries and publishers differ on which of these terms they hyphenate). A **vice** is a clamp with metal blocks that can be tightened with a screw. It is used in carpentry.

vise *noun*, is the AE spelling of a *vice* in the sense of a clamp used in carpentry.

vicinity

See NEIGHBOURHOOD.

vicious, viscous

vicious *adjective*, means violent, aggressive and dangerous. If someone says something with vicious criticism this is full of hatred. It is used in expressions like *vicious circle* or *vicious cycle*, a chain of evil or misfortune that reinforces itself: *They don't have the cash to finance the rebuilding of the team and that can become a vicious circle: poor results, lower crowds, less revenue*.

viscous *adjective*, means thick and sticky: *A hot lava, freshly erupted, is a great deal less viscous than a cold one, and it can therefore flow faster*. This word is normally used in technical contexts.

victim, casualty

victim *noun*, means someone who is attacked, injured or killed as the result of a disease, crime or accident: *The woman who was 79 and a widow became the victim of a series of errors by medical staff*. A **victim** can also be someone who has been tricked: *He is believed to be an innocent victim of a clean-up campaign*.

casualty *noun*, means someone who is injured or killed in a war or accident: *The only casualty came in the first week after the ceasefire last August*. The *casualty unit* or *casualty ward* is the part of a hospital where people requiring emergency treatment are taken. This part of the hospital is also known as **Casualty** or A & E (Accident and Emergency) in BE: *A major Casualty department is no place for children!* In AE this is called the Emergency Room (or ER).

videlicet, viz.

See NAMELY.

view

See OPINION.

vigour, vigor

vigour *noun*, means physical strength, energy and enthusiasm: *They act with vigour, sing with great effect, and the small, but rather loud orchestra, sweep them all along*. Note that the adjective is spelt with only one 'u' – *vigorous*.

vigor *noun*, is the AE spelling of *vigour*. See -OR, -OUR SPELLINGS.

vigorous

See AGGRESSIVE.

village, settlement

village *noun*, means a small community in a country district. The **village** as a singular can refer to the local residents: *The entire village was in the pub*. This is a typical BE expression. In AE, **village** refers to a self-contained unit or community inside a town or city, like *Greenwich Village* or the *student village*. See TOWN.

settlement *noun*, means a previously uninhabited place where people have made their homes: *There was certainly a settlement in the neighbourhood well before the Norman Conquest*. See PAYMENT.

viscous

See VICIOUS.

vise

See VICE.

visible, visual

visible *adjective*, means relating to things that can be seen: *Our landing lights were* *soon visible to air traffic control*. It also means clear and obvious: *Meat must be lean, with all visible fat trimmed before cooking*.

visual *adjective*, means used in seeing or involving sight: *We were soon visual and able to locate the airfield*. *Visual aids* are pictures or videos used in education or training in order to assist learning. *The visual arts* means activities such as painting, sculpture and film.

visit

See STAY.

vital

See ESSENTIAL.

viz.

See NAMELY.

vociferous, voracious

vociferous vŏssíffĕrŭss /vəˈsɪfərəs/ *adjective*, means expressing opinions loudly and strongly: *The politics students thrive on argument and vociferous debate*.

voracious vŏráyshŭss /vəˈreɪʃəs/ *adjective*, means very hungry, never satisfied: *The pizza bar staff tried to keep up with the voracious appetite of the rugby team*. Figuratively, people who have a passionate interest in something are also said to have a **voracious** interest in or appetite for it: *His voracious interest in the arts set him apart from most of the other students*. See GLUTTONOUS.

voluntary

See OPTIONAL.

vortex, vertex

vortex *noun*, is a spinning mass of air or liquid like a whirlwind or whirlpool. The plurals are *vortices*, where the last syllable is pronounced like the word 'seas', or *vortexes*. In literature it describes a feeling or situation that you cannot avoid: *a swirling vortex of emotional confusion*.

vertex *noun*, is the highest point or summit. In geometry it is a point where two lines meet, such as the point of a cone. The plurals are *vertices* (the last syllable is pronounced like the word 'seas'), or *vertexes*.

vote

See ELECTION.

voucher, coupon

voucher *noun*, means a ticket that allows the purchase of goods without money or to get a reduction in the normal price of something: *A sample presentation pack is available, which includes a money-saving voucher*. A *gift voucher* or *gift token* allows someone to buy goods up to the value of the **voucher** in a certain shop or type of shop, or to purchase tickets for a concert or other event. This is called a *gift certificate* in AE.

coupon *noun*, means a ticket that gives the right to a reduction in the price of goods: *You can cut out the coupon opposite and get your first pack at half price*. It can also be a printed form such as *a pools coupon* or one that is cut out from a newspaper in order to enter a competition, order a brochure or goods: *If you'd like to know more about a real cook's kitchen, phone us free or return the coupon today*.

voyage

See TRAVEL.

voyeur, peeping Tom, watcher

V

voyeur vwaa-yúr /vwɑːˈjɜːr/ *noun*, means a person who either gains sexual satisfaction from watching other people who are naked or having sex, or who enjoys finding out details of other people's private lives: *He was a voyeur, an observer of life who never committed himself to becoming part of it*.

peeping Tom *noun*, means someone who enjoys secretly watching others removing their clothes or doing things in private, a *voyeur*: *Peeping Tom is said to have watched Lady Godiva ride naked through Coventry*.

watcher *noun*, means an observer who studies something regularly: *He inevitably became a sunset watcher; there was nothing else to do*. This word usually appears in compounds, such as *birdwatcher, trend watcher, royal watcher*.

Spelling

va**cc**inate	Note the double -cc-
va**c**illate	Note the single -c-
va**cuu**m	Note single -c- but double -uu-
vag**ary**	Note there is no 'u' in this word, and it ends -ary
vag**u**e	Note the -u-
vall**eys**	Note the ending: -eys
vap**or**ous	Note there is no 'u' before the -r-
var**ie**gated	Note the -ie-
vehic**u**l**ar**	Note the -u- and the ending: -ar
v**ei**l	Note 'e' before 'i'
v**ei**n	Note 'e' before 'i'
veng**e**ance	Remember the second -e-
v**er**ge	Note -er-
vet**eri**nary	Note there are two 'r's in this word
vi**c**i**ss**itude	Note the single -c- and double -ss-
vigil**ant**	Note the ending: -ant
vig**o**rous	Note there is no 'u' before the -r-
vin**e**g**ar**	Note the -e-, and that the word ends in -ar
vocabul**ary**	Note the ending: -ary, not -arly
volcan**oes**	Note the ending in -oes
vill**ai**n	Note the -ai-
voll**eys**	Note the ending: -eys
vulg**ar**	Note the ending: -ar

W

wage

See PAY.

waist, waste

waist *noun*, means the area around the middle of the body between the ribs and the hips: *Invest in a money belt that fits round your waist and has zipped compartments*. *Waistline* refers to the measurement of the body around the **waist**: *The waistline is usually the first area where fat accumulates*.

waste *noun*, means using something carelessly so that it is lost, spending money carelessly, or a situation where it is not worth the effort to do something: *It's such a waste of time. The police should be tracking down criminals*. **Waste** also means material that is not wanted, or a by-product. If one specific type of waste is referred to, there is a singular verb: *Three million tonnes of toxic waste is transported for treatment or disposal*. In the plural, *wastes* either means different types of material that are not wanted, such as *industrial wastes*, or areas of uninhabited land: *The wind whipped across the open wastes of moorland*.

> *'In-sink waist disposal.'*
> (Web advert from New Zealand) !

waistcoat

See VEST.

wait, await

wait *verb*, means either to remain in a place: *Do not leave the car: wait for the motorway patrols to find you;* or to postpone an action until something happens: *Wait until 6 before you eat*.

await *verb*, means to wait for an event or somebody or something: *A wealth of inviting attractions await all visitors*. This is a formal word.

> Note that *wait* usually has no object while *await* always takes an object.

waive, wave

waive *verb*, means not to use the legal or official rights one has: *The US government could decide to waive its penalties against UK suppliers*. As **waive** means to not exercise a right, it should not be combined with aside or away. This is a formal word.

wave *verb*, means to move the hand from side to side as a signal or greeting: *The children playfully waved to us as we went by*.

> The phrase *to wave something aside*, meaning dismiss, is sometimes incorrectly confused with *waive*.

waiver, waver

waiver *noun*, is a legal term that refers to a situation in which a person agrees not to exercise a legal right: *The professor signed a waiver giving the university the rights to his invention*.

waver *verb*, means either to sway and be unsteady or to be unable to make a decision: *There will be no wavering from the course of reform*.

wake, awake

wake *verb & noun*. As a verb, this means to stop sleeping or to make someone else stop sleeping: *It is time to wake the baby. Wake up* is often used figuratively to say that someone starts to realize the truth of a situation: *Why did it take so long for the world to wake up to what was going on?* As a noun, **wake** can mean a party in connection with a funeral

> *'There have been a number of offences by the press which have deeply disturbed public opinion; indeed, one cannot just waive them aside.'*
> (House of Lords, Hansard 1998)

where people gather together to reminisce and talk about the deceased. In another context it means the track left behind a boat as it moves through the water and this is the origin of the figurative expression *in the wake of*: *In the wake of the persecutions many fled from Germany in 1938*. See AROUSE (ARISE).

awake *verb & adjective*. As a verb, this means to stop sleeping and is usual in writing especially in the past tense *awoke*: *We awoke to a bright, sunny Sunday morning*. As an adjective it means not being asleep, or figuratively being aware of the situation: *More and more people are awake to the need for energy savings*.

wardrobe

See CLOAKROOM.

warm, hot

warm *adjective*, means at a fairly high temperature that is comfortable: *It all looks very attractive, particularly on a warm evening when you can dine outside*. **Warm** is also used about colours and feelings: *He could feel that she was getting warmer to him*.

hot *adjective*, means at a high temperature. **Hot** is used in many contexts ranging from lust, anger and danger to highly topical things such as *hot tips* or *hot news*. **Hot** combines with many other words to form expressions such as *boiling hot*, *red-hot* and *white-hot*.

warning, caveat

warning *noun*, means any kind of written or spoken statement that something unpleasant may happen so that action can be taken to avoid it: *As the quality of air fell to 'very poor', the government issued a health warning and urged people in London not to use their cars*.

caveat kávvi-at /'kæviæt/ *noun*, means a warning that something needs to be carefully considered before action is taken: *She will be offered hormone treatment – with the caveat that the method has only around a 30 per cent chance of success*. In other cases, **caveat** refers to a reservation: *With this caveat, the President endorsed the general's proposal for resuming the offensive*. This is a formal word.

warranty

See GUARANTEE.

waste

See WAIST.

watcher

See VOYEUR.

waterproof, watertight

waterproof *adjective & noun*. As an adjective, this means not letting water through or not damaged by water: *a waterproof tent*. As a noun it means a jacket treated to resist water. *Waterproofs* means a waterproof jacket and trousers.

watertight *adjective*, means made or sealed so that water cannot get in or out: *The matches were in a watertight container*. Figuratively it refers to an excuse or alibi that cannot be disproved: *The police questioned a couple of suspicious characters but their alibis are watertight*.

wave

See WAIVE.

waver

See WAIVER.

-ways

See -WISE.

WC

See TOILET.

'we' tips

See WRITING SKILLS.

wealth generation

See VALUE CREATION.

wealthy

See RICH.

weather, whether, wether

weather *uncountable noun*, means the meteorological conditions in the atmosphere. Note that 'a' can never be placed before the word **weather**: *What foul weather*.
See HURRICANE, RAIN, SNOW, STORM.

whether *conjunction*, is used for making a choice between alternatives: *She paused, suddenly wondering whether to stick to her* *prepared story, or to change it*. In this use, **whether** is followed by 'or'. It can also express doubt: *It is doubtful whether the benefits justify the cost*.

wether *noun*, is a castrated ram, most commonly seen as part of the word *bellwether*, a male sheep wearing a bell in order to lead the flock, and figuratively as an indicator of what will happen in the future: *The pundits are looking for another bellwether to signal the direction of the market*. Note that there is no 'a' in this word.

> *'The bellweather Dow fell a record 508 points, or 22.5 percent . . .'* (*Chicago Sun Times*) **!**

web addresses

When reading a web address it is recommended to use the terms that are in everyday use internationally:

www is read as 'w, w, w' (this stands for the World Wide Web).

'slash', the / sign, is used to indicate directories and subdirectories in World Wide Web addresses. As the top of the slash leans forwards, it is also called 'forward slash'. If there are two, call them 'double slash'. (Note that web addresses never contain a backslash \.)

'dot' is the way to read a full stop in web and email addresses.

'dash' is the way to read a hyphen in web and email addresses. Thus *s-de* is read as 's, dash, d, e'.

'underscore' is the term to use for letters or spaces that are underlined. Thus *john_smith* is read as 'john, underscore space, smith'.

'tilde' tíldĕ /ˈtɪldə/ is the ˜ sign from Spanish and Portuguese. Thus ˜*xy* is read as 'tilde, x, y'.

A full web address like *http://www.bbc.co.uk* is read as:

> 'h, t, t, p, colon, double slash, w, w, w, dot, b, b, c, dot, kō /kəʊ/, dot, u, k'

See EMAIL ADDRESS.

web forum

See CHAT LINE.

web page, website, home page, World Wide Web

web page *noun*, means a document with one or many pages that can be accessed via the Internet. Each web page has its own address: *Bookmark this web page*.

website *noun*, means a location on the Internet where information about an organization, business or individual is available: *Visit our website for the best holiday deals*. A **website** for a large organization can have thousands of web pages.

home page *noun*, means the start page an organization has on the Internet with connections to other web pages on their website: *Click on our home page bbc.co.uk*. It also means the screen that first appears on a computer when the Internet browser is opened: *He clicked on the house icon to see what they had selected as their home page*.

World Wide Web *noun*, is the widely used information system on the Internet which is also called the *Web*. The most common abbreviation is *www*. This is usually read aloud as 'w,w,w' when giving the address of a web page or website on the Internet.

Some central web terms

web browser *noun*, means a program like Explorer or Firefox that is used to find websites on the Internet.

webcam *noun*, means a camera connected to a computer that records images that can be seen on a website.

webcast *noun*, means a broadcast that is transmitted on the Internet.

web crawler, **web spider** or **web robot** *noun*, all mean a type of software designed to search the Internet automatically to find certain things, usually email addresses. The terms *bot*, *harvester* and *email harvester* also refer to the same thing.

webhead *noun*, means a person who is an active Internet user. This is informal.

weblink *noun*, means a word or symbol with a hyperlink to another web page or website. See HYPERLINK.

webliography *noun*, means a list of websites, web pages or other work that can be accessed electronically, and that focus on a particular subject.

weblog *noun*, is a blog that belongs to a particular person who writes about matters he or she finds interesting. See BLOG.

webmaster *noun*, means a person responsible for a particular website. A webmaster may be either male or female.

webphone *noun*, a phone that uses the Internet for voice messages.

web traffic *uncountable noun*, means the number of people visiting a website.

webzine *noun*, a magazine that is published on the Internet.

Note that most of these terms are written as a single word.

wedding breakfast

See BREAKFAST.

weight, weighting

weight *noun*, means both how heavy something is in physical terms and how influential and important it is: *Although their views appeared to carry little weight, they changed public opinion*.

weighting *uncountable noun*, means giving matters of special importance more weight: *By weighting two important questions we were able to grade the examination papers more accurately*. It also means an allowance such as extra pay that someone receives for living in an area with a high cost of living: *This is partly due to higher wage rates and to the London weighting in salaries*.

well-, well

well- *prefix*, means suitably, comfortably or highly when it is attached to an adjective coming before a noun in phrases like *well-balanced person, well-known person, well-paid person*. Always use a hyphen when such phrases come before a noun.

well *adverb*, means suitably, comfortably or highly when it modifies an adjective coming after a verb in phrases like *this person is well balanced, this person is well known, this person is well paid*. It is not recommended to use a hyphen when such phrases come after a noun.

Welsh, welch

Welsh *adjective & noun*, means someone or the people from Wales. **Welsh** is also the Celtic language spoken there: *About 20 per cent of the people in this part of Wales speak Welsh*. **Welsh** can be combined with other terms to refer to dishes: *Welsh rarebit* (a dish of toasted cheese) or objects such as *Welsh dresser* (an item of furniture).

welch *verb*, means to cheat, such as *to welch on a debt or agreement*, which means not to pay a debt or to ignore a commitment. The spelling **welch** should be used here to avoiding making a negative reference to the *Welsh* people. Although the two words are often pronounced identically, some people pronounce the final '-ch' as they would in 'church'.

west, western

west *noun & adjective*, is the direction of the sunset. When **west** refers to a direction it is not usually capitalized: *The sun sets in the west*. **West** is capitalized when it refers to Europe and North America: *The West and its high technology*; or is part of a continent, country or defined regional name: *West Africa*; *West Indies*; *Gaza and the West Bank*. See CAPITAL LETTERS (WRITING SKILLS).

western *adjective*, can mean in or from the west of a country or place: *They moved to the western part of Canada last year*. **Western** (capitalized) describes a characteristic of life in the West: *The book was full of typical Western ideals*. **Western** is also capitalized when it forms part of a proper noun: *Western Isles*; *Western Australia*.

westerly, westbound, westward, westwards

westerly *adjective & noun*. As an adjective, this means either in a direction *towards* the west: *The annual westerly migration of birds is very late this year*; or describes a wind that is blowing *from* the west: *When they arrived in that part of the Atlantic, they used the westerly winds*. Note that **westerly** is normally followed immediately by a noun. As a noun, this is a wind blowing from the west.

westbound *adjective*, means leading or travelling in a westerly direction: *They patrolled the Central Line trains westbound from Oxford Circus*. This word is almost always connected with transport or traffic.

westward *adjective & adverb*, means in a westerly direction. In both BE and AE, it is used as an adjective: *The westward current brought the ship out of position*. Note that it usually comes before a noun. In AE it is also generally used as an adverb: *They moved westward*.

westwards *adverb*, means moving towards the west: *The army moved westwards*. This is the usual form of the adverb in BE.

wether

See WEATHER.

wharf

See DOCK.

what or which in questions?

Here is a useful rule of thumb:

Use **what** when there is an *open* choice: *What are your favourite books?*

Use **which** when there is a *restricted* choice: *Which of these books do you want to borrow?*

whatever, wherever

whatever *pronoun, determiner & adverb*. As a pronoun, this means everything or anything: *Make whatever you like for dinner*. Used on its own as a complete remark, it means that the speaker has no opinion or preference and is being dismissive: *'Shall we go to the pictures?' 'Whatever.'* This is normally spoken usage. As a determiner, it is used in questions to signal surprise: *Whatever time did you go to bed last night?* As an adverb, it is often used following a negative word, to mean at all: *I had nothing whatever to do with it*.

wherever *conjunction & adverb*, means in whatever place or situation: *Wherever you found this cat, you must return it* (conjunction); *Wherever did you get to last night?* (adverb).

whether

See WEATHER.

which

See THAT.

while, whilst, whereas

while *noun & conjunction*. As a noun, this means a period of time: *The silence held for a while and then she heard a low laugh*. As a conjunction, it means at the same time: *That big yellow beast did this while I was out for a swim*. It can also be used in the same way as *whereas* (see below).

whilst *conjunction*, means at the same time and is a less common alternative to *while*: *No insurance cover is possible whilst the craft is in international waters*. **Whilst** is common in formal BE, but is rarer in AE.

whereas *conjunction*, is used to emphasize contrast: *Taxes were now uniform, whereas previously the self-employed had paid up to three times as much as state employees*. If *while* is used here to replace **whereas**, it does not give such a strong emphasis.

whisky, whiskey

whisky *noun*, from Scotland and Canada is spelt without an 'e': *That malt whisky is best without water*. The plural is spelt *whiskies*.

whiskey *noun*, produced in Ireland and the USA is spelt with an 'e': *He did not recommend Guinness with a whiskey chaser*. The plural is spelt *whiskeys*.

whistle-blower

See INFORMANT.

white

See HAIR COLOUR.

white-collar, blue-collar

white-collar *adjective*, refers to office workers, rather than those who do physical work in factories or construction sites: *White-collar crime is often systematic fraud and fiddling by white-collar, middle-class staff*.

blue-collar *adjective*, refers to those doing physical work in industry: *The overwhelming majority of airport staff are unskilled or semi-skilled blue-collar workers*.

Both these terms must be followed by a noun.

W

whiten

See BLEACH.

White Paper, Green Paper

White Paper *noun*, means a government report that gives a brief statement of policy before a Bill is introduced to Parliament: *The primary official manifestation of this UK commitment to the environment has been the government's White Paper*.

Green Paper *noun*, means a government report distributed for public comment before drafting a new law: *Reaction to the Green Paper was hostile*.

> These are both BE terms and may need an explanation if used with an international audience.

Whitsun, Pentecost

Whitsun *noun*, is the Christian festival on the seventh Sunday after Easter. *Whit* is an abbreviation for **Whitsun** and is used in *Whit Sunday* and *Whit Monday*. The term is common in BE: *The Commons will stage a series of brief debates before MPs break for the Whitsun recess*. The term *Whitsuntide* refers to the period around **Whitsun**.

Pentecost *noun*, is either an alternative Christian name for the *Whitsun* festival, or a Jewish festival 50 days after the second day of Passover. **Pentecost** is used when the intention is to emphasize the religious aspects of the festival: *Speaking in tongues, as the disciples did at the original Pentecost, is said to be commonplace in these ceremonies*.

whizz

See ZOOM.

who, whom

who *pronoun*, refers to a person or people, not things. It is used in questions like *Who am I speaking to?* where 'to' is placed at the end of the sentence. **Who** is also used instead of *that* and *which*. See THAT.

whom *pronoun*, refers to a person who is the object of a verb or preposition. **Whom** is only used in modern English in formal written contexts such as *The people for whom I worked disliked computers*. Note that **whom** is placed after a preposition. *To whom it may concern* is a useful salutation in a letter of recommendation where the addressee is unknown.

> Note that the normal phrase *Who am I speaking to?* has a formal equivalent *To whom am I speaking?* where there is no 'to' at the end.

whose, who's

whose *pronoun & determiner*, is the possessive form of *who* and is used in questions to find out who owns something: *Whose is this book?* (pronoun); *Whose book is this?* (determiner). **Whose** is also used to indicate the person or thing referred to: *He's a footballer whose skill I admire;* or give extra information: *John whose office I am moving into is still in Paris*. **Whose** can refer to things as well as people: *It was like an abandoned village whose streets had turned to pastureland*.

who's is a contraction of *who is* (who's speaking?), *who has* (who's arrived?) or *who does* (who's he think he is?). See CONTRACTIONS.

> Avoid confusing these soundalikes: *Whose is this?* asks who owns something. *Who's this?* (= *who is this?*) asks about a person's identity.

> **!** *'You may see any advisor who's office hours are convenient for you.'*
> (website, California State Polytechnic University)

wide, widely

See BROAD.

wife

See PARTNER.

wilful, willful

wilful *adjective*, means either intentional: *I was charged with wilful damage and assault*; or stubborn: *As a girl she was wilful and headstrong*.

willful *adjective*, is the AE spelling of *wilful*.

will

See SHALL.

window dressing

See LIE[2].

win-win, no-win

win-win *adjective*, refers to a situation where each person or group involved will gain an advantage: *Win-win describes one of three possible outcomes from a transaction between people*.

no-win *adjective*, refers to a situation where whatever is decided things will end badly: *The manager is got at from every angle, from the board of directors, the spectators and the players, and is in a no-win situation*.

wink

See BLINK.

wire, strand, wire rope

wire *noun*, means metal that is pulled into long, thin flexible threads. It can be used to conduct electricity or in fences in the form of *barbed wire* and *wire netting*.

strand *noun*, means a single thin piece of thread or wire such as a *strand of wool*.

wire rope *noun*, means several strands of *wire* that are twisted together: *The anchor chain was fastened by thick wire rope*.

wireless

See RADIO.

wisdom

See KNOWLEDGE.

-wise, -ways

-wise *suffix*, means either in the manner or in the direction of something, such as *clockwise* or *lengthwise*; or it is used informally, meaning referring to, speaking of: *It was a terrible journey time-wise*. The formation of some new words with the **-wise** ending has been criticized, and words such as *saleswise, jobwise* and *newswise* are best avoided in formal writing. **-wise** is also used to form adverbs from adjectives, such as *likewise* (similarly), *otherwise* (apart from that) and *lengthwise* (an alternative form to lengthways).

-ways *suffix*, means the direction or manner of doing something. This ending is added to nouns and is used to form adverbs such as: *lengthways, widthways, edgeways* and *sideways*.

> Both these suffixes are used to form adverbs from nouns.

withdraw

See RETIRE.

with regard to

See REGARDING.

witness, testify

witness *verb & noun*. As a verb, this means either to see something happen such as a crime or an accident: *The whole team witnessed the robbery*; or to sign a document to prove that you saw another person sign it: *The form must be witnessed by two independent witnesses*. In a figurative sense it can indicate that something happened at a particular time: *The 1990s witnessed a rise in environmental concern in most of Europe*. As a noun, it means a person who gives evidence in court: *The judge asked the witness if this statement was accurate*.

testify *verb*, means to give evidence as a witness in court: *The defence produced five witnesses prepared to testify in a court of law to that effect*. This is also used figuratively: *The number of people taking second holidays testified to the general state of the economy*.

> One cannot be asked *to witness in court*. The correct phrase is *to testify in court*.

womanly, womanish, effeminate, effete

womanly *adjective*, refers to the behaviour or appearance associated with a woman rather than a girl: *She looked more adult and womanly than she really was*. This is a term of approval. Note that the adjective girlish suggests a less mature appearance or manner: *Belinda's too girlish and Linda's far more womanly*. See GIRLISH (BOYISH).

womanish *adjective*, can refer unfavourably to stereotypically female behaviour, but is more commonly used to describe men who show such characteristics: *Other people in the show considered him a weak womanish fool*. **Womanish** is not a complimentary term.

effeminate *adjective*, is used of men who are *womanish* or have feminine characteristics: *His hair, in long, effeminate ringlets, was barley-fair, like Oliver's*. It may be considered insulting to use this word.

effete *adjective*, means either weak or powerless: *Designers were effete trendies from art college*; or over-refined: *a rich aroma of manure and wood smoke, pungent to my effete nostrils*. An *effete man* is usually one who looks or behaves like a woman. The speaker usually implies dislike when using this word.

wood, forest

wood *noun*, means a small area of trees. It is often found in the plural, *the woods*: *Winding paths lead into the surrounding woods*.

forest *noun*, means an extensive area of trees: *The forest contains a range of different habitats*. Figuratively, it can refer to a large number of tall narrow objects: *From the façade and sides rise a mass of spires that form a small forest of stone*.

The BE expression: *Cannot see the wood for the trees* means that too much detail or confusing information is making it difficult to understand a situation clearly. It has an AE equivalent: *Cannot see the forest for the trees*. See TIMBER.

work, works

work *verb & uncountable noun*. As a verb, this means to be employed or involved in a specific area: *While working at the cinema, for instance, he tried to repair a cistern and ended up flooding the place*. It can mean to make a considerable effort: *He works too hard*. **Work** can also refer to how something operates: *This mobile is not working*. As a noun, **work** means a job that one is paid for and the tasks at the place of employment: *Everyone has too much work to do*. **Work** can also be the result of physical or intellectual effort: *He regularly has work published in Britain's national newspapers*. See POSITION.

works *noun*, means the complete artistic output of a writer, artist or composer: *the theory of constitutional government in the Collected Works of Jeremy Bentham*. **Works** also refers to activities such as repairing or construction: *Roadworks ahead*. The term *public works* means government spending on building infrastructure such as roads, hospitals and schools: *Neither the Tories nor Labour could find the money for the extensive public works programme*. When **works** refers to a place it usually means a factory or a manufacturing plant. If the definite article is used, **works** can take a singular or plural verb: *The engineering works is/are....* **Works** in this sense is usually restricted to the manufacturing industry.

work experience, internship, placement

work experience *noun*, means the experience and skills acquired in a person's career: *The applicants are mostly graduates with two years' work experience since qualifying*. In BE, the period of time a student or young person spends in a company on a training scheme is also called **work experience**: *A good work experience report from an employer may be a reference in itself*.

internship *noun*, means a period of time when a student or graduate gets practical work experience. This is an AE term. See INTERN (INTER), HOUSE OFFICER (JUNIOR DOCTOR).

placement *noun*, means a job in business or industry that is integrated with a course at college or university in order to give a student work experience. This is known as an *industrial placement* or more usually *work placement*: *The final-year project is based on some aspect of the student's work placement*.

workforce, staff, manpower

workforce *uncountable noun*, means either all the people available for work in an area: *In London 11.3 per cent of the workforce are jobless*; or all the people who work for a particular company or organization: *Contrast this with Porsche, where most of the workforce is skilled*.

staff *noun*, means workers who are employed in a company or organization considered as a group. There may be full-time, part-time, professional, skilled or technical **staff**. Note that in BE the following verb may be singular when referring to the group as one unit: *Their production staff is experienced in a wide variety of techniques*; or plural when referring to the individuals: *The White Hart Lane medical staff are working overtime*. A search in the British National Corpus reveals that the plural verb is more common. In AE usage, however, the verb is always singular. In AE, people working in educational institutions who do not teach students are termed **staff** (the teachers are called faculty). See COLLECTIVE NOUNS (GRAMMAR TIPS).

manpower *uncountable noun*, means the number of people available to work, whether they are employed or not: *The software industry was handicapped by an acute manpower shortage*. The term is disliked as it ignores one sex. *Workforce* and *workers* are alternatives. See SEXIST LANGUAGE (WRITING SKILLS).

> In the MS Word 2003 edition the following sentence generates green lines even though the British spellchecker is operative: *The staff are working*. This is misleading as *staff* can take a singular or plural verb in BE.

workshop

See CONGRESS.

worldly, mundane

worldly *adjective*, refers to ordinary everyday life rather than to philosophical or religious concerns: *When clergymen became involved in worldly affairs, mistakes were inevitable*. One's *worldly possessions*, or *worldly goods*, means everything one owns: *With all my worldly goods I thee endow* (part of the traditional English marriage service).

mundane *adjective*, means ordinary or boring: *She might have preferred a more mundane job, where she could daydream from time to time*.

World Wide Web

See WEB PAGE.

worry

See CONSTERNATION.

worthless

See VALUELESS.

wound, injure

wound *verb & noun*. As a verb this means to cause physical damage to the body by a cut in the flesh as a result of deliberate action, often in battle or surgery: *Many of the soldiers will be killed or seriously wounded by this time tomorrow*. Although **wound** can refer to one person it is generally used to refer to a number of people who are war casualties: *Over 300 soldiers were severely wounded*. As a noun it means a hole made in the skin by a weapon or surgical instrument: *The bullet left only a flesh wound*. The related adjective form *wounded* refers either to physical damage: *a wounded soldier*; or to emotional pain caused by what is said or done to someone: *He remains deeply wounded that the Foreign Office accused him of selling visas for sex*.

injure *verb*, means to cause physical damage to one's self or another person, usually in an accident: *Three were critically injured yesterday when two cars crashed in driving rain*. In a figurative sense it means to damage the reputation or pride of a company or person: *Such espionage activity gravely injured the national interest*. The related noun is *injury*. See DAMAGE.

> Note that one can *wound* someone's pride but never *injure* it. One can *injure* a reputation, but not *wound* it.

wrapped

See RAPT.

wreck, destroy, smash

wreck *verb & noun*. As a verb, this means to damage something severely or destroy it: *Last month, rebels completely wrecked the entire hospital*. It can also mean to spoil something: *The last day was wrecked by fierce, gusting winds but 71 was enough to win*. As a noun, **wreck** means the loss of or severe damage to something such as a ship at sea, a plane or road vehicles. **Wreck** can also apply to people who are in a bad mental condition: *He was left mentally wrecked after a gruelling tour of South America*. In AE, a *car wreck/ train wreck* is an alternative to a *car crash/ train crash*.

destroy *verb*, means to completely damage and ruin something: *The island was destroyed by the storm*. People's hopes can be *destroyed* by others or by bad luck. To **destroy** an animal means to kill it quickly and painlessly because it is dangerous or severely injured or diseased.

smash *verb & noun*. As a verb, this means to break something such as a window violently out of vandalism or in order to gain access: *They smashed the car window in order to steal the radio*. It is a word that conveys the impact of something hitting another surface very hard. As a noun, **smash** can mean a physical impact such as *a car smash* or impact in more general terms such as *a box-office smash*.

write, wright, rite

write *verb*, means to put words on paper or on a computer screen. To *write copy* means to write advertisements for an agency. See TYPE IN, WRITTEN (VERBAL).

wright *noun*, means a maker or builder. The word is classified as archaic when it is used alone. **Wright** is still used in terms such as *playwright* and *shipwright*.

rite *noun*, means a religious ceremony or other ceremonial act, event or custom: *This is a place of legendary prehistoric rites and ceremonies*. The term is mostly used in the plural.

writing on the wall, the

See GRAFFITI.

wreak, wrought

wreak *verb*, means to inflict widespread damage or harm: *Even a typical British summer can wreak havoc with your skin*.

wrought *verb & adjective*. This is one form of the past tense and past participle of *wreak*: *The flash flood that followed wrought havoc on the countryside*. As an adjective it means worked, as in *wrought iron*.

> Some linguists dislike the expression *wrought havoc* but it is found in the British National Corpus. However, *wreaked havoc* is more common.

written

See VERBAL.

Spelling

wear**i**some	Note the -i-
w**ei**rd	Note 'e' before 'i'
wit**hh**old	Note that there is double -hh- in this word
wi**z**ard	Note there is only a single -z-

x-axis, y-axis, z-axis

x-axis *noun*, means the horizontal axis in a system of coordinates. As 'x' is pronounced ecks /eks/, the indefinite article is 'an': *This is how to draw an x-axis*.

y-axis *noun*, means the vertical axis in a system of coordinates. Some people think of the long vertical stroke in 'y' to remind them of which axis is which. As 'y' is pronounced wī /waɪ/, the indefinite article is 'a': *C is the point where the line cuts a y-axis*.

z-axis *noun*, means the third axis in a three-dimensional system of coordinates. See AXIS.

xenon, halogen (headlamps)

xenon *uncountable noun*, is a chemical element (symbol Xe). It is a gas that occurs in limited quantities in the air and is used in some electric lamps. In cars and bicycles, *xenon headlamps* produce more light than standard headlamps of the same wattage and sometimes appear bluish. It is pronounced zénnon /ˈzenɒn/.

halogen *uncountable noun*, is a group of chemical elements including chlorine, iodine and bromine. Standard vehicle headlamps use *halogen bulbs* which are often filled with iodine vapour.

xenophobia

See PHOBIA

Xerox, photocopy

Xerox *noun & verb*. As a noun, this means either a dry copying process involving light or a copy made from this process: *Sit down while I make a Xerox*. This is the trademark for the process. Note the word is capitalized. As a verb, this means to make a copy using the **Xerox** process or similar ones: *We were xeroxing 20 sets when the paper in the machine jammed*. Note that this refers to a general activity and the verb is not capitalized. The pronunciation is zéerocks /ˈzɪərɒks/.

photocopy *noun & verb*. As a noun, this means a dry copying process involving light: *The photocopies of this lecture are on the table over there*. As a verb, this means to make a copy of something using this process: *I have photocopied the lecture notes*. As there is no ownership or legal rights involved with the term **photocopy**, this is a term to use generally when copies are made by machines or processes that are not Xerox. See TRADEMARK.

Xmas, Noel, Yuletide

Xmas *noun*, is an informal expression used as a short form of Christmas that is commonly used in commercial contexts or casual writing. Many people read **Xmas** as Christmas.

Noel nō-éll /nəʊˈel/ *noun*, is a word for Christmas that is often used in songs or on Christmas cards. Note that the stress comes on the second syllable. It is also spelt *Nowell*.

Yuletide *noun*, means the Christmas festival. This is an archaic term mostly found in literature.

X-rated, 18 certificate

X-rated *adjective*, refers to the rating for a film with adult content such as explicit sex or violence, or very strong language. This is a widely recognized term internationally. It is also known as the *X certificate* or *X classification*. In the USA this is not an official film classification but some pornographic films use X, XX and XXX as a marketing device to show how X-rated a film is.

18 certificate *noun*, is usually called an *18 film* and refers to a film that has been rated by the British Board of Film Classification as only suitable for adults; 18 is the lower age limit for renting or buying a film or see an 18 film in a cinema. There is also the *R18 (Restricted 18) certificate*, which is used for films with explicit sexual content that can only be shown in specially licensed cinemas or bought from licensed sex shops. As these are UK terms, *X-rated* may be more informative to non-British people.

> *The passenger complained that he didn't want to be X-rated by Security.* **!**

X-ray, ultrasound

X-ray *noun*, is used for diagnosing internal disorders of the body, or for examining property without opening it: *The airport official gave us directions to gate 6, where we found two gentlemen and an X-ray machine.* Because of the dangers of radiation, medical technology is developing other ways of carrying out internal examinations.

ultrasound *noun*, uses sound pressure to visualize muscles and internal organs. It is also used to visualize the foetus during routine pre-natal care: *If twins are detected by ultrasound scan, parents can prepare themselves for the births and plan accordingly.*

-y, -ey

Adjectives ending in -y can be formed from nouns. Examples are those describing qualities: *dirty* (dirt), *dusty* (dust), *gluey* (glue), *sleepy* (sleep). Some adjectives like this have 'ey' as in *clayey* (clay) and *holey* (hole) where *holy* only means sacred.

What's brown and sticky?
Answer: a stick.

Yankee, Yank

Yankee *noun*, in AE use originally meant a New Englander, or a Northerner in the Civil War.

Yank *noun*, has developed from *Yankee* and both terms are used freely as informal ways of meaning any inhabitant of the USA.

These terms are sometimes used in BE as a sign of disapproval for all Americans. In AE, they are sometimes used by people in the South as an insult to those living in the northern states.

yawn

See GASP.

yea, yeah, nay

yea *noun*, means yes and is old-fashioned except in parliamentary usage. See AYE.

yeah *exclamation*, means yes and is used in writing to express either informal agreement: *Yeah, great let's go to York*; or disbelief: *'She is going to be a star.' 'Oh yeah?'*

nay *noun*, means a negative answer and is also old-fashioned except in parliamentary usage: *This right to say yea or nay clearly indicates the continuing supremacy of the British Parliament*. See NO (AYE).

Other informal forms of *yes* include *yep* and *yup*.

year-old, years old

year-old *adjective phrase*, is a common way to describe the age of someone or something: *We have a nine-year-old Toyota*, also written *9-year-old*. Note that the parts of this adjective phrase are hyphenated and there is no 's' added to year.

years old *noun + adjective*, also means the age of someone or something. Unless the person or thing is only 1 year old, *year* takes a plural 's': *Our Toyota is 9 years old*. Note that there are no hyphens.

yield, relinquish, surrender

yield *noun & verb*. As a noun this means the total amount of profit or product from industrial processes, crops or animals: *In North America the pied Dutch cows were selected for high yield*. As a verb it means either to produce a profit or to allow someone to take control of something previously in your possession: *They are forced to yield ground because of the losses they incur*.

relinquish *verb*, means to give up power or the control of something, especially when this is done unwillingly: *Ukraine was reluctant to relinquish its nuclear arsenal*. This is a formal term.

surrender *noun & verb*. As a noun this means the announcement of defeat and the wish to stop fighting: *In this case, however, unconditional surrender was now required*. As a verb it means to admit defeat and allow someone to catch you. In a more formal context it means to be forced to give up the control of something: *He was examined by the court and he agreed to surrender his property*.

yogurt, yoghurt, yogourt, yoghourt

yogurt, yoghurt, yogourt, yoghourt *noun*. All these refer to the same thing – a thick liquid food based on milk and often flavoured with fruit. The first spelling is the most usual, and the last the rarest.

yoke, yolk

yoke *noun & verb*. As a noun this means a crossbar that is shaped to fit a pair of oxen or other animals. It can also be a piece of wood that is shaped to fit a person's shoulders for carrying heavy or bulky loads. *The yoke of . . .* is a formal term for harsh treatment or something that restricts freedom and makes life very difficult to bear: *'The Glass Menagerie' is relevant to all young people chafing under the yoke of parental control.* As a verb it means to link two animals, people or countries together: *The oxen were yoked together for 12 hours a day.*

yolk *noun*, means the yellow part in the middle of an egg: *Chicken eggs are large because of the yolk which acts as a source of nutrients for the growth of the developing embryo.*

-ys, -ies (in plural nouns)

-ys is added to nouns that end in **-y** if the **y** has a vowel immediately before it: *attorneys, donkeys.*

-ies replaces the **-y** when there is a consonant immediately before it: *cherry ~ cherries, country ~ countries, supply ~ supplies.*

-yse, -yze

-yse *suffix*, is the BE spelling for verbs such as *analyse, catalyse, hydrolyse, paralyse* and *photolyse.*

-yze *suffix*, is the AE spelling of the same verbs: *analyze, catalyze, hydrolyze, paralyze* and *photolyze.* See -IZE, -ISE.

Yuletide

See XMAS.

Spelling

ya**cht**	Note the final -cht
y**ie**ld	Note -i- before -e-

Z

z (pronunciation)

The BE pronunciation of the letter **z** is zed /zed/, and the AE pronunciation of **z** is zee /ziː/.

This is the only letter of the alphabet where there is a clear difference in pronunciation between AE and BE, and care should be taken to pronounce proper nouns or names correctly:

ZZ Top has been performing for over 30 years (pronounced 'zee zee top').

Purves was previously a teacher, and also a straight actor, appearing in 'Z Cars'; and as an assistant in 'Doctor Who' (pronounced 'zed cars').

The case of DMZ ('demilitarized zone') is difficult: it is mostly used in AE, but the DMZ in Korea was set up by the UN, including British forces, so either pronunciation (**dée emm zée** /'diː em 'ziː/ or **dée emm zéd** /'diː em 'zed/) may be used.

zebra crossing

See **PEDESTRIAN CROSSING**.

zenith, nadir

zenith *noun*, means the highest point that a planet, the Sun or Moon reaches in the sky. It is often used in horoscopes: *With Venus at the zenith, the climate is right for success in your worldly endeavours*. It can also be applied to peaks in a person's life: *The zenith of my angling career came when I was about 15 years old*.

nadir *noun*, means the worst moment in a period or situation: *The nadir was reached when at Bannockburn in 1314 the English army was annihilated by the Scots*. **Nadir** is pronounced **náydeer** /'neɪdɪər/.

zero, oh, *nought, naught*, nil

zero *noun & verb*, as a noun, is used in BE for temperature: *It will be below zero all week*; and in numerical amounts: *How many zeroes did you say*? Except in scientific writing, there is no need to add zeroes (0, 00, etc.) in writing when referring to the time or money. For example, 5 p.m. is better than 5.00 p.m. but when using the 24-hour clock it is best to write 17.00 (read as '5 p.m.' or '17 hundred hours' in a military context). The same is true for whole units of money: write £325, not £325.00, except on cheques. In AE, **zero** is widely used when reading the number 0. This is also sometimes used in BE for the sake of clarity. For telephone or bank account numbers, 5112 0400 would be 'five double one two, zero four double zero' in AE. A decimal number like 2.04 in AE is read as *two point zero four*. The plural is either *zeros* or *zeroes*. As a verb, **zero** appears in the phrasal verb to *zero in on* something, which means to focus on the main issue: *Parliament has finally zeroed in on the cost of European expansion*. The verb forms are *zeroes, zeroed, zeroing*. See **ZOOM**.

oh *noun*, is widely used in BE, where AE uses *zero*. In telephone or bank account numbers, 5112 0400 is read: *five double one two, oh four double oh*. A decimal number such as 2.04 is read: *two point oh four*. Except in reported speech (where it is an exclamatory word, and does not mean zero): *Oh yes, he did*, **oh** is not used in writing. See **TELEPHONE NUMBERS**.

nought *noun*, means *zero* in BE in mathematical references: *The student was asked to multiply six by eight, and then add three noughts*. In numbers less than one expressed as decimals the 0 is read as **nought** before the word *point*: *nought point two*. **Nought** also appears as one extreme in a range: *His motorbike could do nought to sixty in seven seconds*.

naught *noun*, is an alternative spelling of *nought*. It also means nothing and is applied both to people: *He's just a naught*; and to situations: *This came to naught, however*.

nil *noun*, is used in some team sports to indicate no score: *Liverpool won 3–0* (read as 'three nil'). In other sports, different terms may be used, such as 'love' in tennis and 'a duck' in cricket. See **ZIP**.

zero tolerance, zero-sum game

zero tolerance *uncountable noun*, means the policy of applying regulations or laws stringently so that they are effective: *Our CO_2 emissions policy is zero tolerance by 2020.*

zero-sum game *noun*, means a win-lose situation so that what one person or group gains involves an equivalent loss for another person or group: *Chess is a typical zero-sum game: it is impossible for both players to win.*

zip, zip fastener

zip *noun & verb*. As a noun a **zip** is a fastening mechanism for trousers, dresses and suitcases. In computing, a *zip file*, or *zipped file*, is one in which data is compressed in order to allow the transfer of large files between computers. Informally, **zip** means speed, energy or excitement: *He's a politician with a lot of zip*. In informal AE, **zip** means nothing: *We beat them six zip* (6–0). As a verb it refers to doing things quickly: *There was little traffic and we zipped along the motorway*. In another sense it means to fasten with a **zip**, and is usually followed by the preposition *up*: *Can you zip up my dress, please?*

zip fastener *noun*, means a *zip* in the sense of something to fasten clothes, bags, etc. This is also called a *zipper*.

ZIP code, postcode

ZIP code *noun*, is the postal codes used by the United States Postal Service. **ZIP** is an acronym for Zone Improvement Plan. The usual format is five digits, hyphen then four digits. The first digit of the **ZIP code** is 0, 1 or 2 for some of the eastern states, and 9 for the states on the western seaboard, Alaska and Hawaii. Thus *ZIP code 02129-1141* is an address in Boston, MA.

postcode *noun*, is the British term for the system used by postal services to identify locations, corresponding to the ZIP code in the US. There are different formats. In most English-speaking countries, the **postcode** forms the last item of the address, whereas the rest of Europe has the **postcode** before the name of the town. Here the first two letters are the ISO 3601 country code, so that an address in Helsinki has the **postcode** *FI-00180*.

zoom, whizz

zoom *verb & noun*. As a verb, this is an onomatopoeic word that resembles engine noise, or the fast movement of traffic: *The cars zoomed around us*. In another sense, **zoom** means to rise quickly: *Oil prices zoomed to record levels in 2007*. The phrasal verb to *zoom in* means either to focus more closely on an image on a computer screen or camera, or to focus on a particular issue: *That newspaper has been zooming in on corruption*. As a noun, a *zoom lens* is a type of camera lens with variable focal length.

whizz *verb*, is also an onomatopoeic word that resembles a high whistling noise: *An arrow whizzed over our heads*. It can also mean to move very quickly: *He whizzed down King's Parade on his bike*. In AE, the verb is spelt *whiz*.

Spelling

z**ea**lous	Note the -ea-
zu**cch**ini	Note the double -cc- and the -h-

Grammar tips

This section only covers some points of grammar that generalize on the matters presented in the rest of this book. For a systematic and thorough review of grammar, we recommend *An Introduction to English Grammar* by Greenbaum and Nelson, Pearson Education, 2002. It has numerous exercises and is ideal for self-study.

Adjective

An adjective is a word that describes an object so that we can identify it more exactly. It may be the colour, size, shape or any other quality of the object being described. Most adjectives fit into sentences in two ways: either immediately before what they are describing (pre-modifying adjective): *a blue car, a simple problem, a brilliant footballer*; or after the verb 'to be': *the table was dirty, the footballer was hot*. Most adjectives can appear in both positions, but some are more restricted. For instance, *nuclear* can only appear before what it is describing: *nuclear weapons*; while on the other hand, *afraid* can only come after the verb 'to be': *the boy was afraid*. See HYPHENATION (PUNCTUATION GUIDE).

Order of adjectives

If you are listing the characteristics of an object, and a string of adjectives is required before it, the following order is generally used:

1. **N**umber
2. **A**ttitude/value
3. **S**ize/length/height
4. **C**olour
5. **O**rigin
6. **M**aterial
7. **P**urpose

(NASCOMP is one way to remember this).

This gives: *three* (1), *perfect* (2), *round* (3), *green* (4), *glass* (6) *spheres*. Another example is: *four* (1), *long* (3), *blue* (4), *steel* (6), *gas-transport* (7) *pipelines*.

Usually only a couple of adjectives will occur before a noun so the above may help decide which order to put them if you are in doubt. Probably the most elegant way to present all the characteristics of the spheres or pipelines in the above is using a list with bullets or rewriting. See LISTS (WRITING SKILLS).

Gradability and comparison of adjectives

Gradability means adding words to intensify or moderate an adjective. If we are discussing the exact extent of the adjective *large*, we can choose from a range of intensifiers such as *extremely, very, moderately, rather* or *fairly large*. There are naturally many other words that might be suitable, so do not just settle for the most common of these words, *very*.

There are two ways to make adjectives comparative. Either use *-er* and *-est*, as in *larger* and *largest* or use *more* and *most* before the adjective, as in *more successful* and *most* *successful*. There is a general rule that adjectives of one syllable like *large* or *rich* use the first type to make comparisons (*larger* and *largest*, *richer* and *richest*), while adjectives with more than two syllables like *difficult* or *successful* use the second type (*more difficult, most difficult* or *more successful, most successful*). Adjectives with two syllables like *clever* can take either type (*cleverer* and *cleverest* or *more clever* and *most clever*). There are a few irregular adjectives such as *good – better – best*.

Absolute adjectives

One of the best examples of an absolute adjective is *unique*, which means the only one of its kind. Therefore, it is recommended that *unique* should not be intensified or compared by words such as *very, more or most*. There are other words in this category such as *absolute, horizontal, infinite, parallel* and *vertical*. Most careful writers consider that if something is *horizontal* or *parallel*, it is simply that, and constructions like 'the most horizontal line' or 'the most parallel lines' should be rewritten.

However, when we are trying to show an approximation to the absolute, constructions with *nearly, almost, close to* are acceptable: *This result was nearly ideal*; *Her performance was almost perfect*.

Adverb

Adverbs add something to a verb, an adjective, an adverb or a whole sentence, but never describe a noun. Many adverbs are formed by adding *-ly* to an adjective, such as *quickly, proudly*. If the adjective ends in *-ic*, the adverb usually ends in *-ically*, such as *economically*. There are also adverbs without the *-ly* ending. This include linking adverbs like *therefore, nevertheless* and *however*; time adverbs like *here, now* and *today* and space adverbs like *here* and *there*. Although *-ly* is a typical adverb ending, some adjectives also end in *-ly* (*a **friendly** dog, a **silly** dog, a **lovely** dog*). Note that these all describe something about a noun, in this case, the dog. See LINK WORDS (WRITING SKILLS).

Order of adverbs

A useful rule to remember is that when more than one adverb or adverbial phrase is used in a phrase or sentence, they tend to come in the order 'manner', 'place', and 'time', which coincidentally is the alphabetical order of these three words ('m', 'p', 't'): *He walked **quickly*** (manner) ***down the street*** (place) ***at five o'clock*** (time).

For stylistic reasons it is best to avoid a string of *-ly* adverbs together: rather than *The email was really exceedingly badly written*; write: *The email was very badly written*. It is not necessary to use hyphens between *-ly* adverbs and a following adjective: *He gave a clearly incorrect answer*. See HYPHENATION (PUNCTUATION GUIDE).

Gradability and comparison of adverbs

Just like adjectives, adverbs can be intensified or moderated and words like *quite* and *very* are often used. If we are discussing the speed of a driver, we can say that *he was driving quite slowly, very slowly* or *extremely slowly when he saw the children on the road*.

When making adverbs into comparatives or superlatives, the short ones usually take *-er* and *-est*, as in *later* and *latest*, and longer adverbs usually have *more* and *most* before them, as in *more cleverly* and *most cleverly*. There are a few irregular adverbs such as *well – better – best*.

Adjective or adverb?
A simple distinction is that adjectives describe a noun. Adverbs, on the other hand, add something to a verb, an adjective, another adverb or a whole sentence, but never describe a noun.

Articles: indefinite

a, an

A is used before words that begin with a consonant sound (not necessarily a consonant letter): *a house, a unit*. **An** is used before words beginning with a vowel sound (not necessarily a vowel letter): *an apple, an hour*. It is the ***sound***, not the ***spelling*** of the first syllable in the following word that follows **a** or **an**, that determines the form of the indefinite article.

Before 'e', 'o', 'h' and 'u'

Most words starting with *e* take **an**, but use **a** before words starting with *eu*, if pronounced 'yoo' as in *a European* and *a euphemism*.

Most words starting with *o* take **an**, but use **a** before *one* and *once* as they are pronounced with an initial 'w' sound, as in *a one-way street, a once-in-a-lifetime opportunity*.

In standard modern English, **a** is used before *h* when the *h* is pronounced: *a hotel, a historic date, a Hispanic,* and **an** before a silent *h*: *an hour, an heir, an honour*.

Use **a** before *u* if it is pronounced 'yoo', which starts with a consonant sound: *a union, a university*. If *u* is pronounced as in 'but', as a vowel sound, it takes **an**: *an underwater vehicle, an umbrella*.

Before abbreviations/acronyms

With abbreviations (which are read letter by letter), it is the sound of the initial letter that determines whether **a** or **an** is used. Thus it is *a Federal Bureau of Investigation report*, but when abbreviated, *an FBI report*. Similarly, it is correct to write *a Master of Science degree* and *a Massachusetts Institute of Technology student*, but when abbreviated, these are: *an MSc degree* and *an MIT student*. The following letters must have **an** before them when they are the first letter in an abbreviation: *A, E, F, H, I, L, M, N, O, R, S, X*.

Note that **an** is used before most acronyms (read as one word) starting with *A, E, I, O*. *An ASCII . . . , an EFTA . . . , an ISO . . . , an OPEC. . . .* See FULL STOP (PUNCTUATION GUIDE).

Numbers

Use **an** with all *eight/eighteen/eighty* combinations: *an 8, 18, 80, 800 . . . degree variation*; **a** is used with all other numbers except 0, when it is pronounced 'oh'.

Articles: definite

'The' with country names

Country names that refer to plural entities have the definite article in running text, but are indexed under the main word, not *the*. Examples are *the United Kingdom, the United States of America* and *the United Arab Emirates* (note the lower case 't' in *the*). Some country names that used to include the definite article no longer do. Examples are *Lebanon, Sudan, Ukraine, Gambia* and *Netherlands*. Although the definite article is no longer part of the official name of the *Netherlands* in English, in running text it is normal to write *the Netherlands*. The same applies to island groups such as *the Philippines, the Maldives, the Channel Islands*

Reference lists and indexing

Most reference lists are in the order: author, date, title. If the title of a book or paper starts with 'The', this should appear in the reference list (Gowers, E. 1973. *The Complete Plain Words*. Penguin Books). However, in an index of books, journals and papers where some of the titles start with 'The', it is usual to ignore the definite article and list the title under the first main word. For example, *The Complete Plain Words* is listed under 'C', even though 'The' is really the first word in the title: *Complete Plain Words, The*. The same is true for proper names. Although the English name of the Dutch town *Den Haag* is *The Hague*, in lists such as indexes it should appear under the letter H: *Hague, The*. Institutions, such as universities, are also listed in this way: *University of Chicago, The*.

Nouns

Collective nouns

Collective nouns are those which have a singular form, but refer to things which by their nature contain more than one item, such as *bank, company, department, family, government, group* or *team*. People have argued for many years about the rights and wrongs of using a singular or plural verb after a collective noun. For instance, should the newspaper headline read *England loses again* or *England lose again*? In BE both solutions are possible, but they have slightly different meanings. When a singular verb is used, the emphasis is on the collective noun as a single unit, so that in the case of *England is winning*, the team (of footballers, for instance) is considered as one single entity. When a plural verb is used, the emphasis is on the individual players: *England are spread all over the pitch*. When a singular verb is used, all further references must also be singular. Similarly with a plural verb, all further references must also be plural: *The Conservative government* ***was*** *first elected in 1979.* ***It*** *then won four elections in a row*, or: *The Conservative government* ***were*** *first elected in 1979.* ***They*** *then won. . . .* Collective nouns are always treated as singular in AE.

Uncountable nouns

One of the many ways in which nouns can be subdivided is into those that can be counted (one cat, two cats, etc.) which are termed **countable nouns** and those that represent a mass and only have a singular form, such as *information*. This group is known as **uncountable nouns**. Uncountable nouns always take a singular verb and cannot have a plural form.

Also they cannot have the indefinite article or words that denote a quantity like *few*, *several* or *many* immediately before them. Uncountable nouns are often the names of qualities, such as *fear* or *hatred*, or of substances of indeterminate amount, such as *beer, hair, knowledge, oil, tea, wheat*.

If the sentence requires some sort of singular concept with an uncountable noun, then longer phrasing must be found: *a grain of rice, a piece of information, a little knowledge, a cup of tea, a feeling of hatred*.

As some nouns like *experience, football* and *tea* can be used in countable and uncountable senses, care has to be taken. *Experiences* is countable and means events in a person's life. *Experience*, on the other hand, in the sense of skills and competence, is an uncountable noun. *Football* and *tea* are both countable nouns when they mean an object to be kicked and two cups of tea or two varieties of tea. The same nouns are uncountable if they refer to the game and tea as a substance respectively.

Most dictionaries use the symbols [C] and [U] after the headword to classify countable and uncountable nouns.

Agreement between subject and verb

In most cases, it is clear that a singular subject must be followed by a singular verb and a plural subject by a plural verb. However, there are some exceptions to this general rule, outlined below, and dealt with in more detail elsewhere in this book.

1. Uncountable nouns are always singular and cannot be preceded by **a/an**: *advice, bread, damage, information, transport, wheat*. They have no plural form, and are always followed by a singular verb.
2. Academic subjects ending in *-ics* are singular: *linguistics, mathematics, physics*. These are followed by a singular verb. The same applies to *athletics* and *gymnastics*.
3. Some nouns ending in *-s* are singular. One such group consists of the names for diseases, such as *measles* and *mumps*. Another such group consists of the names for games, such as *billiards, draughts,* (AE *checkers*) and *dominoes*. There are a few other words that follow this pattern, including *crossroads, means* and *news*. These are all followed by a singular verb.
4. Pairs of things are plural: *binoculars, scales, scissors, trousers*. These are followed by a plural verb but if the phrase *a pair of* is used immediately before them, they are followed by a singular verb.
5. Two singular nouns joined by *and* take a plural verb except when they have become a fixed phrase: *John and David* ***are*** *brothers*, but *fish and chips* ***is*** *a good meal*.
6. Collective nouns may be either singular or plural in BE, but are always singular in AE. Examples are: *company, family, team*.
7. Some nouns ending in *-s* are plural, but have no singular: *antics, oats*. These are followed by a plural verb.
8. Some nouns are plural, even though they do not end in *-s*, and must take a plural verb. Examples are: *cattle, clergy, gentry, people, police, vermin*. These words have no singular form.

See EITHER . . . OR, -ICS, PLURAL NOUNS (WORD FORMATION).

Genitive forms: 's'-genitive and 'of'-genitive

The genitive is the form of a noun that indicates possession or close connection between two things. This can be written as either *John's hat* (the hat belonging to John), which is called the 's'-genitive; or *the people of Paris* (the people who come from Paris), which is called the 'of'-genitive.

The **'s'-genitive** is used to form the possessive of people and animals, as well as things people are fond of. Two general rules are:

1. Place **'s** after singular nouns that end in *s*, or after a noun (singular or plural) that does not end in *s*. (Examples: *the class's teacher, dog's dinner, a child's toys, the children's toys, the boat's performance*.) Names can be an exception to this rule, with the genitive formed by adding an apostrophe but no extra *s*: *Charles's* and *Charles'* are alternatives, and both acceptable.

2. Place an apostrophe after plural nouns that end in *s*. (Examples: *the classes' teacher* and *the dogs' dinner*.)

These rules make it clear whether a teacher looks after one class (*class's teacher*) or more than one (*classes' teacher*), and whether your pet has to share his dinner with others.

Remember to place an apostrophe after the whole of a compound noun, even if the last word is not the headword of the phrase: *The Lord Mayor of London's coach* (the coach is the Lord Mayor's, not London's). See APOSTROPHE (PUNCTUATION GUIDE).

The **'of'-genitive** is used to form the possessive of objects and things. (Examples: *the Tower of London, the people of Paris, toy of the year, a performance of 'Hamlet'*.)

Phrasal verbs

A **phrasal verb** is a verb combined with either a preposition or an adverb to create a new or extended meaning, which may appear to have little to do with the literal meaning of the verb by itself. Some examples with *come* are *come in* (to enter or become fashionable), *come out* (to make an exit or admit to being gay), *come to* (wake up, especially after being unconscious rather than asleep), *come through* (arrive or succeed).

Phrasal verbs often indicate informality. The expression *he sticks by his partner* is unsuitable for formal writing. If you are unsure which word or words could replace *stick by*, check in a dictionary and you will nearly always find a good alternative in the defining sentence for the phrasal verb. *The Longman Dictionary of Contemporary English* defines the phrasal verb *stick by* as: *to remain loyal to a friend*. . . . Thus in a formal context you could write: *he remains loyal to his partner*.

Pronouns

The subject pronouns, *I, you, he, she, it, we, they* are sometimes confused with the object pronouns, *me, you, him, her, it, us, them*. The entry in this book on **I, me** gives further examples of some of the most common problems and how to solve them.

When a personal pronoun is followed by a clause beginning with *who* or *that*, the form of the pronoun is determined by its position in the sentence, and not by its relation to the clause. So, in the sentence *She who must be obeyed was very angry with him*, the form of the personal pronoun is *she*, as it is the subject of the verb (***she** was very angry*). If the sentence reads *He had to please her who must be obeyed*, then *her* is correct as *her* is the object of the verb 'please' (*He had to please **her***). If in doubt, remove the *who* or *that* clause, and it becomes obvious which form is appropriate.

Word formation

Affix, prefix, suffix

Affix *noun*, is a letter or group of letters added to the beginning or end of a word to change its meaning, or to change the way it relates to the rest of the sentence. Thus **affix** means both **prefix** and **suffix**. The word *independent* has the prefix *in-* and *suddenly* has the suffix *-ly*. Both *in-* and *-ly* are affixes.

Prefix *noun*, is a letter or group of letters added to the beginning of a word, such as *co-*, *in-*, *un-* in words like *cooperate*, *independent* and *unhappy*. Separate the two parts by hyphens if there could be confusion, for example, *re-cover* (to cover again) and *recover* (to get better). Conventions about hyphenation here are different in BE and AE, and modern BE dictionaries have different hyphenation than older editions. See **HYPHENATION (PUNCTUATION GUIDE)**.

Suffix *noun*, is a letter or group of letters added to the end of a word, such as *-ly*, *-less* and *-ness* in words like *quickly*, *careless* and *goodness*.

Negative prefixes

Note that there are some exceptions to the following guidelines. One general point is that the prefixes **il-**, **im-**, **ir-** are derived from **in-** by a process of phonetic assimilation. This may be called 'historical laziness', as the easiest way to move from one sound to another.

a- is mostly used in formal or technical words to indicate lacking in or lack of: *amorphous* (lacking in shape), *amoral* (lacking in morals)

dis- is used with verbs, adjectives and nouns to form opposites: *dislike*, *disobedient*, *distrust*

dys- is used with nouns and adjectives to mean abnormal or difficult: *dysfunctional*, *dyslexia*

il- is used to form opposites before the letter **l**: *illogical*

im- is used to form opposites before the letters **b**, **m**, **p**: *imbalance*, *immaterial*, *impossible*

in- is used to form opposites, such as: *inaccurate*, *inexact*

ir- is used to form opposites before the letter **r**: *irregular*, *irresponsible*

non-/non are two of the most used negative prefixes added to nouns, adjectives and adverbs to indicate an absence of something: *a non-drinker*, *a non-slip floor*, or *speaking non-stop*. Most of these 'non'-words are hyphenated in BE: *non-cooperation*, *non-existent* but are spelt as one word in AE: *noncooperation*, *nonexistent*.

un-/un is added to adjectives and indicates the opposite quality from the positive word: *unexpected* = surprising, *unwise* = foolish. See **HYPHENATION (PUNCTUATION GUIDE)**.

The difference between **non-** and **un-** becomes clear by comparing *non-American* (a nationality which is not American) with *un-American activities* (being disloyal to America).

There are also some *false negative prefixes* which may be confusing. See **FLAMMABLE (INFLAMMABLE), HABITABLE (INHABITABLE), VALUABLE (INVALUABLE).**

Suffixes: -er, -or, -ee nouns

The **-er** form is used for both objects and people, such as *silencer, lawnmower, employer, teacher* and *worker*.

The **-or** form is generally used for people: *auditor, author, elector, perpetrator,* but some objects like *generator* have this suffix, so there are no fixed rules about the distribution of these suffixes. In some cases, the **-er** form and the **-or** form exist side by side, as alternative spellings with no difference in meaning: *adviser/advisor*.

The **-ee** form is added to a verb to refer to the person who is the recipient of something. Examples are: *addressee, employee, trainee* (the person who is addressed, employed, trained). Some **-ee** forms have general equivalents for those on the other side of an interaction, where **-er** (or **-or**) is added to equivalent verbs. (But note exceptions such as *escapee* and *escaper*, which are both people who have escaped.) Examples are: *addresser, employer, trainer*. However, not all these **-er** words correspond to an **-ee** form, for instance *lover, teacher, worker*. Some **-ee** words have no equivalent **-er** forms: *attendee, retiree* and *standee*.

WORD FORMATION

Forming new words

There are many ways of forming new words. This section considers three ways in which existing words are modified to form new ones.

Back-formation is a way of forming a new word that is derived from the original word but is shorter and reverses the normal process of word formation. Examples are: *burgle* (from burglar), *diagnose* (from diagnosis), *edit* (from editor), *enthuse* (from enthusiasm), *televise* (from television).

Blend words are words created by combining parts of other words. Some of these are firmly established in English and are found in larger dictionaries, so they may be used freely. Examples include *breathalyser* (breath, analyser), *brunch* (breakfast, lunch), *cheeseburger* (cheese, hamburger), *mechatronics* (mechanical and electronic engineering), *moped* (motor pedal), *motel* (motor hotel), *Oxbridge* (fictitious place, from Oxford and Cambridge universities), *paratroops* (parachute troops), *smog* (smoke, fog), *workaholic* (work addiction, alcoholic). Non-standard blends are common in press headlines but reach the pages of only the largest dictionaries. Before using a blend in this last category, explain it. Otherwise avoid it. Examples are *chocoholic* (chocolate addiction, alcoholic), *infomercial* (information commercial) and *plugmentary* (plug [meaning advertisement] and documentary).

Clipped words are words and phrases that have been shortened in order to save time and energy. Sometimes the beginning of the word has been lost: *loudspeaker* has become *speaker, omnibus* has been shortened to *bus, telephone* to *phone*; but often it is the end of the word that has disappeared: *cabriolet* to *cab, microphone* to *mike* (or *mic*), *taximeter* to *taxi, television* to *telly*. The last of these is a clipped phrase, as *television* is properly the technology, and the box in the corner of the room a *television set*. Other phrases which have been clipped to a single word include *immersion* (from *immersion heater*), *mobile* (from *mobile phone*) and *overhead* (from *overhead projector*).

Plural nouns

Standard formation

Most plural nouns are formed by adding an 's' to the singular form. There are some irregular plurals that have survived from Old English. These include:

brother ~ *brethren* (only for religious orders) *child* ~ *children*
man ~ *men* *woman* ~ *women* (wŏŏmăn /'wʊmən/ ~ wímmin /'wɪmɪn/)

ox ~ *oxen*	*foot* ~ *feet*	*goose* ~ *geese**
tooth ~ *teeth*	*louse* ~ *lice*	*mouse* ~ *mice*

* But note that the plural of *mongoose* is *mongooses*.

-es, -s after nouns ending in -o

-es is added to form the plural of a few nouns: *cargo, domino, echo, embargo, hero, innuendo, motto, Negro, potato, tomato, torpedo, veto*. Of these, *cargo, innuendo* and *motto* may also form their plural without the **e**.

-s is added to form the plural of nouns ending in *-io* or *-eo* such as: *radio, cameo*; to musical terms such as *cello, crescendo, soprano*; to clipped words such as *kilo, photo*; and to newer nouns such as *commando*. There are a few exceptions: always use a spellchecker.

-f, -fe endings in nouns and plurals -fs, -fes, -ves

There are two rules for forming the plural of words ending with **-f** or **-fe**, but their distribution is unpredictable. Some change the **-f** to **-v**, and add an **-e** where there is none in the singular, while others simply add **-s**. Here is a list of some of the most common words that have these endings:

belief ~ *beliefs*
calf ~ *calves*
dwarf ~ *dwarfs/dwarves*
elf ~ *elves*
grief ~ *griefs*
half ~ *halves*
himself/herself/itself ~ *themselves*
hoof ~ *hoofs/hooves*
knife ~ *knives*
leaf ~ *leaves**
life ~ *lives*†
loaf ~ *loaves*
myself ~ *ourselves*
oaf ~ *oafs*
proof ~ *proofs*
relief ~ *reliefs*
roof ~ *roofs*
scarf ~ *scarfs/scarves*
self ~ *selves*
sheaf ~ *sheaves*
shelf ~ *shelves*
staff ~ *staffs*
thief ~ *thieves*
wharf ~ *wharfs/wharves*
wife ~ *wives*
yourself ~ *yourselves*

* The Canadian ice hockey team is the *Toronto Maple Leafs*, not 'Leaves'.
† The plural of the type of painting known as a *still life* is *still lifes*, not 'lives'.

Nouns without a singular

There are several examples of nouns which have no true singular form. Those that represent groups of people can often be made singular by adding *a member of*, for example *he is a member of the clergy*.

cattle	*clergy*	*gentry*
people (but *person* is used)	*police*	*vermin*

Compound nouns

The plurals of compound nouns are formed by adding 's' to the most significant word, not necessarily the last word, often a head noun. Examples:

deputy judges	*lieutenant colonels*	*trade unions*	*higher-ups*
attorneys at law	*lords lieutenant*	*brothers-in-law*	*daughters-in-law*
goings-on	*passers-by*	*lookers-on*	

Foreign plurals

Many nouns of foreign origin have adopted the English plural *-s*: *piano ~ pianos; kilo ~ kilos, sauna ~ saunas*, but nouns borrowed from the classical languages (Latin and Greek) and French often retain the plural spellings of their origins.

Nouns of Latin origin

-a *becomes* **-ae** *(some nouns have an alternative in* **-as***)*
alumna ~ alumnae; antenna ~ antennae (zoological use)/*antennas* (wireless aerials); *formula ~ formulae/formulas*. Note that the plural of *agenda* must always be *agendas*.

-ex *becomes* **-ices** *(some nouns have an alternative in* **-exes***)*
index ~ indices/indexes; vertex ~ vertices; vortex ~ vortices.

-is *becomes* **-es**
analysis ~ analyses; axis ~ axes; basis ~ bases; crisis ~ crises; hypothesis ~ hypotheses; oasis ~ oases; parenthesis ~ parentheses; synopsis ~ synopses; thesis ~ theses.

-ix *becomes* **-ices** *(some nouns have an alternative in* **-ixes***)*
appendix ~ appendices/appendixes; helix ~ helices; matrix ~ matrices; radix ~ radices.

-um *becomes* **-a** *(some nouns have an alternative in* **-ums***)*
consortium ~ consortia; curriculum ~ curricula/curriculums; datum ~ data; equilibrium ~ equilibria; erratum ~ errata; forum ~ forums/fora (*fora* in the archaeological sense of a Roman marketplace); *medium ~ media* (in most senses)/*mediums* (intermediaries with the spirit world); *memorandum ~ memoranda/memorandums; referendum ~ referenda/referendums* (different meanings); *stratum ~ strata; symposium ~ symposia.*

-us *becomes* **-i** *(some nouns have an alternative in* **-uses***)*
alumnus ~ alumni; focus ~ foci/focuses; nucleus ~ nuclei; radius ~ radii/radiuses; stimulus ~ stimuli; syllabus ~ syllabuses/syllabi (rare); *terminus ~ termini.*

-us *becomes* **-ra** *with change of preceding vowel*
corpus ~ corpora; genus ~ genera; opus ~ opera (but *opera* is also a singular noun for a staged musical work, with plural *operas*).

-us *becomes* **-uses**
census ~ censuses; crocus ~ crocuses; octopus ~ octopuses; omnibus ~ omnibuses. Note these are the only standard plurals of these words.

Nouns of Greek origin

-a *may become* **-ata** *with alternative* **-as**
dogma ~ dogmas; stigma ~ stigmas/stigmata.

-on *becomes* **-a**
criterion ~ criteria; oxymoron ~ oxymora/oxymorons; phenomenon ~ phenomena.

Nouns of French origin

-eau *becomes* **-eaux** *(some nouns have an alternative in* **-s***)*
bureau ~ bureaux/bureaus; château ~ châteaux; gâteau ~ gâteaux/gateaus.

Retronyms

There are two meanings of the term **retronym**. First, a word spelt backwards to create a new word. A good example of this is *yob*, a negative term for a male youth, formed by spelling *boy* backwards.

The second interpretation of **retronym** is a new name for something whose original name has become confusing and inadequate because of technological or other developments. An example is *television*. If you want to describe what was originally *television* you have to use the retronym *black-and-white television*, as today *television* means *colour television*. The same has happened in the film industry where the retronym *silent movie* is required if you mean what was originally a *movie*. Once *mail* only had one meaning within communications, now the retronyms *snail mail* and *paper mail* are common to avoid confusion with *electronic mail*. New retronyms are rapidly entering English. Two recent additions are *eyeball search* (as opposed to computerized search) and *natural language* (as opposed to artificial or synthetic speech).

Punctuation guide

Apostrophe (') contractions and pronouns

Contractions such as *I'm* and *don't* are best reserved for informal, conversational writing, and when reporting speech. Although it is correct to use an apostrophe to indicate a missing letter and write: *aren't, can't, isn't, it's*, etc., contractions are to be avoided in official letters, reports, academic papers or theses and other types of formal English. Here, the expected forms are: *are not, cannot* (one word), *is not, it is*. Using contractions wrongly not only looks very informal, it also leads to mistakes like confusing *it's* with the possessive pronoun *its*, which both sound the same. Also, *us* is sometimes contracted with verbs like *let*, as in *Let's go*.

A few pronouns take an apostrophe in the genitive (s-genitive): *some, any, every* and *no* when combined with *-body, -one* and *-thing*. Example: *Someone's life is at stake*. See **GENITIVE (GRAMMAR TIPS)**.

Confusing contractions and their soundalikes

it's (it is or it has) is often confused with the possessive **its**. Compare: *It's time to land* (contraction), *the plane lost its rudder* (possessive).

they're (they are) may be confused with the possessive **their** or even the adverb **there** (all of which may be soundalikes).

you're (you are) may be confused with the possessive **your** (*You're late; has your watch stopped again?*)

who's (who is or who has) may be confused with the possessive **whose**. Compare: *Who's driving to town?* (contraction), *Whose car is that?* (possessive).

It is also necessary to be careful with *is* and *has* when used as auxiliary verbs, since their contracted forms are the same. Compare: *He's finished* (he is finished) and *He's finished* (he has finished). The context should make it clear which verb is being used. Remember that the apostrophe in the contraction indicates that letters have been left out. As there are so many potential confusions and ambiguities, it is best to use the full form of the verb whenever this is suitable.

Dates and abbreviations

A useful rule is to use **'s** to form genitives (*30's* and *IBM's*), and **s** without an apostrophe to form plurals (*30s* and *PCs*). Thus *the 1930s' problems* means *the problems of the 1930s*. The only exception to this is when the plural *s* follows a single letter (in chemical formulas, for instance) when not writing an apostrophe may lead to confusion: *Dot your i's and cross your t's*.

Nouns

Apostrophes are used to form the genitive when the noun refers to people and animals, as well as to things we are fond of and feel close to. See **GENITIVE (GRAMMAR TIPS)**.

Brackets

Different names in BE and AE

BE	*Symbol*	*AE*
round brackets/brackets	(. . .)	parentheses
square brackets	[. . .]	square brackets/brackets
braces/curly brackets	{. . .}	braces
angle brackets	<. . .>	angle brackets

How they are used

Round brackets enclose extra information in a sentence that could be omitted without changing the meaning. They are usual in essays and in more formal writing to add clarification: *Several English teams (Arsenal, Man Utd, Liverpool and Chelsea) usually do well in the Champions League.*

- Round brackets can enclose an extra letter such as the singular or plural option as in *the student(s) who left college last term.*
- Round brackets are also used to enclose abbreviations and acronyms that will be used later in a text: *The remotely operated vehicle (ROV) has a range of . . .*
- Round brackets are used in referencing: *Other researchers (Jones, 2005; Kimberly, 2001) have found that* . . . See **REFERENCES (WRITING SKILLS)**.
- When a set of brackets encloses a complete sentence, the final full stop or question mark is placed inside the final bracket. Otherwise the punctuation follows the final bracket.
- It is recommended to rephrase a sentence if a bracket within a bracket creates a double bracket at the end: *When discussing what to serve, it was tricky (my choice (fish and chips) was impossible to combine with Janet's (paella)).* We suggest a solution such as: *When discussing what to serve, it was tricky. My choice (fish and chips) was impossible to combine with Janet's (paella).*

Square brackets are mainly used to mark off a word that is inserted in a quotation to make it more precise or grammatically correct: *The report focused on [living] standards*, or to indicate a typo *The Millenium* [sic] *Bridge*.

Braces and **angle brackets** are rarely used in general writing and readers are referred to style guides for details.

Brackets or dashes?

Both round brackets and dashes are means of presenting extra information. Round brackets are used in more formal writing than dashes. Dashes can also express a contrast or an afterthought at the end of a sentence: *We're looking forward to meeting up in Devon for a long weekend – hope John doesn't bring his holiday snaps this time*. Brackets should not be used here.

Colon (:)

The colon is used to make a break within a sentence in order to add a clause or phrase that gives more information about what has already been stated. *Take care when handling this liquid: it can burn your skin*. A colon may be followed by a lower-case letter unless an abbreviation, proper noun or speech follows. In this book an example of usage that is a complete sentence starts with a capital letter after the colon. A colon is also used to show that something is to follow. See LISTS (WRITING SKILLS), SEMICOLON, below.

Comma (,)

A **comma** is used to signal a slight pause in a sentence. There are numerous rules, but the basic one is that commas break up a text to make it easy to read. A rule of thumb which is often helpful is to place a comma at a point where someone reading the text aloud should pause, change intonation or take a breath. So, if in doubt, read the text aloud and remember that readers have to breathe. Here are some specific points about comma use.

Using commas with adverbs/adverb phrases

Sentences sometimes start with a single adverb, a link word, or a phrase that states the manner, place, reason or time in relation to the main statement that follows: *Suddenly, . . . ; In London, . . . ; In order to find the solution, . . . ; In 2010, ...*

In speech, the end of such units is signalled by the intonation used and a pause. In writing, readers are given the same signals by a comma at the end of these preliminary units. With no comma in this position, readers may be confused. Compare:

Frequently, adjusted prices for new PCs are misleading (adjusted prices are often misleading).

Frequently adjusted prices for new PCs are misleading (prices that are often adjusted are misleading).

Otherwise, adverbs in mid-sentence have a comma before and after them if this is a natural place to change the intonation or to breathe when reading aloud. Compare:

The temperature was steady when, suddenly, there was an explosion.

The temperature was probably too high.

Using commas with adjectives in a series

Use commas to separate two or more adjectives in a series, when each modifies the noun separately: *a fast, new laptop*. As *and* can be inserted between *fast* and *new*, both these words modify *laptop*. Thus a comma is required. If *and* is inserted between *new* and *laptop*, this does not make sense, so do not put a comma here.

Using commas in lists before 'and' (the 'Oxford comma')

The Oxford comma (in AE, the Harvard comma) is the name given to the comma that sometimes divides the last two items in a list, even when the last item follows the word *and*:

Apples, pears, plums, greengages, and damsons all grew in the garden.

Many style guides recommend that this final comma should be omitted.

However, all style guides agree that when a list contains only two items, there is never a comma to divide them:

Greengages and damsons both make very good jam.

There is also general agreement that the comma should be inserted before 'and' in order to avoid ambiguity:

Our fax machine has the following function messages: Error, Out of Paper, Repeat and Send, and Receive. (There are four functions.)

Without the final comma, the fax might be understood as only having three functions, the last one being: *Repeat and Send and Receive*; or four functions, the last two being: *Repeat, and Send and Receive*.

Using commas in defining and non-defining clauses

A defining clause which is essential to the meaning of a sentence is not separated by commas: *The hotel which is by the beach is expensive*. This refers to a resort where there are many hotels but you are only referring to the one by the beach which is why it is called a defining clause. A non-defining clause gives additional information about a noun and is always placed within commas: *The islands, which are privately owned, are very beautiful*. This refers to a situation where there are no other islands to be considered, consequently this is called a non-defining clause. See THAT.

Do not use commas with numbers in international business

As most European languages use a decimal comma rather than a decimal point, some standardization bodies state that the comma should not be used as a divider in large numbers. Thus for numbers above 9999, a space should be inserted before each group of three digits: Examples: *3000; 30 000; 30 000 000*. This book has followed standard BE usage and inserted commas as dividers.

Example: *the weight is 11 856 kg* can have only one meaning, whereas: *the weight is 11,856 kg* might be confusing for those who are used to the decimal comma.

Dash, en dash, em dash

The **dash** has the same function as a set of round brackets but is more usual in informal writing, texts on the web and journalism. A dash typically adds an extra comment: *Due to policing reasons the Chester and Shrewsbury Town matches will be on Sundays – with midday kick-offs – unless they clash with a rugby international.*

The **dash** occurs in two main forms, the **en dash** and **em dash** which are printers' technical terms. The **en dash** is a short dash, the length of the letter 'n'. This is used in many ways such as creating a break, giving a range or period: *1985 – 1995*, or when there are two units: *The Chelsea – Man Utd. match*. Some publishers dislike a space on each side of the **en dash** (–) but it is the house style for many leading UK publishers and is used in this book. The **en dash** is automatically formed when you type a hyphen in Word then press enter. The **em dash** is a longer dash, the length of the letter 'm' (—). This is an alternative to a pair of commas but many people avoid it as it does not appear automatically on the keyboard and looks very dominant when used. On a PC the **em dash** is made by holding down the ALT key and typing 0151 on the numeric keypad.

One way to distinguish between the en dash and the hyphen is that a dash separates words or indicates missing letters within a word and should have a space on both sides, in the house style that we use; whereas a hyphen connects parts of a word and has no space before or after (except for the suspended hyphen). See HYPHENATION, below.

Exclamation mark (!)

Some writers tend to overuse the **exclamation mark** (**exclamation point** in AE). When it is correctly used, an exclamation mark serves to stress a forceful utterance giving a warning or indicating astonishment, anger and surprise: *Allergy advice: These biscuits contain nuts!*

Exclamation marks express the tone of something and are often used in correspondence between friends. If they are overused, your friends will probably assume that you wrote the message while you were carried away, angry, excited or agitated.

In business contexts, academic and formal writing exclamation marks should be avoided. Emails starting with 'Hi!' that are sent to people you have never met are likely to cause irritation. See EMAILS AND LETTERS (WRITING SKILLS).

The exclamation mark should not be combined with other punctuation. *Fire!, he shouted* is non-standard. Similarly an exclamation mark at the end of a sentence should not be followed by a full stop or question mark.

Full stop (.)

A **full stop** (**period** in AE) marks the end of a sentence. Use full stops also to mark abbreviated words: *Jan., a.m., no.* In BE, it is normal to omit the full stop when the last letter of an abbreviation is used: *Mr, Mrs, Ms, Dr,* and in the abbreviations of degrees: *BA, MSc, PhD*. This is not the case in AE, and *Mr., Dr., M.A.* and *Ph.D.* are typical of AE style.

In BE, abbreviations for names of countries are not punctuated with full stops: *the USA and the UK*. In AE, it is common to insert full stops here: *the U.S.A. and the U.K.* See ABBREVIATION.

Ellipsis

When using a quotation in written work, it is normal to write three dots (. . .) to mark an omission in the middle of a text, and to add a fourth dot if the omission comes at the end of a sentence. For instance: *The teacher told them about comma use and that additional information about a noun is always placed within commas*. This might be shortened to *The teacher told them about comma use.* . . . See ELLIPSIS (ECLIPSE).

Decimal point

The decimal point is a full stop: *25.67 per cent*, and between units of money involving decimals: *£55.50*. See CURRENCY UNITS.

Other uses

When expressing time, BE uses a full stop between hours and minutes: *7.30 a.m.* and AE often uses a colon: *7:30 a.m.*

In lists, there is a full stop at the end of each item if this is a complete sentence. Otherwise, there are no full stops after keywords or at the end of a bulleted list. See LISTS (WRITING SKILLS).

In email and Internet addresses the full stop is used between elements, but is read as *dot*. See EMAIL ADDRESS.

One space or two after the full stop?

In typewriting classes many, many years ago, the convention was to put two spaces after a full stop. Modern word processing systems only put one space and this has become established practice today.

Hyphenation

In individual words

A **hyphen** shows that parts of a word, or two or more words, belong together. Hyphenation has an important function in preventing misunderstandings. Consider a *light-blue compound* meaning a pale blue compound, not one that is lightweight and blue. Similarly, *a high-voltage cable* means a cable that has a high voltage, not one that is high up.

AE traditionally uses fewer hyphens than BE, but modern BE is changing. For example, the spellings *co-operate, co-ordinate* and *e-mail* in BE have been replaced by *cooperate, coordinate* and *email*. Not all *co-* words follow this pattern and both BE and AE have a hyphen in *co-opt* (elect) as in *they co-opted a woman to the committee*. In BE, many words prefixed by *non-* and *semi-* have hyphens. Thus *non-linear* is BE and *nonlinear* is AE spelling. Nevertheless, the *uni-* prefixes are usually written in one word in BE.

In general, as words become more familiar, hyphens tend to be dropped. A typical example is *offshore*, as in *offshore drilling, offshore racing* or *offshore banking*, which used to be spelt *off-shore* (hyphenated) in BE a few years ago. It is difficult to determine any consistency between *off-licence* and *off-peak* which are hyphenated in BE, and *offside* and *offload* which are not. It is advisable to consult the most recent edition of a good dictionary for advice on the current spelling of such words.

One general rule relates to prefixes like *anti-* and *quasi-*, which are hyphenated when they are the first element in compound adjectives, such as *anti-American, quasi-scientific,* and not hyphenated when they form part of a compound noun: *antibody, antifreeze, quasicrystal, quasiparticle*.

Hyphenation should be used if the second element is capitalized, as in: *non-European, pro-Irish*. Some prefixes such as: *all-* (*all-star, all-time*), *ex-* (*ex-marine, ex-works*) and *self-* (*self-suggestion*), are hyphenated in both BE and AE.

Distinguishing between pairs of words

A hyphen can also distinguish between pairs of words that apart from the hyphenation are spelt the same, but have different meanings. When these words are read, the hyphen shows that there is stress on the prefix and on the word after the hyphen:

recover (get well)	*re-cover* (cover again)
reform (correction)	*re-form* (reshape)

As some soccer stars have found out, there is a considerable difference between:

resigning (leaving the club) and *re-signing* (renewing a contract)

Initial adjective phrases

A simple rule with hyphenation in phrases is to decide whether the words are qualifying a noun or not. Consider the difference between *twelve-year-old boys* where the first three words form an adjective phrase that all say something about the noun *boys* and are hyphenated and *twelve year olds* which is a number + noun + adjective-used-as-noun and is not hyphenated. Similarly we have *fifty-odd students* (just over 50 students) with the hyphenated adjective phrase, and *fifty odd students* (50 strange ones) which is a number + adjective + noun.

Hyphens are needed in *state-of-the-art solutions* but if the phrase comes after the verb, there are no hyphens: *These solutions are state of the art*.

Note that if an *-ly* adverb is in this initial position, there is no hyphen: *We are looking for environmentally friendly solutions; He was convicted for extremely dangerous driving*.

Numbers and colours

Use hyphens for number compounds such as: *thirty-three* and *one-third*. Note the hyphens in phrases like *a 70 kilometre-an-hour vessel*.

When a colour is a part of a compound, a hyphen is used:

. . . *a blue-metallic car* (a special shade of blue)

. . . *a greyish-red fluid* (a mix of grey and red)

Suspended hyphens

Suspended hyphens are used to create compounds so that numbers are attached to the correct word. *Tests were at 60-, 75-, and 85-degrees Celsius* (three different sets of readings).

Single capitals

It is normal to put a hyphen after an initial single letter, particularly a capital: *T-shirt, U-turn, X-ray*.

Misleading combinations

Use hyphens to create compounds in which an awkward combination of letters would be formed by joining the words, particularly if there are two similar letters:

animal-like *bell-like* *pre-empt* *water-repellent*

Hyphenation at the end of lines

Dividing a word at the end of a line can make it difficult to read or misleading (*mass-age, rest-less*). This shows that sometimes it is best not to hyphenate. Once in a while our unthinking word processors fail to notice badly placed word divisions such as *the leg-end of Robin Hood*.

If divisions must be made, here are some guidelines:

- Divide according to the origin and meaning of words: *trans-port* (not tran-sport), *tele-phone* (not te-lephone). Otherwise, follow the way a word is pronounced: *Euro-pean, chil-dren, de-scribe, de-pend-ent, thou-sand*. When a group of consonants forms one sound, do not split the group: *fea-ther* (not feat-her), *laugh-able* (not laug-hable), *wash-able* (not was-hable). As a rule of thumb, read the word aloud.
- Avoid divisions that create two confusing words: *re-adjust* (not read-just), *minis-ter* (not mini-ster). Some divisions such as wo-men and fe-male may confuse your readers.
- If words already have a hyphen, only divide at the hyphen: *pseudo-intellectual* (not pseudo-intel-lectual), *anti-American* (not anti-Ameri-can).
- Words ending with *-ing* are usually divided at the end of the stem: *carry-ing, divid-ing, mov-ing*. But, if there is a double consonant before *-ing*, carry the last consonant over (*control-ling, puzz-ling*). However, as word division is largely based on pronunciation, if the double consonants form a single sound divide before -ing (*cross-ing, pass-ing*).
- Make sure that numbers followed by a unit of measurement, value or similar are kept together on the same line: *EUR 15 560* (not EUR 15–560), *55°C* (not 55–°C).

Many English dictionaries mark where words are to be divided by dots in mid-position in the headword, such as *tech·no·logy* and *tech·no·lo·gical*. As the pronunciation is generally the guiding rule in word division, make sure you are using the dictionary that suits the form of English you prefer. Webster's, which reflects American English, suggests *a·lu·mi·num* and *prog·ress*. However, the *Longman Dictionary of Contemporary English* which reflects BE usage suggests *al·u·min·i·um* and *pro·gress*.

Quotation marks, inverted commas

Quotation marks are a pair of punctuation marks that can be either single ('. . .') or double (". . .") enclosing a quotation, a word or a jargon-type expression. **Quotation marks** are also called **inverted commas**, although this term is mainly used in BE. It is common to place a following full stop inside the closing quotation mark in AE: *He enjoyed seeing a rerun of 'Ben Hur.'* In BE, the full stop is placed after the quotation mark: *'. . . Ben Hur'*. If the quotation is a complete sentence, in both BE and AE the following full stop is placed inside the quotation marks: *'This is a written gentleman's agreement.'* The same is true for both question marks and exclamation marks, which are placed inside the quotation marks, with no separate full stop written afterwards. There are several typographical patterns such as the jagged version « » and various curly types of quotation marks " ". See QUOTATION (QUOTE), SO-CALLED.

Semicolon (;)

A **semicolon** separates parts of a sentence that already have commas. This is particularly useful in lists: *Here are the sales figures: Scotland, north +10%, western isles + 5%; Wales, north + 5%, south +15%; Ulster . . .*

The semicolon can join two clauses instead of using words like *and* or *but*: *The car was probably worthless; nevertheless we decided to repair it.*

When a link word or linking phrase like *however, therefore, on the one hand, as a result,* starts the second clause a semicolon is used to divide the two clauses: *A number of players have been sold; however, Man Utd is still expanding its squad.*
See BRACKETS, REFERENCES (WRITING SKILLS).

Symbols on the Internet

Many of these punctuation signs are used in a special way in email and Internet addresses. See SYMBOLS.

Writing skills

This section considers:

A. Correspondence – emails and letters, addresses, titles.
B. CV writing – guidelines and templates.
C. Style – guidelines for reports, theses and dissertations.
D. Style – commenting, link words, lists, numbers, repetition, sexist language.
E. Formal English – avoiding slang and contractions.

A. Correspondence – emails and letters

Guidelines to writing emails, letters and faxes

Irrespective of whether you send an email, or post or fax a letter, these guidelines still apply.

- *Use either the BE or AE standards*. There are differences between BE and AE customs in standard salutations in email and letter writing (see below).
- *Use a salutation*. In most cases this will be 'Dear Mr Jones' or 'Dear John'. Occasionally in emails just use the first name: 'John' The exception is letters of recommendation or similar that usually start: 'To whom it may concern'.
- *Use the ending that matches the salutation*. If you are unsure, follow the guidelines given below.
- *Use '-ing forms' in the verbs at the end*. This stresses that you have an ongoing relationship and that there is unfinished business. Some examples are: 'We are looking forward to receiving your comments on this report, by the end of April.' 'We are considering your proposals and are looking forward to discussing matters with you on 12 April.' Naturally this does not apply to all types of emails.
- *Write the month in letters or use the ISO standard for international contacts*. Use the format, 2 May 2009, or the ISO standard for all-digit dates (CCYY-MM-DD). In ISO 8601, 2 May 2009 is written 2009-05-02. See DATES.
- *Never write a date as 02.05.09 if it is going to read by an international company*. To Europeans, this probably means 2 May 2009; but most Americans will understand it as February 5, 2009.
- *Avoid exclamation marks (!) in formal business letters*. An exclamation mark in English is used to express astonishment or surprise.
- *Avoid short forms like 'I'm' and 'don't' in business letters*. These should only be used in informal, conversational writing and when reporting another person's exact words. Sometimes they are used in personal emails to stress closeness and informality. See CONTRACTIONS.

- *Never treat a business email differently from a business letter*. Although many people try to avoid using the formal salutation (see FORMAL EMAILS AND LETTERS, below), its use is recommended if the name of the recipient is not known. Though emails tend to be friendlier than letters, a salutation should always be used. A typical email starts with 'Dear Mary', or sometimes 'Mary', and ends 'Regards'. A *Financial Times* survey of 2000 business people in the UK a few years ago found that 60 per cent objected to the lack of salutations in emails and were irritated by the use of a casual tone in many mails. Emails from a company or institution should not be too informal and a safe rule is to avoid salutations like 'Hi!' and endings like 'love and kisses'. Some standard salutations and endings are listed below.

Standard openings (salutations) and endings in emails and letters in BE

Formal emails and letters, where you are writing to an institution or an unnamed person

These start with the following salutations:

Dear Sirs,	when you write to a company, organization, university.
Dear Sir,	to an unnamed person, who you know is male.
Dear Madam,	to an unnamed person, who you know is female.
Dear Sir or Madam,	the safe option to an unnamed person, such as a Personnel Manager.
Dear Editor,	in a letter to a newspaper.

These end:

Yours faithfully,

Normal business emails and letters, where you know the recipient's name

These start:

Dear Mr Jones,	to a named man. Never use 'Mister'.
Dear Ms Jones,	to any named woman, without referring to her marital status. This is becoming more and more usual for any woman.
Dear Mrs Jones,	to a named woman who is married. Some women write (Mrs) after their names in letters so that their correspondent knows that this is the expected salutation to use in their reply.
Dear Miss Jones,	to a named woman who is unmarried.
Dear Professor Jones,	used for all professors, including assistant and associate professors. Avoid using the slangy Prof. and always capitalize Professor.
Dear Dr Jones,	can be used for someone holding a PhD or other doctoral degree.

These end:

Yours sincerely,

Note that in British English, you do not use a stop after abbreviations like *Mr*, *Ms* (pronounced miz /mɪz/), *Mrs*, and *Dr*, as is the custom in American English. If you are writing to someone where it is difficult to determine whether you should use *Mr* or *Ms*, one solution is just to use the first and last name: *Dear Sam Smith* or *Dear Li-Ching*.

Emails and letters to colleagues, associates and friends, etc.

These start:

Dear Jim,	if a person signs his email or letter with 'Jim', use this in your reply. If you use 'Dear Mr Jones', you signal coldness and distance to Jim.
Dear Mary,	as for 'Dear Jim'.
Dear colleagues,	useful in group mailings, but you could be more personal.

There are many endings. Here are some on a scale from a businesslike tone to close friendship:

Yours sincerely,	even though you start 'Dear Jim,' you show that this is a businesslike email or letter.
Regards,	although frequently used in emails, this is too informal for most business letters.
Kind regards,	
Best wishes,	used to signal friendliness.
Warm regards,	more friendly, frequently used for friends.
Love,	only used for close friends.

Example of a formal letter

12 Hills Road
Haywards Heath
RH16 4XY

Southern Customer Services
PO BOX 277
Tonbridge TN9 2ZP

12 November 2009

Dear Sir or Madam,

IMPROVED SERVICE ON SOUTHERN RAIL

This is not a letter of complaint about your rail services. In fact, it is quite the reverse. I wish to compliment you on your rail services. Getting to London and back is so much more comfortable than it was a few years ago when another company was running the service. I regularly go to Victoria and your staff are extremely helpful. I have also noted that the service staff keep the carriages clean and tidy. Keep up the good work.

Yours faithfully,

George Smith

Example of a business letter

78 Wingate Road
Trumpington
Cambridge
CB2 2RF

The University of Exeter,
The Queen's Drive,
Exeter,
Devon,
EX4 4QJ

2 November 2009

Dear Ms Smith,

APPLICATION FOR POSITION AS ASSISTANT OFFICE MANAGER IN STUDENT SERVICES, UNIVERSITY OF EXETER

I wish to apply for the above position that was advertised in *The Daily Telegraph* on 28 October 2009. I have a bachelor's degree in business studies from the University of Nottingham in 2005 and since then I have worked at The Grand Hotel in Eastbourne with responsibility for updating their booking systems (2006–2007). At present I am working as an assistant office manager in the RSA Examinations Syndicate at Cambridge. This is only a temporary position until the end of the year.

The position you advertise seems to be an excellent opportunity for me to apply my knowledge of business studies and work in a university environment which is a central objective in my career plans.

I have attached my CV where I feel that my education and skills should make me a candidate worth consideration. I speak and write excellent French which I have noted is one of the skills you require. My computer skills correspond with what you specify in the above advertisement. My tutor and present employer have kindly agreed to provide references and their contact details are given on the CV.

I am a serious-minded person who works conscientiously and diligently. I get on well with colleagues and like to be part of a team. Outside working life I enjoy sports, especially rugby which I play at Old-Boys level, although I have appeared twice for the Eastern Counties team.

I am available for an interview in Exeter at any time in November or December.

I am looking forward to hearing from you.

Yours sincerely,

Colin Slater

Example of an email to a business contact

Subject line: Interview at University of Exeter

Dear Mr Birnet,

Thank you very much for inviting me for an interview. I confirm that I will be at your offices at 10.30 on Thursday 19 November.

I am very grateful that you have offered to cover my travel expenses.

Looking forward to meeting you.

Yours sincerely,
Colin Slater

Example of an email to a friend

Subject line: Exeter calling . . .

Hi Jane,
How are things in Bath? I tried to ring you just now but your mobile must be on the blink so I decided to send this mail. Last week, we talked about spending a weekend together. Guess what? I've been picked for an interview for that job in Exeter. I'll be there on Thursday next week. How about making it a weekend trip and we can see a bit of Devon? I can pick you up on Wednesday afternoon, if you can get time off work.

Love,
Colin

Standard openings (salutations) and endings in emails and letters in AE

Formal emails and letters, where you are writing to an institution or an unnamed person

These start with the following salutations:

Dear Sirs:	when you write to a company, organization, university.
Dear Sir:	to an unnamed person, who you know is male.
Dear Madam:	to an unnamed person, who you know is female.
Dear Madam or Sir:	always the safe option for an unnamed person.

These often end:

Sincerely, / Sincerely yours,

Note the use of the colon after the salutation in AE. Some American letters and emails of this type also omit the 'Dear' in these types of salutations, and just open *Madam or Sir*:

Another such salutation is *Ladies and Gentlemen*: (to a company, etc.) Many feel that *Truly* has become overused as an ending and should be avoided. *Respectfully* is very formal and is rarely used today.

Normal business emails and letters, where you know the recipient's name

These start:

Dear Mr. Jones:	to a named male, never use 'Mister' in a letter.
Dear Ms. Jones:	to a named female, without reference to her marital status.
Dear Mrs. Jones:	to a named female, who is married.
Dear Miss Jones:	to a named female, who is unmarried.
Dear Professor Jones:	use for all professors: also assistant and associate professors. Write *Professor* in full, do not use the slangy *Prof*.
Dear Dr. Jones:	can be used for someone holding a PhD, or other doctoral degree.

These often end:

Sincerely,

Sincerely yours,

Note that in American English, a stop is used after abbreviations like *Mr.*, *Ms.* (pronounced miz /mɪz/), *Mrs.*, and *Dr.*, and a colon placed after the name (as an alternative, a comma is sometimes used). Some Americans use just *Dear M. Jones*: to avoid the gender specific greeting. *Dear M./M. Jones*: is also sometimes used for the same reasons in place of 'Mr. and Mrs.' in emails and letters.

Emails and letters to colleagues, associates and friends, etc.

These start:

Dear Jim,	if a person signs his email or letter with 'Jim', use this in your reply. If you use 'Dear Mr Jones', you signal coldness and distance to Jim.
Dear Mary,	same comments as for 'Dear Jim'.
Dear colleagues,	useful in group mailings, but you could be more personal.

The endings vary on a scale that indicates a business tone to close friendship:

Sincerely,	even though you start 'Dear Jim', you show that this is a businesslike email or letter.
Regards,	although frequently used in emails, this is too informal for most business letters.
Kind regards,	
Best wishes,	used to signal friendliness.
Warm regards,	getting slightly 'hotter', frequently used for friends.
Love,	only used for close friends.

Note that a comma is frequent after such salutations and endings.

Addresses in letters

In modern English, all addresses are written with as few stops and commas as possible. Companies and organizations have their name on the top line of a letterhead followed by the address. However, personal letters only have the address placed at the top. (When the recipient does not know the writer, the writer's name should be printed underneath his or her signature.) The address of the recipient is normally placed under the address of the sender. Many people place both addresses against the left-hand margin of the letter. Note that although the street number is placed before the street name in the UK, the USA and elsewhere, there are many other countries in which this order is reversed. Try to follow the practice of the destination country:

Visclar Ltd.
169 Orange Street
New Haven
CT 06510, USA

Clovn Corporation
Bahnhofstrasse 19–21
DE – 63543 Neuberg, Germany

Common short forms in addresses are: *Ave* (Avenue), *Blvd* (Boulevard), *Rd* (Road), *Sq.* (Square), *St* (Street).

ISO 3166-1 'Codes for the representation of names of countries and their subdivisions – Part 1: Country codes' is a list of the international two-letter codes for about 240 countries (details about ISO can be obtained from www.iso.ch).

Titles for appointed or elected officials

Ambassadors (BE model)

In letters

Envelope: *His Excellency John Smith, Ambassador of the Republic of Ireland, Irish Embassy*

Salutation: *Dear Ambassador,*

Close: *Yours sincerely,*

In meetings

Introduction: *Her Excellency Jane Smith, British Ambassador to Spain*

When meeting her: *Ambassador*

When referring to her: *Your Excellency*

Ambassadors (AE model)

In letters

Envelope: *The Honorable James/Jane Smith, Ambassador of the United States, American Embassy*

Salutation: *Dear Mr Ambassador: / Dear Madam Ambassador:*

Close: *Sincerely yours, / Sincerely,*

In meetings

Introduction: *The Ambassador of the United States of America*

Reference: *Mr Ambassador, Madam Ambassador*

Government ministers (BE model)

In letters

Envelope: *The Rt. Hon. John Smith, MP, Minister for . . .*

Salutation: *Dear Sir, Dear Madam,*

Close: *Yours faithfully,*

In meetings

When meeting: *Minister*

Introducing: *Mr Smith, Minister for . . .*

MPs/MEPs

In letters

Envelope: *Mr John Smith, MP*

Salutation: *Dear Sir, Dear Madam,*

Close: *Yours faithfully,*

In meetings *Mr Smith,*

Senators (AE model)

In letters

Envelope: *The Honorable James/Jane Smith, United States Senate*

Salutation: *Dear Senator Smith:*

Close: *Sincerely yours, / Sincerely,*

In meetings

Introduction: *Senator Smith from Nebraska*

Reference: *Senator Smith*

Representatives (AE model)

In letters

Envelope: *The Honorable James/Jane Smith, United States House of Representatives*

Salutation: *Dear Mr. Smith: / Dear Ms. Smith:*

Close: *Sincerely yours, / Sincerely,*

In meetings

Introduction: *The Representative from New Jersey*

Reference: *Mr Smith, Ms Smith*

B. CV writing – guidelines and templates

A skills-based CV is one way to show what you can offer the job market. There is a template and instructions for completing this type of CV (in most European languages) which can be downloaded at http://europass.cedefop.europa.eu/europass/home/hornav/Downloads/navigate.action.

These notes may also help you to match your skills to the advertised job or appointment.

Use headings, such as:

Personal information
Desired employment
Work experience
Education and training
Personal skills and competences
Social skills and competences
Organizational skills and competences
Technical skills and competences
Computer skills and competences
Artistic skills and competences
Other skills and competences
Additional information – References
Annexes

A CV should be as concise as possible, and limited to a maximum of two pages.

Personal information

Name: (on both pages of the CV)

Address: **Home:** **Term:** (give dates)

Phone: **Email:**

Date of birth:

Work experience

Start with the most recent activities and tailor this section to each job you apply for.

- Use complete sentences and active constructions:

  became proficient in . . .
  gained experience in . . .
  acquired skills in . . .
  responsible for . . .
  conducted research in . . .
  in charge of . . .

- Explain any gaps:

  2006 to 2007 Unemployed, used this time for retraining (ICT skills).

Education and training

- Start with your most recent education.
- Explain grading systems in international CVs.

Personal skills

This is to be written in complete sentences and is where you can describe your transferable skills such as teamwork, adaptability, communication skills, innovative skills, organization skills and leadership.

Language skills

English – native language; German – good; French – basic.

The term *excellent* is often used for language skills that are between *native language* and *good*. Some people rank their written and spoken language skills separately.

The *Europass Language Passport* allows you to describe your language skills and is useful for those interested in studying or working elsewhere in Europe. For details, search for *Europass Language Passport* or http://europass.cedefop.europa.eu/europass/home/vernav/Europasss+Documents/Europass+Language+Passport/navigate.action.

This is based on the *Common European Framework of Reference for Languages* developed by the Council of Europe.

Organizational skills

Use active constructions, such as:

Responsible chemical engineer with good organizational skills (give examples).

The ability to work independently (give examples), *and successful experience of working in a project team* (give examples).

Strong background in ICT (see Skills), *matched by three years of international experience in* (country) *working for* (name) – *a leading software company*.

Choose positive language.

- Your level of expertise:

competent in	*skilled in*	*qualified in*	*specialized in*

- Your type of expertise:

practical	*theoretical*	*analytical*	*responsible*
successful	*articulate*	*informed*	*diplomatic*

- Your outlook on life:

adaptable	*flexible*	*versatile*	*enterprising*
innovative	*creative*	*positive*	*enthusiastic*

Technical skills

List your skills that are relevant to the job advertised: Social science, specializing in . . . ;

Computer skills

Programming experience in C++, desktop publishing.

Artistic skills

Other skills

Your interests indicate a lot about you. Say what you can do, no one else will.

– **sport**	(healthy, well trained)
– **leisure (swimming, snowboarding)**	(healthy, well trained)
– **politics**	(engaged, aware)
– **developing countries**	(engaged, generous)
– **achievements**	(stamina, determined)

Additional information – References (if requested)

- One academic and one personal reference.
- Check that the people you state agree (phone them).
- Take their names and full contact details to the interview.

C. Style guidelines for reports, theses and dissertations

Many journals have their own guide to authors which states how some of the material covered below is to be presented. Some universities also have well-formulated style guidelines for academic writing. Such documents naturally take precedence over the following. These guidelines are suggestions that may help solve a stylistic problem.

Acknowledgements

This is the part of a thesis or report in which the author lists or thanks those who have helped in its production. Remember to be formal in the acknowledgements:

*I **acknowledge** the invaluable assistance of my supervisor Professor John Smith at the Department of XZY, University of Nottingham.*

*I would **also like to thank** . . .*

*I **appreciate** the assistance of . . .*

***Special thanks** are given to . . .*

***Gratitude** is also expressed to . . .*

***I am grateful** for the help of Anne Jones, research technician and other department staff in preparing the FEM analysis.*

*Finally, I **acknowledge** the generous financial support from the . . .*

Capital letters

Always capitalize:

- Proper nouns or adjectives. Use initial capital letters for proper nouns and for adjectives derived from proper nouns (a proper noun is the name and title of a specific person, a company, institution, place, location, country, month, day, or a holiday):

  . . . the volt is named after Count Volta
  . . . he is Professor Gibbs from University College
  . . . Northern Ireland
  . . . French Canadian
  . . . in late December on the Friday before Christmas Eve

- Structural words like:

Appendix	*Chapter*	*Equation*
Figure	*Section*	*Table*

are capitalized when followed by a number or letter: *Equation 3.2 and Section 4.2.*

Do not capitalize:

- Names of elements (except as the first word of a sentence): *This is a mixture of iron, aluminium and copper*.
- Names of methods, unit symbols (except for the proper name part): *pattern recognition, kilometre, degree Celsius*.

Capitalization – the King or the king? The West or the west?

When referring to a specific person, capitalize king, queen, prince, bishop, ambassador, professor and similar titles. References to the institution such as the Crown and the Monarchy are capitalized. However, if a general group is being referred to, use lower case: *all the kings of Spain*; *all the professors in the Department*. A capitalized reference to the Prime Minister means a specific person, but *just like a typical prime minister* means like many of them and is not capitalized.

This is also the general pattern to follow with parts of recognized political units. Thus, Northern Territory, in Australia, is capitalized but northern Queensland is not, as the latter refers to a general area, not a defined political unit. Capitalization is correct for *the West* as a force in American history, the West Bank, the West Country in the UK and the West when it refers to North America and Europe. Otherwise, *west* is lower case when the direction towards the setting sun is being referred to: *They moved west*. Referring simply to *the South* may mean different things to different people: the south-east part of the USA to many Americans, the developing countries to some and the southern hemisphere to others.

Words that are derived from a geographical name where there is only a distant connection with the original place are written in lower case. Examples: *bohemian* (referring to a lifestyle), *italics* (print font) and *morocco* (fine leather). Note that these words are used alone. When such words are used in fixed phrases like *Danish pastry*, *French window*, *Arabic numerals* and *Roman numerals*, upper case should be used for the nationality word. See NATIONALITY WORDS.

Capitalization in report and publication titles

1. Titles of books and reports

The general standard in scientific and academic work is to use upper case for the first letter of the main words in the titles of books and reports. Use lower case for *a, an, the, and, or, for, nor* and prepositions, unless they are the first or last word in a title. Examples:

A Brief History of Time
The History of the New West
Cancer and the Symptoms to Look For

2. Chapters and sections

In scientific and academic papers, reports and doctoral theses, there are few general standards about when to use capitals in chapter or section headings. Follow the Guidelines for Authors of the specific journal, or the house style of the organization. If there are no such guidelines, there is a general trend towards using block letters (all capitals) for the level 1 headings (chapter titles). Level 2 headings (such as Section 2.1, Section 2.2) have the main words capitalized. Level 3 headings (Section 2.1.1, Section 2.1.2) have the first word and only proper nouns capitalized. Examples of level 3 headings: *Section 2.1.1 Modelling of Cartesian coordinates* or *World history from a German perspective*.

3. Brochures, press material, web

Many people feel that capital letters shout at the reader, and that titles without capitals are softer and easier to read. As a result sales brochures, press material and text on the Internet show a clear movement away from capitals in titles when they are optional. A study of various guides to authors shows that some scientific journals are also moving in this direction.

4. Hyphenation and capitalization in report and publication titles

The general rule is to capitalize only the first element in the hyphenated phrase:

Low-pressurized Aircraft Design
Near-critical Values
Moscow's English-speaking Community

There are a couple of exceptions to this rule:

1. Capitalize both the first and second elements in a hyphenated phrase in a title when they have equal force:

   Vapour-Liquid Compounds
   Regional-National Legislation

2. Capitalize the second element in a hyphenated compound in a title when it is a noun or proper adjective:

   Non-American Election Principles
   Anti-Christian Thinking

See HYPHENATION (PUNCTUATION GUIDE).

Equations

References to specific equations are to be capitalized. Many prefer the format 'Equation 2.1'. An alternative is: 'Eq. 2.1.' Do not mix these two formats in the same report.

Verbs that are often combined with 'equation' include: *indicate, establish, present, give, prove*.

Figures

As figures are visual, use the term *figure* for all illustrations that are not tables.

In many major journals, the guidelines to authors suggest that:

- The captions are placed under or at the side of figures.
- In a figure caption, the following model is recommended, note the punctuation:

  'Figure 2. Schematic representation . . .'

- References to specific figures are to be capitalized. Many prefer the format *Figure 2.1*. An alternative is: *Fig. 2.1*. Do not mix these two formats in the same report.

Verbs that are frequently combined with *figure* include: *show, present, illustrate, demonstrate*.

Introduction

The introduction presents what you are writing about

Thus it should **not** contain information you know as a result of having completed the work you are about to report.

The introduction should be a presentation of the nature/scope of the subject matter

- explains what the situation was before you began the work that you are about to report.
- your objectives and strategy in writing the report.
- your assumptions about the audience's expertise/needs.

Relevant literature for guidance

- how the report relates to other sources of information.
- a review of previous work and theoretical considerations.

Explain how the thesis/report is organized

Use variety in your outline of thc chapters in a thesis: too many people use *show* and *describe*. The following link words are useful here:

Chapter 2 ***considers*** *. . . and* ***states*** *how . . .*
Then, Chapter 3 ***turns to*** *the issue of . . . and* ***illustrates*** *how . . .*
After this, Chapter 4 ***demonstrates*** *. . . and* ***provides*** *a comparison with . . .*

This is followed by Chapter 5 which ***presents*** *the conclusions and* ***explains*** *the applications of this work for the . . . industry. Finally, Chapter 6* ***outlines*** *the implications and potential for further work.*

References

In running text

There are two main methods of referencing articles in journals and other publications. These are known as the *Harvard* (author–date) and *Vancouver* (author–number) reference systems. Many journals have their own house style. If you are using the author–date system and a comma is placed between the author and date, a semicolon is necessary between two references. Example: *Other researchers (Jones, 2005; Kimberly, 2001) have found that . . .*

Some style guides suggest that a comma is not to be placed between the author and date and here a comma is necessary between two references. Example: *Other researchers (Jones 2005, Kimberly 2001) have found that . . .*

In the Vancouver system the author–date is replaced by a number which is found in the reference list at the end. In some journals, all these numbers are listed in the reference list in order of appearance in the text. Thus in the text the references will appear as: *This is indicated in another paper (1). Other writers have commented on related issues, notably Smith (2,3) and Jones (4)*. Other journals ask authors to use an alphabetical order for the references in the reference list. This means the references in the text will appear as: *This is indicated in another paper (45). Other writers have commented on related issues, notably Smith (67,68) and Jones (34)*. In other journals the author(s) are not named and the reference number comes in square brackets often in superscript: [34].

In reference lists

All reports and theses should have a reference list that indexes the references in the text. The reference list comes last in the document on a new page with the heading *Reference list* or *References*. In most cases the references are arranged alphabetically according to the family name of the first author. When there are several works by the same author(s), sort them chronologically. If an author has two or more publications in the same year that are both referred to, add lower case a, b, etc. after the year: Smith, Arthur (2007a), Smith, Arthur (2007b).

Note that chapters in books are referenced with the pages following the abbreviation pp.:

Smith, J., ed. *The rise of new governments in Eastern Europe*, pp. 167–173. London: AC Publications.

But papers in journals indicate the page numbers after a colon and do not use pp.:

Smith J., Industrial marketing concepts need revision. *Journal of Marketing Research*, 12(2): 156–157.

While *et al.* is used after the first author in the text if there are three authors or more: Jones *et al.*, 2000, it should not be used in a reference list as all the authors are to be cited.

Referencing electronic documents

As more publications and other documents become available in electronic form, often without a paper version, it is necessary to reference these electronic resources so that researchers are able to document their work. ISO 690-2 has addressed this issue (ISO 690-2: *Information and documentation – Bibliographic references – Part 2: Electronic documents or parts thereof*).

Electronic documents differ from printed publications in a number of ways:

- First, online electronic documents have no page references, volumes or edition numbers; sometimes the absence of publishers means that there has to be a system of identification. The location of the source of the document cited is also to be provided for online documents. This information should be given by the words *available from* or an equivalent phrase. Example:

  Available from Internet: gopher://info.lib.uh.edu.

- Second, online electronic documents can be instantly updated, which necessitates the use of *citation* in references. Citation means the date on which the electronic document was actually seen. The word 'cited' or an equivalent term is written in square brackets before the date. Examples:

  [cited 3 September 2007], [cited 2007-09-03; 21:15 GMT]

- Third, the type of electronic medium has to be established in the reference list. This is to be given in square brackets. The following words or their equivalent should be used:

  [online], [CD-ROM], [magnetic tape], [disk]

  ISO 690-2 gives some examples of how to write references to electronic documents:

- Reference to off-line electronic documents:

  Passano E; Igland R T; Mirza S; Larsen C M. In *Petroleum Abstracts* [CD-ROM]. California: Knight-Ridder Information Inc., 1998. ISBN: 0-7918-1952-3.

- Reference to online electronic documents:

  Talker, Petter. Stochastic resonance in the semiadiabatic limit. In New Journal of Physics [online]. Bristol, UK. Institute of Physics Publishing, 12 March 1999 [cited 2003-07-01]. Available from Internet: <http://njp.org/>. ISSN: 1367–2630.

Structure

In long reports and theses, the **chapter** is the basic structural unit. Chapter is capitalized when it is followed by a number: *This is discussed in Chapter 4*, but not otherwise: *The present chapter contains the conclusions*.

In short reports, the **section** is the basic structural unit: *See Section 1 and Section 4*. Note that this is capitalized when it is followed by a number, but not otherwise. In long reports use **section** for all levels below *chapter*: *See Sections 1.2, 1.3.2 and 3.2.1.4*.

Tables

Use the term *table* for all tabular material. In many journals, the guidelines to authors suggest that:

- Captions are placed over tables
- References to specific tables are to be capitalized. Many prefer the format *Table 2.1*. Note that *Tab. 2-1* is non-standard.

'We' tips for authors

Academic papers, dissertations and theses written by a single author should use the word *we* with care. *We* is a powerful word as it sets the tone. At worst, *we* can irritate readers into thinking the writer has an inflated opinion of himself or herself as it conveys the impression that this is the opinion of the entire department or research group. At best, it can rivet the reader's attention to a valuable contribution to knowledge.

Editorial 'we'

Use *we* when it refers to the view of a board or a collective body: *We recommend this solution. . . .* It is recommended that sentences like *as we have indicated in Section 2* should be avoided and replaced by *as is indicated in Section 2* since it is unnecessary to involve the actor here.

'We' for reader involvement

The use of *us* and *we* in contexts like: *Let us consider these results in detail. . . . We now turn to the applications of this,* is encouraged by many style guides as a way of involving your reader in the discussion.

Royal 'we'

Referring to oneself as *we* is known as the *Royal we*. This used to be a way to distance the monarch from the people. Nowadays this is avoided, even in formal contexts, by the British monarch.

D. Style

Commenting to your readers

Useful words when discussing facts in a paper

This paper starts by . . .
. . . making some observations about . . .
. . . giving some facts about . . .
. . . outlining national policy.

Useful words when presenting a theory

- Useful nouns: *notion, concept, theory, idea, hypothesis, principle, rationale.*

- Useful verbs: *indicate, illustrate, point out, present, develop, embody, elaborate, state, establish, formulate, accept, reject, reveal, support.*

Avoid words such as *thing, tell, say.*

Link words

A moderate use of link words improves the readability of documents.

A simple check of the readability of something you have written is counting how many sentences start with *The*. '***The** paper presents . . .*'. '***The** challenge was . . .*'. '***The** work involved . . .*'. One way to liven up such 'machine-gun' style is to use link words or transitions that give signposts to your reader. However, do not throw the baby out with the bathwater. A text where every sentence starts with a link word is just as difficult to follow as a road where the signposting is overdone. Note that the typical position of a link word is at the beginning of a sentence, but this is not compulsory. The advantage of the preliminary link word is that the reader is not slowed down by a comma, link word and a second comma in mid sentence. Compare: '*Research in reducing emissions, as a rule, has provided . . .*' with: '*As a rule, research in reducing emissions has provided . . .*'. Here are some examples of link words and where to use them.

- When **comparing** things, useful link words include:

By contrast,	*Conversely,*	*However,*	*In contrast,*
In spite of,	*Instead,*	*Likewise,*	*Nevertheless,*
Otherwise,	*On the contrary,*	*On the one hand,*	*For the most part,*

- When **generalizing**, use:

As a rule,	*As usual,*	*For the most part,*	*Generally,*
In general,	*Ordinarily,*	*Usually,*	

- When **describing a sequence**, useful link words for a linear progression are:

First, . . .	*Second, . . .*	*Third, . . .*	*Next, . . .*
Then, . . .	*Finally, . . .*		

  Note that most English style guides recommend: *First, . . . Second, . . . Third, . . .* rather than: *Firstly, . . . Secondly, . . . Thirdly, . . .*

  Also, once *First, . . .* is used as a link word, your reader will expect *Second, . . . Third, . . .* and *Next*

- Sequences can be signposted by link words that point backwards, like:

  Having completed step one, the next step is . . .   *After stage one, . . . Previously, . . .*

- Link words to describe simultaneous actions include:

  During this stage . . .   *While . . .*   *At the same time . . .*   *Simultaneously . . .*

- Finally, there are link words to end a sequence. Make sure that these are used at the very end:

  Finally, . . .   *In the last stage, . . .*   *The report finishes with, . . .*   *In conclusion, . . .*

Lists

Use a colon to introduce a list. If the items in a list are in a sequence or hierarchy, show this by numbering them:

1. *time*
2. *money*
3. *skilled staff*

or by placing a lower-case letter before each item:

(a) *time*
(b) *money*
(c) *skilled staff*

Do not place commas, semicolons or stops after keywords in a list or at the end of the list. If the items in a list are separate and parallel, but in no significant order or hierarchy, use bullets, dashes, or some other symbol before each item.

In modern English style, the items in a list are only followed by a stop if they are full sentences:

- *Sufficient time will be allocated for training.*
- *This is backed by the financial resources to give adequate training.*
- *The staff we recruit have a sound academic education and relevant work experience.*

Numbers in numerals or words

It is normal to write numbers as Arabic numerals in scientific and technical contexts. Otherwise, a general rule is to write numbers below 10 as words and larger numbers as numerals. Avoid mixing numerals and words in the same range: *The boys were from 7 to 15* (not from seven to 15). However, large numbers are written as words at the beginning of a sentence: *Seventy-two thousand people are in hospital.* To avoid starting a sentence with *72,000*, which is generally considered poor style, the sentence can be rephrased either by starting *A total of 72,000* . . . or by moving the number to another part of the sentence: *The hospitals have admitted 72,000 people.*

The house style used for this book has the comma as a thousand marker which is customary in BE. However, when writing for an international audience where many languages use the comma as a decimal marker, the figure 3,456 could be understood as a decimal rather than almost three and a half thousand. See **COMMA (PUNCTUATION GUIDE)**.

The ISO standard 31-0 (1992), tries to resolve this by recommending the use of a space as the thousand/million/billion marker: 35 500 and 45 500. Another convention is to use a space for thousands, millions, etc., only for numbers greater than 9999.

Numerals – Arabic and Roman

Arabic numerals such as 1, 2, 3, 4 etc. are almost always preferred to Roman numerals – I, II, III, IV, etc. or i, ii, iii, iv, etc. which are only used in limited applications. These include designating the number of names of kings, queens, emperors, popes, etc.: Henry IV and Henry V are also plays by Shakespeare (read as 'Henry the Fourth', 'Henry the Fifth'); giving dates of films, and paginating the numbers of introductory pages in books. When filmmakers produce a sequel to an earlier film, the title is often written in Roman numerals (Rocky II, Rocky III, etc.) but is read as 'Rocky Two', 'Rocky Three', etc. The pronunciation of the number in a ship's name indicates the origin of the name: the Queen Mary II, for instance, is pronounced 'Queen Mary Two', rather than 'Queen Mary the Second', because there was a previous ship called 'Queen Mary', and not because of the British Queen Mary the Second who reigned 1688–94.

Repetition of words

- Repeat a keyword rather than use another term such as 'it' that might be misunderstood:

  The technical malfunction began before the last inspection, a month before the breakdown. It was an obvious human error ('It' refers to what? The malfunction, inspection or breakdown?)

  The advert below shows the confusion that can result from not repeating a keyword.

- Avoid placing similar sounding words together if they have different meanings:

  Figure 7 ***showed*** *that the temperature* ***showed*** *an increase* (use 'indicated', 'increased by').

  These clear ***effects*** *will* ***affect*** *our budget* (use 'effects', 'influence').

- Avoid repetition of several words containing the same sounds:

  *There is to be no vari**ation** in hyphen**ation** and capitaliz**ation*** (use 'in the use of hyphens and capitals').

  Many major man-machine manifestations may . . . (rewrite).

Although repetition is often boring, it can be used for a special effect. An example is one of Churchill's speeches in the Second World War: 'We shall fight on the beaches, we shall

WRITING SKILLS

fight on the landing grounds, we shall fight in the fields and in the streets, we shall fight in the hills; we shall never surrender.'

> *'German Shepherd for sale, obedient and will eat anything. Fond of children.'*
> (Classic dog ad.) **!**

Sexist language

Sexist language is to be avoided in politically correct, modern English. Here are some of the problem areas and solutions.

Generic terms like ***mankind*** and ***man*** when used to mean people of both sexes are criticized because they are old-fashioned, and also because they make males more central than females. One solution is to use *people, humanity* and *humankind* instead. *Humankind* is not a new term. It has existed since the seventeenth century. Today, ***mankind*** should be used for males exclusively.

It follows from this that 'the man in the street' could be replaced by *the average person*; 'a man–machine interface' could be *a human–machine interface*; 'manpower' could be *workforce, workpower, personnel* or *human resources*; 'man's achievements in space' could be *human achievements*. When ***man*** occurs in expressions such as 'time and tide wait for no man' this could be rephrased into *time and tide wait for nobody*.

-man also occurs in some occupations or roles. Modern dictionaries suggest that unless you mean a male and only a male, 'businessman' becomes *business person*, 'chairman' becomes *chair/chairperson* (*chair* is now the official designation adopted by some British societies), 'fireman' becomes *firefighter*, 'foreman' becomes *supervisor*, 'layman' becomes *layperson*, 'policeman' becomes *police officer*, 'postman' becomes *postal worker* and 'sportsman' becomes *sportsperson*, and so on. Even though 'a Frenchman and Frenchwoman are present' is better than using 'Frenchman' for both sexes, another solution is writing *two French people are present*.

The verb ***to man*** is more difficult to replace by a single standard accepted alternative. Unless you are referring only to males, it should be avoided. Here are some suggestions. An office can be *staffed*, a phone service can be *operational*, not *manned*. Avoid 'manning a ship' by rephrasing and use *the ship's crew* or *the crew on the ship*.

-ess is a feminine suffix which has never been used widely, and is quickly losing ground. *Actor–actress, author–authoress, steward–stewardess* are all pairs which are being replaced, either by *actor, author* (whether a man or a woman) or by another term completely, such as *flight attendant* for *air steward(ess)*. The pairs *host–hostess* and *governor–governess* still show useful distinctions in meaning and there is no real masculine equivalent for the term *seamstress*. However, some titles such as *duchess, marchioness, countess, viscountess* and *baroness* still survive. See AUTHOR, HOST, GOVERNOR.

Examples of sexist writing and how to avoid it

Man and *his* intellectual development. (Use: *People and their intellectual development*. Alternatively: *Intellectual development in humans*.)

The *men* and *girls* in the office. (Use parallel terms: *men and women*, or *boys and girls*, perhaps even reverse the traditional order.)

The *girls* at the reception desk. (Use: *secretaries, office assistants* or just *staff*.)

Woman doctor, lady lawyer. (Use: *doctor, lawyer*. If it is necessary to mention the sex of the person, use *female doctor* and *female lawyer*.)

The *child* may notice *his* surroundings. (Change *his* to *its*.)

Each person was interviewed and *his* statement was checked. (Use the plural: *people . . . their statements were*. Otherwise, keep the singular and use *his or her*.)

The traditional use of *Mr and Mrs James Green* is found on wedding invitations and in other formal contexts. Otherwise use *Mr and Mrs Green* or *James and Mary Green* in less formal contexts.

The traditional use of *Mrs James Green* may be found on wedding invitations and in other very formal contexts. Otherwise use *Mrs Green*, if she still uses 'Mrs', *Ms Green*, or *Mary Green*, which is the most informal of these.

E. Formal English

The formal, written English that is expected in reports, business correspondence and documents is different from spoken everyday English. Here are three features of formal English.

Suitable vocabulary

Formal vocabulary is mainly based on classical words. These are more often found in written English.	Informal vocabulary is mainly short Anglo-Saxon words. These are typical of spoken English or used in informal notes.
arrange (dinner)	*lay on (dinner)*
by coincidence	*by chance*
collect (someone)	*pick up (someone)*
commence	*begin, start*
conceal	*hide*
consider	*weigh up*
construct	*build*
donation	*gift*
endeavour	*try*
enquire	*ask*
finalize (a contract)	*tie up (a contract)*
inspect	*look over*
reserve	*book*
position	*job*
purchase	*buy*
review (problems)	*look at (problems)*
settle (matters)	*sort out (matters)*

Avoiding slang expressions or jargon

Slang and jargon are typical characteristics of oral English. They are verbal short cuts when speakers and their audience share common assumptions and knowledge. Using slang can cause irritation and make what is written appear very casual. Compare the formal, *please do this as soon as possible* with *do this ASAP*; or the formal *we will rectify the malfunction in the computer system* with *we will fix the hard disk foul up*. Slangy expressions like *belt and braces* (meaning taking extra care to make sure something is successful) and the use of text messaging abbreviations from mobile phones can also cause misunderstanding. Thus a formal report, a letter or even an email written as a representative of a company or organization is no place for smiley symbols such as :-) or :-(or cryptic SMS (Short Message Service) abbreviations like *Which one r u?* See **JARGON, SLANG**.

Avoiding contractions (I'm . . . won't . . . , etc.)

Contractions or short forms are to be avoided in official letters, reports and other types of formal English. They should only be used in informal, conversational writing and when reporting speech. Compare the formal English with corresponding contractions:

We are looking forward to this	*We're looking forward to this*
The contract does not commence until . . .	*The contract doesn't start until . . .*

Using short forms in the wrong context looks sloppy and may also lead to mistakes such as confusing *it's* with the identical sounding possessive pronoun *its*. See **CONTRACTIONS, ITS**.

Bibliography

Accents of English, (1982). J.C. Wells. Cambridge University Press, Cambridge.

BBC Pronouncing Dictionary of British Names, 2nd edition (1983). G.E. Pointon (ed.). Oxford University Press, Oxford.

British National Corpus. http://www.natcorp.ox.ac.uk.

Chicago Manual of Style, 13th edition (1982). The University of Chicago Press, Chicago

Dictionary of Differences, (1989). Laurence Urdang. Bloomsbury Publishers, London

The Economist Style Guide, 6th edition (2000). The Economist/Profile Books, London.

English Pronouncing Dictionary, 15th edition (1997). Peter Roach and James Hartman (eds). Cambridge University Press, Cambridge.

The Financial Times Style Guide, (1994). Colin Inman. Pitman Publishing, London.

Getting Your English Right, 3rd edition (2005). Stewart Clark. Tapir Academic Press. Trondheim, Norway.

Hart's Rules for Compositors and Readers at the University Press Oxford, 39th edition (1999). Oxford University Press, Oxford.

An Introduction to English Grammar, 2nd edition (2002). Sidney Greenbaum and Gerald Nelson. Longman, Harlow, England.

Longman Dictionary of Contemporary English, 4th edition (2005). Pearson Education, Harlow.

Longman Guide to English Usage, (1988). Sidney Greenbaum and Janet Whitcut. Longman, Harlow.

Longman Pronunciation Dictionary, 3rd edition (2000). J.C. Wells. Pearson Education, Harlow

Mind the Gaffe, (2001). R.L. Trask. Penguin Books, London.

The New Fowler's Modern English Usage, 3rd edition (1996). R.W. Burchfield (ed.). Oxford University Press, Oxford.

The New Oxford Dictionary of English, (1998). Oxford University Press, Oxford.

The New Penguin English Dictionary, 2nd edition (2000). Robert Allen (ed.). Penguin Books, London.

The New Shorter Oxford English Dictionary, 4th edition (1993). Oxford University Press, Oxford.

Oxford Advanced Learners Dictionary, 7th Edition, (2005). Oxford University Press, Oxford.

Oxford Collocations Dictionary, (2002). Oxford University Press, Oxford.

The Oxford Dictionary of Pronunciation for Current English, (2001). Clive Upton, William A. Kretzschmar, Jr and Rafal Konopka. Oxford University Press, Oxford.

Oxford Idioms Dictionary, (2001). Oxford University Press, Oxford.

The Oxford Companion to the English Language, (1996). Oxford University Press, Oxford.

Oxford Dictionary for Writers and Editors, 2nd edition (2000). Oxford University Press, Oxford.

Practical English Usage, 2nd edition (1995). Michael Swan. Oxford University Press, Oxford.

Room's Dictionary of Confusibles, (1979). Adrian Room. Routledge and Kegan Paul, London.

Troublesome Words, 3rd edition (2001). Bill Bryson. Penguin Books, London.

Webster's Encyclopedic Unabridged Dictionary of the English Language, (1989). Gramercy Books, New York.

Word for Word, (2003). Stewart Clark and Graham Pointon. Oxford University Press, Oxford.

Standardization organization

International Organization for Standardization (ISO), Geneva, Switzerland. (www.iso.ch)